Microsoft®

Microsoft®
Systems Management Server 2.0 Administrator's Companion

Steven D.
Kaczmarek

PUBLISHED BY
Microsoft Press
A Division of Microsoft Corporation
One Microsoft Way
Redmond, Washington 98052-6399

Library of Congress Cataloging-in-Publication Data
Kaczmarek, Steven D.
    Microsoft Systems Management Server 2.0 Administrator's Companion / Steven D. Kaczmarek.
        p. cm.
    ISBN 0-7356-0834-2
    I. Title

                                                                              99-089287

Printed and bound in the United States of America.

1 2 3 4 5 6 7 8 9   WCWC   5 4 3 2 1 0

Distributed in Canada by Penguin Books Canada Limited.

A CIP catalogue record for this book is available from the British Library.

Microsoft Press books are available through booksellers and distributors worldwide. For further
information about international editions, contact your local Microsoft Corporation office, or contact Microsoft Press International directly at fax (425) 936-7329. Visit our Web site at
mspress.microsoft.com.

Acquisitions Editor: David Clark
Project Editor: Julie Miller
Technical Editor: Julie Xiao
Manuscript Editor: Jennifer Harris

Dedication

I would like to dedicate this book to my parents, who proudly tell anyone who will listen that there is an author in the family. I am especially grateful to my partner, William, for his support and encouragement and to Scruffy, our cairn terrier, who kept me from working too many continuous hours at my three (count 'em!) computers by subtly reminding me of the importance of the occasional walk.

Contents at a Glance

Table of Contents

Part II
Resource Discovery,
Client Installation, and Remote Control

Part III
Software and Package Management

Part IV
Site Database Maintenance and Recovery

20 Microsoft Windows 2000 and Microsoft Systems Management Server 2.0   860

Part VI
Appendixes

Acknowledgments

Having authored and participated in the publication of several books in recent years, I can assert with conviction that the process takes the commitment of many people. This book was certainly no exception.

First and foremost, many thanks to the editorial team at Microsoft Press. Their dedication and hard work were outstanding in every respect. The editorial review process can be frustrating, but they made it comfortable for me and I greatly appreciate their efforts, their comments, and their patience. In particular, thanks to David Clark for accepting my book proposal and to Julie Miller, Jennifer Harris, Julie Xiao, and Cheryl Penner, the excellent editorial team who made sure I dotted the i's and crossed the t's.

Special thanks to Jeff Sparks, a colleague and friend from Productivity Point International, for his contributions to the chapters about remote control, SMS Installer, and SQL Server maintenance. I appreciate the time and effort he committed in assisting me with this material. I would also like to express my gratitude to all my training and consulting colleagues. It is through the healthy and often spirited exchange of information in a variety of forums—along with my own training and consulting experiences—that I have developed a deeper appreciation for this product and gained greater insight into its strengths and foibles. In this vein, a special thank you to the contributors of the SMS MCT forum for your generous commitment to keeping the SMS community informed about SMS.

Introduction

Microsoft has traditionally geared its development of Microsoft BackOffice applications toward providing network administrators with tools that can facilitate the functionality and management of their Microsoft Windows NT networks. For example, applications such as Microsoft Exchange 5.5 and Microsoft SQL Server 7.0 provide exceptional mail and database support through centralized management. Microsoft Systems Management Server (SMS) 2.0 is just such a product. In this current release, especially with the application of Service Pack 1, you have a superior product that provides centralized management and support for your install base of computers. Those of you who have grown up with SMS will be particularly impressed with the improvements made in this version that enhance the product's functionality and scalability within large enterprise networks.

This book is designed to provide you with both a learning and practical guide to the administrative tasks you'll be performing with SMS 2.0. You'll find "real world" examples that illustrate how to apply a concept in a realistic scenario, "tips," "cautions," and resource suggestions for obtaining more information about a topic. Where appropriate as SMS 2.0 performs a specific function or process, the process flow and its components will be outlined, monitoring techniques will be suggested, and troubleshooting considerations will be highlighted. Many chapters include a "Checkpoints" section, in which potential problem areas are reviewed and new troubleshooting tips are presented. You'll also find references to enhancements provided by Service Pack 1 throughout this book.

Part I: Installation, Planning, and Management

Part I introduces the reader to SMS 2.0, outlining its features and functionality and comparing and contrasting it to the previous version, SMS 1.2. This part also covers a wide range of topics specific to the installation and planning of an SMS site. Chapter 1 presents an overview of SMS 2.0. Chapter 2 provides a detailed discussion of the installation process for an SMS primary site, including preinstallation requirements as well as post-installation system modifications. You'll also learn how to navigate administrative functions using the SMS Administrator Console, which uses the new Microsoft Management Console (MMC) format. In Chapter 3, you'll learn how to define and configure the SMS site and site systems. Chapter 4 suggests planning considerations for a multiple-site structure, including developing parent-child relationships among primary sites, creating secondary sites, and establishing SMS 2.0 communication mechanisms between sites. Chapters 5 and 6 introduce the reader to the various tools available in SMS 2.0 that enable the administrator to monitor activity in the SMS site, track the flow of information, and analyze network and server performance. These tools will be examined in more detail in subsequent chapters.

Part II: Resource Discovery, Client Installation, and Remote Control

Part II discusses three main areas of client system support through SMS 2.0: resource discovery, client installation, and remote control. Chapters 7 and 8 describe the discovery and assignment process for SMS client systems. Before a client can be installed as an SMS client, it must be discovered and assigned to an SMS 2.0 site. The three client setup methods are described, along with their process flow. SMS 2.0 now supports software inventory as well as enhanced hardware inventory, and the collection process for the various SMS client types is defined for both hardware and software inventory in Chapter 9. In Chapter 10, you'll learn how to remotely monitor and troubleshoot a client system through the SMS Administrator Console.

Part III: Software and Package Management

Part III discusses what is probably an SMS administrator's primary reason for purchasing SMS 2.0—the distribution of software and other packages to client systems through the network with little or no user intervention, and the management of that software once it's installed. This part is divided into four areas of concern. Chapter 11 explains the concept of a collection in SMS 2.0 and describes how collections are created and maintained. Chapter 12 describes the package distribution process, including creating packages and programs, identifying package recipients through collections, and executing package commands at the client system. Chapter 13 illustrates the use of SMS Installer 2.0 to script an installation process and make it potentially invisible to the user. Chapter 14 discusses a new feature introduced in SMS 2.0: software metering, which enables SMS to monitor and regulate software usage on client systems, including validation of licenses and restriction or prohibition of nonstandard software products such as games.

Part IV: Site Database Maintenance and Recovery

Part IV covers a wide variety of topics related to the SMS 2.0 database. Because the database itself must be maintained on a server running Microsoft SQL Server 6.5 or 7.0, this part approaches database management from two perspectives: management and reporting from within the SMS 2.0 Administrator Console, and maintenance and events related directly to SQL Server. In Chapter 15, you'll learn how to query for and report on information kept in the database from within the SMS Administrator Console. In Chapter 16, we'll look at securing access through Windows NT and through custom consoles, and in Chapter 17, we'll examine disaster recovery techniques. Chapter 18 covers SQL Server topics, including event triggers, SQL Server resources and components used by SMS 2.0, maintenance and optimization techniques, and SQL Server backup and restore methods. Part IV is not intended as a primer for SQL Server; instead, it is designed to provide the SMS administrator with a basic understanding of SQLServer–related maintenance tasks. Since SMS supports both version 6.5 and version 7.0 of SQL Server, any differences in maintenance tasks between these versions are noted.

Part V: Supporting Microsoft Systems Management Server 1.2 and Microsoft Windows 2000

Part V covers two main areas of discussion: support for SMS 1.2 and support for Windows 2000. Chapter 19 covers the topic of migration from SMS 1.2 to SMS 2.0. In addition to describing the migration process, this chapter also identifies planning considerations, discusses post-migration issues, and describes client handling and upgrading as well as supporting mixed SMS 1.2 and 2.0 environments. Chapter 20 then takes a look at how SMS 2.0 features compare to similar features in Windows 2000. We'll see how SMS 2.0 can be used to ready a network for Windows 2000 and explore some Windows 2000 deployment options using SMS 2.0. We'll discuss how the product compliance database feature of SMS 2.0 can be used to assist you in developing a Windows 2000 upgrades strategy. And we'll take a look at future plans for SMS 2.0 in the Windows 2000 environment.

Appendixes

Two appendixes are included with this book:

- **Appendix A: Sample Backup Control File**   Contains the code for the backup control file used by the SMS Site Backup service when performing a site server backup scheduled through the SMS Administrator Console, as discussed in Chapter 17

- **Appendix B: Recommended Internet Sites**   Lists some of the Web sites that the author considers particularly useful for gathering additional information about or obtaining support products for SMS 2.0

Companion CDs

This book includes two CDs. The first contains a 120-day trial version of SMS 2.0 that you can use to explore the features and management methods discussed in the text. The second contains an online version of this book, two Microsoft white papers, and four demo applications from Computing Edge, a leading developer of SMS enhancement products.

The white papers included on the CD are:

- **Integrating Microsoft Systems Management Server 2.0 with Novell NetWare**   Discusses how to integrate SMS 2.0 with Novell NetWare 3.x (Bindery) and NetWare 4.x (NDS and Bindery emulation). This document covers requirements needed to successfully implement SMS 2.0 in a Novell environment, such as security, supported client versions, NDS name space specifications, and so on.

- **Windows Management Instrumentation: Background and Overview**   Serves as an introduction to Web-Based Enterprise Management (WBEM). This document discusses Microsoft's implementation of this technology, known as Windows Management Instrumentation (WMI).

The demo applications included on the CD are:

- **Web**   Lets you access and administer an SMS 2.0 site using your Web browser
- **Web Reports**   Extends the functionality of Web Administrator by integrating over 100 report templates to the data provided through Web Administrator
- **Download +Solution**   Enables you to install software and run scripts on a Windows NT or Windows 2000 system without having to log on as the administrator
- **Serial Number +Plus**   Enables you to record and track serial number data from your SMS client computers

This book is designed to provide you with a comprehensive discussion of SMS 2.0 and its administrative and management potential for your organization, along with a set of tools and suggestions to facilitate your use of SMS 2.0. We hope you will enjoy the book and find it to be a useful and productive tool in itself!

Part I
Installation, Planning, and Management

Chapter 1
Overview

Welcome to the wonderful world of Microsoft Systems Management Server (SMS) 2.0. This book provides you with the insight and tools necessary to successfully administer SMS 2.0. We will explore the many components and features of SMS, including package distribution, hardware and software inventory, remote diagnostics, and software metering. We will discuss the installation procedures for site systems and clients, and we'll walk through the implementation of an SMS site hierarchy. We'll also look at relevant SMS 1.2 migration and at disaster recovery and database maintenance recommendations. Since SMS 2.0 was first released in March 1999, Microsoft has issued SMS 2.0 Service Pack 1. The enhancements included with Service Pack 1 are incorporated into the discussion throughout this book. This chapter introduces SMS 2.0 and describes what SMS 2.0 is all about.

What Is Systems Management Server 2.0?

The computing industry has undergone many changes since the days of UNIVAC. In the early 1980s, the desktop computer as a viable business tool was relatively new. In fact, typical corporate discussions at the time centered around issues such as whether to purchase a desktop computer with a 10-MB disk drive at an additional cost of $1,700 because "users will just never need that much space."

Since that time, the desktop computer as a productivity tool has become a necessity in most organizations as well as in schools and at home. The need to provide processing power at the user's fingertips is a foregone conclusion. As a result, desktop computing has grown into a major industry, and consequently a potentially huge administration headache. Desktop computer users can be territorial about their systems and the applications they run. It's not unheard of to have an information systems (IS) group that supports a user running three different word processing programs in several different versions because that user is unwilling to risk converting documents to a single word processing version. While this is an unusual case (we hope), it does exemplify the fact that supporting multiple desktop computers installed with a variety of program applications can be a challenge for even the best-equipped and well-funded IS support groups.

In addition to application support, IS groups often provide hardware support for their organization's users. This too can be a daunting prospect when the install base of computers is in the thousands or tens of thousands, deployed within different departmental, geographic, or international locations. It is not always practical—or even possible—to physically access every computer in an organization.

Recently IS managers have acknowledged the need to provide standards for desktop computing and now have begun to look for and to implement some kind of centralized desktop management system. IS support groups need to be able to respond actively and proactively to their users' requests for assistance as quickly, effectively, and consistently as possible. IS support groups should be able to perform as much user desktop management as possible while sitting at their own desktop computers. The key to effective remote desktop management is to provide a reliable set of remote management tools that enable an IS support group to be as effective as if they had actually laid hands on the user's desktop.

Microsoft has long recognized this need and has responded by providing tools to assist IS groups in centralizing desktop management. These tools include the use of Microsoft Windows NT 4.0 system profiles and policies to provide standard desktop environment settings and registry values. Microsoft Zero Administration Kits for Windows NT Workstation 4.0 provide customizable policy templates to further "lock down" desktop settings, such as which programs appear in the Control Panel. Microsoft Windows 2000 and the Windows Management Instrumentation (WMI) services provide a robust schema for managing desktop configurations from a central location.

SMS 2.0 is a powerful Microsoft BackOffice tool that offers a rich set of desktop management features, providing IS managers with perhaps their most effective centralized management tool to date. With SMS 2.0, you will be able to remotely diagnose and troubleshoot desktop systems, install applications, and manage software.

With these general specifications in mind, let's take a closer look at the various features offered by SMS 2.0.

Features and Functions

SMS 2.0 offers remote desktop administration in four primary areas:

- **Inventory and resource management**   The ability to gather and maintain a workstation's hardware and software configuration in a central database that is easy to access and interpret
- **Diagnosis and troubleshooting**   The tools to effectively analyze hardware and software concerns on remote workstations
- **Package distribution**   The ability to install applications and updates and execute programs on a remote workstation
- **Application management**   The ability to track, restrict, and license application usage on a user's workstation as well as to monitor product compliance issues

We will explore these SMS features more closely throughout this book. First let's look at the various SMS components; we will refer to these components as we look at features.

Components

The term "SMS component" refers to a program that performs a specific SMS task. In this section, we will review some basic SMS 2.0 terms and component definitions. If these descriptions seem brief, don't despair! Each component is discussed in detail later in this book.

SMS Site

An *SMS site* defines the computers, users, groups, and other resources that will be managed by SMS so that SMS can remotely control a Windows NT workstation, advertise a package to a user, view all Internet Protocol (IP) devices, or inventory system resources. An SMS site is defined first and foremost by IP subnet address, which means that you can manage computers based on their subnet address rather than simply by their domain membership. This computer managing feature allows SMS 2.0 to scale more efficiently to your enterprise network. An SMS site consists of an SMS site server, SMS site systems, and SMS clients and resources.

SMS Site Server

The *SMS site server* is the Windows NT 4.0 server on which SMS 2.0 has been installed and that manages the SMS site and all its component attributes and

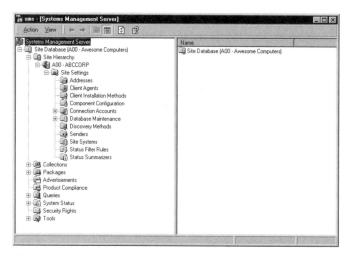

Figure 1-1. *A representative SMS Administrator Console displaying the different top-level objects that can be managed by the SMS administrator.*

Table 1-1. Top-level SMS objects

Object	Description
Site Hierarchy	Displays the site hierarchy and contains site properties and component configurations such as client agents, installation methods, discovery methods, site systems, status filters, and summarizers.
Collections	Predefined or SMS administrator–defined groupings of SMS resources. Collections can consist of any SMS-discovered resources.
Packages	Display package and program settings. A *package* is a set of files, programs, or commands that you want executed on an SMS client. Package programs are advertised to collections. Package files are stored in distribution points.
Advertisements	The means by which you let an SMS client know that a package is available for it. An advertisement can be offered not only to SMS client computers, but also to any users or user groups that have been discovered by SMS. Advertisements are maintained on CAPs.
Product Compliance	Defines a list of products and their Y2K-compliance level.
Queries	Provide a means of displaying database information based on a set of predefined criteria. Several queries are defined by default, and the SMS administrator can also create new queries.

Table 1-1. *continued*

Object	Description
System Status	SMS equivalent to the Windows NT Event Viewer. Virtually every SMS service or process generates a robust set of status messages that outline the progress of that service or process. The information provided by the *System Status* object is the best place for an SMS administrator to begin troubleshooting.
Security Rights	Provide the capability to define and refine the level of access that users have when working with SMS objects. This gives you the ability to delegate specific tasks to specific groups of users.
Tools	Four primary tools can be utilized through this object: Network Monitor, for network traffic analysis; SMS Service Manager, for monitoring component status and logging; Software Metering, for monitoring and maintaining product usage and licensing; and Reports for creating database reports using Crystal Info.

SMS Site Hierarchy

An *SMS site hierarchy* resembles an organizational flowchart and exists whenever two or more SMS sites have been defined in a parent-child relationship. SMS site hierarchies provide a means of extending and scaling SMS support across a wide variety of organizational structures.

Parent and child sites are defined by their relationship within an SMS site hierarchy. A *parent site* is any site with at least one child site defined and has the ability to administer any child site below it in the SMS site hierarchy. A *child site* is any SMS site that has a parent defined. Child sites send discovery, inventory, and status information up to the parent site. Any SMS primary or secondary site can also be a child site. An SMS primary site can have a child site reporting to it, but an SMS secondary site cannot.

Primary Site   An *SMS primary site* is an SMS site that has access to a SQL Server database. An SMS primary site can be directly administered through the SMS Administrator Console as well as by any SMS site above it in the SMS site hierarchy. An SMS primary site can also administer any child site below it in the site hierarchy. SMS primary sites can be children of other primary sites. They can also have child sites of their own.

Secondary Site   An *SMS secondary site* is an SMS site that does not have access to a SQL Server database. An SMS secondary site is always a child of a primary site and is administered solely through its parent or through another primary site above it in the SMS site hierarchy. A secondary site cannot have child sites of its own.

Central Site   An *SMS central site* is an SMS primary site that resides at the top of the SMS site hierarchy. Inventory data, status messages, site control data, and discovery data roll from child to parent and are collected ultimately at the central site's SMS database. An SMS central site can administer any site below it in the SMS site hierarchy.

Figure 1-2 illustrates a simple SMS hierarchical model showing both primary and secondary sites as child sites of a central site. An SMS site system's roles do not all have to be enabled on the site server. CAPs, distribution points, and software metering servers can all be enabled on member servers in the domain. Logon points will be enabled on all domain controllers in the specified domain.

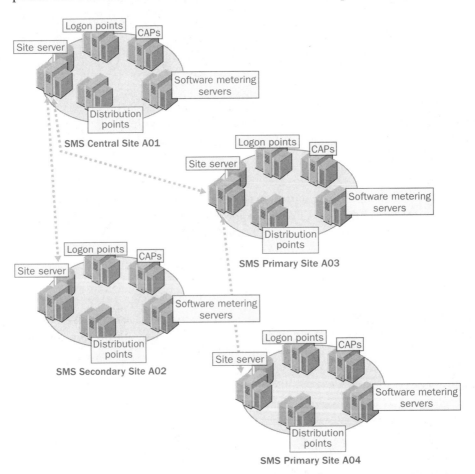

Figure 1-2. *Various site system roles that can be assigned within an SMS site and a representative SMS site hierarchy.*

That's it for general terminology. All these components and terms will be explored in more detail as we progress through the book.

Inventory and Resource Management

SMS 2.0 can collect and display resources deployed within your network. These resources include, of course, the workstations and servers that have been installed. You also have the ability to discover and view your Windows NT domain users and global groups, as well as any IP-addressable component connected to your local area network (LAN) or wide area network (WAN). SMS 2.0 offers several configurable discovery methods. While not all discovered resources may be manageable, some basic properties can be displayed and viewed by the administrator. For example, a computer's discovery data includes its IP address, network card address (the media access control [MAC] address), its computer name, and the domain of which it is a member. The process of discovering resources will be discussed at length in Chapter 7.

> **Note** The process of discovering a resource such as a computer does not automatically mean that SMS is installed on that computer. Nor does it mean that inventory is collected. Rather, it means that the "fact" of the resource being there is recorded along with some basic properties of that resource.

In addition to discovery data, SMS 2.0 can collect hardware and software data from an SMS 2.0 client. Two of the many client agents that can be installed on an SMS client computer are the Hardware Inventory Client Agent (also sometimes referred to as the Hardware Inventory Agent) and the Software Inventory Client Agent (also sometimes referred to as the Software Inventory Agent). Both are enabled and configured by the SMS administrator and then installed on an SMS client. Collected inventory is stored, viewed, and maintained in the SMS database. This database is created on a computer with SQL Server installed. The SMS Administrator Console acts as a front end to this database and provides the SMS administrator with the tools to manage that data. For example, an SMS client's inventory is viewed through the SMS Administrator Console using a tool called the Resource Explorer.

When troubleshooting needs to be performed, it is not always possible, or even appropriate, that users have full knowledge of their hardware or software configuration. Having an SMS client's inventory readily available and up-to-date, however, provides an administrator with the computer configuration data needed to assist a user with a problem.

The Hardware Inventory Client Agent executes according to an administrator-defined frequency and collects system configuration data such as hard disk space, processor type, RAM size, CD type, monitor type, and so on. In addition, the Hardware Inventory Client Agent can be configured to collect more granular information from 32-bit clients such as Windows 98 and Windows NT 4.0 Workstation, including the install date of the BIOS, program group names, and printers installed. It does so by using the Windows Management Service. Windows Management is Microsoft's implementation of Web-Based Enterprise Management (WBEM). (You'll learn more about these services in the section "Understanding WBEM and WMI" later in this chapter.) Briefly, Windows Management allows for detailed system configuration data to be reported and stored on the workstation for use by management applications such as SMS. Once the Hardware Inventory Client Agent on a 32-bit client has collected the full inventory, only changes to the inventory on the client will be reported in subsequent inventories. This feature is a welcome change from SMS 1.2, in which a complete inventory was always generated and reported at every hardware inventory interval. The hardware inventory process and configuration are discussed thoroughly in Chapter 9.

The Software Inventory Client Agent also executes according to an administrator-defined interval and essentially audits the SMS client for applications installed on its local hard disks. The SMS administrator can configure the Software Inventory Client Agent to audit other file types, as well as to collect copies of specific files. As with the Hardware Inventory Client Agent, the first time the Software Inventory Client Agent runs, a complete software audit or file collection takes place and the full inventory is gathered and reported. At each successive inventory interval, only changes to the audited files will be reported. The software inventory collection and configuration process is discussed more completely in Chapter 9.

Diagnosis and Troubleshooting

Several tools provided through the SMS Administrator Console can help the SMS administrator diagnose problems in the SMS site, with communications within and among sites, and with SMS client computers. These tools can also help the SMS administrator troubleshoot those problems with little direct physical intervention.

HealthMon

This utility presents an at-a-glance view of the current status of Windows NT 4.0 computers in the site. Through settings prescribed by the SMS administrator, HealthMon can generate events based on specific thresholds that are met or surpassed. For example, HealthMon can be set to display a warning indicator for a computer when its processor utilization exceeds 75 percent and a critical indicator when processor utilization exceeds 90 percent. See Chapter 6 for more information about working with HealthMon.

Network Monitor 2.0

This utility provides the means to track, capture, and analyze network traffic that occurs between individual client computers or within the network itself. This version has been enhanced both in functionality and security. Experts have been added to assist you in tracking down and parsing events such as top users, protocol distribution, and so on. In addition, the SMS Administrator Console provides seven Network Monitor Control tools that enable the SMS administrator to identify activities and specific problem situations, such as rogue Dynamic Host Configuration Protocol (DHCP) servers or connections from disallowed IP subnets, through real-time tracking routines. Network Monitor is discussed in detail in Chapter 6.

Network Trace

This utility offers a snapshot flowchart of the SMS site system structure that maps the communication path of each site system, checks for communication status between site systems, and displays the status of SMS components running on each site system. Think of Network Trace as a miniature Simple Network Management Protocol (SNMP) manager. See Chapter 6 for more information about working with Network Trace.

Performance Monitor

When SMS has been installed on a site server, it also adds several new objects that contain counters to the Windows NT Performance Monitor utility. These objects are listed here:

- *SMS Discovery Data Manager*
- *SMS Executive Thread States*
- *SMS In-Memory Queues*
- *SMS Inventory Data Loader*
- *SMS Software Inventory Processor*
- *SMS Standard Sender*
- *SMS Status Messages*

These objects and their corresponding counters, along with the traditional Windows NT objects and their counters (*Processor*, *Process*, *Memory*, *Logical Disk*, *Physical Disk*, and so on) can be used to assist the SMS administrator in performance testing site systems and determining optimization alternatives. See Chapter 6 for more information about working with Performance Monitor.

Remote Tools

This utility is perhaps the most appreciated feature of SMS 2.0. Remote Tools enables the SMS administrator to gain keyboard and mouse control of an SMS client from the administrator's workstation. Through a video transfer screen, the administrator can "see" the user's desktop and diagnose and troubleshoot problems without having physical access to the remote client. The administrator can also "talk" to the user through a remote chat screen, execute programs on the remote client, transfer files to and from the remote client, and restart the remote client. As with the Hardware Inventory Client Agent and the Software Inventory Client Agent, the amount of remote access that can be initiated is configured by the SMS administrator and rendered on the client by a Remote Tools Client Agent (also sometimes referred to as the Remote Tools Agent).

The Remote Tools utility also includes remote diagnostic utilities specific to Windows NT 4.0 and other Windows operating systems that provide real-time access to system attributes such as interrupt usage, memory usage, services running, and device settings. This feature is discussed more thoroughly in Chapter 10.

SMS Trace

This utility allows the SMS administrator to view one or more SMS log files in real time in order to follow, diagnose, and troubleshoot service activity. You can use SMS Trace to search for text strings and to highlight found values. See Chapter 5 for more information about SMS Trace.

SNMP Traps and the Event to Trap Translator

SNMP Traps is a tool developed to monitor and troubleshoot IP-addressable devices in a network. Status and event information about these devices is both requested by and reported to an SNMP management server. The SMS 2.0 Event to Trap Translator lets you generate SNMP traps out of Windows NT events logged through Windows NT's event service and send them on to a defined SNMP management system such as Hewlett-Packard's OpenView or Compaq's Insight Manager. It does so by utilizing the SNMP Service, which can be added to any Windows NT computer. Chapter 6 discusses the Event to Trap Translator in more detail.

SMS services also create and update a wide variety of log files and generate detailed event status messages. These files and messages provide the SMS administrator with an extensive source of diagnostic data that is critical to the successful maintenance of the SMS site, as well as providing an ideal means to learn about the inner workings of SMS.

Package Distribution

One important way of reducing the total cost of owning and maintaining client computers is to minimize the amount of time an administrator needs to physically spend at a computer. When part of the administrator's job involves installing and upgrading software at a computer, the amount of time spent at each computer can be significant. We've already looked at some of the remote tools available to reduce the time spent at a user's computer. Another way to reduce this time is to acquire the ability to remotely install, maintain, and upgrade software. SMS 2.0 enables you to do just that. Through its package distribution feature, you can run programs on client computers to install and upgrade software, update files, execute tasks such as disk optimization routines, and modify configuration settings such as registry entries or INI files.

The SMS administrator defines a package's properties, including the location of source files, sending priority, where the package should be stored and shared on the distribution point, and version and language values. The SMS administrator identifies which distribution points should receive the package and also creates one or more programs for the package that define how the package should be executed at a client computer. For example, a software application installation may have several types of installs that can be run, such as Typical, Custom, and Laptop. Each of these installs would represent a program that the SMS administrator would create for the package. The same package definition could then be used to install the application in different ways on different clients.

Clients are made aware of the existence of a program through advertisements. An *advertisement* is created by the SMS administrator and identifies both the program that should be executed by the target resources and the SMS collection that defines the target resources. Programs can be advertised only to collections, and a valid collection can consist of SMS clients, Windows NT users, or Windows NT global user groups. The advantage of this arrangement is that when a new computer, user, or global user group is added to a collection, it will automatically receive any advertisements for that collection. Packages and advertisements are discussed in detail in Chapter 12.

Application Management

SMS 2.0 offers several tools for managing applications installed on SMS clients. Perhaps the most distinctive new tool is the software metering server. The software metering server provides two main functions: application usage tracking and application licensing. Whenever an application is executed at the client, a client agent reports that fact to the software metering server. This information is passed to the SMS site server and stored in its own SQL database. The data can then be summarized and displayed for the SMS administrator through the SMS Administrator Console. The SMS administrator is capable of excluding applications from monitoring. For example, you probably would not be interested in knowing every time the Clock accessory was run. If you exclude the Clock application, the client agent will then ignore any instance of Clock that is run on the client.

An application can also be registered by the SMS administrator. When an application is registered, the SMS administrator can set restrictions on it or enforce tracking of licenses. For example, an organization might allow FreeCell to be played on company computers only at lunchtime. The SMS administrator can register FreeCell and restrict its execution to a designated time period—say, from 12:00 PM to 1:00 PM. Or the SMS administrator could bar the execution of any applications that are not Y2K-compliant or Euro-compliant. An application can also be restricted by user, group, or client, much like creating an access control list (ACL) for a Windows NT folder.

When the restricted or licensed application is run on a client, the client agent checks for restrictions or licenses on the software metering server. If a restriction exists, the client will receive a message stating that the application cannot be run, and the client agent will shut down the application. Similarly, if the application has been licensed, the client agent will check to see whether any licenses are available for the application. If no licenses are available, the client agent will shut down the application and display a message to that effect. The client agent will also offer a callback option to the user, which means that the user doesn't have to keep retrying the application until a license becomes available on the software metering server. Instead, if the user requests a callback, the software metering server will reserve a license for that user for a default period of time when a license becomes available. The client agent checks the software metering server periodically for available callbacks and notifies the user when a license is available.

Note As with all SMS site systems, you can have multiple software metering servers. SMS will automatically balance available licenses across all the software metering servers based on the license usage data it collects.

An additional application management tool, the product compliance database, is an optional feature that can be installed with SMS. The product compliance database was originally intended to be used to provide a list of Microsoft applications and their level of Y2K compliance. You can add your own product information to this database and use it to identify other compatibility issues, such as Windows 2000 compatibility of the existing clients and software applications, before you implement a Windows 2000 upgrade strategy.

This identification process actually involves several SMS features. The Software Inventory Client Agent can be used to collect a list of programs installed on each client. This list is compared to the product compliance database using SMS queries. Once you have identified the programs that need to upgraded, you can use the package distribution process to send and apply the appropriate upgrades. The product compliance database is discussed in Chapter 20.

Understanding WBEM and WMI

WBEM is an industry initiative adopted by the Desktop Management Task Force (DMTF) to implement a common interface between management applications, such as SMS, and management entities, such as SMS objects. SMS objects include discovery data, client computers, packages, advertisements, sites, and site control information. This common interface is called the Common Information Model (CIM) repository. It defines a standard schema for storing and exposing object data. Providers are components that collect object information from managed objects and store them in the CIM repository. A management application can then obtain that information from the CIM repository and make it available for view and analysis.

This interface feature is similar to installing a Windows device driver such as a printer driver. The print device manufacturer provides a printer driver that is compatible with Windows operating systems. All Windows-based applications use this same printer driver to generate print jobs on the print device. Using a similar premise, with the WBEM interface installed, any management application program should be able to obtain workstation data from any workstation running any operating system. The implementation of the WBEM interface into a particular operating system environment is the responsibility of the operating system manufacturer. Microsoft's implementation of WBEM, the WMI, provides its own CIM Object Manager, or repository. Providers can be written to store and expose data in the CIM repository, and management applications (written with Microsoft

Visual Basic, SQL Server, Java, ODBC, Active Directory Service, and so on) can be created to obtain that data from the CIM repository.

To illustrate, suppose a hardware provider on the SMS client stores SMS object information such as hardware inventory in the CIM repository. SMS agents such as the Hardware Inventory Client Agent extract that data from the CIM repository and report it to the SMS database. The SMS Provider, which can be installed on the SMS site server or the SQL Server, accesses the SMS database to provide the data to the SMS Administrator Console. Figure 1-3 demonstrates this relationship.

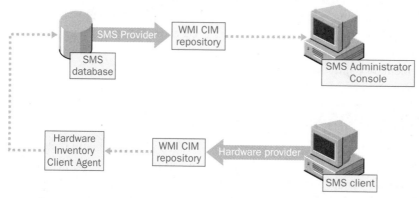

Figure 1-3. *Relationship between the SMS Provider, the WMI, and the SMS database.*

The SMS database objects, views, and tables are not directly accessible or modifiable except through the WMI layer. SMS provides an open architecture, however, which makes it possible to create tools other than the SMS Administrator Console that can access and manipulate the SMS database objects. In essence, any WBEM-compliant and ODBC-compliant application can be used to access these objects. So you could view the data with a Web browser using ActiveX controls or Java, through applications written using C++, Visual Basic, or the Component Object Model (COM).

WMI is installed on all 32-bit SMS clients, including Windows 95/98, Windows NT 4.0 or later, and requires about 8 MB of disk space. The registry is modified to reflect the WMI component installation, and the Windows Management Service is installed and started.

More Info For more information about Microsoft Windows Management Instrumentation see the white paper "Microsoft Windows Management Instrumentation: Background and Overview" on one of the companion CDs included with this book.

What's Changed Since Systems Management Server 1.2?

SMS 2.0 differs from SMS 1.2 in several key areas. First and foremost, SMS 2.0 represents a fundamental regeneration of the program code. Most services and processes have been completely reworked to provide a higher level of performance and a more efficient load balancing of resources. For example, whereas the SMS 1.2 Executive service managed about 10 SMS process components, the SMS 2.0 Executive service manages 42 process components. At first glance, you might infer that this proliferation of process components would in fact reduce performance rather than improve it. In actuality, overall performance does improve because the various SMS tasks are being carried out by their own individual process components. In SMS 1.2, each process component might be responsible for handling many SMS tasks.

Another major performance change from SMS 1.2 comes through the use of SQL stored procedures and triggers. Process components and services in SMS 1.2 would wake up and carry out a task based on a sometimes configurable polling cycle. This cycle would necessarily cause delays in the completion of a task such as processing a change to a site's properties or updating the database with inventory changes.

SMS 2.0 installs SMS SQL Monitor on the SQL Server computer. With nearly 200 different SQL triggers and stored procedures, SMS 2.0 uses SQL Monitor to wake up process components, allowing a task to be carried out immediately rather than waiting for the next polling cycle to occur. To visualize how SMS 1.2 carried out a task, imagine the workings of an old mechanical clock tower. Before the minute hand can move, several gears and cogs must engage and click and move. In contrast, SMS 2.0's clock tower model has a refined quartz movement.

Some other differences between SMS 1.2 and 2.0 come from feature changes, as you have probably already noticed. The more notable of these differences are listed in Table 1-2.

Table 1-2.   Feature changes between SMS 1.2 and SMS 2.0

Feature Change	SMS 1.2	SMS 2.0
Software inventory implementation	Simulates a software inventory through the use of software inventory packages and audit rule files. This manual process requires that you know some unique characteristics of the software in question, such as file size or cyclic redundancy check (CRC) value.	Adds true software inventory capabilities through a simple configuration process and reports the application name and version where possible as well as the executable file name.
Client support	Supports OS/2, Macintosh, and MS-DOS platform computers as manageable clients.	No longer supports OS/2, Macintosh, and MS-DOS platform client computers.
Shared network application	Provides support for shared network applications, which allows the administrator to use SMS to install a network version of an application and then provide access to the application by creating a program group and shortcut on the client's desktop.	No longer provides this support directly through the SMS site server as a configurable option, although it can be duplicated through other SMS 2.0 components.
Administrative tools	Uses the SMS 1.2 Administrator window.	Uses the SMS Administrator Console, which is a snap-in for MMC. This console is far more customizable than the SMS 1.2 Administrator window.
Security level	When accessing the SMS database through the SMS 1.2 Administrator window, the administrator has to provide the account and password that would be used to open the database. Some additional security roles can be assigned to various users, but this is basically as secure as you can get with SMS 1.2.	Adds object-level security through the SMS Administrator Console to provide a true method for locking down a console, delegating administrative tasks, and creating streamlined custom consoles for specific tasks as opposed to the single logon access to the SMS 1.2 Administrator window. For example, if a selected group of help desk users need to perform Remote Tools tasks for a specific group of clients, a custom console can be created that displays only the collection for that group of clients. A thorough implementation of object security enables that group of users to see only the collection they need to use in the SMS Administrator Console.

Table 1-2.   *continued*

Feature Change	SMS 1.2	SMS 2.0
Package delivery	Uses jobs to deliver packages to other sites, distribution servers, and clients.	Merges elements of the job process into its packages and advertisements. Part of the package definition, for example, now includes the DPs for the package files and the priority level for sending the package. The advertisement includes the target resources (grouped by collection), the program to be executed, and any mandatory time assignments.
Package recipients	Packages can be sent only to target SMS client computers.	A package is advertised to a collection, and an SMS collection can include SMS client computers as well as discovered users and user groups. This capability allows you to send a package directly to a user regardless of what computer that user is sitting at.
Status messaging system	Uses the SMS 1.2 Event Viewer.	Uses a more robust and detailed status messaging system named Status Message Viewer.
Package target management	Uses machine groups, which are created and maintained manually. If a new client computer is added to the site or to a machine group, the administrator will have to create a separate job to distribute any packages that the client requires.	Uses collections based on SMS queries. Thus, when the query result changes, the collection is updated automatically. This feature greatly simplifies package management in SMS 2.0. Because packages are advertised to collections, when the collection membership is updated, any new members automatically receive the advertisement, and any members removed no longer see the advertisement.
Hardware inventory implementation	Before an administrator can perform any client or package management, SMS has to be installed on the client, and the client's hardware inventory has to be in the SMS database.	Implements hardware inventory as an option rather than a requirement for installing the SMS client, advertising programs, and initiating a Remote Tools session.

(continued)

Table 1-2. *continued*

Feature Change	SMS 1.2	SMS 2.0
Site boundary	Determines site boundaries based on domain structure and management requirements.	Bases a site's boundaries on network topology using IP subnet addresses or Internet Protocol Exchange (IPX) network numbers to assign clients and resources to the site and therefore is not constrained by the Windows NT domain structure.
Sender support	LAN Sender, RAS Asynchronous Sender, RAS ISDN Sender, RAS X.25 Sender, SNA Batch Sender, and SNA Interactive Sender.	Standard Sender (LAN Sender in SMS 1.2), RAS Asynchronous Sender, RAS ISDN Sender, RAS X.25 Sender, SNA RAS Sender (replacing the SMS 1.2 SNA Senders), and Courier Sender.
Remote control	Remote Control settings cannot be preset by the SMS administrator before installing the Remote Control Agent on the client. The settings are configured at each client through the help desk program. Users can potentially modify these settings.	Remote Tools settings—such as which remote options are enabled and requiring permission—can be predefined by the SMS administrator before the Remote Control Agent is installed on the SMS client. Additionally, the Remote Control Agent can now be configured so that the user cannot make any changes to the settings.
Database maintenance	Database maintenance tasks are manual.	Provides scheduled database maintenance routines. Tasks such as backing up the database and site server can now be automated through the SMS Administrator Console.
Network monitoring	Network Monitor Agent needs to be installed as a service on remote clients.	Network Monitor has been enhanced to include experts and monitors to assist the administrator in identifying problem areas in the network infrastructure. No longer needs Network Monitor Agent.

In addition to these feature changes, SMS 2.0 now supports eight site system roles—three more than SMS 1.2. These are described in Table 1-3.

Table 1-3. Server role changes between SMS 1.2 and SMS 2.0

SMS 1.2 Server Role	SMS 2.0 Server Role
Site server Domain controller.	**Site server** Domain controller or member server.
Site database server Any Windows NT 4.0 server running SQL Server 6.0 or later. Does not support SQL Server 7.0.	**Site database server** Any Windows NT 4.0 server running SQL Server 6.5 with Service Pack 4 or later. Supports SQL Server 7.0.
Logon server Domain controller.	**Logon point** Domain controller.
Distribution server Any Windows NT 4.0 server.	**Distribution point** Any Windows NT 4.0 server.
Helper server Any Windows NT 4.0 server; used primarily to designate servers for sender support, such as installing one of the RAS senders on a separate Windows NT RAS server.	**Site system** Any Windows NT 4.0 server running the SMS Executive; used primarily to designate servers for sender support, such as installing one of the RAS senders on a separate Windows NT RAS server.
N/A	**CAP** Any Windows NT 4.0 server; used as the main point of interchange between the client and the site server. These functions were provided by the logon server in SMS 1.2.
N/A	**Software metering server** Any Windows NT 4.0 server
N/A	**Software metering database server** Any Windows NT 4.0 server running SQL Server 6.5 with Service Pack 4 or later. Support SQL Server 7.0.

Note The server roles referred to in Table 1-3 are roles maintained on Windows NT servers. NetWare servers are also supported for some of these roles. The level of support provided by NetWare servers will be referenced as we discuss each role in more detail in later chapters.

Changes have also occurred on the client side with SMS 2.0. Perhaps the most noticeable change has to do with disk space requirements. The SMS 2.0 client installation will require from 12 MB to 15 MB of disk space, depending on the components that are installed. This requirement is largely due to changes made in the way client components function. Unlike the components in SMS 1.2, SMS 2.0 client components run almost entirely as services or service processes on 32-bit clients (Windows 95/98, Windows NT, and Windows 2000). While this change does require additional resources on the client computers, it also results in increased functionality and less user interaction.

Much of the component processing has been implemented as scheduled events on the client computer. For example, hardware inventory frequency in SMS 1.2 was configured at the site server and collected largely as a function of the user logging in and initiating a hardware inventory collection process from the logon server. In SMS 2.0, the Hardware Inventory Client Agent and Software Inventory Client Agent are enabled and configured at the site server and installed on the SMS client. The agents then run on the client computer and collect inventory according to the configured frequency. After the first complete inventory is processed and copied to the CAP, the agent maintains inventory history on the client and sends only changes in subsequent collection cycles. This process results in a significant reduction in network bandwidth utilization and a marked decrease in the amount of time it takes the user to log in.

Note In switching from SMS 1.2 to SMS 2.0, 16-bit client computers (Windows 3.1 and Windows for Workgroups 3.11) will see little change in function. Inventory, for example, will still be initiated during logon and will still collect and send a complete inventory file at each collection cycle.

The SMS client program group is no longer created in SMS 2.0. Instead, any SMS client agents that require any kind of user interaction will be accessible through program icons added to the Control Panel. The SMS.ini file has also been eliminated on 32-bit clients (yeah!). Instead, all SMS client configuration settings are maintained in the registry under the HKEY_LOCAL_MACHINE\SOFTWARE\ MICROSOFT\SMS and NAL keys. In SMS 1.2, the MS\SMS subdirectory structure created when the SMS client is installed was placed in the root directory. In SMS 2.0, this directory structure is created in the operating system directory. This makes the structure less obvious to the user and less tempting for them to erase (double-yeah!).

Summary

As you can see, SMS 2.0 represents a significant advance from previous versions of SMS. It has a robust feature set, increased functionality, improved client support, and extensive status messaging and troubleshooting tools. We've reviewed most of the differences that an SMS 1.2 administrator will encounter when implementing and managing an SMS 2.0 environment. We'll look at more of these changes as we progress through this book.

By now you may be thinking that this all sounds too good to be true. You, of course, will be the ultimate judge as to this product's effectiveness within your own environment. Certainly the product is not flawless. In fact, as with all new version releases of products, there are some, er, um, eccentricities with SMS 2.0. These too will be pointed out as we continue our journey through the world of SMS. But by the time you finish this book, you'll probably agree that SMS 2.0 is rich with features and functions that make it—among products of its kind—the product of choice. Onward, now, to installation!

Chapter 2
Primary Site Installation

This chapter focuses on the process of installing a Microsoft Systems Management Server (SMS) 2.0 primary site server. SMS is relatively easy to install, but its implementation is far from trivial—as you'll see in the course of reading this book. Because the creation of an SMS site requires a great deal of thought, this chapter begins with a discussion of planning considerations. This planning includes identifying such issues as your current network and domain structures, which SMS features you plan to install, and personnel and training concerns. Next we will review preinstallation considerations, including hardware and software requirements and Microsoft SQL Server setup issues. We then look at the installation process itself, examining both express and custom setups. This installation discussion includes instructions for upgrading the site server with SMS 2.0 Service Pack 1. Then we review changes that take place after installation, such as adding SMS services, modifying the Microsoft Windows NT registry, and creating service accounts. We'll also take our first look at the SMS 2.0 directory structure. Last you'll learn how to navigate the SMS Administrator Console and how to remove SMS from the server if necessary.

Planning Considerations

Perhaps the most commonly heard complaint at training sessions for new users of SMS is, "I installed SMS out of the box and I can't get it to work." Unlike Microsoft Word or Microsoft Excel, products that you can install and begin using almost immediately, SMS 2.0 is a more complex application. As we've seen, it contains many features and functions and requires more than just a casual walk-through. Indeed, the importance of determining where and how you will deploy SMS 2.0 can't be stressed enough. In short, planning, planning, planning!

The *Systems Management Server Administrator's Guide* included with SMS 2.0 has an excellent chapter (Chapter 3) that outlines a deployment strategy, so there is really no need for us to reinvent the wheel in that respect. Read that chapter first for the details of SMS planning and site designing. Here we'll look at a few main points that any deployment strategy should take into consideration.

Network Infrastructure

The first, and probably the most important, information you'll need is about your network's infrastructure (boundaries, hierarchy, and connectivity). You should have concise answers to each of the following questions:

- How is your network structured? Is it one large LAN, or is it segmented by routers and remote links into a WAN? This information will influence your placement of SMS sites and site systems.

- What network protocols are you employing? SMS 2.0 requires the use of IP or IPX.

- Into how many subnets is your network divided? Can you identify departments, regions, or other organizational divisions by their subnet? SMS 2.0 assigns clients based on IP address or IPX network number.

- How reliable is your network infrastructure? SMS 2.0 will make the most of well-maintained and optimized networks but will exploit poorly maintained networks. For example, if you are using 100-MB switches but have installed 10-MB network cards in your computers, your throughput will be only 10 MB.

- What Windows NT domain model is in use in your organization? Although not strictly speaking a network infrastructure issue, the Windows NT domain model is generally influenced by the network topology. The Windows NT domain model in use may influence the design of your SMS site hierarchy. If your Windows NT domain structure is no longer efficient or appropriate for your organization's needs, now would be a good time to reconsider and restructure your Windows NT domains.

Once you have a clear understanding of your network infrastructure, you will be better equipped to make other deployment decisions.

Systems Management Server 2.0 Functionality

Next you should consider SMS 2.0 functionality—which is to say you must determine what SMS 2.0 features and functions you intend to implement, and where. You might decide to deploy SMS 2.0 to distribute packages to clients and to collect hardware inventory. Perhaps some clients need to be remotely managed by a help desk while others do not. Perhaps certain departments or regions need to handle their own packages and advertisements. An organization with more diverse requirements may require more SMS 2.0 sites to be installed. For example, client options such as Remote Tools are sitewide options. You cannot deploy Remote Tools for only some clients in a site; instead, you must deploy Remote Tools for *all* clients in a site. This is where a good understanding of your network infrastructure will be beneficial. It may be possible to use your network's subnets to your advantage. In the Remote Tools scenario, if the clients that require Remote Tools support can be segmented to their own subnet, a separate SMS 2.0 site can be installed to provide Remote Tools support.

As another example, suppose the finance department requires that its employees maintain and deploy their own packages within their department. Their packages are specific to their environment and their users. You could manage all the packages from a central site, but doing so would mean that the finance-specific packages might also need to move through a wider network path than is necessary. If the finance department is defined by its own subnet, it can be given its own SMS 2.0 site. Employees can then deploy their packages only within their own subnet and not affect the rest of the network. Remember that creating multiple sites like this is not always desirable, or even practical. These examples simply demonstrate that you need to focus your thinking as you develop a deployment strategy for SMS 2.0.

Another consideration along these lines, and tying in network infrastructure concerns as well, involves the placement and communication of SMS sites and site systems. In general, SMS site systems, such as client access points (CAPs), logon points, and distribution points, should reside within the same LAN as the site server and SMS database server, or they must at least have reliable, high-speed connections available if they are located remotely. This requirement is due largely to the amount of information that is transferred between these site systems and the site server. The network traffic involved will be discussed as we talk about enabling and managing each SMS feature later in this book. For now, let's look at one scenario.

Hardware inventory is collected on the SMS client by the Hardware Inventory Client Agent, with changes copied to a CAP. The CAP, in turn, sends the changes on to the site server. The site server updates the SMS database with the change information. The amount of data that is generated, and the corresponding network bandwidth that will be used, will be determined by the number of clients involved and how frequently inventory information is collected. Bandwidth considerations will generally be less of a concern within a local network than across a wide area link. In other words, it will be more efficient and perhaps less disruptive to the network to collect this inventory if the client, CAP, site server, and database are all located in the same LAN.

Now suppose that your company needs to send packages from a central location to various geographic regions around the world. Package files are copied to distribution points within the SMS site. These files include source files, programs, and installation scripts and can represent a fairly large amount of data. Microsoft Office, for example, could require more than 200 MB of storage space. This data must be moved across the network to the distribution points, and generally moves in an uncompressed state. You could certainly plan for one large SMS 2.0 site, with distribution points in each geographic region. Your packages will then need to be copied to these distribution points across WAN links and will have to contend with any other WAN traffic that may be occurring. Alternatively, you could plan for an SMS site in each geographic region. Each SMS site can have one or more local distribution points. Package files are compressed before they are sent from one site to another. Also, you can adjust how much bandwidth is actually used when communicating from one site to another. This arrangement should significantly improve WAN performance related to package distribution.

Personnel, Training, and Testing

As you develop your deployment strategy, keep in mind who needs to use SMS 2.0. The features and functions of SMS 2.0 can easily be delegated to various users. Help desk personnel, for example, can be given access to Remote Tools but not to any other features. An SMS administrator in the finance department might be given the ability to create packages and advertisements and to deploy them only to finance department users. This distribution of tasks is an essential part of determining where and how to implement SMS 2.0 and to establish the appropriate levels of training and security required. Security options are explored in Chapter 16.

Another consideration might be staffing issues. In a small site, one person may be responsible for most or all SMS-related support issues, including not only things like package distribution and remote control, but also site design, database maintenance, network analysis and troubleshooting, status message analysis, SQL administration, package scripting, and general troubleshooting. But in a medium-sized SMS site structure—let's say three SMS sites with perhaps a thousand clients—one person will be hard-pressed to adequately maintain all aspects of the SMS sites. In fact, each site should have at least one SMS administrator assigned. In an ideal setting, SMS 2.0 will be provided with a support team among whose members tasks will be divided throughout the SMS site structure. Remember that SMS 2.0 is designed to be a network management tool. This product is not trivial to set up or to maintain. Treat it with the same consideration that you give your Windows NT domain support and your network infrastructure support. It truly requires no less.

Along with appropriate staffing comes appropriate training. Even if management and budget constraints would prefer it otherwise, SMS 2.0 is definitely not the kind of product that you can install out of the box and begin using immediately. (You will hopefully come to this conclusion yourself by the end of this book.) And while you could teach yourself how to use SMS 2.0, the most effective learning environment will be one that is structured and controlled, and one in which you can freely destroy SMS if you like!

Several Microsoft-certified training centers offer courses in SMS 2.0. Other training centers offer their own versions of SMS 2.0 training. You should seriously consider some kind of formal training for yourself and your staff before rolling out SMS 2.0. This training might cover administrative tasks for those users involved in the day-to-day operations of SMS 2.0, such as using Remote Tools or creating advertising packages. For those staffers involved in the background support of SMS 2.0, training should include a thorough review of SMS services and processes, security, site system roles, network traffic considerations, and performance issues. Guides such as this book will serve to supplement and reinforce that training.

More Info   For information about courses, certifications, and training providers, refer to Microsoft's training Web page, at *www.microsoft.com/train_cert*.

Consider too the possibility of instituting a lab environment in which you can simulate your network environment, experiment with different site and site system configurations, perform stress testing on site systems and network load—without worrying about damaging SMS. Such an undertaking is not always possible, of course, but think of how much time, energy, and expense you might save by testing your SMS strategy in a lab rather than in live production.

Client and Server Configuration

The configuration topic includes two areas of concern: current configuration and standard configuration. SMS 2.0 does have some specific hardware and software requirements for both the server and the client computers. As part of your deployment strategy, it would be more than prudent to canvass your current install base of computers and determine which ones meet the requirements to be SMS clients and SMS site systems. You can then identify those computers that require upgrades in software or hardware and those instances in which an investment in new equipment is preferred. With the help of SMS 2.0, you can establish hardware and software standards for your organization that will be applicable to all new computers purchased, and you can identify those current computers to which the standards must be applied. As you continue to test and refine your network infrastructure, again with the help of SMS 2.0, these standards may be extended to include recommendations for network devices, protocols, and communication links as well.

Preinstallation Requirements

In this section, we'll explore the specific hardware and software requirements for SMS sites and site systems, beginning with Microsoft SQL Server because it is an integral part of SMS and because the SQL Server database serves as the repository for most of the data that SMS collects. To that end, we will explore database size and security considerations as well as SQL Server optimization considerations. We will also explore the hardware and software requirements of the Windows NT server that will become your SMS site server.

SQL Server Requirements

SMS 2.0 requires a server running SQL Server 6.5 with Service Pack 4 or later applied or SQL Server 7.0. In SQL Server 6.5, databases and their corresponding transaction logs are created and maintained in devices. A *SQL device* represents a placeholder, or predefined storage space, for the database and for its transaction log. SMS requires separate devices for the SMS database and for the transaction log. As with SMS 1.2, if SQL Server is installed on the same computer as the SMS site server, SMS can create the database and log devices for you. If SQL Server is installed on a separate computer, you must create the database and log devices before you install SMS 2.0.

> **Note**   If you are using SQL Server 6.5 with Service Pack 4, you will also need
> to copy an updated file from the SMS 2.0 CD to avoid potential general protection
> faults. Copy the file Sqlcrt60.dll from the Sqlsetup\Sqlhotfix\<*platform*> folder
> on the SMS 2.0 CD to the Mssql\Binn folder on the SQL server. SQL Server 6.5
> with Service Pack 5 and SQL Server 7.0 are not affected.

SQL Server 7.0 does not require the creation of devices for the database and log
files. Instead, the database and transaction logs are maintained in separate files.
Again, if SMS 2.0 is to be installed on the same computer as SQL Server, SMS 2.0
can create the database and log files for you. If not, you will need to create the
files ahead of time.

If you install SMS 2.0 on the same computer as SQL Server, SMS 2.0 will not only
create the devices for you, but it will also tune SQL Server for use with SMS 2.0.
This does not, of course, relieve you of all responsibility for maintaining the SQL
server, but it does ease some of the setup concerns regarding SQL Server, which
is especially helpful if you have little experience with SQL Server.

> **More Info**   While a working knowledge of SQL Server is not required to install
> and work with SMS 2.0, in the long run, you will need a good working knowledge
> of at least SQL Server administration tasks. SMS 2.0 is not itself a database
> server; rather, it acts as a front end to the SMS database maintained in
> SQL Server. Therefore, many database maintenance tasks will need to be initi-
> ated through SQL Server. Consider taking a class in SQL Server administration,
> such as Microsoft-certified course 832, "System Administration for Microsoft
> SQL Server 7.0," or 867, "System Administration for Microsoft SQL Server 6.5."

If SQL Server is not already installed on the proposed site server, the SMS 2.0
installation process will prompt you for the SQL Server 6.5 or 7.0 source files and
will install a dedicated SQL Server database for itself. In the case of SQL Server 6.5,
the installation will also automatically apply SQL Server Service Pack 4.

The burning question then becomes, "Which is better: installing SQL Server on
the same computer as the site server, or installing it on a separate server?" Well,
it all depends. Microsoft recommends that you have a dedicated installation of
SQL Server just for SMS 2.0. This is because of the significant increase in information SMS 2.0 now stores in the database, the over 200 SQL transactions and
triggers related to SMS 2.0 processes and services, the 50 connection accounts
required just for the site server, the resource requirements of SQL Server itself,

and the fact that SMS 2.0 installs Windows Management Instrumentation (WMI) on the SQL Server and uses it to provide access to the database for the SMS Administrator Console.

Installing SQL Server on the same computer as the site server will provide more efficient access to the database for the site server and will significantly reduce network traffic involved with SMS-SQL transactions. However, this arrangement will also require an increased investment in hardware on the proposed site server computer to accommodate the resource requirements for both SMS 2.0 and SQL Server. This cost will be felt in three areas:

- **Processing memory (RAM)**   SMS 2.0 requires a minimum of 64 MB of RAM, with 128 MB recommended and, quite frankly, 256 MB standard. SQL Server requires a minimum of 32 MB of RAM and is driven largely by the size of the databases it will maintain. So the total RAM requirement will be significant. On the other hand, RAM is relatively inexpensive.

- **Disk storage and I/O**   SMS 2.0 requires a minimum of 1 GB of disk storage, with a recommended size of 6 GB. SQL Server can require up to 266 MB, depending on the type of installation, and this does not take into account the amount of storage required for the database itself. SMS 2.0 has an automatic minimum of 50 MB for the database and 20 MB for the transaction log. Most SMS 2.0 and SQL processes are disk intensive, so the faster the disk access, the better the performance gained. Unlike RAM, disk upgrades can be costly. For example, hardware-based redundant array of independent disk (RAID) systems offering disk mirroring (RAID 1) and/or disk striping with parity (RAID 5) provide excellent I/O performance as well as fault tolerance in the event of a disk failure. However, such a system can cost $10,000 or more.

- **Processor**   The type of processor used will obviously affect the performance of the site server. SMS 2.0 requires at least a 133-MHz processor, while SQL Server 7.0 requires at least a 166-MHz processor. Both support the Alpha platform, which provides better performance and more efficient processing. However, you may lose some SMS 2.0 functionality. For example, software metering is not supported on an Alpha-platform site server. The newer Pentium III 500MHz processors in a dual-processor system would be preferable for optimum performance. Again, these types of systems are not inexpensive.

Ultimately you will need to balance resource requirements, network traffic concerns, and overall performance considerations when deciding whether to use a single computer for both SQL Server and SMS 2.0 or to use separate computers.

Sizing the Database

SMS 2.0 requires a minimum database device size (for SQL Server 6.5) or file size (for SQL Server 7.0) of 50 MB and a transaction log device or file size of 20 MB. Microsoft recommends anticipating between 100 KB and 200 KB per client for the database. The transaction log should be at least 20 percent of the database size. Additional factors in determining the amount of database space required include the amount of hardware and software inventory collected, the number of packages, programs and advertisements that will be deployed, the size and number of collections, the type and number of discovered resources, and the number of queries and status messages to be maintained.

The Microsoft Systems Management Server Version 2.0 Release Notes offer the following formula for determining database size:

$$7.4 \text{ MB} + (x * 70 \text{ KB}) \text{ where } x = \text{number of clients}$$

This formula is based on a weekly hardware and software inventory schedule, default aging (the number of days)of discovery and inventory out of the database, and 20 status messages reported by each client each week. If we apply this formula to a single site with 1000 clients, we get:

$$7.4 \text{ MB} + (1000 * 70 \text{ KB}) = 77.4 \text{ MB}$$

Using the base value of 100 KB per client, we would require 100 MB. As you can see, sizing the database is not an exact science, and it will require that you monitor database usage periodically.

Tip The Microsoft Systems Management Server Version 2.0 Release Notes comes on the SMS 2.0 CD and is installed with SMS 2.0. You can access it through the Systems Management program group.

As if this weren't enough to consider, don't forget your site hierarchy. If you have identified child sites, these sites will report their inventory, discovery records, status messages, and site configuration to their parent site. You must allow space for this additional information in the parent site's SMS database. Needless to say, the greatest cause for concern regarding database space will be at the central site, as it will collect and maintain database information for every site below it in the site hierarchy.

Database Security

Two basic types of security are available for the SQL Server database: integrated and standard. *Integrated security* indicates that SQL Server will use a Windows NT domain account to provide access to the database. *Standard security* indicates that you will create or identify a SQL login ID within SQL Server itself that will provide access to the database. The default SQL login ID is sa, which stands for *system administrator* and has no password assigned.

If you use integrated security, you can create a Windows NT account that SMS will use to create and access the database in SQL Server and then map that account to the sa account using the SQL Security Manager, or you can let SMS use the existing SMS Service account. The SMS Service account (named *SMSService* by default) is created when you install SMS and is the default account that site server services use to manage Windows NT site systems. By default, all members of the Administrators group in the SQL Server are mapped to the sa account. If the SQL Server is a member of the same domain as the SMS site server, SMS can use the SMS Service account to access the database, as this account becomes a member of the Domain Admins global group in the Windows NT domain, which is, by default, a member of the local Administrators group on every member server in the domain. If the SQL Server is not a member of the same domain, you can either establish a trust relationship between the domain in which the SQL Server resides and the domain in which the SMS site server resides, and add the Domain Admins group from the SMS domain to the Administrators local group on the SQL Server, or you can explicitly create a duplicate account (and password) in the SQL domain so that Windows NT pass-through authentication can allow access to the SQL Server and thus the database.

If you use standard security, use the SQL Server Enterprise Manager to create the SQL login ID and assign it access to the database. You will then provide the SQL login ID to SMS 2.0 during setup.

Tuning SQL Server

If you install SQL Server as part of the SMS 2.0 setup process, SMS will set SQL Server parameters to their optimum settings for you. However, if you install SQL Server yourself you should pay attention to some specific SQL Server configuration parameters and set them appropriately before installing SMS 2.0. Table 2-1 lists these parameters and provide guidelines as to how they should be set.

Table 2-1. **SQL Server configuration parameters**

Parameter	Guidelines
User Connections	SMS 2.0 requires a minimum of 40 user connections for the site server and 2 connections for each SMS Administrator Console you plan to install. It also requires 5 additional user connections for each instance of the SMS Administrator Console, if more than five consoles will be running concurrently on your site. You can set SMS 2.0 to calculate this number and configure it automatically during setup. Each installation of SMS 2.0 requires 20 user connections. In SQL Server 6.5, each user connection allocates 40 KB of RAM. In SQL 7.0, this allocation is made dynamically at the time of the connection, providing more efficient memory management.
Open Objects	This parameter indicates the number of tables, views, stored procedures, and the like that can be open at a time. If you exceed the specified number of open objects, SQL Server must close some objects before it can open others, resulting in a performance hit. For most sites, although the default is *500*, you may want to set this parameter to *1000*. For large sites, this number could be *5000* or more. Use SQL Server Performance Monitor counters to track the number of open objects in use to determine the optimum number for the SMS site. Note that SQL Server 7.0 sizes this number automatically.
Memory	This parameter indicates the amount of RAM that should be used for database caching and management. SMS automatically allocates 16 MB of RAM for SQL Server use. In SQL Server 6.5, memory is allocated in memory units of 2 KB. Set this value to at least *8192* (16 MB). Increasing this number may improve SQL Server performance, but it may also detract from other server operations (such as SMS site server).

SQL Server 7.0 allocates memory dynamically in 8-KB units. You can define a range for SQL Server to use. |
| *Locks* | This parameter prevents users from accessing and updating the same data at the same time. Because of the volume of information contained in the database, Microsoft recommends setting this value from *5000* to *10,000* depending on the size of the database and the number of SMS Administrator Consoles. |
| *tempdb Size* | The temporary database and log are used to manage queries and sorts. By default, the tempdb database and log information are maintained in the same SQL device. (Please see Chapter 18 for details on the SQL device.) For best performance, both should be kept in this default location. Note that this is contrary to what the *Systems Management Server Administrator's Guide* recommends for high volumes of activity. This recommendation was later corrected in the Microsoft Systems Management Server Version 2.0 Release Notes.

Set the tempdb data device size in SQL Server 6.5 to at least 20 percent of the SMS database device size. Set the tempdb log device size to at least 20 percent of the tempdb data device size. In SQL Server 7.0, as you have by now surmised, the tempdb database is sized dynamically. |

While system clock synchronizing is not a function of SQL Server per se, it is nevertheless important that you synchronize the system clocks between the SQL Server and the SMS site server if they are installed on separate computers. When an SMS service or process schedules a task, it will use the SQL Server's system clock to trigger the task.

Real World   Synchronizing System Clocks

Conventional and unconventional wisdom alike suggest that you identify a time server for your SMS site that synchronizes the system clocks not only between the SQL Server and the SMS site server, but also among all SMS site systems and SMS clients. This should be an essential part of your deployment strategy for SMS 2.0. SMS services use the SQL Server system clock when scheduling tasks. However, SMS clients and site systems will look to their own system clocks when determining when scheduled tasks should run. Scheduling tasks is perhaps most critical with SMS clients.

When you advertise a program to a collection of SMS clients, you can assign a schedule for that program to run, or you can make the program mandatory to run at an assigned time. Advertised Programs Client Agent, the SMS client agent that checks for available advertisements, will determine whether the program is scheduled to run at an assigned time or a mandatory time. However, the agent will determine this schedule based on the system clock of the SMS client. If the system clock is inaccurate for some reason, the program may not run at the expected time, and may never run.

Here's an example. Suppose you have a user who obtains trial software that is time-stamped to run for a specific trial period—say, 120 days. The user decides that she likes the product, but she does not want to actually buy it. To keep using the software beyond the proscribed time period, the easy thing to do is to set the system clock back—perhaps a couple months, or perhaps a year. Not touching on the legal or ethical issues involved here, this tampering can wreak havoc on your advertised programs. As you can see, something scheduled to run today may in fact never run on this user's SMS clients.

The steps involved in creating devices, databases, security accounts, and so on are outlined in Chapter 18.

Caution A final thought about SQL Server preparations: be sure to set SQL Server services to autostart after installing SQL Server manually. If you don't, you could be in for a big surprise after you install SMS 2.0 and then restart the server.

Site Server Requirements

SMS 2.0 site servers have specific hardware and software requirements, including disk space, memory, processor, and operating system requirements. In this section, we'll examine these requirements, as well as explore other platform considerations, such as Windows Terminal Server and Cluster Server support.

Hardware Requirements

SMS 2.0 has the following hardware and platform requirements:

- Be sure that your computer hardware is included on the Windows NT Hardware Compatibility List (HCL). It is sometimes possible to install Windows NT Server 4.0 on computers whose hardware components may not be on the HCL. However, when you install a Microsoft BackOffice product onto such a server, you may experience anomalous activity—such as the "blue screen of death." It's not worth the gamble.

- The server platform can be Intel, Alpha, or a compatible system.

- SMS 2.0 requires a minimum processor type of Pentium 133 MHz. The more powerful (and plentiful) the processor, the better performance you will see. A dual-processor Pentium III 500 MHz is recommended if your budget allows, or a dual-processor Alpha-based server.

- SMS 2.0 requires a minimum of 64 MB to 96 MB of RAM. Of this, 16 MB is automatically allocated to SQL Server. SMS 2.0 running on a 64-MB server is not a pretty sight. As RAM is a relatively inexpensive upgrade, you should install at least 256 MB, testing performance under various load conditions and then upgrading RAM as necessary.

- SMS 2.0 must be installed on a Windows NT file system (NTFS) partition. SMS 2.0 uses NTFS permissions to secure access to SMS directories and shares.

- SMS 2.0 requires that a minimum of 500 MB of hard disk space be available on the NTFS partition, as well as 100 MB of free space on the operating system partition. While SMS 2.0 will install under this configuration, this configuration also implies that you are working with a relatively small stand-alone SMS site. Microsoft recommends starting at 1 GB and working up from there, depending on such factors as the system roles the site server will employ, the number of clients and resources that will be managed, and the number of packages, programs, and advertisements that will be generated. For example, 2 GB of free space may be sufficient if the site server functions as a logon point and a CAP in a medium-sized stand-alone site. However, if the site server will also function as a distribution point, you will almost certainly require additional disk space for storing the package files.

Note A medium-sized stand-alone site refers to a site with a few thousand clients that is collecting hardware and software inventory, status messages, and discovery data based on the SMS 2.0 default settings. The assumption is that the site averages two to three packages a week of about 20 to 30 MB in size, and two to three advertisements a week. These examples should be taken as soft guidelines only. As always, you must test your SMS 2.0 configuration within the unique requirements of your own organization and modify it to provide you with satisfactory performance parameters.

- Microsoft also recommends a higher video resolution than you might have on most servers running Windows NT 4.0. SMS 2.0 will function just fine with a standard VGA resolution monitor. However, if you plan to use the SMS Administrator Console on the site server itself for regular site tasks, consider setting video resolution to at least 256 colors, 800 by 600 pixels.

- Microsoft also always mentions the following two devices in its requirements list, although it's hard to imagine purchasing a server nowadays without them: a mouse and a CD-ROM drive. (Performing SMS 2.0 tasks using only keyboard shortcuts is possible, but would be ill-advised.)

SMS 2.0 and Alpha-Platform Support

SMS 2.0 does support the Alpha-platform computer system, but keep the following limitations in mind:

- SMS 2.0 supports Alpha servers using Windows NT 4.0 only if Windows NT 4.0 Service Pack 4 or later has been applied, as well as Microsoft Windows 2000 servers that are not running Active Directory.

- SMS 2.0 does not support Alpha servers or workstations if they are using Windows NT 3.51 or earlier.

- Alpha site systems do not support the software metering function of SMS 2.0. However, Alpha clients using TCP/IP are supported as valid software metering clients.

- If a parent or child site to an Alpha site server has enabled software metering, the Alpha site server will be unable to forward software metering data from either the parent or the child.

Software Requirements

In addition to the hardware requirements already outlined, you need to consider the following software requirements before beginning the SMS installation process:

- The SMS 2.0 site server must be installed on a server running Windows NT 4.0 that is fully Y2K-compliant, meaning that Windows NT 4.0, Service Pack 4 must be applied. The server must have Microsoft Internet Explorer 4.01 with Service Pack 1 or later. SMS 2.0 uses Internet Explorer for its online help. Also, the server must be running Microsoft Data Access Components (MDAC) 2.0 with Service Pack 1. Microsoft has included all these on the SMS 2.0 CD. When you insert the CD, it will autorun and display four options. Choose the Install NT 4.0 SP4a option, as shown in Figure 2-1. (Alternatively, you could install these options directly from the Ntqfe\Nt4sp4a\I386 or Alpha directories on the SMS 2.0 CD.)

Caution If Windows NT 4.0 Service Pack 5 is used to install the SMS 2.0 server, you must install MDAC 2.0 Service Pack 1 because it is not included in Windows NT 4.0 Service Pack 5.

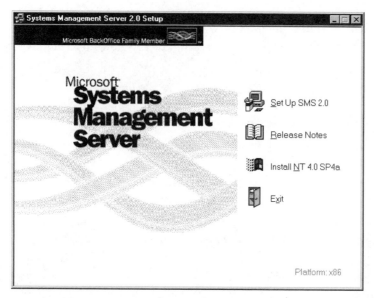

Figure 2-1. *The autorun screen that appears when you insert the SMS 2.0 CD.*

- The SMS site server can also be installed on servers running Windows NT 4.0, Enterprise Edition (again fully Y2K-compliant), and Windows 2000 servers that are members of an existing Windows NT 4.0 domain. SMS 2.0 does not currently support Windows 2000 servers running Active Directory for any site system role. Site servers cannot be implemented on any Novell NetWare platform.

- SMS 2.0, as we've seen, requires SQL Server 6.5 with Service Pack 4 or later applied, or SQL Server 7.0. Either can be installed as part of the SMS 2.0 setup routine. See the section "SQL Server Requirements" earlier in this chapter for a discussion of the merits of having SMS 2.0 perform the SQL Server installation for you.

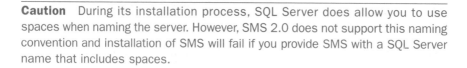

Caution During its installation process, SQL Server does allow you to use spaces when naming the server. However, SMS 2.0 does not support this naming convention and installation of SMS will fail if you provide SMS with a SQL Server name that includes spaces.

The SMS 2.0 CD also contains a Windows NT 4.0 hotfix file that rectifies a memory leak that is sometimes caused by running the SNMPTest utility to obtain a load signature for the Windows NT Simple Network Management Protocol (SNMP) agent. As with all such hotfixes, this one should be applied only if you encounter this problem. Otherwise, wait for the next Windows NT Service Pack, which will include the same hotfix fully regression-tested. The file is named Smsfix.exe and can be found in the Ntqfe\Nthotfix\I386 or Alpha directory on the SMS 2.0 CD.

More Info   This memory leak issue and the hotfix are discussed in Microsoft Knowledge Base Article #Q196270. You can find this article at *http://support.microsoft.com/support/kb/articles/q196/2/70.asp*.

Windows NT Terminal Server and Cluster Server Considerations

SMS 2.0 provides only limited support for Windows NT 4.0 Terminal Server in both server and client roles. The only site system role that SMS 2.0 supports is distribution point. Only five client features are supported: hardware inventory, software inventory, Network Monitor, remote Windows NT client installation, and manual client installation (provided the CHANGE USER /INSTALL command is executed on the client first).

SMS 2.0 does not directly support Cluster Server. If you do install SMS 2.0 on a Windows NT 4.0 Enterprise server using Cluster Server, be sure to take the following precautions:

- Do not install the site server or any site systems on the shared drive of any cluster.

- Install the site server or any site systems on only one side of a cluster. If one side of a cluster is a site system, the other side must be an SMS client.

- Do not install SMS 2.0 at all if the domain controllers in the site are clustered. If you enable either the Windows Networking Logon Discovery or Windows Networking Logon Client Installation method, SMS 2.0 will by default set up *all* domain controllers as logon points, which would violate the second item in this list.

Installing a Primary Site Server

Now that you have created a viable deployment strategy for your SMS 2.0 site, decided how to install and configure your SQL Server, and confirmed the hardware and software requirements necessary for a successful installation of SMS 2.0, it's time to begin the installation process itself. This section will concentrate on the installation of an SMS 2.0 primary site server. Installing secondary site servers and other site system roles will be discussed in Chapters 3 and 4.

Installation Options

You can install your SMS 2.0 site server using a variety of techniques and options. You may install directly from the CD, or you can first copy the source files from CD to the local hard disk of the proposed site server or a network drive. If you choose to copy the source files to a drive location, be sure to copy the entire SMS 2.0 CD, as the installation process does require files located in the Alpha directories.

Once you have located the source files, you can run the installation interactively through the Systems Management Server 2.0 Setup Wizard by inserting the SMS 2.0 CD and choosing Set Up SMS 2.0 from the autorun menu shown in Figure 2-1, or you can run the installation from a Windows NT command line. The command-line syntax is shown here:

SETUP [/?] [/SCRIPT *scriptname*] [/UPGRADE] [/NODISKCHECK] [/NOACCTCHECK]

The command-line method provides five switch options to initiate the setup process under different circumstances, as outlined in Table 2-2. If you execute the SMS 2.0 setup from the command line, you will still launch the SMS 2.0 Setup Wizard, which presents you with a series of nice, "user-friendly" installation screens that guide you every step of the way.

Two installation options are available once you begin the setup process: Express Setup and Custom Setup. Express Setup installs SMS 2.0 with a complete set of SMS 2.0 components and features including Crystal Info; Custom Setup lets you choose which components and features to install.

Table 2-2. Command-line switch options

Switch	Description
/?	Displays a pop-up dialog box listing and describing each switch along with the command-line syntax.
/SCRIPT *scriptname*	Allows you to specify a path and script file, which provides the different pieces of information required during setup for unattended installation.
/UPGRADE	Allows to you specify an unattended upgrade from an earlier version of SMS.
/NODISKCHECK	Allows you to perform the installation without having SMS 2.0 check for available disk space first. Assumes you have already confirmed that you have the required amount of disk space available.
/NOACCTCHECK	Allows you to perform the installation without having SMS 2.0 check the specified service account for the appropriate level of permission and rights. Assumes that you have already created the account and have given it the appropriate administrative permissions and the Logon As A Service user right.

Caution Don't use Express Setup for sites with more than 500 clients. If you choose to install Crystal Info as one of your options in Custom Setup, the Setup Wizard will display a message box describing a Crystal Info limitation. In brief, the version of Crystal Info supplied with SMS 2.0 is meant for single SMS sites with fewer than 500 clients. It is a sample snap-in only. If you intend to use Crystal Info with larger sites, do not select Crystal Info for installation on your site server. Instead, create a separate site server for which the only optional SMS component you will select is Crystal Info. You will then need to make this site an SMS parent site for the actual site. Refer to the Microsoft Systems Management Server Version 2.0 Release Notes for more information about this workaround.

Table 2-3 outlines the SMS components and features that are installed and the default values that are set for each. Features, discovery methods, installation methods, and client agents have additional options that can be configured; these elements are discussed in their respective chapters later in this book.

Table 2-3. SMS 2.0 components installed during setup

Component	Express Install	Default Value	Custom Install
SMS 2.0 Features			
SMS site server	Installed	N/A	Installed
SMS Administrator Console	Installed	N/A	Installed
Crystal Info	Installed	N/A	Optional
NetWare Bindery support	Not installed	N/A	Optional
NetWare NDS support	Not installed	N/A	Optional
Network Monitor	Installed	N/A	Optional
Package automation scripts	Installed (Note: only scripts, not source files)	N/A	Optional
Product compliance database	Installed	N/A	Optional
Remote Tools	Installed	N/A	Optional
SMS Installer	Installation point created	N/A	Optional
Software metering	Installed	Enabled	Optional
Discovery Methods			
Windows Networking Logon Discovery	Enabled	Every logon; Modify Logon Script option disabled	Disabled
Windows NT User Discovery	Enabled	Once a day at midnight	Disabled
Windows NT User Group Discovery	Enabled	Once a day at midnight	Disabled
NetWare NDS Logon Discovery	Disabled	N/A	Disabled
NetWare Bindery Logon Discovery	Disabled	N/A	Disabled
Heartbeat Discovery	Enabled	Once a week for Custom Setup; once a day for Express Setup	Enabled
Network Discovery	Disabled	N/A	Disabled

Table 2-3. *continued*

Component	Express Install	Default Value	Custom Install
Installation Methods			
Windows Networking Logon Client Installation	Enabled	N/A	Disabled
NetWare Bindery Logon Client Installation	Disabled	N/A	Disabled
NetWare NDS Logon Client Installation	Disabled	N/A	Disabled
Windows NT Remote Client Installation	Enabled for servers, workstations, and domain controllers running Windows NT	N/A	Disabled
Client Agents			
Advertised Programs Client Agent	Enabled	Polls every 60 minutes for advertised programs; scheduled programs have 5-minute countdown	Disabled
Event To Trap Translator Client Agent	Enabled	N/A	Disabled
Hardware Inventory Client Agent	Enabled	Once a week	Disabled
Software Inventory Client Agent	Enabled	Once a week	Disabled
Remote Tools Client Agent	Enabled	All remote options enabled; user permission required; user notified; user can make changes	Disabled
Software Metering Client Agent	Enabled	Polls for configuration changes every 4 hours (240 minutes); licensing not enforced	Disabled

Express Setup is a fast and easy way to install SMS 2.0 and is recommended for small stand-alone sites or test environments. Express Setup also installs a dedicated SQL Server 6.5 (with Service Pack 4 automatically applied) or SQL Server 7.0 on the same server; creates and configures SQL Server data devices for SQL Server 6.5, database files for SQL Server 7.0, and SQL Server parameters (as discussed in the section "SQL Server Requirements" earlier in this chapter); and creates all necessary service accounts. When installation is complete, the site server will assume the site system roles of CAP and distribution point. It will also assume the role of logon point if the site server is also a Windows NT domain controller. If it is not, Express Setup will configure all domain controllers in the site server Windows NT domain as logon points for the site.

> **Note**   The Express Setup method is supported for servers running Windows NT Enterprise Edition and for servers running SQL Server 6.5, but not for servers running both applications together.

The Custom Setup option installs SMS 2.0 with the basic site server and SMS Administrator Console installed. All other SMS 2.0 features and components are options that can be selected as desired. You can always leave an option unselected and install it at a later time. If the option is selected, it will be installed, but not enabled by default. Once an option is installed, it cannot be uninstalled without removing and reinstalling SMS 2.0. The site server will assume the site system roles of CAP and distribution point. However, unlike Express Setup, if the site server is a domain controller, it will not assume the role of logon point until Windows Networking Logon Discovery or Windows Networking Logon Client Installation has been enabled.

Like Express Setup, Custom Setup installs a dedicated SQL Server 6.5 (with Service Pack 4 automatically applied) or SQL Server 7.0 on the same server; creates and configures SQL Server data devices for SQL Server 6.5, database files for SQL Server 7.0, and SQL Server parameters; and creates all necessary service accounts. If SQL Server has already been installed and configured on the proposed site server computer, you will be presented with only the Custom installation option.

Running Setup

To install a primary site server, follow these steps:

1. Either execute Setup.exe from the command line, by inserting the SMS 2.0 CD and choosing Set Up SMS 2.0 from the autorun menu (shown in Figure 2-1), or enter the path to the SMS 2.0 source files and execute Autorun.exe to display the autorun menu.

2. The welcome screen appears, as shown in Figure 2-2.

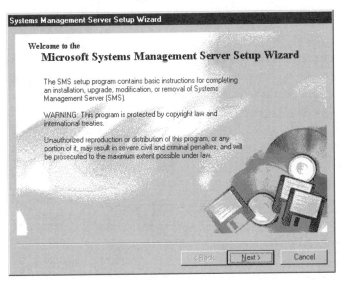

Figure 2-2. *The Setup Wizard welcome screen.*

3. Click Next to display the System Configuration screen, shown in Figure 2-3. At this time, Setup checks to see if you have any earlier versions of SMS installed or if the server is already functioning as an SMS site system.

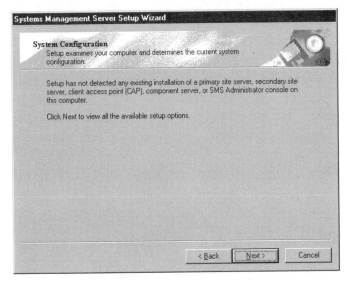

Figure 2-3. *The System Configuration screen.*

4. Click Next to display the Setup Options screen, as shown in Figure 2-4. If no current installation of an SMS site server or site system is detected, the first three options will be enabled. You can install a primary site, a secondary site, or just the SMS Administrator Console. If an existing SMS 2.0 site server is detected, the last three options will be enabled. In this case, you can upgrade the existing installation by adding additional SMS components, remove SMS 2.0, or modify or reset the installation—for example, by changing service account names and passwords or re-building a site control file. If the Setup Wizard detects a site server installation for an earlier version of SMS, only the Upgrade An Existing SMS Installation option will be enabled. In this case, select Install An SMS Primary Site and click Next.

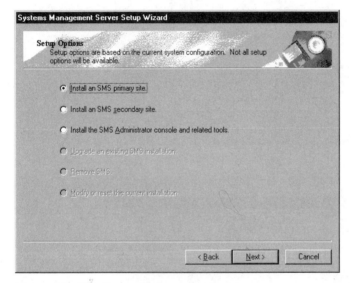

Figure 2-4. *The Setup Options screen.*

Note If the Setup Wizard detects an existing installation of an SMS site system such as a CAP or a logon point, you will not be able to continue the installation until you remove that site system from the SMS site it is a member of.

5. If you have not already installed SQL Server on the same server as the proposed site server, the Installation Options screen will appear, as shown in Figure 2-5. Choose Express Setup or Custom Setup.

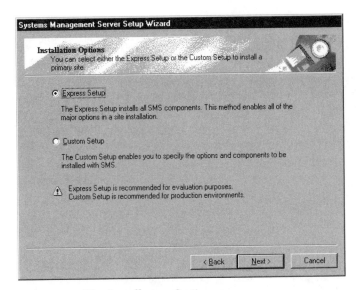

Figure 2-5. *The Installation Options screen.*

6. Click Next to display the License Agreement screen, shown in Figure 2-6. Read this agreement carefully, and signify your acceptance by selecting I Agree.

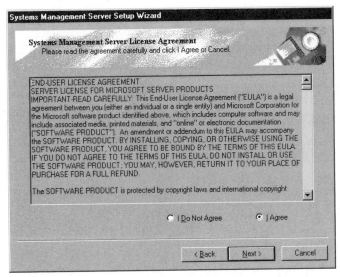

Figure 2-6. *The Systems Management Server License Agreement screen.*

7. Click Next to display the Product Registration screen, shown in Figure 2-7, and enter the name, the organization name, and the CD key located on the back of your SMS 2.0 CD case.

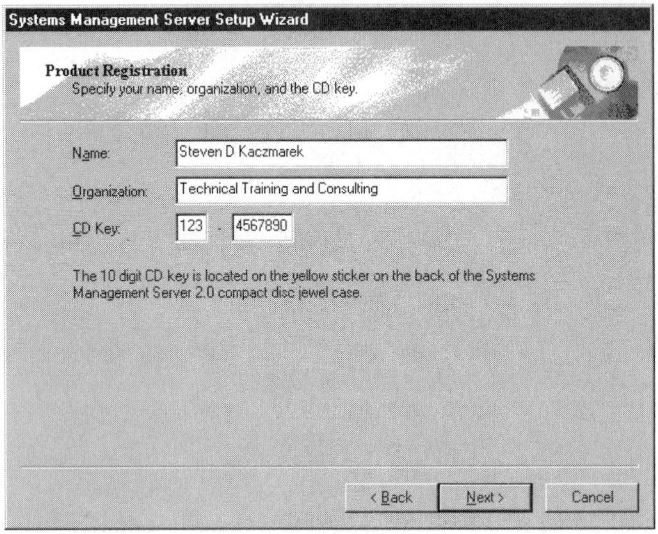

Figure 2-7. *The Product Registration screen.*

8. Click Next to display the SMS Site Information screen, shown in Figure 2-8, which asks you to supply the three-character site code you want to assign to this site, a descriptive site name, and the Windows NT domain in which you are installing the site.

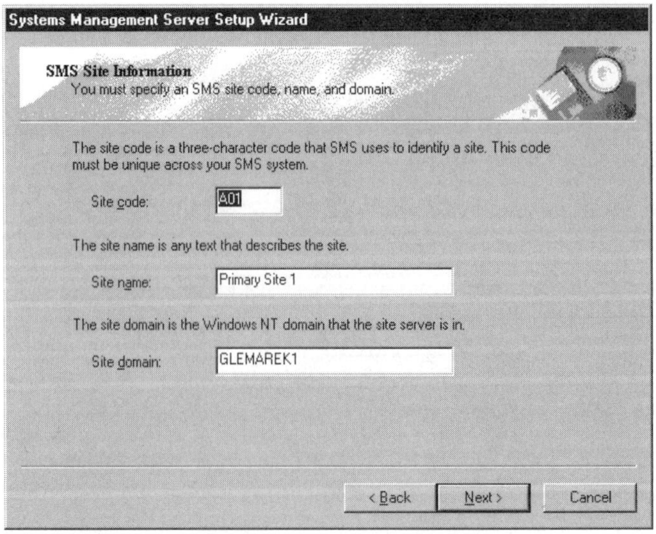

Figure 2-8. *The SMS Site Information screen.*

The site code is limited to three characters and must be unique across your SMS hierarchy. The site name is descriptive, limited to 50 characters (including spaces) and should reflect the location or function of the site, such as *Awesome Computer Central Site* or *Finance Primary Site*. It is usually a good idea to specify whether the site is central, primary, or secondary. Once this information is entered, it sticks—with the exception of the site name, which is merely descriptive. If you need to change the domain name or the site code later, you will need to remove this installation of SMS and reinstall it.

9. Click Next to display the SMS Service Account Information screen, shown in Figure 2-9. Here you will need to specify the name and domain of the SMS Service account you will be using. If you have not created one yourself, either accept the default account *SMSService* or enter the name of the account you would like SMS to create. SMS will automatically assign it the appropriate group memberships and user rights. If you have already created this account using User Manager For Domains in Windows NT, specify it here using the convention *domain\account*. Be sure you have already assigned the account the appropriate group memberships in the SMS site domain (Domain Admins, Domain Users, and Administrators) and have given the account the Logon As A Service user right using the User Rights policy in Windows NT. Enter and confirm a password (preferably something other than *password*).

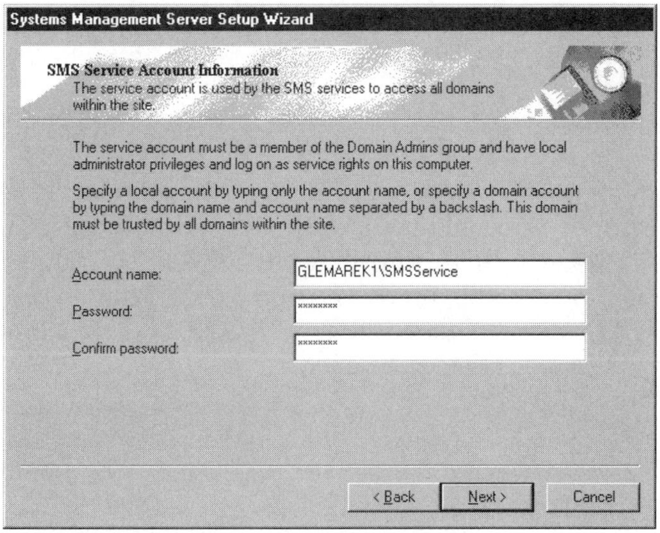

Figure 2-9. *The SMS Service Account Information screen.*

10. Click Next to display the SMS Primary Site Client Load screen, shown in Figure 2-10. Enter the number of SMS clients that this site will manage, as you determined in your deployment strategy. The number that you enter here ultimately affects the size of the SQL database that SMS will create or that you have created ahead of time. An incorrect database device or file size will cause the installation to fail.

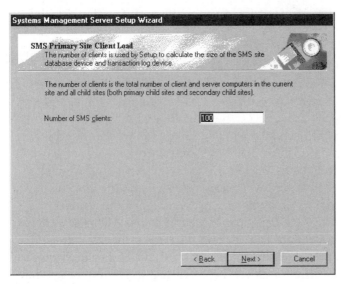

Figure 2-10. *The SMS Primary Site Client Load screen.*

At this point, the installation process will vary depending on whether you have choosen Express Setup or Custom Setup. Let's continue first with the Express installation options and then look at the Custom installation options.

Express Installation

1. On the SMS Primary Site Client Load screen, click Next to display the SQL Server Administrator Account screen, shown in Figure 2-11. Since Express installation assumes that you will install a dedicated SQL Server on this same server, it will prompt you only for the SQL Server sa account password. It will not prompt you for any SQL database information. The Setup Wizard determines the database size based on the number of clients you entered in the previous screen, and it uses the default data and log names of SMSDATA and SMSLOG. Enter and confirm the password if necessary.

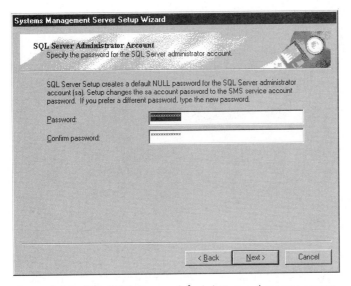

Figure 2-11. *The SQL Server Administrator Account screen.*

2. Click Next to display the Concurrent SMS Administrator Consoles screen, shown in Figure 2-12, and enter the number of concurrent SMS Administrator Consoles you expect to be running in the site. SMS will add 5 user connections for each instance of the SMS Administrator Console to its default of 50 when configuring this parameter in SQL Server.

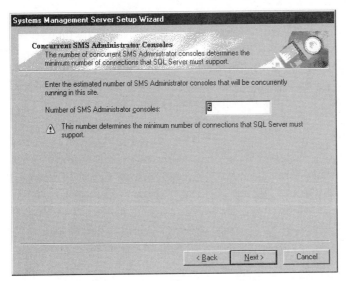

Figure 2-12. *The Concurrent SMS Administrator Consoles screen.*

3. Click Next to display the Completing The Systems Management Server Setup Wizard screen, as shown in Figure 2-13. Confirm your settings, and then click Finish. You can click the Back button from this and any previous screens to go back and modify your entries—and even to switch from Express to Custom installation.

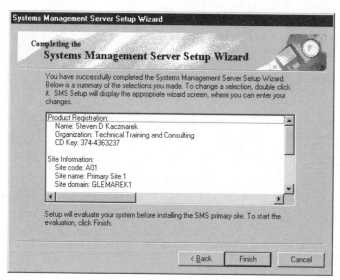

Figure 2-13. *The Completing The Systems Management Server Setup Wizard screen.*

4. The Setup Wizard will ask whether it should create the SMS Service account for you, if you have not already created it. Choose Yes. SMS Setup will then prompt you for the SQL Product ID and the path to the SQL source files, as shown in Figure 2-14. After SMS Setup finishes installing SQL Server, it will complete the SMS installation.

Custom Installation

1. If you are performing a Custom installation, the next screen you will see after the SMS Primary Site Client Load screen will be the SMS Server Platform screen, shown in Figure 2-15. The platform check box that is checked matches the platform of the server on which you are performing the site server installation. If you expect to support a site with mixed-platform site systems or clients, check the appropriate option.

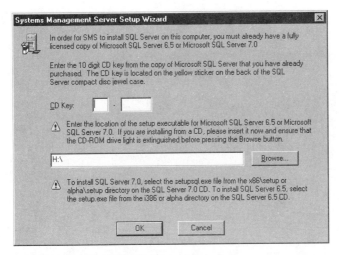

Figure 2-14. *The SQL Server setup screen.*

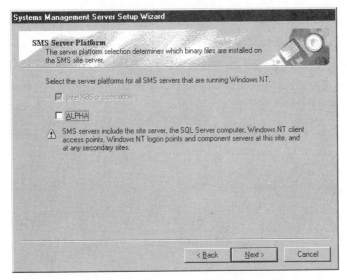

Figure 2-15. *The SMS Server Platform screen.*

2. Click Next to display the Setup Installation Options screen, shown in Figure 2-16. You can select which SMS components you want to install

at this time. As you check each option, a brief description is displayed in the Description box.

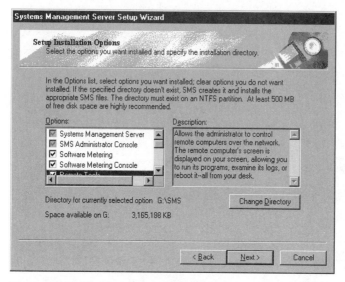

Figure 2-16. *The Setup Installation Options screen.*

The Setup Wizard will automatically select the NTFS partition with the most free disk space as the installation directory. Click the Change Directory button to select a different location.

3. Click Next to display the Dedicated Copy Of SQL Server screen, shown in Figure 2-17. This screen lets you specify whether the Setup Wizard should install a dedicated copy of SQL Server on the site server for you or whether you have already installed SQL Server yourself. Select Yes or No as appropriate.

Once again, the setup process branches depending on whether you choose Yes or No in the Dedicated Copy Of SQL Server screen. Let's proceed with the options you set when you choose Yes. Then we'll see what happens when you choose No.

Choosing to Install a Dedicated Local Copy of SQL Server

1. Choose Yes, and click Next to display the SQL Server Administrator Account screen, shown in Figure 2-18. Since SMS will install SQL Server for you, you need to confirm the SQL Server sa account password.

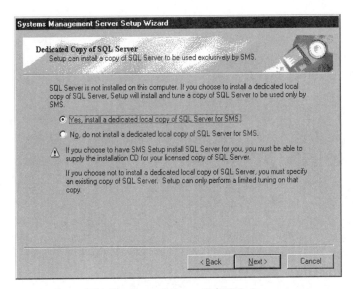

Figure 2-17. *The Dedicated Copy Of SQL Server screen.*

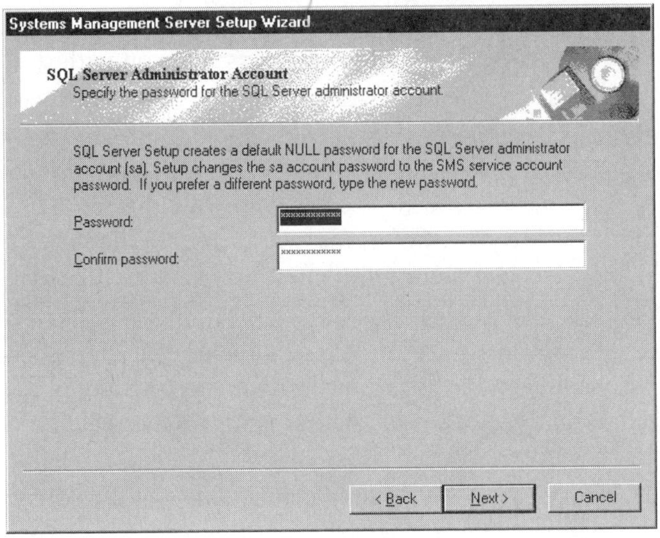

Figure 2-18. *The SQL Server Administrator Account screen.*

2. Click Next to display the SQL Server Installation screen, shown in Figure 2-19. Identify the installation drive and directory in which the Setup Wizard should install SQL Server. Once again, the Setup Wizard chooses the drive with the most free space.

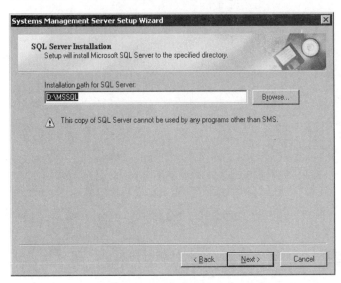

Figure 2-19. *The SQL Server Installation screen.*

3. Click Next to display the Concurrent SMS Administrator Consoles screen, shown in Figure 2-12, and enter the number of concurrent SMS Administrator Consoles you expect to be running in the site. SMS will add 5 user connections for each instance of the SMS Administrator Console to its default of 50 when configuring this parameter in SQL Server.

4. Click Next to display the Completing The Systems Management Server Setup Wizard screen, shown in Figure 2-13. Confirm your settings, and then click Finish. You can click the Back button from this and any previous screens to go back and modify your entries—and even to switch from Express to Custom installation.

5. The Setup Wizard will ask whether it should create the SMS Service account for you. Choose Yes. Setup will then prompt you for the SQL Product ID and the path to the SQL source files, as shown in Figure 2-14. After the Setup Wizard finishes installing SQL Server, it will complete the SMS installation.

Choosing to Not Install a Dedicated Local Copy of SQL Server

1. Choose No in the Dedicated Copy Of SQL Server screen (Figure 2-17) and click Next to display the SQL Server Information For SMS Site Database screen, shown in Figure 2-20. Since choosing No implies that

you have already installed SQL Server, this screen requires that you identify the name of the computer running SQL Server, which version (6.5 or 7.0) is installed, and whether SMS should use standard or integrated security. Make your selections as appropriate and click Next.

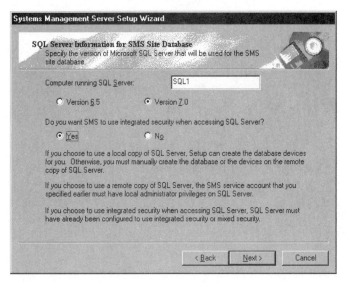

Figure 2-20. *The SQL Server Information For SMS Site Database screen.*

2. If you choose standard security, you need to specify the SQL Server login ID and password for SMS to use, as shown in Figure 2-21.

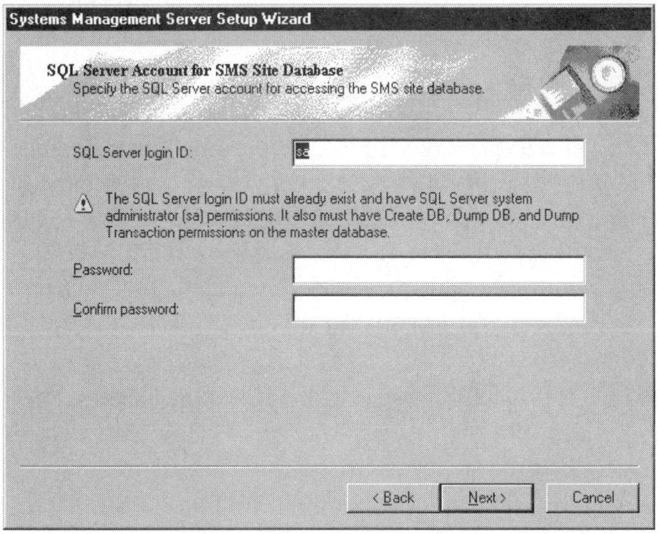

Figure 2-21. *The SQL Server Account For SMS Site Database screen.*

3. Click Next to display the SQL Server Devices For The SMS Site Database screen, shown in Figure 2-22. Here you'll be asked whether the Setup Wizard should create the database and any necessary devices. Choose No if you have already created the database and devices; otherwise, choose Yes.

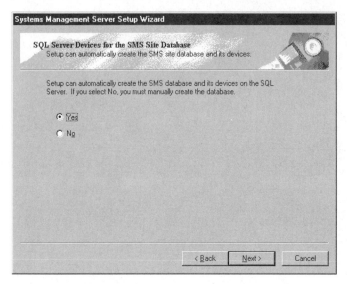

Figure 2-22. *The SQL Server Devices For The SMS Site Database screen.*

SQL 7.0 Installations   If you chose Yes in the previous screen, click Next to display the default database name the Setup Wizard has created in the SMS Site Database Name screen, shown in Figure 2-23. The default name is in the form SMS_*sitecode,* where *sitecode* represents the three-character site code that you assigned to this site.

If you chose No in the SQL Server Devices For The SMS Site Database screen, the Setup Wizard will display a similar screen, also named the SMS Site Database Name screen, this time asking you to confirm the name of the database you already created and warning you as to size requirements. The minimum database and log file sizes are 50 MB and 20 MB, respectively. The numbers displayed will be calculated based on the number of clients you entered previously. The Setup Wizard allocates 100 KB per client.

SQL 6.5 Installations   If you chose Yes in the SQL Server Devices For The SMS Site Database screen, the Setup Wizard will display the default database, database device, and log device names it will create in the SMS Site Database And Device Names screen, shown in Figure 2-24. The defaults are SMS_*sitecode*, SMSData_*sitecode*, and SMSLog_*sitecode*, where *sitecode* represents the three-character site code that you assigned to this site.

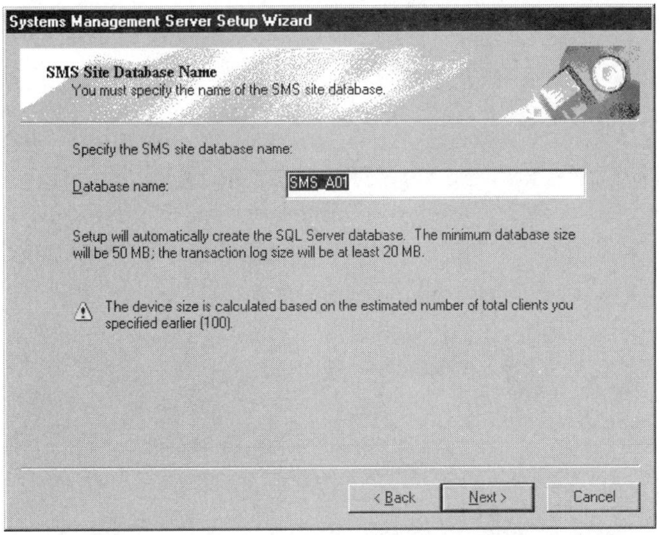

Figure 2-23. *The SMS Site Database Name screen.*

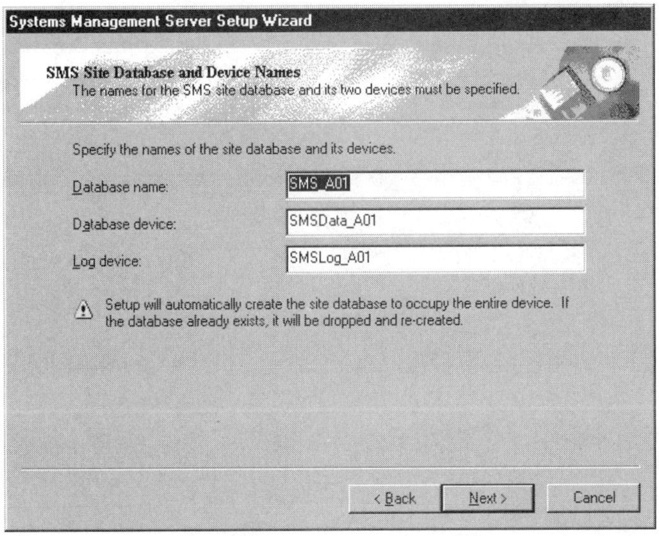

Figure 2-24. *The SMS Site Database And Device Names screen.*

If you chose No in the SQL Server Devices For SMS Site Database screen (Figure 2-22), the Setup Wizard will first display a message screen warning you as to size requirements. The minimum database and log device sizes are 50 MB and 20 MB. The numbers displayed will be calculated based on the number of clients you entered previously. SMS allocates 100 KB per client. Click Next to display the SMS Site Database And Device Names screen, as shown in Figure 2-24.

4. Choose Yes in the SQL Server Device For The SMS Site Database screen and click Next twice to display the SQL Server Device Directory Path For SMS Site Database screen, shown in Figure 2-25. Enter the location and path to the directory in which you intend to store the database and devices. Again, the Setup Wizard chooses the partition with the most free disk space.

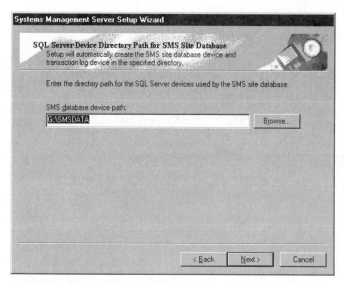

Figure 2-25. *The SQL Server Device Directory Path For SMS Site Database screen.*

5. The software metering feature of SMS 2.0 requires its own SMS database. If you chose to install this option, clicking Next will display the SQL Server Information For Software Metering Database screen, shown

in Figure 2-26. Here you'll be asked for the name of the SQL Server you'll be using for the software metering database and whether to use integrated or standard security, as you were when you set up the SMS database. Make your selections as appropriate, and click Next.

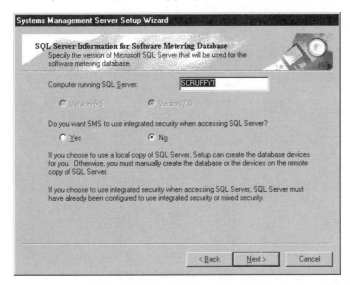

Figure 2-26. *The SQL Server Information For Software Metering Database screen.*

6. If you choose to use standard security, the next screen will ask you to confirm the SQL Server login ID account and password, as you did earlier.

7. Click Next to display the SQL Server Devices For The Software Metering Database screen, shown in Figure 2-27. This screen asks whether the Setup Wizard should create the software metering database and any necessary devices. Choose Yes or No as appropriate.

SQL 7.0 Installations If you chose Yes in the previous screen, the Setup Wizard will display the default database name that it will create in the Software Metering Database Name screen, shown in Figure 2-28. The default is SMS_*sitecode*_LicDB, where *sitecode* represents the three-character site code that you assigned to this site.

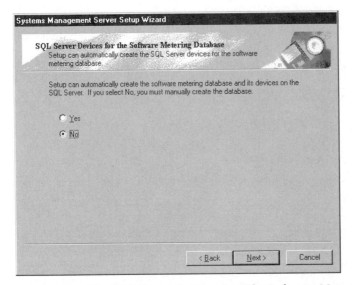

Figure 2-27. *The SQL Server Devices For The Software Metering Database screen.*

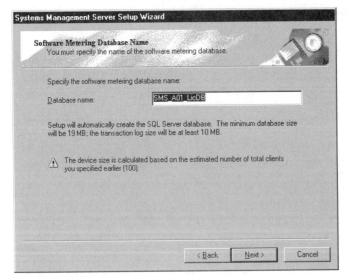

Figure 2-28. *The Software Metering Database Name screen.*

If you chose No in the SQL Server Devices For The Software Metering Database screen (Figure 2-27), the Setup Wizard will display a screen similar to the one shown in Figure 2-28, this time asking you to confirm the name of the database you already created and warning you as to size requirements. The minimum database and log file sizes are 19 MB and 10 MB.

SQL 6.5 Installations If you choose Yes in the SQL Server Devices For The Software Metering Database screen and click Next, the Setup Wizard will display the default database, database device, and log device names that it will create in the Software Metering Database And Device Names screen, as shown in Figure 2-29. The defaults are SMS_LicDB_*sitecode*, LicData_*sitecode,* and LicLog_*sitecode,* where *sitecode* represents the three-character site code that you assigned to this site.

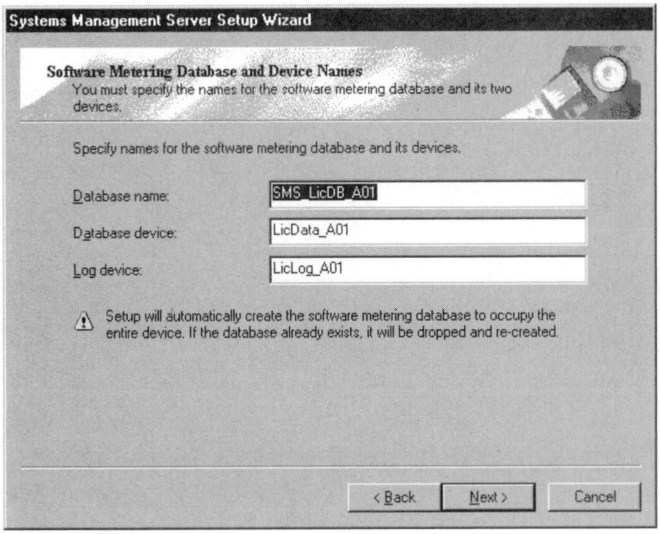

Figure 2-29. *The Software Metering Database And Device Names screen.*

If you choose "No" in the SQL Server Devices For The Software Metering Database screen, the Setup Wizard will display a message screen warning you as to size requirements. The minimum database and log device sizes are 19 MB and 10 MB, respectively. Click Next to display the screen shown in Figure 2-29.

8. Click Next to display the Concurrent SMS Administrator Consoles screen, shown in Figure 2-30, and enter the number of concurrent SMS Administrator Consoles you expect to be running in the site. SMS will add 5 user connections for each instance of the SMS Administrator Console to its default of 50 when configuring this parameter in SQL Server. If you leave the check box checked that allows the Setup Wizard to automatically configure SQL Server for the correct number of user connections, SMS will dynamically fill in the correct number in the Minimum Number Of SQL Server Connections text box. If you uncheck the check box, be sure to enter an appropriate number of user connections or your site server might not be able to access the SMS database.

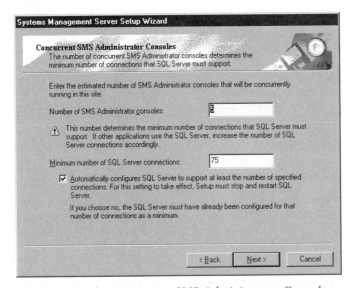

Figure 2-30. *The Concurrent SMS Administrator Consoles screen.*

9. If SQL Server has been installed on the same server as your site server, proceed to step 10. If SQL Server has been installed on a different server, clicking Next will take you to the SMS Provider Information screen, shown in Figure 2-31.

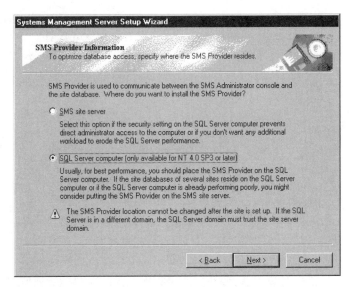

Figure 2-31. *The SMS Provider Information screen.*

Recall from Chapter 1 that the SMS Provider accesses the SMS database through the WMI Common Information Model (CIM) repository for the SMS Administrator Console. In this screen, you specify whether to install the SMS Provider on the site server or the SQL server. In general, optimum performance access is achieved when the SMS Provider is installed on the SQL server. However, if doing so would result in poorer performance, if the SQL server is home to other SMS site databases, or if security on the SQL server prevents the administrator from directly accessing that computer, you should place the SMS Provider on the site server.

10. Click Next to display the Completing The Systems Management Server Setup Wizard screen, shown in Figure 2-13, and confirm your choices. You can click the Back button in any of these screens to return to a previous screen and modify your entries—and even to switch from Express to Custom installation. Click Finish to complete the installation.

11. The Setup Wizard will ask whether it should create the SMS Service account for you, if you have not already done so. Choose Yes. The Setup Wizard will proceed to install SMS 2.0.

If you have followed these steps closely, you have now successfully installed an SMS 2.0 primary site server on your Windows NT server! If you performed a custom installation, you made choices as to which SMS components you wanted to install. The next section discusses the process of adding components to your site server.

Planning: Installing Service Pack 1

As we all know, products such as SMS will continue to mature over time. As SMS becomes more widely used in different networking environments, unusual or anomalous activity, affectionately referred to by many of us as "undocumented user features," will be discovered and addressed. Short-term fixes for problems of this nature usually come in the form of patches. Longer-term fixes, including product enhancements, usually take the form of a service pack.

In July 1999, Microsoft issued SMS 2.0 Service Pack 1. This service pack includes several patches and other fixes for known issues that were recorded in the initial release. It also includes enhancements to SMS that add additional functionality and configuration options. These fixes and enhancements include an updated version of the online *Systems Management Server Administrator's Guide* and are documented in detail in the Microsoft Systems Management Server Version 2.0 Service Pack 1 Release Notes. Here we'll go over the process of installing the service pack on your site server.

First you need to obtain the Service Pack 1 source files. These can be ordered on CD from Microsoft or downloaded through the SMS Web page, at *http:// www.microsoft.com/smsmgmt*. The source files will also be available through the various Solution Provider programs offered by Microsoft. Future releases of the SMS 2.0 source file CD will include Service Pack 1, and setup from this CD can proceed as described in this chapter when we talk about how to install a primary site server.

You need to provide the service pack utility with the location of the original SMS 2.0 source files. It will copy these source files to a server location you specify and then update them with the service pack version. The updated source files can then be used to either install new SMS site servers or update existing sites.

If you downloaded the service pack from a Web site, follow these steps to update your source files:

1. Execute the self-extracting file Smsupdi.exe. This file will expand the service pack source files and launch the SMS 2.0 CD Image Update Utility Installation Wizard, shown in Figure 2-32.

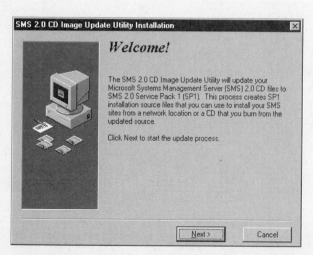

Figure 2-32. *The SMS 2.0 CD Image Update Utility Installation Wizard Welcome screen.*

2. Click Next to display the License Agreement screen, shown in Figure 2-33, and click the Display License Agreement button to display the license agreement for the service pack. After reading the license agreement, click the Agree button to close the display.

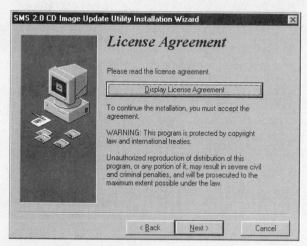

Figure 2-33. *The License Agreement screen.*

3. Click Next to display the Select Destination Directory screen, shown in Figure 2-34. Here you will provide the service pack utility with the location of the SMS 2.0 source files to be updated. The source files must be located on a local or network drive. If the source files are on CD, choose the option The SMS CD Image Is Not On A Local Or Network Drive. This will cause the utility to first copy the source files to a designated local or network directory and then update them with the service pack. If you have already copied the SMS 2.0 source files to a local or network drive, choose the option The SMS CD Image Is On A Local Or Network Drive. Click the Browse button to identify the local or network location that will host the updated source files.

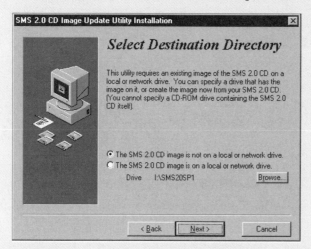

Figure 2-34. *The Select Destination Directory screen.*

4. Click Next. If you chose the first option in step 3, the Copy The SMS 2.0 CD Image screen shown in Figure 2-35 is displayed. (If you chose the second option, proceed directly to step 5.) Use the Browse buttons to identify the location of the CD files and to specify or verify the destination directory for the updated source files.

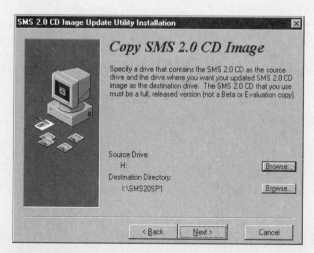

Figure 2-35. *The Copy The SMS 2.0 CD Image screen.*

5. Click Next to display the Ready To Install! screen, shown in
Figure 2-36. This screen indicates that the update process will take about
20 minutes to complete. Click Next to begin the process.

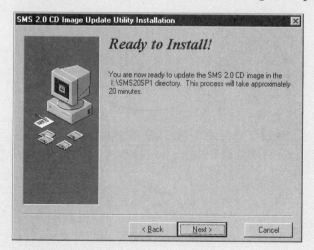

Figure 2-36. *The Ready To Install! screen.*

After the original SMS 2.0 source files have been updated, you can either install a new primary site server following the steps outlined earlier in the "Installing a Primary Site Server" section, or update the existing site server. Follow these steps to update the existing site:

1. Using Windows Explorer, navigate to the updated source file directory (by default, Sms20sp1). Launch the SMS 2.0 Setup Wizard either by executing Smssetup\Bin*platform*\Setup.exe, where *platform* refers to i386 or Alpha, or by running Autorun.exe from the main source file directory.

2. The usual welcome screen and System Configuration screen will be displayed. Click Next on each screen until the Setup Options screen is displayed, as shown in Figure 2-37. Verify that the option Update An Existing SMS Installation is selected.

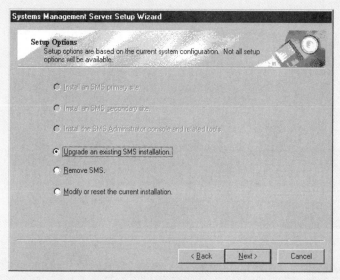

Figure 2-37. *The Setup Options screen.*

3. Click Next to display the Completing The Systems Management Server Setup Wizard screen (Figure 2-13). Click Finish on this screen to begin the update process.

A progress bar will track the progress of the update process. You'll notice that SMS components and services are first stopped, then the source files are updated, and last the SMS components and services are restarted. When the process is complete, your site will have been successfully updated with SMS 2.0 Service Pack 1.

When you have finished installing Service Pack 1, open and read the updated Microsoft Systems Management Server Version 2.0 Release Notes to review the changes that have been made to the product. Throughout the rest of this book, we will assume that you have applied SMS 2.0 Service Pack 1 to your site server and we will approach SMS features and functionality with that focus.

Modifying the Installation

When you first install SMS 2.0, you may decide to include only those components or features that you know you will be using right away. For example, you may decide to install the Hardware Inventory Client Agent, the Software Inventory Client Agent, and Remote Tools, but nothing else initially. At a later time, your needs or the needs of your organization may change, and you may find that you need to enable software metering for your site. Or you might need to move the SMS database to a different SQL Server or change SQL Server security. To modify your installation, follow these steps:

1. Either insert the SMS 2.0 CD, or run SMS 2.0 Setup.exe from the Smssetup\Bin\<*platform*> directory. The SMS Setup Wizard welcome screen is displayed as it was during the actual installation. Click Next.

2. Because the Setup Wizard detects that you have already installed an SMS 2.0 site server on this computer, it displays that information in the System Configuration screen, shown in Figure 2-38.

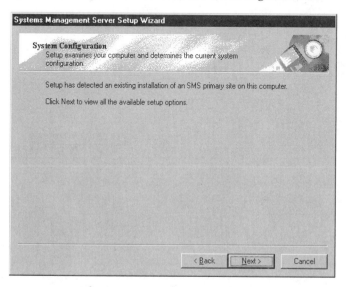

Figure 2-38. *The System Configuration screen.*

3. Click Next to display the Setup Options screen, shown in Figure 2-39, and choose Modify Or Reset The Current Installation.

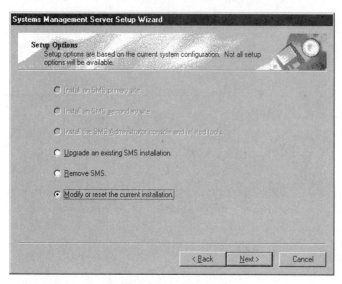

Figure 2-39. *The Setup Options screen.*

4. Click Next to display the SMS Server Platform screen, shown in Figure 2-40. If you need to include additional platform support, check the appropriate check box.

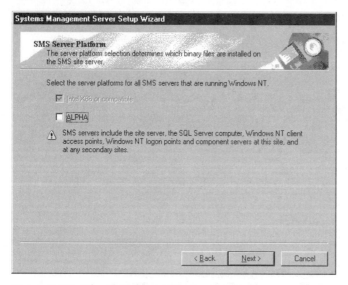

Figure 2-40. *The SMS Server Platform screen.*

5. Click Next to display the Setup Installation Options screen, shown in Figure 2-41, and select the additional SMS 2.0 components or features you want to install. Note that even though the instructions on this screen imply that you can clear options you do not want installed, you cannot actually remove an option once it has been installed without removing SMS 2.0 and reinstalling it. The instructions here merely remind you that you can both select and deselect *available* options while on this page.

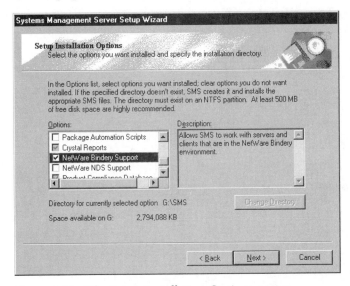

Figure 2-41. *The Setup Installation Options screen.*

6. Click Next to display the SMS Service Account Information screen, shown in Figure 2-42, where you can modify the SMS Service account name or password.

7. Click Next to display the Database Modification screen, shown in Figure 2-43. Make any SMS or software metering database modifications here. Note that you must first use SMS Service Manager to stop all SMS services before running the Setup Wizard if you choose to modify database information. This screen also assumes that you have already modified the databases in SQL Server.

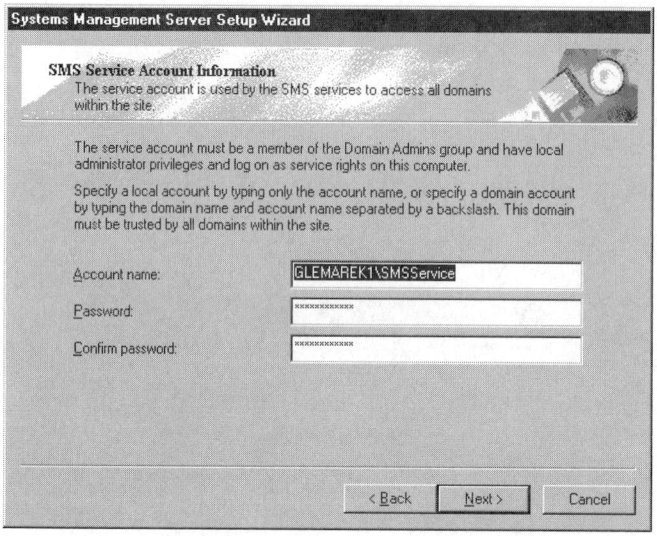

Figure 2-42. *The SMS Service Account Information screen.*

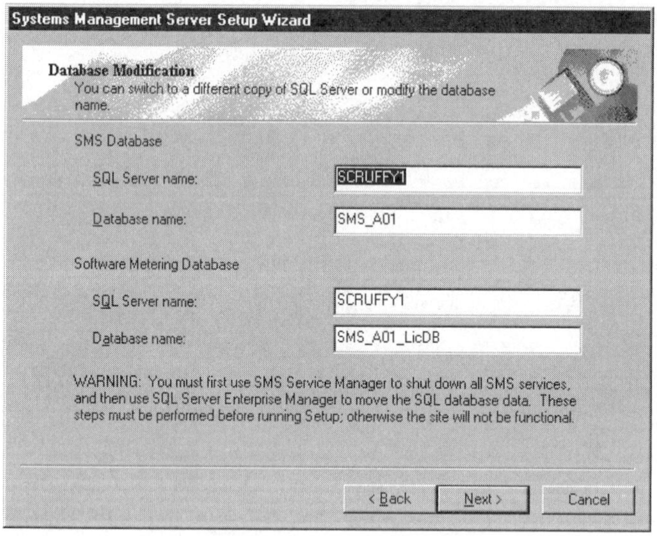

Figure 2-43. *The Database Modification screen.*

8. Click Next to display the Integrated Security For SMS Site Database screen, shown in Figure 2-44. This screen gives you the opportunity to switch between integrated and standard security for accessing the SMS database. As with other database changes, you need to make the appropriate security and account changes in SQL Server before you make any changes here.

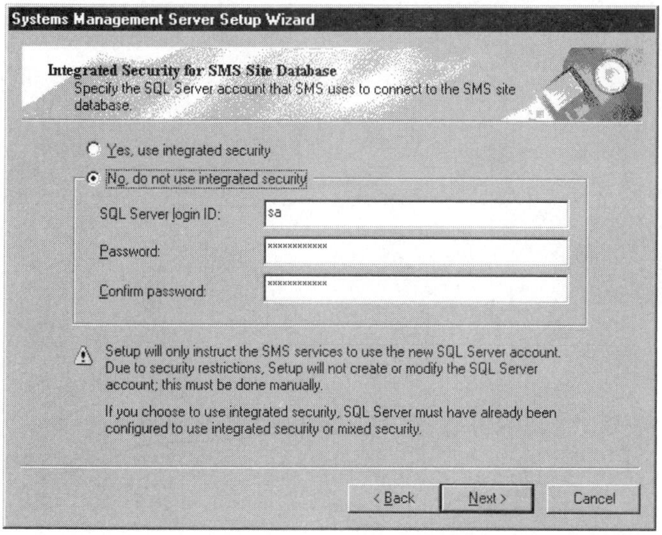

Figure 2-44. *The Integrated Security For SMS Site Database screen.*

9. Click Next to display the Integrated Security For Software Metering Database screen, as shown in Figure 2-45, which enables you to switch between integrated and standard security for accessing the SMS software metering database. As with other database changes, you need to make the appropriate security and account changes in SQL Server.

10. Click Next to display the Completing The Systems Management Server Setup Wizard screen, shown in Figure 2-13. Remember that you can click the Back button from any of these wizard screens to return to a previous screen and modify your entries. Confirm your choices and then click Finish.

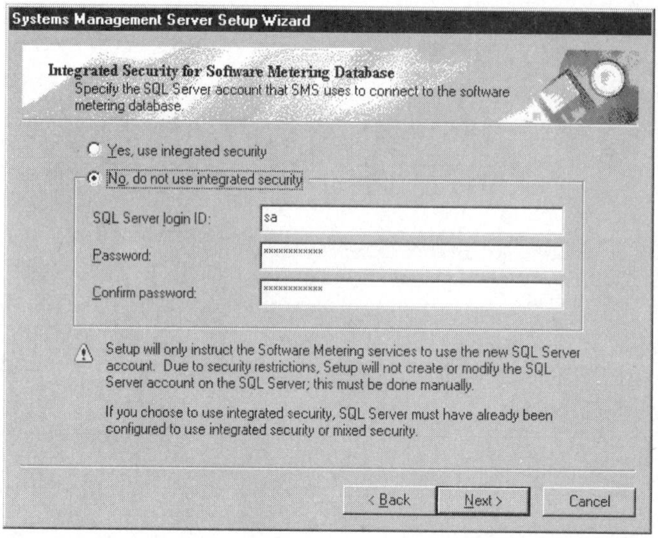

Figure 2-45. *The Integrated Security For Software Metering Database screen.*

The Setup Wizard will proceed to add components and modify parameters as you specified. If it encounters any problems—for example, if you forgot to modify SQL Server security before running Setup—SMS will display a warning message giving you the opportunity to exit the Setup Wizard and correct the problem.

Server Modifications After Installation

The SMS 2.0 Setup program makes several modifications to your Windows NT Server upon completion. It automatically installs the SMS client software components in the \MS\SMS folder it creates in the operating system root, including installing and starting any default client agents that have been enabled, such as the Hardware Inventory Client Agent or Remote Tools. It loads and starts the SMS Client Service, which in turn starts additional client processes and modifies the registry accordingly. The client installation process for the primary site is essentially the same as for any other 32-bit SMS client and is discussed in detail in Chapter 8.

Additional modifications are made in the following areas:

- Program group
- Services
- Directory

- Shares
- Windows NT Registry

In this section, we'll look at each of these areas of modification in detail.

Program Group

After the primary site server installation is complete, the Setup Wizard adds the Systems Management Server program group to the Start menu. The shortcuts created and displayed in the Systems Management Server program group will vary depending on the components you chose to install. Table 2-4 describes the program group shortcuts that are created in an Express installation and represents the most common entries created.

Table 2-4.   Systems Management Server program group shortcuts

Shortcut	Description
Network Monitor	Launches the Network Monitor utility, which is used to track and analyze network traffic and usage.
Network Monitor Control Tool	Launches the Network Monitor Control Tool, which allows you to set custom network tracking tools to identify and alert certain network events.
SMS Administrator Console	Launches the SMS Administrator Console, which is used to access and administer the SMS database and its site components.
SMS Administrator Guide	Launches the online version of the *Systems Management Server Administrator's Guide*, which contains the same material in searchable format as the print version that comes boxed with the SMS 2.0 CD.
SMS Release Notes	Launches the Microsoft Systems Management Server Version 2.0 Release Notes, additional reference notes, workarounds, and technical pointers that supplement and correct the *Systems Management Server Administrator's Guide*.
SMS Setup	Launches the SMS 2.0 Setup Wizard, through which you can modify and reset site settings, such as the service account name and password, and remove SMS.
SMS Courier Sender	Launches the SMS Courier Sender Manager, which creates and receives parcels from packages using the Courier Sender. The Courier Sender can be used to send packages between sites that have slow or unreliable network links, although it is not meant to be used exclusively in place of other network connections.

Tip After you install your SMS 2.0 primary site server, be sure to print out the 86 pages of Microsoft Systems Management Server Version 2.0 Release Notes and read through them. Not only is it a terrific cure for insomnia, but it is also an invaluable source of additional information about and corrections to the *Systems Management Server Administrator's Guide*. This book incorporates the most significant entries.

Services

During the SMS installation, SMS services, or processes, are installed and enabled. By default, the SMS Setup program will load and start five new services on a primary site server: SMS Executive, SMS Site Component Manager, SMS SQL Monitor, SMS Site Backup, and Windows Management Service (if WMI has not been previously installed). If you installed Crystal Info as an option, Setup will also load and start three Crystal Info services: Info Agent, Info APS, and Info Sentinel. These services run in the background; to view their running status, select Services in the Control Panel in Windows NT.

The SMS Executive is the primary SMS service—sort of like the CIO for the SMS site. It accesses and updates the database, and it manages up to 42 different process threads, depending on the components installed. These process threads are listed here:

- Client Configuration Manager
- Client Install Data Manager
- Collection Evaluator
- Courier Sender Confirmation
- Despooler
- Discovery agents
  - NetWare Bindery Logon Discovery
  - NetWare NDS Logon Discovery
  - Network Discovery
  - Windows NT Logon Discovery
  - Windows NT Server Discovery
  - Windows NT User Account Discovery
  - Windows NT User Group Discovery

- Discovery managers
  - NetWare Bindery Logon Manager
  - NetWare NDS Logon Manager
  - Windows NT Logon Manager
- Discovery Data Manager
- Distribution Manager
- Hierarchy Manager
- Inbox Manager
- Inbox Manager Assistant
- Inventory Data Loader
- Inventory Processor
- Installation managers
  - NetWare Bindery Installation Manager
  - NetWare NDS Installation Manager
  - Windows NT Logon Installation Manager
- License Metering
- License Server Manager
- Offer Manager
- Replication Manager
- Scheduler
- Senders
  - Asynchronous RAS Sender
  - Courier Sender
  - ISDN RAS Sender
  - SNA RAS Sender
  - Standard Sender
  - X.25 RAS Sender
- Site Control Manager

- Status summarizers
  - Advertisement Status Summarizer
  - Component Status Summarizer
  - Site System Status Summarizer
- Software Inventory Processor
- Status Manager

You'll learn about the significance of each of these process threads as we encounter them in future chapters.

The Site Component Manager carries out site configuration requests posted in the database and written to the site's site control file. This service is similar to the Site Configuration Manager service installed in SMS 1.2.

The SMS SQL Monitor acts as a wake-up service for the SMS Executive and its process threads. Based on SQL event triggers and stored procedures, the SMS SQL Monitor writes a wake-up file to the inbox of the SMS process that needs to carry out a specific task. Through this service, SMS 2.0 becomes event-driven rather than cycle-driven, as in earlier versions of SMS.

The Windows Management Service manages the WMI CIM repository and gives access to any WMI providers and agents.

The three Crystal Info services are specific to Crystal Info's function. Info Agent uses the most recent instance of a report to send back data to Crystal Info. Info APS manages the configuration, scheduling, creation, and security of reports generated by Crystal Info. Info Sentinel maintains communication between the Crystal Info components and the SMS database.

Real World   What If the Info APS Service Fails to Start?

The Info APS service is set to start up automatically when a system boots, and it uses the SMS Service account as its service account. However, you will find that instead of starting up, it times out (after several minutes) and causes Windows NT to display the familiar "Service or Dependency Failed to Start" message. (This problem no longer occurs if you have installed SMS 2.0 Service Pack 1.) During the time-out period, the SMS Administrator Console will be delayed in connecting to the SMS database, and the Windows NT service database will be locked. A further review of the Windows NT Event Viewer will reveal that a Service Control Manager error with event ID 7000 is generated with a description, as shown in Figure 2-46.

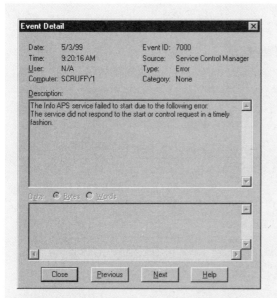

Figure 2-46. *The Event Detail dialog box.*

In the initial release of SMS 2.0, the Info APS service includes a shipping bug that causes this error. Officially, the workaround is to manually start the service after rebooting. In practice, you may have to try starting it a couple times before it actually starts. This, of course is not always practical, especially if your servers are not easily accessible. The good news, perhaps, is that the Info APS service affects only Crystal Info—and nothing else.

Here is another workaround. The Info APS service has three dependencies—that is, it depends on three other services starting before it can start: EventLog, Info Sentinel, and NM. (NM is the Network Monitor agent that SMS 2.0 installs for remote monitoring of computer systems using Network Monitor.) However, when Info APS is installed, it fails to add the NM dependency to the list. Consequently, Info APS times out because it tries to start before the third dependency service NM has itself started up. To modify the Info APS service dependencies, follow these steps:

1. Start the Windows NT Registry Editor (Regedt32.exe).

2. Find the key HKEY_LOCAL_MACHINE\System\CurrentControlSet \Services\Crystal Info APS.

3. Find the *DependOnService* value, and double-click on it. The Multi-String Editor dialog box will appear, containing two entries: EventLog and Crystal Info Sentinel.

4. Add NM at the end of the list, as shown in Figure 2-47, and click OK.

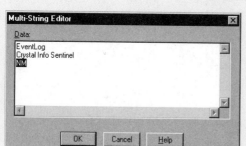

Figure 2-47. *Adding NM in the Multi-String Editor dialog box.*

5. Close the Windows NT Registry Editor.

After you restart your server, the Info APS service will start up just fine.

Directory Structure and Shares

When you run the SMS Setup program, it creates the registry, shares, and services needed to make configuration changes. Among the items created are two SMS directories: \SMS and \CAP_*sitecode*. The \SMS directory is the main SMS installation directory. It contains all the site component files, inboxes, system files, data files, and so forth needed to maintain and service the SMS site. It is shared as SMS_*sitecode*, where *sitecode* represents the three-character site code you assigned to the site.

The \CAP_*sitecode* directory is created on every site system configured as a CAP. The site server becomes a CAP by default. This directory contains all the client component configuration files, advertisements, site assignment lists, component inboxes for client data, and any other instruction files the client might require. It is shared as CAP_*sitecode*.

If the site server is configured as a logon point, as it would be automatically if you performed an Express installation and the site server were also a domain controller, Setup would create the \Smslogon directory and share, which would contain the site list, site assignment list, CAP list, and client configuration files. In this scenario, the Winnt\System32\Repl\Export\Scripts directory is shared as REPL$ (if directory replication is not already enabled on the server) for use in replicating discovery and client installation files to all domain controllers.

The Setup program also shares the SMS\Inboxes\Despoolr.box\Receive directory as SMS_*site*. SMS site servers use this share to connect to another site and to copy package information and other data to that site. If Crystal Info has been installed, the directory containing its support files for creating, scheduling, and running reports—\SMS\CInfo—is shared as CInfo.

Suffice it to say that the Setup program creates no superfluous directories. Every SMS component and thread has its directory or directories, and every directory has its component or thread.

Windows NT Registry

The Setup program creates and configures four main areas of the Windows NT registry—specifically in the HKEY_LOCAL_MACHINE subtree. Setup adds the Network Access Layer (NAL) and SMS keys to HKEY_LOCAL_MACHINE \Software\Microsoft in the registry. The NAL key contains information relating to logical disk and network providers used by SMS, connection account information, and CAP lists. The SMS key contains all the site configuration and control information, including components installed, site parameters, SQL information, and so on. If Setup installs WMI, it adds a Web-Based Enterprise Management (WBEM) key as well, which contains the configuration and access information needed by Windows Management. Additionally, Setup will add the appropriate service-related keys to HKEY_LOCAL_MACHINE\System\CurrentControlSet\Services.

As always, it is possible, and sometimes necessary for you, the SMS administrator, to modify SMS site and component settings through the Windows NT Registry Editor. As always, please use due caution when making changes. Before browsing the registry to look up current settings or to determine whether a change should or could be made, it would be wise to set the Registry Editor to read-only mode. This precaution will prevent you from accidentally modifying an existing entry, adding an incorrect entry, or deleting a significant entry from the registry—the results of which could range from minor annoyance to critical disaster. This is not a lesson you want to learn the hard way.

Navigating the SMS Administrator Console

The SMS Administrator Console is actually a snap-in to the Microsoft Management Console (MMC) version 1.1. As you are probably aware, MMC is a productivity utility that enables you to customize management tools for your environment. The idea is to have all your management tools accessible through a single interface. So you can add in the snap-ins you need or display only the functionality of the snap-in you require. SMS 2.0 third-party utilities will largely be available as snap-ins to the SMS Administrator Console.

The SMS Administrator Console, like any MMC, can be run in Author mode. To run the SMS Administrator Console in Author mode, right-click on the console's title bar, choose User Options, and check the Always Open Console Files In Author Mode option. You will need to close the SMS Administrator Console and reopen it to enable Author mode. Author mode lets you customize the console. For example, SQL Server 7.0 also uses MMC to run the SQL Server 7.0 Enterprise Manager. To simplify your administrative tasks, you might decide to add the SQL Server 7.0 Enterprise Manager to the SMS Administrator Console. We'll spend more time on the subject of customizing and securing the SMS Administrator Console in Chapter 16. The purpose of this section is to familiarize you with the SMS Administrator Console and how to navigate it.

The SMS Administrator Console is installed to run with Author mode turned off by default. It is launched from the Systems Management Server program group, or by choosing Start from the taskbar, choosing Run, and then entering *d*:\SMS \Bin*platform*\Sms.msc, where *d* represents the drive on which SMS was installed on, and *platform* is either i386 for Intel or Alpha.

As shown in Figure 2-48, the SMS Administrator Console looks very much like an Windows Explorer window. Objects that can be accessed and managed by the SMS administrator are displayed in the left pane, which is also called the console tree. As you select each object in the left pane, the contents of that object are displayed in the right pane. These contents generally consist of additional objects that can be accessed and maintained.

Notice that highlighting the *Collections* object in the left pane displays the twelve default collections that SMS 2.0 created during setup in the right pane. Refer back to Table 1-1 for descriptions of each top-level object.

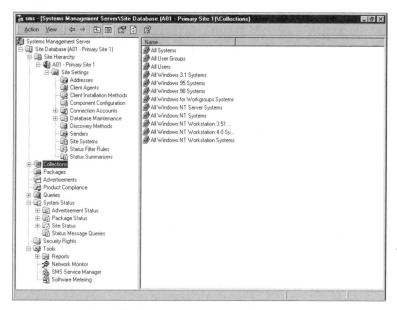

Figure 2-48. *The default SMS Administrator Console, displaying all top-level objects that can be accessed by the SMS administrator.*

You navigate through the objects as you would navigate through the Windows Explorer screen—the same keyboard shortcuts apply. For example, click on a plus sign or a minus sign to expand or collapse an object or a folder. Or double-click on the object or folder name to expand or collapse it. Press the Tab key to move between panes, or to move from entry to entry in a dialog box.

The SMS Administrator Console has two menus: Action and View. Selecting an object and choosing the Action menu will display the Action menu options for that object. These options may include opening the item (same as double-clicking on it), refreshing the object (updating its contents or properties), deleting the object, or performing some additional task such as displaying messages or launching a tool. Most objects have Properties windows in which you can view and change an object's attributes. Right-clicking on an object displays the object's context menu, which lists the same options as the Action menu.

The View menu is active only if the SMS Administrator is run in Author mode. This menu lets you customize how the console appears. For example, you can show or hide the description bar, status bar, or console tree and you can decide which toolbars to display, including menus or buttons from other snap-ins.

In addition to the two menus, the SMS Administrator Console provides six toolbar buttons, shown in Figure 2-49. The blue left and right arrows are jump buttons that switch you backward and forward through the last console tree selections you made. The yellow folder with the up arrow lets you navigate up one object or folder level from where your cursor is currently placed. The list with an arrow next to it toggles the left pane on and off for easier reading of the right pane. The white paper with revolving green arrows is the Refresh button. Because the SMS Administrator Console is not dynamically updated, remember to refresh your screen to view new and updated data. You can also refresh any object by highlighting it and pressing F5 on the keyboard, or by right-clicking on the object and then choosing Refresh. Of course, there is also the Help button—the one with the yellow question mark. This button invokes SMS help for whichever object you have highlighted.

This seems like an ideal opportunity to put in a plug for SMS 2.0's help engine. Compared to other help products you may have used (even from Microsoft), this one is really quite good. Combined with the online *Systems Management Server Administrator's Guide* and the Microsoft Systems Management Server Version 2.0 Release Notes, you will have the resources you need to answer the majority of your questions about SMS. Get yourself the SMS 2.0 Resource Kit which is located in the \Support\Reskit directory in the SMS 2.0 CD and the Software Development Kit (SDK) through the Microsoft Developer Network (MSDN) program, and you'll be on your way to becoming an SMS guru. For more information on the MSDN program, please check the Web site at *http://msdn.microsoft.com*.

That's all there is to it. Navigating the SMS Administrator Console is actually quite easy once you get used to it. The hardest part is finding out where to look for various SMS component settings. If you come from a current SMS 1.2 environment, you might find yourself becoming a little frustrated at first because you will be so used to the old SMS Administrator utility. Give yourself a little extra time to become comfortable with the new MMC. After a while, you'll wonder how you got along without it. Indeed, going back to the old SMS Administrator utility may seem like going back to File Manager after using Windows Explorer.

Removing a Primary Site

At some point, you might need to remove an SMS 2.0 site server for one reason or another. Perhaps you are moving your site server to another computer, or perhaps you need to remove a component. The removal process consists of three main parts: removing the site server client software, removing the SMS site server components, and cleaning up the server. This last task generally consists of removing any leftover folders and files, registry keys, and SMS accounts.

Removing the Site Server Client Software

When SMS 2.0 installs your site server, it also installs the SMS client software. The site server automatically becomes a client to the SMS 2.0 site. The first step in uninstalling your primary site, therefore, is to remove the client piece. To do so, follow these steps:

1. Start the Windows NT Registry Editor (Regedt32.exe).

   Caution Modifying the Windows NT Registry without due caution is like signing your server's death warrant. Be careful!

2. Find and highlight the following key: HKEY_LOCAL_MACHINE \Software\Microsoft\SMSClient\Configuration\Client Properties.

3. Choose Edit from the Registry Editor menu, and then choose Add Value to open the Add Value dialog box. Enter SMS Client Deinstall as the value name, select REG_SZ as the data type, and click OK to open the String Editor dialog box.

4. In the String Editor dialog box, enter True and then click OK.

5. Close the Windows NT Registry Editor.

6. Open the Control Panel in Windows NT, and start the Services program.

7. Find and highlight the SMS Client Service option.

8. Click Stop to stop the SMS Client Service. After the service stops, click Start to start the SMS Client Service. Restarting the SMS Client Service causes it to reread the registry to find the deinstall value you entered. It will then begin the deinstall process. Once the service starts, close the Services program.

You will notice that the deinstall process has begun. This may take several minutes to complete—when the SMS Client Service is no longer running, the deinstall process will be complete. To see whether this service is running, check the Control Panel again or check the Task Manager for the absence of the process file Clisvcl.exe.

This same process can actually be used to remove the SMS client software from any Windows NT computer. Once the client components have been removed from the site server, you can proceed to the next task at hand—removing the site server components.

Removing the Primary Site

To remove a primary site, follow these steps:

1. Initiate SMS 2.0's uninstall process by executing SMS 2.0 Setup from the SMS 2.0 CD, or by running the SMS Setup program from the Systems Management Server program group on the site server.

2. From the Setup Options screen, shown in Figure 2-40, select Remove SMS.

3. Click Next to display the SMS Database Deinstallation Options screen, shown in Figure 2-49. Here you are given the opportunity to also delete the SMS and software metering databases. Uncheck these check boxes if your intent is to reinstall the site server and point it to the existing databases.

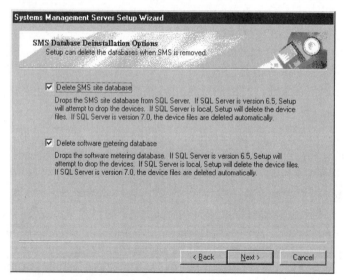

Figure 2-49. *The SMS Database Deinstallation Options screen.*

4. Click Next and then click Finish to complete the removal process.

The SMS 2.0 removal process will uninstall SMS services and components, remove the SMS Administrator Console, and remove the Systems Management Server program group. However, it will not completely remove all vestiges of SMS 2.0 from your server. There are three areas of cleanup which you will need to attend to: removing folders and files, removing Windows NT registry keys, and removing SMS accounts and groups. We'll look at how to perform this cleanup next.

Removing Folders and Files

Use the Windows Explorer to search for the drive on which SMS 2.0 was installed. You will still see the SMS folder. Delete it and all its subdirectories. Remember that any non-SMS files or folders in the SMS folder will be removed also. To avoid the removal of non-SMS data, install SMS in a folder that doesn't hold any other data. You might also find the following folders on this drive: CAP_*sitecode,* if the site server was assigned the CAP site system role; SMSLogon, if the site system was assigned the logon point site system role; and one or more SMSPkg*x*$ directories (*x* represents the drive letter) if the site system was assigned the distribution point site system role. The CAP and logon point folders should all have been removed when you ran the Remove SMS option in Setup. Nevertheless, be sure to confirm that they are gone.

When SMS 2.0 sets up your site server, it also installs the site server as a site client. The client component files are stored in a subfolder named MS created in the operating system folder—for example, WINNT\MS. The client removal process should have already cleaned out all the subfolders below \MS, but not the \MS folder. You will need to delete this subfolder yourself.

In the C root, delete all SMSSetup.* files. In the operating system folder root, delete SMSCFG.ini. After these folders and files have been deleted, you must turn your attention to the registry. SMS does add several entries to the registry; however, the uninstall process does not completely remove them. The next section discusses how to clean up the registry.

Removing SMS Windows NT Registry Keys

Using the Windows NT Registry Editor (with all due caution, of course), find the HKEY_LOCAL_MACHINE\Software\Microsoft key. Within this key, remove the following subkeys if they exist:

- MMC
- NAL
- SMS
- SNMP_EVENTS

Then find the HKEY_LOCAL_MACHINE\System\CurrentControlSet\Services key and be sure to delete any service keys beginning with *SMS* if any exist.

Now that we have cleaned up the leftover folders, files, and registry keys, we have one last job. SMS uses many different accounts and groups to perform different tasks. So far, we have looked only at the SMS Service account. Other accounts are described throughout this book, especially in Chapter 16. You should remove these accounts and groups to complete the cleanup process.

Removing Accounts and Groups

Through the User Manager For Domains in Windows NT member servers, find and remove any user accounts that begin with *SMS*. You should find at least five accounts, depending on how you configured your primary site. Also remove the groups SMSAdmins and SMSInternalCliGrp. If you created any additional accounts of your own for use with SMS, be sure to delete those as well.

After you perform these cleanup steps successfully, your server should be free of any leftover SMS folders, files, registry keys, and accounts. Be sure to review the entire process before you remove your site servers and perhaps create a checklist for yourself of the tasks involved. Always pay particular attention when editing or deleting any registry key to avoid errors.

Summary

This chapter explored the ins and outs of the installation process for an SMS primary site server. We took a close look at the prerequisite issues involved in planning your installation, including not only domain and network considerations but also hardware and software requirements. We have thoroughly examined the installation process itself, highlighting changes made to the server through services loaded; files, folders, and shares created; and registry keys added. You've even learned how to remove SMS from the server if the need arises.

Chapter 3 focuses on the different functional roles that the site server and other identified site systems can assume. We'll define these roles and examine how to assign them to servers within our growing SMS site. Then in Chapter 4 we'll look at how to link SMS sites to create a management hierarchy.

Chapter 3
Site Systems

Now that you have successfully installed your Microsoft Systems Management Server (SMS) primary site server, the next step in your deployment strategy is to begin configuring your site. This configuration may consist of two parts. Certainly, you will need to configure the single SMS site. This means identifying which components should be enabled, what the SMS site boundaries should be, and what additional servers should be enabled as component or site systems for the site. You may also need to establish an SMS site hierarchy for your organization. This means, among other things, identifying parent-child relationships, establishing a reporting and administration path, configuring communication mechanisms, and identifying primary and secondary sites.

This chapter concentrates on the first part of the configuration process—that is, configuring the single SMS site, including setting site boundaries, monitoring status and flow, and identifying site systems. In Chapter 4, you'll learn how to implement a site hierarchy.

Defining and Configuring the SMS Site

The first step in configuring your new SMS 2.0 site is to identify which clients should become members of the site. SMS 2.0 determines which clients should be assigned to the site according to the site boundaries you configure. SMS 2.0 site boundaries are defined by either an IP subnet address or an IPX network number. A subnet is a segment of a network whose members share the same network address; it is distinguished from other subnets by a subnet number.

For example, in a network using TCP/IP, two typical network host addresses might be 192.168.20.35 and 192.168.30.147, both with a subnet mask of 255.255.255.0. The subnet mask determines the subnet address for that segment of the network. In this case, the subnet address for the first host device would be 192.168.20.0, and the subnet address for the second host device would be 192.168.30.0. The first two positions in this address identify the network address (192.168.0.0), and the third identifies the subnet within that network where you can find that particular host device. The fourth position is the actual device address. In other words, the device with address 192.168.20.35 and the device with address 192.168.30.147 are on two separate subnets within the same IP network. If you want the clients whose addresses begin with 192.168.20 to become SMS clients in the new SMS 2.0 site you just created, you need to add 192.168.20.0 as a site boundary for the site. If you want to include clients in both subnets as SMS clients in the new site, add both 192.168.20.0 and 192.168.30.0 as site boundaries for the site.

A valid site boundary could also be an IPX network number. In Novell NetWare networks using IPX, the IPX network number performs the same function as an IP subnet does in an IP network. Both are methods of segmenting clients by network location.

Don't confuse site assignment with the discovery process. SMS uses any of several configurable discovery processes to "look for" and record an instance of a resource. A resource might be a client computer, but it might also be a user, a global group, or an IP-addressable device such as a switch or a network printer. A resource does not become an SMS client just because it has been discovered by the SMS site server. A client computer cannot become an SMS client until it has been assigned to an SMS site. Once it has been assigned, it can then be installed with the SMS client software. To summarize, clients can be discovered as a site resource by the SMS site server, but not necessarily installed. On the other hand, they can be installed as SMS clients without first being discovered. But in all cases, a client must be assigned to an SMS site before it can be installed. The discovery process is explored in detail in Chapter 7.

When you configure the site boundaries for a site, all the client agent settings that you define will be applied to all the assigned clients when the SMS software is installed. In other words, agent and component settings are sitewide settings and apply equally to all members of the site. If different sets of clients require different client components, you need to create a separate site for those clients. For example, if 100 out of 1000 clients require Remote Tools to be enabled, and the remaining clients do not, you need to segment these clients into their own subnet, create an SMS site for that subnet, assign those 100 clients to that site, and enable Remote Tools for that site. This is one of the reasons a well-conceived deployment strategy will be extremely valuable to you as you construct your SMS site hierarchy.

Clients can also be assigned to more than one site, although doing so is not recommended. If two or more sites include the same subnet in their site boundaries, it is possible for a client to be assigned and installed as a valid SMS client to both sites. The benefit of doing this is to ensure that the client can be managed from whatever network location the client connects from. For example, a laptop user who travels to different company offices in different network locations still needs to be managed by an SMS site. Each office has its own network subnet address. It is not practical or advisable to maintain one large SMS site for a WAN-based organization. So, you can implement SMS sites at each company office and allow the laptop user to be assigned to each site, ensuring that the user can receive advertisements, be managed remotely, and so on.

On the down side, if each site has its own client agent settings, conflicts can arise as SMS tries to determine the scope of functionality that should be enabled. Figure 3-1 demonstrates such a scenario for Remote Tools. Notice that if Remote Tools is enabled at any one site, it is installed on the client. However, the Remote Tools options—remote control, remote chat, remote file transfer, and so on—are evaluated on a most-restrictive basis among the sites. For example, if one site allows the remote control option, but at least one other site does not, the SMS administrator from either site can't establish a remote control session.

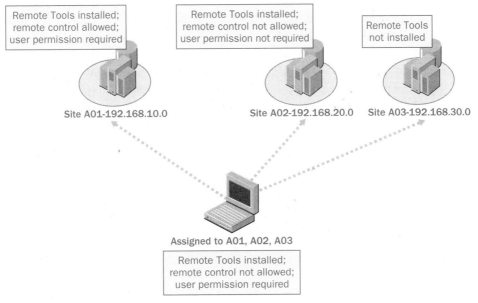

Figure 3-1. *Remote Tools access when a client is assigned to and installed on more than one site.*

Real World **Site Boundaries and Subnet Masks**

When SMS 2.0 determines whether to assign a client to a site, it checks the client's discovery record to see whether the client's IP address falls within the IP boundaries set by the SMS administrator. It does so by checking the client's subnet mask. (The *subnet mask* determines the subnet address for that segment of the network.) Checking the client's subnet mask is significant because many companies do not use a subnet mask of 255.255.0.0 or something similar to define their network segments. In fact, they very likely will use a mask such as 255.255.248.0 to segment the network into different subnets for organizational reasons, network routing considerations, security, localization of resources, and so on.

Using a subnet mask such as 255.255.0.0 makes it easy for us to identify the subnet address. With this particular mask, every number in the third and fourth octets will constitute a host device address. Every number in the first and second octets will constitute a different IP subnet address. For example, consider these two IP addresses: 172.16.10.50 and 172.16.20.50. Using subnet mask 255.255.0.0, it is easy to see that they are both in the same subnet. If you set the SMS site boundary to 172.16.8.0, you will be sure to discover and assign both clients.

Now take the same two IP addresses, but use subnet mask 255.255.248.0 instead. This subnet mask places each client address into a different subnet. The site boundary 172.16.8.0 will discover and assign clients whose IP addresses fall within the range 172.16.8.1 through 172.16.15.254. Thus the client with address 172.16.10.50 would be assigned and the client with address 172.16.20.50 would not. To include the latter client, you would need to add its subnet address— 172.16.16.0—to the site boundaries.

You might need to review your IP addressing skills to fully appreciate the significance of subnet masking and SMS 2.0. But rest assured, the subnet mask does make a difference.

Configuring Site Properties

In SMS 2.0, you can configure site boundaries and other site properties, including site accounts and security. In this section, you'll learn how to configure all of these properties.

To display the site properties for an SMS site:

1. Open the SMS Administrator Console.

2. Under the Systems Management Server group, expand the Site Database folder, and then expand the Site Hierarchy folder to display the site object (in the form *sitecode - sitename*).

3. Right-click on the site object and choose Properties from the context menu. Or select the site object and choose Properties from the Action menu to display the Site Properties window for the site, as shown in Figure 3-2.

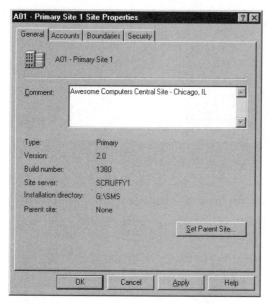

Figure 3-2. *The Site Properties window for the site.*

Let's begin by configuring site boundaries on the Boundaries tab.

The Boundaries Tab

To configure the site boundaries, follow these steps:

1. Click on the Boundaries tab in the Site Properties window, shown in Figure 3-3. The IP subnet address or IPX network number of the segment in which the site server was installed will be displayed by default.

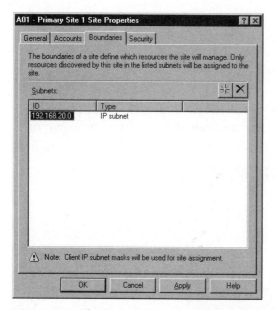

Figure 3-3. *The Boundaries tab of the Site Properties window.*

2. To add a new IP subnet address or IPX network number, click the New button (the yellow star) to open the New Subnet dialog box, shown in Figure 3-4. Select a subnet type from the drop-down list, and enter the subnet ID (either an IP subnet address or an IPX network number). Then click OK.

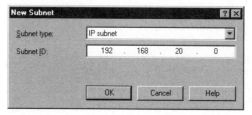

Figure 3-4. *The New Subnet dialog box.*

3. The new boundary will be displayed in the Subnets list on the Boundaries tab. Click OK or Apply to save your changes.

The General Tab

Let's take a moment to examine the other tabs in the Site Properties window, beginning with the General tab shown in Figure 3-2. There are really only two things you can do on the General tab: enter a descriptive comment about the site, and identify the parent site for your site. We'll talk about creating parent-child relationships in Chapter 4.

Descriptive comments always add value to objects in SMS 2.0, as they help to provide additional information that might otherwise not be available. In this case, we can use the Comment text box to indicate the name of the company (Awesome Computers), its site hierarchy role (central site), and its location (Chicago, IL).

The Accounts Tab

SMS 2.0 makes use of several different accounts to access other sites, install clients, install packages, access the database, generate reports, and so on. The Accounts tab, shown in Figure 3-5, provides the SMS administrator with the means of modifying three accounts specific to the site itself: the SMS Service account, the SMS Client Remote Installation account, and the SQL Server account.

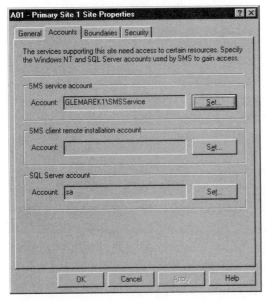

Figure 3-5. *The Accounts tab in the Site Properties window.*

SMS Service Account   The SMS Service account, named *SMSService* by default, is created by SMS during setup and is the primary service account for the SMS site. It provides the site server with access to most SMS services running on the site server as well as on other site systems. These SMS services include SMS Executive, SMS Site Backup, SMS Site Component Manager, and SMS SQL Monitor. If you installed Crystal Info, its three services (Info Agent, Info APS, and Info Sentinel) also use the SMS Service account to access the database to generate reports.

You don't need to create the account and assign permissions in User Manager For Domains if you want to use the SMS Service account for the SMS site. During the

SMS installation process, the SMS Service account is made a member of the local Administrators group on the site server and the Microsoft Windows NT domain's Domain Users and Domain Admins global groups. It is granted the Log On As A Service and Act As Part Of The Operating System user rights for the site server as well. The SMS Service account is created during the SMS setup process; it can be modified later. Follow these steps to modify the SMS Service account name and password:

1. Create the new account through User Manager For Domains. Be sure that the new account is a member of the local Administrators group and the Windows NT domain's Domain Admins and Domain Users global groups. Also be sure that you have given the account the Log On As A Service and Act As Part Of The Operating System user rights on the site server.

2. On the Accounts tab, click the Set button in the SMS Service Account section of the dialog box to display the Windows NT Account dialog box, shown in Figure 3-6.

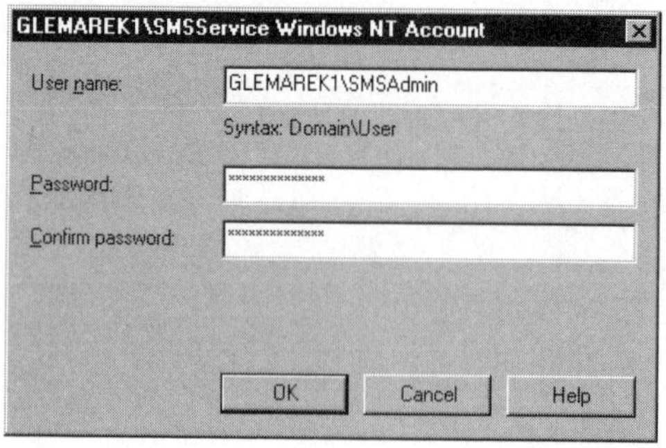

Figure 3-6. *The Windows NT Account dialog box.*

3. Enter the new account name in the form *domainname\username*, and then enter and confirm a password. Click OK to save your changes, then click OK again to close the Site Properties window.

Alternatively, you can let SMS create the new account for you by running the SMS Setup program in the Systems Management Server program group. To do so, follow these steps:

1. Choose Programs from the Start menu, and then choose Systems Management Server and SMS Setup.

2. From the Setup Wizard welcome screen, click Next twice to get to the Setup Options screen. Select the Modify Or Reset The Current Installation option, as shown in Figure 3-7.

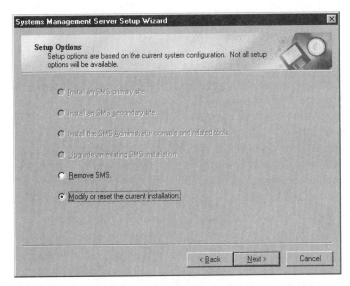

Figure 3-7. *The Setup Options screen.*

3. Click Next to display the SMS Service Account Information screen, as shown in Figure 3-8. Enter the new account and password that you want SMS to create for you.

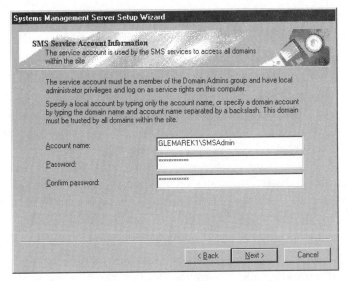

Figure 3-8. *The SMS Service Account Information screen.*

4. Click Next to pass through the rest of the screens (unless you need to make other modifications), and then click Finish on the final screen. SMS will prompt you to confirm the creation of the new account. Click Yes.

SMS will create the account, make it a member of the appropriate groups, grant it the appropriate rights, and reset the service account for the site server and its services.

> **Tip** As with all administrative-level accounts, exercise appropriate security with the SMS Service account. It does, after all, have administrative access across the domain as well as in the SMS site. Use an identifiable name as well as a long and secure password, preferably using some combination of alphanumeric and special characters (for example, gle43kaz$) In addition, consider making the SMS Service account a direct member of the local Administrators group on each site system (CAP, logon point, and so on). By doing this, you can remove the account from the Domain Admins global group for the domain so that the account won't affect the security of other systems in the domain.

Not all SMS services use this account by default, however. As we'll see in the section "Site System Connection Accounts" later in this chapter, specific accounts are preferred for specific access. For example, SMS prefers a separate connection account to NetWare Novell Directory Services (NDS) site systems that has the appropriate level of access defined in NetWare. Nevertheless, because the SMS Service account has administrative rights throughout the domain, it could be used in place of most other SMS accounts.

When SMS attempts to access a site system in another Windows NT domain, SMS uses the SMS Service account you specified to complete its tasks. If your site server and site systems are in separate Windows NT domains, the SMS Service account you specify must have access to the other Windows NT domains. This access can be accomplished by using Windows NT trust relationships or pass-through authentication.

If the Windows NT domain that contains the site system trusts the site server Windows NT domain, you can use the same SMS Service account you (or SMS) created in the site server Windows NT domain to access the site system. All the rules apply, of course. Be sure that the SMS Service account from the trusted domain is a member of the trusted domain's Domain Admins global group, or make it an explicit member of the local Administrators group on the site system in the trusting domain, and grant it the appropriate user rights.

If no trust relationship exists between the two Windows NT domains, you must duplicate the SMS Service account in the site system's Windows NT domain, giving it the appropriate group access and user rights. Duplicating the account means creating an account with the same name and password so that SMS can use pass-through authentication to access the site system.

SMS Client Remote Installation Account The SMS client installation process involves installing .DLL files and loading and starting services. As you may know, such installations require administrative access to the desktop on a Windows NT 4.0 platform. Because many organizations choose not to allow users administrative access to their local Windows NT 4.0 workstations, these users will not have adequate permission on their own to complete the SMS client installation. This is not something for you to be terribly worried about, however. You should expect few, if any, obstacles to getting SMS installed on Windows NT 4.0 workstation clients.

SMS 2.0 offers you two solutions—one is using the SMS Service account to install the SMS client software; the other is creating the SMS Client Remote Installation account, which gives you more control. The SMS Client Remote Installation account is used by SMS—or, more specifically, by Client Configuration Manager, to perform the SMS client software installation on Windows NT 4.0–platform computers. It is used in situations in which the user does not have the appropriate level of permission to complete the installation. It is also used when there is no user logged on, as with a Windows NT 4.0 server kept in a secure location, or for installing the SMS client on new site systems that, of course, need to become SMS clients when they become site systems.

You create the SMS Client Remote Installation account yourself through User Manager For Domains and then give it local administrative permissions on the Windows NT 4.0 member computers in the domain. When a Windows NT computer joins a domain, the Domain Admins global group for that domain automatically becomes a member of the computer's local Administrators group. So, the easy thing to do is to make the SMS Client Remote Installation account a member of the Domain Admins global group. Of course, to be more secure, you could add the account explicitly to the local Administrators group on each Windows NT client.

If you don't create the SMS Remote Client Installation account yourself, never fear! Client Configuration Manager will simply use the SMS Service account to complete the installation.

Caution To use the SMS Service account to complete the SMS client installation, you must not have altered the default group memberships in any way. By default, the SMS Service account is a member of the Domain Admins group that is itself, by default, a member of the local Administrators group on every Windows NT computer that joins the domain. If you have altered this scenario in any way such that the SMS Service account does not have local Administrator access to the client, the client installation will fail.

After you have created the SMS Client Remote Installation account in User Manager For Domains and given it the appropriate level of permissions and user rights, you must follow these steps to tell SMS to use it:

1. On the Accounts tab, click the Set button in the SMS Client Remote Installation Account section to display the Windows NT Account dialog box, which looks similar to the one shown in Figure 3-6.

2. Enter the new account name in the form *domainname\username*, and then enter and confirm a password. Click OK to save your changes, and then click OK again to close the Site Properties window.

You've now finished configuring the SMS Client Remote Installation account to ensure that your Windows NT clients can be installed with the SMS client software components. Next we'll look at how to configure the SQL Server account.

SQL Server Account   The SMS 2.0 site server uses the SQL Server account to gain access to the SMS database and the software metering database if software metering has been installed. The same account could be used for accessing both the SMS database and the software metering database, or, for added security, you could create separate accounts for each.

The SQL Server account is created during setup and varies with the type of SQL Server security implemented during setup. If SQL Server is using standard security, you could specify the default sa account or another SQL login ID that you create and configure. If SQL Server is using integrated security, SMS will use whatever account the SMS administrator logs on with to access the database.

> **Note**   If SMS 2.0 is installed using Express Setup, SMS uses the SQL sa login ID as the SQL Server account by default.

There should be little need to modify this account. However, if you must change the account that SMS uses, you must first create it with User Manager For Domains and configure it for SQL Server. If your site server and SMS site database are in different domains, you must establish a trust relationship between the domains or duplicate the account and password for the SQL Server account in the domain containing the database for pass-through authentication between domains. After you do so, you can follow these steps to instruct SMS to use the account:

1. On the Accounts tab, click the Set button in the SQL Server Account section to display the Windows NT Account dialog box, which resembles the one shown in Figure 3-6.

2. Enter the new SQL account user name, and then enter and confirm a password. Click OK to save your changes, and then click OK again to close the Site Properties window.

> **Tip** If your working knowledge of how to create the SQL Server account falls short, you may want to attend a training class on SQL Server, as mentioned in Chapter 2.

The Security Tab

The Security tab, shown in Figure 3-9, displays the current security rights for the *Site Properties* object. Every object in the SMS database has both class and instance security that can be applied. Applying security to SMS objects is similar to creating an access control list (ACL) for Windows NT files, folders, or shares. To set object class security rights, click the New button in the Class Security Rights section to display the Object Class Security Rights Properties window. You can specify permissions such as Administer, Create, or Delete by checking the check boxes in the Permissions section. To set object instance security rights, click the New button in the Instance Security Rights section and follow the same procedure for setting the class security rights.

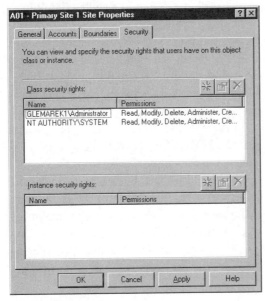

Figure 3-9. *The Security tab of the Site Properties window, showing the two default accounts granted permissions to manage the Site Properties object class.*

Class security rights indicate the access granted to all objects of this type. In the example displayed in Figure 3-9, the class security rights apply not only to this specific site, but also to any other site that may enter into a parent-child relationship with this site.

Instance security rights indicate the access granted to a specific instance of an object. In this example, the instance security right apply only to this particular site (A01 - Primary Site 1).

As another example, consider the *Collections* object. The class security rights indicate which users and groups have been granted specific permissions for working with *all* collections. Each individual collection, however, has an instance security right that identifies which users or groups have been granted specific permissions to that *one* collection.

By default, the administrative-level account that was used to perform the SMS site server installation as well as the local system account (Windows NT Authority\ System) are granted full class security rights for all SMS objects in the database. The list of permissions that are granted, or that can be granted, vary from object to object. Full permissions for the *Site Properties* class include Administer, Create, Delete, Modify, and Read. Full permissions for the *Collections* class include Administer, Advertise, Create, Delete, Delete Resource, Modify, Modify Resource, Read, Read Resource, Use Remote Tools, and View Collected Files.

So, permissions granted to a user for a class of object will apply to all objects of that class. Permissions granted to a user for a specific object in a class will apply to that object alone. If a user is a member of two or more groups, each with different permissions, permissions are cumulative for the user—that is, the least restrictive of the permissions will apply. For example, if the user is a member of a specific help desk group named FINHELP that has Read permission assigned to it and a member of a group named FINMGRS that has Full permissions assigned to it, the user's permissions are Full permissions. The least restrictive permission prevails. However, permissions at the instance level of an object will override the class permissions granted. For example, suppose you want the FINHELP group to be able to initiate Remote Tools sessions only with the clients in the *Finance* collection. You would grant FINHELP no permission for the *Collection* class, but Full permission for the *Finance* collection. This would not only restrict members of FINHELP to only the *Finance* collection, but also their SMS Administrator Consoles would display only the *Finance* collection. As you can see, class and instance security give the SMS administrator far more control over securing objects in the SMS database than in earlier versions of SMS. Chapter 16 explores class and instance security and other security options in more detail.

Site Settings

In SMS 1.2, the SMS administrator modified component attributes of the site such as inventory frequency, site addresses, logon servers, helper servers, and client components to be installed by opening the Site Properties window for the site. As we've seen, these other settings are not part of the Site Properties window for an SMS 2.0 site. The SMS 2.0 Site Properties window should be thought of as relating more to object properties than to component settings.

To access the component settings, expand the Site folder in the console and then expand the Site Settings folder. Under the Site Settings folder, you will find SMS 2.0 component settings similar to those you may have configured in SMS 1.2. Each of these site settings will be discussed in detail in later chapters. Remember that these site settings are integral and unique to each specific SMS site and can rightly be termed properties of the site.

Site Configuration Process Flow

Different SMS 2.0 services and processes carry out different tasks depending on the site property or site setting you enable or configure. However, there is still one basic process flow that takes place when any site setting changes: the change is made, the change is carried out, the database is updated with the change. Let's explore this process more closely.

Site settings are stored in the site control file. This file is named Sitectrl.ct0 and is maintained in the SMS\Inboxes\Sitectrl.box directory on the site server. This file is a text file that you can view using any text editor. The beginning of a representative site control file is displayed in Figure 3-10. The file is quite complete and detailed. It is the single most significant file for the site apart from the database itself because it contains every site setting parameter.

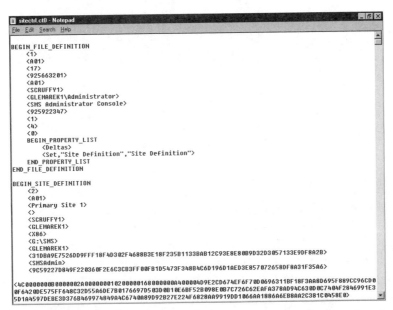

Figure 3-10. *An example of some of the site properties contained in the site control file, showing the site code and site name (A01 and Primary Site 1), the site server platform (X86), the installation directory (G:\SMS), and the site control file serial number (17).*

The site control file can be modified either through a change initiated by the SMS administrator or through a change initiated by an SMS component. Figure 3-11 outlines the process flow for initiating and carrying out a change to the site control file. The SMS SQL Monitor service and the Hierarchy Manager and Site Control Manager threads are the three SMS 2.0 components responsible for maintaining and updating the site control file.

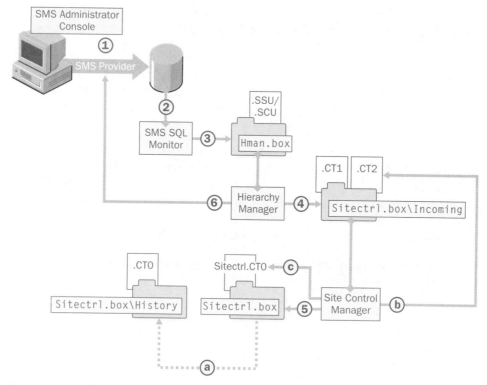

Figure 3-11. *The process flow for carrying out changes to the site control file in an SMS site.*

This process is broken down into the following steps:

1. When the SMS administrator makes a change to a site setting, the SMS Provider updates the SMS database through Windows Management Instrumentation (WMI). The SMS Provider matches the change against the current database settings, called the site control image, and then creates a delta site control image, which contains the changes to be made.

2. A SQL stored procedure is triggered, which wakes up SMS SQL Monitor.

3. SMS SQL Monitor, in turn, writes a wake-up file to Hierarchy Manager's inbox, SMS\Inboxes\Hman.box. This filename is in the form *sitecode*.ssu or *sitecode*.scu, where *sitecode* is the three-character code you assigned to the site during setup.

4. The Hierarchy Manager thread accesses the database and looks for any proposed changes to the site settings. If a delta image exists in the database, Hierarchy Manager creates a delta site control file with the extension .CT1 and writes this file to Site Control Manager's inbox, SMS\Inboxes\Sitectrl.box\Incoming.

5. When this file is written, the Site Control Manager thread wakes up, reads the .CT1 file, and performs three actions:

   a. It copies the current Sitectrl.ct0 file to the SMS\Sitectrl.box\History directory. SMS retains the last 100 site control files. As you'll discover, these files can multiply quickly.

   b. It merges the changes into the current site control file and creates a .CT2 file in Hierarchy Manager's inbox, SMS\Inboxes\Hman.box.

   c. It creates a new Sitectrl.ct0 file in the SMS\Sitectrl.box directory.

6. Hierarchy Manager wakes up when the .CT2 file is written to its inbox and updates the SMS database with the new site control data.

Note Hierarchy Manager and Site Control Manager wake up whenever a file is written to their respective inboxes on the site server. However, they also have wake-up cycles. Hierarchy Manager will wake up every 60 minutes by default, and Site Control Manager will wake up once a day at midnight by default to generate a heartbeat site control file for Hierarchy Manager.

Site Control Filenames

As you monitor the Hierarchy Manager and Site Control Manager inboxes, you will see the .CT1 and .CT2 files created. You will also notice the rather strange filenames that are assigned to these files. When the files are created, they are assigned randomly generated filenames. This is done both to ensure uniqueness and to provide security. By scanning the status messages that are generated, or the log files, for Hierarchy Manager and Site Control Manager, you will be able to follow the creation of these files as they move from inbox to inbox.

The history copy of the site control file that Site Control Manager writes to the SMS\Inboxes\Sitectrl.box\History folder, however, has a very definite naming convention. Here each site control history file is named *.ct0, where * represents the site control file serial number in hexadecimal format. Thus site control file 9 would be saved with the filename 00000009.ct0, and site control file 10 would be saved with the filename 0000000A.ct0.

The serial number of the site control file is simply its sequential order in relation to other site control files. The site control file created during setup is serial number 0. The next one representing a change in site settings would be serial number 1, and so on. The serial number is recorded in the sixth line of the site control file, which can be read using any text editor.

This is not the whole story, of course. When you initiate a change, you may be asking SMS to enable a component, schedule a task, or initiate discovery or installation. Other SMS components also monitor the Sitectrl.ct0 file for changes. When Site Control Manager writes the new site control file, these other components wake up, read the file for changes that pertain to that component, and then carry out the change. These same components may themselves create .CT1 files to update the site control file with changes that have been carried out.

Those of you familiar with earlier versions of SMS will recognize this process flow, since it is similar to that carried out by the old Hierarchy Manager and Site Configuration Manager services. The main difference is that this process was largely cycle-driven in earlier versions of SMS. That is, after the SMS administrator proposed a change to the site control file, you had to wait for Hierarchy Manager to wake up from its sleep cycle before the change would be processed. In SMS 2.0, the Site Control Manager process is event driven, meaning that services and threads wake up when a change is detected. This greatly enhances the performance of SMS 2.0.

Monitoring Status and Flow

SMS 2.0 offers an excellent set of tools for monitoring the status and flow of the site configuration process: site status messages and site component log files. Together, these tools provide you the means not only to effectively troubleshoot an SMS process, but also to learn the process and become familiar with the way SMS components interact with, and react to, each other.

Status Messages

Each of the SMS components responsible for carrying out the site configuration process generates a set of status messages specific to this process. To view these status messages, expand the System Status folder in the SMS Administrator Console, expand Site Status, and then expand your site. Click on Component Status to view a list of status messages for all the components, as shown in Figure 3-12. You will find entries for Hierarchy Manager and Site Control Manager listed here.

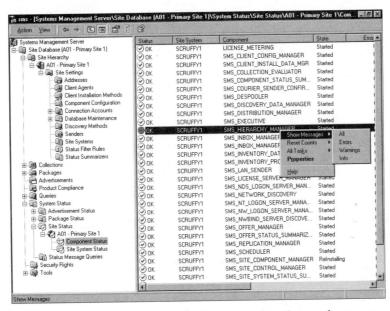

Figure 3-12. *The Site Component Status window, listing the status messages for all the SMS components.*

To view the detailed status messages for a component, right-click on the component, choose Show Messages from the context menu, and then choose All. SMS will display the rich set of detailed messages that that component has generated during a predefined period. Figures 3-13 and 3-14 show the messages generated by Hierarchy Manager and Site Control Manager, with the content of one message displayed. Message content can be viewed by double-clicking on the message or by positioning your cursor on the description area of each message to open a pop-up window. Viewing and configuring status messages are discussed in detail in Chapter 5.

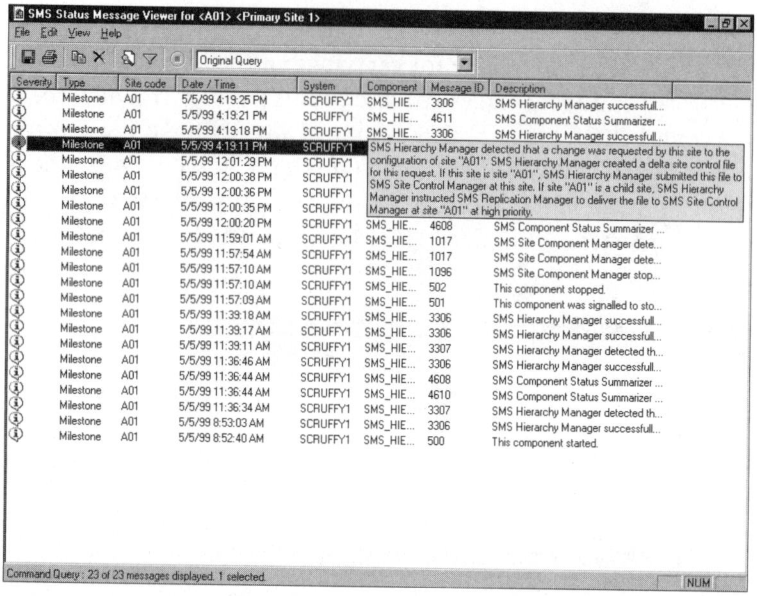

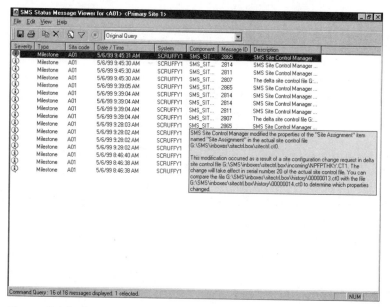

Figure 3-13. *Status messages generated by Hierarchy Manager. Message IDs 3306 and 3307 (displayed) are specific to the Site Control Manager process.*

Figure 3-14. *Status messages generated by Site Control Manager. Message IDs 2807, 2811, 2814 (displayed), and 2865 are specific to the Site Control Manager process.*

Log Files

In addition to status messages, each component can also be configured to create and maintain log files. Unlike status messages, which are generated automatically and enabled by default, log files are not automatically enabled for the site server in SMS 2.0. This is a notable change from earlier versions of SMS. Logging component activity does require additional resources on the site server. Depending on the SMS 2.0 features you installed and the components you have enabled and configured, SMS could generate 30 or more log files—more than twice as many as were generated in SMS 1.2.

Needless to say, it is not always practical, or even necessary, to enable logging for every SMS component. Logging is intended primarily as a troubleshooting tool. However, you would do well to practice using logging in a test environment to learn how the SMS components interact with each other. Logging is certainly not the most exciting activity you could engage in, but nevertheless this exercise will be very enlightening from an SMS perspective.

Enabling SMS 2.0 Log Files

SMS 2.0 component log files are enabled through the SMS Service Manager utility launched in the SMS Administrator Console. Follow these steps to enable SMS 2.0 component log files:

1. Expand the Tools folder in the SMS Administrator Console.

2. Right-click on SMS Service Manager, choose All Tasks from the context menu, and then choose Start SMS Service Manager, as shown in Figure 3-15. SMS will launch the SMS Service Manager utility. Notice that it makes its own connection to the SMS database.

3. Expand the site server entry and select Components, as shown in Figure 3-16.

4. Right-click on the component for which you want to enable logging—for example, SMS_Hierarchy_Manager—and then choose Logging from the context menu to display the SMS Component Logging Control dialog box, as shown in Figure 3-17.

5. Check the Logging Enabled check box. Note the location and name of the log file that will be created. Modify this entry only if you need to. Note also the default log size of 1 MB. This setting ensures that the log does not compromise disk storage space. Again, you can modify this entry (in MB) if you need to.

6. Click OK, and then close the SMS Service Manager window.

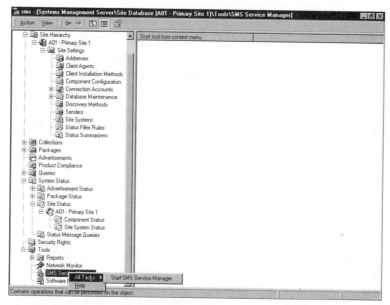

Figure 3-15. *Launching SMS Service Manager.*

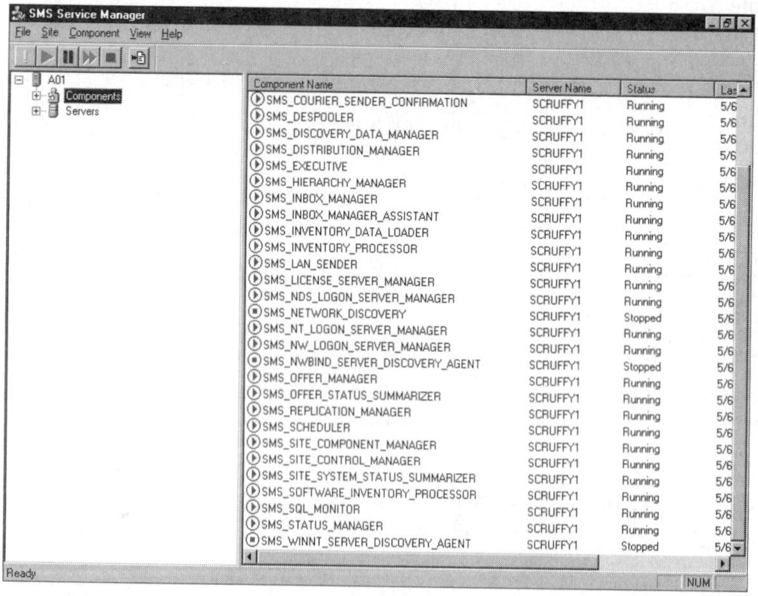

Figure 3-16. *The SMS Service Manager window.*

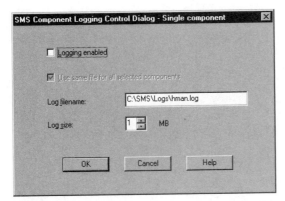

Figure 3-17. *The SMS Component Logging Control dialog box for a single component.*

Real World   Enabling Logging for Multiple Components

Obviously, there's much more to SMS Service Manager, which we'll look at more closely in Chapter 5. However, one feature that is definitely applicable here is the ability to enable logging for multiple SMS components at one time.

You can enable logging for multiple components at one time by holding down the Ctrl key and clicking on the components you want to log, just like selecting multiple files in Windows Explorer. You can enable logging for all components by choosing Select from the Component menu in the SMS Service Manager window and then choosing Select All, or by right-clicking on a component and choosing Select All from the context menu. With all the components selected, you can either right-click on any one of them and choose Logging from the context menu or choose Logging from the Component menu and then enable logging as described earlier.

When you enable logging for multiple SMS components in this way, the option Use Same File For All Selected Components will be selectable in the SMS Component Logging Control dialog box, as shown in Figure 3-18.

Checking this option will cause the components that you selected to write their logging data to a single file. With more than two or three components, this log file can become confusing and somewhat unwieldy. Nevertheless, for something like the site configuration process, in which two SMS threads are involved, this file can provide a single source of tracking information.

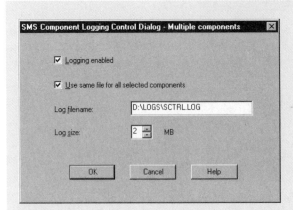

Figure 3-18. *The SMS Component Logging Control dialog box for multiple components.*

Log files are text files that are written, by default, to the SMS\Logs folder. You can save these files anywhere you want when you enable logging, but unless you have disk space concerns, why make changes? Log files can be viewed using any text editor or using the SMS Trace utility included on the SMS 2.0 CD. The advantage of using SMS Trace is that it displays one or more log files in real time—that is, while they are being updated. A text editor will display the file only as it appears up to that point in time. For details on how to install the SMS Trace utility and all its features, refer to Chapter 5.

Defining and Configuring Site Systems

New site systems for the SMS site are defined as site settings for the site. As such, you could consider these site systems to be properties of the site as well. In this section, we will review the site systems that you can define and examine how each becomes a site system for your SMS site. The various site roles that can be assigned to an SMS 2.0 site system are listed here (with abbreviations corresponding to those in Table 3-1):

- Site server
- Site database server (site DB server)
- SMS logon point (logon point)
- SMS client access point (CAP)
- SMS distribution point (SMS distrib. point)
- SMS software metering server (SWM)

- SMS software metering database server (SWM DB server)
- SMS component server (comp. server)

Each of these roles is supported to a greater or lesser extent depending on the operating system platform the site system is using (Windows 2000 and SMS 2.0 compatability issues are discussed in Chapter 20). Table 3-1 outlines the site system roles supported by each platform.

Table 3-1. Site system roles and their supported platforms

Platform	Role Supported							
	Site Server	Site DB Server	Logon Point	CAP	Distrib. Point	SWM	SWM DB Server	Comp. Server
Windows 2000 (version limited)	X	X	X	X	X	X	X	X
Windows NT 4.0, Enterprise Edition	X		X	X	X	X		X
Windows NT 4.0, Terminal Server Edition					X			
Windows NT 4.0, Service Pack 4 or later	X	X	X	X	X	X	X	X
Windows NT 4.0, Service Pack 3 (x86)			X	X	X			
Windows NT 4.0					X			
Windows NT 3.51 Service Pack 5 or later (x86)			X		X			
NetWare Bindery 3.12 or later			X	X	X			
NetWare NDS 4.1x			X	X	X			

Note CAPs and distribution points created on NetWare NDS servers must be defined in the same container as the logon point volume; otherwise, Windows clients will be unable to access them.

We've already looked closely at installing and configuring the site server and the site database server (the SQL server). Let's now focus on the other site system roles. Some site system roles are assigned by the SMS administrator. The SMS administrator can assign CAPs, distribution points, and software metering servers.

Other site system roles are assigned automatically when another component is enabled. When you first install the site server, it is automatically assigned as a CAP and distribution point. If you install SMS 2.0 using the Express Setup option and the site server is also a domain controller, it is also assigned as a logon point.

When a sender is installed on a server, or when the CAP role is assigned to a site system, that site system is automatically assigned the role of component server. A *component server* is any site system running the SMS Executive service. When a client discovery or installation method is enabled, SMS automatically assigns the logon point site system role to the Windows NT domain controllers for the domain specified by the SMS administrator or to the NetWare Bindery or NDS servers defined by the SMS administrator.

In either case, you must be sure that the proposed site system meets the platform requirements outlined in Table 3-1. In addition, check for space and partition requirements as outlined in the relevant sections later in this chapter for each site system role. For example, both logon points and CAPs require an NTFS partition because of security that SMS 2.0 applies to the directories it creates on those site systems. Clients must be able to access site systems such as logon points, CAPs, and distribution points in order to execute the SMS login script, access advertisements and client component files and configuration updates, write discovery and inventory data, and read and execute package scripts. In large part, SMS 2.0 assigns the appropriate level of permissions, but this does not totally absolve you from checking and testing permissions and access.

> **Planning** If you plan on including NetWare Bindery servers or NetWare NDS servers as site systems, you must first install a connection service for the NetWare servers. NetWare NDS servers require that Novell IntranetWare Client be installed on the site server before you assign any site system roles to them. NetWare Bindery servers require that either Novell IntranetWare Client or Windows NT Gateway Services for NetWare (GSNW) be installed on the site server, with the recommended preference being Novell IntranetWare Client. Of course, you will also need to install the NWLINK IPX/SPX Compatible Transport protocol on the site server. Refer to the *Microsoft Systems Management Server Version 2.0 Service Pack 1 Release Notes* topic "Supported NetWare Redirectors" for a list of supported redirectors.

Site System Connection Accounts

SMS 2.0 uses site system connection accounts, also called server connection accounts, to establish communications between the site server and site system services. When you installed SMS 2.0 on the site server, the Setup program created the SMS Service account. Among other tasks, this account is used by the site server to connect to site systems. You can, however, create additional accounts, called

SMS Site System Connection accounts, depending on the security requirements of your site. You do so through User Manager For Domains. An SMS Site System Connection account must be a member of the site system's local Administrators group and must be granted the Log On As A Service user right. It should also have the Password Never Expires option selected since service accounts cannot change their own passwords. The site server uses SMS Site System Connection accounts to connect to the site systems to transfer data. In particular, the site server requires SMS Site System Connection accounts for accessing NetWare Bindery or NDS servers.

When you identify and assign site system roles, the site server automatically creates an SMS Server Connection account named SMSServer_*sitecode*. Site systems such as CAPs and logon points use this account to connect to the site server and transfer data such as inventory and discovery data. SMS creates and maintains this account on its own, so do not modify it in any way. With Windows NT site systems, SMS will attempt a connection first through any existing service connection. It then tries the SMS Site System Connection account if one exists. If the attempt fails, SMS tries the SMS Service account. Typically, SMS will use the SMS Service account because current connections with that account are likely to exist.

The connection process with NetWare servers is similar, but with two exceptions. A NetWare NDS or NetWare Bindery Site System Connection account must be created by the SMS administrator. You must create the account or accounts on the NetWare NDS or NetWare Bindery server first, and then assign the accounts the appropriate level of permissions. For the NDS servers, the accounts must have Admin permissions for the appropriate container object and volume. For the Bindery servers, the accounts must have Supervisor permissions or the equivalent. Then you must identify the account or accounts to the SMS site server as NetWare NDS or Bindery Server connection accounts. If the connection accounts for the NetWare Bindery servers do not exist, however, SMS will then try the SMS Service account before giving up on the connection attempt. If the connection accounts do not exist for NetWare NDS servers, SMS site system management components won't attempt to use the SMS Service account.

After you have created the connection account either through User Manager For Domains or on the NetWare servers, identify the account to the SMS site server using the following method:

1. In the SMS Administrator Console, navigate to the Site Settings folder, and expand it.

2. Then expand the Connection Accounts folder and highlight the Site System folder, as shown in Figure 3-19.

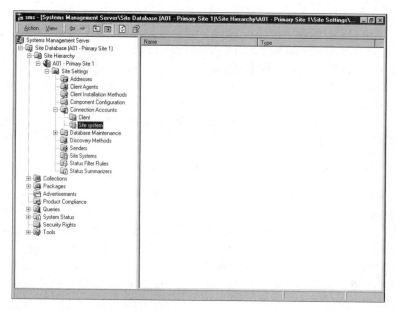

Figure 3-19. *The SMS Administrator Console, showing the Site System folder selected.*

3. Right-click on the Site System folder, and choose New from the context menu to display a list of connection account types, as shown in Figure 3-20.

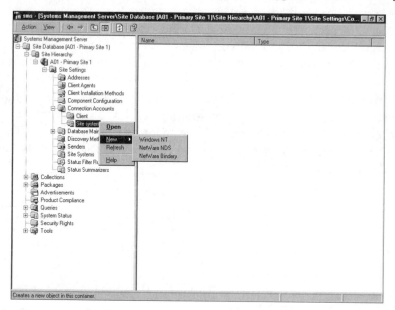

Figure 3-20. *The SMS Administrator Console, showing the connection account types for the* Site System *object.*

4. Choose an account type to display the Connection Account Properties window. In this window, click the Set button to display the account information dialog box.

   For a Windows NT connection account, enter the account name in the form *domainname\username*, and enter and confirm a password, as shown in Figure 3-21. Choose OK.

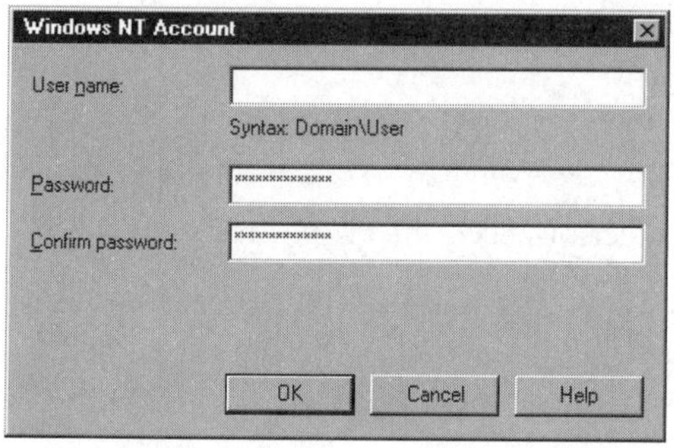

Figure 3-21. *The Windows NT Account dialog box.*

For a NetWare NDS connection account, enter the account name and tree reference using the syntax indicated in Figure 3-22, and then enter and confirm a password. Click OK.

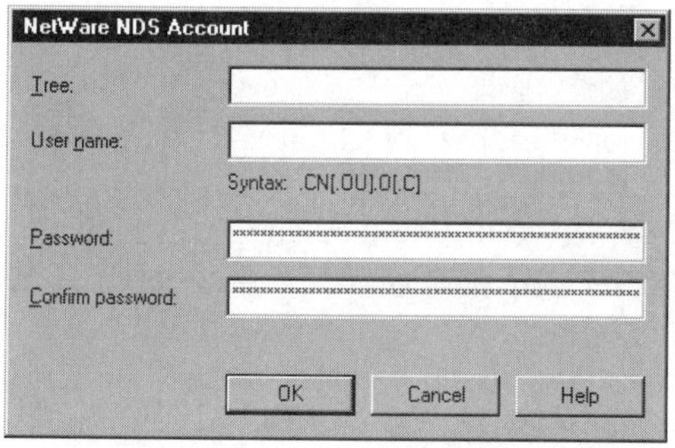

Figure 3-22. *The NetWare NDS Account dialog box.*

For a NetWare Bindery connection account, enter the account name using the syntax indicated in Figure 3-23, and then enter and confirm a password. Click OK.

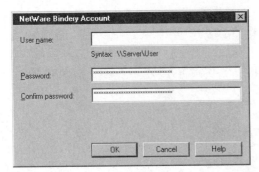

Figure 3-23. *The NetWare Bindery Account dialog box.*

5. Click OK again to close the Connection Account Properties window.

Now that you have identified the servers that will become site servers and created any necessary connection accounts, you must tell SMS that the server should be considered a site system. To do so, follow these steps:

1. In the SMS Administrator Console, navigate to the Site Settings folder and expand it.

2. Select the Site Systems folder. Initially, the only entry you will see is the site server itself.

3. Add a new site system by right-clicking on the Site Systems folder and choosing New from the context menu to display the New Site System options list, as shown in Figure 3-24.

4. Choose either Windows NT Server or Windows NT Share. If you installed NetWare support during installation, you may also choose NetWare Bindery Volume and NetWare NDS Volume. The main difference between the Windows NT Server and Windows NT Share options is that by creating a share first and defining it as the site system, you can direct where SMS will create and write the support files for the CAP and distribution point roles. The software metering server role does not support the Windows NT Share option. However, if you use Windows NT Share, SMS will not create a discovery record for that site system.

Tip If you need a discovery record for the site system created as a Windows NT share, perhaps because you want to use the Network Trace utility to monitor its health, create the site system as both a Windows NT share and a Windows NT server. Simply assign the CAP and distribution point roles to the Windows NT share site system entry; do not assign any site system roles to the Windows NT server site system entry. Refer to Chapter 7 for details on discovery records.

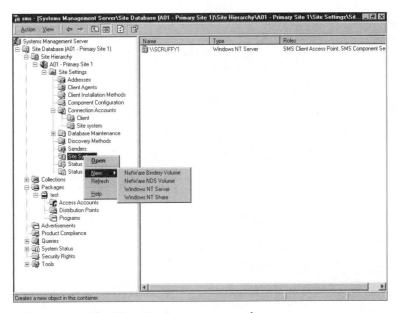

Figure 3-24. *The New Site System options list.*

- Choosing Windows NT Server will display the Site System Properties window shown in Figure 3-25. Click Set and enter the name of the Windows NT server that you want to define as a site system. Then click OK.

Figure 3-25. *The Site System Properties window for Windows NT Server.*

- Choosing Windows NT Share will display the Site System Properties window shown in Figure 3-26. Click Set and enter the name of the server and share (which you have already created) that you want to define as a site system. Then click OK.

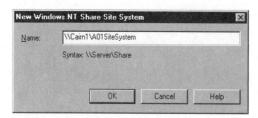

Figure 3-26. *The Site System Properties window for Windows NT Share*

- Choosing NetWare Bindery Volume will display the Site System Properties window shown in Figure 3-27. Click Set and enter the NetWare server name and volume. Click OK.

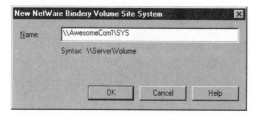

Figure 3-27. *The Site System Properties window for NetWare Bindery Volume.*

Note NetWare Bindery volumes support the CAP and distribution point roles, but not the software metering server role. They can also be assigned the logon point role by enabling the NetWare Bindery Logon Discovery or NetWare Bindery Logon Client Installation methods.

- Choosing NetWare NDS Volume will display the Site System Properties window shown in Figure 3-28. Click Set and enter the NetWare NDS tree and volume, following the syntax provided. Click OK.

Figure 3-28. *The Site System Properties window for NetWare NDS Volume.*

5. Click OK to close the Site System Properties window and save your new site system.

> **Note** NetWare NDS volumes also support the CAP and distribution point roles, but not the software metering server role. They can also be assigned the logon point role by enabling the NetWare NDS Logon Discovery or NetWare NDS Logon Client Installation methods.

The new site system still has to be assigned the role or roles that you want it to play in your SMS site. We'll discuss these roles in the following sections.

Client Access Points

Recall that a CAP is an SMS site system and functions as the exchange point between SMS clients and the SMS site server. Components of SMS clients are installed from a CAP. Inventory, status, and discovery information is collected to a CAP. Advertisement information and other client instructions are obtained from a CAP. When a client receives an advertisement for a program, it will also include a list of distribution points at which the client can find the package files.

When the site server is installed, it becomes a CAP by default. Typically, however, you will want to assign other site systems as CAPs and remove this role from the site server to reduce its resource requirements and improve its performance. CAPs are installed through the SMS Administrator Console as a site system setting. To assign the CAP role, follow these steps:

1. In the SMS Administrator Console, navigate to the Site Settings folder and expand it.

2. Select the Site Systems folder to display the list of site systems you have defined.

3. Right-click on the site system you want to assign as a CAP, and choose Properties from the context menu to display the Site System Properties window, shown in Figure 3-29.

4. Select the Client Access Point tab, shown in Figure 3-30. Check the Use This System As A Client Access Point check box, and then click OK.

5. Click OK again to save this setting and begin the site configuration process that will set up the new CAP.

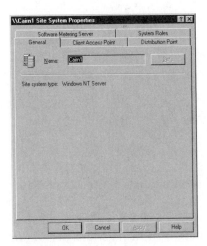

Figure 3-29. *The General tab of the Site System Properties window.*

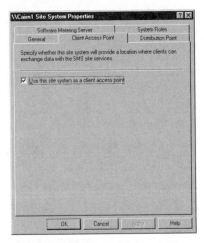

Figure 3-30. *The Client Access Point tab of the Site System Properties window.*

If you want to remove the CAP role from the site server, right-click on the site server, and follow the same procedure you used to assign a CAP role to the site system. In this case, however, you should uncheck the Use This System As A Client Access Point check box on the Client Access tab.

When you enable a new CAP, you have identified a change to the site control information for the site. A new site control file will be created according to the process described in the section "The Site Configuration Process Flow" earlier in this chapter. Recall that during that process, after the new site control file is generated, other components wake up and read the file to determine whether they need to perform any tasks. One of these components is Site Component Manager.

In this scenario, Site Component Manager wakes up and installs the SMS Executive service and the Inbox Manager Assistant thread on the new CAP if it is a Windows NT server. SMS Executive runs Inbox Manager Assistant, which is used to copy inventory files, discovery records, and so on from the CAP to the site server. In addition, the Inbox Manager thread on the site server wakes up and creates the directory structure and share needed on the CAP for both Windows NT and NetWare servers, as shown in Figure 3-31. The directory name and share is CAP_*sitecode*. This directory includes all the inboxes needed for client agents to write information generated on the client to the CAP, and to write instructions needed by the client from the site server to the CAP. As you can see, the folder names in the CAP directory structure are fairly descriptive of the data that is written.

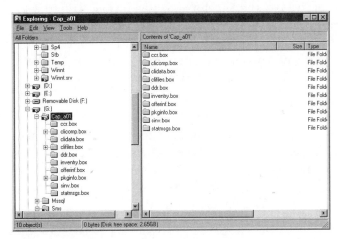

Figure 3-31. *The CAP directory structure, which contains the inboxes needed to write data from both the client and the site server.*

Inbox Manager and Inbox Manager Assistant

Those of you that come from an SMS 1.2 or earlier environment may recognize Inbox Manager and Inbox Manager Assistant. These two SMS 2.0 threads carry out similar functions to that of the Maintenance Manager thread in SMS 1.2. Like Maintenance Manager, both Inbox Manager and Inbox Manager Assistant are responsible for writing information from the site server to the CAP (Inbox Manager) and from the CAP to the site server (Inbox Manager Assistant), maintaining the integrity of the data and ensuring that it is written to the appropriate inbox on the appropriate server.

Inbox Manager copies client component and configuration information, the site assignment list, advertisements, package instructions, and the SMS_def.mof file (hardware inventory definition) to the CAP. It also copies client data files from NetWare servers defined as CAPs since Inbox Manager Assistant would not be running on these site systems. It wakes up when the site control file changes and when any inbox is written to or modified, and it reports status messages and logs activity in the Inboxmgr.log file if logging was enabled for this thread.

Inbox Manager Assistant copies client data records from the client inboxes on the CAP (Ccr.box, Ddr.box, Inventry.box, Sinv.box, and Statmsgs.box) to their counterpart inboxes on the site server. It wakes up when an inbox on the CAP has been written to or modified, reports its status messages, and logs activity to the Inboxast.log file on the CAP if logging was enabled for this thread.

For example, Ddr.box, Inventry.box, and Sinv.box are used by the client to write discovery data records, hardware inventory files, and software inventory data. Clicomp.box, Offerinf.box, and Pkginfo.box are used by the site server to write client configuration parameters, instruction and offer files for advertisements and packages, and package contents and location information.

CAPs require 27 MB of disk space on an NTFS partition and will generate about 35 MB of network traffic to complete installation. The time the installation takes will, of course, depend on the performance level of your network and on whether the installation will need to take place across a WAN connection. As with all site systems, Microsoft strongly suggests that CAPs be located on the local LAN, or be accessible through a fast and reliable remote connection.

The actual number of CAPs that you create will depend on several factors. Perhaps the most significant factor will be the number of clients that the site manages. Recall that CAPs provide the main point of contact between the SMS client and the SMS site. The CAP provides client component configuration, advertisement, and package information to the client, and it records and relays inventory, discovery, and status information from the client. The more clients managed, the greater the resource requirement on the CAP. From another perspective, the larger the number of packages and advertisements the site generates, the greater the resource requirement will be at the CAP. In other words, there is no cookie-cutter approach in determining the optimum number of CAPs that should be created. You need to monitor resource usage on the CAP itself (using the

Windows NT Performance Monitor utility), monitor the network traffic that is generated (using Network Monitor), and consider the needs of the site and your organization.

Distribution Points

The distribution point is an SMS site system that stores the package files, programs, and scripts necessary for a package to execute successfully at an SMS client computer. When the site server is installed, it becomes a distribution point by default. As with CAPs, however, you will want to assign other site systems as distribution points and remove this role from the site server to reduce its resource requirements and improve its performance. Distribution points are installed through the SMS Administrator Console as a site system setting.

To assign the distribution point role, follow these steps:

1. In the SMS Administrator Console, navigate to the Site Settings folder and expand it.
2. Highlight the Site System folder to display a list of the site systems you have defined.
3. Right-click on the site system you want to assign as a distribution point, and choose Properties from the context menu to display the Site System Properties window.
4. Select the Distribution Point tab, shown in Figure 3-32. Select the Use This Site System As A Distribution Point check box, and then click OK.

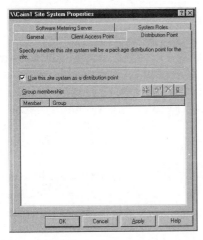

Figure 3-32. *The Distribution Point tab of the Site System Properties window.*

5. Click OK again to save this setting and begin the site configuration process that will set up the new distribution point.

If you want to remove the distribution point role from the site server, right-click on the site server, and follow the same procedure you used to assign a distribution point role to the site system. In this case, however, you should clear the Use This System As A Distribution Point check box on the Distribution Point tab.

When you enable the new distribution point, you have identified a change to the site control information for the site. A new site control file will be created according to the process described in the section "The Site Configuration Process Flow" earlier in this chapter. However, no SMS components are installed on the distribution point.

The distribution point is not written to until a package is actually distributed. At that time, the Distribution Manager thread on the site server checks the distribution point for the partition with the most free space. On that partition, it creates a shared folder named SMSPkg$x$\$$, where x is the drive letter of the partition. The share is a hidden share—a change from earlier versions of SMS. Then Distribution Manager copies the package and program files to a subfolder beneath SMSPkg$x$\$$. If in the course of copying packages to the distribution point you begin to run low on disk space, Distribution Manager will find the next partition with the most free space and create another shared SMSPkg$x$\$$ folder there. We will encounter Distribution Manager again in Chapter 12.

Tip   If you want or need to specify where the package files will be copied on the distribution point, create the SMSPkg$x$\$$ folder and share yourself. Be sure to give your users at least Read access to the folder, and give the SMS Service account Full Control access.

You can also use the Distribution Point tab in the Site Properties window to create what are known as *distribution point groups*. Basically, *distribution point groups* let you group your distribution points into more manageable units. Packages can then be targeted to a distribution point group rather than to individual distribution points.

To create a distribution point group, follow these steps:

1. In the SMS Administrator Console, navigate to the Site Settings folder and expand it.

2. Select the Site System folder to display a list of the site systems you have defined.

3. Right-click on any site system you have assigned as a distribution point and choose Properties from the context menu to display the Site System Properties window.

4. Select the Distribution Point tab, shown in Figure 3-32.

5. In the Group Membership section, click the New button to display the Distribution Point Group Properties window, as shown in Figure 3-33.

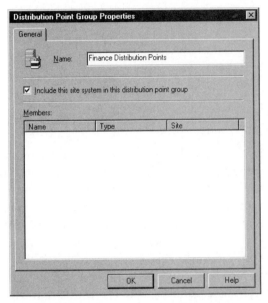

Figure 3-33. *The Distribution Point Group Properties window.*

6. Enter the name of the distribution point group you want to create. If you want the site system you selected to be included in the group you are creating, check the Include This Site System In This Distribution Point Group check box. Then click OK.

7. Click OK again to save this setting and begin the site configuration process that will set up the new distribution point group.

Now when you create a new distribution point or display the properties of an existing distribution point site server, any distribution point groups you created will be displayed in the Group Membership list on the Distribution tab of the Site Systems Properties window, as shown in Figure 3-34, and you will have the opportunity to include the distribution point in one or more of the distribution point groups.

Figure 3-34. *The Group Membership list on the Distribution Point tab.*

Unlike CAPs, distribution points can be shared among SMS 2.0 sites. This sharing enables you to leverage equipment and place distribution points closer to the users and clients that will need to access them. The most significant resource consideration for a distribution point is disk space. Since you are copying source files and scripts for package installation there, you will need enough disk space to accommodate all the packages. The next most significant resource consideration will be network access and traffic. You can use Network Monitor to track and gauge this factor. This tool can also help you determine when an additional distribution point may be necessary. The amount of network traffic that is generated will depend on the size of your packages, the number of clients accessing the distribution point to execute a program, and whether you scheduled the package to run at an assigned time.

Software Metering Server

The SMS software metering server is an SMS site system that enables you to track application usage on SMS clients, restrict application usage, and grant or deny licenses for applications running on an SMS client. This feature of SMS requires its own SQL database for storing usage and license data. This site server role is assigned in the same way you assigned the CAP and distribution point roles.

To assign the software metering server role, follow these steps:

1. In the SMS Administrator Console, navigate to the Site Settings folder and expand it.

2. Select the Site Systems folder to display a list of site systems you have defined.

3. Right-click on the site system you want to assign as a software metering server, and choose Properties from the context menu to display the Site System Properties window.

4. Select the Software Metering Server tab, shown in Figure 3-35. Select the Use This Site System As A Software Metering Server check box, and then click OK.

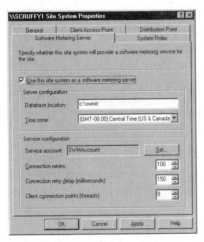

Figure 3-35. *The Software Metering Server tab.*

5. Optionally specify the drive and folder in which you want the software metering data cache to be created, the correct time zone, the service account you want to use, and the connection settings. Click OK.

6. Click OK again to save this setting and begin the site configuration process that will set up the new software metering server.

The complete installation process, including the SMS components that are used and installed and the network traffic that is generated, is covered in detail in Chapter 14. In brief, the License Server Manager thread does most of the work, including creating the Swmtr directory structure and files, sharing the Swmtr folder as Licmtr, loading and starting the SMS_License Server service on the software metering server, and initiating the Install_ODBC process. Install_ODBC installs the Open Database Connectivity (ODBC) support needed to access the software metering SQL database and a local data cache used to collect metered data from the clients. Inbox Manager also gets involved here, creating inboxes in the Swmtr directory. All in all, about 10 MB of disk space is required to complete the installation as well as enough space to store metered data from the clients. The amount of space needed will, of course, vary greatly depending on how many applications you intend to meter and how many clients are involved.

Component Server

Any site system that runs SMS Executive is considered a component server. As we've seen, the CAP is also considered a component server for this reason. The other type of component server that you may define in your site would support the site server by running senders. *Senders* are communication routines used by one site server to contact another site server in a site hierarchy in order to transfer information. For example, a child site will send inventory data, discovery data, status messages, and site control information to its parent via a sender. A parent site will send package information, advertisements, collections, and configuration data to its child sites via a sender.

When a sender is installed on another Windows NT 4.0 server (with Service Pack 4 or later applied), the SMS Executive service and all required support files for that sender are copied to the server and the server becomes a component server—a site system for that SMS site. The best example of using a component server effectively in a production environment is when a Remote Access Service (RAS) connection is required or is available as an alternative connection mechanism between two sites. It would probably not be practical or advisable to install the SMS site server on the Windows NT RAS server. The combined resource requirement would no doubt result in reduced performance. So with RAS on one server and SMS on another, the RAS server could be installed with an SMS RAS sender, making it a component server for the SMS site. Outside of this scenario, the network traffic that might be generated between the site server and the component server (depending on the size and number of packages, advertisements, and so on) might counterbalance any positive benefit derived from having the additional sender capability. We'll look at senders more closely in Chapter 4.

Logon Points

The logon point is an SMS site system that becomes the first point of contact between a client computer and the SMS site. Using a logon script (SMSls.bat), the logon point collects discovery information about the client, determines the client's site assignments, and provides the client with a list of CAPs. Actual installation of the client takes place from the CAP.

A logon point is implemented when either Windows Networking Logon Discovery or Windows Networking Client Logon Installation is enabled by the SMS administrator. All domain controllers in the Windows NT domains identified by the SMS administrator will be installed as logon points. It is not possible to install only specific domain controllers, even if the SMS site server is itself only a member server. If you installed SMS using the Express Setup option, both Windows Networking Logon Discovery and Windows Networking Logon Client Installation are enabled by default. If SMS was installed on a domain controller, all domain controllers for that Windows NT domain will be set up as logon points for that site by default. If you installed SMS using the Custom Setup option, by default neither Windows Networking Logon method is enabled.

If you enable the NetWare NDS or NetWare Bindery Logon Discovery method, or the NetWare NDS or NetWare Bindery Logon Client Installation method, you can identify which NetWare servers to install as logon points. All these discovery methods and installation methods will be addressed in more detail in Chapters 7 and 8. For now, let's review the basic steps for enabling these methods and explore the process behind setting up the logon point site system.

Windows Networking Logon Discovery

To enable Windows Networking Logon Discovery, follow these steps:

1. In the SMS Administrator Console, navigate to the Site Settings folder and expand it.

2. Expand the Discovery Methods folder.

3. Right-click on Windows Networking Logon Discovery and choose Properties from the context menu to display the Windows Networking Logon Discovery Properties window, shown in Figure 3-36.

4. On the General tab, select the Enable Windows Networking Logon Discovery check box.

Note If you installed the site server using the Express Setup option, this discovery method will be enabled already by default.

5. The Keep Logon Point Lists For Discovery And Installation Synchronized option is enabled by default and ensures that the domain entries in the Logon Points list box are the same for both the Windows Networking Logon Discovery and Windows Networking Logon Client Installation methods. If you intend to use this discovery method to discover resources only and not necessarily install them, clear this option. (See Chapter 7 for more information.)

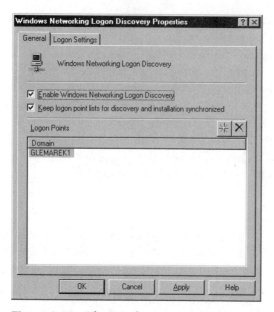

Figure 3-36. *The Windows Networking Logon Discovery Properties window.*

6. Click the New button in the Logon Points section of the Properties window to display the New Windows Networking Logon Point dialog box, shown in Figure 3-37. Enter a domain name and click OK to add a Windows NT domain to the list. Note that every domain controller in the domains specified will be installed as logon points for the SMS site.

Figure 3-37. *The New Windows Networking Logon Point dialog box.*

7. Click OK again to begin the site configuration process that will cause the logon point to be installed.

NetWare Bindery Logon Discovery

To enable NetWare Bindery Logon Discovery, follow these steps:

1. In the SMS Administrator Console, navigate to the Site Settings folder and expand it.

2. Expand the Discovery Methods folder.

3. Right-click on NetWare Bindery Logon Discovery and choose Properties from the context menu to display the NetWare Bindery Logon Discovery Properties window, shown in Figure 3-38.

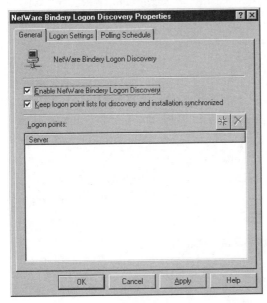

Figure 3-38. *The NetWare Bindery Logon Discovery Properties window.*

4. On the General tab, select the Enable NetWare Bindery Logon Discovery check box.

5. The Keep Logon Point Lists For Discovery And Installation Synchronized option is enabled by default and ensures that the NetWare Bindery server entries in the logon points list box are the same for both the NetWare Bindery Logon Discovery and NetWare Bindery Logon Client Installation methods. If you intend to use this discovery method to discover resources only and not necessarily install them, clear this option. (See Chapter 7 for more information.)

6. Click the New button in the Logon Points section to display the New NetWare Bindery Logon Point dialog box, shown in Figure 3-39. Enter a server name and click OK to add a NetWare Bindery server to the Logon Points list.

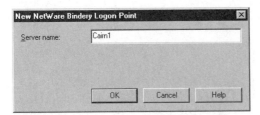

Figure 3-39. *The New NetWare Bindery Logon Point dialog box.*

7. Click OK again to begin the site configuration process that will cause the logon point to be installed.

NetWare NDS Logon Discovery

To enable NetWare NDS Logon Discovery, follow these steps:

1. In the SMS Administrator Console, navigate to the Site Settings folder and expand it.

2. Expand the Discovery Methods folder.

3. Right-click on NetWare NDS Logon Discovery and choose Properties from the context menu to display the NetWare NDS Logon Discovery Properties window, shown in Figure 3-40.

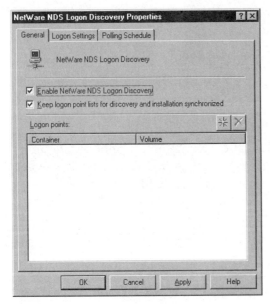

Figure 3-40. *The NetWare NDS Logon Discovery Properties window.*

4. On the General tab, select the Enable NetWare NDS Logon Discovery check box.

5. The Keep Logon Point Lists For Discovery And Installation Synchronized option is enabled by default and ensures that the NDS container entries in the Logon Points list box are the same for both the NetWare NDS Logon Discovery and NetWare NDS Logon Client Installation methods. If you intend to use this discovery method to discover resources only and not necessarily install them, clear this option. (See Chapter 7 for more information.)

6. Click the New button in the Logon Points section to display the New NetWare NDS Logon Point dialog box, shown in Figure 3-41. Enter the appropriate tree, container, and volume settings and click OK to add a new NDS container to the list.

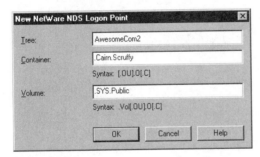

Figure 3-41. *The New NetWare NDS Logon Point dialog box.*

7. Click OK again to begin the site configuration process that will cause the logon point to be installed.

Windows Networking Logon Client Installation

To enable Windows Networking Logon Client Installation, follow these steps:

1. In the SMS Administrator Console, expand the Site Settings folder.

2. Expand the Client Installation Methods folder.

3. Right-click on Windows Networking Logon Client Installation and choose Properties from the context menu to display the Windows Networking Logon Client Installation Properties window, shown in Figure 3-42.

4. On the General tab, select the Enable Windows Networking Logon Client Installation check box.

Note   If you installed the site server using the Express Setup option, this installation method will be enabled already by default.

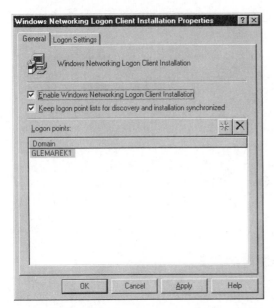

Figure 3-42. *The Windows Networking Logon Client Installation Properties window.*

5. The Keep Logon Point Lists For Discovery And Installation Synchronized option is enabled by default and ensures that the domain entries in the Logon Points list box are the same for both the Windows Networking Logon Client Installation and Windows Networking Logon Discovery methods.

6. Click the New button in the Logon Points section to display the New Windows Networking Logon Point dialog box, shown in Figure 3-43. Enter a domain name and click OK to add a Windows NT domain to the list. Note that every domain controller in the domains specified will be installed as a logon point for the SMS site.

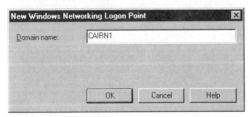

Figure 3-43. *The New Windows Networking Logon Point dialog box.*

7. Click OK again to begin the site configuration process that will cause the Logon Point to be installed.

NetWare Bindery Logon Client Installation

To enable NetWare Bindery Logon Client Installation, follow these steps:

1. In the SMS Administrator Console, navigate to the Site Settings folder and expand it.

2. Expand the Client Installation Methods folder.

3. Right-click on NetWare Bindery Logon Client Installation, and choose Properties from the context menu to display the NetWare Bindery Logon Client Installation Properties window, shown in Figure 3-44.

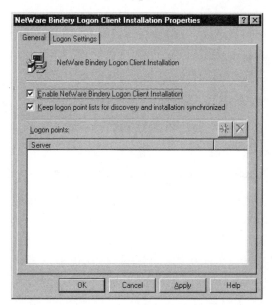

Figure 3-44. *The NetWare Bindery Logon Client Installation Properties window.*

4. On the General tab, select the Enable NetWare Bindery Logon Client Installation check box.

5. The Keep Logon Point Lists For Discovery And Installation Synchronized option is enabled by default and ensures that the NetWare Bindery server entries in the Logon Points list are the same for both the NetWare Bindery Logon Installation and Discovery methods.

6. Click the New button (the yellow star) in the Logon Points section to display the New Server dialog box, shown in Figure 3-45. Enter a server name and click OK to add a NetWare Bindery server to the Logon Points list.

Figure 3-45. *The New Server dialog box.*

7. Click OK again to begin the site configuration process that will cause the Logon Point to be installed.

NetWare NDS Logon Client Installation

To enable NetWare NDS Logon Client Installation, follow these steps:

1. In the SMS Administrator Console, navigate to the Site Settings folder and expand it.

2. Expand the Client Installation Methods folder.

3. Right-click on NetWare NDS Logon Client Installation, and choose Properties from the context menu to display the NetWare NDS Logon Client Installation Properties window, shown in Figure 3-46.

4. On the General tab, check the Enable NetWare NDS Logon Client Installation check box.

5. The Keep Logon Point Lists For Discovery And Installation Synchronized option is enabled by default and ensures that the NDS container entries in the Logon Points list are the same for both the NetWare NDS Logon Client Installation and NetWare NDS Logon Discovery methods.

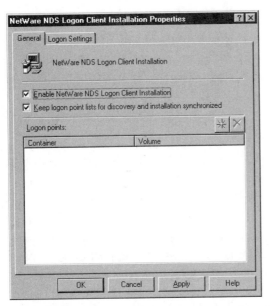

Figure 3-46. *The NetWare NDS Logon Client Installation Properties window.*

6. Click the New button in the Logon Points section to display the New NetWare NDS Logon Point dialog box, shown in Figure 3-47. Enter the appropriate tree, container, and volume values and click OK to add a new NDS container to the Logon Points list.

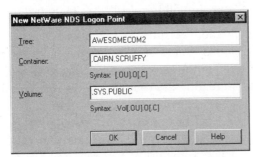

Figure 3-47. *The New NetWare NDS Logon Point dialog box.*

7. Click OK again to begin the site configuration process that will cause the logon point to be installed.

Logon Point Site Server Installation Process

As with other site server installations, the enabling of a logon discovery or logon installation method triggers a change in the site control file for that site. Whenever a site control file changes, as we have seen, other SMS components read it to determine whether they need to carry out any changes of their own. In this scenario, SMS Logon discovery managers and SMS Logon installation managers read the modified site control file to determine whether there are any changes that affect them. If you enabled a logon discovery method, an appropriate SMS Logon discovery manager will initiate the process of installing the logon points. Similarly, if you enabled a logon client installation method, an appropriate SMS Logon installation manager will initiate the process of installing the logon point(s). SMS Logon Server Manager actually carries out the installation of the logon point.

SMS Logon Server Manager creates and shares the folder SMSLogon on the logon point, applies the necessary permissions, and copies the appropriate files to that directory structure. These files include the site list, the CAP list, the logon script, and support programs to initiate client discovery and installation routines and detect slow network speeds. About 15 MB of disk space is required, with a corresponding amount of network traffic generated. On Windows NT logon points, an NTFS partition is also required. The time it takes to complete the installation will, of course, depend on when the process takes place, and what other kinds of network traffic are being generated. Also, the number of logon points that need to be installed will affect the time and the network traffic generated. Recall that all Windows NT domain controllers in a Windows NT domain will be installed as logon points.

Each logon discovery and installation method has an SMS Logon discovery manager, SMS Logon installation manager, and SMS Logon server manager. As shown in Figure 3-48, when a change is detected in the site control file, the SMS Logon discovery managers and SMS Logon installation managers wake up and read the file to determine whether the change applies to them. If it does, the appropriate discovery or installation manager creates a *.pcf file in the appropriate SMS Logon server manager's inbox. This file contains the files required for performing logon discovery and a list of discovery properties, or the list of files required for logon installation. When this file is written to Logon Server Manager's inbox, Logon Server Manager wakes up, reads the files, and proceeds to install the Logon Point.

On Windows NT logon points, SMS Windows NT Logon Server Manager installs and starts the SMS_NT_Logon_Discovery_Agent, an SMS component that discovers computers running Windows as they log on to Windows NT domains in an SMS site. No SMS services or threads are installed on a NetWare server.

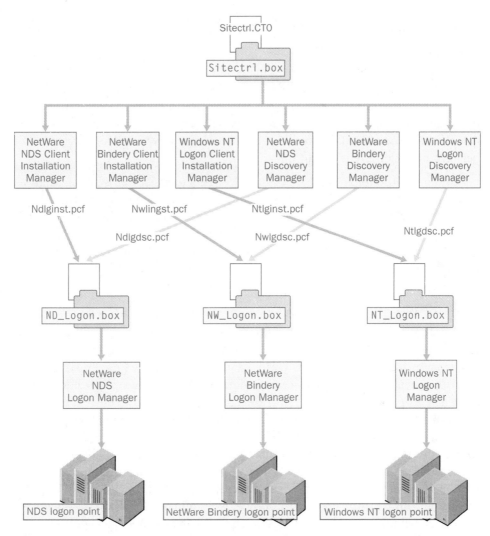

Figure 3-48. *The Logon Point Site Server Installation process.*

Checkpoints

If you've been reading carefully, you'll have encountered several notes and cautions describing situations that if not considered can result in strange and unusual things happening in your site. These administrative lapses might be called "gotchas" because of the sneaky way they have of jumping up to get you. Let's recap the most significant gotchas here.

Planning and Identifying Site Systems

First and foremost, be sure that your deployment strategy has identified which servers will serve as site systems, how many servers you may need, and which roles they will play. Your answers will depend on the size of your site; the number of clients, packages, advertisements, and so on involved; and the current state of your network and network traffic. The soundest approach is to test, track, and analyze. Use the tools available to learn how your site server and site systems will perform under different conditions.

Performance Monitor is an ideal Windows NT tool to assist you with this analysis on Windows NT servers. Use Network Monitor to track and analyze traffic generated between the site server and its site systems. Identify, wherever possible, those times when site traffic might take advantage of lighter traffic loads. As we delve more deeply into SMS processes such as inventory collection and package distribution, you'll learn how to identify and analyze network traffic.

Disk Space

The amount of disk space required for each type of site system has been identified in the section "Defining and Configuring Site Systems" earlier in this chapter. Be sure that the site systems you have in mind have adequate disk space to carry out their function and store their data. CAPs, for example, need space to store inventory data, discovery data, and status messages from clients, as well as package information, advertisements, site lists, and client configuration files. We know that CAPs need about 27 MB of disk space for installation, but you will need additional space for the client data and package and advertisement information. Of course, the number of clients you are managing and the number of packages and advertisements that you generate will affect the disk space requirements, but this quantity can—with some effort and resource analysis—be determined. Distribution points require as much disk space as each package you store. Again, with some calculation effort and forward planning, you can determine the amount of disk space needed.

Connection Accounts

Connection accounts were discussed in detail in the section "Site System Connection Accounts" earlier in this chapter. For Windows NT site servers, additional connection accounts beyond the default account that SMS creates or the SMS Service account are really not required unless you have specific security issues to address on specific site systems.

On the other hand, connection accounts for NetWare Bindery or NDS servers are not created by default, and they are most assuredly required in order for SMS components to be able to install the site system roles and collect data from these servers. NetWare servers support only the logon point, CAP, and distribution point site server roles. Recall from the section "Defining and Configuring Site Systems" that you must have installed some redirection service such as GSNW or the IntranetWare Client (necessary for accessing NDS containers) on the site server. Next, you must have already created the account on the NetWare server and assigned it the appropriate permissions. Admin or Supervisor equivalence will do, but you can apply only those permissions that are actually needed to provide a higher level of security.

More Info   For the most current information about using SMS 2.0 in a NetWare environment, visit the Systems Management Server Web site at *http://www.microsoft.com/smsmgmt.*

Summary

In this chapter, you learned how to identify and configure site systems for your SMS site. The site server can be assigned all site system roles, of course, and in many environments this may be appropriate. However, other concerns might cause you to assign one or more site system roles to other servers in your site. These concerns, as we have seen, include performance limitations of the site server, the number and location of clients and users, network infrastructure, and network traffic patterns. Now that you understand how to manage systems within your site, we can explore the process of joining different SMS sites in an enterprise-wide site hierarchy—the topic of Chapter 4.

Chapter 4
Multiple-Site Structures

For most large organizations, maintaining a single Microsoft Systems Management Server (SMS) site to manage all network resources will not be practical. In an organization whose network infrastructure consists of subnets that communicate through WAN connections, routers, and so on, implementing multiple SMS sites may well prove to be the stronger strategy. With that in mind, in this chapter, we'll examine the strategies and processes involved in designing and implementing a site hierarchy for your organization. We will explore the concepts of parent-child relationships and secondary sites, and we'll look at methods of communicating between sites. We'll also examine the factors that will affect your site structure strategy, such as network performance, domain model, number and location of clients, and the client components you want to install. Let's begin with the basic building block of the SMS site structure—the parent-child relationship.

Defining Parent-Child Relationships

Parent sites and child sites are defined by their relationship within an SMS site hierarchy. We've already explored the related terms and concepts in Chapter 1. Let's review these terms and then examine them in more detail. A *parent site* is any site with at least one child site defined; the parent site has the ability to administer any child sites below it in the SMS hierarchy. A *child site* is any SMS site that has a parent defined.

An SMS *primary site* has three main distinguishing characteristics:

- It is an SMS site that has access to a Microsoft SQL Server database.
- It can be directly administered through the SMS Administrator Console as well as by any SMS sites above it in the site hierarchy. A primary site can also administer any child sites below it in the site hierarchy.
- It can be a child of other primary sites, and it can have child sites of its own.

The requirement that a primary site have access to a SQL Server database may translate into an additional investment in hardware and software for each SMS site and/or site server. On the other hand, because a primary site can be both a parent site and a child site, it is relatively easy to restructure your site hierarchy if all your sites are primary sites, as we will see in the section "Implementing a Parent-Child Relationship Between Primary Sites" later in this chapter.

An SMS *secondary site* is also distinguished by three main characteristics:

- It does not have access to a SQL Server database.
- It is always a child of a primary site and is administered solely through its parent, or through another primary site above it in the SMS site hierarchy.
- It cannot have child sites of its own.

Because a secondary site does not require access to a SQL Server database, it might not command the same investment in hardware and software as a primary site. However, a secondary site can be administered only through its parent site or through another primary site above it in the site hierarchy. If an SMS administrator on the same local subnet as the secondary site wants to administer the site, that SMS administrator will first need to connect to the site database for the secondary site's parent site. If the SQL database for the parent site is accessed across a WAN link, response may be slow or inefficient. On the other hand, if there is no local SMS administrator available the secondary site can be rather easily managed by a remote SMS administrator in the same manner.

Caution To switch primary and secondary site roles, you must first uninstall and then reinstall SMS.

A *central site* is an SMS primary site that resides at the top of the SMS hierarchy. Database information rolls from child to parent and is collected ultimately at the central site's SMS database. A central site can administer any site below it in the SMS hierarchy and can send information down to its child sites.

Figure 4-1 shows a typical SMS site hierarchy model. In this site hierarchy, site A01 is the central site. All information rolls up to this site. Sites A02, A03, and A04 are primary sites, since they have access to a SQL database for SMS. Site A05 is a child site to site A03; it is also a secondary site, since it does not have access to a SQL database for SMS.

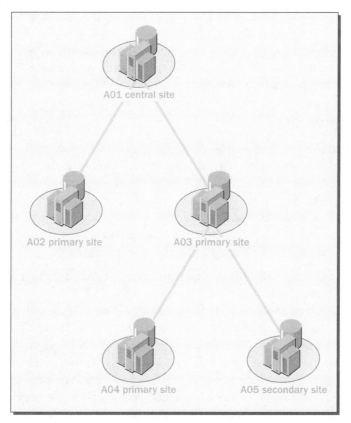

Figure 4-1. *A typical SMS site hierarchy.*

Child sites send inventory data, discovery data, site control data, and status messages to their immediate parent sites. A child site never sends information to its "grandparent" site. Parent sites, in turn, send information about collections, package definitions, advertisements, and site control files to their child sites. Although child sites send data only to their immediate parent, a parent site can send information to any child below it in the SMS site hierarchy, provided it has an address for that site.

Because child sites send inventory data to their parent sites, database storage space becomes a greater concern at the parent sites at each successive layer in the hierarchy. In the hierarchy shown in Figure 4-1, site A04 reports its inventory data to site A03. Site A03's database needs to be large enough to accommodate its own information plus the information coming from site A04. Similarly, site A03 reports its inventory data to site A01. Site A01's database therefore needs to be large enough to accommodate its own information plus that of both sites A03 and A04.

Tip Try to keep your site hierarchy as flat as possible. A flatter hierarchy will require information to flow through fewer layers (sites) before reaching the central site. Child site information will be reported to the central site more quickly and efficiently. In addition, the flatter the hierarchy, the less concern you will have about database space requirements at parent sites at each level of the hierarchy.

Installing a Secondary Site

In Chapter 2, you learned how to install an SMS 2.0 primary site. In this section, we'll explore the process of installing an SMS 2.0 secondary site. In earlier versions of SMS, the secondary site was created as a property of a parent primary site through the Site Properties window of the SMS Administrator window. The SMS 2.0 secondary site should also be considered a property of a primary site. It can be a child only of a specific primary site, and it is managed primarily through that primary site or through any site above it in the site hierarchy.

As in earlier versions of SMS, an SMS 2.0 secondary site installation can be initiated through the SMS Administrator Console. However, in SMS 2.0, a secondary site can also be installed directly from the SMS 2.0 CD. The Setup program gives you the option of installing a secondary site. You might choose this option if you need to install the secondary site but do not yet have a WAN connection available to the primary site, or if the existing WAN connection is "network traffic challenged" and you want to avoid the additional traffic involved in performing the installation from the primary site server. Also, when you install a secondary site from the CD, you will be able to choose which SMS components you want to install on the secondary site server, much like the Custom installation we reviewed in Chapter 2. When you install the secondary site from the parent site, all SMS components are installed on the secondary site server.

Installing the Secondary Site from Its Parent Primary Site

Follow these steps to install an SMS 2.0 secondary site server from a primary site:

1. In the SMS Administrator Console, navigate to the site entry folder and right-click on it, choose New from the context menu, and then choose Secondary Site. The Welcome To The Create Secondary Site Wizard screen will appear, shown in Figure 4-2.

2. Click Next to display the Site Identity screen, shown in Figure 4-3. Enter a three-character site code, a descriptive name for the site, and optionally a descriptive comment.

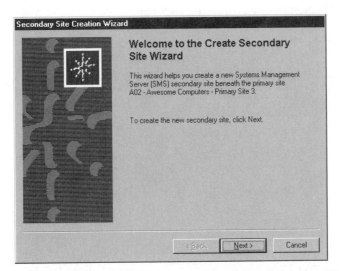

Figure 4-2. *The Welcome To The Create Secondary Site Wizard screen.*

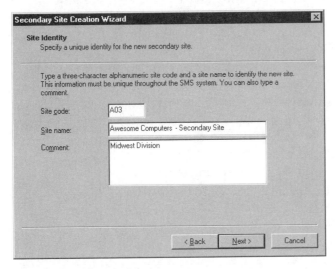

Figure 4-3. *The Site Identity screen.*

3. Click Next to display the Site Server screen, shown in Figure 4-4. Enter the name of the domain in which the secondary site server is located, the server name, the processor platform (Intel or Alpha), and the NTFS installation directory (be sure that you reference an NTFS directory).

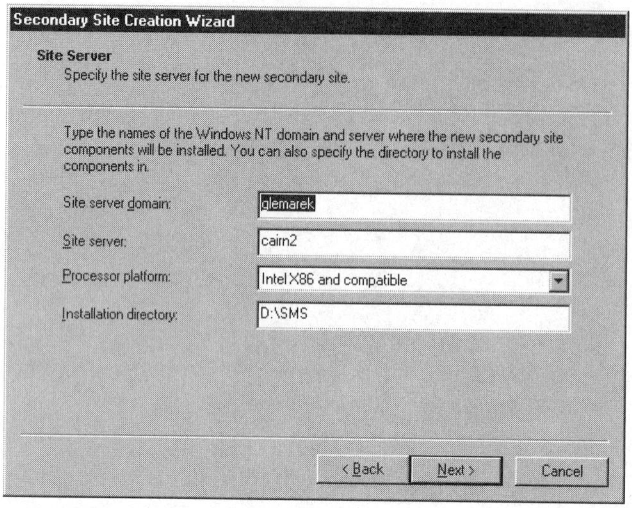

Figure 4-4. *The Site Server screen.*

4. Click Next to display the Installation Source Files screen, shown in
    Figure 4-5. This screen lets you specify where the source files for install-
    ing the secondary site reside. If you select the Transfer Installation Source
    Files From Parent Site Server check box, Setup will obtain the installation
    files from the primary site server and transfer them across the network
    to the target secondary site. This option will, of course, generate a fair
    amount of network traffic. If you select the Installation Source Files Are
    On A CD-ROM At Secondary Site Server check box, Setup will look for
    the installation files on the SMS CD on the local (secondary site) server.
    This option assumes, of course, that you have inserted the SMS 2.0
    CD in the CD-ROM on the target secondary site server.

5. Click Next to display the SMS Service Account screen, shown in
    Figure 4-6. Enter the name of the SMS Service account (which you
    have already created) that the secondary site server will use, and
    confirm the password.

Caution   The SMS Service account you specify during the installation of the
SMS 2.0 secondary site must already have been created for the target server,
as we discussed in Chapter 3. Be sure to make the account a member of the
Domain Admins global group in the secondary site's Windows NT domain. Also
be sure that the account is a member of the local Administrators group on the
secondary site server itself—either explicitly or by virtue of its being a member
of the Domain Admins global group—and that it has the Log On As A Service user
right on the secondary site server. If any of these prerequisites is not met, the
installation process will fail—miserably!

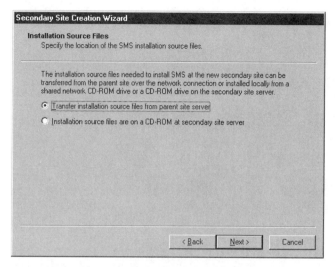

Figure 4-5. *The Installation Source Files screen.*

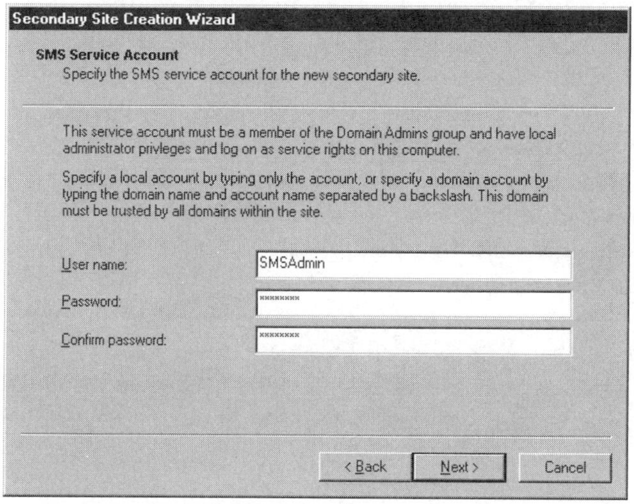

Figure 4-6. *The SMS Service Account screen.*

6. Click Next to display the Addresses To Secondary Site screen, shown in
   Figure 4-7. If you have already created one or more addresses to the target secondary site—for example, using Standard Sender (through LAN
   or WAN connections) or Asynchronous RAS Sender (through a dial-up
   connection)—these will be listed in the Addresses To list. Select the No
   option and proceed to step 9. If you have not already created an address
   to the secondary site, or if you want to create a new address, select the
   Yes option.

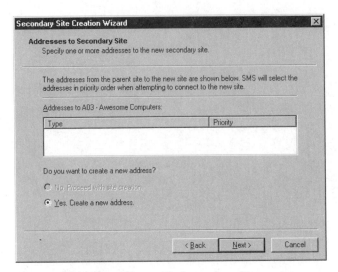

Figure 4-7. *The Addresses To Secondary Site screen.*

7. If you chose Yes in the preceding step, clicking Next will take you to the
New Address To Secondary Site screen, shown in Figure 4-8. Here you
must select a sender address type, confirm the secondary site server
name, and identify the name of the account on the secondary site server
that you want the primary site to use when connecting to the secondary
site. This account will generally be the SMS Service account, but it can
be any account that has at least Change permission for the SMS_SITE
share. Once again, this account must have been created before you
begin the secondary site installation.

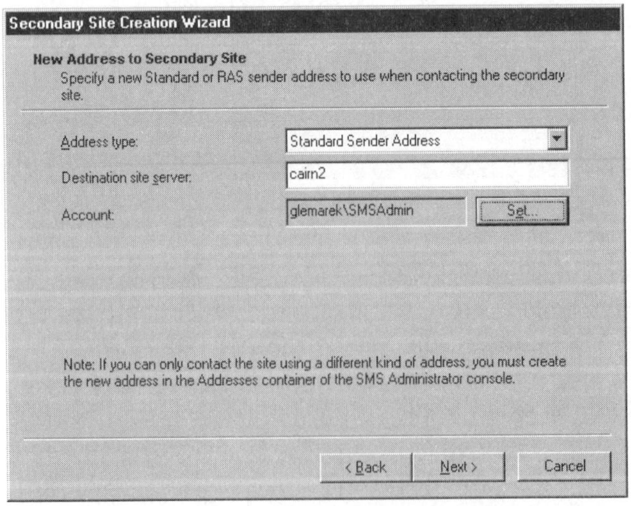

Figure 4-8. *The New Address To Secondary Site screen.*

Note When you create an address using Setup, you will have only the options Standard Sender Address and Asynchronous RAS Sender Address on this screen. If you choose to use a RAS sender, RAS must be installed on the server you will use for the secondary site server or on another server accessible to the proposed secondary site server. If you need any other sender type, you must create the address through the SMS Administrator Console before beginning the secondary site installation process.

8. Click Next to display the New Address To Parent Site screen, shown in Figure 4-9. Specify a sender address type, confirm the primary site server name, and identify the name of the account on the primary site server that you want the secondary site to use when connecting to the primary site. This account will generally be the SMS Service account, but it can be any account that has at least Change permission for the SMS_SITE share on the primary site server. Once again, this account must have been created before you begin the secondary site installation.

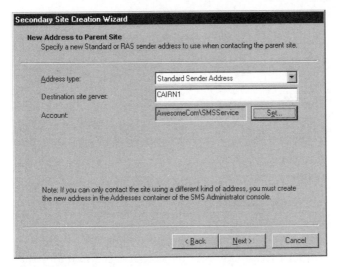

Figure 4-9. *The New Address To Parent Site screen.*

9. Click Next to display the Completing The Create Secondary Site Wizard screen. Review your selections in the New Secondary Site Characteristics section, and then click Finish to begin the installation process. You can also click Back to return to previous screens to make changes.

Installing the Secondary Site Locally from the SMS CD

Follow these steps to install an SMS 2.0 secondary site server from the SMS CD:

1. Begin Setup from the SMS CD. You will see the Systems Management Server Setup Wizard welcome screen, as you did when you were installing the primary site.

2. Click Next until the Setup Options screen is displayed, shown in Figure 4-10. Select the Install An SMS Secondary Site option.

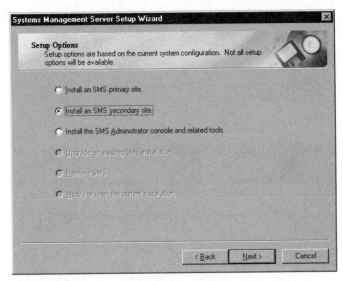

Figure 4-10. *The Setup Options screen.*

3. Click Next to display the Product Registration screen, shown in Figure 4-11, and enter the name, organization, and CD key information.

4. Click Next to display the SMS Site Information screen, shown in Figure 4-12. Enter the three-character site code you will assign to the secondary site server, a descriptive name for the site, and the name of the Windows NT domain in which the secondary site server is located.

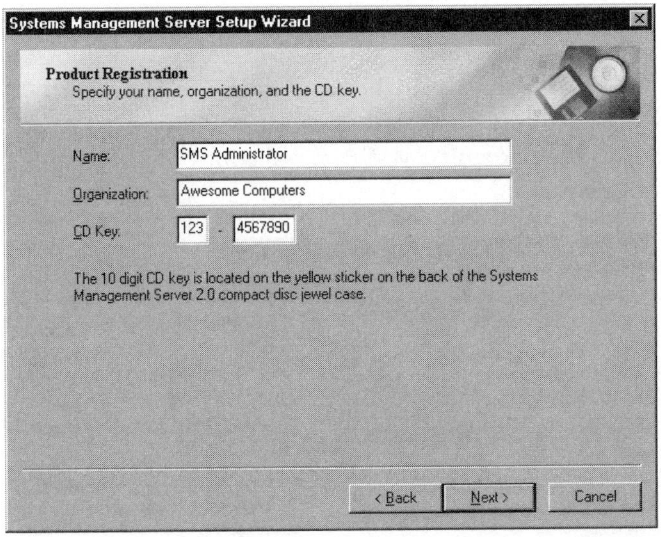

Figure 4-11. *The Product Registration screen.*

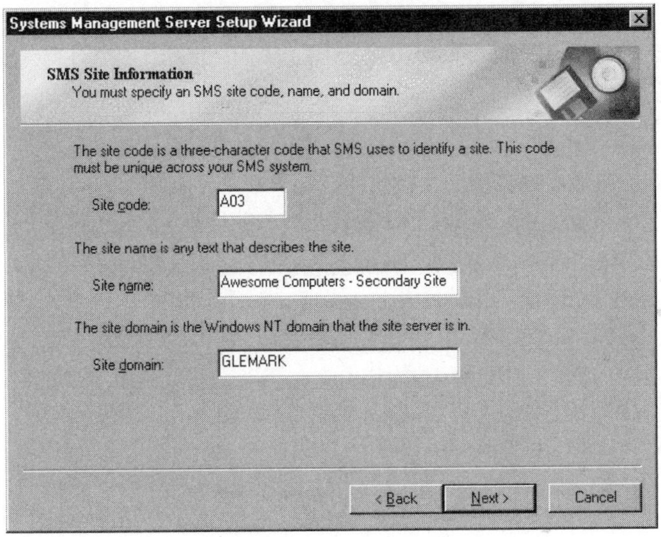

Figure 4-12. *The SMS Site Information screen.*

5. Click Next to display the SMS Service Account Information screen, shown in Figure 4-13. Enter the name of the SMS Service account (which you have already created) that the secondary site server will use, and enter and confirm the password. If you haven't created a service account, either use the default *SMSService* account or enter an account name and password.

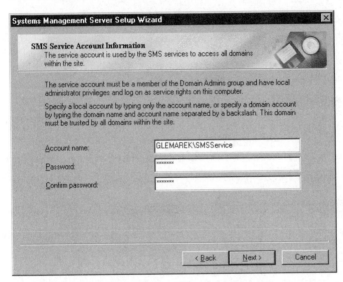

Figure 4-13. *The SMS Service Account screen.*

6. Click Next to display the SMS Server Platform screen, shown in Figure 4-14. Select an alternate platform file support if your secondary site will support a mixed platform environment.

7. Click Next to display the Setup Installation Options screen, shown in Figure 4-15. Select the SMS 2.0 options that you want to enable on the secondary site server. You can also change the directories in which the components are installed on your site server.

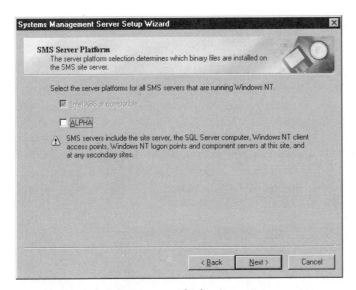

Figure 4-14. *The SMS Server Platform screen.*

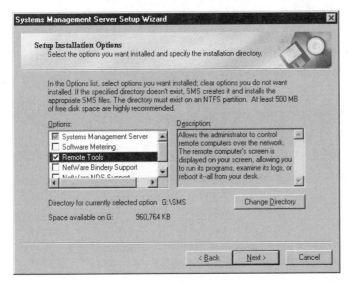

Figure 4-15. *The Setup Installation Options screen.*

Note When installing SMS from the CD, you can select which SMS options you want to install, much like a Custom installation for a primary site server. Notice, however, that only those options that do not require access to a SQL SMS database or that are applicable to the SMS Administrator Console are listed as valid options. Missing from the list are the SMS Administrator Console, Crystal Info, Software Metering Console, SMS Installer, Network Monitor, Package Automation Scripts, and Product Compliance Database.

8. Click Next to display the Parent Site Information/Identification screen, shown in Figure 4-16. Enter the site code and server name of the parent primary site, and select the network connection type that the secondary site will use to connect to that parent site.

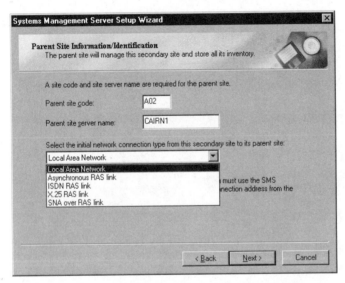

Figure 4-16. *The Parent Site Information/Identification screen.*

Caution You will still need to create a valid address at the primary site server that identifies connection parameters that allow the primary site to connect back to the secondary site server. Address creation will be discussed in the section "Creating an Address" later in this chapter.

9. Click Next to display the Connection Account Information screen, shown in Figure 4-17. Here you must enter the name and password of the account that the secondary site server will use to connect to the parent site. This account will generally be the SMS Service account, but it can

be any account that has at least Change permissions for the SMS_SITE share on the primary site server. Once again, this account must have been created before you begin the secondary site installation.

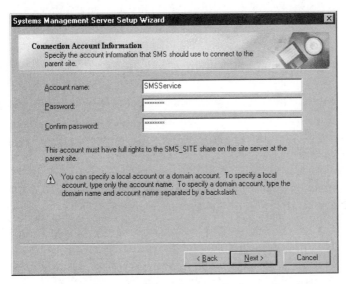

Figure 4-17. *The Connection Account Information screen.*

10. Click Next to display the Completing The Systems Management Server Setup Wizard screen, review your selections, and then click Finish to begin the installation process. Again, you can click the Back button from this screen or any previous screen to go back and modify your entries. As with the primary site installation, if the service account has not been created ahead of time, Setup can create an account for you. Setup will display a dialog box prompting you to do so; choose Yes.

Planning   To upgrade your secondary site server to SMS 2.0 Service Pack 1, first upgrade its parent primary site. When you right-click on the secondary site folder in the SMS Administrator Console for the primary site, the context menu will appear. Choose All Tasks from the context menu, and then choose Upgrade Site. The Upgrade Secondary Site Wizard will walk you through the upgrade process.

The Secondary Site Installation Process Flow

The process of installing a secondary site from the SMS CD is relatively uninteresting. Setup simply creates the subdirectory structure, loads services and components as necessary, and connects to the parent site to complete the parent-child relationship. This process is remarkably similar to the primary site server installation. However, installing a secondary site from a primary site server involves SMS primary site server components, network traffic, and installation routines installed and executed on the secondary site server. This section provides a basic overview of that process.

When you initiate the installation of a secondary site through the SMS Administrator Console, you are in effect making a change to the primary site's properties, and the site configuration process flow described in Chapter 3 is initiated. Hierarchy Manager wakes up and queries the sites table and site control file in the SMS SQL database. From this information, it determines that a secondary site installation process needs to be initiated and generates a request to do so in Scheduler's inbox (Schedule.box). Scheduler, in turn, creates the package and instruction files that support the installation and that need to be sent to the secondary site server and creates a send request file for the sender that will connect to the secondary site server. The sender will be the same connection mechanism you chose when you initiated the setup process.

The sender connects to and copies the package and instruction files to the secondary site server and loads a bootstrap service, which creates the SMS directory structure, starts the setup process, and loads and starts SMS Site Component Manager. Site Component Manager completes the installation and configuration of SMS components, loads and starts the SMS Executive service, and generates a new site control file. Finally the connection back to the parent site is configured, and a minijob is created by SMS Replication Manager to send the new secondary server site control information back to the parent site via Scheduler and sender at the secondary site.

You can follow the flow of this process by monitoring the status messages and log files (if enabled) on the primary site server for Hierarchy Manager, Site Control Manager, Discovery Data Manager, Scheduler, and the appropriate sender, such as SMS Standard Sender.

Differences Between Primary and Secondary Sites

The SMS 2.0 secondary site server is installed much like the SMS 2.0 primary site server. Setup builds the SMS and CAP_*sitecode* directory structures (where *sitecode* represents the three-character site code of the secondary site), including the component support files and inboxes, and installs the secondary site server as an SMS client. Setup installs the secondary site as a site system with the client access point (CAP) and distribution point roles assigned by default, and does not enable any discovery or installation methods or client agents until the SMS administrator does so through the SMS Administrator Console. The SMS Executive, SMS Site Component Manager, SMS Client Service, and Windows Management services are loaded and started, and the SMS, Network Access Layer (NAL), Web-Based Enterprise Management (WBEM), and SMS service keys are added to the Windows NT server registry. The same shares are created on the secondary site server as on the primary site server.

However, the secondary site server is fully administered through a parent site, as shown in Figure 4-18. Thus, no Systems Management Server program group is created, and no SMS Administrator Console is installed. The SMS SQL Monitor service is not installed, nor are any references to SQL Server or SQL Server triggers placed in the Windows NT server registry. Also missing from the SMS directory structure are folders and/or files that reference SMS components, and options that are not applicable to the secondary site such as the product compliance database.

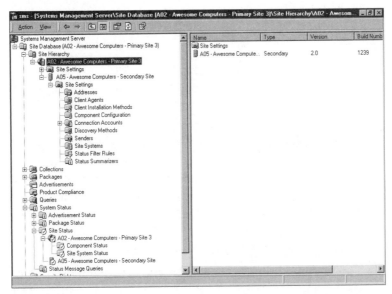

Figure 4-18. *The SMS Administrator Console, showing the secondary site.*

Because the secondary site is administered through its parent site, site property changes will take place across the network, generating some network traffic. This network traffic generally includes writing the change to the site control file on the secondary site server or writing a file to a component inbox on the secondary site server. The secondary site server will experience performance similar to the primary site server, and you should plan your hardware investment for a secondary site server in much the same way as you would for a primary site server. Since you do not have the added overhead of SQL Server database access, the resource requirements for the secondary site server will not be as high as for a primary site server. Nevertheless, you will sell yourself, your company, and the secondary site short if you do not include the same planning and testing strategies when implementing the secondary site as you do when implementing a primary site.

Implementing a Parent-Child Relationship Between Primary Sites

When you install an SMS 2.0 secondary site, it becomes a child of the primary site it is installed from, and *voilà!*, you have a parent-child relationship. As we've seen, however, primary sites can also enter into parent-child relationships. Two main requirements must be met to successfully implement a parent-child relationship between two primary sites: each site must have an address to the other site, and the child must identify its parent.

Creating an Address

An address in SMS 2.0 is yet another site setting—that is, a property of the site. A site server needs to know which other site servers it needs to communicate with—for sending package information, inventory data, status messages, and site control information—and how to establish that communication.

The parent and the child need each other's address. The child sends inventory data, status messages, discovery data, and site control information to its immediate parent. The parent site sends package, collection, advertisement, and site control information to its child. A parent site can also send this information to any other site below it in the hierarchy. It does so by routing the information through its child sites, or by configuring an address directly to the other site.

This flow of information is illustrated in Figure 4-19. Sites A04 and A05 will report data directly to their parent, site A03. Site A03 will, in turn, report its data (which includes the data from sites A04 and A05) directly to its parent, central site A01, as will site A02. Sites A04 and A05 need an address to site A03, and sites A02 and A03 need an address to site A01. Similarly, site A01 needs an address to sites A02 and A03, and site A03 needs an address to sites A04 and A05. Site A01 can administer any site below it in the hierarchy. It can send package and advertisement information to sites A04 and A05 by routing that information through site A03, for which it has an address. However, if the SMS administrator configures an address in site A01 for site A04, site A01 could send information directly to site A04.

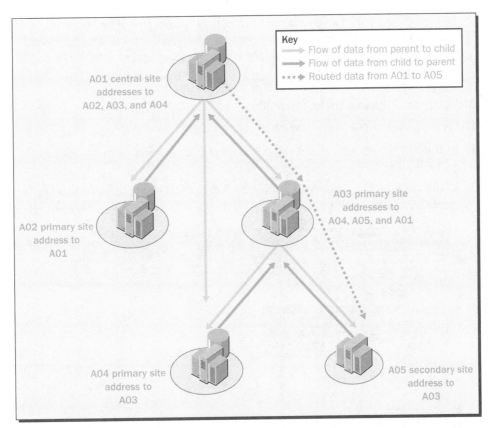

Figure 4-19. *Information flow in a site hierarchy.*

An SMS 2.0 site delivers information to another site by connecting to that site using a communications mechanism called a sender. The five available senders are Standard Sender (regular LAN/WAN connection), Asynchronous RAS Sender, ISDN RAS Sender, X.25 RAS Sender, and SNA RAS Sender. These senders, along with a sixth sender named Courier Sender, will be discussed in detail in the section "Communicating Through Senders" later in this chapter.

These senders connect to a default share on the target site named SMS_SITE. This share references the SMS\Inboxes\Despoolr.box\Receive directory and is created automatically during the installation of a primary or secondary site server. The SMS administrator must identify a connection account that has at least Change permission for this share. That could, of course, be the SMS Service account, but it doesn't have to be. Using this account to access the target site server share, the sender copies the data in question to the target site, keeping track of its progress. When it has finished, the sender disconnects from the target site.

> **Tip** Since the SMS Service account is a domain administrator as well, it is not
> the most secure account to use. The more secure approach would be to create
> a new account (just a regular user), password-protect it, and give it Change per-
> mission for the SMS_SITE share.

Creating an Address to Another Site

To create an address to another site, follow these steps:

1. In the SMS Administrator Console, navigate to the Site Settings folder
   and expand it.

2. Right-click on the Addresses folder, and choose New from the context
   menu. A list of sender address types is displayed, as shown in Figure 4-20.

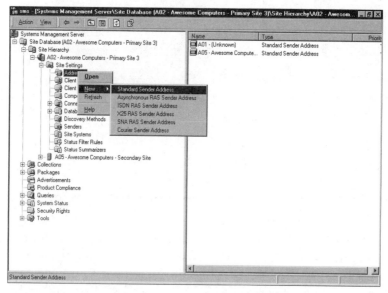

Figure 4-20. *Displaying a list of sender address types.*

3. Choose the sender address type you need to display its Properties window. Fill in the General tab in the appropriate Properties window as
   follows:

   - In the Standard Sender Address Properties window, shown in Fig-
     ure 4-21, enter the three-character site code for the target site. In the
     Destination Access section, enter the NetBIOS name of the target site's
     site server and the server's domain. Click the Set button to specify the
     name and password of the account on the target site that has at least
     Change permission for the SMS_SITE share on the target site.

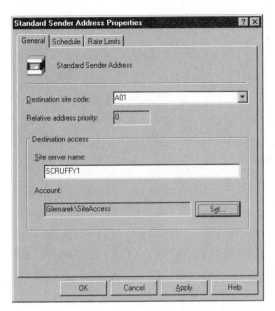

Figure 4-21. *The Standard Sender Address Properties window.*

- In the Asynchronous RAS Sender Address Properties window, shown in Figure 4-22, enter the three-character site code for the target site. In the RAS Access section, enter the RAS phone book entry that references dial-up information for accessing the target site. Click the Set button to specify the dial-up access account and phone number to be used when dialing in to the target site. In the Destination Access section, enter the NetBIOS name of the target site's site server and the domain of which it is a member. Click the Set button to specify the name and password of the account on the target site that has at least Change permission for the SMS_SITE share on the target site.

- In the ISDN RAS Sender Address Properties window, shown in Figure 4-23, enter the three-character site code for the target site. In the RAS Access section, enter the RAS phone book entry that references dial-up information for accessing the target site. Click the Set button to specify the dial-up access account and phone number to be used when dialing in to the target site. In the Destination Access section, enter the NetBIOS name of the target site's site server and the domain of which it is a member. Click the Set button to specify the name and password of the account on the target site that has at least Change permission for the SMS_SITE share on the target site.

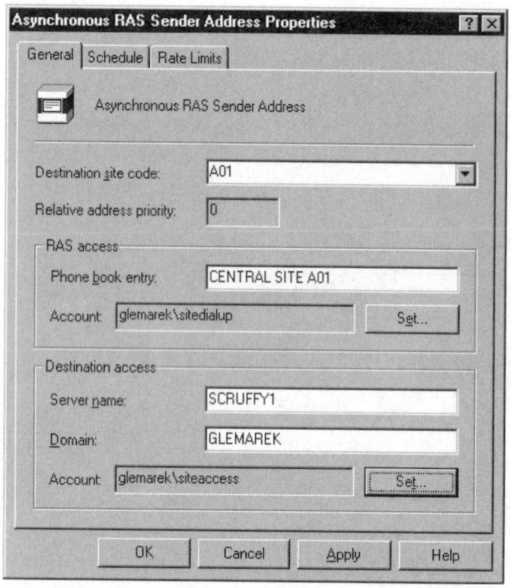

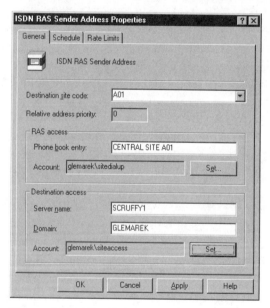

Figure 4-22. *The Asynchronous RAS Sender Address Properties window.*

Figure 4-23. *The ISDN RAS Sender Address Properties window.*

- In the X.25 RAS Sender Address Properties window, shown in Figure 4-24, enter the three-character site code for the target site. In the RAS Access section, enter the RAS phone book entry that references dial-up information for accessing the target site. Click the Set button to specify the dial-up access account and phone number to be used when dialing in to the target site. In the Destination Access section, enter the NetBIOS name of the target site's site server and the domain of which it is a member. Click the Set button to specify the name and password of the account on the target site that has at least Change permission for the SMS_SITE share on the target site.

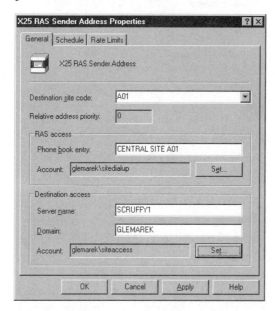

Figure 4-24. *The X.25 RAS Sender Address Properties window.*

- In the SNA RAS Sender Address Properties window, shown in Figure 4-25, enter the three-character site code for the target site. In the RAS Access section, enter the RAS phone book entry that references dial-up information for accessing the target site. Click the Set button to specify the dial-up access account and phone number to be used when dialing in to the target site. In the Destination Access section, enter the NetBIOS name of the target site's site server and the domain of which it is a member. Click the Set button to specify the name and password of the account on the target site that has at least Change permission for the SMS_SITE share on the target site.

- For details on how to create a Courier Sender address, refer to the section "Courier Sender" later in this chapter.

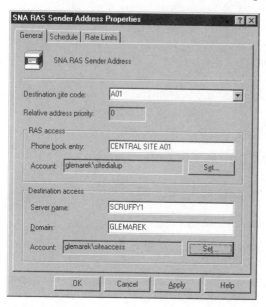

Figure 4-25. *The SNA RAS Sender Address Properties window.*

4. Select the Schedule tab, shown in Figure 4-26. As you can see, by default the sender is available for all priority send requests at all times. Select the time period you want to modify by highlighting it using the mouse. In the Availability list, select the appropriate option: Open For All Priorities, Allow Medium And High, Allow High Only, or Closed. The priority of a send request such as a package is set when the package is created. Choose Closed for periods when you do not want the sender to send anything, such as during regular backup times. If there are multiple addresses to a target site, SMS will automatically choose the next sender in order of priority (based on the Relative Address Priority setting on the General tab) if the current sender is unavailable for some reason. Select the Unavailable To Substitute For Inoperative Addresses check box to prevent this sender from being used as an alternative sender.

5. Select the Rate Limits tab, shown in Figure 4-27. Notice that by default SMS can use as much bandwidth as it wants when transferring data to the target site. Select the Limited To Specified Maximum Transfer Rates By Hour option and highlight the period of time you want to modify using the mouse. In the Rate Limit For Selected Time Period section, select a preferred bandwidth percentage from the drop-down list.

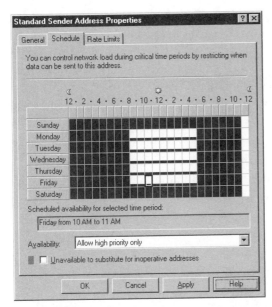

Figure 4-26. *The Schedule tab of the Standard Sender Address Properties window.*

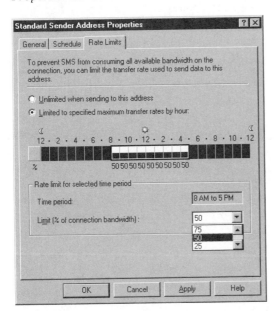

Figure 4-27. *The Rate Limits tab of the Standard Sender Address Properties window.*

6. Click OK to create the address.

If multiple addresses exist for a target site, the order of priority in which SMS will use them to connect to the target site is the order in which the addresses were created. This is known as the *relative address priority*—that is, the priority of one address relative to another. You can change the relative priority of an address by right-clicking on one of the addresses in the Address window of the SMS Administrator Console and choosing either Increment Priority or Decrement Priority from the context menu.

Multiple addresses to the same target site provide SMS with alternative ways of connecting to a site and transferring data if one sender is busy or unavailable. This flexibility can improve performance in the sending process, but with one caveat. Only one sender of each type can be installed on the same site server. For example, you cannot install two Standard Senders on the same site server, but you can install the Standard Sender once on as many component site systems as you want.

Real World   Alternative Senders to a Target Site

A more likely scenario is this: You will use Standard Sender on your site server to connect to a target site. Another server in the domain is already being used as a RAS server. A RAS server also exists in the target site server's domain. To provide an alternative means of connecting to the target site and transferring data, you install SMS Asynchronous RAS Sender on the RAS server and create an Asynchronous Sender Address to the target site. Now SMS can use Standard Sender, Asynchronous RAS Sender, or both to connect to the target site and transfer data.

You will want to closely monitor the traffic generated between the site server and the RAS server—which, in this case, is functioning as a component server for the SMS site. Assuming that both servers are on the same subnet, the traffic should not be significant. Nevertheless, you don't want to find yourself in a situation where the benefit you gain in improved sending performance to the target site is negated by excess traffic or denigrated network performance between the site server and the RAS server.

Identifying the Parent Site

Before you identify a site's parent, you must have created an address to that parent site. The child site will use that address to connect to the parent and transfer its site control information—including the fact that the parent now has a new child site. You can then set the parent site by following these steps:

1. In the SMS Administrator Console, navigate to the site entry and choose Properties from the context menu.

2. The Site Properties window will appear, as shown in Figure 4-28. On the General tab, click the Set Parent Site button.

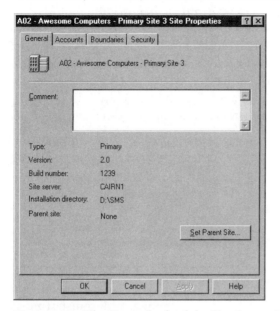

Figure 4-28. *The General tab of the Site Properties window.*

3. In the Set Parent Site dialog box, shown in Figure 4-29, select the Report To Parent Site option, enter the three-character site code of the parent site, and click OK to return to the Site Properties window.

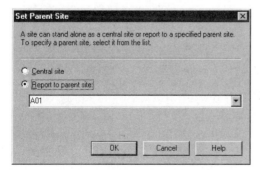

Figure 4-29. *The Set Parent Site dialog box.*

4. Click OK again to set the parent site, which starts the site configuration process.

The site configuration process includes not only updating the child site's database with the new parent site information, but also sending data to the parent site and updating the parent site's database and site control information. This process should not take more than a few minutes, but factors such as the resource capabilities of both the child and parent sites, available bandwidth, and other database activity will affect the length of time it takes for the parent-child relationship to be established and "recognized" by both parent and child. When you first create the address entry for the parent or the child, the site entry should include the site code and should indicate that the site name is unknown. After the relationship has been established and site control data has been transferred, this information will be updated to reflect the actual site name of the addressed site.

You can follow the flow of the site configuration process and the transfer of information that takes place by monitoring the status messages that the SMS components record at each point in the process. A detailed explanation of how to view status messages can be found in Chapter 3. Table 4-1 lists the SMS components and the status messages that relate to this process.

Table 4-1. Status messages generated during the establishment of a parent-child relationship

SMS Component	Status Message Codes	Description
Discovery Data Manager	2603, 2607	Transferring discovery data to the parent site
	2611, 2634	Updating child discovery data (at the parent site)
Inventory Data Loader	2708, 2709, 2711, 2713	Transferring inventory data to the parent site
Replication Manager	4000	Creating jobs to send data to parent site
Hierarchy Manager	3306, 3307	Processing site control files (at the parent site)

You can also monitor the log files associated with the appropriate SMS components for information regarding the flow of this process if you have enabled logging. These log files can be found in the directory SMS\Logs and would include Hman.log (Hierarchy Manager), Sched.log (Scheduler), Sender.log (Sender), Ddm.log (Discovery Data Manager), and Replmgr.log (Replication Manager), depending on which components you have enabled logging for.

These log files are text-based and can be viewed using a text editor such as Notepad. They can also be viewed using the SMS Trace utility, which is included on the SMS 2.0 CD. Refer to Chapter 5 for details regarding how to use SMS Trace.

Developing Site Hierarchies

In Chapter 2, you learned about the importance of developing a viable deployment strategy for SMS 2.0. A significant part of that design process should include determining the kind of site hierarchy—if any—you need to implement for your organization. An SMS site hierarchy exists whenever two or more SMS sites have been defined in a parent-child relationship; its structure resembles an organizational flowchart. Site hierarchies provide a means of extending and scaling SMS support across a wide variety of organizational structures. Figure 4-30 illustrates what our completed SMS hierarchy looks like when viewed through the SMS Administrator Console from the central site server. As you can see, the central site has the ability to view and manage any site below it in the hierarchy.

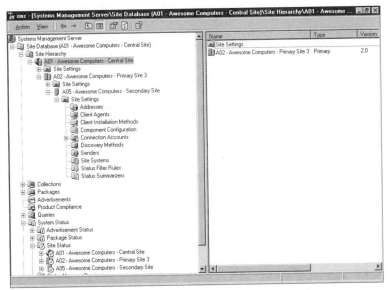

Figure 4-30. *The SMS hierarchy viewed through the SMS Administrator Console.*

SMS sites, as we have seen, are identified by the site boundaries you assign. Clients are assigned to an SMS site based on either IP or IPX subnet addresses. As such, a multinational organization with locations in different countries could be managed by one large SMS site or by individual SMS sites in each location connected to a central site. Figure 4-31 illustrates an example hierarchy. Awesome Computers has a corporate office in Chicago and regional offices in New York, London, and Tokyo. Each office has its own IP subnet. The single SMS site, located in Chicago, could manage all Awesome Computers locations because it includes all the IP subnets in its site subnet boundaries.

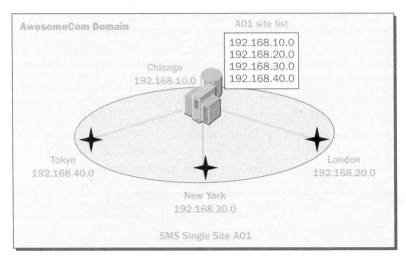

Figure 4-31. *The Awesome Computers site hierarchy, with one SMS site.*

In contrast, Figure 4-32 shows the same organization, but this time with individual SMS sites in each region, each reporting back to a central site located at Awesome Computers headquarters in Chicago.

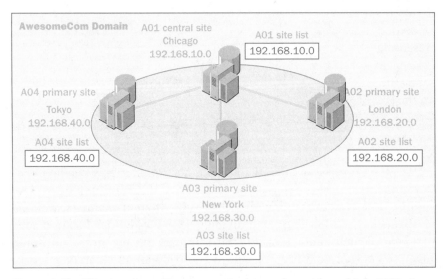

Figure 4-32. *The Awesome Computers site hierarchy, with multiple SMS sites.*

Many factors and circumstances can affect your site structure strategy. Each must be considered carefully before you implement the hierarchy. These factors are likely to include, but are certainly not limited to, the following:

- Network performance
- SMS client components
- Location and number of clients
- International site considerations
- Administrative model
- Windows NT domain model

Let's look at each of these factors in detail.

Network Performance

Network performance issues will no doubt be the single most significant factor in determining what your site structure should look like. Varying amounts of network traffic are generated among SMS site servers, SMS site systems, and SMS clients. Site servers communicate package, advertisement, and site configuration data to their site systems. The amount of traffic that is generated depends on the nature of the data being sent. For example, a site that distributes three packages a day with an average size of 50 MB to 10 distribution points is generating 500 MB of network traffic three times a day. This traffic could be significant on an already crowded network infrastructure. Or suppose that hardware inventory files representing only changes that have occurred are collected from a group of 32-bit SMS clients. If inventory is collected once a week from 5000 clients, the amount of traffic generated is probably not going to be significant. Even at 100 KB per client, the size of a full default inventory file, this traffic would total 500 MB once a week.

Network traffic concerns are particularly significant when SMS traffic must cross WAN connections. You might ask yourself whether the existing WAN connections are fast, reliable, and efficient enough to handle the traffic generated between the proposed SMS site systems or whether it would make more sense to create an additional SMS site at the other end of a WAN connection. Let's return to our Awesome Computers example. Suppose that you need to send a 50-MB package from the site server in Chicago to 10 distribution points in New York, as illustrated in Figure 4-33. This transaction will generate about 500 MB of package distribution traffic across the WAN connection between Chicago and New York because SMS must deliver the entire package to each distribution point within the same site—generally in an uncompressed state.

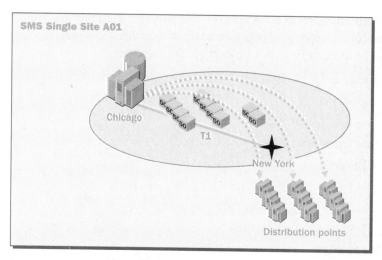

Figure 4-33. *A package distributed from a site server to multiple distribution points.*

On the other hand, SMS sends packages from one site to distribution points in another site by sending the package to the target site once and letting the target site distribute the package to its local distribution points. Furthermore, SMS generally sends the package to the target site in a compressed format. As illustrated in Figure 4-34 , the amount of WAN traffic generated for the same package scenario is considerably less—only about 25 MB as opposed to around 500 MB. Your deployment strategy should already have assessed and predicted how you will use SMS and the amount of data that you will be generating within the site. Armed with this information, consider its effect on the current network traffic patterns and volumes, especially across WAN links, when deciding whether to implement one large SMS site or several SMS sites participating in a site hierarchy.

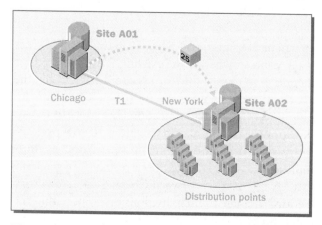

Figure 4-34. *Package distribution between different sites.*

Tip   Microsoft recommends implementing a single SMS site only if the WAN links are fast and reliable and can handle network traffic within acceptable thresholds (as identified by you, of course).

Client Components

Client component settings within a given SMS 2.0 site apply to all the clients assigned to that site—they are sitewide settings. As such, there is no means of installing certain components on one set of clients and other components on another set. For that matter, there is no means of enabling one set of attributes for a component for some clients and a different set of attributes for the same component for other clients.

The most frequent example of this situation concerns the Remote Tools component. If Remote Tools is enabled as a client agent for the SMS site, all SMS clients will be installed with Remote Tools. If the Do Not Ask For Permission option is disabled for the Remote Tools Client Agent, permission will be required on all clients before a Remote Tools session can be established. In other words, if your site has 1000 clients and 100 do not require Remote Tools, or if 100 do not require permission to establish a Remote Tools session, you cannot accommodate those clients. They must all either have Remote Tools installed or not. They must all either require permission or not. Chapter 10 discusses the Remote Tools Client Agent and its configuration options in detail.

One solution would be to create one SMS site for those clients that require Remote Tools (or that require permission to establish a Remote Tools session) and another SMS site for those clients that do not require Remote Tools (or that do not require permission to establish a Remote Tools session) and to enable Remote Tools appropriately. The same reasoning applies to all the client component options.

Real World   Enabling Client Features as Sitewide Settings

At first glance, it might seem that enabling client features as sitewide settings is not that big a concern. Consider this case, however: suppose you choose to enable Remote Tools for your SMS site and require that permission at the client be granted before a Remote Tools session can be established. Of course, all clients will be installed with the Remote Tools Agent and all will be required to grant permission before the Remote Tools session can be established. So far, so good.

You also have a need, however, to establish Remote Tools sessions with your Windows NT servers, which are also clients in your SMS site. As SMS clients, they too will have been installed with Remote Tools and will require that permission be granted before a Remote Tools session can be established. The latter ➤

setting will cause problems at the servers because typically no user is logged on at a Windows NT server to grant the permission request.

One solution, of course, would be to create a separate SMS site to manage the Windows NT servers. This would involve being able to identify the servers on a subnet or subnets separate from those that the other SMS clients are segmented on. This segregation may also involve a separate investment in hardware and software to install the SMS site server for that site, which may not be practical. Another solution would be to *not* require permissions at any of the clients in your site—which could raise other security or privacy concerns—or to forgo the use of Remote Tools for your servers altogether.

A third solution might be to require permission but also allow the user to change Remote Tools options at the client. This would let you as the administrator turn off the permission requirement at each Windows NT server. Unfortunately, this solution also lets users modify Remote Tools attributes without regulation, which could pose other Remote Tools problems on a client-by-client basis.

Location and Number of Clients

Another factor that might affect the structure of your SMS site hierarchy is the number and location of SMS clients and resources. Microsoft recommends between 10,000 and 30,000 clients per SMS site. But if you think this gives you license to create one large site and be done with it, go back and read the section "Network Performance" earlier in this chapter.

The true number of clients that any one SMS site server will be able to manage will be dictated more realistically by the server hardware—how powerful it is—as well as by the number of SMS features and options you have decided to enable on that server. The minimum hardware requirements for an SMS site server are a 133-MHz Pentium processor, 96 MB of RAM, and a recommended 1 GB of disk space. Let's say that you have two site servers with this configuration. Suppose you install only the basic site server and enable Remote Tools on one server, and install all options and enable all client components on the other. The resource requirements for the latter site server will obviously surpass those of the former server. It follows logically, then, that the second site server could manage fewer SMS clients than the first site server (perhaps 10 as opposed to 20—which also gives you some idea of how minimal the minimum hardware requirements are).

Location of clients can also be a factor, as it was with network performance. Your site server can easily manage 10,000 SMS clients or more. However, their location in the network may suggest the creation of multiple SMS sites depending on the SMS features you are implementing, the amount of network traffic generated, the efficiency of your WAN link, and the number of clients that need to be managed. For example, suppose you have three regional locations. If these are relatively small offices—say, 10 to 20 clients—with a modest WAN link between them and the corporate SMS site server, you might create a single SMS site, perhaps placing a distribution point, a logon point, and a CAP in each local subnet. On the other hand, if these regional locations had 100 or more clients, you might begin to weigh the possibility of creating separate SMS sites in each location and linking them together into a site hierarchy—depending, of course, on what features (such as package distribution) you have enabled, the size of packages, the frequency of advertisements, and so on.

International Site Considerations

Just as Windows NT supports a wide variety of language versions in its operating system, so too does SMS 2.0 support a wide variety of language versions for both the site server and SMS clients. SMS 2.0 site servers support the following languages:

- Chinese (simplified and traditional)
- English
- French
- German
- Japanese
- Korean

Each of these site server languages, with the exception of French, supports clients in its language, as well as English-language clients. Note also that English is the default language for the server-side user interfaces for Chinese and Korean site servers, but you can choose to display the local language characters instead. The client-side user interfaces have been localized to the local language. In addition to English, SMS 2.0 clients are available in 23 language versions:

- Arabic
- Chinese (simplified and traditional)
- Czech
- Danish
- Dutch
- Finnish
- French
- German
- Greek
- Hebrew
- Hungarian
- Italian
- Japanese
- Korean
- Norwegian
- Polish
- Portuguese (Brazilian)
- Portuguese (Iberian)
- Russian
- Spanish
- Swedish
- Turkish

For the most part, you can create a site hierarchy with any combination of language versions. Keep in mind, however, that some data that is recorded in one language version will be transferred between sites in that language version. For example, site code, collection, package, and advertisement names and MIF files will always be transferred in the language version in which they were created. This untranslated information can cause a problem if the parent and child site servers are using different language code pages. If they are using the same code pages, data will be passed on and displayed correctly. If not, the names may appear corrupted.

Default collection names are defined at each site; however, in a parent-child relationship, the default collection names from the parent site overwrite those of the child sites. Again, if both sites are using the same code page to view the default collection names, the names will be displayed correctly. If the child site is using a different code page, the default collection names may be corrupted.

If the site servers are using different code pages, you do have a couple of options. You could use all ASCII characters or a combination of ASCII and the language characters in the Name or Comments field of collections, advertisements, packages, and programs to provide easier identification. You could also use a separate Windows NT workstation running the SMS Administrator Console with the appropriate code page enabled. Keep in mind that extended and double-byte character names are not supported in domain and site server names. When your sites represent a mix of languages, use ASCII characters when naming domains and site servers.

More Info Both the *Systems Management Server 2.0 Administrator's Guide* and the Microsoft Systems Management Server Version 2.0 Service Pack 1 Release Notes discuss language considerations; consult these references for more specific information. If language versions are a concern within your organization, you should also periodically review the Knowledge Base articles published for SMS 2.0 for references to specific issues you may be encountering. (See *http://support.microsoft.com/search/www.microsoft.com/smsmgmt.*)

Planning If you have installed an International Client Pack (ICP) for your SMS 2.0 site and are planning to upgrade to SMS 2.0 Service Pack 1, be sure to upgrade your ICP with the service pack version as well. If you do not, the ICP files will be overwritten and only English-language clients will be supported.

Administrative Model

The structure of your corporate Information Services (IS) support (as well as company politics) will no doubt influence your SMS site structure. Whether or not a proposed SMS site has a designated SMS administrator locally may determine, for example, whether you install a primary or a secondary site at that location. The size and location of the administrative staff may also determine the number of child sites in the hierarchy, as well as its depth.

This is a good opportunity to make a recommendation regarding SMS administrative staff. The reality of many corporate environments is that a small number of people manage large numbers of computers and networks and typically fulfill many roles: database administrator, network administrator, mail server administrator, and so on. The role of the SMS administrator is just as significant and time-consuming. As you've already seen, implementing SMS 2.0 is far from trivial. A successful installation requires a significant amount of planning and testing.

The ongoing management of SMS clients and resources, troubleshooting, and maintenance are no less trivial. Therefore, you could recommend that many SMS tasks be delegated to other support personnel. For example, help desk staff might be given the ability to initiate Remote Tools sessions to facilitate their task of troubleshooting client problems. Resource administrators in specific departments might be given the ability to create and distribute packages to users and clients within their departments. Nevertheless, these are administrative tasks, and they make up only a small percentage of the overall management of an SMS site or an SMS site hierarchy.

Windows NT Domain Model

As with earlier versions of SMS, the Windows NT domain model that supports your organization will no doubt influence your SMS 2.0 hierarchical structure. You may, from an administrative point of view, decide to simply let your SMS structure reflect your domain model. This kind of model may or may not be efficient for managing SMS resources. In fact, if your current Windows NT domain model is "messy," you might want to consider cleaning it up before you implement your SMS site hierarchy.

Consider too the issue of Windows Networking Logon Client Installation and Windows Networking Logon Discovery. If either of these two methods is enabled, every domain controller for the domain specified will be assigned the logon point site system role. If your domain model is a single domain with several WAN links, a fair amount of network traffic will be generated across those WAN links to configure and install the domain controllers located across those links if you choose to create a single SMS site. Conversely, the same domain model could result in having domain controllers become logon points for multiple SMS sites if you choose to create an SMS site at each WAN link location.

Communicating Through Senders

As we've seen, SMS uses a sender to connect to another site and transfer information to that site. A sender is a highly reliable and fault-tolerant communication mechanism that transfers data in 256-KB blocks, making it more efficient than dragging and dropping or using an XCOPY command. Senders can communicate using the standard LAN/WAN connection that exists between two sites, or they can use one of four RAS sender types: Asynchronous RAS Sender, ISDN RAS Sender, X.25 RAS Sender, or SNA RAS Sender. There is also a Courier Sender type, which enables you to create and send package information to another SMS site if you have a slow or unreliable link between a site and its parent. You will use the RAS sender types for most intersite communication.

Sender Process Flow

Three main SMS components are involved in sending data from one site to another: Replication Manager, Scheduler, and a sender. With the exception of Courier Sender, the sender component wakes up when it receives a send request file in its outbox. The process begins earlier than that, however, as illustrated in Figure 4-35. When a request to send data is made, an SMS component will create a replication file and place the file in Replication Manager's inbox. When the parent-child relationship is established, for example, the Inventory Data Loader places an .MIF file in Replication Manager's inbox (in the SMS\Inboxes\Replmgr.box\Outgoing directory) so that it can send the child site's inventory data to the parent site. As another example, when a package is identified for distribution to another site, Distribution Manager places a replication object file (.RPL or .RPT) in Replication Manager's inbox.

Replication Manager will in turn bundle the data if necessary and then create a minijob for Scheduler. Scheduler creates packages, the instructions needed for sending the data in question, and a send request file (.SRQ) for the sender. The package and instruction files are placed in the SMS\Inboxes\Schedule.box\Tosend directory. The send request file is an instruction file for the sender that contains information such as the priority of the request, the site code and preferred address of the target site, a job identifier, the location of the sender's outbox, the location and names of the package and instruction files, action codes, and routing information if a direct address to the target site does not exist. This file is written to the preferred sender's outbox (SMS\Inboxes\Schedule.box\Outboxes*sender,* where *sender* is the sender folder, such as LAN, RASAsynch, RASISDN, and so on).

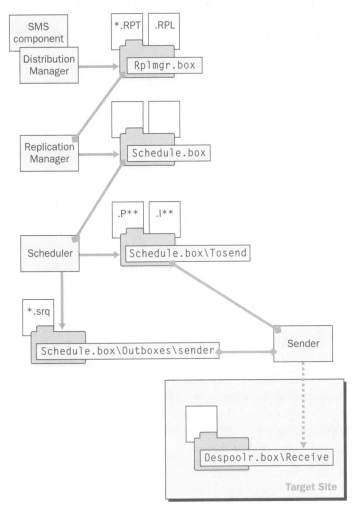

Figure 4-35. *The sender process flow, showing the flow of information among SMS components.*

When this file is written, the sender wakes up and reads the send request file. It also checks to see whether the address properties have placed any restrictions on when requests of this priority can be sent and whether any bandwidth limits have been set. The sender then changes the extension of the send request file to .SRS and writes status information to the file, including when the sending process started, when it ended, and how much data has been transferred at a particular point in time.

> **Note**   The Total Bytes To Send and Bytes Left To Send values in the send request file serve an important fault-tolerance role. If the sending process is interrupted for any reason—for example, if a send request of higher priority is created—the sender knows how to pick up where it left off.

The sender connects to the target site's SMS_SITE share—the SMS\Inboxes\ Despoolr.box\Receive directory—where the Despooler component will complete the processing of information at the target site. If the sender comes across an error while transferring the data, it will write an error status message to the .SRS file. When the data has been completely transferred, the send request file is updated to Completed status and is then deleted.

> **Tip**   As always, monitor the appropriate SMS component status messages and log files to follow the progress of a send request. The SMS CD includes a utility named Dumpsend.exe that can be used to display the contents of a send request file. You'll find this utility in the Support\Reskit\Bin\Platform\(*I386* or *Alpha*)\ Diagnose folder. You'll need to make a copy of the send request file (.SRQ or .SRS) and then execute the command *dumpsend filename.srq|more* at a command prompt to display the file's contents.

Defining a Sender

When the SMS site server is first installed, Setup creates Standard Sender and Courier Sender by default. The SMS administrator can then choose to install additional senders as necessary. As mentioned, only one sender of each type can be installed on the same server. However, you can install multiple instances of the same sender type on individual servers. These servers will become SMS component servers when you install a sender on them.

There is nothing special involved in adding an additional Standard Sender on an SMS component server. The only requirement is that you have an existing LAN or WAN connection between the Standard Sender component server and the target site server. Then, of course, you must configure an additional address to the target site using the new Standard Sender.

Enabling the use of one or more of the other four RAS sender types—Asynchronous RAS Sender, ISDN RAS Sender, X.25 RAS Sender, and SNA RAS Sender—

assumes that you have already established a RAS server at each site installed with the appropriate hardware and software support. That is, a modem, ISDN, X.25, or SNA connection. It is not necessary or even desirable that the site server itself be installed as a RAS server; it is only necessary that the site server for each site have access and connectivity to a RAS server (appropriately configured) on their local networks.

Senders on Other Servers

When you install a sender on another server, such as the Asynchronous RAS Sender on a RAS server, that server becomes an SMS component server. SMS Executive, the support files, and the directories for the sender are installed as well. Since the sender does not reside on the site server, it will not wake up when a send request file is created. Instead, the sender wakes up on a 5-minute polling cycle.

This polling cycle will require some additional resources on the sender's server. Also, network traffic will be generated between the site server and the sender server to transfer send request, package, and instruction data. The ultimate effect on the network's and sender server's performance will depend on the amount of usage the sender will experience and, of course, the current usage of the server itself. Alternative senders do provide a means for Scheduler to improve sending performance from one site to another. The SMS administrator will need to determine the significance of any trade-offs between having an alternative sending mechanism and the network and server performance hits that may occur.

New senders are added to the site through the SMS Administrator Console as a site setting. To establish a new sender, follow these steps:

1. In the SMS Administrator Console, navigate to the Site Settings folder and expand it, and select the Senders folder. One sender will be displayed—Standard Sender installed by default. (Note that Courier Sender isn't displayed. Although Courier Sender is installed by default, it can't be modified. For details, refer to the section "Courier Sender" later in this chapter.)

2. Right-click on the Senders folder, and choose New from the context menu to display the five sender type options, as shown in Figure 4-36. Select the type of sender you want to establish.

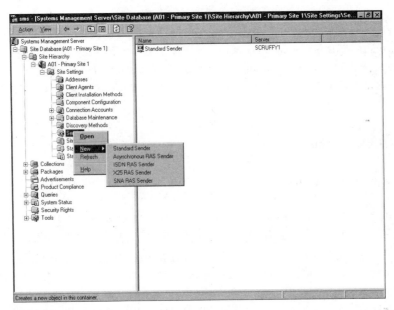

Figure 4-36. *The list of sender type options.*

> **Note** Because all the sender types will display a similar series of Properties window screens, we'll show only the screens for Asynchronous RAS Sender here.

3. On the General tab of the Sender Properties window, shown in Figure 4-37, enter the name of the server on which you want to create the sender—in this case, the name of the RAS server. (By default, the site server runs the sender.)

4. Select the Advanced tab, as shown in Figure 4-38, and enter values for the Maximum Concurrent Sendings and Retry Settings options.

   Maximum Concurrent Sendings represents the number of concurrent transmissions that can be made to all sites via this sender or to any single site (Per Site). The Per Site setting is set to 1 and disabled for RAS senders by default. The Retry Settings options consist of the number of retries to attempt if a connection fails and the number of minutes to wait between retries (Delay Before Retrying). Your settings for these options will depend primarily on the kind of network connection you have between the sites. For example, if you have a fast, reliable network connection and the amount of bandwidth used is low, you might increase the Maximum Concurrent Sendings value and decrease the Retry Settings options.

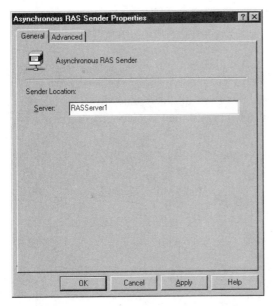

Figure 4-37. *The General tab of the Sender Properties window.*

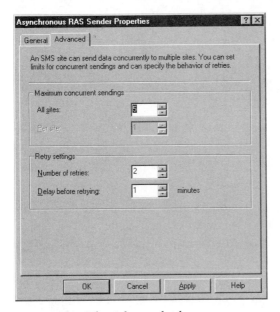

Figure 4-38. *The Advanced tab.*

5. Click OK to begin the site configuration process.

Establishing a new sender initiates the same site configuration process we've seen in earlier examples. Part of this process includes creating an outbox for the sender in the SMS\Inboxes\Schedule.box\Outboxes directory. If the sender is being installed on another server, the process will include installing SMS Executive on the sender server (making it a component server), installing the sender support files and the sender's support directory, and then updating the site server's site control file appropriately. Status messages for the new sender will include a notice of successful installation, as shown in Figure 4-39. Of course, you can also follow the process by checking status messages and logs for Hierarchy Manager, Site Control Manager, and Site Component Manager.

Figure 4-39. *Status message indicating that the RAS sender has been successfully installed on the component server.*

Courier Sender

As mentioned, Courier Sender enables you to create and send package information to another SMS site through non-network channels, such as regular postal service or a package delivery service, if you have a slow or unreliable link between a site and its parent. It can also be used to send packages that are so large an existing address might not provide adequate performance levels. It is not, however, meant to be used as a consistent alternative to existing network communications mechanisms.

As with other senders, to use Courier Sender as an alternative means of sending packages, you must create an address to the target site using Courier Sender as the sender type. We've seen how to create an address to the target site using other sender types in the section "Creating Address to Another Site" earlier in this chapter. A similar process is used here:

1. In the SMS Administrator Console, navigate to the Site Settings folder and expand it.

2. Right-click on the Addresses folder, and choose New from the context menu, and then choose Courier Sender Address to display the Courier Sender Address Properties window, as shown in Figure 4-40.

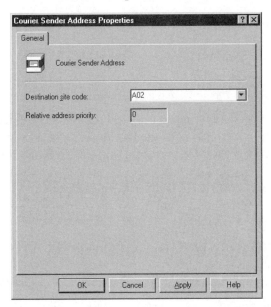

Figure 4-40. *The General tab of the Courier Sender Address Properties window.*

When you create the package, you can also identify Courier Sender as the preferred sender type for that package, as shown in Figure 4-41. (For details on creating packages, refer to Chapter 12.)

You will also need to identify the target site as a distribution point for the package. Refer back to Chapter 3 for details.

Tip If you have more than one address to a target site and you want to send a package using Courier Sender, choose Courier Sender as the preferred sender type when you create the package.

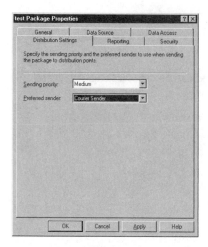

Figure 4-41. *The Distribution Settings tab of the Package Properties window.*

When you use Courier Sender as the sending mechanism to transfer a package, the package files are compressed into a single package (.PCK) and placed in the SMS\Smspkg directory. A send request file is also created and placed in Courier Sender's outbox. Because no automatic connection needs to be made to the target site, you must next launch Courier Sender Manager from the Systems Management Server programs group on the Start menu. To create outgoing parcels, follow these steps:

1. In Courier Sender Manager, choose Create Outgoing Parcel from the File menu.

2. Select your package from the list and click Next.

3. In the Parcel Properties section, enter the name of the package, a tracking name, the method you are using to send the parcel (for example, UPS or Federal Express), and a descriptive comment. Click Next.

4. Enter the path where you want to save the parcel. The default is SMS\Inboxes\Coursend.box\Out. Click Next.

5. Click Finish to create the parcel (.PCL) file.

You can now copy this parcel to some other medium, such as CD-ROM, and then send it on via some non-network method, such as the U.S. Postal Service. The SMS administrator at the target site will in turn copy this parcel to a directory on the target site server. (The default used by Courier Sender Manager is SMS\Inboxes\Coursend.box\In.) The SMS administrator will then launch Courier

Sender Manager on the target site server, essentially reversing the sending process. To receive the parcel, follow these steps:

1. In Courier Sender Manager, choose Receive Incoming Parcel from the File menu to display the Receive An Incoming Parcel screen of the Courier Sender Wizard.

2. Click Browse, select the package from the list, and click Open.

3. Click Next and then Finish to complete the package receiving process.

Courier Sender Manager will process this parcel as though a package had been sent using one of the other senders. If necessary, a SMSPkg$x$$ directory (where x stands for the drive letter) will be created, and the package files will be uncompressed and copied to a subfolder below the directory. When the process has been completed, you can check the parcel's status by choosing Parcel Status from Courier Sender Manager's File menu. (Refer to Chapter 12 for details on Distribution Manager status messages.)

Summary

In this chapter, you've explored how to implement multiple-site structures. Various factors mitigating your choice of site hierarchy have been introduced and discussed. We have also examined the concept of parent-child relationships in SMS 2.0 and you've learned how to establish that relationship through addresses and senders. You've also learned how to install a secondary site and the site configuration process involved. Last we looked at defining and implementing SMS senders and traced the sending process. Chapters 5 and 6 will introduce several diagnostic tools that will become invaluable to you as you maintain and troubleshoot your site.

Chapter 5
Analysis and Troubleshooting Tools

In the preceding chapters, we've viewed log files and status messages as a way of interpreting and troubleshooting process flows and component activity in your Microsoft Systems Management Server (SMS) 2.0 site. In this chapter, we'll spend a little more time exploring the uses of these tools, and we'll look at some additional tools that will help you maintain your site. In particular, you'll learn how to view status messages, use status summarizers, filter status messages, report status to other SMS components, and use queries to customize the status messages displayed. You'll also learn how to use SMS Service Manager to start, stop, and monitor the status of the components as well as to enable logging, and how to use the SMS Trace utility to view log files.

Working with Status Messages

Virtually every SMS 2.0 component and service generates status messages as it goes about its business. These messages are not the sometimes vague or unhelpful variety you may have come to dread in the Windows NT Event Viewer. On the contrary, SMS 2.0 status messages are rich with details. In the event of error messages, the details very often offer potential reasons for the error and suggest possible remedies.

Status messages represent the flow of process activity for each site system and client. They are automatically consolidated and filtered for display using status summarizers and status filters (discussed in detail in the sections "Understanding Status Summarizers" and "Filtering Status Messages" later in this chapter). As you'll see throughout this book, these status messages will provide your first and often best insight into how a process or task works and what to do in the case of a problem.

There are three levels of severity for status message in SMS 2.0: informational, warning, and error messages. *Informational messages* are just that—informational. They simply record the fact of an event occurring, such as a service or component starting, or the successful completion of a task, and so on. *Warning messages* are of concern, but they do not necessarily indicate problems that are fatal to the operation of the site server. They generally indicate potential problems, such as low disk space, a component that has failed or that is retrying a task, or a file that has been corrupted. *Error messages* are usually of great concern, as they indicate problems that could harm the SMS site. These require the attention of the SMS administrator for resolution. Error messages include authentication problems, the complete failure of a service or component to complete a task, database access problems, and so on.

Every status message that is generated will fall into one of three message type categories: milestone, detail, and audit. *Milestone message types* usually relate to the start or completion of a task. For example, a successful completion would generate a milestone info message, whereas an unsuccessful task would generate a milestone warning or error message. *Detail message types* generally refer to the steps in a process and make sense only in the context of the status message process flow. Again, these might be informational, warning, or error messages depending on the nature of the situation being reported. *Audit message types* refer to objects being added, deleted, or modified in some way, usually by the SMS administrator—for example, a site system role being assigned or a collection membership being modified.

Tip Status messages sometimes stand alone and can be readily interpreted from the detail message. In many cases, however, a status message will make sense only in the context of a process flow. It is always a good idea, therefore, to look not only for a specific message reference, but also at the status messages preceding and following the reference to gain further insight into the specific message. Throughout this book, when we explore process flows, you should review the status messages for *all* the SMS components and services involved to develop a well-rounded understanding of the process.

Status messages can be viewed through the System Status folder in the SMS Administrator Console, as shown in Figure 5-1. From this folder, you can view the advertisement status, the package status, the component status, and the site system status for the SMS site, and you can execute status message queries. We'll discuss status messages for advertisements and packages as we get to those topics in Chapter 12.

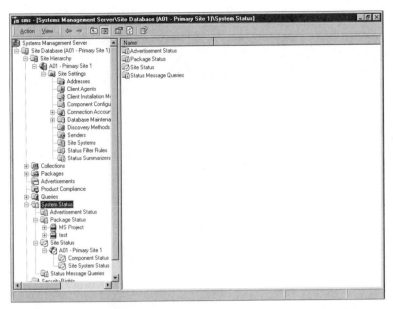

Figure 5-1. *The expanded System Status folder in the SMS Administrator Console.*

Viewing Site Status Messages

Site status messages fall into two categories: component status and site system status. If all is well with your site, you should see a green check mark (an OK indicator) to the left of each folder, as in Figure 5-1. If any problems have been detected, this check mark might change to an exclamation point in a yellow triangle (a Warning indicator) or a red "x" (a Critical indicator) based on the thresholds you set. (For a detailed discussion of thresholds, see the section "Status Message Thresholds" later in this chapter.) The icons for OK, Warning, or Critical indicators will help you determine which components need attention.

You will always begin troubleshooting by viewing the summary information. First click on Component Status in the Administrator Console to display a list of all SMS components and services and a summary of their current status, as shown in Figure 5-2. In the Component Status window, you can see at a glance the component status; the site system on which the component is running; the component name; its current state; the number of error, warning, and informational messages that have been generated; how the component wakes up; when a scheduled component next runs; the last time the component woke up; and the last time a message was written. In this case, all the SMS components are running properly.

The Show/Hide Console Tree icon

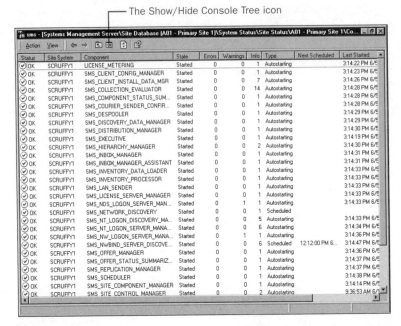

Status	Site System	Component	State	Errors	Warnings	Info	Type	Next Scheduled	Last Started
OK	SCRUFFY1	LICENSE_METERING	Started	0	0	1	Autostarting		3:14:22 PM 6/5
OK	SCRUFFY1	SMS_CLIENT_CONFIG_MANAGER	Started	0	0	1	Autostarting		3:14:23 PM 6/5
OK	SCRUFFY1	SMS_CLIENT_INSTALL_DATA_MGR	Started	0	0	7	Autostarting		3:14:26 PM 6/5
OK	SCRUFFY1	SMS_COLLECTION_EVALUATOR	Started	0	0	14	Autostarting		3:14:28 PM 6/5
OK	SCRUFFY1	SMS_COMPONENT_STATUS_SUM...	Started	0	0	1	Autostarting		3:14:28 PM 6/5
OK	SCRUFFY1	SMS_COURIER_SENDER_CONFIR...	Started	0	0	1	Autostarting		3:14:28 PM 6/5
OK	SCRUFFY1	SMS_DESPOOLER	Started	0	0	1	Autostarting		3:14:29 PM 6/5
OK	SCRUFFY1	SMS_DISCOVERY_DATA_MANAGER	Started	0	0	1	Autostarting		3:14:29 PM 6/5
OK	SCRUFFY1	SMS_DISTRIBUTION_MANAGER	Started	0	0	1	Autostarting		3:14:30 PM 6/5
OK	SCRUFFY1	SMS_EXECUTIVE	Started	0	0	1	Autostarting		3:14:19 PM 6/5
OK	SCRUFFY1	SMS_HIERARCHY_MANAGER	Started	0	0	2	Autostarting		3:14:30 PM 6/5
OK	SCRUFFY1	SMS_INBOX_MANAGER	Started	0	0	1	Autostarting		3:14:31 PM 6/5
OK	SCRUFFY1	SMS_INBOX_MANAGER_ASSISTANT	Started	0	0	1	Autostarting		3:14:31 PM 6/5
OK	SCRUFFY1	SMS_INVENTORY_DATA_LOADER	Started	0	0	1	Autostarting		3:14:33 PM 6/5
OK	SCRUFFY1	SMS_INVENTORY_PROCESSOR	Started	0	0	1	Autostarting		3:14:33 PM 6/5
OK	SCRUFFY1	SMS_LAN_SENDER	Started	0	0	1	Autostarting		3:14:33 PM 6/5
OK	SCRUFFY1	SMS_LICENSE_SERVER_MANAGER	Started	0	0	1	Autostarting		3:14:33 PM 6/5
OK	SCRUFFY1	SMS_NDS_LOGON_SERVER_MAN...	Started	0	1	1	Autostarting		3:14:33 PM 6/5
OK	SCRUFFY1	SMS_NETWORK_DISCOVERY	Started	0	0	1	Scheduled		
OK	SCRUFFY1	SMS_NT_LOGON_DISCOVERY_MA...	Started	0	0	5	Autostarting		3:14:33 PM 6/5
OK	SCRUFFY1	SMS_NT_LOGON_SERVER_MANA...	Started	0	0	6	Autostarting		3:14:34 PM 6/5
OK	SCRUFFY1	SMS_NW_LOGON_SERVER_MANA...	Started	0	1	1	Autostarting		3:14:36 PM 6/5
OK	SCRUFFY1	SMS_NWBIND_SERVER_DISCOVE...	Started	0	0	6	Scheduled	12:12:00 PM 6...	3:14:47 PM 6/5
OK	SCRUFFY1	SMS_OFFER_MANAGER	Started	0	0	1	Autostarting		3:14:36 PM 6/5
OK	SCRUFFY1	SMS_OFFER_STATUS_SUMMARIZ...	Started	0	0	1	Autostarting		3:14:37 PM 6/5
OK	SCRUFFY1	SMS_REPLICATION_MANAGER	Started	0	0	1	Autostarting		3:14:37 PM 6/5
OK	SCRUFFY1	SMS_SCHEDULER	Started	0	0	1	Autostarting		3:14:38 PM 6/5
OK	SCRUFFY1	SMS_SITE_COMPONENT_MANAGER	Started	0	0	1	Autostarting		3:14:14 PM 6/5
OK	SCRUFFY1	SMS_SITE_CONTROL_MANAGER	Started	0	0	2	Autostarting		9:36:53 AM 6/1

Figure 5-2. *The Component Status window in the SMS Administrator Console.*

Tip Click on the Show/Hide Console Tree icon (third from the right on the toolbar at the top of the SMS Administrator Console) to hide the console tree so that you can more easily view the Component Status window.

Click on the Site System Status folder to display a list of all the site systems identified for the site and their summary status by site system role, as shown in Figure 5-3. In the Site System Status window, you can view the site system status, the site system name, the role that has been assigned to the site, the location of the storage object (partition and folder or database), total and free storage space, free space represented as a percentage of the total, and whether the system has been down. In this case, all site systems are running properly.

The detailed information behind each message summary entry in the Component Status window pertains specifically to that component. However, the detailed messages behind each summary entry in the Site System Status window reference messages from any number of SMS components and services that are running on or that affect that particular site system.

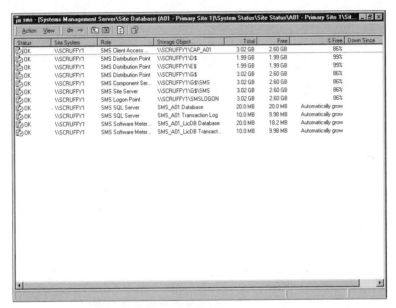

Figure 5-3. *The Site System Status window.*

We examined how to view status messages in Chapter 3; let's review here. To view the detailed information about the selected message for a specific component in the Component Status window, follow these steps:

1. Right-click on the component's summary entry, and choose Show Messages from the context menu to display a list of message types, as shown in Figure 5-4.

2. The All option displays all messages collected for this entry, Errors displays only error messages, Warnings displays only warning messages, and Info displays only informational messages. For this example, choose Info. The SMS Status Message Viewer will appear, as shown in Figure 5-5.

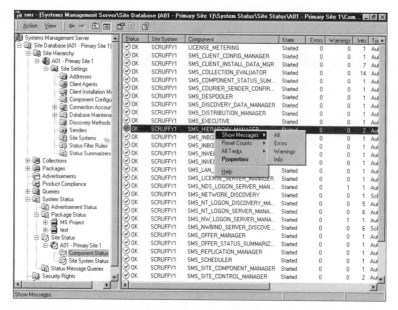

Figure 5-4. *Displaying a list of message type options.*

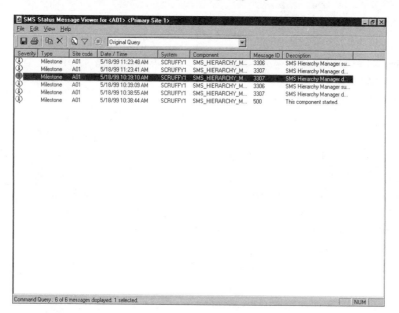

Figure 5-5. *The Status Message Viewer.*

3. To view a detailed description of the message, position the mouse pointer over the Description field to display a pop-up window, shown in Figure 5-6.

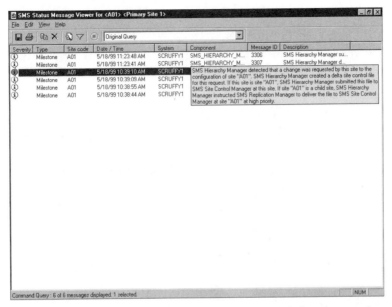

Figure 5-6. *A pop-up window containing a detailed description of a status message.*

Alternatively, you can double-click on the message to display the Status Message Details dialog box, shown in Figure 5-7. This dialog box provides you with more specific details about the message. It also contains buttons that enable you to view the previous and following messages. Click OK to close the dialog box.

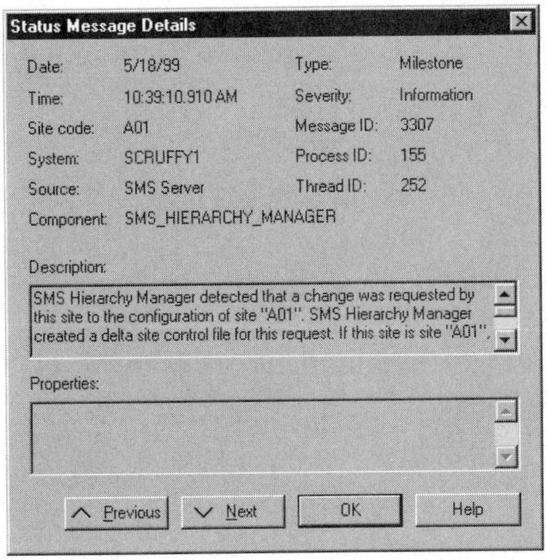

Figure 5-7. *The Status Message Details dialog box.*

4. Close the Status Message Viewer when you have finished reviewing the message details.

To view the detailed information about the selected message for a site system in the Site System Status window, follow these steps:

1. Right-click on the site system's summary entry and choose Show Messages from the context menu to display a list of message types.

2. Choose All to display all messages collected for this entry, choose Errors to display only error messages, choose Warnings to display only warning messages, or choose Info to display only informational messages.

3. After you choose an option, the Set Viewing Period dialog box is displayed, as shown in Figure 5-8.

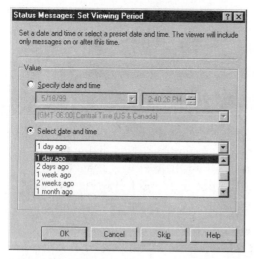

Figure 5-8. *The Set Viewing Period dialog box.*

Select the Specify Date And Time option to display only messages generated after the date and time you enter. Select the Select Date And Time option to display messages generated within a more generic time period, from 1 hour ago to 1 year ago.

4. Click OK to display the Status Message Viewer, shown in Figure 5-9. You can also click Skip if you prefer not to limit the scope of the messages displayed.

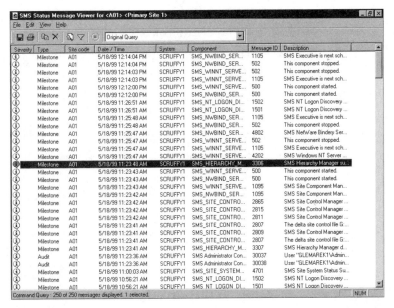

Figure 5-9. *The Status Message Viewer displaying the detailed messages for a Site System Status summary entry.*

5. View the detailed description for each message either by positioning your mouse pointer on the message's Description field to display a pop-up window or by double-clicking on the message to display the Status Message Details dialog box.

6. Close the Status Message Viewer when you have finished reviewing the message details.

7. Now that you know how to view status messages, let's look at how to configure the Status Message Viewer.

Setting Status Message Viewer Options

When status messages are generated by SMS components or services, they are written to the site database. The Status Message Viewer uses the SMS Provider to query the database for the detailed messages when you use the technique described in the preceding section.

As shown in Figure 5-9, the Status Message Viewer for the site system status displays all the SMS components that are running on that site system or that affect it in any way. These messages are the same as those displayed for each component in the Component Status window. For example, the selected Hierarchy Manager message in Figure 5-9 is the same as the first message listed in Figure 5-5.

Regardless of whether you are viewing component status or site system status, the Status Message Viewer always displays the following information:

- **Severity**   Specifies whether the message category is informational, warning, or error
- **Type**   Specifies whether the message type is milestone, detail, or audit
- **Site Code**   Specifies the three-character site code of the site for which the message was generated
- **Date/Time**   Specifies the time and date stamp indicating when the message was generated
- **System**   Specifies the server name of the site system for which the message was generated
- **Component**   Specifies the name of the SMS component or service that generated the message
- **Message ID**   Specifies the numeric code related to the task performed by the SMS component or service that generated the message
- **Description**   Provides a detailed description of the message

The Status Message Viewer provides many features that can facilitate your analysis of messages. Let's begin with some of the GUI features. You can change the sort order of each column simply by clicking on the column header. Each column has three sort options: click once to sort from lowest to highest, click again to sort from highest to lowest, and click once again to return to the default column order. The columns can, of course, be resized by clicking on the border between each column heading and dragging to make the column wider or narrower. You can also move the columns to customize the display simply by dragging and dropping a column header to a new position.

By right-clicking on any message entry to display its context menu, you can copy it, delete it, or display its Status Message Details window. You can also set a filter for the Status Message Viewer or refresh all the messages from this menu. Multiple messages can be selected for copying, deleting, and printing by using the old Windows Explorer Ctrl-click method.

The Status Message Viewer also provides a variety of options and features that are enabled through the menus on its menu bar. Because most of these settings are self-evident, here we'll look only at those that are unique or of special interest to the SMS administrator—in particular, the options in the Status Viewer Options window and the Filter Status Messages window.

The Status Viewer Options Window

Let's start by looking at the Status Viewer Options window. Choose Options from the View menu to display the Status Viewer Options window, shown in Figure 5-10.

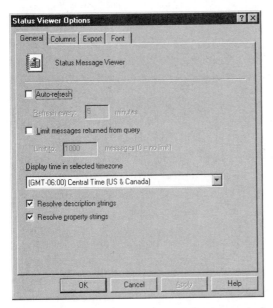

Figure 5-10. *The Status Viewer Options window.*

The General Tab   The Status Message Viewer does not refresh the interface with new messages by default unless you tell it to—for example, by pressing F5. The General tab, shown in Figure 5-10, lets you enable auto-refresh and specify a refresh interval. However, having the viewer automatically refresh itself will incur additional resource cost, so you shouldn't select this option unless you intend to leave the viewer open for a long period of time—perhaps to follow the flow of a task or the generation of messages. You can also limit the number of messages that are collected and displayed.

Caution   The Status Message Viewer might leak virtual memory if you keep it open for long periods of time. Don't forget to close the viewer when you aren't using it.

The Status Message Viewer displays messages stamped with the local time and date. The General tab lets you specify different time zones if you want to see when a message was generated on a site or site system in a different geographic location.

Most status messages are generated based on generic text strings in which variables have been inserted to customize the data to a specific component, time, and so on. For example, message ID 4611 for SMS Component Status Summarizer contains the text:

```
SMS Component Status Summarizer reset the status of component %1,
running on computer %2, to OK.
```

This message always reads the same, except that the percent values are replaced with a specific SMS component value and server value. Displayed in the Status Message Viewer for SMS Site Component Manager on site server Scruffy1, this message would read:

```
SMS Component Status Summarizer reset the status of component
"SMS Site Component Manager", running on computer "Scruffy1", to OK.
```

If you clear the Resolve Description Strings and Resolve Property Strings check boxes on the General tab, the status messages would resolve more quickly but would leave empty quotation marks in the variable positions, rendering the messages not especially helpful to the SMS administrator.

The Columns Tab The Columns tab of the Status Viewer Options window, shown in Figure 5-11, enables you to customize the information displayed in the Status Message Viewer by adding columns to view thread and process IDs or by removing columns that may not be of interest.

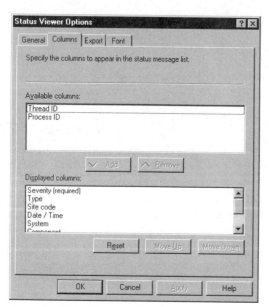

Figure 5-11. *The Columns tab of the Status Viewer Options window.*

The Export Tab   By default, status messages are deleted after seven days, but you can adjust this setting to suit your needs. Because some components can generate a multitude of messages, you may decide to delete messages more frequently to better manage database space. If you need to save or copy status messages to a file for future reference and analysis or to print them out, the Export tab of the Status Viewer Options window, shown in Figure 5-12, provides options for doing so.

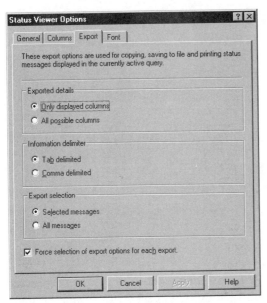

Figure 5-12. *The Export tab of the Status Viewer Options window.*

The Exported Details section lets you specify whether to include all possible data about a status message or only the data associated with the displayed columns. Under Information Delimiter, you can identify whether columns should be exported as tab delimited or comma delimited. This option is helpful if you expect to import this data into some other reporting or analysis tool such as Microsoft Excel or Microsoft Access. The Export Selection section lets you specify whether to export only messages that you have highlighted in the viewer or all messages. By default, every time you choose to copy, print, or save a message, the Export tab will be displayed, allowing you to modify the options before continuing. If you want the same options to apply to every copy, print, or save operation, clear the Force Selection Of Export Options For Each Export check box.

The Font Tab   The Font tab, shown in Figure 5-13, enables you to set the typeface, style, and size of the font that will be used to display messages in the Status Message Viewer. Be careful to choose something readable. A decorative font may look pretty at first, but if you'll be scrutinizing messages for long periods of time, a poorly chosen font can give you a headache.

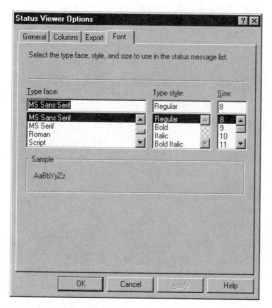

Figure 5-13. *The Font tab of the Status Viewer Options window.*

Filter Options

Another neat feature of the Status Message Viewer is the set of filter options, which let you customize which messages are displayed in the Status Message Viewer. If you've used the filter options in Windows NT Event Viewer, these filter options will be familiar. To set the filter options, choose Filter from the View menu to display the Filter Status Messages window, shown in Figure 5-14.

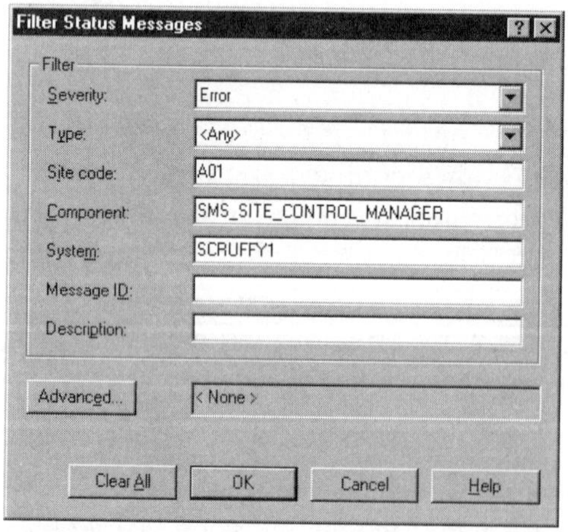

Figure 5-14. *The Filter Status Messages window.*

You can filter messages based on the specified criteria. Figure 5-14 shows a filter that displays error messages of any type (milestone, detail, and audit) for site A01 that have been generated by SMS Site Control Manager on site system Scruffy1. Click the Advanced button to display the Advanced Options dialog box, where you can also specify filtering based on thread ID and process ID, message properties, and a range of time.

Real World   Using Queries to Customize the Status Message Viewer

The status messages that are displayed for a particular component, site system, package, advertisement, and so on are built based on an SMS query for that status message object. By default, the original query is listed in the drop-down list on the Status Message Viewer toolbar. To view the original query's criteria, choose Query Information from the View menu to display the Query Information dialog box, shown in Figure 5-15.

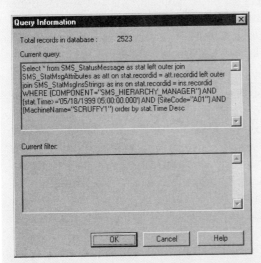

Figure 5-15. *The Query Information dialog box.*

The original query usually shows all messages for a specific component on a specific site system. However, there are many predefined queries that you can run against any status message object; we'll look at some of these predefined queries later in this section.

You can display and compile the status messages based on a query by selecting the query you want from the drop-down list of queries on the Status Message Viewer toolbar. For example, Site Component Manager status messages may include messages generated on several site systems in your site as well as on child sites. Perhaps you need to see only the status messages for your site or for a specific site system. Status message queries are available for both of these situations: All Status Messages From A Specific Component At A Specific Site and All Status Messages From A Specific Component On A Specific System. To resolve these queries, select a query from the drop-down query list to display its corresponding query resolving window, enter the requested values, and then click OK to execute the query. The Status Message Viewer screen will be refreshed accordingly.

Understanding Status Summarizers

Status messages can be configured in a variety of ways. For the most part, the default configuration of the status message system will serve the average site quite well and will generate a sufficient number of messages to facilitate reporting and troubleshooting. However, you might need to modify or enhance the reporting of status messages. One way to control the way messages are displayed in the SMS Administrator Console is by using status summarizers.

Status summarizers provide a mechanism to consolidate the copious amounts of data generated by status messages into a succinct view of the status of a component, a server, a package, or an advertisement. In the Component Status window (shown in Figure 5-2), for example, you are presented with a single entry for each component that indicates the component's status (OK, Warning, or Critical), its state (Started or Stopped), and the number of error, warning, and informational status messages that have been generated. Remember that behind each of these entry summaries can be a host of detailed information about the selected messages. Let's explore some techniques for modifying how the status summarizers consolidate and display the data you see in the SMS Administrator Console.

Display Interval

The status messages that are displayed are filtered first by a display interval. By default, only status messages generated since the most recent midnight are displayed. This limitation does not mean that all previous status messages have been deleted. On the contrary, all status messages are written to the SMS database by default. (You'll learn more about the status message reporting process in the section "Status Message Process Flow" later in this chapter.) The display interval merely facilitates your view of recent messages. You can modify the display interval for status summaries displayed in the Component Status folder and the

Advertisement Status folder. Since summaries displayed in the Site System Status folder and the Package Status folder are based solely on state, you cannot modify the display interval for these status messages.

To modify the display interval, right-click on the Component Status folder or the Advertisement Status folder and choose Display Interval from the context menu to display a list of interval options, as shown in Figure 5-16.

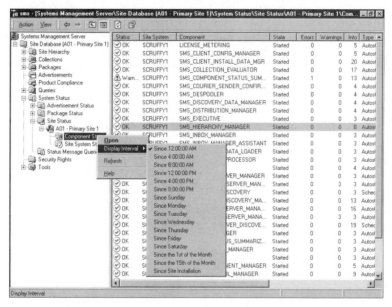

Figure 5-16. *Displaying the list of display interval options.*

Select the interval option that best suits your viewing needs. Be aware that choosing an interval such as Since Site Installation is likely to net you a significant number of messages to scroll through when you choose Show All Messages from the context menu.

Strictly speaking, the display interval is not so much an attribute of the status summarizer mechanism as it is a way to facilitate your view of the status messages kept in the database. Package status can also be viewed based on display interval; we will discuss package and advertisement status in detail in Chapter 12.

Status Message Thresholds

A *status message threshold* is a limit that defines when the status summary for a component or site system should indicate OK, Warning, or Critical. This threshold is set by determining the number of actual informational, warning, and error messages that have been generated for each component or site system. When a predetermined number of messages has been collected, the status changes from OK to Warning or from Warning to Critical.

For example, consider the Status Threshold Properties window shown in Figure 5-17. To access this window, right-click on a status summary entry in the Component Status window and choose Properties from the context menu. The Status Message Threshold settings indicate that if one error status message is generated for SMS Site Component Manager, the status summarizer will change the component's status summary from OK to Warning. If five error status messages are generated, the component's status summary will change from Warning to Critical. Similarly, if 2000 informational status messages are generated for SMS Site Component Manager, the status summarizer will change the status summary of SMS Site Component Manager from OK to Warning, and if 5000 informational status messages are generated, the status summary will change from Warning to Critical.

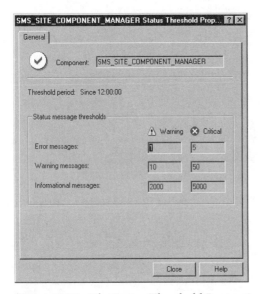

Figure 5-17. *The Status Threshold Properties window.*

Status thresholds for site system status are calculated similarly, but are based on available free space in the SMS site system and the site and software metering databases. Figure 5-18 shows the Free Space Thresholds Properties window, which you can access by right-clicking on the status summary entry in the Site System Status window and choosing Properties from the context menu. Notice that the free space thresholds change the storage object's status to Warning if free space falls below 20 MB and to Critical if free space falls below 10 MB.

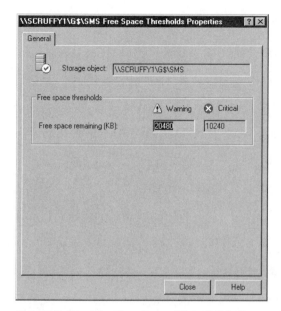

Figure 5-18. *The Free Space Thresholds Properties window.*

Other thresholds are specific to the databases based on a percentage of the database size. You'll learn how to modify these values or add new threshold values in the next section.

Configuring Status Summarizers

You can configure three status summarizer components: Component Status Summarizer, Site System Status Summarizer, and Advertisement Status Summarizer. To access these status summarizers, in the SMS Administrator Console expand the Site Settings folder and then expand the Status Summarizers folder. We'll look at the specific property settings for each of these status summarizers in the following sections.

Component Status Summarizer

To configure the Component Status Summarizer, follow these steps:

1. Right-click on Component Status Summarizer in the Status Summarizers folder and choose Properties from the context menu to display the Component Status Summarizer Properties window, shown in Figure 5-19.

   Notice that the Enable Status Summarization and Replicate To Parent Site options on the General tab are selected by default. You can also specify the replication priority on this tab and the display interval, here called the threshold period.

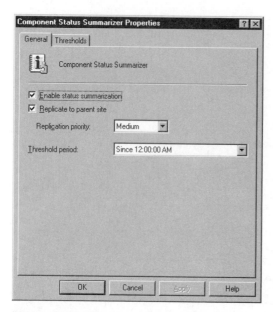

Figure 5-19. *The General tab of the Component Status Summarizer Properties window.*

2. Select the Thresholds tab to configure summary thresholds for each component, as shown in Figure 5-20.

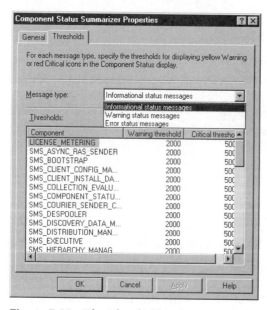

Figure 5-20. *The Thresholds tab.*

3. Select the message type you want to set the threshold for—informational, warning, or error—from the drop-down list and then double-click on the component whose thresholds you want to change to display the Status Threshold Properties window.

The default status message thresholds differ for each message type. Figure 5-21 shows the default settings for informational status messages.

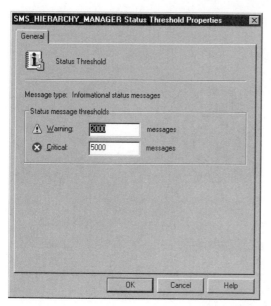

Figure 5-21. *The default status message thresholds for informational status messages.*

Figure 5-22 shows the default settings for warning status messages.

Figure 5-23 shows the default settings for error status messages.

4. Specify the number of warning and error messages that need to be generated (the threshold) before the Component Status Summarizer changes the status summary from OK to Warning or to Critical.

5. Click OK to close the Status Threshold Properties window, and then click OK in the Component Status Summarizer Properties window to save your modifications.

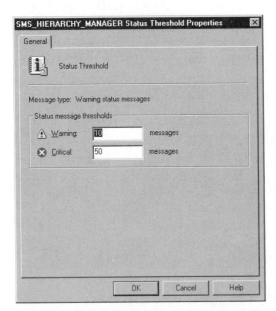

Figure 5-22. *The default status message thresholds for warning status messages.*

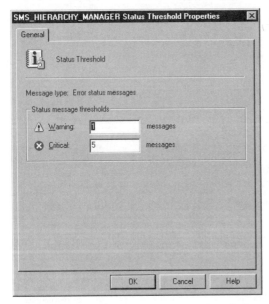

Figure 5-23. *The default status message thresholds for error status messages.*

Site System Status Summarizer

1. To configure the Site System Status Summarizer, follow these steps: Right-click on Site System Status Summarizer in the Status Summarizers folder and choose Properties from the context menu to display the Site System Status Summarizer Properties window, shown in Figure 5-24.

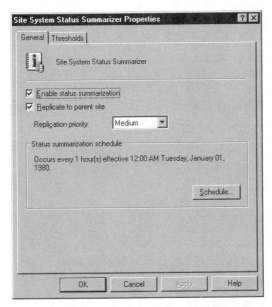

Figure 5-24. *The General tab of the Site System Status Summarizer Properties window.*

Notice that the Enable Status Summarization and Replicate To Parent Site options on the General tab are checked by default. The replication priority can also be set here. Click the Schedule button to display the Schedule dialog box, where you can specify a schedule for when and how often site system status summarization takes place.

2. Select the Thresholds tab to configure space thresholds for each database and for each site system, as shown in Figure 5-25.

SMS has already set general default values for site systems. You can modify these settings by entering new values in the Warning or Critical text boxes. SMS has also defined default space threshold values for the SMS database and the software metering database. If you need to change these values, double-click on the entry to display the Free Space Threshold Properties window, where you can specify the values you prefer.

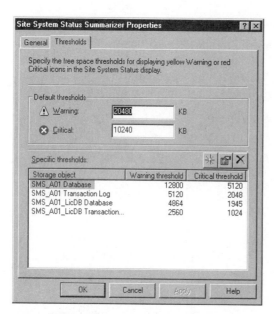

Figure 5-25. *The Thresholds tab.*

3. To add a specific site server to monitor its status, click the New button (the yellow star) in the Specific Thresholds section to display the Free Space Threshold Properties window, shown in Figure 5-26.

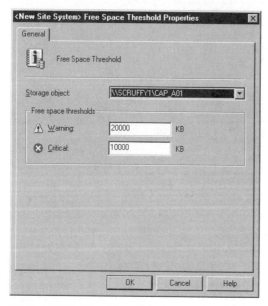

Figure 5-26. *The New Site System Free Space Threshold Properties window.*

Select the site system to monitor from the Storage Object drop-down list, enter the desired free space thresholds to monitor for in the Warning and Critical text boxes, and click OK.

4. Click OK again to save your changes.

Advertisement Status Summarizer

To configure the Advertisement Status Summarizer, follow these steps:

1. Right-click on Advertisement Status Summarizer in the Status Summarizers folder, and choose Properties from the context menu to display the Advertisement Status Summarizer Properties window, shown in Figure 5-27.

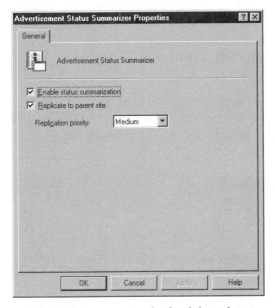

Figure 5-27. *The General tab of the Advertisement Status Summarizer Properties window.*

Notice that the Enable Status Summarization and Replicate to Parent Site options on the General tab are checked by default. You can also specify the replication priority on this tab.

2. Choose OK to save your modifications.

Status summarizers help us define how component, system, and advertisement status are displayed to the SMS administrator based on their message type—informational, warning, or error. In the next section, we'll look at further refining which status messages are captured and displayed in the Status Message Viewer.

Filtering Status Messages

SMS components and site systems generate a constant stream of status messages. Most of these messages will prove to be extremely helpful in resolving issues or troubleshooting problems you may be having with your SMS site. Some messages, however, may simply be flooding the Status Message Viewer with interesting but not particularly useful information, or too much information, or not the kind of information you are looking for.

There are several ways to filter status messages and display just the status information of interest. We looked at one technique in the section "Setting Status Message Viewer Options" earlier in this chapter. Status filtering can also be accomplished in a more global fashion by modifying the status reporting properties or by defining status filter rules.

Configuring Status Reporting Properties

To configure the status reporting component properties, in the SMS Administrator Console, expand the Site Settings folder and then expand the Component Configuration folder. Right-click on Status Reporting and choose Properties from the context menu to display the Status Reporting Properties window, shown in Figure 5-28.

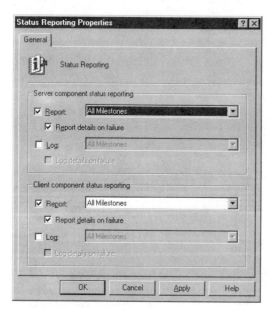

Figure 5-28. *The Status Reporting Properties window.*

By default, reporting is enabled for both the site server and the client components for the following types of messages:

- All milestones
- All milestones and all details
- Error and warning milestones
- Error milestones

By selecting the appropriate message types from the drop-down lists, you can control how much data is reported. For example, to filter out all milestone messages that are not errors or warnings, select the Error And Warning Milestones option.

Caution   The default settings for message reporting are considered appropriate for most SMS sites. Enabling too many messages or filtering out too much information can make the status message system less effective as a problem-solving tool.

The Report Details On Failure option is also selected by default. This powerful feature ensures that when a failure occurs or an error is reported, the affected component reports details as to the nature of the failure as well as possible causes and remedies. You will probably not want to disable this feature—unless, of course, you can troubleshoot without knowing the details of a problem.

You can also enable logging for the same message types to the Windows NT Event Log and include failure details in the log.

Status Filter Rules

The second way to globally affect how status messages are reported is by using status filter rules. SMS creates fifteen status filter rules of its own to control how status messages are reported and viewed, as shown in Figure 5-29. To access this list, in the SMS Administrator Console, expand the Site Settings folder, and then expand the Status Filter Rules folder. These default status filter rules are used to control how many and which status messages are reported and displayed in the Status Message Viewer.

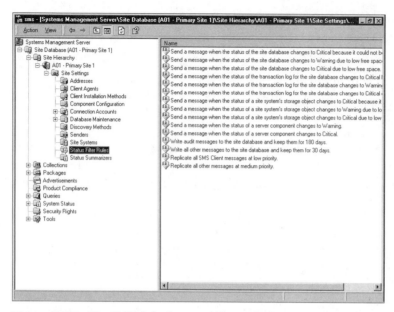

Figure 5-29. *The SMS default status filter rules.*

When a status message is generated by an SMS component, Status Manager tests the message against these status filter rules to determine how that message should be handled. Status Manager then performs one or more of the following actions:

- Writes the message to the SMS database
- Writes the message to the Windows NT Event Log
- Replicates the message to the parent site
- Sends the message to a status summarizer
- Executes a program

Most of the default status filter rules generate a system message that is displayed on the site server using a NET SEND command. You should not fool around with any of these default status filter rules. Each has been created for a reason, and they are all significantly useful. But you may find that you want to create additional status filter rules. You can customize status filter rules to discard certain types of messages that you don't want or need to see, to replicate certain types of messages to a parent site at a higher priority than others or not replicate certain messages at all, and to execute a program based on a message type.

Begin by deciding just what messages you need to see and what messages you do not need to see. For example, if your site participates in a parent-child relationship but is fully administered within the site—that is, no administration occurs at the parent site—it may be unnecessary to replicate any status messages to the parent site. Eliminating this replication would certainly decrease the amount of network traffic generated between the parent site and your site.

> **Caution**   Do not modify existing status filter rules or define any new status filter rules until you are fully comfortable with and knowledgeable about the status message system. If you make a change without knowing its full effect, you could render the status message system useless to you as a troubleshooting tool.

Follow these steps to create a new status filter rule:

1. In the SMS Administrator Console, expand the Site Settings folder.

2. Right-click on Status Filter Rules, choose New from the context menu, and then choose Status Filter Rule to display the Status Filter Rule Properties window, shown in Figure 5-30.

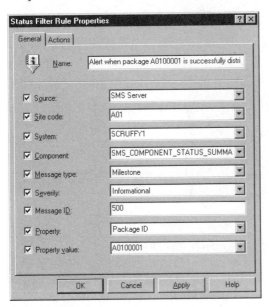

Figure 5-30. *The General tab of the Status Filter Rule Properties window.*

3. On the General tab, enter a descriptive name for your filter.

> **Tip** The status filter name should adequately explain the function and purpose of the status filter rule you are creating. Use the default status filter names as a guideline.

You can narrow your filter criteria further by selecting any combination of options available on the General tab. These options are described in Table 5-1.

4. Select the Actions tab, shown in Figure 5-31, and specify what Status Manager should do when the message criteria defined on the General tab are met.

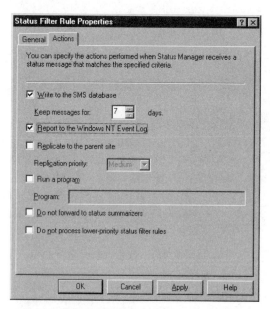

Figure 5-31. *The Actions tab.*

In this example, Status Manager has been instructed to write the message to the SMS database as well as to the Windows NT Event Log. By default, the message will also be forwarded to the appropriate status summarizer to be included in the Status Message Viewer.

5. Click OK to save the new filter rule.

Table 5-1.   Status filter rule options

Option	Description
Source	The source of the status message: SMS site server, SMS client, or SMS Provider
Site Code	The site code corresponding to the source of the status message
System	The name of the SMS client or server that generates the status message
Component	The name of the SMS component that generates the status message
Message Type	The status message type: milestone, detail, or audit
Severity	The message severity: informational, warning, or error
Message ID	The specific status message ID you are reporting on—for example, an ID of 500 generally relates to a component starting up
Property	The name of a specific property, such as Advertisement ID, Package ID, Collection ID, or User Name, that may be present in some status messages you want to report on
Property Value	A specific property attribute for the property name you specified, such as Advertisement ID, Package ID, Collection ID, or User Name, that may be present in some status messages you want to report on

The new status filter rule will be added at the end of the list of existing rules. The order in which the rules are listed is determined by their relative priority. Status messages will be passed through all the filters if you don't select the Do Not Process Lower-Priority Status Filter Rules check box for a filter on the Actions tab. If you do select this option for a filter, the message won't pass through any filters below this one in the filter list. You can change the order of filter processing by right-clicking on a filter, choosing All Tasks from the context menu, and then choosing Increment Priority to move the filter up in the list or Decrement Priority to move the filter down in the list.

Tip   The Run A Program option on the Actions tab can be a useful alert tool if you are using a Microsoft Windows NT–compatible paging application. You can then enter the command-line sequence for executing a page to notify you when a specific status message is generated. Consult Appendix F in the *Systems Management Server Administrator's Guide* for a more complete discussion of the use of command-line sequences for customized status programs.

Real World   Using Status Filter Rules

Chapter 20 of the *Systems Management Server Administrator's Guide* contains several useful example status filter rules. The status filter rule for discarding status messages from a component that is flooding the system is particularly useful. After you have become comfortable with the status message system and the way in which the various SMS components work and interact, you may want to filter out simple informational messages such as messages generated when a component starts or wakes up. Follow the steps outlined earlier to define this simple filter. On the General tab, specify a name in the form "Discard message *xyz* from component *abc* on server *123*." Fill in the System, Component, and Message ID fields as shown in Figure 5-32. For this example, we are excluding startup messages for Site Control Manager.

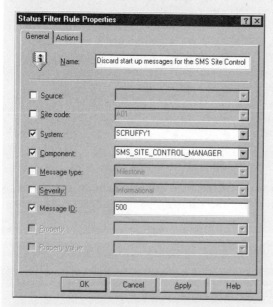

Figure 5-32. *Defining a sample status filter rule.*

On the Action tab, select the Do Not Forward To Status Summarizers check box. This setting will ensure that the message is disregarded and that it will not be displayed in the Status Message Viewer. Depending on where this new rule sits in relation to the other rules, you may also want to check the Do Not Process Lower-Priority Status Filter Rules check box to prevent any subsequent filters from picking up this message and possibly writing it to the database or displaying it in the Status Message Viewer.

Working with Status Message Queries

You already know how to effectively use the Status Message Viewer to customize status messages and troubleshoot components and site systems. The Status Message Viewer displays messages on a per-component or per-system basis. Sometimes, however, you might need to see all messages of a specific type generated across all the site systems or from several components.

The SMS 2.0 development team, being one step ahead of the rest of us in this thinking, created status message queries as a means of accomplishing just that. In fact, there are nearly seventy existing default queries that may well satisfy most of your message viewing needs. These queries are listed in the Status Message Queries window, shown in Figure 5-33. To display this window, in the SMS Administrator Console, navigate to the System Status folder and expand it, and then highlight the Status Message Queries folder. For example, the query highlighted in Figure 5-33 will generate a list of all SMS clients on which the Hardware Inventory Client Agent was unable to create the Management Information Format (MIF) file needed to report the client's hardware information to the site database. Running this query is certainly easier than scanning for the error status message for every client reporting messages to the Component Status Summarizer.

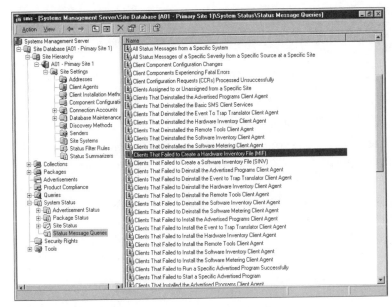

Figure 5-33. *The Status Message Queries window.*

Most of these default queries are prompted—meaning that you must provide information such as a site code, the server name, and so on. To execute a status message query, right-click on the query in the Status Message Queries window, and choose Show Messages from the context menu. Any values that need to be resolved will be listed, and you must enter the information or values requested.

You can also create your own status message queries. To do so, follow these steps:

1. Right-click on Status Message Queries, choose New from the context menu, and choose Status Message Query to display the Status Message Query Properties window, shown in Figure 5-34.

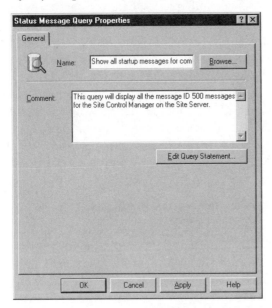

Figure 5-34. *The Status Message Query Properties window.*

2. Enter a descriptive name for your query and a comment that further explains the query's purpose. Then click the Edit Query Statement button to display the Query Statement Properties window.

   By default, a status message query displays only status messages in its results window, thus all the options on the General tab are unavailable, as shown in Figure 5-35.

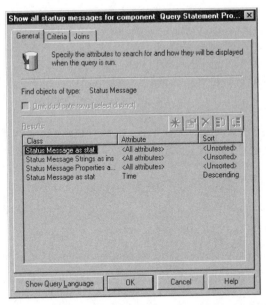

Figure 5-35. *The General tab of the Query Statement Properties window.*

3. Select the Criteria tab to create the query statement. Click the New button to display the Criterion Properties window, shown in Figure 5-36.

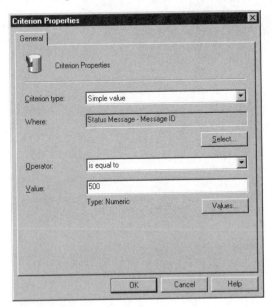

Figure 5-36. *The Criterion Properties window.*

4. Select the criterion type (in most cases, this will be Simple Value) from the drop-down list, and specify the attribute and the attribute class by clicking the Select button. The attributes describe an SMS object type and are grouped into one or more attribute classes. In this example, the attribute class *Status Message* consists of attributes that include component, machine name, severity, and site code, any of which can be used to qualify the results of the query. Next specify an operator by choosing one from the drop-down list. Click on the Values button to display all the values related to the attribute you selected that have been recorded in the SMS database.

5. Click OK.

6. To add criteria to your query, repeat steps 3, 4, and 5 for each additional criterion. When you have finished, click OK twice to save your query.

The new status message query will now be available in the Status Message Queries window. Figure 5-37 shows the results of running our sample query by right-clicking on the sample query and choosing Show Messages from the context menu. Notice that the result of the query is to display the message "This component started" for every component on the site server.

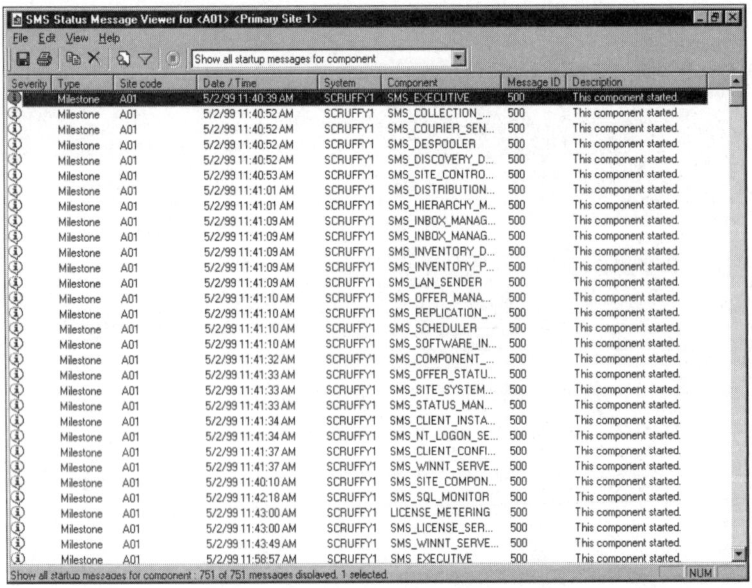

Figure 5-37. *The results of running a sample status message query.*

Status Message Process Flow

Now that we've examined the different tools for handling status messages, let's look at the status message process flow. Nearly every SMS 2.0 service and component generates status messages. Not only does the site server itself generate messages, as one would expect, but the components and services running on site systems (logon points, client access points, and so on) and agents running on SMS clients also generate status messages. The status message system in SMS 2.0 has the capacity to generate a multitude of messages; however, status summarizers and filters keep these messages to a manageable level by default. Nevertheless, status message reporting can add to your existing network traffic bandwidth issues.

Reporting Status on Site Servers and Site Systems

Status messages generated on the site server are processed within the site server itself and then updated to the SMS database. If the SMS database resides on the same server, no additional network traffic is generated. However, status messages that are generated by SMS services and components on site systems are copied to the site server so that they can be updated to the SMS database. Figure 5-38 illustrates the process flow for status messages generated on the site server and site systems.

As mentioned in the section "Configuring Status Reporting Properties" earlier in this chapter, several options are available to the SMS administrator when configuring status message reporting. Remember that one option enables the SMS administrator to specify whether to convert the status message to a Windows NT event. When a status message is generated by an SMS service or thread, its properties are checked by that service or thread to see whether this option has been set. If it has, the status message is first converted to a Windows NT event and written to the Windows NT Event Log. If no other reporting options have been configured, the process stops here. If other reporting options have been configured, the status message must be handed off to the Status Manager component on the site server. If the server on which the status message was generated is the site server, the status message is placed either in Status Manager's in-memory queue if the message was generated by a thread component or in Status Manager's inbox (SMS\Inboxes\Statmgr.box\Statmsgs) as an .SVF file if the message was generated by a service component. If the server on which the status message was generated is a site system, the status message is copied to Status Manager's inbox on the site server. If for some reason the component is unable to copy the status message to the site server, it stores the status message in the WINNT\System32\Smsmsgs subdirectory on the site system and retries until it can successfully copy the status message to Status Manager's inbox on the site server.

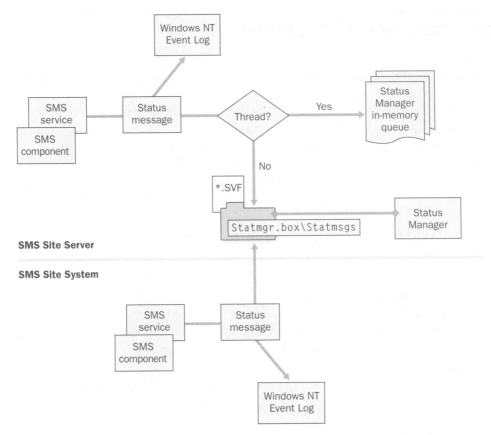

Figure 5-38. *Status message process flow for status messages generated on the site server and site system.*

Reporting Status from Clients

As we've seen, SMS components and agents residing on SMS clients also generate status messages, and these messages too must be reported back to the site server for updating to the SMS database. Figure 5-39 illustrates the flow of status messages from the client to the site server.

Status information is collected not only from SMS client components and agents, but also as the result of application installations in the form of status MIFs. For example, both the package program created through the SMS Administrator Console and the packages compiled through SMS Installer have the ability to generate status .MIF files upon the execution of the program or package.

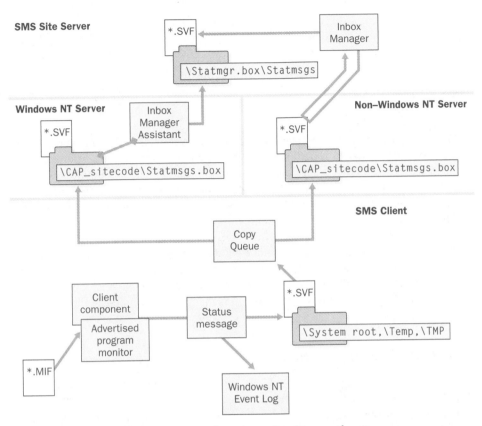

Figure 5-39. *Status message process flow from the client to the site server.*

When a status message is generated on the SMS client by an SMS client component, the message's properties are checked by that component to determine whether the message needs to be converted to a Windows NT event. If so and if the SMS client is also a Windows NT client, the status message is written to the Windows NT Event Log. Next the status message and status .MIF files are written to an .SVF file and stored in the system root (Windows or WINNT, for example) or in the Temp or TMP directory. The client component then initiates a request for the Copy Queue on the client to move the .SVF file to Status Manager's inbox on the CAP (CAP_*sitecode*\Statmsgs.box). Copy Queue is an SMS client component that writes data to CAPs and logon points reliably. When Copy Queue has trouble writing its error messages to the CAP, it will write them to the CQMgr32.log file instead.

At this point, if the CAP is a Windows NT server, the Inbox Manager Assistant thread wakes up and moves the .SVF file to Status Manager's inbox on the site server. If the CAP is not a Windows NT server—that is, it is a NetWare server or an NDS server—the Inbox Manager thread on the site server will copy the .SVF file from that server to Status Manager's inbox on the site server at its next polling cycle. Inbox Manager, by default, polls these CAPs once every 15 minutes.

Tip Each client component generates a log file in the MS\SMS\Logs directory on the client computer by default. Check these log files to determine whether the .SVF file was created during troubleshooting of status message generation. Additionally, in the log file of the component that should have generated the status message, look for a line that begins with "STATMSG" from around the time the status message should have been generated. If that line doesn't exist, or if the next line begins with the text "CServerStatusReporter," the component may have had trouble generating and reporting the status message. Refer to Chapter 23 of the Microsoft Systems Management Server 2.0 Resource Guide (part of the *Microsoft BackOffice 4.5 Resource Kit*, available through Microsoft Press) for a complete discussion of the status message reporting process and troubleshooting tips.

Reporting Status to the SMS Database

Once the status message is written to its in-memory queue or to its inbox, Status Manager wakes up and reads the status message or .SVF file. It evaluates the message against the status filter rules established by SMS during setup and those modified by the SMS administrator. Remember, a status message can be handled in one of five ways, as shown in Figure 5-40.

The status message could be written to the SMS database, converted to a Windows NT event and written to the Windows NT Event Log, or handed to a status summarizer to be condensed for viewing through the SMS Administrator Console. If a parent site exists, the message could be sent to the parent site for inclusion in its SMS database or viewing through its SMS Administrator Console. The SMS administrator could also configure a program to be executed upon receipt of a status message. This program might be a system pop-up notification on the SMS administrator's Windows NT workstation desktop, the execution of a batch file, or a notification using paging software.

As you can see, the status messaging system in SMS 2.0 is quite robust and is capable of inundating you with information about your site server, site systems, and clients. Fortunately, you can control which status messages are reported and how these messages are handled, and you can tailor their generation to fit your specific reporting needs.

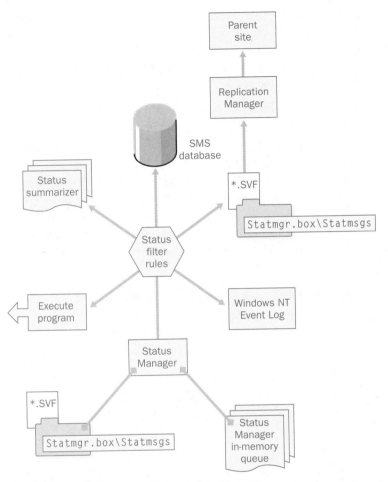

Figure 5-40. *Using status filter rules to handle a status message.*

Using SMS Service Manager

Status messages will be and should be your first stop when you are trying to understand an SMS process or to troubleshoot a problem on your site. However, in addition to status messages, you can also study the log files that can be generated by each component. Log files provide an even greater level of detail in describing how an SMS component is functioning, especially in relation to other components.

Remember from Chapter 3 that log files are not enabled in SMS 2.0 by default—a departure from earlier versions of SMS. This change was made to conserve server resources. After all, there are now over forty SMS components and services that can generate log files. On the other hand, log files are enabled on SMS clients by default because the number of client agents is considerably less (six) and so that the SMS administrator does not have to visit a client to enable the log files. We also explored using SMS Service Manager to enable SMS 2.0 log files in the SMS Administrator Console in Chapter 3.

SMS Service Manager is also used to monitor the status of components. Unlike Status Message Viewer, SMS Service Manager provides an at-a-glance view of SMS components and services running on the site server and on each site system. As shown in Figure 5-41, you can see the status of each component (represented both as an icon preceding each entry and in the Status field), the server the component is running on, the last time the component was polled, and the component type. The status icon for an entry appears only after you query each component for its current status by right-clicking on it and choosing Query from the context menu. Using the same technique, you can also stop, pause, and resume component activity.

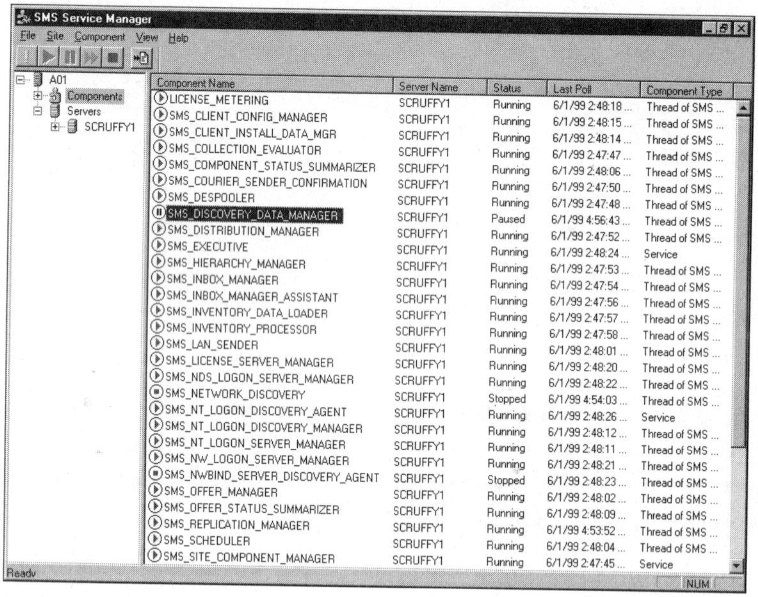

Figure 5-41. *SMS Service Manager, displaying a list of components and services running on the site server.*

Tip If you want to stop all the SMS Executive threads, stop SMS_SITE_COMPONENT_MANAGER first and then stop SMS_EXECUTIVE using SMS Service Manager because Site Component Manager might attempt to restart the SMS_Executive if it is stopped. The Windows NT Services application also enables you to stop these services; however, using SMS Service Manager is the preferred method.

Just because an SMS component is listed as stopped does not necessarily mean that there's a problem with the service. Some services run on a predetermined or administrator-defined schedule. It's important to familiarize yourself with viewing status messages and log files so that you can determine whether a component problem exists.

Using SMS Trace

As discussed in Chapter 3, log files are simply text files that can be read using any text editor. However, trying to scroll through several long log file entries using Notepad can become tedious, if not frustrating. Fortunately, SMS 2.0 includes an updated version of the SMS Trace utility that provides a nicer interface for viewing log files. Each log entry is easily readable, ordered, and time-stamped. In addition, the view is dynamically updated as components modify the log file. You can even view multiple log files at one time—a great way to learn how various components interact with each other.

Installing SMS Trace

SMS Trace is not installed by default when you install your SMS site server. However, it can be installed on any site server or site system or, preferably, on the Windows NT workstation running the SMS Administrator Console. SMS Trace is located on the SMS 2.0 CD in the directory Support\Reskit\Bin*platform*\SMSTrace, where *platform* represents either the Alpha or i386 platforms. To install the SMS Trace utility, follow these steps:

1. From this directory, execute Traceinst.exe to launch the SMS Trace Installation Wizard. The Welcome screen will appear, as shown in Figure 5-42.

Figure 5-42. *The SMS Trace Installation Wizard Welcome screen.*

2. Click Next to view descriptive information about SMS Trace. Click Next again to display the Select Destination Directory screen, shown in Figure 5-43, where you can confirm or select a destination directory. Click Next twice to perform the installation.

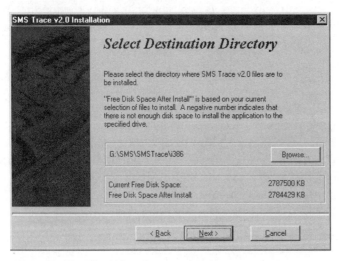

Figure 5-43. *The Select Destination Directory screen.*

3. When the installation is complete, a message box will appear telling you so. Click OK.

Planning

As you learned in Chapter 2, the process that updates SMS 2.0 with Service Pack 1 involves creating updated source files. When this occurs, the SMS 2.0 support tools are also updated. However, the support tools that previously could be found in the Support\Reskit\Bin*platform*\ directory on the source file CD now appear in a self-extracting file named Support.exe in the Support folder created by the service pack update.

To locate the SMS Trace utility and other support tools, you need to extract the SMS support tools. Follow these steps to extract the SMS support tools:

1. Navigate to the Support folder in the updated source file location.

2. Double-click on Support.exe to launch the SMS 2.0 Supportability Files Installation Wizard. The Welcome screen will appear, as shown in Figure 5-44.

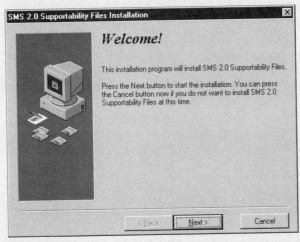

Figure 5-44. *The SMS 2.0 Supportability Files Installation Wizard Welcome screen.*

3. Click Next to display the Select Destination Directory screen, shown in Figure 5-45. Click the Browse button to select the drive and directory location where you'd like the files copied.

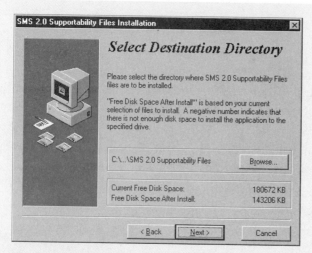

Figure 5-45. *The Select Destination Directory screen.*

4. Click Next to display the Ready To Install screen, shown in Figure 5-46. Click Next once more to begin the installation process.

Figure 5-46. *The Ready To Install screen.*

5. When the installation is complete, the wizard will display the Installation Completed screen, shown in Figure 5-47. Click Finish to end the setup process.

Figure 5-47. *The Installation Completed screen.*

Unless you modified the default directory name and location, you will be able to find the updated SMS 2.0 support tools in the C:\Program Files\SMS 2.0 Supportability Files directory. Expand this folder to find the Reskit\Bin*platform* directory and the subdirectories that contain the SMS 2.0 support tools, and then install the SMS Trace utility as described earlier.

When specific SMS 2.0 support tools are referenced in future chapters, be sure to look for them in the SMS 2.0 Supportability Files directory if you have installed SMS 2.0 Service Pack 1.

The SMS Trace utility is added to the Systems Management Server program group and is launched from there. To use SMS Trace to view log files, follow these steps:

1. Start SMS Trace from the Systems Management Server program group. The SMS Tracer window will appear, as shown in Figure 5-48.

2. Choose Open from the File menu or click the File Open icon on the toolbar to display the Open dialog box. SMS Trace will automatically default to the SMS\Logs directory.

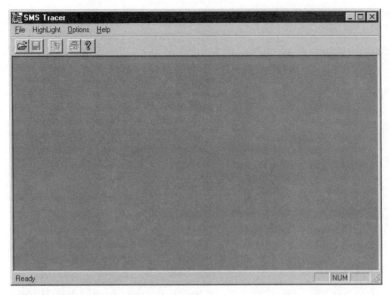

Figure 5-48. *The SMS Tracer window.*

3. Select the log file you want to open and click Open, or double-click on the filename. The contents of the log file will be displayed in the SMS Tracer window, as shown in Figure 5-49.

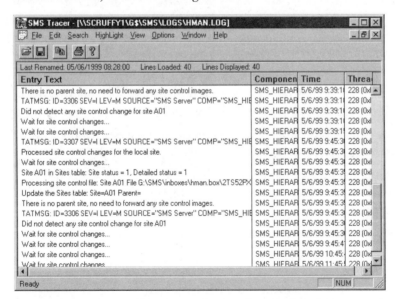

Figure 5-49. *The log file contents displayed in the SMS Tracer window.*

Notice how nicely this utility displays the contents of the log file. Each entry is easy to read, ordered, and time-stamped. In addition, the view is dynamically updated as the component modifies the log file. Compare this window to the same log file opened in Notepad, shown in Figure 5-50.

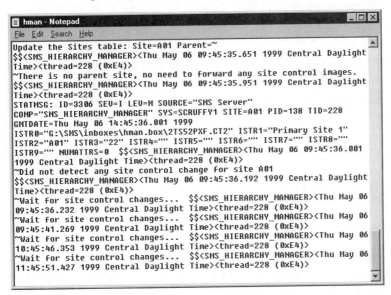

Figure 5-50. *The log file contents displayed using Notepad.*

The SMS Trace interface offers several nice features. You can of course print the log file and modify how much data appears on the screen. SMS Trace also lets you search for text, highlight text, and filter what is displayed on screen.

Searching for Text

If you are looking for a particular text string—perhaps a filename, an extension, a package ID, or an advertisement ID—you can ask SMS Trace to find the log entry that contains that text string. To do so, follow these steps:

1. Start SMS Trace and open the log file you want to search. Select the first log entry.

2. Choose Find from the Search menu to display the Find dialog box, shown in Figure 5-51.

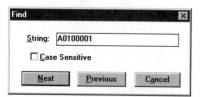

Figure 5-51. *The Find dialog box.*

3. Enter the text string you want to search for. This can be a partial string. To make this a case-sensitive search select the Case Sensitive check box.

4. Click Next. The entry that contains the text string you entered will be highlighted if it exists.

5. To view the next entry with this text string, choose Find from the Search menu and then click on Next in the Find dialog box, or simply press F3. To view the previous entry, click on Previous in the Find dialog box, or simply press F4.

Highlighting Text

Perhaps, as you open multiple log files, you would like to highlight any entry that references a particular text string. For example, when a site setting is modified, Hierarchy Manager and Site Control Manager both create and reference files back and forth. While monitoring the flow of this interaction, you might choose to highlight the lines that reference specific files or file extensions to better view how the two components work with each other and hand files back and forth. To use SMS Trace to specify text that should be highlighted as it occurs in the log file, follow these steps:

1. Start SMS Trace.

2. Choose Highlight from the Highlight menu to display the HighLight dialog box, shown in Figure 5-52.

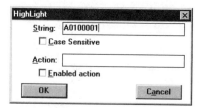

Figure 5-52. *The HighLight dialog box.*

3. Enter the text string you want SMS Trace to look for. This can be a partial string. To make this a case-sensitive search, select the Case Sensitive check box.

4. You can also have SMS Trace initiate a simple command-line action, such as a NET SEND, by entering the command in the Action text box and then selecting Enabled Action.

5. Click OK.

6. Open the desired log file or files. As the log files are opened, any entry that contains the referenced string will be highlighted with a box surrounding the entry.

Caution The Action option is really only useful for strings that appear once or twice in the log file. The action will be executed for every occurrence of the text string. Since log files are updated within SMS Trace dynamically, you might use this option to alert the administrator via a NET SEND action when a particular string occurs—for example, when a package ID is picked up by a component and referenced by the log.

Filtering the SMS Trace View

Log files can get filled up quickly and can contain hundreds of entries. Perhaps you are interested only in certain types of entries—for example, status message entries or entries that contain a reference to a particular package ID. SMS Trace provides a filter tool that can facilitate your view of these kinds of entries. To filter the SMS Trace view, follow these steps:

1. Start SMS Trace and open the log file or files you want to filter.

2. Choose Filter from the View menu to display the Filter dialog box, shown in Figure 5-53.

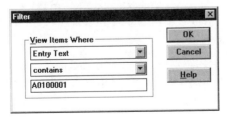

Figure 5-53. *The Filter dialog box.*

3. In the first text box under View Items Where, choose the column through which you want to apply the filter. For example, if the package ID appears in the Entry Text column, choose Entry Text from the drop-down list.

4. In the second box under View Items Where, choose the appropriate operator. For example, if you are looking for a partial entry text string such as a package ID within a log entry, choose Contains rather than Is Equal To.

5. In the third box under View Items Where, enter the string value that you are filtering for, such as the package ID.

6. Click OK. SMS Trace will refresh the screen and show only the entries you filtered for.

Note Once you have filtered a log in this manner, you cannot turn off the filter without first closing the log file. After you close the log file, you can go back into the filter, choose the option <No Filter>, and then reopen the log file.

Tracer.exe

When you install the SMS Trace utility, SMS also installs the companion tool Tracer.exe in the SMS\SMSTrace\i386 directory. This is a command-line tool that is used to open individual log files. This tool differs from the SMS Trace utility in that the log file records the new entries as they are generated from the point where you opened the log rather than showing the entire log and all its entries (which include both the new entries and the entries generated before starting SMS Trace). This feature is useful if you want to follow the flow of a specific process and note the entries as they are created.

Tracer provides a continuously scrolling set of entries in a command window. It does not maintain history, so it may not be very effective for monitoring SMS components that generate large numbers of entries. You can open as many Tracer windows as you want to monitor different log files. You can also associate the log files with Tracer.exe so that when you double-click on a log file you automatically launch the Tracer tool.

Start Tracer by entering the following command line at a Windows NT command prompt or by choosing Run from the Start menu:

*d:\SMS\SMSTrace\i386\Tracer.exe d:\SMS\Logs*filename.log

The variable *filename.log* represents the name of the log file you want to monitor. If you move Tracer.exe to the SMS\Logs directory, you can eliminate some of the path references.

Summary

In this chapter, we've examined two of the most useful troubleshooting and learning tools you will have at your disposal through SMS: status messages and log files. While status messages will provide you with most of the information you will need to successfully monitor and troubleshoot SMS component activity, the log files, when enabled, will give you that extra level of granularity that can so often provide the elusive bit of data needed to pull all the pieces of a puzzle together.

In Chapter 6, we will continue our exploration of troubleshooting and analysis tools as we discuss HealthMon, Network Trace, Network Monitor, and other helpful utilities.

Chapter 6
System Performance and Network Analysis

In Chapter 5, we began a discussion about monitoring and troubleshooting Microsoft Systems Management Server (SMS) 2.0 using status messages and log files. In this chapter, we'll round out that discussion by looking at some additional tools that can be used to assist SMS administrators as they monitor the performance of their systems and networks. We'll start with a brief review of the Windows NT Performance Monitor utility and the SMS performance objects that are added during SMS setup. Then we'll look at how to use HealthMon and Network Trace to determine the status of site systems and how to configure the Event to Trap Translator to interact with a Simple Network Management Protocol (SNMP) management system. Last we will examine the Network Monitor utility and the new control tools included with SMS 2.0.

Performance Monitor

Windows NT Performance Monitor tends to be an underappreciated utility—generally because administrators haven't taken the time to learn how to use it effectively. With a product such as SMS 2.0, which requires significant resources to function efficiently, Performance Monitor can be one of the most effective tools at your disposal for identifying server resource usage and load. Let's approach this discussion, therefore, with two objectives: to reintroduce the Performance Monitor tool and ensure that you understand how to navigate it, and to identify some Performance Monitor objects and counters that can be of specific use when you are monitoring resource usage and load on your site systems.

Using Performance Monitor

One of the more important tasks in troubleshooting problems on your server, whether it is a Windows NT server or an SMS site system, is to spot potential problem sources and develop and analyze trends before the problems materialize. Achieving this kind of analysis is a two-step process of baseline creation and real-time tracking. You should always create a baseline chart or log of "normal" activity on your server. In our case, this chart should include the objects and counters specific to SMS 2.0 server activity. When you are analyzing performance, you can create real-time charts using the same objects and counters you used for your baseline chart and then compare the real-time charts to the baseline to determine how server performance has been affected.

> **Note** Throughout this book, references to a Performance Monitor object and one of its counters will appear in the form *Object:Counter*. For example, the *Processor* object has several counters that you can chart, one of which is the *% Total Processor Time* counter. This object and counter set would be referred to as *Processor:% Total Processor Time*.

Windows NT initially includes about twenty Performance Monitor objects. These objects facilitate the monitoring of basic system resources, including memory, processor, disk, and network. You will want to monitor these four areas on any given Windows NT server, especially your SMS servers. In addition to these default objects, other objects and their corresponding counters are added when other applications—for example, SMS 2.0 or Microsoft SQL Server 7.0—are installed. These objects represent additional items that you can monitor to get more information about a specific resource situation.

> **Tip** Monitoring *Object:Counter* values alone without gathering any other object data to reference against is a futile exercise for the administrator—you cannot obtain any useful or specific information. For example, if the *Processor:% Processor Time* value is consistently higher than 80 percent, you might conclude that the processor is overutilized. However, you have no information as to what may be overutilizing the processor. To determine which process is causing the problem, you should track *Process:% Processor Time* for suspected processes. You will then have data connected to each suspected process, and you can base your analysis on this data comparison.

Baselines are also important in determining when a given system is being "resource-challenged." It should be obvious, but it bears repeating that unless you know what normal resource utilization is like on any given system, you cannot begin to analyze problems or bottlenecks, develop trends, or implement load balancing across systems.

Creating a Performance Monitor Chart

To create a Performance Monitor chart, follow these steps:

1. Start Windows NT Performance Monitor.

2. Choose Add To Chart from the Edit menu to display the Add To Chart dialog box, shown in Figure 6-1.

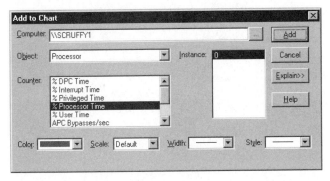

Figure 6-1. *The Add To Chart dialog box.*

3. Confirm the name of the system you are monitoring in the Computer text box. You can also click the Browse button to select from a list of systems, or type in the name of the system you want to monitor.

> **Tip**   Because running Performance Monitor on a Windows NT server requires additional resources in and of itself, you could remotely monitor your systems from your Windows NT workstation rather than at the actual system in question.

4. Select an object, a counter, and an appropriate instance, if necessary.

5. Specify the desired color, scale, width, and style for your chart lines.

6. If you're unsure of the purpose or function of a counter, select it and click the Explain button to display a brief description at the bottom of the dialog box.

7. Click Add to begin charting information for the objects you selected.

Figure 6-2 shows a representative chart. Here three *Object:Counter* sets are being monitored: *Processor:% Processor Time, Process:% Processor Time* for the

SMS Executive instance (smsexec), and *Memory:Pages/Sec.* In this example, where the values were generated by updating the collection memberships in the SMS Administrator Console, the peaks in the chart show the point at which the update has taken place through activity monitored by the three counters. For detailed information about updating the collection memberships in the SMS Administrator Console, see Chapter 11.

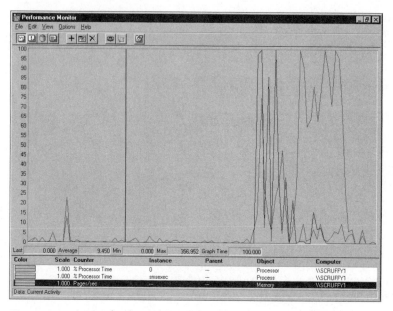

Figure 6-2. *A simple chart that continually monitors three* Object:Counter *values.*

Tip The more objects monitored in a chart, the busier the chart becomes. To facilitate the reading of chart lines, turn on the highlight feature. With the chart open, press Ctrl-H or Backspace. Then when you select a line on the chart, it will be displayed as a heavy white line, making it easier to read. Press Ctrl-H or Backspace again to turn off the highlight feature.

SMS 2.0 performance, like that of most Windows NT systems, tends to revolve around a specific set of system resources that can be monitored and analyzed with the help of Performance Monitor. These resources include processor, disk, memory, and network. Table 6-1 outlines the more useful objects and counters for tracking and analyzing SMS site system server performance using Performance Monitor.

Table 6-1.   Suggested Performance Monitor objects and counters

Object:Counter	Description	Instance	Threshold Suggestions
Memory: Committed Bytes	Represents the amount of virtual memory that has been committed for use for paging RAM	N/A	This value should be less than the amount of physical RAM. The higher the value, the more likely that the system is experiencing a high level of paging and thrashing.
Memory: Page Reads/Sec	Represents the frequency at which data had to be read from the page file back into RAM to resolve page faults	N/A	A value less than or equal to 5 generally represents acceptable performance. Values over 5 may indicate a need for more RAM.
Network Segment: Total Bytes Received/Second	Represents the number of bytes received per second on this network segment	Each network card	This value should remain relatively consistent and reflect average network traffic being generated. Prolonged increases in this value may indicate that a process or server on the segment is generating additional traffic and using potentially more bandwidth.
Network Segment: Total Frames Received/Second	Represents the number of network frames received per second on this segment	Each network card	Same as the threshold suggestion for *Network Segment: Total Bytes Received/Second*.
Physical Disk: % Disk Time	Represents the amount of time the disk is engaged in servicing read and write requests	Each physical disk	Levels less than or equal to 80 percent generally represent acceptable system performance.
Physical Disk: Current Disk Queue Length	Represents the number of read and write requests currently waiting to be processed on the physical disk	Each physical disk	Subtract from this value the number of spindles on the disks. (A RAID device would have two or more spindles.) The resulting value should average less than 2.
Process: % Processor Time	Represents the percentage of time spent by the processor or processors executing threads for the process selected	Total, or for each process currently running	Use with *Processor:% Processor Time* to determine which SMS process in particular is utilizing processor time and to what extent.
Processor: % Processor Time	Represents the percentage of time spent by the processor or processors executing nonidle threads	Total, or for each installed processor	Levels less than or equal to 80 percent generally represent acceptable system performance.

(continued)

Table 6-1 *continued*

Object:Counter	Description	Instance	Threshold Suggestions
SQL Server: Cache Hit Ratio	Represents how often SQL Server requests could be resolved from the SQL Server cache rather than having to query the database directly	N/A	This value should be very high—98 percent or greater, which indicates efficient and responsive processing of SQL queries.
System: % Total Processor Time	Represents the average amount of productive time spent by all processors executing nonidle threads	N/A	Levels less than or equal to 80 percent generally represent acceptable system performance. Use this object while also monitoring the *SMS Executive Thread States* object.
System: Processor Queue Length	Represents the number of threads waiting to be processed	N/A	There should generally be no more than two requests waiting to be processed. Use this object while also monitoring the *SMS Executive Thread States* object.
Thread: Context Switches/Sec	Represents the number of context switches between threads; a thread switch might be caused by one thread requesting information from another or yielding to a higher priority thread	Total	The lower the value, the better.

These and other Performance Monitor objects and counters are meant to be used together to determine overall system performance as well as limit problem processes and potential resource bottlenecks.

As mentioned, you cannot perform effective problem or trend analysis of a system if you do not have statistics relating to normal performance of that system. To get this baseline data, you should create chart information during periods of normal and peak performance and then save this information as Performance Monitor logs.

Creating a Performance Monitor Log

To create a Performance Monitor log, follow these steps:

1. Start Windows NT Performance Monitor.

2. Choose Log from the View menu to display the Performance Monitor Log window, shown in Figure 6-3.

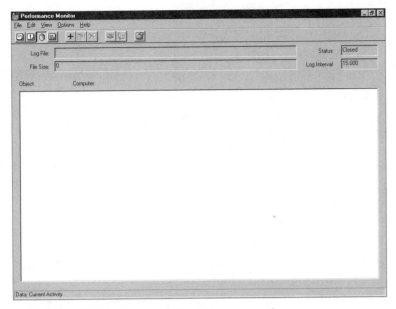

Figure 6-3. *The Performance Monitor Log window.*

3. Choose Add To Log from the Edit menu to display the Add To Log dialog box, shown in Figure 6-4. This dialog box displays the name of the computer from which you will gather data and a list of objects whose data you can collect.

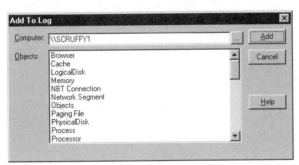

Figure 6-4. *The Add To Log dialog box.*

4. Select each object for which you want to collect data and click Add. Click Done when you have finished to return to the Performance Monitor Log window.

5. Choose Log from the Options menu to display the Log Options dialog box, shown in Figure 6-5.

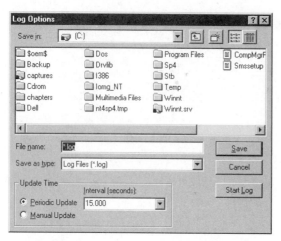

Figure 6-5. *The Log Options dialog box.*

6. Enter a name for the log file, and specify the locations where you'd like to store the log. Change the update interval if you want.

7. Click Start Log to return to the Performance Monitor Log window and begin collecting data. You can monitor the size of the log file in the File Size box.

8. When you have collected the amount of data you need, choose Log from the Options menu once again, and click Stop Log in the Log Options dialog box.

9. Choose Log from the Options menu one more time, and click Save in the Log Options dialog box to save the log file.

Creating a Chart from a Log File

Unlike a typical chart, log files do not let you specify which counters to monitor for each object you add to the log. You do that when you create a chart from the collected log data. To create a chart using log file data, follow these steps:

1. Start the Windows NT Performance Monitor.

2. Choose Data From from the Options menu to display the Data From dialog box, shown in Figure 6-6.

Figure 6-6. *The Data From dialog box.*

3. Enter the name of the log file you created and click OK to return to Performance Monitor.

4. Choose Add To Chart from the Edit menu to display the Add To Chart dialog box, shown in Figure 6-1. The only objects that will be available are those you added to the log file. All the counters corresponding to those objects will be available. Build your chart just as before.

Figure 6-7 shows a chart created from a log file, which is a static chart. It represents values collected by the objects over a specific period of time. As with the chart shown in Figure 6-2, the values in this chart were generated by updating collection membership through the SMS Administrator Console.

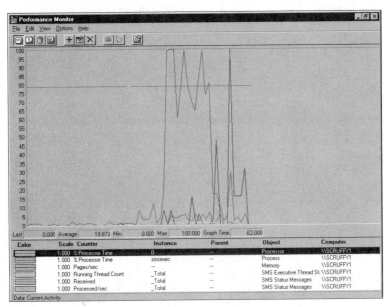

Figure 6-7. *A sample static chart created from a log file.*

You can compare this chart to a dynamic current chart on the same system to determine whether current activity falls within acceptable normal limits.

Specific Objects and Counters

When SMS 2.0 is installed, the Setup program adds a set of SMS-specific objects and counters to the Windows NT Performance Monitor that can be used to assess performance levels of your SMS site system. These objects and counters are available only when Performance Monitor is started on an SMS site server and the SMS Executive service is running on that site server. Table 6-2 describes these added objects and some of their more useful counters.

Table 6-2. SMS-specific Performance Monitor objects and counters

Object	Counter	Description
SMS Discovery Data Manager	*Total DDRs Processed*	Total number of discovery data records (DDRs) processed by Discovery Data Manager during the current session. This value should generally be high when one or more discovery methods have been enabled. If this value is low, you may need to check the discovery process to determine whether it is processing normally. Refer to Chapter 7 for a discussion of the discovery process.
SMS Executive Thread States	*Running Thread Count*	When using the _Total instance, this value indicates the total number of SMS threads currently running. By examining specific instances, you can assess thread count on a per-thread basis. You can also monitor sleeping threads, which are blocked by the *Yield* function, and yielding threads, which are ready to run but not allowed to due to the need to limit running threads.
SMS In-Memory Queues	*Total Objects Dequeued*	Represents the total number of objects added to the queue by a specific component since the component last started. The number of objects can be monitored for each component by selecting the component in the instance list.
SMS Inventory Data Loader	*Total MIFs Processed*	Represents the total number of inventory records processed by Inventory Data Loader during the current session. You can also monitor the number of MIFs processed per minute during the monitoring session and the number of bad MIFs processed during the current session.
SMS Software Inventory Processor	*Total SINVs Processed*	Represents the total number of software inventory records (SINVs) processed by the Software Inventory Processor during the current session. You can also monitor the number of software inventory records processed per minute during the monitoring session and the number of bad records processed during the current session.
SMS Standard Sender	*Average Bytes/Sec*	Represents the average throughput of the sender. Generally, this value should be high since you want to process the greatest amount of information in the shortest amount of time. If the value is low, you might suspect network or card problems. You can also monitor total bytes attempted, failed, and sent in order to establish baselines for the sender.

Table 6-2   *continued*

Object	Counter	Description
SMS Standard Sender	*Sending Thread Count*	Represents the number of threads currently sending to a destination. You can monitor the total number of threads sent to all sites or monitor threads on a per-site basis by selecting the appropriate instance.
SMS Status Messages	*Processed/Sec*	Represents the number of status messages Status Message Manager has processed per second. Depending on the instance selected, you can monitor the total number of status messages processed or break down messages into those processed from the in-memory queue and from Status Manager's inbox.

Some of these objects are informational, providing additional data to help you understand how a component is working. By and large, they all can assist you in establishing how resources are being utilized on your SMS servers. Remember, the idea here is to use these SMS-specific objects and counters along with the traditional objects and counters used to monitor processor, memory, disk, and network performance to establish a baseline of normal activity on your SMS servers. You then use that baseline to help you determine when performance is inside the norm and when it becomes unacceptable.

Note   By default, disk performance object counters are *not* enabled on Windows NT systems, reducing the number of resources monitored and the overhead needed to monitor them. If you create a chart using disk objects such as *Logical Disk* and *Physical Disk*, no data will be created until you enable disk counters. To do this, enter the following command at a Windows NT command prompt: *DISKPERF -Y*. You will need to restart the system in question before the disk counters are enabled. Enter *DISKPERF -N* to disable the disk counters when you have finished, again remembering to restart your system to make the change take effect.

More Info   Performance Monitor contains many additional features and options. For a complete discussion of Performance Monitor, attend Microsoft Official Curriculum (MOC) 689 "Supporting Microsoft Windows NT 4.0 Server Enterprise Technologies" or refer to the Windows NT 4.0 Administrator's Guide in the Readme file for Windows NT 4.0.

HealthMon

HealthMon is an add-on tool for SMS 2.0 that offers the SMS administrator a real-time at-a-glance view of the status of any Windows NT 4.0 or Windows 2000 computer. As with status messages, the "health" of a system is graphically represented by a green check mark for OK, a yellow triangle for Warning, and a red "X" for Critical status.

HealthMon includes several built-in monitored objects that look suspiciously like the Performance Monitor objects we saw in the preceding section. In fact, Health-Mon uses Performance Monitor objects and counters to collect data and determine status thresholds. These status thresholds are known as *monitoring policies* and are, of course, configurable by you, the SMS administrator. HealthMon also includes monitors specific to the Microsoft BackOffice application services. Table 6-3 lists the HealthMon objects and the Performance Monitor counters associated with them—or, in the case of a BackOffice application, the services associated with them.

Table 6-3. HealthMon objects and their associated counters

Object	Counter or Service
Processor	*Interrupts Per Second* *Percent Total System Time*
Memory	*Available Memory Bytes* *Page Reads Per Second* *Pages Per Second* *Percent Committed Bytes to Limit* *Pool Non-Paged Bytes*
Paging File	*Percent Peak Usage* *Percent Usage*
Logical Disk	*Percent Free Disk Space*
Physical Disk	*Disk Queue Length* *Diskperf Driver Started* *Percent Disk Time*
Network Interface	*Excessive Network Traffic Bytes Total/Sec*
Server Work Queues	*Context Blocks Queued/Sec* *Processor Queue Length*
Security	*Errors Access Permission* *Errors Logon*
Fault	*Pool Non-Paged Failures* *Pool Paged Failures* *Sessions Errored Out*

Table 6-3. *continued*

Object	Counter
SQL Server	*MSDTC Service Started* *MSSQL Server Service Started*
IIS Server	*IIS Service Started*
Exchange Server	*MSEXCHANGEDS Service Started* *MSEXCHANGEIS Service Started* *MSEXCHANGEMTA Service Started* *MSEXCHANGESA Service Started*
SNA Server	*Host Connection Status* *SNABASE Service Started*
SMS	*SMS_Executive Service Started* *SMS_Site_Component_Manager Service Started* *SMS_SQL_Monitor Service Started*

Installing HealthMon

HealthMon is not installed as part of the regular SMS 2.0 setup; instead, it is included on the SMS 2.0 CD as an add-on utility. HealthMon is itself a Microsoft Management Console (MMC) snap-in and as such could be added later to the SMS Administrator Console to keep all your SMS 2.0 utilities in one place. You can add the HealthMon snap-in to the SMS Administrator Console when you run the console in the Author mode. For more information on adding an MMC snap-in, refer to Chapter 16 and to the MMC online documentation.

HealthMon consists of two components: the client agent and the console. Each system that will be monitored must have the HealthMon Agent installed on it. You will most likely install the HealthMon Console on the SMS administrator's Windows NT workstation.

To install the HealthMon Agent and HealthMon Console, follow these steps:

1. Navigate to the Healthmon folder on the SMS 2.0 CD or in your up-dated SMS 2.0 Service Pack 1 source file directory, and expand the folder to your appropriate platform folder—Alpha or i386.

2. Expand the platform folder, expand the 00000409 folder, and open the Agent folder.

3. In the Agent folder, double-click on Setup.exe to launch the Microsoft SMS HealthMon Agent Installation Wizard. The installation instructions are straightforward and self-explanatory, so we won't go through them here. You do have the option of turning on disk performance

counters during this setup, but you shouldn't do so because Windows Management Instrumentation (WMI) will freeze when you restart the computer. You can enable the disk performance counters later when you need to use them.

4. On the last screen of the Installation Wizard, click Finish. The Health-Mon Agent will start automatically. If you turned on disk counters, you will be required to restart the system.

5. Return to the 00000409 folder and open the Console folder.

6. Again, double-click on Setup.exe to launch the Microsoft SMS HealthMon Console Installation Wizard, which installs the HealthMon Console. HealthMon will, by default, appear in the Systems Management Server program group.

Now that you've installed the HealthMon Agent and HealthMon Console successfully, let's look at how to run HealthMon on the monitored system.

Using HealthMon

The first time you run HealthMon, the HealthMon Console will open but no systems will be displayed, as shown in Figure 6-8.

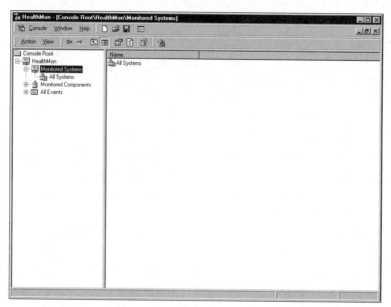

Figure 6-8. *The HealthMon Console.*

To specify the Windows NT systems that you want the utility to monitor, follow these steps:

1. Right-click on Monitored Systems in the HealthMon Console, choose New from the context menu, and then choose System to display the New Monitored System dialog box, shown in Figure 6-9.

Figure 6-9. *The New Monitored System dialog box.*

2. Enter the name of the Windows NT 4.0 or Windows 2000 system you want to monitor and then click OK.

3. Expand the new system entry to view its component status and events.

Figure 6-10 shows the HealthMon Console with an SMS site server added to it. The server's component status is displayed. In this example, a Warning icon appears next to the Logical Disk entry. As you can see, each component in the Components window corresponds to a HealthMon object listed in Table 6-3.

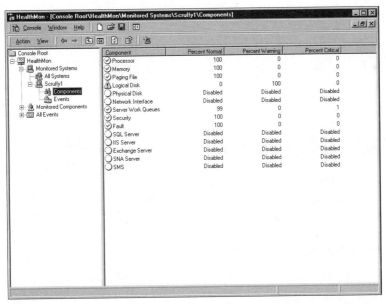

Figure 6-10. *The HealthMon Console with an SMS site system named Scruffy1 added.*

A value of *100* appears in the Percent Warning column. If we switch to the Events folder for the same system, as shown in Figure 6-11, the same Warning icon will appear, but with a more understandable message—namely, that drive C has less than 10 percent free disk space available. Normally, you would want to open the Components folder for a quick scan of components and then switch to the Events folder for a more detailed description of a specific event or message. With the HealthMon Console open and the Events folder in view, events will be displayed dynamically as they occur.

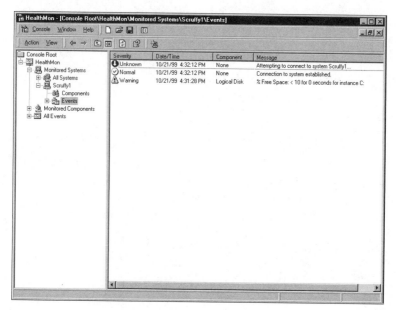

Figure 6-11. *The HealthMon Events folder for a Windows NT system.*

HealthMon and WBEM

The HealthMon Agent, which is installed on all systems that need to be monitored, uses Windows Management Instrumentation (WMI) to collect data through Performance Monitor. WMI is, of course, Microsoft's implementation of Web-Based Enterprise Management (WBEM). Because HealthMon is a WBEM-compliant application, it is capable of monitoring activity from any device or application that includes a WBEM provider to collect health data. For information about WBEM providers and other WBEM-related components and terms, refer to Chapter 1.

Research into creating and marketing WBEM-compliant hardware such as computer motherboards is currently underway. Such devices will expose to the WMI layer on Windows 2000 systems events such as the computer chassis being opened, the fan stopping, or the processor chip exceeding acceptable heat levels. Such technology will make it possible for network administrators to closely monitor all aspects of their systems, from resource utilization to hardware functionality and specification.

Configuring HealthMon

As mentioned, the components you monitor can also be configured by you, the administrator. You can enable the components you want to monitor using one of two methods and then configure the components you enabled. The first method is shown here:

1. Right-click on the system entry in the HealthMon Console and choose Properties from the context menu to display the System Properties window, shown in Figure 6-12.

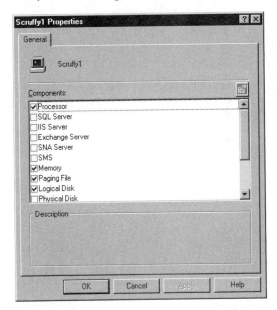

Figure 6-12. *The System Properties window.*

2. To enable monitoring, check the components you want to monitor.

3. Double-click on an enabled component to display its Properties window, where you can configure the component's properties.

4. Choose OK when you have finished.

The second method is shown here:

1. Select the Components folder under the appropriate system entry in the HealthMon Console.

2. Right-click on the component you want to enable, and choose Enable from the context menu.

3. Right-click on the component again, and choose Properties from the context menu to display its Properties window, where you can configure the component's properties.

4. Click OK when you have finished.

Regardless of which technique you choose to enable components, configuring a component's properties will always be done in the Properties window for that component. For example, you would configure the logical disk from the Logical Disk Properties window, shown in Figure 6-13.

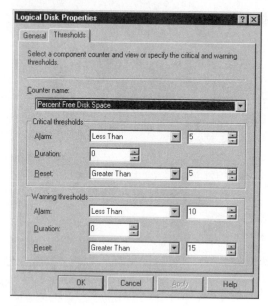

Figure 6-13. *The Thresholds tab.*

The General tab of the Logical Disk Properties Window simply lists the Performance Monitor counters that are used to generate events and gives a brief explanation of the purpose of each counter. The Thresholds tab, however, provides your configuration options. Here you can set the Critical and Warning alarm thresholds for each component counter.

In this example, if the *Logical Disk* counter detects that less than 10 percent of free disk space is available on any logical drive, a Warning message will be generated. If the value subsequently goes above 15 percent, the warning is reset. If you delete or move files from the monitored drive to create more free space, you can eventually get the Warning message to go away. Similarly, if the amount of free space falls below 5 percent, a Critical message will be generated. The Duration value represents the number of seconds over which the condition must be met before the messages are generated. This setting ensures that messages are not generated for momentary spikes and other anomalies. In this case, the value is set to 0 because any loss of free space on a disk—especially on an SMS site server—can be detrimental and ought to be investigated.

> **Note**   Enabling the *Physical Disk* object requires that you first enable the disk performance counters in Performance Monitor using the DISKPERF command at a Windows NT command prompt. (See the section "Specific Objects and Counters" earlier in this chapter for details.)

Network Interface counters are disabled by default. To enable them, you should install the Windows NT 4.0 Resource Kit counters component from the Windows NT 4.0 CD or install the SNMP Service using the Network option in the Control Panel. If you install SNMP, remember to also reapply the Windows NT Service Pack 4.0 or later to your system.

When you enable Microsoft BackOffice objects, remember that you are simply monitoring to determine whether the application's services are running. Be sure that you have enabled the appropriate services through the application before you enable monitoring of those services—for example, be sure to install Microsoft Exchange Server before trying to monitor its services. Otherwise, you will always display critical error messages.

> **Planning**   If you installed SMS 2.0 Service Pack 1, SMS Setup disables Performance Monitor counters for SQL Server 6.5 if SQL Server and SMS Provider are located on the same computer. Because of this, Performance Monitor, HealthMon, and other applications will be unable to access SQL Server counters. To enable the counters, you will need to modify the following registry key: HKEY_LOCAL_MACHINE\System\CurrentControlSet\Services\MSSQLServer\Performance. Double-click on the parameter entry Library, and change the value to *Sqlctr60.dll* to enable the SQL performance counters. To disable these performance counters when you have finished your analysis, reset the Library value to "" by double-clicking on the reference to Sqlctr60.dll and then deleting it.
>
> Making this change may result in random WMI or SMS Administrator Console errors. Restarting the SMS Administrator Console should clear up the problem. However, for this reason, you should only enable the SQL Server performance counters when it is necessary to analyze a suspected performance-related issue. SQL Server 6.5 with Service Pack 5 and SQL Server 7.0 are not affected by this change.

Network Trace

Some of you might work with an SNMP management application. These types of applications are used to map out and monitor IP-addressable hardware devices such as routers, switches, and printers. Often these applications can provide you with a graphical map of what your network infrastructure looks like.

The Network Trace utility is similar to SNMP in that it can help you map out and monitor your SMS site system structure—kind of like "reduced-calorie" SNMP. Network Trace provides the following features:

- A graphical map of the relationship between the SMS site server and its site systems, including subnets
- A graphical view of the assigned role of each site system
- A polling mechanism to check the running status of SMS components on each site system
- A polling mechanism to check the connectivity between site systems

This utility can be accessed through the SMS Administrator Console by navigating to the Site Systems folder under Site Settings and right-clicking on any site system. Choose All Tasks from the context menu, and then choose Start Network Trace. A site map similar to that shown in Figure 6-14 will be generated.

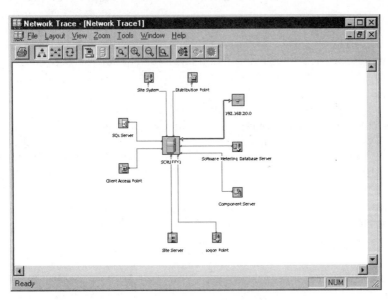

Figure 6-14. *A Network Trace utility site map.*

In this particular mapping, only one site system exists; it is named Scruffy1. This site system has been assigned the roles of site server, CAP, distribution point, logon point, and software metering database server. It is also the SQL server and is part of the subnet 192.168.20.0.

The Network Trace interface is fairly easy to navigate. You can, of course, print the map, which is actually quite convenient, especially for documentation purposes. You can also switch between Trace view and Site view. Trace view is the default view, as displayed in Figure 6-14. Site view reconfigures the map to show all the elements of the site. You can also zoom in and out to view the map more easily or to display more detail.

The monitoring aspect of this utility is accessed through the Tools menu. Two connectivity options are available: Ping All Servers And Routers and Ping Selected Servers And Routers. Both options will generate a network connectivity check to determine whether the site systems can be accessed across the network. The result of the ping test is a green check mark on top of each site system that was successfully accessed, as shown in Figure 6-15, and a red "X" on top of those systems that could not be accessed.

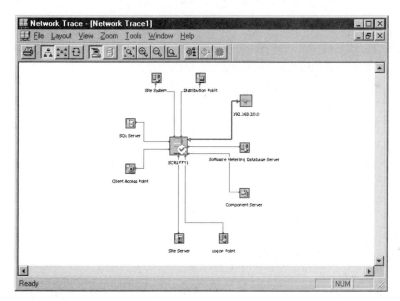

Figure 6-15. *The results of a ping test, indicating which site systems could be successfully accessed across the network.*

Network Trace also provides a component check option. Click on a site system in the Network Trace map, and then choose Poll Components Of Selected

Server(s) from the Tools menu to display the Component Poller window, shown in Figure 6-16. In this window, you can select a specific component or several components and then click Poll Selected to check the running status of particular SMS components on that particular site system. To check the running status of all components, click Poll All. (Figure 6-16 shows the result of clicking Poll All.) The status of each component is listed, along with the last time it was polled, the name of the site system, and whether the component is a service or a thread.

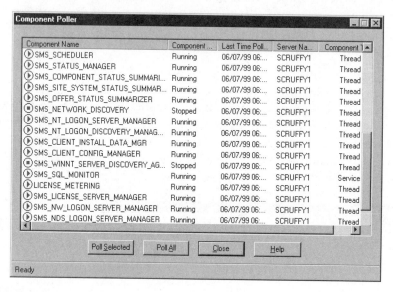

Figure 6-16. *The Component Poller window.*

In this example, two components—SMS Network Discovery and SMS WINNT Server Discovery Agent—show a status of Stopped. These components run on predetermined schedules and at the time of the poll, they were simply not scheduled to run. As you've probably discerned, the status of a component as displayed in the Component Poller window may or may not be indicative of a problem with the component. To get to that next level of information, the savvy SMS administrator would check the status messages for those components, and perhaps the log files, to determine whether a problem exists.

The purpose of this utility then is to convey a high-level view of the status and mapping of an SMS site and its site systems. Network Trace is one more tool—a neat one, at that—available to SMS administrators as they balance day-to-day administration with the wider issues of site structure, connectivity, and interaction.

Event to Trap Translator

If you currently use or have used an SNMP management application, the information in this section may be interesting because SMS 2.0 includes a means of collecting SNMP information. In this section, we will briefly review the concept behind SNMP management and then see how SMS 2.0 can add value to SNMP management.

SNMP and Systems Management Server 2.0

SNMP is actually part of the TCP/IP protocol suite. Contrary to popular thinking, TCP/IP consists of several protocol components that together provide connection mechanisms among computers and other devices. SNMP is used primarily for monitoring IP-addressable devices such as routers, gateways, hubs, switches, network printers, and mini and mainframe computers as well as Windows NT computers.

Agents running on these devices respond to requests for information or generate information based on events that occur at that device. The information is then forwarded to a configured SNMP management server, which organizes it in a reportable fashion, generating graphical maps of the network infrastructure, notifying administrators of events, and so on. This type of information is known as a *trap*. For example, when a computer is running low on disk space, or when a switch has experienced a port failure, a trap is generated and forwarded to an SNMP manager for action.

Microsoft does not itself offer an SNMP management application as part of its product line. However, it does provide SNMP services that can be installed on Windows NT computers to generate traps for other SNMP management applications and respond to requests for information from those applications. For example, Windows NT computers can report DHCP lease information or WINS name registrations and resolutions.

> **Note**   The SNMP Service must be installed on a Windows NT computer to enable TCP/IP counters in Performance Monitor, even if the computer is not participating in an SNMP community.

So what does all this have to do with SMS 2.0? Plenty, actually. SMS 2.0 provides the Event to Trap Translator, which can translate any configured Windows NT event into an SNMP trap that can then be forwarded to an SNMP management server. Essentially, any Windows NT event recorded by the Windows NT event log can be translated by this utility into an SNMP trap. Because such events can contain large amounts of text, the Event to Trap Translator truncates the string-based trap to 4 KB to avoid using unnecessary bandwidth.

For the Event to Trap Translator to work, the following conditions must be met:

- Your system must be running Windows NT 3.51 with Service Pack 4 or later or Windows NT 4.0 with Service Pack 3 or later.
- Your system must be using TCP/IP as its network protocol.
- The SNMP Service must be installed and configured for the SNMP community and manager it will communicate with.

Caution   As with any other Windows NT service, after you install the SNMP Service, be sure to reapply the Windows NT Service Pack before restarting your computer, since you added a service from the original Windows NT 4.0 CD. Remember that when you install a new component from the original Windows NT source files, one or more files that were upgraded by the service pack may get overwritten by old files. Also, verify that the SNMP Service is configured to start up automatically. Otherwise, you will have to manually start it each time you restart your system. Refer to the Windows NT 4.0 Administrator's Guide in the Readme file for Windows NT 4.0 for more information about the SNMP Service.

Because the Event to Trap Translator Client Agent (also sometimes referred to as the Event to Trap Translator Agent) is installed on SMS 2.0 clients by default, you need to perform an update configuration or repair installation operation on the client to initiate the client agent. This initiation process is discussed in detail in Chapter 8. For now, here's a brief overview of the procedure to perform on the SMS client:

1. On the client computer, open the Control Panel and double-click on the Systems Management icon to display the Systems Management Properties window.
2. On the Components tab, select NT Event To SNMP Trap Translator and click Repair Installation to initiate the client agent reinstallation.
3. Click OK to close the Systems Management Properties window.

Note   In general, it is incumbent upon you as the SMS administrator to keep the site systems and clients up to date with the most current service packs and fixes appropriate to your particular SMS sites.

Real World   Is the Event to Trap Translator Installed on the Client?

If you have not deployed SMS 2.0 Service Pack 1, you may experience a failure in enabling the Event to Trap Translator on some SMS clients. In this case, the Systems Management application in the Control Panel will still show the Event to Trap Translator as uninstalled. The other way to confirm the problem is through the Windows NT registry. In the registry, navigate to the following key:

HKEY_LOCAL_MACHINE\System\CurrentControlSet\Services\SNMP\ Parameters\ExtensionAgents

Look for the value *SOFTWARE\Microsoft\SNMP_EVENTS\Eventlog*, which represents the Event to Trap Translator utility. If this value does not appear, the client agent has not been installed. The first course of action in solving this problem is to perform a repair installation operation as described earlier or to shut down and restart the client to force a client component update.

If this doesn't work, you can enable the agent manually by executing the Stsinstl.exe program to run the SMS NT Event To SNMP Trap Translator Installation Wizard. This program is located in the SMS\Inboxes\Clicomp.src\Snmpelea*platform* directory, where *platform* is either Alpha or i386. Running this simple wizard will ensure that the Event to Trap Translator will be installed on the SMS 2.0 client. If you recheck the registry entry and the Systems Management application in the Control Panel, you will see that the agent has been successfully installed.

Configuring the Event to Trap Translator

To avoid network traffic issues, no Windows NT or SMS events are converted to SNMP traps by default. It is entirely up to the SMS administrator to determine just what events should be configured, and how.

Events are configured on a per-computer basis. More specifically, only computers that have installed the SNMP Service can generate successful SNMP traps. To select these computers and configure trap translation on them through the SMS Administrator Console, follow these steps:

1. Navigate to the Collections folder and select an appropriate collection, such as All Systems.

2. Right-click on the name of the computer for which you want to configure the Event to Trap Translator, choose All Tasks from the context menu, and then choose Start Event to Trap Translator to display the Event To Trap Translator window, as shown in Figure 6-17.

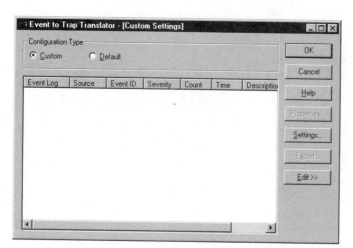

Figure 6-17. *The Event To Trap Translator window.*

3. Select Custom and then click Edit to expand the window and add events, as shown in Figure 6-18.

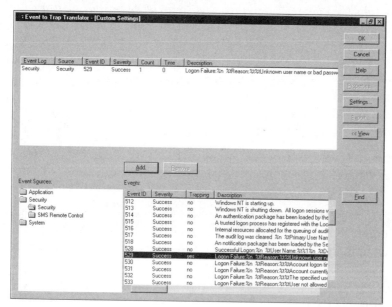

Figure 6-18. *The expanded Event To Trap Translator window.*

4. The Event Sources section contains three folders related to the three Windows NT event logs: Application, Security, and System. Select Windows NT events to translate into SNMP traps by navigating through these folders, selecting the events you want from the Events

list, and clicking Add. In Figure 6-18, Windows NT security event ID 529 (a logon failure due to unknown user name or bad password) has been selected and added to the list of events to be translated.

5. When you add an event, that event's Properties window is displayed, as shown in Figure 6-19.

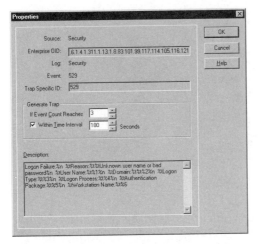

Figure 6-19. *The Event Properties window.*

This window includes the SNMP mapping for the event object known as the Enterprise OID, the log that the event is written to, the event and trap–specific IDs, and a description of the event. None of these settings can be configured.

6. You can set a threshold before the event is translated, however. In the If Event Count Reaches text box, enter the number of this kind of event that must be generated. If you enable the Within Time Interval option, enter the number of seconds within which the specified number of events must occur before the event is translated into an SNMP trap. In this example, if three bad logon attempts occur within 3 minutes (180 seconds), the bad logon event will be translated into an SNMP trap.

7. Click OK to save your changes. The Event To Trap Translator window will reflect the changes you made.

8. In the Event To Trap Translator window click Settings to display the Settings dialog box, shown in Figure 6-20.

Here you can change the default string length limit of 4 KB (4096 bytes) and control how many traps are sent by modifying the Trap Throttle settings. Click OK to close this dialog box.

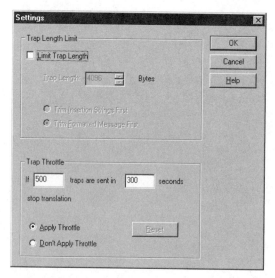

Figure 6-20. *The Settings dialog box.*

9. In the Event To Trap Translator window, click Export to display the Export Events dialog box, where you can export the translated events to a text file or to a Config Tool (.CNF) format file containing the Windows NT events that the Event to Trap Translator should translate into SNMP traps. You can use these export files for the SNMP manager if it requires configuration to receive and display these traps properly or to configure the Event to Trap Translator to trap the same events on other SNMP clients. Click Save to close the dialog box.

10. Click OK to close the Event To Trap Translator window.

Unlike SMS 1.2, SMS 2.0 does not provide an SNMP Trap Receiver, which means that you have no way to actually record the trapped event and view it through the SMS 2.0 database. The only way to be certain that the event was generated is to check through the SNMP manager for the trap or to use a traffic analysis tool such as Network Monitor to identify the creation and sending of an SNMP frame from the computer generating the trap to the SNMP manager.

Real World   Configuring Multiple Clients for SNMP Traps Remotely

The configuration process we've been looking at involves selecting individual clients through the Collections folder and launching the Event to Trap Translator. The Export feature in the Event To Trap Translator window, however, also produces a .CNF file, which can be used to advertise the same event to trap configuration to several clients using SMS advertisements.

To configure multiple clients for SNMP traps, first you need to create the .CNF file. Click the Export button in the Event To Trap Translator window, and save the file as a .CNF file. Next create an SMS package using this file and the Remote Configuration Tool (Eventcmt.exe). This command-line tool can be found in the SMS\Scripts\00000409\Eventcmt folder under the appropriate platform directory; it enables you to automatically configure many clients with the same configuration. The package would be created with the command Eventcmt.exe *filename*.cnf. Command-line options for Eventcmt.exe include the following:

- /NOMIF   Suppresses the creation of a status MIF for SMS
- /NOLOG   Suppresses the writing of an Eventcmt log for the client
- /DEFAULT   Directs Eventcmt to run only if the configuration file is not designated as Custom
- /SETCUSTOM   Changes the current configuration designation to Custom
- /NOSTOPSTART   Directs Eventcmt to not stop and restart the SNMP Service on the client when the configuration file is applied.

By default, the Remote Configuration Tool will generate a status MIF for SMS to indicate whether the events were configured successfully as well as write a more detailed log file (Eventcmt.log) in the *System Root*\MS\SMS\Logs folder on the SMS client.

The configuration files can also be created manually. Like all other script-like files, this process requires learning some additional script commands. If this prospect appeals to you, you can refer to the SMS online help for more information about creating your own configuration files.

Network Monitor

The Microsoft utility Network Monitor 2.0 included with SMS 2.0 is yet another SMS administrator tool that enables you to analyze and monitor network traffic among computers in your network. Network Monitor is similar in function to other, more expensive hardware-based tools currently on the market. It is used to identify heavily used subnets, routers, and WAN connections; to recognize bottlenecks and potential bottlenecks; and to develop trends to optimize the network infrastructure and placement of computers, servers, and in our particular case, SMS site systems.

There are actually two parts to this tool: the Network Monitor interface itself and the Network Monitor Agent. Unlike SMS 1.2, with SMS 2.0 the Network

Monitor Agent no longer needs to be installed as a service on the computer to be monitored. Instead, it is initiated at the time the remote connection is made to begin capturing data.

Note Network Monitor 2.0 should not be confused with the version that can be installed on any Windows NT 4.0 server. The version that comes with Windows NT 4.0 servers is a feature-limited copy of the earlier version of Network Monitor and allows monitoring of traffic only for traffic originating from or received by the server in question.

Network Monitor 2.0 provides the following functions:

- Captures, filters, and displays network frames
- Edits captured frames and forwards them
- Monitors traffic for remote computers
- Determines which users and protocols used the most bandwidth
- Determines the location of routers
- Resolves device names to MAC addresses

Network Monitor 2.0 also includes experts. These are not little network gurus that come popping out of the box—*experts* are post-capture analysis tools that can facilitate the administrator's understanding of the data collected. Table 6-4 lists these experts and describes what they are designed to accomplish.

Table 6-4.   Network Monitor 2.0 experts

Expert	Description
Average Server Response Time	Identifies the average time each server in the capture took to respond to requests
Property Distribution	Calculates protocol statistics for a specified protocol property in a capture
Protocol Coalesce Tool	Combines all the frames of a single transaction that may have been fragmented into a single frame and creates a new capture file using this information
Protocol Distribution	Calculates which protocols generated the most traffic during the capture session
TCP Retransmit	Identifies which TCP frames were transmitted more than once during the capture, indicating congestion or connectivity issues
Top Users	Identifies the senders and recipients of frames that generated the most traffic during the capture session

In addition to the Network Monitor utility and its features and experts, the SMS Administrator Console offers *monitors*—analysis tools that can be used prior to capturing frames to monitor for specific types of network activity. (The next section covers capturing frames in more detail.) Once the monitors have been configured, they generate events based on criteria supplied by the SMS administrator. Table 6-5 describes the available default monitors that are installed if you chose Network Monitor as an Install option during setup.

Table 6-5.   Network Monitor 2.0 monitors

Monitor	Description
ICMP Redirect Monitor	Generates an event each time an unauthorized or improperly configured router redirects Internet Control Message Protocol (ICMP) frames.
IP Range Monitor	Generates an event when a frame has an IP address outside the specified valid range.
IP Router Monitor	Generates an event when a specified IP router fails.
IPX Router Monitor	Generates an event when a specified IPX router fails.
Rogue Monitor	Generates an event when invalid, unauthorized DHCP or WINS servers are found on the network.
Security Monitor	Generates an event when unauthorized users are detected using Network Monitor to capture frames on the network. Security Monitor prevents these users from capturing data.
SynAttack Monitor	Half-open, unresponsive, or other suspicious connections are made to identified servers on the network.

Using Network Monitor 2.0

To run Network Monitor 2.0, you and your computer must meet the following requirements:

- Your computer must be running Windows NT 4.0 with Service Pack 3 or later and Microsoft Windows Internet Explorer 4.01 or later.

- You must have local Administrator privileges on the computer running Network Monitor 2.0 and/or local Administrator privileges on the remote computer that will be monitored using the Network Monitor Agent.

- Your computer must have a network interface card (NIC) that supports Promiscuous mode (meaning that it is able and ready to receive any and all frames).

- Windows Management must be installed and running.
- You must have already installed Network Monitor 2.0 (by running Setup from the SMS 2.0 CD).

Network Monitor 2.0 has its own online help, which can assist you with the more detailed uses of the product. For now, let's look at some of the more common uses and features and some fundamentals for using Network Monitor 2.0.

Planning SMS 2.0 Service Pack 1 includes upgrades to Network Monitor 2.0. If you install Network Monitor using the Setup.exe file found in the Nmext folder of the service pack source files, the Setup program will uninstall any previous Network Monitor 2.0 external installation. (An *external installation* is one performed outside the SMS Setup program. See Chapter 2 for a discussion of the SMS Setup program.) Previous versions of Network Monitor are not automatically upgraded to Network Monitor 2.0. To upgrade a previous version, specify that the installation directory for Network Monitor 2.0 be the same as the previous version. Refer to the *Microsoft Systems Management Server Version 2.0 Service Pack 1 Release Notes* for more information about these issues, as well as other issues regarding the use of Network Monitor 2.0 with various network cards and drivers.

Capturing Data

Network Monitor's primary function is to capture network traffic for analysis and troubleshooting. To use Network Monitor to capture data, follow these steps:

1. Start Network Monitor using one of the following techniques:
   - From the Systems Management Server program group, select Network Monitor.
   - In the SMS Administrator Console, open the Tools folder, right-click on Network Monitor, choose All Tasks from the context menu, and then choose Start Network Monitor.

2. The Network Monitor Capture window is displayed, as shown in Figure 6-21. Each section of the Network Monitor Capture window will reflect various aspects of the captured data, but the window is dataless until a capture session is initiated. We'll examine this window in more detail in the section "Viewing Captured Data" later in this chapter. For now, choose Start from the Capture menu to display the captured frames.

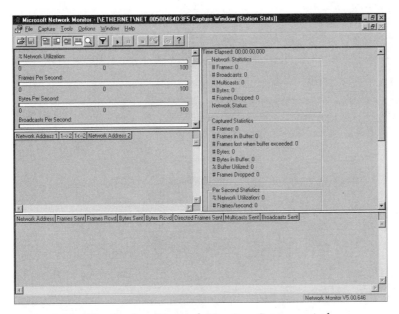

Figure 6-21. *The dataless Network Monitor Capture window.*

3. When you have captured enough data, choose Stop from the Capture menu to end the capture session. You can then view the captured frames by choosing Display Captured Data from the Capture menu, or save the captured data as a file for viewing individual frames later.

    Alternatively, you can choose Stop And View from the Capture menu to end the capture session and immediately view the individual frames that were captured.

Without any further filtering, all frames generated on the network and received by the monitored computer will be captured and potentially saved and displayed. The captured frames can add up quickly, as any network administrator can attest. Frequently, you will be interested in viewing the traffic generated between two specific computers—for example, between the site server and the SQL server hosting the SMS database, between the site server and its site systems, or between an SMS client and a CAP. This task can be easily accomplished by adding a filter before initiating a capture session. Filters can be based on protocols used, a specific frame property such as SAP or Etype, or the originating or destination address. You can also filter based on network segment if you are capturing data remotely.

To establish a capture filter, follow these steps:

1. Start the Network Monitor.

2. Choose Filter from the Capture menu to display the Capture Filter window, as shown in Figure 6-22.

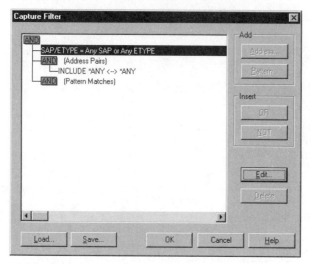

Figure 6-22. *The Capture Filter window.*

3. Select the property you want to filter against.

   If you choose SAP/ETYPE, you can then click Edit to display the Capture Filter SAPs And ETYPEs dialog box, shown in Figure 6-23, where you can specify the protocols that will be captured during the capture session. By default, all protocols are enabled.

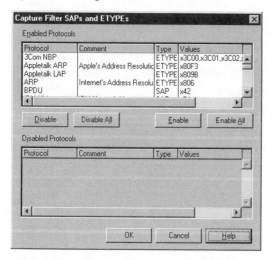

Figure 6-23. *The Capture Filter SAPs And ETYPEs dialog box.*

If you select INCLUDE under Address Pairs, you can click Edit or Address to display the Address Expression dialog box, shown in Figure 6-24, where you can modify the computers monitored from the default setting of ANY to a specific set of addresses.

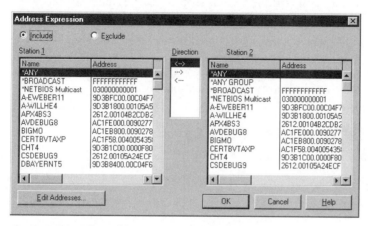

Figure 6-24. *The Address Expression dialog box.*

If you choose Pattern Matches, you can click Pattern to display the Pattern Match dialog box, shown in Figure 6-25, where you can specify that only frames containing a particular pattern of ASCII or hexadecimal data be captured. This pattern can start at the beginning of the frame or at a specified offset.

Figure 6-25. *The Pattern Match dialog box.*

4. Choose OK in the Capture Filter window to start your capture session. Only frames that meet your criteria will be collected during the capture session.

Establishing Capture Triggers

You can also configure Network Monitor to perform an action when the capture file fills to a certain level or when a particular pattern match is detected. This trigger action can sound an audible signal, stop capturing data at that point, or execute a command-line program or batch file.

To establish a capture trigger, follow these steps:

1. Start Network Monitor.

2. Choose Trigger from the Capture menu to display the Capture Trigger dialog box, shown in Figure 6-26. By default, no triggers are enabled.

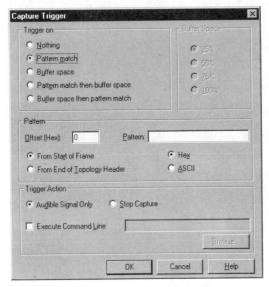

Figure 6-26. *The Capture Trigger dialog box.*

3. Select the type of trigger you want to enable. "Buffer" refers to the filled size of the capture file, and "pattern match" refers to those frames that contain a particular pattern of ASCII or hexadecimal data The pattern can start at the beginning of the frame or at a specified offset.

   If you choose a buffer trigger, specify the desired percent of buffer space.

   If you choose a pattern match trigger, enter the hexadecimal or ASCII text pattern that you want to match, and an offset value if necessary.

4. Select a trigger action. These options are fairly self-explanatory. An example of a command-line action might be a NET SEND command to

the SMS administrator noting that a capture trigger event occurred—for instance, *net send SMSAdmin1 Capture Trigger Event Occurred.*

5. Click OK to close the dialog box.

Viewing Captured Data

When you stop a capture session, you can view capture statistics in the Network Monitor Capture window, as shown in Figure 6-27. This window is divided into four sections, or panes. The top left pane, referred to as the Graph pane, contains five graphical charts of the frames generated and received during the capture session. This pane is dynamic and only active during the capture session itself. The data monitored is self-explanatory.

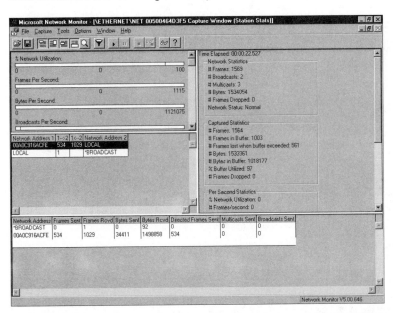

Figure 6-27. *The Network Monitor Capture window, showing captured data.*

The middle left pane, called the Session Statistics pane, displays a summary of the frames sent and received between this computer and any other specified computers. In this example, 534 frames were sent from a computer with MAC address 00A0C916ACFE to the local server, and 1029 frames were sent from the local server to the other computer.

The bottom pane, called the Station Statistics pane, displays more detailed frame information on a per-computer basis—specifically, the number of frames sent and received, bytes sent and received, directed frames sent, multicast frames sent, and broadcast frames sent.

The right pane, referred to as the Total Statistics pane, displays summary information about the capture session as a whole. This summary information is divided into Network Statistics, Captured Statistics, Per Second Statistics, Network Card Statistics, and Network Card Error Statistics sections.

You probably noticed in Figure 6-27 that Network Monitor identifies source and target computers primarily by their MAC address, which is the network card address, of course. You can make this window as well as the Frames view easier to read by helping Network Monitor to resolve the MAC address to a NetBIOS name. To do so, follow these steps:

1. Choose Addresses from the Capture menu to display the Address Database window, shown in Figure 6-28.

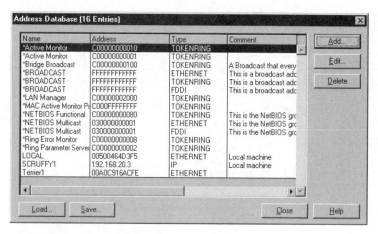

Figure 6-28. *The Address Database window.*

2. Click Add to display the Address Information dialog box, shown in Figure 6-29.

Figure 6-29. *The Address Information dialog box.*

3. Enter the NetBIOS name, or whatever name you want, in the Name text box. Enter the MAC address in the Address text box, and select a network type from the Type drop-down list if necessary.

4. Click OK to return to the Address Database window.

5. Click Close to close the Address Database window and use the name values for this session, or click Save to save the name values to facilitate viewing of future captures.

Caution   The maximum size for a capture file is 1024 MB. As you generate capture files that approach this size, Windows may experience low levels of virtual memory or may even run out . As virtual memory runs low, Network Monitor will continue to capture data, although some frames may be dropped due to a corresponding reduction in system performance. If you must generate and view large capture files, be sure to increase the size of the virtual memory page file. Refer to your Windows documentation for instructions on how to modify the page file size. In addition, save the capture file before viewing it, restart Network Monitor, and then open the file.

This statistical information can certainly help identify the amount of traffic generated, but there are still the frames themselves to view. By viewing the frames that were captured, you can understand the type of traffic that was generated and which frames are associated with certain kinds of activity on various servers. For example, you can determine when the CAP forwarded discovery data to the site server and how much traffic was generated as a result.

Frames can be viewed by opening a saved capture file or by choosing Stop And View from the Capture menu when ending a capture session. Figure 6-30 shows a sample capture file of individual frames. In this view, you can see the frames generated and received between the two servers SCRUFFY1 (the local server) and Terrier1.

This screen begins with a frame number, a time offset, the source and destination MAC addresses (which can be resolved to readable names as they have been here), the protocol type of the frame, a brief description of the frame, and the MAC address resolved to a NetBIOS name or IP address.

Each frame is "viewable" in that if you double-click on a frame, you can view the contents of the frame in the Frame Details window, as shown in Figure 6-31.

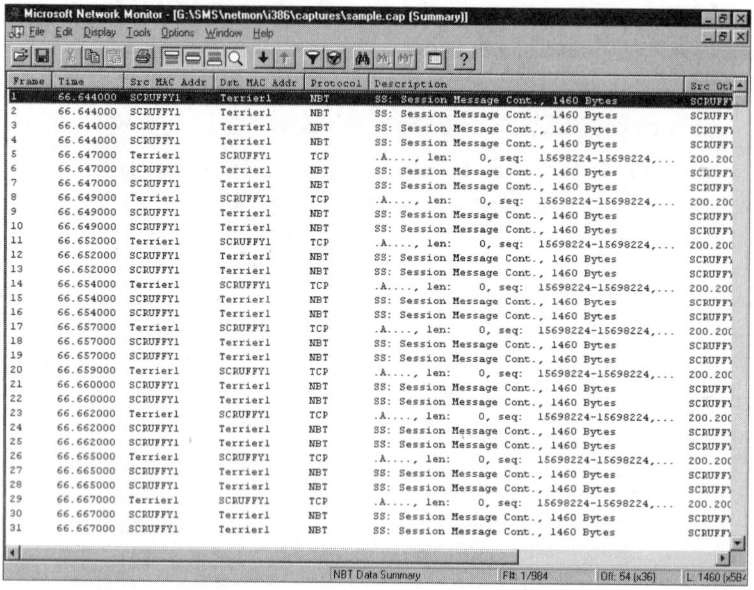

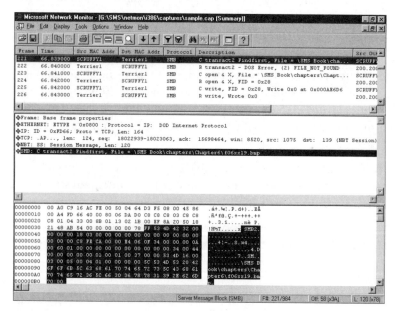

Figure 6-30. *A sample capture file showing individual frames that were captured between two computers on a network.*

Figure 6-31. *The Frame Details window.*

At the top is the Summary pane, a tiled view of the capture file we started from. The middle pane is the Detail pane, which provides an expandable view of the contents of the frame currently selected in the Summary pane, including the frame's size, Ethernet information such as MAC address, IP information such as IP address, and Server Message Block (SMB) information such as the frame offset and flags if the frame is part of a fragmented group of frames and the frame data. You can double-click the plus sign (+) or minus sign (–) to expand or collapse the levels of detail that appear in this pane. The bottom pane is the Hex pane, which displays the frame contents in both hexadecimal and text where possible. In this example, the frame is part of a file copy routine that is copying a file named F06xx19.bmp from SCRUFFY1 to Terrier1. The filename can be seen in both the Detail and Hex panes.

> **More Info**   We won't spend a lot of time here exploring every nuance of using Network Monitor or interpreting frames, especially because there are two Microsoft certified classes that cover the use of Network Monitor in significant detail—MOC 689, "Supporting Microsoft Windows NT Server 4 Enterprise Technologies," and MOC 828, "Planning, Implementing, and Supporting Systems Management Server 2.0." However, we will cover the traffic generated by specific SMS components and agents as well as specific frames to look for as appropriate throughout this book.

Using Experts

We do want to take the time to examine how to use the new experts that come with Network Monitor 2.0 (see Table 6-4), as they are appropriate to our discussion of SMS 2.0. As mentioned, these experts are post-capture analysis tools designed to help facilitate your understanding of the data you collect.

To enable the experts, follow these steps:

1. Open a capture file.
2. Choose Experts from the Tools menu in the Frame Details window to display the Network Monitor Experts dialog box, shown in Figure 6-32.
3. Select the expert you want to enable—in this case, Average Server Response Time—and click Configure Expert to display the Average Server Response Time Configuration dialog box, shown in Figure 6-33. With this expert, you can add and delete TCP/IP port numbers and IPX socket numbers. Other experts will offer other configuration options.

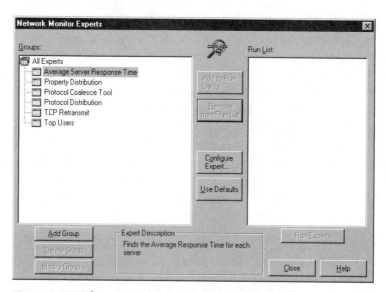

Figure 6-32. *The Network Monitor Experts dialog box.*

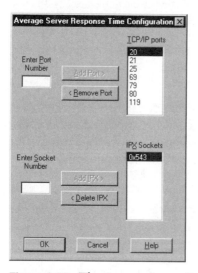

Figure 6-33. *The Average Server Response Time Configuration dialog box.*

4. Click OK to return to the Network Monitor Experts dialog box, and then click Add To Run List.

5. When you are ready to run the expert, click Run Experts.

6. When the expert has completed processing, a Network Monitor Event Viewer window will be displayed similar to the one shown in Figure 6-34,

containing the information you requested. In this example, all experts were selected to run. You can access the result of each expert by clicking on its respective tab in the Event Viewer window.

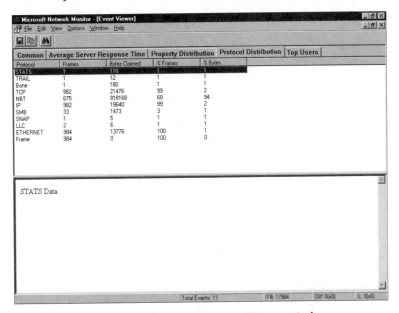

The following table appears within the figure:

Protocol	Frames	Bytes Claimed	% Frames	% Bytes
STATS	1	110	1	1
TRAIL	1	12	1	1
Bone	1	180	1	1
TCP	982	21476	99	2
NBT	675	918168	68	94
IP	982	19640	99	2
SMB	33	1473	3	1
SNAP	1	5	1	1
LLC	2	6	1	1
ETHERNET	984	13776	100	1
Frame	984	0	100	0

STATS Data

Figure 6-34. *The Network Monitor Event Viewer window.*

> **Note** If your capture file consists of a large number of SMB frames, the Average Server Response Time expert may return incorrect averages because it fails to discard duplicate requests. In general, the larger the capture file, the less accurate the averages will be.

Using the Control Tool

As mentioned, this new version of Network Monitor also includes control tools, or monitors, that are properly used as precapture analysis tools. The seven monitors described in Table 6-5 are installed by default; you can also add third-party monitors or create your own custom monitors.

When you configure a monitor, it examines network traffic on the local network segment in real time, watching for specified conditions or frame properties. When a match is found, the monitor generates an event that the SMS administrator can view using the Monitor Control Tool. As with other SMS Administrator Console tools, the Monitor Control Tool uses Windows Management to collect and expose the required information to be viewed through the interface.

To configure and enable monitors, follow these steps:

1. In the SMS Administrator Console, navigate to and expand the Tools folder, right-click on Network Monitor, choose All Tasks from the context menu, and then choose Start Network Monitor Control Tool to display the Monitor Control Tool window, shown in Figure 6-35.

   Alternatively, you can start the Network Monitor Control Tool from the Systems Management Server program group.

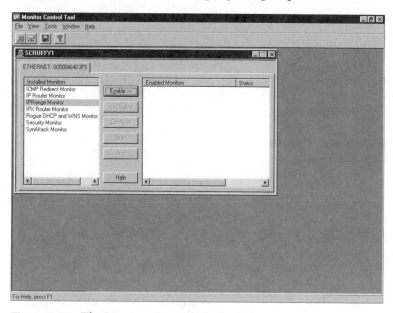

Figure 6-35. *The Monitor Control Tool window.*

2. If you want to monitor a remote computer, choose Remote Computer from the File menu to open the Remote Computer dialog box, supply the NetBIOS name or IP address of the computer in question, and then click OK.

3. Select the monitor you want to enable from the Installed Monitors list and click Enable. A message box will appear, informing you that the monitor has not yet been configured. Choose Yes to configure the monitor. If you choose No, you can configure the monitor later by selecting it in the Enabled Monitors list and clicking Configure.

4. Each monitor will have a different, easy-to-understand configuration screen. You can also press F1 from any configuration screen to access help. Here are three examples:

- Figure 6-36 shows the IP Range Monitor Configuration screen. Recall that this monitor generates an event when an IP address outside a valid identified range generates traffic on the network. Configure this monitor by supplying a range of valid addresses or invalid addresses, depending on whether you want to find any invalid frames or those from a specific address range.

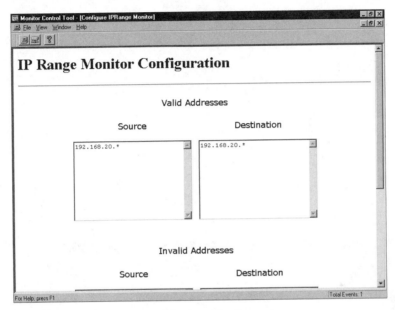

Figure 6-36. *The IP Range Monitor Configuration screen.*

- Figure 6-37 shows the IP Router Monitor Configuration screen. This monitor generates an event when a specified IP router fails (that is, the router is quiet for a specified period of time). Enter the IP addresses of the routers you want to monitor and the amount of time in seconds (10 to 600) that a router must be quiet to be considered nonfunctioning.

- Figure 6-38 shows the Security Monitor Configuration screen. This monitor enables you to specify which computers can run Network Monitor on the local subnet and to disallow any other computers from being able to run it. Enter the MAC addresses of the computers that should run Network Monitor, and specify whether to log IP addresses for those computers, whether to shut down the capture session on invalid computers, and the number of minutes allowed between event notifications that are reported to the Event Viewer window.

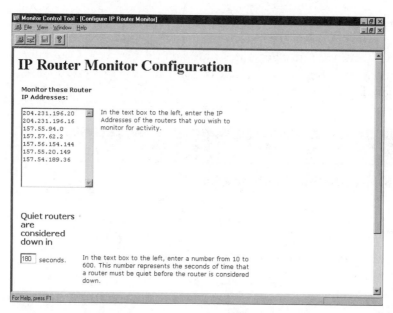

Figure 6-37. *The IP Router Monitor Configuration screen.*

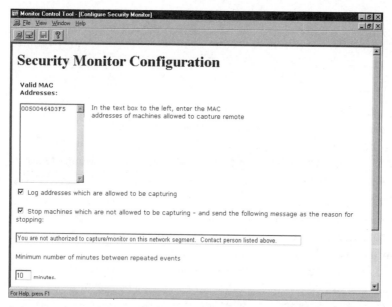

Figure 6-38. *The Security Monitor Configuration screen.*

5. When you have finished setting monitor options, click the Set Monitor Configuration button, located at the bottom of each configuration screen, to return to the Monitor Control Tool window.

6. When you have configured your monitors, select each one in the Enabled Monitors list, and click Start to start the monitor.

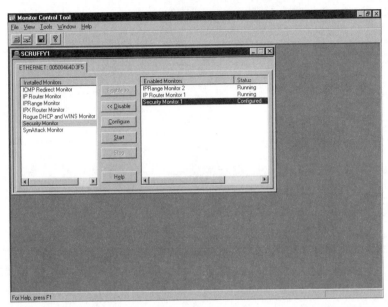

Figure 6-39. *The Monitor Control Tool window, showing enabled monitors.*

As an event is generated by the monitor, the Event Viewer window appears. Alternatively, you can view the event by choosing Events from the View menu in the Monitor Control Tool window. Figure 6-40 shows an example of events generated by the Monitor Control Tool monitors enabled using the procedure described above.

> **Caution** Security Monitor monitors only the local network segment. If your routers do not forward multicast frames, Security Monitor will not be able to watch other segments. To ensure that Security Monitor can watch other segments, install Network Monitor (and WMI) on a computer in each affected segment and enable Security Monitor on each.

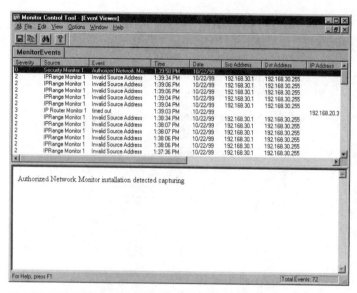

Figure 6-40. *The Event Viewer window, listing all events generated by the configured monitors in the order in which the frames were received.*

Summary

You should now have a full set of tools to help you understand, monitor, analyze, and troubleshoot your SMS site and site systems. This chapter reacquainted you with Performance Monitor as a server optimization tool, including several objects and counters that can help you assess the performance of your SMS site systems. HealthMon and Network Trace provide a high-level view of the health of a system and a site map. The Event to Trap Translator adds value to a network using SNMP services by translating Windows NT events into SNMP traps that can be forwarded to an SNMP manager. Network Monitor offers a rich network of frame analysis tools to assist you in determining the health of your network, including locating congested segments or unresponsive routers. Network Monitor has been updated to include experts and monitors to facilitate frame analysis and highlight specific events.

Part II will concentrate on the discovery of resources in your SMS site and, at long last, the client installation, inventory collection, and remote control services.

Part II
Resource Discovery, Client Installation, and Remote Control

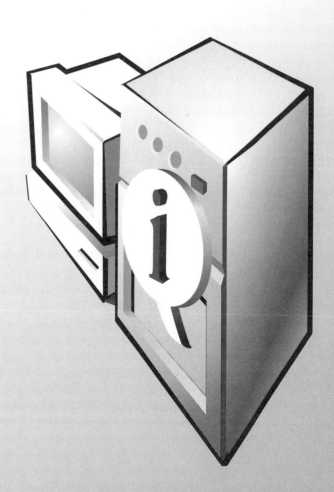

Chapter 7
Resource Discovery

Now that our SMS site has been implemented and our monitoring, analysis, and troubleshooting tools are ready and at our disposal, it's time to begin adding resources and clients to our site. After all, we can't use any of the neat features we've been talking about—package delivery, remote control, software metering—unless we identify and install valid Microsoft Systems Management Server (SMS) 2.0 clients. In Part II, we'll focus primarily on discovery methods and client installation and look at two specific client management options—inventory collection and remote control.

The installation process, as we'll see in Chapter 8, consists of discovering a client, assigning it to an SMS site, and then installing SMS client components on that computer. In this chapter, we'll look specifically at the resource discovery methods and process and Discovery Data Manager.

Overview

When we talk about the SMS 2.0 database, we are generally referring to the population of client computers in our environment. These clients are probably the most significant resources that we deal with in our SMS sites on a day-to-day basis. In fact, with SMS 1.2 and earlier, you really couldn't do anything at all unless the client computer was not only "discovered" and installed, but also inventoried into the SMS database.

With SMS 2.0, our computer clients are still our most significant resource. However, the processes of discovering, installing, and inventorying these clients are now separate and distinct functions. For example, it is no longer necessary to complete an inventory of a client before an SMS administrator can initiate a Remote Tools session with that client or advertise a program to it. Indeed, a client computer can be discovered without ever being installed.

In addition to discovering client computers, we can also discover other resources and add them to the SMS database. These other resources include user and global groups from the Microsoft Windows NT domain account database, other site systems, routers, hubs, switches, network printers, and any other IP-addressable devices on the network. They could even include mainframe computers or UNIX workstations.

Of course, we won't be able to send a package of TrueType fonts to that network printer that SMS discovers—not yet, anyway. But, we can know that the printer is there and make it part of the database of information about our network. More significantly, unlike earlier versions of SMS, we now have the ability to advertise programs not only to clients, but also to users and groups. As an SMS administrator, having access to those two new resources might become as important to you as your SMS client computers.

When a resource is discovered by an SMS discovery method, a record is created for it and included in the SMS database. This record is called a discovery data record (DDR), and the DDR file generated by the discovery method has a .DDR extension. The information that is "discovered" varies depending on the resource, but it might include such data as the NetBIOS name of a computer, IP address and IP subnet of a computer or device, user name, SMS unique identifier (SMSUID), operating system, MAC address, Windows NT account domain, and so on.

The seven methods that can be used to discover resources are:

- Site system discovery (Windows NT Server Discovery and NetWare Bindery Server Discovery)
- Logon discovery (Windows Networking Logon Discovery, NetWare Bindery Logon Discovery, and NetWare NDS Logon Discovery)
- Windows NT User Account Discovery
- Windows NT User Group Discovery
- Network Discovery
- Heartbeat Discovery
- Manual discovery

Most of these discovery methods are configurable by the SMS administrator. The logon discovery methods have corresponding client installation methods. When a DDR is created, SMS assigns that resource an SMSUID to distinguish it from other resources in the database. Depending on the discovery method chosen, discovery records are periodically regenerated to keep the discovery data up-to-date in the database and to verify that the resource is still a valid resource within the site.

Recall that when you install SMS using the Custom Setup option, none of the discovery methods are enabled except for site system discovery, which is automatic and can't be configured. Therefore, the SMS administrator must determine which methods to use and how to configure them. When SMS is installed using the Express Setup option, however, Windows Networking Logon Discovery, Windows NT User Account Discovery, Windows NT User Group Discovery, and Heartbeat Discovery are all enabled by default.

Tip   Table 2-2 in Chapter 2 lists the SMS 2.0 features and components that are installed or enabled during Express and Custom setup and their main default values.

Resource Discovery Methods

In this section, we'll examine the individual discovery methods. You'll learn how to configure each discovery method if applicable, the mechanics involved in carrying out the discovery process, the network traffic generated, and the elements you might need to troubleshoot when you work with each discovery method.

Site System Discovery

There are two site system discovery methods: Windows NT Server Discovery and NetWare Bindery Server Discovery. Both methods are designed to automatically create discovery records for Windows NT and NetWare Bindery servers that have been assigned a site system role such as logon point, client access point (CAP), distribution point, and so on. Both methods are nonconfigurable, and they do not appear in the SMS Administrator Console. Instead, they are automatically initiated by the WINNT Server Discovery Agent and the NetWare Bindery Server Discovery Agent. These discovery agents are SMS threads that discover Windows NT or NetWare Bindery site systems to ensure that their discovery data is updated in the SMS site database.

Site System Discovery Process

Each method generates about 30 KB of network traffic, and the resulting discovery data includes the server name, operating system, version, and platform. In addition, both discovery agents generate status messages when a new Windows NT or NetWare Bindery site system is discovered or a discovery record is generated.

For the WINNT Server Discovery Agent, look for status messages with code range 4200 through 4202, and for the NetWare Bindery Server Discovery Agent, look for status messages with code range 4800 through 4802, indicating the creation of DDRs for these servers. Refer to Chapter 3 for information about viewing status messages.

SMS client software is automatically installed on Windows NT site systems when they are discovered, provided the server lies within the site boundaries. If the site system doesn't lie within the site boundaries, DDRs will be generated but the SMS client software will not be installed. If you want to include those site systems as clients for the SMS site, you will need to install the SMS client software using a different method. SMS client software is not installed on NetWare Bindery servers or NetWare NDS servers.

Checkpoints

The most common source of problems with the site system discovery methods is the inability of the agent to connect to the server in question. In this case, you should take a look at the site system connection account. As we saw in Chapter 3, the successful creation of a site system requires a valid site system connection account or that you assign the SMS Service account administrative permissions (or Supervisor equivalence, in the case of NetWare Bindery servers) on the site system. This account will be used by SMS to contact the site system. Without a valid site system connection account, the discovery agent won't connect to the site system.

Logon Discovery

The Windows Networking Logon Discovery method is designed to generate discovery records for all resources that log on to the Windows NT network and that are running supported SMS operating systems (Microsoft Windows 3.x and later, that is). The NetWare Bindery and NetWare NDS Logon Discovery methods are designed to generate discovery records for all NetWare client resources that log on to a NetWare Bindery or NDS server. With the exception of inboxes and agents, these two discovery methods function in much the same way.

Enabling and configuring the three logon discovery methods involves two main tasks. The first is to identify and assign logon points. The second is to enable the logon process by modifying users' logon scripts. Both tasks can be accomplished by enabling the discovery method through the SMS Administrator Console.

In Chapter 3, we explored the process of installing and configuring a logon point. Let's review the basic steps here and go one step further, enabling logon scripts.

Enabling Logon Discovery and Logon Scripts

To enable logon discovery and logon scripts, follow these steps:

1. In the SMS Administrator Console, navigate to the Site Settings folder, expand it, and then expand the Discovery Methods folder.

2. Select the discovery method you want to enable. The procedures for enabling Windows Networking Logon Discovery, NetWare Bindery Logon Discovery, and NetWare NDS Logon Discovery are essentially the same. For this example, select Windows Networking Logon Discovery, right-click on it, and choose Properties from the context menu to display the Windows Networking Logon Discovery Properties window, shown in Figure 7-1.

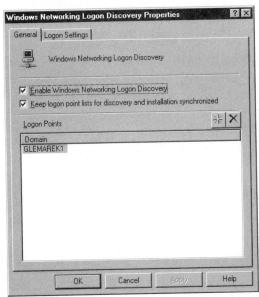

Figure 7-1. *The Windows Networking Logon Discovery Properties window.*

3. On the General tab, select the Enable Windows Networking Logon Discovery check box. (This option will vary depending on the discovery method you've chosen.)

4. The Keep Logon Point Lists For Discovery And Installation Synchronized option is enabled by default and ensures that the domain entries in the Logon Points list box are the same for both the discovery and installation methods. If you intend to use this discovery method to discover resources only and not necessarily install them, clear this check box.

5. To add a Windows NT domain to the list, click the New button (the yellow star) in the Logon Points section to display the New Windows Networking Logon Point dialog box. Then enter a domain name and click OK to close the dialog box. Note that every domain controller in the domains specified will be installed as logon points for the SMS site.

If you chose to enable the NetWare Bindery or NDS Logon Discovery, you can also add a new NetWare Bindery server or NDS container to the Logon Points list by clicking the New button to display the New NetWare Bindery (or NDS) Logon Point dialog box. Enter the appropriate server or tree, container, and volume entries, and then click OK.

6. Click the Logon Settings tab, shown in Figure 7-2. If you want SMS to automatically modify users' logon scripts to include the SMSls.bat script used to initiate logon discovery, select the Modify User Logon Scripts check box.

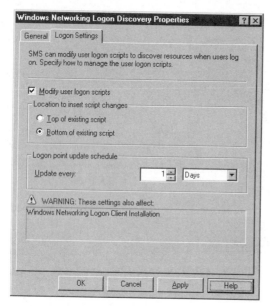

Figure 7-2. *The Logon Settings tab.*

Notice that you can have SMS add its script to the top or bottom of existing logon scripts.

7. Modify the Logon Point Update Schedule setting if necessary. This setting defines the frequency at which logon scripts will be updated.

8. Click OK to begin the setup process.

Caution Only existing logon scripts that have a filename extension will be modified by this process. A logon script that does not have an extension will be ignored.

Modifying the user logon script in this manner is an automatic process and ensures that all existing users' logon scripts will reflect the SMS script. If you don't already use a logon script, or if your existing logon scripts are fairly straightforward, go ahead and use this method. However, if your existing logon scripts are more complex, having SMS append its script to the top or bottom of an existing script would probably not be a good idea. In that case, it would be wise to not enable the Modify User Logon Scripts options and instead modify the logon scripts yourself.

Tip It's a good idea to modify NetWare logon scripts yourself simply because they use a different set of script commands than the Windows NT logon script, and you'll have more control over what happens if you make the modifications yourself.

Real World   Modifying Logon Scripts Manually

Many organizations prefer to handle the SMS script by modifying their own logon scripts. This approach can be useful for a variety of reasons. Suppose you support dial-in access to your network for several users. Because client settings for an SMS site are sitewide, dial-in clients and local network clients would have the same configuration for receiving packages, collecting inventory, and so on. When users access the network through a dial-in connection, you might not want their computers to be installed into the SMS site. Or perhaps you don't want advertisements to be made available when a user is dialed in from a client machine because of the line speed. For various reasons, it is not always possible or practical to segment these users into their own subnet.

A common solution involves creating a logon script that tests Windows NT environment variables to determine whether a user is dialed in from a client machine to the network. If a dial-in client is detected, you could then direct the script to skip the SMS portion—which in the case of discovery would effectively keep that client from being discovered by the SMS site.

Logon Discovery Process

The discovery process for NetWare logon points is remarkably similar to that for Windows NT logon points. The primary exception is in the support files that are executed by the SMS script to check for slow network speed and to install Cliex32.dll.

When a user logs in and the SMS logon script is executed, the script initiates a series of boot processes that create the MS\SMS\Core directory on the client and install some basic data files (SMSboot1.exe and Boot32wn.exe for Windows NT clients, SMSnw1.exe and Boot32nw.exe for NetWare Bindery clients, and SMSnds1.exe and Boot32nd.exe for NetWare NDS clients). If the client is a 32-bit client (Windows 95 and later) it installs a .DLL file named Cliex32.dll on that client. This .DLL generates the DDR and stores it on the client computer. If the client is a 16-bit client (Windows 3.x and Windows for Workgroups), Boot16wn.exe is run on the client to generate the DDR.

Although this DDR differs slightly between client types, it always contains the following information:

- SMS Unique Identifier
- NetBIOS Name
- IP Addresses
- IP Subnets
- IPX Addresses
- IPX Network Numbers
- MAC Addresses
- Resource Domain
- Operating System Name
- Last Logon User Name

This information is saved in a DDR on the client as SMSDisc.ddr. It is then copied to the logon point's SMSLogon\Ddr.box folder and given a new unique filename.

If you are enabling Windows Networking Logon Discovery, the DDR is forwarded by the Windows Networking Logon Discovery Agent from the logon point to Discovery Data Manager's inbox on the site server (SMS\Inboxes\Ddm.box). Discovery Data Manager in turn updates the site database with the new information.

Because NetWare servers do not run Windows NT services, there is no agent capable of forwarding the DDR to the SMS site server. Instead, NetWare Bindery Logon Manager and NetWare NDS Logon Manager scan the SMSLogon\Ddr.box for DDRs once per day and copy them to Discovery Data Manager's inbox on the site server (SMS\Inboxes\Ddm.box). Discovery Data Manager in turn updates the site database with the new information.

DDRs generated for computers and other devices are automatically made members of the *All Systems* collection, which is viewable through the SMS Administrator Console. They are also added to the other default collections based on the operating system of the resource (Windows 3.1, Windows 95, and so on). To view the properties and values of all the collected data for a selected resource, right-click on the computer entry under All Systems in the SMS Administrator Console, and choose Properties from the context menu to display the Resource Properties window, shown in Figure 7-3.

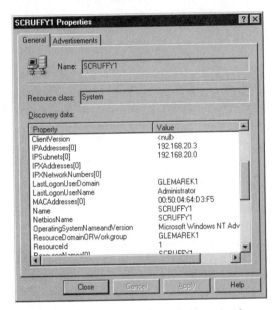

Figure 7-3. *The Resource Properties window.*

Each client that is discovered using these discovery methods will have the MS\SMS\Core directory created and some data files installed. Altogether, the client footprint is just over 5 MB; the bulk of this is an executable named Clicore.exe, which does the installing of Cliex32.dll. The DDRs themselves are only about 1 KB in size. Each client's DDR is stored in the MS\SMS\Core\Data directory on the client as SMSDisc.ddr. The DDR is also copied to the logon point (or to the CAP, when the client is also installed) and to the site server. At 1 KB per record, we're not talking a significant amount of data. However, if ten thousand clients are hitting the same logon points, CAPs, or site server, that adds up to about 10 MB of storage space.

Tip Refer to Chapter 3 for a complete discussion of the logon point setup process and the SMS components involved.

Checkpoints

Outside of the logon discovery method not being enabled or configured correctly, there are not too many areas for failure when you use the Windows Networking Logon Discovery method or the NetWare Bindery and NetWare NDS Logon Discovery methods. The most likely problem may involve slow networks. As it happens, part of the client setup process involves running a check for a slow network connection. If SMS detects that the network speed is less than 40 KB per second, the discovery process will simply stop.

Another possible area of failure is access to the logon point. The SMS script initiates processes that read information from and write discovery data to the SMSLogon share created on the logon point when it was defined as a site system. Make sure that the logon points are accessible and that the permissions to this share have not been altered.

Windows NT User Account and User Group Discovery

The Windows NT User Account Discovery and Windows NT User Group Discovery methods are designed to discover domain user accounts and domain global group accounts and to add them as resources to the SMS database. When you enable either of these discovery methods, you can specify which Windows NT domains to poll for user and group account information. A corresponding DDR is generated for each user and group account discovered. By default, these resources will be added to the *All Users* and *All User Groups* collections, which can be viewed through the SMS Administrator Console.

The primary purpose in enabling either of these discovery methods is to provide the SMS administrator with an alternative target for advertising programs through SMS. Although we haven't discussed package distribution in great length yet, we have talked briefly about the advertisement process. (Chapter 12 covers the details of package distribution.) As we saw in Chapter 1, in SMS 2.0 a package reaches a target destination by advertising a program associated with that package. This program might be a Typical installation of Microsoft Office, for example, or a Custom installation of Microsoft Project. Programs are always advertised to collections. If you want a specific group of SMS clients to receive a particular program, you must create a collection that contains those clients and then advertise the program to that collection.

Real World   Packages for Discovered Users or User Groups

The beauty of SMS 2.0 in the context of package distribution is that you can also advertise programs to collections that contain discovered users or user groups. This gives the SMS administrator an alternative target for certain packages. For example, suppose you have a budget spreadsheet that must be distributed and available to all finance department users regardless of which computer they are logged into. If you have discovered those users through SMS or discovered a Windows NT global group named Finance that contains these users, you can create an SMS collection with those users or that group as its members. You can then create a package that contains the spreadsheet and advertise it to your user or group collection. Whenever a member of that collection checks for advertisements on whatever SMS client the member happens to log in on, that spreadsheet will be made available. Furthermore, if the collection gains any new members, those users (or group members) will automatically receive all advertisements targeted to that collection.

Enabling Windows NT User Account and User Group Discovery

To enable the Windows NT User Account Discovery and Windows NT User Group Discovery methods, follow these steps:

1. In the SMS Administrator Console, navigate to the Site Settings folder, expand it, and then expand the Discovery Methods folder.

2. Right-click on Windows NT User Account Discovery or Windows NT User Group Discovery, as appropriate. The two procedures are essentially the same, so in this example, we'll select User Account Discovery. Choose Properties from the context menu to display the Windows NT User Account Discovery Properties window, shown in Figure 7-4.

3. On the General tab, select the Enable Windows NT User Account Discovery check box (or Enable Windows NT User Group Discovery, if you're enabling the other discovery method).

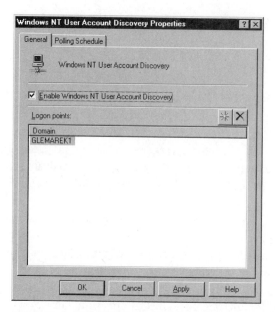

Figure 7-4. *The Windows NT User Account Discovery Properties window.*

4. Click the New button in the Logon Points section of the Properties window to add a Windows NT domain to the list for the discovery agent to poll. The New Domain dialog box will appear, as shown in Figure 7-5.

Figure 7-5. *The New Domain dialog box.*

Enter the name of the Windows NT domain for which you want to discover user accounts, and then click OK.

5. Click on the Polling Schedule tab, shown in Figure 7-6.

6. Click the Schedule button to display the Schedule dialog box, shown in Figure 7-7.

7. Define the frequency with which the User Account Discovery Agent or User Group Discovery Agent should poll the specified domains for user accounts, and then click OK.

8. Click OK to begin the discovery process.

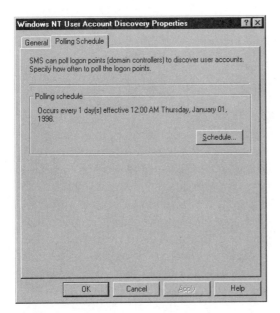

Figure 7-6. *The Polling Schedule tab.*

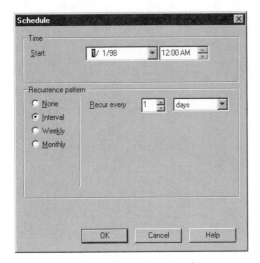

Figure 7-7. *The Schedule dialog box.*

Windows NT User Account and User Group Discovery Process

The discovery process for these two methods is fairly straightforward as SMS processes go. When you enable either method, the corresponding discovery agent on the site server makes a secure connection to the primary domain controller of the Windows NT domain you specified, and according to the schedule you specified when you enabled the discovery method.

The discovery agent enumerates the user accounts or global groups in the Windows NT domains and generates a DDR for each one it discovers. These DDRs are written directly to Discovery Data Manager's inbox on the site server (SMS\Inboxes\Ddm.box). Discovery Data Manager in turn updates the SMS database with the new discovery information. User resources are automatically added to the *All Users* collection, viewable through the SMS Administrator Console, and user group resources are automatically added to the *All User Groups* collection. To view this discovery data, right-click on the user resource under All Users in the SMS Administrator Console, and choose Properties from the context menu. A sample user resource discovery record is shown in Figure 7-8.

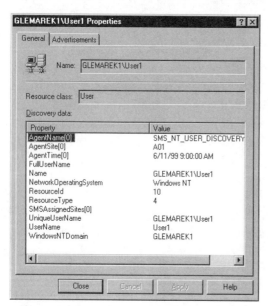

Figure 7-8. *A sample user resource discovery record Properties window.*

In terms of network traffic, each user and group will generate, on average, 2 KB of traffic. If your Windows NT account database contains, say, 10,000 users and 100 groups, you will experience around 20 MB of network traffic to generate the corresponding DDRs. The frequency at which this traffic is generated, of course, depends on the polling schedule you have defined. If your Windows NT account databases are relatively stable and rarely change, you do not have to poll frequently, and network traffic relating to user or user group discovery will be largely a one-time experience. On the other hand, if your Windows NT account database is volatile, you may need to enumerate users and groups more frequently, and, of course, you will generate a corresponding amount of network traffic.

Each agent generates status messages when it starts, stops, and generates DDRs. These status messages can be viewed through the SMS Administrator Console. Look for messages in the 410x range for SMS_NT_USER_GROUP_ DISCOVERY_AGENT and messages in the 430x for SMS_NT_USER_ DISCOVERY_AGENT. The sample status message window shown in Figure 7-9 tells us that in this case four Windows NT user groups were enumerated and discovered. These agents also write detailed processing information to their respective log files (Ntuser.log and Ntusrgp.log) if you have enabled logging through the SMS Service Manager tool in the SMS Administrator Console.

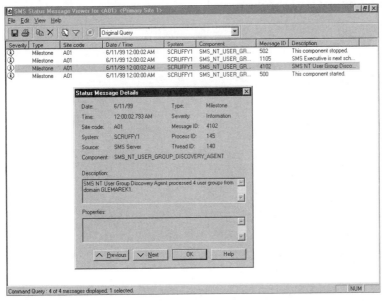

Figure 7-9. *A sample status message window, and the Status Message Details dialog box.*

Checkpoints

The main problems you may encounter with these discovery methods have to do with access. The SMS Service account must have Administrator rights on the primary domain controller that it is polling for resources. If this condition is not met, user and group discovery will fail. Other possible problems, of course, are that the discovery agent has not been enabled or that the scheduled polling time has not yet been encountered.

Network Discovery

The Network Discovery method is designed to provide the SMS administrator with the means of discovering any network resources that are IP addressable, which means that you can discover not only computers, but also printers, routers, bridges, and so on. The discovery that takes place using this method can be far reaching. You can discover these resources on the local subnet in which the site server resides, or you can discover resources throughout your enterprise network using DHCP, SNMP, and other mechanisms. Resources discovered using this method are automatically added to the *All Systems* collection, which is viewable through the SMS Administrator Console.

Network Discovery includes the following information as part of the discovery record:

- SMS Unique Identifier
- NetBIOS Name
- IP Addresses
- IP Subnets
- IPX Addresses
- IPX Network Numbers
- Last Logon User Domain
- Last Logon User Name
- MAC Addresses
- Name
- Resource Domain
- User Domain
- Operating System Name and Version
- Resource ID

- SMS Assigned Sites
- SNMP Community Name
- System Roles

This discovery method can be useful in a variety of contexts. It can be used, for example, to find computers that could become SMS clients. When a computer is discovered, its IP address and subnet mask are included in the discovery record. This information can help you identify where your potential SMS clients are located and how they are distributed among the subnets, enabling you to formulate a more specific plan for locating and implementing your SMS sites, site servers, and site systems.

You can also use this information to plan the best client installation method for implementing SMS 2.0 on those computers. As mentioned at the beginning of this chapter, some discovery methods have corresponding client installation methods associated with them. Network Discovery is associated with the Windows Remote Client Installation method, which we'll look at in detail in Chapter 8. Briefly, the Windows Remote Client Installation method is a kind of "push" installation that can install the SMS client components automatically on discovered Windows NT 4.0 and Windows 2000 client computers. So, you could enable Network Discovery to "find" potential SMS clients and enable Windows Remote Client Installation to automatically install the SMS client components on the Windows NT 4.0 and Windows 2000 computers that Network Discovery finds. If you did not want such an automatic and "intrusive" combination, you could enable a different client installation method, perhaps based on the computer's domain membership or subnet mask.

Network Discovery can also make your Network Trace map more meaningful. As we saw in Chapter 6, the Network Trace utility provides a graphical mapping of your SMS site structure showing the routes between site systems and site servers. This mapping can include any routers, switches, and the like that the route between systems encounters.

If you don't enable Network Discovery to discover these links between systems, they will be represented in the Network Trace window as "clouds." The Network Trace map is built based on the DDRs that have been generated for site systems and devices on the network. Again, since Network Trace provides a means of testing connectivity, problem links can be more easily identified if all possible routes between systems are displayed in the Network Trace window. As you can see, some unique benefits can be gained by enabling the Network Discovery method.

Enabling Network Discovery

Like the other discovery methods, Network Discovery is enabled through the SMS Administrator Console. To enable Network Discovery, follow these steps:

1. Expand the Site Settings folder, and then expand the Discovery Methods folder.

2. Right-click on Network Discovery, and choose Properties from the context menu to display the Network Discovery Properties window, shown in Figure 7-10.

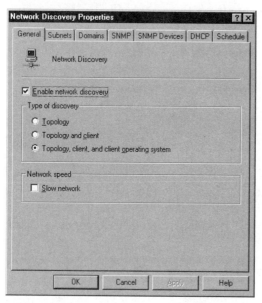

Figure 7-10. *The Network Discovery Properties window.*

3. On the General tab, select the Enable Network Discovery check box.

4. Specify the type of discovery you want. Selecting the Topology option will cause Network Discovery to discover IP-addressable resources such as subnets and routers using SNMP. (You would also configure options on the Subnets, SNMP, SNMP Devices, and DHCP tabs, as we'll see shortly.) The Topology And Client option additionally discovers computers and resources such as printers and gateways using SNMP, DHCP, and the Windows NT Browser. Topology, Client, And Client Operating System also picks up the computer's operating system name and version using SNMP, DHCP, Windows NT Browser, and Windows Networking calls.

5. Select the Slow Network check box for networks with speeds less than 64 Kbps. This option will cause Network Discovery to decrease the number of outstanding SNMP sessions it generates by doubling SNMP time-outs.

6. Select the Subnets tab, shown in Figure 7-11. Here you can add, Click on , enable, and disable the subnets you want Network Discovery to search. By default, Network Discovery will search the local subnet in which the site server is a member. If you want to ignore that subnet, clear the Search Local Subnets check box.

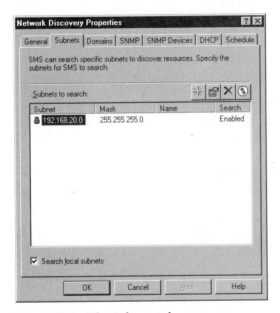

Figure 7-11. *The Subnets tab.*

Network Discovery will display the subnets it discovered during each previous search. As it discovers the subnets, it marks them with a lock to indicate that they cannot be modified or deleted—in fact, subnets discovered by Network Discovery, unlike those you add yourself, cannot be modified or deleted once they have been discovered. However, you can enable or disable those subnets that you want Network Discovery to search on subsequent cycles.

7. To add subnets to the list, click the New button to display the New Subnet Assignment dialog box, shown in Figure 7-12. Provide the appropriate subnet address and subnet mask and click OK.

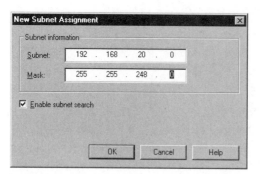

Figure 7-12. *The New Subnet Assignment dialog box.*

8. If you have selected a discovery type other than Topology on the General tab, click on the Domains tab, shown in Figure 7-13, and enter the name of the Windows NT domain that you want to search for resources.

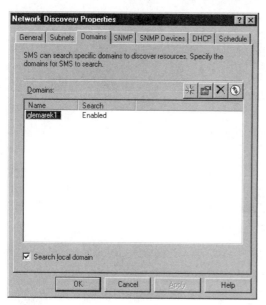

Figure 7-13. *The Domains tab.*

By default, the local Windows NT domain to which the site server belongs will be searched. If you want to ignore that domain, clear the Search Local Domain check box.

Note Network Discovery can find any computer that you can find using Network Neighborhood to browse the network. Once it finds a computer, it still must obtain its IP address and will use one of the other methods (DHCP, SNMP, and so on) to do so. Network Discovery will ping each computer to determine whether it is active, find its subnet mask, and generate a DDR for it.

9. To add Windows NT domains to the list, click the New button to display the Domain Properties dialog box, shown in Figure 7-14. Enter the appropriate domain name. The domain must be accessible through the network. By default, the Enable Domain Search check box is selected. This option enables Network Discovery in the domain. Click OK to close the dialog box.

Figure 7-14. *The Domain Properties dialog box.*

10. Click on the SNMP tab, shown in Figure 7-15, and specify the SNMP community you want Network Discovery to search.

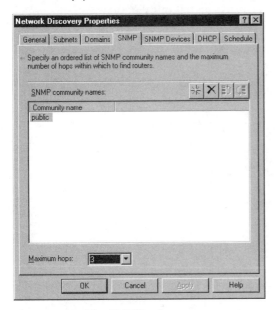

Figure 7-15. *The SNMP tab.*

11. To add SNMP communities, click the New button to display the New SNMP Community Name dialog box, shown in Figure 7-16. Enter the appropriate community name and click OK to return to the SNMP tab.

If you enter multiple communities, you can specify the order in which you want them searched by using the two Order buttons.

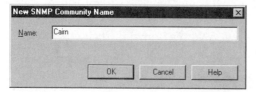

Figure 7-16. *The New SNMP Community Name dialog box.*

 Note It's not necessary to have the SNMP Service installed on the site server performing Network Discovery. This discovery method uses its own SNMP stack to make requests and discover data.

12. Network Discovery attempts to access the local router to obtain IP addresses and data from the device. If the Maximum Hops value is set to *0*, Network Discovery will search only the default gateway. You can set this value as high as *10*. Each successive increment extends discovery to another set of routers. For example, setting Maximum Hops to *1* enables Network Discovery to search the default gateway and any routers connected to it.

13. Click on the SNMP Devices tab (a companion to the SNMP tab) shown in Figure 7-17.

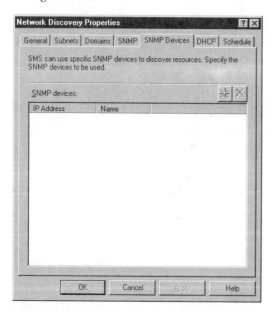

Figure 7-17. *The SNMP Devices tab.*

On this tab, you can identify specific SNMP devices that you want to discover by clicking the New button and supplying the IP address or name of the device. The SNMP devices can include routers, hubs, and token-ring media access units.

14. Click on the DHCP tab, shown in Figure 7-18, and identify which Microsoft DHCP servers you want Network Discovery to query for a list of IP addresses leased to computers.

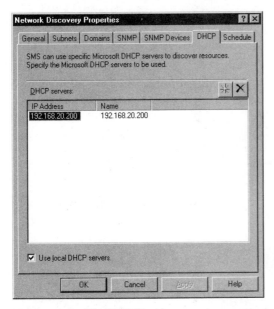

Figure 7-18. *The DHCP tab.*

If the site server is itself a DHCP client, Network Discovery will automatically query the site server's DHCP server. If you want to ignore that DHCP, clear the Use Local DHCP Servers check box.

Tip   Network Discovery uses RPC calls to retrieve information from the DHCP database. Because of this, the SMS Service account must be listed as a domain user in the DHCP server's Windows NT domain.

15. To add Microsoft DHCP servers to the list, click the New button and provide the appropriate subnet address or server name.

16. Click on the Schedule tab, shown in Figure 7-19, and identify the frequency at which you want Network Discovery to run.

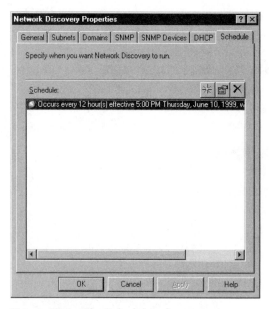

Figure 7-19. *The Schedule tab.*

17. To add a new schedule, click the New button to display the Schedule dialog box, shown in Figure 7-20.

Figure 7-20. *The Schedule dialog box.*

18. To modify a schedule's properties, click the Properties button (the hand holding a piece of paper) to display the same Schedule dialog box.

In the Schedule dialog box, enter the time you want discovery to begin. You can also specify a Recurrence pattern. Selecting None directs Network Discovery to search only one time for resources. You might select this option as a first pass, to find all subnets, for example. The other options direct Network Discovery to perform subsequent searches according to your specified schedule. Duration indicates the period of time Network Discovery has to complete its search for resources. On a local subnet, two hours might be sufficient. However, if you are performing a search of an enterprise network across several router hops with several thousand potential resources, you may need to increase this number so that Network Discovery has enough time to complete its search. If Network Discovery runs out of time, it will log a message to that effect and complete DDRs only for the part of the search that was completed.

19. Click OK twice to save your settings and initiate the Network Discovery process.

Note Network Discovery is the only discovery method that isn't enabled automatically when you run Express Setup to install SMS. As we saw in Chapter 3, no discovery methods are enabled for Custom Setup.

Network Discovery Process

The discovery process itself is once again fairly straightforward. Depending on the discovery options you enabled, Network Discovery will attempt to search for subnets, routers, computers, and other devices. It needs to retrieve an IP address and subnet mask for each resource in order to generate a DDR for it. Network Discovery uses the information it receives from DHCP servers and SNMP to communicate directly with a device, such as a router, and then uses the router's ipNetToMedia table and Router Interface table to obtain subnet masks. It also uses Router Information Protocol (RIP), SNMP, and Open Shortest Path First (OSPF) multicast addresses to discover routers.

Network Discovery uses Windows Management Insrtumentation (WMI) to store discovered resource information and generates DDRs based on this information. When Network Discovery generates a DDR, it writes the DDR to Discovery Data Manager's inbox (SMS\Inboxes\Ddm.box). Discovery Data Manager in turn adds the record to the SMS database.

Network Discovery is capable of discovering literally thousands of devices on your network, and in doing so, it can generate a fair amount of network traffic. For this reason, your choice of schedule will be significant. If you need to find large numbers of devices, you may opt to schedule Network Discovery to run during quiet periods on the network. And as suggested earlier, the Duration value (shown in Figure 7-20) may also need to be increased to accommodate processing of larger numbers of resources.

Tip Discovery Data Manager processes DDRs at an average rate of two to five per second.

Like the other discovery methods, Network Discovery generates status messages that can be viewed through the SMS Administrator Console. Figure 7-21 shows a representative set of messages generated by Network Discovery. Messages in the 13*xx* range relate specifically to the discovery of resources.

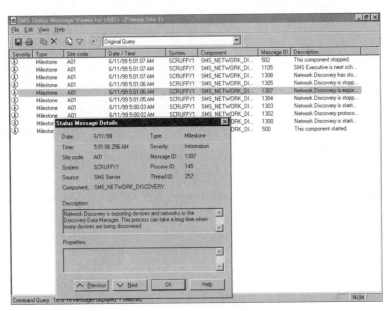

Figure 7-21. *A sample status message window for Network Discovery, showing the Status Message Details dialog box.*

Also, if you have enabled logging for Network Discovery, more detailed information will be written to the Netdisc.log file.

Checkpoints

When you are performing a Topology, Client, And Client Operating System search, the operating system on Windows 95 and Windows 98 clients will be returned only if file sharing has been enabled on those computers. In addition, the operating system will be returned as Windows 9*x* until the SMS client software has been installed.

When using DHCP to retrieve IP addresses, it is important to note that unless SMS 2.0 Service Pack 1 is installed, Network Discovery ignores reserved IP addresses and those that are part of an excluded range and will not retrieve any resources from the DHCP server if the DHCP has been configured to offer unlimited leases.

Remember that the SMS Service account must be a domain user for the domain in which the DHCP server is a member. Network Discovery uses existing trust relationships or pass-through authentication to authenticate its connection to the DHCP server.

Finally, verify that you have identified not only the correct subnet address to search, but also the correct subnet mask. Network Discovery is more concerned with the subnet mask when retrieving device IP address information.

The *All Systems* collection displays discovered system resources. System resources include any IP-addressable device. Network Discovery also discovers logical networks and subnets. To view these resources, you will need to create a query to display the logical networks and subnets that were discovered. Refer to Chapter 15 for more information about creating queries in SMS 2.0.

Heartbeat Discovery

Heartbeat Discovery is designed to keep DDRs up-to-date for computers that either do not use any other method of discovery or, in the case of logon discovery, have users that either seldom log on (namely, servers) or seldom log off. This discovery method is significant because it ensures that resource records will not be accidentally aged out of the SMS database.

By default, SMS periodically executes a maintenance routine that deletes records whose discovery data is older than 90 days out of the database. For computers such as Windows NT servers, to which users should seldom log on, it could be problematic for users to be deleted from the database. Heartbeat Discovery is designed for just these types of situations.

Enabling Heartbeat Discovery

Heartbeat Discovery is enabled by default and generates DDRs from each client every seven days. If you choose to disable Heartbeat Discovery, you will need to have enabled some other discovery method to keep the DDR information up-to-date. Furthermore, Heartbeat Discovery is active only on computers that have already been installed as SMS clients.

To configure Heartbeat Discovery, follow these steps:

1. In the SMS Administrator Console, expand the Site Settings folder and then expand the Discovery Methods folder.

2. Right-click on Heartbeat Discovery, and choose Properties from the context menu to display the Heartbeat Discovery Properties window, shown in Figure 7-22.

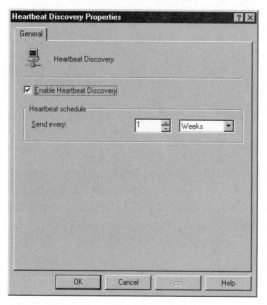

Figure 7-22. *The Heartbeat Discovery Properties window.*

If you want to disable Heartbeat Discovery, clear the Enable Heartbeat Discovery check box.

3. Specify the frequency at which you want Heartbeat Discovery to generate DDRs.

4. Click OK to implement your schedule.

Heartbeat Discovery Process

Heartbeat Discovery runs on installed SMS clients according to the schedule you specified. With this method enabled, Client Component Installation Manager (CCIM) on the client causes the Cliex32.dll to generate a DDR, which is written to the CAP by the Copy Queue component (refer to Chapter 8 for details on Copy Queue). The network traffic generated is the size of a normal DDR—that is, about 1 KB per client.

Checkpoints

The only potential problem here is ensuring that Heartbeat Discovery has in fact been enabled and not disabled by accident. Also, be sure that the schedule you create causes the DDRs to be generated frequently enough that the DDR is not accidentally deleted from the SMS database.

Manual Discovery

Manual discovery is just that—a discovery method that is initiated by you on a per-client basis to generate DDR information for that client. This method is predominantly used as part of a manual client installation process. Part of this process actually ends in installing the SMS software on the client if the client can be assigned to the SMS site.

Initiating Manual Discovery

To initiate manual discovery, follow these steps:

1. Make a network connection to the SMSLogon share, volume, or directory on an SMS logon point.

2. Navigate to the appropriate *platform*.bin directory (Alpha.bin or X86.bin), and open the \00000409 directory.

3. In this directory, run the appropriate wizard or program for that client's operating system. The available programs are listed here:

   * Manboot.exe for MS-DOS clients
   * SMSMan.exe for 32-bit clients
   * SMSMan16.exe for 16-bit clients

In this example, we've run SMSMan.exe to display the Systems Management Installation Wizard welcome screen, shown in Figure 7-23.

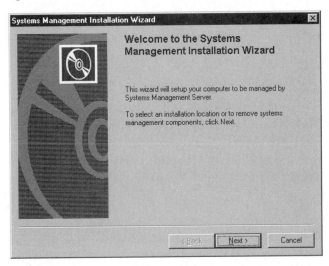

Figure 7-23. *The Systems Management Installation Wizard welcome screen.*

4. Click Next to display the Select A Systems Management Installation Option screen, shown in Figure 7-24. If the client can be assigned to an SMS site, specify the appropriate logon point or domain name from which to initiate the client installation, or let SMS make the assignment.

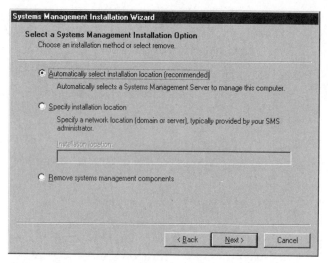

Figure 7-24. *The Select A Systems Management Installation Option screen.*

5. Click Next to display the Completing The Systems Management Installation Wizard screen.

6. Click Finish to start the installation process.

> **Note** Alternatively, you can run SMSMan.exe from a floppy disk, from any of the potential client's local or network drives, or from an e-mail message. Refer to Chapter 8 for detailed information about the executable file.

Manual Discovery Process

When the program executes, a DDR will be generated just as it would if you had used a logon discovery method. The DDR will be stored on the client as SMSDisc.ddr in the MS\SMS\Core\Data directory. It will be copied to the discovery data inbox on the logon point (SMSLogon\Ddr.box) and then forwarded to Discovery Data Manager's inbox on the site server (SMS\Inboxes\Ddm.box). Discovery Data Manager in turn will update the SMS database with the new record.

> **Note** The Manboot.exe program can be used only to generate a DDR for an MS-DOS client. MS-DOS clients are not supported as valid SMS client computers and cannot be installed using SMS client software.

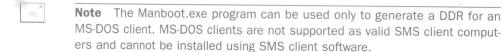

Checkpoints

There are no real "gotchas" in manual discovery—you either run it or you don't. The main thing to remember is that if the client is also assigned to an SMS site, it will be installed as an SMS client as part of this process. If the client is not assigned to an SMS site, only the DDR will be generated.

Discovery Data Manager

The most prominent and common SMS site server component in the discovery process is Discovery Data Manager. Its role is to process DDRs written to its inbox on the site server (SMS\Inboxes\Ddm.box) and to create site assignment rules based on the site boundaries as specified in the site control file. It also forwards the site assignment rules to secondary sites and creates Client Configuration Request (CCR) files for discovered Windows NT 4 and Windows 2000 clients if Windows Remote Client Installation has been enabled. (*Site assignment rules* are the list of subnets and IPX network numbers that define the site boundaries to determine whether discovered computers are assigned to SMS sites. See Chapter 8 for details.) Discovery Data Manager will also forward discovery information via Replication Manager to the parent site, if one exists.

Since it is a site server component, Discovery Data Manager generates status messages and writes more detailed information to its log file (SMS\Logs\Ddm.log) if logging has been enabled for this component. Look for status messages in the 26*xx* range for specific information related to the processing of DDRs.

Summary

This chapter explored the first step in populating the SMS database and installing SMS clients—discovering resources. We looked at a variety of discovery methods that can be used to carry out the discovery process. Some of these discovery methods are paired with corresponding client installation methods—for example, each logon discovery method has a corresponding client installation method. In Chapter 8, we'll examine the various client installation methods available to the SMS administrator.

Chapter 8
Client Installation Methods

In Chapter 7, you learned how Microsoft Systems Management Server (SMS) discovers resources and then adds them to the SMS database. To manage a computer resource, however, you must make that computer an SMS client, which means installing SMS client components on it. In this chapter, we'll focus on the installation process. We'll begin by exploring the concept of site assignment. Then we'll look at the installation methods, and you'll learn how to manage the client configuration and how to remove SMS from the client if necessary.

Site Assignment

Before a computer can be installed as an SMS client, it must first be assigned to an SMS site. A computer's site assignment is determined by its IP subnet address and mask or its IPX network number. (Refer to Chapter 3 for detailed information on subnet addresses and subnet masks.) If the computer is assigned to the site, installation continues. If not, the installation process stops. Site assignment depends on the site boundaries configured for your SMS site. This group of site boundaries is also known as the site assignment rules—the list of subnets and IPX network numbers for defining the site boundaries of an SMS site. These rules are maintained at the site server level and are written to the client access points (CAPs) and logon points.

Site boundaries determine only which clients are to be installed as SMS clients to the site. They are not used to specify which site systems can be assigned site roles in the site. In fact, site systems can be members of other accessible subnets.

> **Caution** Microsoft recommends that subnets identified as site boundaries all be local to the site and that site boundaries not span WAN connections unless the link is fast and reliable. Network and site server performance could be adversely affected if the WAN connection is already heavily utilized.

Setting Site Boundaries

The site assignment rules are created by setting the site boundaries for the site. Site boundaries are a property of the site and are set through the SMS Administrator Console. To set site boundaries, follow these steps:

1. In the SMS Administrator Console, navigate to your site entry in the Site Hierarchy folder. Right-click on the site entry, and choose Properties from the context menu to display the Site Properties window.

2. Click on the Boundaries tab, shown in Figure 8-1.

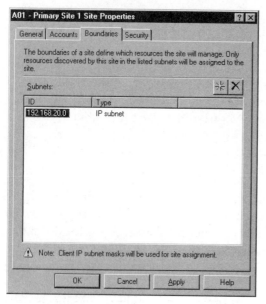

Figure 8-1. *The Boundaries tab of the Site Properties window.*

3. To add a subnet to the Subnets list, click the New button (the yellow star) to display the New Subnet dialog box, shown in Figure 8-2.

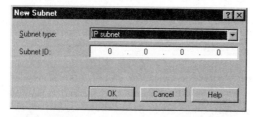

Figure 8-2. *The New Subnet dialog box.*

4. Select a subnet type from the drop-down list—either IP Subnet or IPX Network Number.

5. In the Subnet ID text box, enter the IP subnet address or IPX network number, and then click OK to close the dialog box.

6. Click OK again to begin the site control process, which will update the site assignment rules.

Multiple-Site Membership

A client can be a member of multiple sites. This situation can occur either by plan or by accident. For example, two SMS sites can include the same subnet in their site boundaries. This practice is not recommended because it can confuse the client. Recall that client agent settings are sitewide settings. When enabled, these settings apply to all the SMS clients of that site. If a client belongs to more than one site, SMS will have to apply some rules to determine which agents are enabled on the clients and which agent settings will take precedence. For example, suppose that a computer named Clientx belongs to SMS sites A and B. The SMS administrator for site B enables the Remote Tools Client Agent (also sometimes referred to as the Remote Tools Agent) to be installed on all clients for that site. The SMS administrator for site A chooses not to enable the Remote Tools Client Agent. Because the Remote Tools Client Agent was enabled on one site, and because Clientx belongs to that site, the Remote Tools Client Agent will be installed on Clientx even though the agent was not enabled on the other SMS site.

Let's look at this from a different perspective. Returning to the preceding example, suppose that the Remote Tools Client Agent was enabled on both SMS sites. However, on SMS site A, the Remote Chat feature was enabled, and on site B the Remote Chat feature was disabled. The site settings conflict. The client agent will evaluate the conflicting security permissions and obtain the more restrictive of the two settings. In this example, the Remote Chat feature won't be available to the administrator of either site.

Real World Joining Multiple Sites

At times, you might have a client join multiple SMS sites by design. For example, if a client has two network interface cards (NICs), each NIC could connect to a different subnet. If each subnet is identified as a site boundary to its own SMS site server, the client would also be assigned to each SMS site.

Suppose an organization, Awesome Computers, finds itself in a support scenario with a local university. Awesome Computers supplies Microsoft Windows NT workstations that the university uses to connect to a support database at Awesome Computers and retrieve information. Both Awesome Computers and the university use SMS 2.0 to manage their equipment. Both need to be able to manage these particular Windows NT workstations. The solution in this case is to install two NICs on each Windows NT workstation. One NIC is connected to the local university's network, the other to Awesome Computers' network. This setup also ensures that each Windows NT workstation is assigned and installed as a client to both the university's and Awesome Computers' SMS sites, and thus both sites can manage the same clients.

Client Installation Process Flow

Suppose Windows Networking Logon Discovery and Windows Networking Logon Client Installation are both enabled. When a user logs on to a logon point, the SMSls.bat script is executed. This script initiates a process that installs the discovery agent on the client, as illustrated in Figure 8-3.

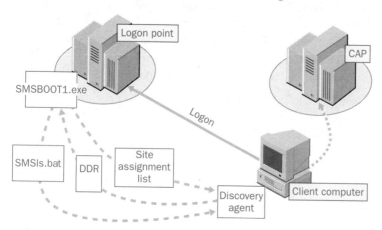

Figure 8-3. *The client installation process.*

The discovery agent generates a discovery data record (DDR) file and copies it to the logon point. The discovery agent checks the client's IP subnet address and subnet mask against the site assignment rules. If the client can be assigned to the site, the client is directed to connect to a CAP to begin the component installation process. If the client cannot be assigned to a site, the installation process stops.

Note Client discovery does leave a footprint on the discovered computers. About 5 MB of data is copied to the client during discovery, including the discovery agent itself and the programs needed to complete installation when the client is assigned to an SMS site.

Each client installation process varies slightly, but all perform the same basic tasks:

- Bootstrap
- Discovery
- Assignment
- Installation

Because logon client installation is the most common installation method, as we'll see in the section "Installation Methods" later in this chapter, we will concentrate here on that process. Figure 8-4 outlines the logon client installation process in detail.

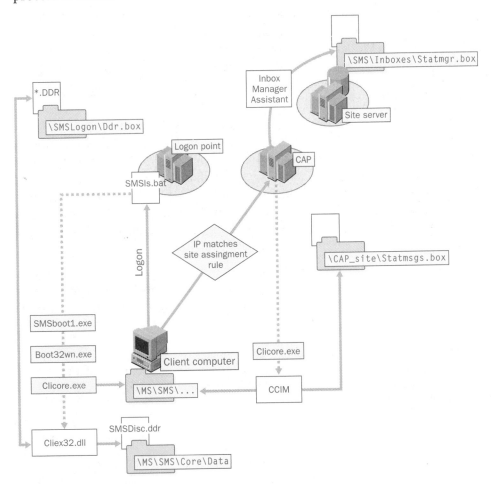

Figure 8-4. *The installation process flow in more detail.*

Client installation begins with the bootstrap phase. A 16-bit executable, SMSboot1.exe, is started. This application performs one task. It copies and starts the bootstrap program on the client—Boot32wn.exe for 32-bit clients or Boot16wn.exe for 16-bit clients.

The bootstrap program launches Clicore.exe. This program creates the MS\SMS\ Core directory structure, copies and installs the discovery agent support files, and starts Cliex32.dll to begin the discovery phase of installation. Cliex32.dll generates a DDR file, saves it as SMSDisc.ddr in the client's MS\SMS\Core\Data folder, and copies it with a randomly generated filename to the SMSLogon\Ddr.box folder on the logon point.

The assignment phase is next. Cliex32.dll checks the client's IP subnet address and subnet mask against the site assignment rules, stored in Netconf.ncf in the SMSLogon\Sites*sitecode* folder. If the client can be assigned to the site, the client is directed to connect to a CAP to begin the component installation process. The site assignment for the client is recorded in the WN_Logon.log in the MS\SMS\ Logs folder on the client.

As the installation phase begins, the bootstrap program writes the list of CAPs (Caplist.ini) found in the SMSLogon\Sites*sitecode* folder on the logon point to the client's registry. It then starts Clicore.exe again to copy base SMS client files and to load and start Client Component Installation Manager (CCIM). CCIM builds the rest of the MS\SMS folder structure and copies the SMS client components to the client. CCIM will subsequently wake up every 23 hours to connect to a CAP and update the client with any changes to the configuration that have been made, including the removal of client components.

After the client has been installed, CCIM generates status messages and writes them to the CAP_site\Statmsgs.box folder on the CAP. Inbox Manager Assistant then moves the status messages to Status Message Manager's inbox (SMS\Inboxes\ Statmgr.box) on the site server.

Note The installation process for 16-bit clients is remarkably similar to that for 32-bit clients. The main difference is that 16-bit versions of the bootstrap, client installation, discovery agent, and CCIM programs are used. These versions are named Bootwn16.exe, Clicor16.exe, Cliex16.dll, and CCIM16.exe.

Installation Methods

Just as several discovery methods are available for adding resources to the SMS database, several client installation methods are available for loading the SMS client components on computers that have been assigned to the SMS site. The three client installation methods are as follows:

- Logon client installation (Windows Networking Logon Client Installation, NetWare Bindery Logon Client Installation, and NetWare NDS Logon Client Installation)
- Windows NT Remote Client Installation
- Manual client installation

As we saw in Chapter 7, some discovery methods are paired with a client installation method—meaning simply that certain installation methods are more likely to use a corresponding discovery method to generate a DDR for the resource. For example, Windows Networking Logon Discovery is paired with Windows Networking Logon Client Installation, and Network Discovery is paired with Windows Remote Client Installation.

It's interesting to note, however, that it is not necessary for a resource to have been discovered before it can be installed. The installation process will automatically generate a DDR for the client if Heartbeat Discovery is enabled or when inventory is collected. The client will be fully functional whether or not a DDR has been generated.

While not essential to the successful installation of an SMS client, it would be productive to configure the client agents that you intend to enable prior to installing the client computers. Doing so will ensure that all the agents and their properties will be installed at one time. If you enable a client component later, the client update process will update the client on its next polling cycle—every 23 hours—or when the update is forced on the client.

These client agents include:

- Advertised Programs Client Agent
- Event to Trap Translator Client Agent
- Hardware Inventory Client Agent

- Remote Tools Client Agent
- Software Inventory Client Agent
- Software Metering Client Agent

Tip Client agents are enabled by default when you install SMS using the Express Setup option. No client agents are enabled if you performed a Custom installation.

The process of enabling and installing each of these agents on your SMS clients will be covered in later chapters, with the exception of the Event to Trap Translator Client Agent, which is installed by default and was discussed in Chapter 6.

Logon Client Installation

There are three types of logon client installation: Windows Networking Logon Client Installation, NetWare Bindery Logon Client Installation, and NetWare NDS Logon Client Installation. All are configured similarly, and all follow pretty much the same process flow to install the SMS clients. These installation methods rely on the execution of the SMSls script commands for initiating the installation process. Windows NT servers will use the SMSls.bat file; NetWare servers will add a call statement to existing NetWare scripts to the SMSls.scr file.

We've discussed how to enable logon client installation methods in Chapter 3. Let's review briefly. To enable one of the logon client installation methods, follow these steps:

1. In the SMS Administrator Console, expand the Site Settings folder and then expand the Client Installation Methods folder.

2. Right-click on the appropriate logon client installation method (Windows Networking Logon Client Installation, NetWare Bindery Logon Client Installation, or NetWare NDS Logon Client Installation), and choose Properties from the context menu to display its Properties window. In the example in Figure 8-5, we'll use the Windows Networking Logon Client Installation option.

3. On the General tab, select the Enable Windows Networking Logon Client Installation check box. (This option will change depending on the installation you've chosen.)

4. If you've enabled the corresponding discovery method—Windows Networking Logon Discovery, NetWare Bindery Logon Discovery, or NetWare NDS Logon Discovery—select the Keep Logon Point Lists For Discovery And Installation Synchronized check box. This option will

ensure that the logon point lists maintained for both the installation and discovery methods are the same. In other words, any changes made to the list in one method will be reflected in the other method's list.

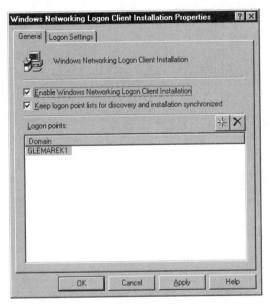

Figure 8-5. *The Windows Networking Logon Client Installation Properties window.*

5. To add logon points, click the New button to display the New Windows Networking Logon Point dialog box. Enter the appropriate information (server name for Windows NT and NetWare Bindery servers; volume, organizational unit, and so on for NetWare NDS servers), and then click OK to return to the Properties window.

Note SMS 2.0 supports the creation of SMS logon points on NTFS partitions only, not on FAT.

6. Click on the Logon Settings tab, as shown in Figure 8-6. Select the Modify User Logon Scripts check box if you want SMS to automatically use the SMSls.bat file as the default logon script for users who do not have a logon script specified in their user profiles, or to append the SMS script to the top or bottom of the existing logon script.

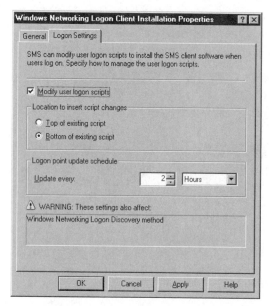

Figure 8-6. *The Logon Settings tab.*

Existing logon scripts are often well planned and can be complex. Therefore, it may not be practical or desirable to let SMS simply add its script changes to the top or bottom of an existing logon script. In this case, do not enable the Modify User Logon Scripts option. Instead, modify the logon scripts yourself to call the SMS script as appropriate.

Caution SMS will ignore existing logon scripts that do not include a file extension.

7. Enter an appropriate schedule for updating the logon scripts.
8. Click OK to begin the site update process.

Note When these installation methods or their corresponding discovery methods are enabled, SMS will first implement the logon points. Refer to Chapter 3 for a complete discussion of this process.

With Windows Networking Logon Client Installation, the account that is used to install the SMS components on Windows NT clients must have administrative privileges because DLLs and agents are installed and loaded. More frequently than not, the user logged onto the Windows NT computer will not have administrative privileges. In these instances, the client configuration cannot continue because CCIM initially runs in the same security context as the logged on user.

This scenario is illustrated in Figure 8-7. In this case, CCIM will create a Client Configuration Request (CCR) for the Client Configuration Manager service on the site server to restart CCIM using an account that does have appropriate administrative privileges on the Windows NT client. CCIM writes the CCR file to Client Configuration Manager's inbox on the CAP (CAP_site\Ccr.box). Inbox Manager Assistant in turn moves that file to Client Configuration Manager's inbox on the site server (SMS\Inboxes\Ccr.box). Client Configuration Manager then initiates an update process, which starts CCIM on the client using an account that has appropriate administrative privileges.

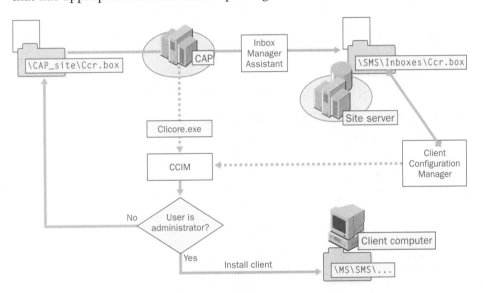

Figure 8-7. *The Client Configuration Manager process flow.*

By default, Client Configuration Manager will use the SMS Service account to run CCIM. That account, as you no doubt recall, is a member of the Domain Admins global group for the Windows NT domain. Domain Admins is automatically made a member of the local Administrator's group on every Windows NT computer that joins the Windows NT domain. So the SMS Service account will have appropriate privileges to complete the SMS installation on the client. If the Windows NT clients are not members of the domain, or if for reasons of security the Domain Admins global group is *not* a member of the local Administrator group, the installation will fail. You need to ensure that the SMS Service account is a member of the local Administrator group on every Windows NT client that needs to be installed as an SMS client.

One way to accomplish this is to create a separate client installation account, called the SMS Client Remote Installation account, for SMS to use when installing the SMS components on a client. You must first create an account through User Manager For Domains and ensure that it is made a member of the local Administrator group on the Windows NT client in question. After you create this account, you need to tell SMS to use the account when installing the SMS components on Windows NT clients. To do so, follow these steps:

1. In the SMS Administrator Console, navigate to your site entry in the Site Hierarchy folder.

2. Right-click on your site entry, and choose Properties from the context menu to display the Site Properties window, shown in Figure 8-8.

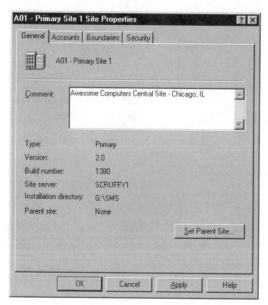

Figure 8-8. *The Site Properties window.*

3. Click on the Accounts tab, shown in Figure 8-9.

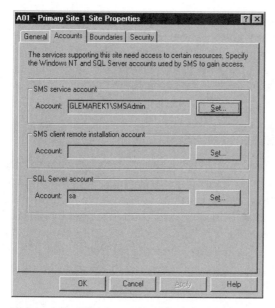

Figure 8-9. *The Accounts tab.*

4. In the SMS Client Remote Installation Account section, click the Set button to display the Windows NT Account dialog box, shown in Figure 8-10.

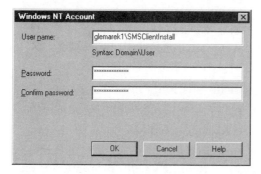

Figure 8-10. *The Windows NT Account dialog box.*

5. Enter the user name for the account you created, in the form *Domain\ User*. Enter and confirm a password for the account, and then click OK.

6. Click OK again to begin the site update process.

Tip If your SMS site includes Windows NT domains that do not participate in trust relationships, you will need to create a matching installation account and password for each Windows NT domain in which you are installing SMS clients. SMS will use Windows NT's pass-through authentication process to connect to clients in untrusted domains, so the installation accounts and passwords must be duplicated in each domain.

Windows NT Remote Client Installation

This installation method is more of a push-type installation. It is meant to facilitate the installation of SMS components on clients running Windows NT for which no other installation method is appropriate. For example, Windows NT servers generally are not left in a logged-on state, and therefore they would probably not be effectively installed using the Windows Networking Logon Client Installation method. Perhaps some users do not execute the SMS logon script—or any logon script, for that matter. This installation method could be used to ensure that their Windows NT computers become SMS clients.

By default, Windows NT Remote Client Installation is not enabled. This is a good thing, actually, because this method is designed to find every Windows NT client that has not already been assigned and installed and install SMS on it. The process is relatively straightforward, but it can also result in Windows NT computers that you did not intend to become clients being set up as SMS clients, such as servers in other administrators' domains. You can configure the method to find and install Windows NT servers, workstations, or domain controllers. The Windows NT Site System Discovery method uses Windows NT Remote Client Installation to install SMS site systems as SMS clients.

To enable Windows NT Remote Client Installation, follow these steps:

1. In the SMS Administrator Console, expand the Site Settings folder and then expand the Client Installation Methods folder.

2. Right-click on Windows NT Remote Client Installation, and then choose Properties to display the Windows NT Remote Client Installation Properties window, shown in Figure 8-11.

3. Check the Enable Windows NT Remote Client Installation check box.

4. The System Types section offers three options: Windows NT Server, Windows NT Workstation, and Domain Controllers. All are enabled by default. Clear the check boxes for options you do not require.

5. Click OK.

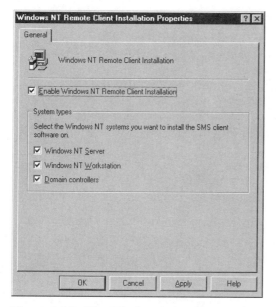

Figure 8-11. *The Windows NT Remote Client Installation Properties window.*

As with the other installation methods, you must provide SMS with administrative-level access on all the Windows NT computers that you intend to install using this method, either by creating and assigning an SMS Client Remote Installation account or by using the SMS Service account. Also, the client must have already been discovered using one of the discovery methods described in Chapter 7.

When an appropriate client is found using this method, Discovery Data Manager generates a CCR for the Client Configuration Manager service on the site server. The CCR is written to Client Configuration Manager's inbox on the site server (SMS\Inboxes\Ccr.box). Client Configuration Manager initiates an update process, which starts CCIM on the client using an account that has appropriate administrative privileges and then installs the SMS components on the client as described earlier in this chapter.

Manual Client Installation

The third method of installing SMS components on a client is manual client installation. You need to use this installation method for those clients that cannot be installed using any other installation method. Using this method, you or the user must manually connect to a logon point for the SMS site from a client machine and execute a setup program. There are two setup programs: SMSMan16.exe for 16-bit operating systems (Microsoft Windows 3.1 and Windows for Workgroups), and SMSMan.exe for 32-bit clients (Windows 95, Windows 98, Windows NT, and Windows 2000). You may recall from Chapter 7 that these setup programs are located in the SMSLogon*platform*.bin\00000409 folder on the logon point, where *platform* represents either Alpha or X86.

Both programs initiate the Systems Management Server Installation Wizard. SMSMan16.exe requires the user to specify the name of the logon point or Windows NT domain to connect to. SMSMan.exe allows the user to specify the name of the logon point or Windows NT domain, but it can also choose a logon point for you. SMS can also be uninstalled from 32-bit clients using SMSMan.exe.

The two setup programs can be scripted using the command-line switches listed in Table 8-1. When either program is started, it launches the SMSboot1.exe program, and the installation proceeds just as described earlier in this chapter. The syntax for running SMSMan.exe or SMSMan16.exe from a command line is shown here:

> SMSMAN.EXE *[switch option]* *[/Q]*

or

> SMSMAN16.EXE *[switch option]* *[/Q]*

Tip If the client needs to become a member of multiple SMS sites, it will be necessary for you or the user to connect to a logon point for each SMS site.

Table 8-1. SMSMan.exe and SMSMan16.exe command-line switches

Switch	Description
/A (SMSMan only)	Automatically selects an installation location and displays results to the user
/B [*server**volume*]	Specifies a NetWare Bindery server logon point
/C [*tree.org.orgunit*] (SMSMan only)	Specifies a NetWare NDS volume as a logon point
/D [*domainname*]	Specifies a Windows NT domain that contains a logon point
/H or /?	Displays a Help screen
/Q	Quiet mode; no messages are displayed on the screen during installation or removal
/S [*servername*]	Specifies the name of a Windows NT server assigned the logon point role
/U	Uninstalls SMS components from the client

Understanding and Managing the Client Configuration

Now that you have finished installing SMS on your clients, let's explore what happened on the client. Just what have we accomplished here? Actually, all we've done is make the client ready to receive any of the optional client agents that allow you to more fully manage the client. (As mentioned, all the client agents except the Event to Trap Translator Client Agent will be discussed individually in later chapters.)

SMS administrators coming from an SMS 1.2 or earlier environment will notice a major change here. In earlier versions of SMS, the installation process included the generation of a complete hardware inventory record for the client—in other words, hardware inventory was "enabled" by default. Not so with SMS 2.0. You no longer have to complete a hardware inventory of the client before you can manage the client.

Changes to the Client

So what does happen to the client? The installation process causes several changes to occur on the client, affecting its directory structure and disk space, its services, its registry, and its Control Panel. Let's start by looking at changes to the client's directory structure.

Directory Structure Changes

First and foremost, perhaps, is the creation of an SMS directory structure within the operating system directory. The default operating system directory name is *Windows* for computers running Windows 95 and Windows 98 and *WINNT* for computers running Windows NT; these names can be changed during installation.

The SMS directory structure takes a form similar to that shown in Figure 8-12. Base and optional client component support files installed on the computer are stored in their respective folders under \MS\SMS\Clicomp. Client installation history and its DDR are maintained in the \MS\SMS\Core\Data folder. SMS sites that the client has been assigned and installed to are reflected under \MS\SMS\Sitefile. Client components and services generate their log information in files written to the \MS\SMS\Logs folder. The \MS\SMS\IDMifs and NOIDMifs folders are used for customizing entries to the SMS database. As you can see, just like the SMS directory structure on the site server or any site system, there are no superfluous directories. Each has a purpose and, in this case, is monitored or used by one or more client components.

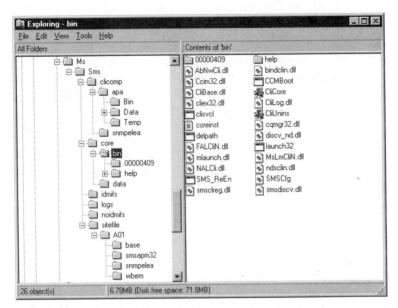

Figure 8-12. *The directory structure created under the operating system directory.*

Service and Component Changes

As we've seen in our examination of logon discovery and logon client installation processes in Chapter 7 and in this chapter, several .EXE and .DLL files are installed and loaded to aid in the discovery and installation process. These files include Clicore.exe (installs Cliex32.dll, which generates the client's DDR) and the client base components outlined in Table 8-2.

Registry Changes

In addition to the directories created and the services and components installed, the client installation process adds three keys to the client's registry under HKEY_LOCAL_MACHINE\Software\Microsoft: NAL\Client, SMS\Client, and WBEM. The installation process also adds client service entries under HKEY_LOCAL_MACHINE\System\CurrentControlSet\Services.

The NAL\Client key records network connections made by the client to site systems such as CAPs, logon points, and distribution points. The SMS\Client key maintains all client component configuration settings—both configurable and nonconfigurable by you, the administrator. The WBEM key, of course, supports the Windows Management implementation on the client. The Services key contains service-specific information such as startup parameters and service accounts for the SMS Client Service and the Windows Management Service. You can find this information in the the two subkeys of the Services key: the Clisvc subkey and the Winmgmt subkey.

Table 8-2.   SMS client components

Client Base Component	Description
Available Programs Manager (SMSapm32.exe)	Executes the installation process for optional client components. Also runs advertised programs when the Advertised Programs Client Agent has been enabled. Uses Launch32.exe to determine whether any advertisements have been offered to the client, user, or user group.
Client Component Installation Manager (CCIM32.exe)	Monitors the client's configuration status; installs, updates, or removes optional client components; and keeps client and site server data synchronized. Runs on a 23-hour polling cycle.
Copy Queue (CQMgr.exe)	Copies client data such as discovery data, inventory, and status messages to the CAP.
SMS Client Service (Clisvcl.exe on Windows NT computers; Clisvc95.exe on Windows 95 and Windows 98 computers)	Monitors the state of client agents and ensures that they run as configured. Responsible for CCIM and Copy Queue as well.
Windows Management Service (Winmgmt.exe)	Implements, monitors, and manages the Web-Based Enterprise Management (WBEM) layer installation.

Control Panel Changes

Last but by no means least, the client installation process updates the client's Control Panel to include the Systems Management applet, as shown in Figure 8-13. This program is used to install, update, or repair components on the client. The only other applets that can be added to the Control Panel are the Remote Tools applet and the Advertised Programs applet, if these optional components have been enabled and installed on the client. Administrators familiar with earlier versions of SMS will notice that the old SMS Client program group is no longer added to the client's Start menu. In fact, in SMS 2.0, user access to and control of SMS client components is far more limited than it was in earlier client installations.

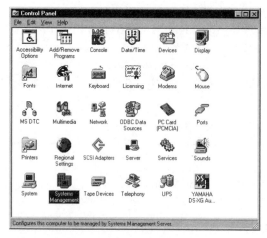

Figure 8-13. *The updated Control Panel.*

All these changes combined require about 14 MB of disk space on the client computer—not exactly a small footprint, especially in comparison to the 4-to-5-MB footprint in earlier client versions.

Systems Management Applet

The Systems Management applet is used to install, update, and repair SMS components installed on the client. Double-clicking on its icon in Control Panel will display the Systems Management Properties window. The applet consists of three management tabs: General, Sites, and Components.

Viewing Discovery Data and Enabling Traveling Mode

The General tab, shown in Figure 8-14, displays a list of the client's system properties. This is a subset of the discovery data reported to the site server and includes the client's IP address and subnet, MAC address, operating system, and domain or workgroup membership—and the SMS globally unique identifier (GUID) assigned to the client. This GUID is a randomly generated, 32-character identifier used internally by SMS to identify the client. Unlike in earlier versions of SMS, the SMS 2.0 administrator does not need to refer to the client by its GUID at any time. You can use the discovered information to manage and troubleshoot your computer.

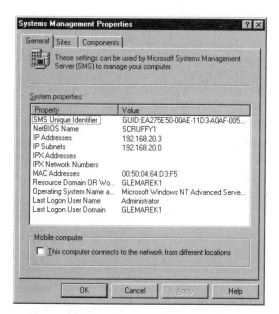

Figure 8-14. *The General tab of the Systems Management Properties window.*

The General tab also provides a mobile computing option that you can enable if the client will be connecting to the network—and potentially to different SMS sites—from different subnets. Recall that SMS uses subnet addresses and the client's subnet mask to assign clients to SMS sites. If a client connects to the network from a subnet managed by a different SMS site, the client could find itself a member of multiple SMS sites, or it could be uninstalled from its original site and installed to the new site. Conversely, if the subnet the client is connecting from is not assigned to any SMS site, the client could be uninstalled.

You can enable the traveling mode by selecting the This Computer Connects To The Network From Different Locations check box. If this mode is enabled, the user will be presented with a dialog box when the client connects to a logon point in a different subnet. The user can either change to the new site (become a member of a different SMS site) or keep the installation intact. If the user does not install to the new site, he or she will not be prompted again for a period of 30 days.

Note If you are running Windows NT, you can't enable or disable the traveling mode if you don't have Administrator permission.

Updating the Client Configuration

The Systems Management applet also lets you update the client configuration. The Sites tab of the Systems Properties window, shown in Figure 8-15, displays all the SMS sites to which the client has been assigned. Unless the client is a member of multiple sites, there will be only one entry here. If the list contains multiple entries, you can use the Move Up and Move Down buttons to change the order of the list and define how SMS evaluates certain component configuration parameters. The entry at the top of the list is designated the *principal site*.

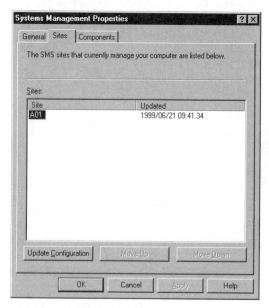

Figure 8-15. *The Sites tab.*

In the case of inventory collection, for example, if each site to which the client belongs has a different inventory collection schedule enabled, the schedule configured at the principal site will take precedence—that schedule will be used by the client to report inventory back to *all* the sites to which it belongs.

As we've seen, CCIM polls the CAP every 23 hours to see whether there are any new components to install, components to remove, or components whose configurations need to be modified in some way. As you enable and configure components on the site server, you can be assured that the client will be updated on a daily basis. However, if you want or need to update the client immediately, you can force CCIM to perform an immediate update by clicking the Update Configuration button at the bottom of the Sites tab.

> **Tip**   If the client belongs to multiple sites, the Update Configuration button will refresh the client components from all the sites.

Real World   **When Does "Immediate" Mean Immediate?**

CCIM will connect to the CAP, check for any configuration changes that need to be made on the client, and carry them out. The amount of time that will elapse before the changes are effected at the client will depend on the components involved and the number of changes that need to be made. In general, use the Kaczmarek rule of thumb for timing: "Immediate" in SMS generally means over the next few minutes (or hours). All kidding aside, even if it seems as if nothing is happening on the client, if you monitor client component logs or view the Processes tab in the Windows NT Task Manager, you will see that things are indeed happening under the hood.

As an example, let's say that you have changed the inventory frequency at the site server. You then go directly to your client and click Update Configuration. When should you expect to see the changes on the client? In this case, probably not until tomorrow—that's right, 23 hours from now. Remember, CCIM is going to check the CAP for updates. You initiated the change at the site server. Even though that change is event driven, we have to wait for several SMS site server components to wake up, process the change, and write it to the CAP before CCIM knows about it.

In particular, the regular site update process involving Hierarchy Manager and Site Control Manager (described in detail in Chapter 3) will take place. When the site control file (Sitectrl.ct0) is updated, Client Install Data Manager will read the file, identify client agent updates, and write configuration and offer files to the SMS\Inboxes\Clicfg.src folder on the site server. Inbox Manager forwards these files to the CAP_Site\Clicomp.box folder on the CAP. Only after this happens (you can view the date and time stamps on the appropriate files in these directories to confirm) can you update the client configuration through the Systems Management applet on the client computer.

Repairing the Configuration

You can repair the configuration through the Components tab of the Systems Management applet. The Components tab, shown in Figure 8-16, displays a list of components that have been installed on the client, their version numbers, and their current status.

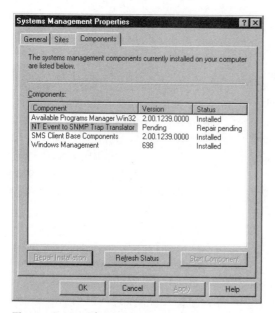

Figure 8-16. *The Components tab of the Systems Management Properties window.*

A basic installation of SMS on the client will result in the following components being installed:

- Available Programs Manager
- Event to Trap Translator
- SMS Client Base Components
- Windows Management

Recall that Available Programs Manager manages the programs available to run on the client. It is not the same as the Advertised Programs Client Agent, which is used to run advertised programs. This entry represents the SMSapm32.exe that is used to run installation programs for various client components.

Note The Event to Trap Translator utility is installed but not enabled on the Windows NT client unless the Microsoft SNMP Service has been installed. If the SNMP Service has not been installed on the client, this component's status will be represented in the Systems Management applet as Not Available. Once the SNMP Service has been enabled on the client, you can update and repair the Event to Trap Translator utility. Refer to Chapter 6 for a complete discussion of trap translation.

As you enable additional client components and they are installed, they will be displayed in this list as well. Installing all client components will require approximately 20 MB of storage space on the client computer.

At the bottom of the Components tab are three buttons: Repair Installation, Refresh Status, and Start Component. Clicking Refresh Status will cause the client components to be rechecked and their status updated. Table 8-3 describes the different status indicators you might see.

Table 8-3. Client component status indicators

Status	Description
Installed	The component has been successfully installed on the client.
Install Pending	SMSapm32.exe has initiated the installation process for the component, but it has not yet been completed.
Repair Pending	CCIM is verifying the component and reinstalling it.
Reboot Required	The component has been repaired, but it will not initialize until a reboot has taken place on the client.
Not Available	The component, although enabled at the site server, is not compatible with this computer's current configuration. Could also indicate that the client's IP address no longer falls within the site assignment rules for the SMS site and that the client components have been subsequently uninstalled.

If you suspect or determine that you are having a problem with a particular component—for example, if yesterday the component's status was Installed and today it is Not Available—you can select that component and click Repair Installation. This will cause that component's status to change to Repair Pending, while CCIM attempts to verify and reinstall that component. This technique is the best way to recover from corrupted component support files. You can either keep clicking Refresh Status until the status changes to Installed, or close the Systems Management applet and wait a few minutes for CCIM to complete the reinstallation.

Tip You can observe the CCIM and SMSapm32 processes through Windows NT Task Manager to gauge when the repair starts and finishes.

Removing Systems Management Server from the Client

At some point, you may need to uninstall SMS from the clients. Removing an individual component is simply a matter of disabling that client agent at the site server. Since client agent settings are sitewide in nature, disabling a client agent at the site server will cause that component to be removed from all clients assigned to that SMS site. There is no way to install or remove client agents on individual clients within the same SMS site.

Your intention, however, may be to remove SMS entirely from all your SMS clients or from individual SMS clients. The easiest way to remove SMS from a large number of clients at one time is to change the site server's site boundaries so that the clients' subnets are no longer represented, meaning that the client is no longer assigned to the site. During the client's next maintenance interval, the SMS components will be uninstalled from the client.

A couple of techniques are available for uninstalling SMS from individual clients. You could run the SMSMan.exe or SMSMan16.exe programs as described earlier in this chapter. Uninstall options are available both through the Systems Management Server Installation Wizard and through command prompt switches. These options can be accessed by connecting to the SMSLogon share on the logon point or by navigating to the *System root*\MS\SMS\Core\Bin\00000409 folder on the client itself. However, neither of these methods is terribly "clean," meaning that some files are left behind for you to remove yourself.

A more thorough method of uninstalling SMS from the clients is through a registry modification made on the client, as we saw in Chapter 2. To use this method, follow these steps:

1. As an administrator, open the client's registry.

2. In the Registry Editor, navigate to the HKEY_LOCAL_MACHINE\ Software\Microsoft\SMS\Client\Configuration\Client Properties key, as shown in Figure 8-17.

3. Select the Client Properties key, and choose Add Value from the Edit menu to display the Add Value dialog box, shown in Figure 8-18. In the Value Name text box, enter *SMS Client Deinstall*. Leave the Data Type setting as REG_SZ. Click OK to return to the Registry Editor.

4. In the String Editor dialog box, shown in Figure 8-19, enter *TRUE* in the String text box, and then click OK.

5. Close the Registry Editor to save your changes.

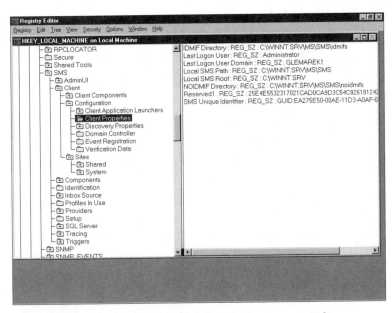

Figure 8-17. *The Client Properties key in the Registry Editor.*

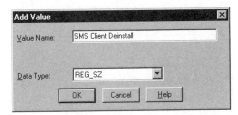

Figure 8-18. *The Add Value dialog box.*

Figure 8-19. *The String Editor dialog box.*

6. From the Control Panel, select the Services applet, select SMS Client Service, and click Stop. After the service has stopped, click Start. The SMS Client Service will read the new registry entry and initiate an uninstall bootstrap process.

Regardless of the method you choose, the uninstall process may take several minutes depending on the number of components installed.

Although the registry method of uninstalling SMS from the client is cleaner than the SMSMan method, you will still have the following cleanup duties to perform:

- Delete the \MS folder. It will be empty, but it is still there.
- Remove the NAL and SMS registry keys under HKEY_LOCAL_ MACHINE\Software\Microsoft.
- Remove the SNMP_Events key, if it exists.
- Although not necessary, you can remove the WBEM registry key if no other applications or components require it. This task, of course, would not apply to computers running Windows 98 or Windows 2000.
- Find the Windows\CurrentVersion\SharedDlls key and remove any values related to SMS.
- Find the Windows\CurrentVersion\Uninstall key and remove any values related to SMS.
- Delete the SMScfg.ini file created in the operating system directory and any .MIF files left over there.

After you have performed all these steps, SMS should have been completely removed from the client computer.

Checkpoints

If you've read this chapter carefully, you've already compiled a list of potential problems regarding client installation. The most obvious sources of error occur in four areas:

- Be sure that an appropriate client installation method or methods have been enabled and properly configured. It would be a good idea to review all your clients (servers and workstations) to determine whether your enabled installation method actually "hits" all your clients. For example, a logon installation method may not be appropriate for installing SMS on Windows NT servers at which administrators rarely or never log on locally.
- Be sure that the client can actually be assigned to your SMS site by confirming the site boundaries. Remember that SMS uses not only the subnet address of the client, but also its subnet mask to determine a client's site assignment.
- Be sure that you have enough free disk space on the client to complete installation of all enabled client components. Recall that you may need

anywhere from 14 MB to 20 MB of disk space. And, of course, this should not be your *last* 14 or 20 MB of available disk space.

- Be sure that whatever client installation account you are using—the SMS Service account or your own designated SMS Client Remote Installation account—has local administrative rights on the client.

The Microsoft Systems Management Server 2.0 Resource Guide

If at all possible, you should obtain the Microsoft Systems Management Server 2.0 Resource Guide. This guide is part of the *Microsoft BackOffice 4.5 Resource Kit* available from Microsoft Press. It is also included as part of the Microsoft Tech Net CD subscription and other partner programs with Microsoft. The *Microsoft BackOffice 4.5 Resource Kit* contains several utilities that can facilitate your management of SMS clients in your site, including the following:

- **Client Cleaner tool (20CliCln.bat)** Removes all SMS 2.0 components from the client

- **Client Utilities tool (Cliutils.exe)** Lets you start, stop, and schedule processes on the client

- **Set Client Event tool (SetEvnt.exe)** Enables you to initiate components based on events—in particular, to trigger a CCIM maintenance cycle

- **Set Preferred Distribution Point and CAP tool (PrefServ.exe)** Enables you to designate a preferred distribution point or CAP for each client.

Summary

In this chapter, we have thoroughly explored the client installation methods and enabled them and our client installation accounts accordingly. We've examined the installation process and seen too how that process ties in to the discovery and site assignment processes. We've noted the changes that take place on the client after SMS has been installed, including modifications made to the client's registry and the amount of disk space required. We've even seen how to go about removing SMS from the client should the need arise. Now that we have installed our clients, the next step is to enable and configure the client agents that will enable us to more completely manage these clients—agents such as the Remote Tools Client Agent and the Advertised Programs Client Agent. We'll begin with the inventory agents in Chapter 9.

Chapter 9
Inventory Collection

Collection of hardware and software inventory from Microsoft Systems Management Server (SMS) clients is certainly one of the more popular client options that SMS administrators can enable for their SMS sites. Inventory collection offers the obvious advantage of reporting to a central database certain specific pieces of information that can be of interest or use to the SMS administrator. Data such as disk space, memory, processor type, network interface card (NIC), operating system, IP address, and software installed can be reported to the SMS database. You might then use that information to identify which clients need an upgrade or a patch for a particular piece of software or an upgrade to Microsoft Windows 2000, for example, or to identify which clients have the hardware requirements to support the upgrade.

In this chapter we'll explore the inventory collection process for hardware and software, including how to enable the hardware inventory and software inventory, how to view inventory, and how to customize the hardware inventory. As in previous chapters, we'll also look at the log files and status messages that are generated throughout the inventory collection process and discuss how to interpret them.

Hardware Inventory

The Hardware Inventory Client Agent (also sometimes referred to as the Hardware Inventory Agent) collects a broad assortment of hardware properties from the client. When we think of hardware inventory, most of us, especially those of us familiar with earlier versions of SMS, think of the basic data: disk information such as space used and space available; memory, video, processor, and operating system data; and MAC, IP, and subnet addresses. To be sure, some of this hardware information sounds a lot like the discovery data stored in the discovery data records (DDRs) we looked at in Chapter 7. However, hardware inventory is *nothing* like discovery data.

In fact, a great deal more hardware information is collected than just these basics. The hardware inventory process for 32-bit clients, for example, is designed to query the Windows Management Instrumentation (WMI) that is part of the SMS client installation to obtain its data. Windows Management itself can expose a vast amount of information about the client, obtaining information from various providers, including the WIN32 subsystem of Windows NT, the registry, the BIOS of the computer, and so on. As a result, the amount of data reported about each of the basic hardware components is more extensive and can actually be extended further. This extension is done by modifying the Managed Object Format (MOF) file stored on the site server.

Data not normally collected as part of the basics can also be reported as part of the hardware inventory. For example, you could report on program groups created on the client, or network printer connections, or account information such as the user's full name or security ID (SID). This reporting is accomplished through the creation of text files known as Management Information Format (MIF) files that you present to SMS as an update to the database.

If information is not available directly through the Hardware Inventory Client Agent, you can update client records with your own manually generated data— or even create whole new classes of object types, such as "multimedia equipment." Or you can obtain one of several new third-party add-ons to SMS 2.0 to obtain data such as OEM-specific DMI-based information. Once hardware inventory has been collected at the client, it is passed on to the client access point (CAP). The CAP, in turn, forwards the hardware inventory to the site server. Hardware inventory is ultimately stored in the SMS database, so it is important to draw a distinction between primary and secondary site servers. As we saw in Chapter 4, the main difference between a primary and a secondary site server is that a primary site server maintains access to an SQL Server database.

In the case of hardware inventory, this does not mean that you cannot enable the Hardware Inventory Client Agent on a secondary site server for its clients. In point of fact, you can, and the agent's configuration settings can even be different from the secondary site's parent site. When hardware inventory is passed to the secondary site server by the CAP, the secondary site server forwards the information to its parent primary site, where it can be added to the SMS database.

Enabling Hardware Inventory

Let's begin by getting the Hardware Inventory Client Agent enabled and installed on our SMS clients. Then we'll explore how inventory is actually collected. You can enable the Hardware Inventory Client Agent through the SMS Administrator Console. To do so, follow these steps:

1. Under Site Settings, navigate to the Client Agents folder and expand it.

2. Right-click on Hardware Inventory Client Agent, and choose Properties from the context menu to display the Hardware Inventory Client Agent Properties window, shown in Figure 9-1.

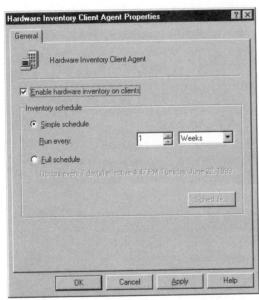

Figure 9-1. *The Hardware Inventory Client Agent Properties window.*

3. Select the Enable Hardware Inventory On Clients check box.

4. The default inventory collection schedule on the client is once a week. With the Simple Schedule option, you can specify collection to run once every 1 to 23 hours, 1 to 31 days, or 1 to 4 weeks. Or you can select Full Schedule and then click the Schedule button to display the Schedule dialog box, shown in Figure 9-2. Here you can designate a more specific start time and recurrence pattern. When you have finished, click OK.

5. Click OK again to begin the site update process.

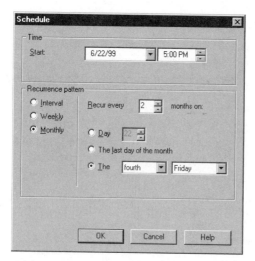

Figure 9-2. *The Schedule dialog box.*

When you enable the Hardware Inventory Client Agent, you are of course making a change to the site properties, and the site's site control file (Sitectrl.ct0) will be updated as a result (as described in Chapter 3). The following three files are written to the SMS\Inboxes\Clicfg.src directory on the site server:

- **Hinv.cfg** Contains the Hardware Inventory Client Agent configuration settings

- **Hinv.nal** Contains the CAPs from which the Hardware Inventory Client Agent can be installed

- **Hinv.pkg** Contains the instructions for installing the Hardware Inventory Client Agent on the client for various platforms

In the same directory, the client offer (.OFR) file is also updated to indicate that the Hardware Inventory Client Agent needs to be installed on all SMS clients for the site. This file is named Cli_*xxx*.ofr, where *xxx* represents the client operating system platform. The *client offer file* is used by the site server to notify its clients of any client components that need to be installed, updated, or removed. It is created on the site server and copied to each CAP for the site.

As you know, SMS clients are installed from a CAP or CAPs for the SMS site. Inbox Manager copies these files to the CAP_site\Clicomp.box directory on the CAPs. At the next Client Component Installation Manager (CCIM) cycle on the client (every 23 hours, or when an update is forced through the SMS 2.0 Resource Guide utility Client Utilities tool (Cliutils.exe) or the Systems Management

Control Panel applet), CCIM will connect to the CAP and read the client offer file. CCIM will then proceed to initiate the installation of the Hardware Inventory Client Agent. This agent is installed by launching Inhinv32.exe or Inhinv16.exe (depending on the platform), both of which can be found in the CAP_site\ Clicomp.box\Hinv*platform* folder, where *platform* is either Alpha or i386.

At this time, the SMS_def.mof file is compiled into the WMI layer on the client, the agent support files are installed, the hardware inventory log files are updated, and the agent is started. Ten minutes after the Hardware Inventory Client Agent is started, the first complete inventory is collected from the client as specified by the SMS_def.mof file through WMI and is then copied to the CAP.

Client Requirements and Inventory Frequency

The client computer will require about 400 KB for the Hardware Inventory Client Agent support files. A complete default inventory will generate a hardware information file 100 KB to 200 KB in size. A copy is stored on the client as part of the WMI Common Information Model (CIM) repository. The initial inventory is also passed to the CAP and then to the site server. Subsequent inventory files generally report only changes to the hardware inventory, however, so you can expect a corresponding amount of network traffic associated with the installation (one time), with the first complete inventory (one time), and with subsequent delta inventories (according to your schedule). The *delta inventory* is an inventory cycle that creates a delta inventory file containing the information that has changed since the previous inventory.

The schedule you specify should reflect the frequency with which you need to collect or update the inventory record of your clients. If your clients have fairly standard hardware installations and do not make or are not allowed to make substantial changes on their own, you could collect inventory less frequently— say, once a week or even once a month.

However, if your client computers are volatile regarding hardware changes, you may need to report changes to the inventory more frequently—perhaps once a day or once every 12 hours. The more frequent the inventory, the more potential network traffic will be generated. SMS 1.x administrators will notice that the option to collect inventory at every logon is no longer available. This is because the Hardware Inventory Agent now runs as a background process on the client computer rather than as a logon server–based process triggered by the SMS script file. In fact, the Hardware Inventory Client Agent will continue to run and report inventory regardless of whether a user is actually logged on to the client.

Tip   The Hardware Inventory Client Agent can be forced to run through the Systems Management applet in the Control Panel. Double-click on the applet to display the Systems Management Properties window, and select the Components tab. Select the Hardware Inventory Agent entry in the Components list, and then click the Start Component button.

Caution   Inventory stored in the SMS database is historical in nature, meaning that it is only as accurate as the last time you collected the inventory record. If your clients are volatile, as described earlier, and you rely on the inventory to identify clients' available disk space for installation applications, you may require an inventory schedule that is more frequent.

Multiple Sites and Hardware Inventory

In Chapter 8, we saw that a client can be assigned to more than one SMS site. Recall that in this situation, SMS will follow predefined rules to determine which agent properties from which SMS site take precedence over the others. If hardware inventory is enabled on any one site, it will be installed on the client. Inventory frequency, however, is determined by the principal site. If the principal site has disabled hardware inventory, inventory will still be collected according to the schedule of the site that has hardware inventory enabled.

The principal site for each client can be set through the Systems Management Control Panel applet installed on each SMS client. To set the principal site, double-click on the Systems Management applet on the client in question and select the Sites tab in the Systems Management Properties window. The Sites tab displays all the SMS sites to which the client has been assigned. Unless the client is a member of multiple SMS sites, only one site will be listed here. If multiple entries are shown, the entry at the top of the list is designated the principal site. To specify a new principal site, use the Move Up and Move Down buttons.

Hardware Inventory Collection Process Flow

Now let's explore the hardware inventory collection process in more detail. In this section, we'll look at the process from the perspectives of both 32-bit clients (Microsoft Windows 95, Windows 98, Windows NT, and Windows 2000) and 16-bit clients (Microsoft Windows 3.1 and Windows for Workgroups).

32-Bit Clients

Recall that the Hardware Inventory Client Agent uses WMI to obtain hardware inventory data about various classes of objects designated in the SMS_def.mof file. When the Hardware Inventory Client Agent (Hinv32.exe) is scheduled to run, it reads the SMS_def.mof file and queries the CIM Object Manager component of WMI for the object properties it needs to report on. The CIM Object Manager, in turn, retrieves the current information from the appropriate object providers, such as WIN32, and then passes the data to the Hardware Inventory Client Agent. This process is illustrated in Figure 9-3.

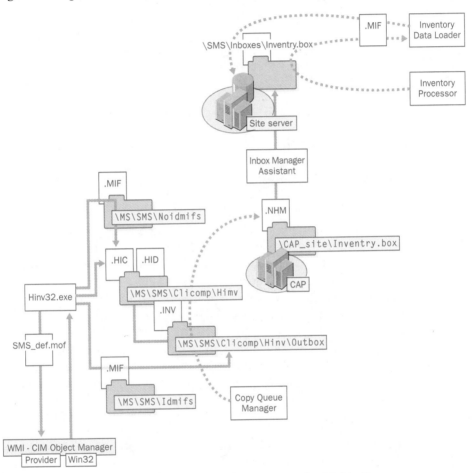

Figure 9-3. *The hardware inventory collection process for 32-bit clients.*

The first time the Hardware Inventory Client Agent runs—approximately 10 minutes after its installation —a complete inventory is collected and its history is maintained in the CIM repository on each client. Each subsequent inventory generates a delta file only, detailing only those inventory properties that have changed since the last interval. When a complete inventory file is generated, Hinv32.exe writes a temporary hardware inventory complete (.HIC) file to the

\MS\SMS\Clicomp\Hinv folder on the client. For subsequent inventory cycles, this delta file will have a hardware inventory delta (.HID) extension.

At this time, Hinv32.exe looks for any NOIDMIFs that might reside in the \MS\SMS\Noidmifs folder on the client. Refer to the section "MIF Files" later in this chapter for details about MIF files. If the client deems a NOIDMIF valid, it is included as part of the .HIC or .HID file. If not, it is written to the \MS\SMS\Noidmifs\Badmifs folder. Hinv32.exe also looks for any IDMIFs stored in the \MS\SMS\Idmifs folder on the client. If an IDMIF is deemed valid, it is moved to the \MS\SMS\Clicomp\Hinv\Outbox folder. If not, it is written to the \MS\SMS\Idmifs\Badmifs folder.

> **Note** The Badmifs folder is created only if a bad NOIDMIF or IDMIF is detected. By default, the MIF file size is set to 250 KB. A NOIDMIF or an IDMIF is considered bad if it exceeds 250 KB in size or if it cannot be parsed successfully because of syntax errors or because, in the case of IDMIFs, it is being used to update the system architecture for an existing client record.

Hinv32.exe renames the .HIC or .HID file with the extension .INV and copies it to the \MS\SMS\Clicomp\Hinv\Outbox folder, which is monitored by Copy Queue Manager (Cqmgr32.dll). Copy Queue Manager renames the file with a unique filename and changes the extension to .NHM (no history MIF). It then copies the file to the CAP_site\Inventry.box folder on the CAP. At this point, the hardware inventory process is complete on the client. The SMS Client Service will start the Hardware Inventory Client Agent again at the next scheduled interval.

> **Note** Once Copy Queue Manager copies the inventory file to the CAP, the temporary files (.HIC, .HID, .INV) are deleted. This process generally happens in a matter of seconds, so you may not see the files unless you are watching closely.

Inbox Manager Assistant running on the CAP in turn moves the file to Inventory Processor's inbox (the SMS\Inboxes\Inventry.box folder) on the site server. If the site server is a primary site server, Inventory Processor adds a binary header to the .NHM file, renames it with the extension .MIF and moves it to Inventory Data Loader's inbox (the SMS\Inboxes\Dataldr.box folder). Inventory Data Loader then reads the .MIF file, parses the data, and writes it to the SMS database on the SQL server. If a parent site exists, Inventory Data Loader forwards the .MIF file to Replication Manager, which forwards it to Inventory Data Loader's inbox on the parent site server.

If the site server is a secondary site server, Replication Manager forwards the .MIF file to the parent primary site server's Inventory Data Loader inbox, where it is processed as described earlier.

16-Bit Clients

The hardware inventory collection process on 16-bit clients, as illustrated in Figure 9-4, is similar in many respects to the process described for 32-bit clients, with two major exceptions. The first, of course, is the absence of Windows Management since these clients do not support WMI. Because of this, no history is maintained on the client, and—here is the second exception—a complete, albeit significantly smaller, inventory is generated at each inventory cycle.

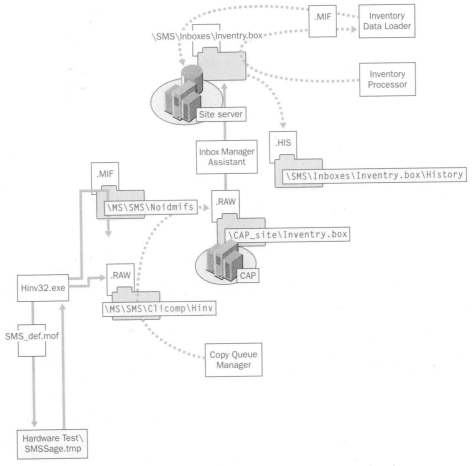

Figure 9-4. *The hardware inventory collection process flow for 16-bit clients.*

When hardware inventory is installed on a 16-bit client, a 16-bit agent (Hinv16.exe) is provided by SMS. The first time the Hardware Inventory Client Agent runs—approximately 10 minutes after its installation—a complete inventory is collected. Each subsequent inventory also generates a complete inventory.

Hinv16.exe will still read the SMS_def.mof file, but it will collect only the classes of objects listed here, with limited properties. (SMS 1.x administrators should immediately recognize this list, as these are the same objects collected from SMS 1.x clients.)

- *Disk*
- *Device Drivers*
- *IRQ Resources*
- *Memory*
- *Name*
- *Network*
- *Operating System*
- *Pointing Devices*
- *Printer Ports*
- *Processor*
- *Serial Ports*
- *TSR*
- *Video Configuration*

Hinv16.exe actually tests for each of these objects. It creates a temporary file named SMSSafe.tmp in the \MS\SMS\Core\Data directory in which it records any failed hardware tests. Failed tests are noted in the client's SMS.ini file until the SMS administrator resolves them and removes their references.

When the complete inventory file is generated, Hinv16.exe writes a file with a .RAW extension to the \MS\SMS\Clicomp\Hinv folder on the client. The .RAW file represents a complete hardware inventory stored in a binary format rather than an .MIF format. At this time, Hinv16.exe will also look for any NOIDMIFs that might reside in the \MS\SMS\Noidmifs folder on the client. Unlike with 32-bit clients, there is no syntax checking of the NOIDMIF here. The .MIF file is included as part of the .RAW file. There is no support for IDMIF processing on 16-bit clients.

Copy Queue Manager (Cqmgr16.dll) copies the file to the CAP_Site\Inventry.box folder on the CAP provided the user is logged onto the network. If not, the .RAW files will stack up on the client (depending on the collection frequency you specify) until the user next logs onto the network. At this point, the hardware inventory process is complete on the client.

> **Note**   Once Copy Queue Manager copies the inventory file to the CAP, the .RAW file is deleted. This process generally happens in a matter of seconds, so you may not see the file unless you are watching closely.

Inbox Manager Assistant running on the CAP in turn moves the file to Inventory Processor's inbox (the SMS\Inboxes\Inventry.box folder) on the site server. If the site server is a primary site server, Inventory Processor receives the .RAW file. If this is the first inventory file received for the client, Inventory Processor creates a history file (.HIS) for it on the site server and maintains the file there in the SMS\Invproc.box\History folder. Inventory Processor then generates an .MIF file from the .RAW file and moves it to Inventory Data Loader's inbox (the SMS\Inboxes\Dataldr.box folder). If a history file already exists for the client, Inventory Processor will compare the .RAW file against the history file and generate a delta .MIF file, again moving it to Inventory Data Loader's inbox.

Inventory Data Loader then reads the .MIF file. At this point, Inventory Data Loader will perform a syntax check on the .MIF file to determine whether it is a valid MIF. If it is, Inventory Data Loader parses the data and writes it to the SMS database on the SQL server. If a parent site exists, Inventory Data Loader forwards the .MIF file to Replication Manager, which forwards it to Inventory Data Loader's inbox on the parent site server. If the file is not a valid MIF, Inventory Data Loader moves it to the Badmifs folder (SMS\Inboxes\Dataldr.box\Badmifs).

If the site server is a secondary site server, Replication Manager forwards the inventory .MIF to the parent primary site server's Inventory Data Loader inbox, where it is processed as described earlier.

Hardware Resynchronization

Occasionally, Inventory Data Loader may determine that the inventory data it receives is somehow "bad," or out of sync with the SMS database. In these instances, a resynchronization (resync) will be triggered automatically. *Resync* is a corrective process that can cause the client agent to ignore the history file and collect a complete hardware inventory. Specific events that trigger hardware inventory resync include the following:

- The inventory MIF contains updates for a database record that does not exist.
- The MIF itself contains bad or corrupted data.
- The client has attached to a new SMS site.

Note Resync doesn't change the hardware inventory schedule—the next inventory cycle will start at the scheduled time.

When a resync is triggered, Inventory Data Loader creates a .CFG file for the client and writes a resync request to it. This file is maintained in the SMS\Inboxes\ Clidata.src folder on the site server. Inbox Manager writes this file to the corresponding folder on the CAP (CAP_Site\Clidata.box). The next time CCIM runs (on its 23-hour cycle or when an update is forced), the .CFG file is read, the client's registry is updated with the resync information (on 32-bit clients), and the SMS Client Service directs the Hardware Inventory Client Agent to generate a complete hardware inventory.

The hardware inventory collection process proceeds as described earlier for 32-bit and 16-bit clients. For 16-bit clients, the resync flag is contained within the .RAW file so that it is treated as a complete inventory file by Inventory Processor.

Note If the client belongs to multiple sites, the complete inventory triggered by a resync event will be forwarded to all the sites the client belongs to.

Status Messages and Log Files for Hardware Inventory

Status messages and log files are generated throughout the inventory installation and collection process. Let's begin with the log files. Unlike log files generated on the site server, client logs are enabled by default and written automatically to the \MS\SMS\Logs folder on each client. When monitoring hardware inventory, you should view the Ccim32.log file for entries related to the detection of the Hardware Inventory Client Agent offer. For example, the notification that the Hardware Inventory Client Agent needs to be installed is made to the client through the client offer file, as discussed in the section "Enabling Hardware Inventory" earlier in this chapter. Monitor the SMSapm32.log file for entries related to Advertised Programs Monitor scheduling the installation of the Hardware Inventory Client Agent. Inhinv32.log tracks the installation of the agent. Figure 9-5 shows examples of the entries you might find in these logs using SMS Trace.

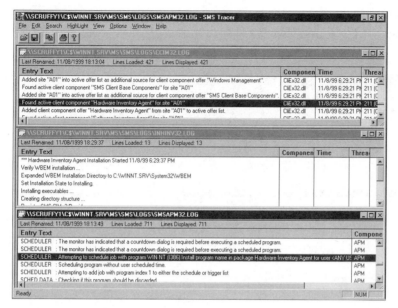

Figure 9-5. *Sample entries for Ccim32.log, Inhinv32.log, and SMSapm32.log in SMS Tracer.*

Hinv32.log tracks the generation of inventory files as well as updates to the SMS_def.mof file, as illustrated in Figure 9-6. Notice the start of the inventory cycle as well as the enumeration of object classes.

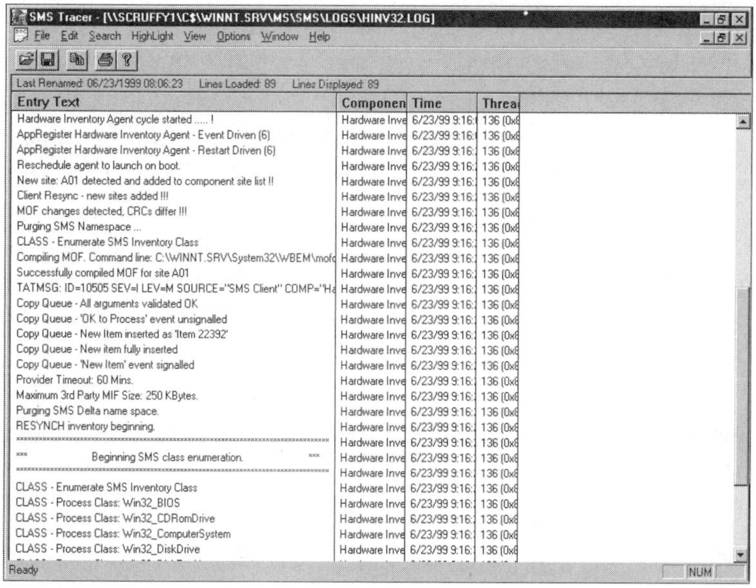

Figure 9-6. *Sample entries for Hinv32.log in SMS Tracer.*

Cqmgr32.log tracks the copying of inventory and status messages to the CAP, as illustrated in Figure 9-7. Notice when the client connects to the Inventry.box folder on the CAP.

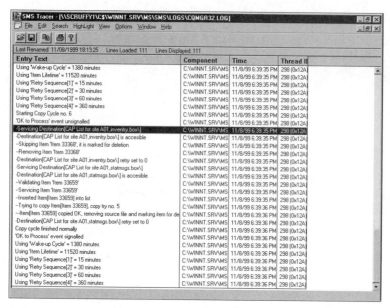

Figure 9-7. *Sample entries for Cqmgr32.log in SMS Tracer.*

You should also monitor the respective log files for Inventory Processor (Invproc.log), Inventory Data Loader (Dataldr.log), Inbox Manager (Inboxmgr.log), and Inbox Manager Assistant (Inboxast.log) to monitor their part in the inventory collection process.

Within 60 minutes of installation, CCIM will generate a status message announcing the successful installation of the Hardware Inventory Client Agent. The Hardware Inventory Client Agent itself will generate a status message after the first inventory collection, and again after every subsequent collection. Copy Queue Manager forwards these status messages to Status Manager's inbox on the CAP (CAP_Site\Statmsgs.box), and of course Inbox Manager Assistant forwards them from the CAP to Status Manager's inbox on the site server (SMS\Inboxes\ Statmgr.box).

You can view these status messages by running a status message query through the SMS Administrator Console. To do so, follow these steps:

1. Navigate to the System Status folder, expand it, and select the Status Message Queries folder.

2. Right-click on the query All Status Messages From A Specific System, and choose Show Messages from the context menu to display the All Status Messages From A Specific System window, as shown in Figure 9-8.

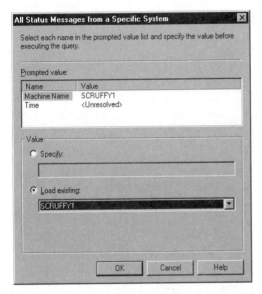

Figure 9-8. *The All Status Messages From A Specific System window.*

3. In the Prompted Value list, select Machine Name. Click Specify and enter the name of the client computer you want to report on, or click Load Existing to have SMS query the database and compile a list of all client names it has recorded.

Note   This process can take a while for large databases.

---

4. Select Time in the Prompted Value list. The options in the Value section will change. Either specify a starting date and time from which you want to see status messages or choose Select Date And Time to enter a range of hours (1, 2, 6, or 12 hours ago).

5. Click OK. The SMS Status Message Viewer will display all the status messages recorded for that client during the period specified.

Figure 9-9 displays an example of status messages generated by the installation of the Hardware Inventory Client Agent and the collection of the inventory from the client. Look for message IDs of 10500, indicating that inventory has been successfully collected; 10505, indicating that the inventory schema (SMS_def.mof) has been updated; and 10204 from CCIM (selected in Figure 9-9), reporting that the Hardware Inventory Client Agent was successfully installed. Note that CCIM made this report an hour later, which is its verification cycle.

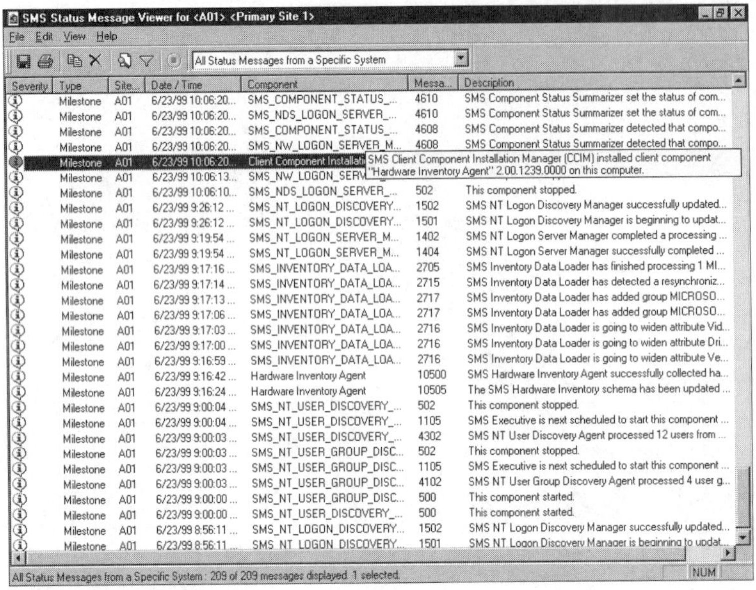

Figure 9-9. *The Status Message Viewer, showing that the Hardware Inventory Client Agent has been installed and that inventory has been collected for this client.*

For a list of clients that have installed the Hardware Inventory Client Agent, run the status message query Clients That Installed The Hardware Inventory Client Agent. To view status messages for clients based on their collection membership, run the status message query All Status Messages For A Specific Collection At A Specific Site. Of course, you could create your own status message query as well. Refer back to Chapter 5 for more information on how to create status message queries.

On the site server, monitor the status messages of Inventory Data Loader. Look for messages in the $27xx$ range identifying successful processing of MIFs. Monitor the status messages for Inventory Processor for resynchronization or the processing of .RAW files from 16-bit clients, and monitor status messages for Replication Manager for forwarding of MIF files to a parent site.

Viewing Hardware Inventory

Hardware inventory is viewed through the SMS Administrator Console. The process is shown here:

1. Navigate to the Collections folder and expand it.

2. Select the collection that contains the client or clients whose inventory you want to view.

3. Right-click on the appropriate client entry in the right pane, choose All Tasks from the context menu, and then choose Start Resource Explorer.

4. In the Resource Explorer window, expand Hardware to view a list of object classes for which properties have been collected, as shown in Figure 9-10. Select each object to view its instances and properties.

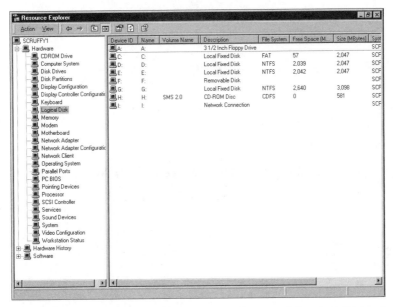

Figure 9-10. *The Resource Explorer window, with Logical Disk selected.*

The Resource Explorer window lists properties horizontally across the viewing screen, requiring you to scroll across to see all the properties. However, if you right-click on an object and choose Properties from the context menu, you can view the same properties listed in a vertical column, as shown in Figure 9-11.

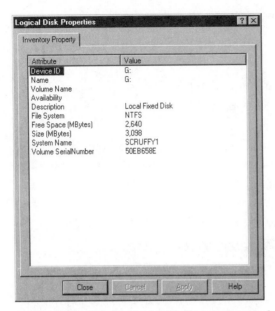

Figure 9-11. *The Logical Disk Properties window.*

5. Expand Hardware History to view information collected from previous inventories such as Logical Disk History, Memory History, and Operating System History, as shown in Figure 9-12.

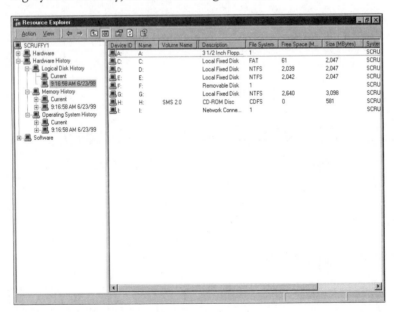

Figure 9-12. *The Resource Explorer window, with Hardware History expanded.*

Tip You could use Hardware History to develop resource usage trends for your clients—for example, to track how much disk storage is utilized over a period of time or whether paging might be excessive due to a lack of RAM.

The entries listed under Hardware in the Resource Explorer window represent the object classes identified through the SMS_def.mof file and any MIF files that were created to be appended to or modify the client's inventory record. As you can see, it is quite a thorough list. You can actually collect more than ten times the amount of data than you could through the hardware inventory process in earlier versions of SMS.

Customizing Hardware Inventory

There are two ways to customize the inventory that you collect from a client or add to the database as a new class of object: you can modify the default SMS_def.mof file, or you can create custom MIF files. Either method will require some planning and testing on the part of you, the SMS administrator. As we've seen, the default SMS_def.mof file collects a large amount of data—100 to 200 KB per client. Modifying the file could result in larger amounts of data to track, more network traffic when sending the data to the CAPs and site server, and so on. Adding an MIF file can also result in additional inventory data being reported. Also, while the SMS_def.mof exists as a template that can be modified, in general, MIF files must be created.

SMS_def.mof

As mentioned, you can consider the SMS_def.mof file a template that defines for Windows Management on SMS clients which inventory objects, or hardware classes, should be queried and how much data should be collected for each. The master SMS_def.mof file is maintained in the SMS\Inboxes\Clifiles.src\Hinv folder on the site server. This file is copied to the CAP (CAP_Site\Clifiles.box\Hinv) and ultimately to each client (\MS\SMS\Sitefile*site*\Hinv).

Included with SMS 2.0, but not installed by default, is a utility called MOF Manager. This tool gives you the ability to enable or disable hardware classes and their properties through an easy-to-navigate interface. Using this tool, you can enable additional object classes beyond those already collected, disable object classes to stop collecting their properties, and specify which properties to collect or ignore on a per-object basis.

The installation setup file for MOF Manager is included on the SMS 2.0 CD in the folder Support\Reskit\Bin*platform*\Mofman, where *platform* is either Alpha or i386. Simply execute the Setup.exe found there and follow the simple MOF Manager Setup Wizard instructions. By default, the MOF Manager shortcut icon will be created in a program group named SMS 2.0 Resource Kit; you can add the icon to the Systems Management Server program group if you prefer.

Planning When you upgrade the site server with SMS 2.0 Service Pack 1, the original utilities found in the \Support folder are replaced with an updated version contained in a self-extracting executable file named Support.exe. Executing this file creates a new folder named SMS 2.0 Supportability Files (placed by default in the C:\Program Files folder). The MOF Manager setup file can be found in the Reskit\Bin\platform\Mofman subdirectory under SMS 2.0 Supportability Files.

After you launch the MOF Manager, open the SMS_def.mof file found in the SMS\Inboxes\Clifiles.src\Hinv folder. Figure 9-13 shows a sample SMS_def.mof file.

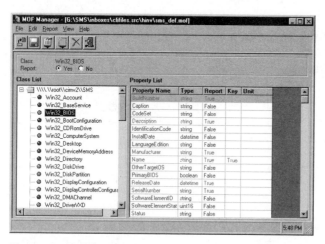

Figure 9-13. *The MOF Manager window, showing a sample SMS_def.mof file.*

Every hardware class that has a green indicator (with Yes selected for the Report option) represents a hardware class for which one or more properties can be collected. As you select each hardware class, you can see at a glance which of its properties is set to be collected—all those highlighted in green or set to True. As you can see, a fair amount of data is collected by default.

In Figure 9-13, the hardware class *WIN32_BIOS* is selected. This object is set to report BIOS information for properties such as *BuildNumber*, *Manufacturer*, *ReleaseDate*, and *Version*. You can disable any of these properties if you don't require that information. You can also enable any additional property you want to report on—for example, you might choose to enable *InstallDate* or *CodeSet*. To change the status of a class property, double-click on that entry in the Properties list or select the entry and select the Yes option at the top left of the MOF Manager screen.

Caution   It bears repeating that your choice of objects and their properties can generate a very large inventory file. If for some reason you feel tempted to turn on and collect every possible object and property, remember that the inventory process was not designed to support that scenario, nor would it be very practical for you as an administrator in the long run.

Some hardware classes that you enable may result in additional network traffic generated to find or resolve resources. For example, *WIN32_LogicalDisk* will report not only local partitions, but also any current network connections. Properties for *WIN32_Desktop* and *WIN32_Environment* may require a connection to a domain controller to validate a username to its SID.

Before you roll out significant changes to the SMS_def.mof file, be sure to test the file on a few sample clients to be sure that you are collecting the information you expected to collect and that the network traffic generated as a result falls within acceptable limits for your network.

Tip   The *Systems Management Server Administrator's Guide* provides a short list of the more common Web-Based Enterprise Management (WBEM) object classes and their properties. The Systems Management Server 2.0 Resource Guide (part of the *Microsoft BackOffice 4.5 Resource Kit* available through Microsoft Press) provides a complete list; see appendixes B and C. Although not compiled specifically for use with MOF Manager, these lists explain the hardware classes and their attributes, making your use of MOF Manager more meaningful.

MIF Files

Another way to modify the hardware inventory is through the creation of MIF files. MIF files modify the database by creating architectures, object classes, and attributes. Architectures define entire new classes of objects, whereas object classes and attributes are generally added to existing architectures.

Two types of MIF files can be created: NOIDMIFs and IDMIFs. NOIDMIFs are used to modify or append object classes and properties to existing client inventory records—hence the term "no id." You are not creating a new architecture;

you are simply appending to an existing architecture—namely, System Resources. You could use a NOIDMIF to add a client system's asset number, information about peripheral devices attached to the computer, or even the department name or code to the existing client record.

IDMIFs, on the other hand, are used to create new architectures of object classes and attributes. For example, suppose you want to report on all the multimedia equipment you have within your organization. Through an IDMIF, you could create a new architecture (say, Multimedia Equipment) with its own object classes—(perhaps *Audio*, *Video*, *CD*, *Tape*, *PC Conferencing*), each of which would have one or more attributes (*Model*, *Manufacturer*, *Asset number*, *Cost*, and so on). IDMIFs can also be used to update existing architectures—for example, to add stand-alone computers to the database or to associate an architecture with existing computer records for the purpose of creating queries and collections that can be linked to unique properties.

More Info Although it would be nice to present examples showing how each of these types of MIFs can be used and explain their basic structure, we don't want to reinvent the wheel here with an in-depth explanation of MIF usage and interaction. That level of detail can be found in the Systems Management Server 2.0 Resource Guide (part of the *Microsoft BackOffice 4.5 Resource Kit* available through Microsoft Press) and also through Microsoft TechNet and the various partner programs offered by Microsoft. Be sure to read Chapter 10 of the Resource Guide, which discusses customizing hardware inventory, if you want to use MIF files to their greatest advantage.

The basic structure of IDMIFs and NOIDMIFs is essentially the same. Because they are text files, they can be created using any text editor. Actually, most third-party add-ons for SMS 2.0 are capable of generating MIF files that update the database with various kinds of information. SMS Installer notifies the site server about the successful or failed installation of an application through a status MIF file. The MIF file format is an industry standard format. If you have created any kind of scripts or batch files in the past, you will find it easy to create an MIF file. Let's start with the NOIDMIF.

Creating a NOIDMIF NOIDMIFs are perhaps the most commonly used MIF file because they add to existing computer records and they are easiest to create. Figure 9-14 shows a sample of a NOIDMIF designed to add the client computer's department name and department code to its existing hardware record in the SMS database.

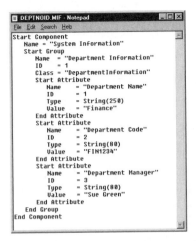

```
DEPTNOID.MIF - Notepad
File  Edit  Search  Help
Start Component
    Name = "System Information"
    Start Group
        Name  = "Department Information"
        ID    = 1
        Class = "DepartmentInformation"
        Start Attribute
            Name    = "Department Name"
            ID      = 1
            Type    = String(250)
            Value   = "Finance"
        End Attribute
        Start Attribute
            Name    = "Department Code"
            ID      = 2
            Type    = String(80)
            Value   = "FIN1234"
        End Attribute
        Start Attribute
            Name    = "Department Manager"
            ID      = 3
            Type    = String(80)
            Value   = "Sue Green"
        End Attribute
    End Group
End Component
```

Figure 9-14. *A sample NOIDMIF file.*

NOIDMIFs always begin with Start Component and a general component name. The next step is to create an object class. You do this by adding the Start Group statement, a Name describing the group, an ID, and a class. The *Name* attribute is the string displayed in the Resource Explorer that refers to this class. The *ID* attribute represents this group in relation to any other group in this MIF. For example, if you add another group, you would give it an ID of 2, and so on—the number is unique. The *Class* attribute is used by SMS internally for processing the group information.

Next you list each attribute that you are adding for this object. In this case, we are adding three attributes: *Department Name*, *Department Code* and *Department Manager*. Each attribute entry begins with Start Attribute and ends with End Attribute. For each attribute, you must provide at a minimum *Name*, *ID*, *Type*, and *Value* settings. These attributes are fairly self-explanatory. *Name* is a descriptive attribute name. *ID* represents the attribute in relation to other attributes. *Type* indicates whether the value is a text string, a number, or a list, and gives the value's length when appropriate. *Value*, of course, is the current value you are assigning to the attribute. You end the MIF file with End Group and End Component statements.

Save the NOIDMIF with a descriptive filename and the .MIF extension. The file must be placed in the \MS\SMS\Noidmifs folder on each client you want to update. You can do this using SMS 2.0's package distribution process, which will be discussed in Chapter 12. At the next hardware inventory cycle, the MIF file will be read, evaluated for syntax, and added to the client's inventory file, as described in the section "Hardware Inventory Collection Process Flow" earlier in this chapter, and then updated to the client's SMS database record. It can then be viewed through Resource Explorer, as shown in Figure 9-15.

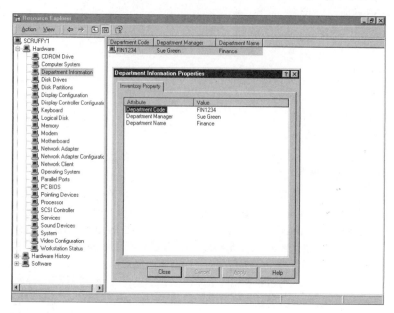

Figure 9-15. *A sample NOIDMIF viewed through Resource Explorer.*

Caution Be sure that the MIF file you create using a text editor is saved with the .MIF extension. Text editors such as Notepad append a .TXT extension. It's easy to miss this, and if you do, you will spend an inordinate amount of time trying to figure out why the MIF file is not working.

Creating an IDMIF   As mentioned, the basic structure of an IDMIF is similar to that of a NOIDMIF. The main difference comes at the beginning of an IDMIF file, as you can see in the example shown in Figure 9-16.

IDMIFs require that you include the following two statements at the top of the MIF:

- **//Architecture**   Identifies the name of the new architecture (object class) you are creating
- **//UniqueID**   Defines a single unique value that identifies this specific instance of the architecture in the database

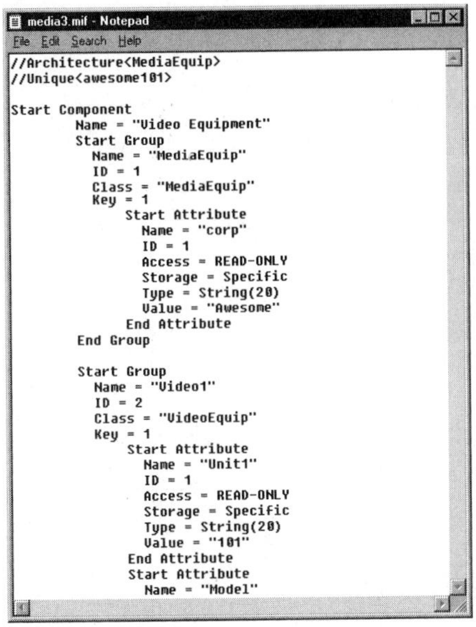


```
//Architecture<MediaEquip>
//Unique<awesome101>

Start Component
        Name = "Video Equipment"
        Start Group
          Name = "MediaEquip"
          ID = 1
          Class = "MediaEquip"
          Key = 1
              Start Attribute
                Name = "corp"
                ID = 1
                Access = READ-ONLY
                Storage = Specific
                Type = String(20)
                Value = "Awesome"
              End Attribute
        End Group

        Start Group
          Name = "Video1"
          ID = 2
          Class = "VideoEquip"
          Key = 1
              Start Attribute
                Name = "Unit1"
                ID = 1
                Access = READ-ONLY
                Storage = Specific
                Type = String(20)
                Value = "101"
              End Attribute
              Start Attribute
                Name = "Model"
```

Figure 9-16. *A sample IDMIF file.*

IDMIFs also require that you include a top-level group that has the same name as the architecture and that has at least one attribute defined. Also, if a class has more than one instance within an architecture, you must have defined at least one key attribute to avoid overwriting previous instances with subsequent information. A key value is simply one of the group attributes. As with NOIDMIFs, you must save the file with an .MIF extension. You can place the file in the \MS\SMS\Idmifs folder on any SMS client.

Viewing an IDMIF Unlike NOIDMIFs, which are associated with specific clients, IDMIFs generally add new object classes to the database. Therefore, you cannot view this information through Resource Explorer. Instead, you must create a query to extract and view the relevant data from the SMS database. For details on creating such queries, refer to Chapter 15.

As mentioned, NOIDMIFs are generally associated with individual client records, and as such, they must be placed in the \MS\SMS\Noidmifs folder on each client. Of course, you can use SMS package distribution to accomplish this. IDMIFs can also be placed in the Idmifs folder on the SMS client. However, since IDMIFs generally are not associated with any one client, you can place an IDMIF in the Idmifs folder on any SMS client. For that matter, you could also place the IDMIF in the CAP_Site\Inventry.box folder on the CAP or in the SMS\Inboxes\ Inventry.box folder on the site server. The end result will be the same.

MIF Tools in the *Microsoft BackOffice 4.5 Resource Kit* The *Microsoft Back-Office 4.5 Resource Kit* CD contains several tools that can assist you in the process of creating MIF files. The first tool, MIFCheck, is also included on the SMS 2.0 CD in the Support\Reskit\Bin*platform*\Diagnose folder on the CD. This is a command-line tool that you can use to determine whether your MIF file is syntactically correct. The MIFCheck.exe and MIF files must both be in the same directory. To run MIFCheck.exe, at a command line execute the command:

> *Mifcheck* filename.*mif*

If MIFCheck finds an error, it will specify the error and the line on which it occurred. You can then go back to the MIF file, fix the problem, and rerun MIFCheck to check for additional errors. Figure 9-17 illustrates how to use this tool.

Figure 9-17. *The MIFCheck command running in the Command Prompt window.*

> **Tip** MIFCheck will find only one error at a time, so you must rerun MIFCheck after you fix each error to be sure that the MIF file is error-free.

The *Microsoft BackOffice 4.5 Resource Kit* contains two additional tools that should be familiar to SMS 1.x administrators: MIF Form Generator (MIFGen.exe) and MIF Entry (MIFWin.exe). MIF Form Generator allows you to create an MIF form using a GUI, use SMS or some other method to deliver the form to the client, and then have a user fill out the form using MIF Entry. MIF Entry would generate the actual MIF and place it in the \MS\SMS\Noidmifs folder on the client.

MIF Form Generator and MIF Entry were left out of the RTM version of SMS 2.0, but thanks to popular demand, they have been included with the *Microsoft Back-Office 4.5 Resource Kit*—updated to support SMS 2.0, of course.

Because they are Resource Kit tools and are well-documented there, we won't look at them in detail here. However, let's take a moment to look at the MIF Form Generator and MIF Entry interfaces, as well as the resulting MIF file.

Figure 9-18 shows a completed form that includes three fields (attributes)— *Department Manager*, *Department Code*, and *Department Name*.

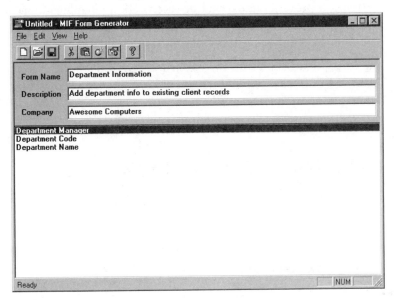

Figure 9-18. *Sample form screen.*

Figure 9-19 shows the properties of one of the fields, a list type.

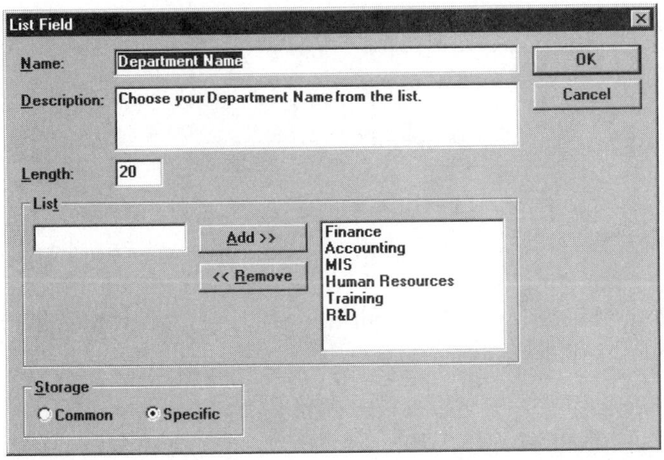

Figure 9-19. *Sample list field properties.*

There is nothing elegant here. You are building a simple form that either you or your user will fill out. Notice that you can include directions for the user, and in some cases, default values for a field.

If your intention is to create the form using predefined values, generate an MIF file from it, and distribute the MIF file to the client's MS\SMS\Noidmifs folder using the SMS distribution process (which will be discussed in Chapter 12), select the Read-Only option in the Properties window for each field. If you intend to have your users fill in the form, leave this option unselected.

When you save the form, it will be given the extension .XNF. This file can be distributed to the \MS\SMS\Bin folder on each client computer after you have installed the MIF Entry tool on the client. When the user runs this tool (or you execute it via a package), the user can select each field and enter the appropriate values, as shown in Figure 9-20.

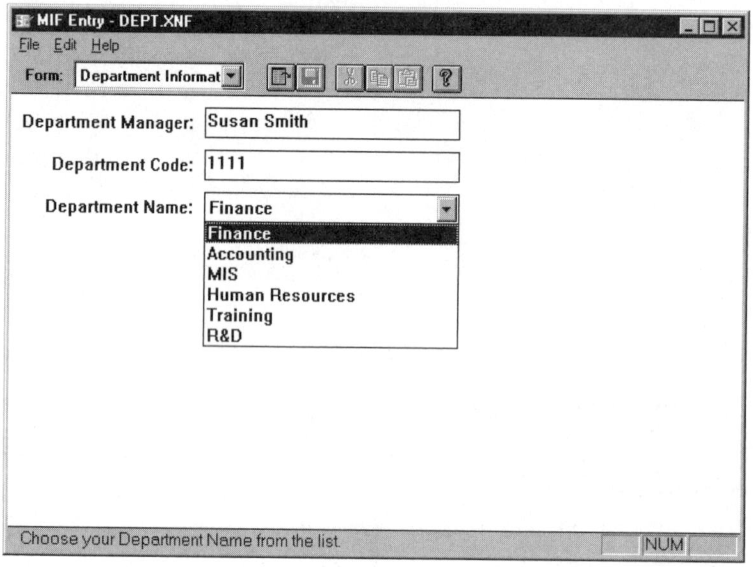

Figure 9-20. *Sample MIF Entry form.*

When the user saves the form, it is automatically saved as an MIF file in the \MS\SMS\Noidmifs folder on that client and will be reported on the next hardware inventory cycle. Figure 9-21 shows the resulting MIF file. Looks similar to the one we created manually, doesn't it?

Of course, you don't have to ask your users to fill out the MIF forms at all. You could generate the MIF files yourself using the MIF Entry tool and then distribute them to the individual clients, as discussed earlier.

```
dept.mif - Notepad
File  Edit  Search  Help
Start Component
  Name = "Machine"
  Start Group
    Name = "Department Information"
    ID = 1
    Class = "Awesome Computers|Department Information|1.0"
    Start Attribute
      Name = "Department Manager"
      ID = 1
      Type = String(35)
      Storage = Specific
      Value = "Susan Smith"
    End Attribute
    Start Attribute
      Name = "Department Code"
      ID = 2
      Type = Counter
      Storage = Specific
      Value = 1111
    End Attribute
    Start Attribute
      Name = "Department Name"
      ID = 3
      Type = String(20)
      Storage = Specific
      Value = "Accounting"
    End Attribute
  End Group
End Component
```

Figure 9-21. *Sample MIF file generated by the MIF Entry tool.*

Software Inventory

Software inventory is a new addition to SMS 2.0. It may be sacrilegious to say so, but as most SMS administrators knew from SMS 1.x, true software inventory capabilities just didn't exist, and what did exist was largely inadequate. Almost always the SMS 1.x administrator would turn to a third-party add-on to collect true software inventory.

SMS 2.0 offers greatly enhanced software inventory capabilities. Actually, the developers completely reengineered the software inventory client component, and it works quite well. A third-party add-on might still provide some extra bells and whistles for you, but the client component is quite robust.

Like its hardware counterpart, the Software Inventory Client Agent (also sometimes referred to as the Software Inventory Agent) runs automatically on the client according to a schedule you create and collects information according to options you select. However, unlike the Hardware Inventory Client Agent, the Software Inventory Client Agent processes data the same way on both 16-bit and 32-bit clients. This is because the Software Inventory Client Agent scans local drives rather than querying the WMI.

The Software Inventory Client Agent collects application information that includes the following data:

- Filename, version, and size
- Manufacturer name
- Product name, version, and language
- Data and time of file creation (presumably at installation)

The Software Inventory Client Agent can also collect copies of specific files.

As with hardware inventory, once software inventory has been collected at the client, it is passed on to the CAP. The CAP in turn forwards the information to the site server. Software inventory is ultimately stored in the SMS database, so it is again important for us to draw a distinction between primary and secondary site servers. Recall that the main difference between a primary and a secondary site server is that a primary site server maintains access to an SQL Server database.

As with hardware inventory, you can enable the Software Inventory Client Agent for the clients on a secondary site. As a matter of fact, the configuration settings for the Software Inventory Client Agent can even be different from the secondary site's parent site. When software inventory is passed to the secondary site server by the CAP, the secondary site server forwards the information to its parent primary site, where it can be added to the SMS database.

Enabling Software Inventory

To begin, let's get the Software Inventory Client Agent enabled and installed on our SMS clients. Then we'll explore how inventory is actually collected. To enable the Software Inventory Agent through the SMS Administrator Console, follow these steps:

1. Under Site Settings, navigate to the Client Agents folder and expand it.
2. Right-click on Software Inventory Client Agent, and choose Properties from the context menu to display the Software Inventory Client Agent Properties window, shown in Figure 9-22.
3. Select the Enable Software Inventory On Clients check box.
4. Notice that the default inventory collection schedule on the client will be once a week. You can specify from 1 to 23 hours, 1 to 31 days, or 1 to 4 weeks under Simple Schedule. Or you can select Full Schedule and then click the Schedule button to display the Schedule dialog box, shown in Figure 9-23. Designate a more specific start time and recurrence pattern, and then choose OK.

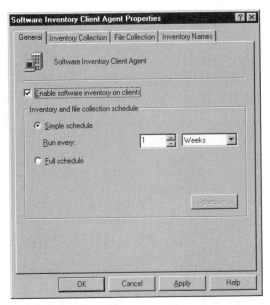

Figure 9-22. *The Software Inventory Client Agent Properties window.*

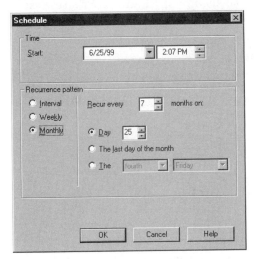

Figure 9-23. *The Schedule dialog box.*

5. Select the Inventory Collection tab, shown in Figure 9-24.

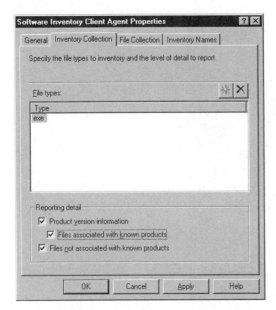

Figure 9-24. *The Inventory Collection tab.*

6. Notice that the default files that the agent will scan for are those with an .EXE extension. You can click the New button (the yellow star) to add additional files. Wildcard characters are acceptable to narrow the scan.

7. Check the appropriate options under Reporting Detail. These three options can tailor how data is collected and represented to you:

  • **Product Version Information** Reports information that the agent can read from the file header of "known" products, including company name, product name, version, and language. For example, the program executable for Microsoft Word 97 is Winword.exe. Winword.exe contains binary header information that identifies the manufacturer, product name, and version associated with the Microsoft Word 97 program.

  • **Files Associated With Known Products** Additionally reports the filename (and other file information) associated with the inventoried product—for example, Resource Explorer would associate Winword.exe with Microsoft Word. This option is available only when Product Version Information is selected.

  • **Files Not Associated With Known Products** Reports filename and other information for files for which the header information contains no product information—for example, some game files. These files will be displayed in the Resource Explorer Unknown list.

You must enable at least one of the three options to enable SMS to report information on inventoried files. By default, all three options are enabled.

8. Click on the File Collection tab, shown in Figure 9-25, if you want to also collect a copy of specific files from each client.

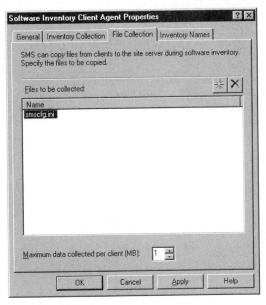

Figure 9-25. *The File Collection tab.*

9. To add the name of a specific file, click the New button to display the New File dialog box, and enter the name of the file. Wildcard characters are acceptable. Then click OK to return to the File Collection tab.

10. Specify a value in the Maximum Data Collected Per Client (MB) edit box. This option lets you identify how much total file data can be collected from the client during a software inventory cycle. This value can be as large as 20 MB. Keep in mind, especially if you are using wildcard characters, that collected files can generate a larger amount of additional network traffic than the basic software inventory.

11. Click on the Inventory Names tab, shown in Figure 9-26, to standardize the names of the company or product that are displayed when you view software inventory information. Sometimes, as companies update their software applications or create new versions, the developers include variations on the company's or the product's name in the header information included in the program executable. Of course, when you view the

software inventory, the products will be sorted and displayed according to each variation of the company or product name. This can make it difficult for you to find all versions of the product.

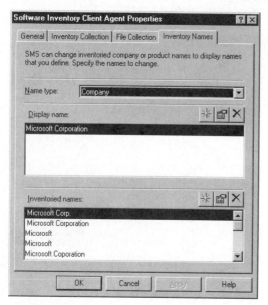

Figure 9-26. *The Inventory Names tab.*

This example lists several variations of the company name for Microsoft—Microsoft Corp., Microsoft Corporation, Microsoft, and so on—that will be displayed as Microsoft Corporation when viewing software inventory information.

12. Select which name type you want to standardize; your choices are Product or Company. In the Display Name section, click the New button to display the Display Name Properties dialog box. Enter the name you want to be displayed on the product information screen, and click OK to return to the Inventory Names tab. In the Inventoried Names section, click the New button to display the Inventoried Name Properties dialog box. Enter the names that have been inventoried by the Software Inventory Client Agent that you want standardized to the display name you entered in the Display Name section and click OK to return to the Inventory Names tab.

13. Click OK to begin the site update process.

Collected files are stored on the site server in the SMS\Inboxes\Sinv.box\FileCol folder. If the file changes at all on the client, the Software Inventory Client Agent will collect it again at the next cycle. By default, SMS will retain the last five copies of the file that were collected. Think about that. At 1 MB per file and five collected copies per client, for 1000 clients you would require 5 GB of storage space just for your collected files. Not pretty! Obviously, you would not use this as an alternative backup process. However, it can be used to look for files that should *not* be on a client, like a game executable. The number of such collected files ought to be significantly smaller. All collected files are kept in the database for 90 days before they are aged out.

> **Note** To modify the number of copies of collected files maintained at the site server, you need to modify the following registry entry: HKEY_LOCAL_MACHINE\ Software\Microsoft\SMS\Components\SMS_Software_Inventory_Processor. Look for the value *Maximum Collected Files*, and change it as desired.

When you enable the Software Inventory Client Agent, you are making a change to the site properties, and the site's site control file (Sitectrl.ct0) will be updated as a result (as described in Chapter 3). The following three files are written to the SMS\Inboxes\Clicfg.src directory on the site server:

- **Sinv.cfg** Software Inventory Client Agent configuration settings
- **Sinv.nal** CAPs from which the agent can be installed
- **Sinv.pkg** Instructions for installing the agent on the client for various platforms

In the same directory, the client offer file is also updated to indicate that the Software Inventory Client Agent needs to be installed on all SMS clients for the site. The offer file is Cli_*xxx*.ofr, where *xxx* indicates the client operating system platform.

Inbox Manager copies these files to the CAP_site\Clicomp.box directory on the CAPs. At the next CCIM cycle on the client (every 23 hours, or when an update is forced through the SMS 2.0 Resource Guide Client Utilities tool (Cliutils.exe) or the Systems Management Control Panel applet), CCIM will connect to the CAP, read the client offer file, and proceed to initiate the installation of the Software Inventory Client Agent by launching Insinv32.exe or Insinv16.exe (depending on the platform). You can find these two files in the CAP_site\Clicomp.box\ Sinv*platform* folder, where *platform* is either Alpha or i386.

Thirty minutes after the Software Inventory Client Agent is started, the first complete inventory is collected from the client as specified by the inventory and collected files options you specified.

Client Requirements and Inventory Frequency

The client computer will require about 200 KB for the Software Inventory Client Agent support files. A complete default inventory will generate a software information file of about 100 KB in size, depending on what you told the agent to scan for and how much data it found. Software inventory history is maintained on each client in the \MS\SMS\Clicomp\Sinv\Sinv.his file. The initial inventory is also passed to the CAP and then to the site server. Like hardware inventory, subsequent software inventory cycles generally report only changes to the inventory. Therefore, you can expect a corresponding amount of network traffic associated with the installation (one time), with the first complete inventory (one time), and with subsequent delta inventories (according to your schedule).

As with hardware inventory, the schedule you choose should reflect the frequency with which you need to collect or update the inventory record of your clients. If your clients have fairly standard software installations and do not make or are not allowed to make substantial changes on their own, you could collect inventory less frequently—say, once a week or even once a month.

If your client computers keep changing in terms of software installations, updates, and uninstalls, you may need to report changes to the inventory more frequently—perhaps once a day or once every 12 hours. The more frequent the inventory is collected, the more potential network traffic will be generated. Like the Hardware Inventory Client Agent, the Software Inventory Client Agent will continue to run and report inventory regardless of whether a user is actually logged onto the client.

> **Tip** Software inventory can be forced to run through the Systems Management Control Panel applet. Double-click on the applet to display the Systems Management Properties window, and click on the Components tab. Select the Software Inventory Agent entry in the Component list, and then click Start Component.

Multiple Sites and Software Inventory

Earlier in this chapter, we talked about the possibility of a client being assigned to more than one SMS site and the effect on hardware inventory. Recall that in this situation, SMS will follow predefined rules to determine which agent properties from which SMS site take precedence over the others. If software inventory is enabled on any one site, it will be installed on the client. Inventory frequency is determined by the principal site. If, however, the principal site has disabled software inventory, inventory will still be collected according to the schedule of the next site that has software inventory enabled.

The principal site for each client can be set through the Systems Management Control Panel applet installed on each SMS client. To set the principal site, open the Systems Management applet on the client in question and select the Sites tab to view a list of all the SMS sites to which the client has been assigned. Unless the client is a member of multiple SMS sites, only one site will appear here. If the list contains multiple entries, the entry at the top of the list is designated the principal site. To change the principal site, use the Move Up and Move Down buttons.

In addition, the Software Inventory Client Agent will report on all file types configured on all the sites to which the client is assigned—that is, if site A reports on .EXE files and site B reports on .DLL files, the Software Inventory Client Agent will scan for both .EXE and .DLL files. The same is true for collected files specified in multiple sites. The amount of data collected and reported will represent the highest level of detail specified at any of the sites.

Software Inventory Collection Process Flow

Now let's explore the software inventory collection process in more detail. This process is illustrated in Figure 9-27. Remember that the inventory collection process is the same for both 16-bit and 32-bit clients.

The first time inventory collection runs—30 minutes after installation of the Software Inventory Client Agent—a complete software inventory is collected and its history is written to the \MS\SMS\Clicomp\Sinv\Sinv.his file on the client. Each subsequent inventory generates a delta file, containing the details for only those inventory properties that have changed since the last interval. When a complete inventory file has been generated, Sinv32.exe writes a temporary file with an .SIC (software inventory complete) extension to the \MS\SMS\Clicomp\Sinv folder on the client. For subsequent inventory cycles, this delta file will have an .SID (software inventory delta) extension.

Copy Queue Manager renames the file with a unique filename but retains the file extension (.SIC or .SID). It then copies the file to the CAP_site\Sinv.box folder on the CAP. At this point, the software inventory process is complete on the client. The SMS Client Service will start the Software Inventory Client Agent again at the next scheduled interval.

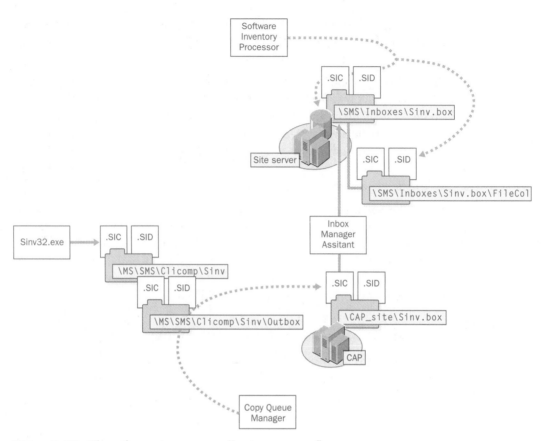

Figure 9-27. *The software inventory collection process flow.*

Note Once Copy Queue Manager copies the inventory file to the CAP, the temporary files (.SIC and .SID) are deleted.

Inbox Manager Assistant running on the CAP in turn moves the file to Software Inventory Processor's inbox (the SMS\Inboxes\Sinv.box folder) on the site server. If the site server is a primary site server, Software Inventory Processor writes the data to the SMS database on the SQL server. If the file is deemed corrupt, it is written to the SMS\Inboxes\Sinv.box\Badsinv folder. If a parent site exists, Software Inventory Processor forwards the MIF file to Replication Manager, which forwards the file to the Software Inventory Processor inbox on the parent site server. Collected files are removed from the inventory file and written to the SMS\Inboxes\Sinv.box\FileCol\ID folder. Files collected from SMS clients are stored in a separate ID folder for each client. The ID folder name represents the resource ID assigned to the client when the client was discovered.

> **Tip** You can find each client's resource ID by viewing its discovery data in the Collections folder in the SMS Administrator Console or by creating a query to display the resource IDs for all the clients.

Software Resynchronization

Occasionally, Software Inventory Processor may determine that the inventory data it receives is somehow "bad," or out of sync with the SMS database. In these circumstances, a resync will be triggered automatically. The following events can trigger a software inventory resync:

- Software Inventory Processor tries to update data that does not exist in the SMS site database.

- The inventory data has been corrupted.

- The client computer has attached to an SMS site different from the one shown in the last inventory.

When one of these events triggers a resync, Software Inventory Processor creates a .CFG file for the client and writes a resync request to it. As with the hardware inventory, this file is maintained in the SMS\Inboxes\Clidata.src folder on the site server. Inbox Manager writes this file to the corresponding folder on the CAP (CAP_Site\Clidata.box). The next time CCIM runs (on its 23-hour cycle or after a forced update), the .CFG file is read, the client's registry is updated with the resync information (on 32-bit clients only), and the SMS Client Service directs the Software Inventory Agent to generate a complete software inventory.

Status Messages and Log Files for Software Inventory

As we've seen, status messages and log files are generated throughout the inventory installation and collection process. As we did for hardware inventory, let's begin here with the log files. As you know, client logs are enabled by default and are written automatically to the \MS\SMS\Logs folder on each client. As you monitor the installation of the Software Inventory Client Agent, look for entries related to the detection of the Software Inventory Client Agent offer in the Ccim32.log file. Monitor the SMSapm32.log file for entries that show when the Advertised Programs Monitor scheduled the installation of the Software Inventory Client Agent on the client. Insinv32.log tracks the agent installation. Figure 9-28 shows examples of the entries you might find in these logs using SMS Trace.

To track the generation of software inventory files on the client, monitor the Sinv32.log. Cqmgr32.log tracks the copying of inventory and status messages to the CAP. Monitoring the log files for Software Inventory Processor (Sinvproc.log),

Inbox Manager (Inboxmgr.log), and Inbox Manager Assistant (Inboxast.log) can help you determine the role of these files in the software inventory collection process.

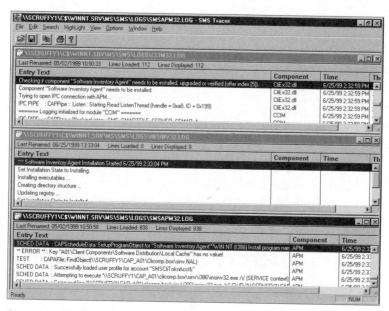

Figure 9-28. *Sample entries for Ccim32.log, SMSapm32.log and Insinv32.log.*

Within 60 minutes of installation, CCIM will generate a status message announcing the successful installation of the Software Inventory Client Agent. The Software Inventory Client Agent itself will generate a status message after the first inventory collection and again after every subsequent collection. Copy Queue Manager forwards these status messages to Status Manager's inbox on the CAP (CAP_Site\Statmsgs.box), and Inbox Manager Assistant forwards them from the CAP to Status Manager's inbox on the site server (SMS\Inboxes\Statmgr.box). You can view these status messages by running a status message query through the SMS Administrator Console using a process similar to that for hardware inventory.

Figure 9-29 shows an example of status messages generated by the installation of the Software Inventory Client Agent and the collection of the inventory from the client. These messages are obtained after running the status message query All Status Messages From A Specific System. The message with ID 10600 indicates that inventory has been successfully collected; 10605 indicates that a file has been collected; 10204 from CCIMreports that the Software Inventory Client Agent was successfully installed. Notice that CCIM reported the installation 60 minutes later, in accordance with its verification cycle.

On the site server, monitor the status messages of Software Inventory Processor. Look for messages in the 37*xx* range, which identify successful processing of MIF files. Also monitor status messages for Replication Manager for forwarding of MIF files to a parent site.

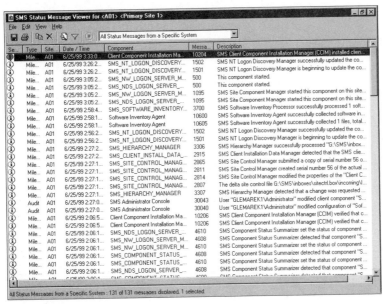

Figure 9-29. *The SMS Status Message Viewer window.*

Viewing Software Inventory

You can view software inventory through the SMS Administrator Console in much the same way as you view hardware inventory. The procedure is described here:

1. Navigate to the Collections folder and expand it.

2. Select the collection that contains the client or clients whose inventory you want to view, right-click on the client entry, choose All Tasks from the context menu, and then choose Start Resource Explorer to display the Resource Explorer window, shown in Figure 9-30.

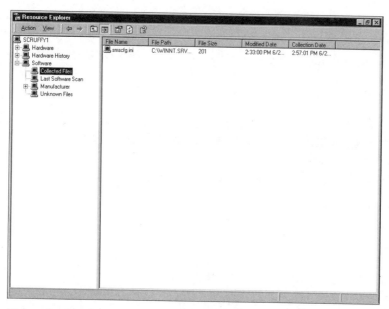

Figure 9-30. *The Resource Explorer window.*

3. Expand Software, and select Collected Files to view a list of files collected for the client.

> **Tip** Properties are listed horizontally across the viewing screen, requiring you to scroll across to view all the properties. If you right-click on an object and choose Properties from the context menu, you can view the same properties listed vertically in a Properties window.

4. Select Last Software Scan to determine the last time the agent ran, as shown in Figure 9-31.

5. Expand Manufacturer to view the product data collected by the Software Inventory Client Agent, as shown in Figure 9-32. Expand each entry to see more specific version information. As you select each version, you can view the filename (and other attributes) associated with this product, assuming that you enabled the Files Associated With Known Products option for the agent.

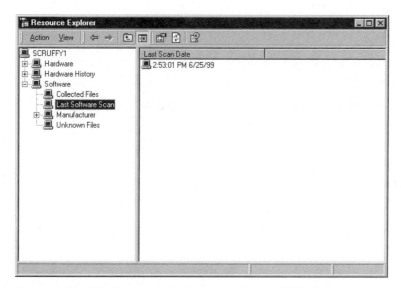

Figure 9-31. *The Resource Explorer window, with Last Software Scan selected.*

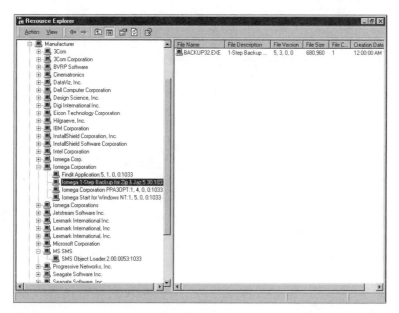

Figure 9-32. *The Resource Explorer window, with Manufacturer expanded.*

6. Select Unknown Files to view a list of those files for which the agent could not obtain product information (if you selected the Files Not Associated With Known Products option when you configured the agent), as shown in Figure 9-33.

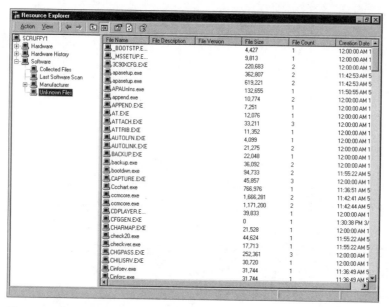

Figure 9-33. *The Resource Explorer window, with Unknown Files selected.*

Real World   **File Path Queries for Collected Files**

You've probably noticed that when you view Collected Files through the Resource Explorer, you do not see the path—that is, the directory on the client in which the files were found. This information is stored with the file information in the SMS database, however, which means that it can be queried. To view the path information, you need to create a query.

To create a simple query to display all the properties of the selected file, follow these steps:

1. In the SMS Administrator Console, navigate to the Queries folder.

2. Right-click on Queries, choose New from the context menu, and then choose Query to display the Query Properties window, shown in Figure 9-34.

Figure 9-34. *The Query Properties window.*

3. On the General tab, enter a descriptive name for the query and a comment if desired. From the Object Type drop-down list, select System Resource.

4. Click Edit Query Statement to display the Query Statement Properties window, as shown in Figure 9-35.

   On the General tab, you define the query results view—that is, which attributes you want displayed when you run the query. Click the New button to display the Result Properties window.

5. Click the Select button to display the Select Attribute dialog box, shown in Figure 9-36.

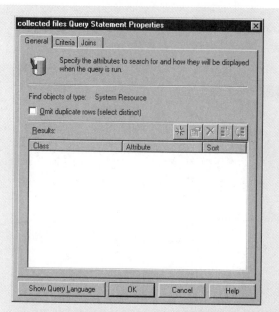

Figure 9-35. *The Query Statement Properties window.*

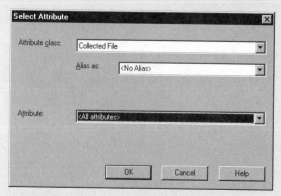

Figure 9-36. *The Select Attribute dialog box.*

6. Select the attribute class *Collected Files* and the attribute (*File Name, File Path, File Size,* and so on) you want to display. Then click OK.

   Repeat this process until you have added all the attributes you are interested in displaying when you run the query, or choose All Attributes as your Attribute option to display all the attributes.

7. Click OK again to return to the Query Statement Properties window. On the Criteria tab, you will define what the query should look for.

8. Click the New button to display the Criterion Properties window, shown in Figure 9-37.

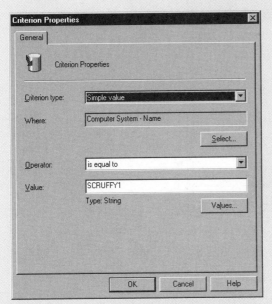

Figure 9-37. *The Criterion Properties window.*

9. Click the Select button once again to display the Select Attribute dialog box, and select an attribute class and an attribute to search on. Since you want to list all collected files for a specific client in this example, select Computer System as your attribute class and Name as the attribute, and click OK to return to the Criterion Properties window.

10. Select an operator from the drop-down list, and enter a value to search on or click the Values button to view the current values in the database. Then click OK.

11. Choose OK to return to the Query Statement Properties window, as shown in Figure 9-38, and click OK again to save your query.

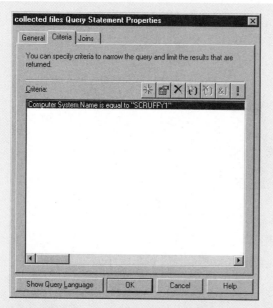

Figure 9-38. *The Query Statement Properties window.*

To execute your new query, follow these steps:

1. In the SMS Administrator Console, navigate to the Queries folder and expand it.

2. Select your new query, right-click on it, and choose Run Query from the context menu. The query result is displayed with the result attributes you selected, as shown in Figure 9-39.

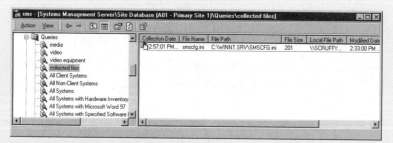

Figure 9-39. *The SMS Administrator Console showing the query results.*

You will now see the path included as part of the query results. With a little modification, you can make this query more generic and useful by having it prompt you for the client name when you execute it.

Summary

Well that's it for the inventory collection process. As you can see, SMS 2.0 can report on a lot of "stuff"—both hardware-related and software-related. Using MOF Manager and customized NOIDMIF and IDMIF files, you can append data to the existing client architecture and add new architectures, object classes, and attributes to the database. You can view inventory through Resource Explorer, and you can further refine what you see through the use of queries.

> **Note**   Because the inventory process is fairly straightforward, this chapter did not include a "Checkpoints" section. Any problems you might encounter can be easily spotted and corrected by monitoring the log files and status messages. You're more likely to encounter issues as you work with MOF Manager and create custom MIF files, and in that regard, there are no better resources than the *Systems Management Server 2.0 Administrator's Guide* and the Microsoft Systems Management Server 2.0 Resource Guide.

In Chapter 10, we'll continue our exploration of client management tools as we look at Remote Tools.

Chapter 10
Remote Control of Client Systems

As most of us know from experience, many computer-related problems can be solved only through a hands-on approach. We have to see the error message displayed, or re-create the scenario that caused a crash, or watch the user perform a task. So it is no surprise that being able to remotely control client systems appeals to the typical administrator. Tools that provide remote access and diagnostic abilities have actually been around for a while. Some are built into existing tools, such as User Manager For Domains in Microsoft Windows NT, which allows the administrator to connect to a different domain for which permission has been granted to administer accounts. Some tools are separate applications that provide a broader scope of functionality.

Remote control has long been a key feature of Microsoft Systems Management Server (SMS) and has been enhanced in SMS 2.0 with Service Pack 1 applied. With SMS 2.0's Remote Tools, the SMS administrator can remotely diagnose a client, start and stop services, view the user's desktop, run programs, transfer files, and specify how much control to allow the user over the session. The user also can be given the ability to determine who can access the client and what remote functions are made available.

In this chapter, you'll learn about the remote control tools available with SMS 2.0 and how to use them. We'll look at the configuration of remote control for the client, including system requirements, protocol considerations, and configuring the remote options at the client system. Then we'll take a look at the Remote Tools installation process itself and how to monitor status of the remote client and network performance. Last, we'll explore several *Microsoft BackOffice 4.5 Resource Kit* utilities and look at some troubleshooting issues.

Configuring a Client for Remote Control

SMS Remote Tools enables you to deliver help desk support from your (the SMS administrator's) desktop to all supported SMS 2.0 clients. As with other SMS components, you begin with configuring the client component through the SMS Administrator Console. Keep in mind that, like other client agent settings, the Remote Tools Client Agent (also sometimes referred to as the Remote Tools Agent) settings are configured and effective on a sitewide basis.

If you enable Remote Tools for a site, the Remote Tools Client Agent is enabled and installed on all SMS clients that belong to that SMS site—with no exceptions. If you require users to give permission for an administrator to initiate a Remote Tools session, permission will be required on all SMS clients that belong to that site. This is the nature of all SMS client agents. Fortunately, the *Microsoft BackOffice 4.5 Resource Kit* (available through Microsoft Press) includes several utilities on its companion CD that alter how the Remote Tools Client Agent functions on different SMS clients. We'll look at these utilities in the section "Resource Kit Utilities" later in this chapter.

Let's begin our discussion of configuration by looking at the client system requirements, including network connection considerations. Then we'll look at the configuration of the Remote Tools Client Agent and the remote options.

Client System Requirements

Clients must meet the following general requirements to use Remote Tools for monitoring and control:

- The client must be installed as an SMS client. This will allow the client to receive and run the Remote Tools Client Agent.

- The Remote Tools Client Agent must be installed and started on the client computer. Each client platform uses different agents, services, or utilities to support remote functions.

- Access to the client must be allowed. The level of remote access to the client must be defined, including who has the ability to initiate a session.

- The SMS Administrator Console computer and the client must use a common protocol. This can be either the same NetBIOS protocol (NetBEUI or TCP/IP) or IPX; 32-bit Microsoft Windows clients also allow Windows Sockets over TCP/IP.

> **Note** SMS can remotely monitor and control clients that are connected to the network locally or via a WAN. SMS can also perform remote functions when an SMS administrator connects to the client's network using Remote Access Service (RAS) through a minimum 28.8-Kbps connection; however, performance degrades significantly for connections lower than 56 Kbps.

If your clients meet these requirements, you can proceed with enabling and configuring the Remote Tools Client Agent, as we'll see in the next section.

Configuring the Remote Tools Client Agent

The Remote Tools Client Agent is the only component that needs to be configured to enable remote control functionality for your site. To verify that you have installed this agent when you installed your site server, check the list of client agents in the Client Agents folder under Site Settings in the SMS Administrator Console, as shown in Figure 10-1. If you don't see the Remote Tools Client Agent listed there, rerun the SMS Setup application from the SMS 2.0 CD to add the component to your site server. (Refer to Chapter 2 for more information about the installation process.)

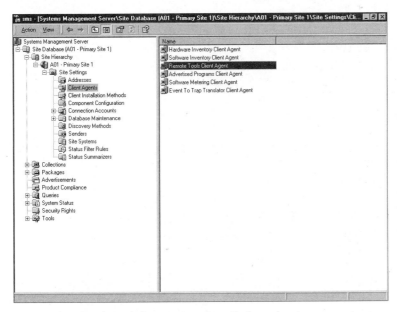

Figure 10-1. *A list of client agents installed on the site server.*

> **Note** If you install SMS using the Express Setup option, Remote Tools will be installed and enabled automatically. If you choose the Custom Setup option, you must choose the Remote Tools option; Custom installation does not enable Remote Tools by default.

Once the Remote Tools component has been installed, we must specify what remote features we want to enable for the clients in our site and how the Remote Tools sessions should be established. To enable and configure the Remote Tools Client Agent, follow these steps:

1. In the SMS Administrator Console, navigate to the Site Settings folder and expand it, and select the Client Agents folder to display the list of client agents (Figure 10-1).

2. Right-click on Remote Tools Client Agent, and choose Properties from the context menu to display the Remote Tools Client Agent Properties window, shown in Figure 10-2.

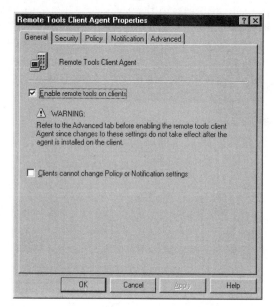

Figure 10-2. *The Remote Tools Client Agent Properties window.*

3. On the General tab, select the Enable Remote Tools On Clients check box.

4. In SMS 2.0, you now have the ability to "lock" your configuration of Remote Tools so that users cannot arbitrarily change your settings. If you want to enable this feature, select the Clients Cannot Change Policy Or Notification Settings check box.

5. Click on the Security tab, shown in Figure 10-3. Here you create the Permitted Viewers list. This list defines which users or user groups are allowed to perform remote functions on Windows NT clients. Before a Remote Tools session can be established on a Windows NT client, the client agent will evaluate this list to determine whether the administrator initiating the session is a valid member.

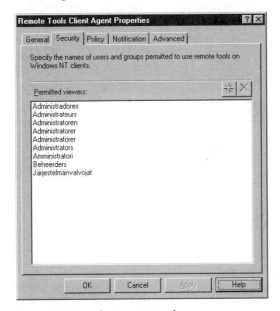

Figure 10-3. *The Security tab.*

Notice that by default the local Administrators group—in every language supported by Windows NT—is listed under Permitted Viewers. For network performance reasons, you may want to keep this list lean and mean—in other words, include only the users or user groups that are responsible for remote support.

6. To add users or user groups to this list, click the New button (the yellow star) to display the New Viewer dialog box, and enter the name of the Windows NT user or global group.

Note   If you use more than 512 characters in the Permitted Viewers list, you won't be allowed to carry out any remote control functions on Windows NT or Windows 2000 clients. The Permitted Viewers list starts and ends with a null character, and a null character appears between each entry in the list. When you count characters, remember to include these null characters.

7. Click on the Policy tab, shown in Figure 10-4. This tab contains settings that define the scope of remote access and the permission level.

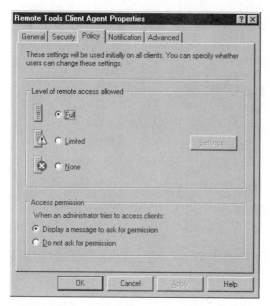

Figure 10-4. *The Policy tab.*

Three levels of access are available:

- **Full**   Allows all remote functions and diagnostics to be run
- **Limited**   Selects individual functions
- **None**   Prohibits remote control

8. If you choose Limited, click the Settings button to display the Default Limited Remote Tools Settings dialog box, shown in Figure 10-5, which contains a list of remote functions to enable or disable.

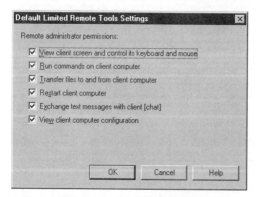

Figure 10-5. *The Default Limited Remote Tools Settings dialog box.*

As you can see, all of these options are enabled by default. Each of the options you select here generates a different level of network traffic, and the first option probably generates the most traffic. Click OK to return to the Policy tab.

9. In the Access Permission section, you can indicate whether you want the user to give permission for the Remote Tools session to be initiated. If you select Display A Message To Ask For Permission, the user will have to respond Yes or No in a pop-up message box before the session can begin. This option may be required in organizations that must comply with C2-level security guidelines.

10. Click on the Notification tab, shown in Figure 10-6. On this tab, you specify how the client will be notified that a Remote Tools session has been established.

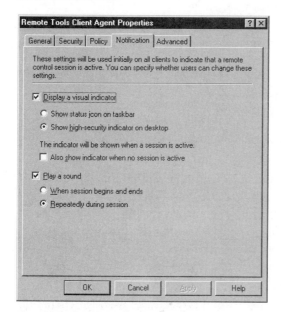

Figure 10-6. *The Notification tab.*

By default, both a visual and an audible indicator will be enabled on the client. The visual indicator can be either a taskbar status icon or a high-security icon that appears in the top-right corner of the user's desktop and cannot be hidden. You can optionally have the indicators display when no Remote Tools session is active. Audible indicator choices include playing a sound when the session begins and ends or repeatedly throughout the session (the default).

11. Click on the Advanced tab, shown in Figure 10-7. This tab allows you to specify several advanced feature settings that affect the performance of remote functions.

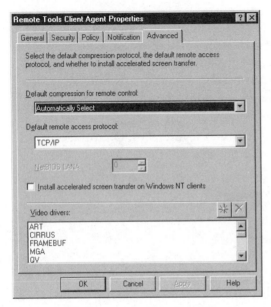

Figure 10-7. *The Advanced tab.*

12. Remote Tools uses low-compression and high-compression methods to control the demands on network bandwidth generated during Remote Tools sessions. Using the Default Compression For Remote Control option, you can select either method for all clients to follow, or you can allow SMS to select the optimal compression method on a per-client basis. By default, the agent will negotiate for the most appropriate compression method based on the processor speed of the client.

If you select Low (RLE), SMS uses the Run Length Encoding (RLE) compression method. This setting should typically be used for clients with CPUs that are slower than a 150-MHz Pentium processor. This method works well on slower CPUs because of the lower demand on CPU cycles. It can also help resolve video transfer problems that may arise from hardware incompatibilities on the client.

If you select High (LZ), SMS uses the Lempel-Ziv (LZ) compression method. This is a math-intensive compression algorithm, and therefore it requires more intensive CPU processing. This method of compression should be configured for clients with 150-MHz Pentium processors or higher. This setting minimizes network utilization; however, it may also impact client performance during the Remote Tools session.

13. From the Default Remote Access Protocol drop-down list, choose the protocol for use with clients. By default, clients will use TCP/IP, but you can choose IPX or NetBIOS. If you specify NetBIOS as the default protocol, you can also set the LANA bound protocol number. Normally this will be set to 0, but if you are using multiple network cards or protocols on your client you can specify the LANA number (0 through 7) that will have the NetBIOS protocol bound to it.

14. For your Windows NT clients, you can optionally enable the Install Accelerated Screen Transfer On Windows NT Clients option. Choose a driver from the Video Drivers list, a list of drivers that have been tested by Microsoft and that can run with the screen transfer "wrapper" Idisntkm.dll that SMS installs on the client when this option is enabled. The *wrapper* is a piece of program code that helps to speed up the screen transfer during a Remote Tools session.

> **Caution** You can add drivers to this list by clicking the New button. However, the screen transfer software works only with the video drivers listed and any other drivers compatible with those listed. If you add a driver to the list, be sure to test and ensure that the Remote Tools session works properly.

15. Click OK to begin the site update process.

As usual, the Remote Tools Client Agent will be installed on the SMS clients during the next update cycle on the client or when the client forces an update through the Systems Management applet in the Control Panel. At this point, an SMS administrator will be able to initiate a Remote Tools session according to the options you configured for the agent.

> **Caution** If you make changes to any of the options on the Advanced tab of the Remote Tools Client Agent Properties window after the Remote Control Client Agent has been installed on the clients, the clients will not receive the new settings. In this case, you could uninstall the agent by disabling it at the site server, updating the clients, and then reenabling the agent so that the clients can get the new settings.

Remote Tools Client Agent Installation Process Flow

Until the Remote Tools Client Agent is enabled for a site, no Remote Tools client components are installed on the clients in that site. If the Remote Tools Client Agent is enabled for a site, the client components are installed on each client in the site at the next client maintenance update cycle (every 23 hours) or when an update is forced using the Systems Management applet in Control Panel

When either of these update events occurs, the client executes either Remctrl.exe (on 32-bit clients) or Remc16.exe (on 16-bit clients). These programs install the Remote Tools Client Agent and its support files, including 32-bit or 16-bit versions of Remote Control support (Wuser32 or Wuser), the File Transfer Slave Agent (Wslave32 or Wslave16), and Remote Chat support (Wchat32 or Wchat16). All in all, about 1.8 MB of disk space will be required on the client, and a corresponding amount of network traffic will be generated.

Depending on the client platform, the Remote Tools Client Agent is installed and started. On Windows NT and Windows 2000 clients, Wuser32 is installed as a service, the appropriate registry keys are created and updated, and Launch32 starts Wuser32. Additionally, two other services are loaded to support virtual keyboard and mouse devices—KBStuff.sys and RCHelp.sys. On Windows 95 and Windows 98 clients, Wuser32 is installed as a client service (a pseudo-service), the appropriate registry keys are created and updated, and Clisvc95.exe starts Wuser32. On Windows 3.x clients, Wuser is installed as a client service, SMSrc16.ini is created and updated, Vuser.386 is loaded into System.ini, and Launch16.exe starts Wuser. SMSrc16.ini acts as an initialization file for storing Remote Tools properties since Windows 3.x clients do not have a registry.

The Remote Control application contains two programs, Hardware Munger and Security Munger. A *munger* basically reconciles configuration settings relating to network interface cards (NICs) and protocols on the client with settings from multiple sites that the client may belong to. The Hardware Munger runs once at installation or when a Repair Installation procedure is run through the Systems Management applet in Control Panel. The Hardware Munger is responsible for determining the default protocol to use for Remote Tools sessions, the compression type, and video acceleration. If different compression, protocol, or acceleration configurations exist on the multiple sites to which the client belongs, the Hardware Munger is also responsible for reconciling those settings. For example, if the client belongs to three sites with two sites identifying TCP/IP as the default protocol and the other using IPX, TCP/IP will win by majority. If there is no clear winner, the Hardware Munger favors TCP/IP, then NetBIOS, then IPX.

The Security Munger runs whenever a change is made to the SMS-related registry keys on the client. It updates the Remote Tools Client Agent settings on the client, and if the client belongs to multiple sites, it reconciles remote agent settings from multiple SMS sites. In general, the Security Munger will always reconcile disparate settings in favor of the most restrictive or most secure setting. For example, if the client belongs to three sites and one site requires user permission while the other sites do not, the client will be set to require user permission before a Remote Tools session can occur.

> **Tip** For more information about mungers and other processes related to Remote Tools, refer to Chapter 9 of the Microsoft Systems Management Server 2.0 Resource Guide (part of the *Microsoft BackOffice 4.5 Resource Kit*).

Each step in the installation process is recorded on the client in the MS\SMS\Clicomp\RemCtrl\Install.log file as well as in the MS\SMS\Logs\Remctrl.log, as shown in Figures 10-8 and 10-9. Notice in Figure 10-9 the notation regarding the initialization of the Hardware Munger (Rchwcfg.exe) process.

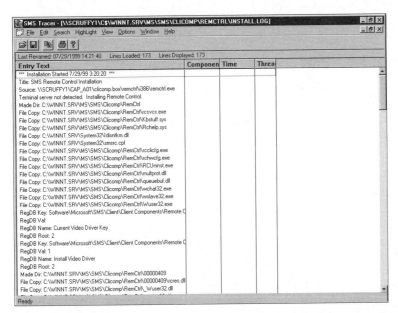

Figure 10-8. *Sample Install.log file, showing the installation process for Remote Tools.*

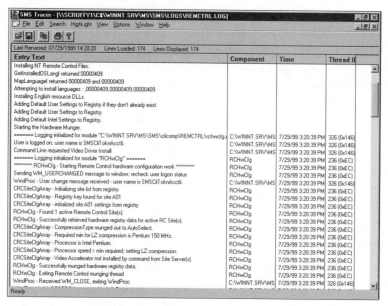

Figure 10-9. *Sample Remctrl.log file.*

Setting Remote Options at the Client System

If the SMS administrator does not enable the option Clients Cannot Change Policy Or Notification Settings on the General tab of the Remote Tools Client Agent Properties window, the user at the client computer will be able to choose some site settings for the Remote Tools session. For example, the user can specify which remote functions to enable, whether permission for the Remote Tools session must be granted first, and how the Remote Tools session will be announced on the client system. The user can modify the remote control options on the client from the Remote Control applet in Control Panel, which is added when the Remote Tools Client Agent is installed, as shown in Figure 10-10. The client's policy settings will take precedence over the site's default settings. You'll have to determine whether allowing the user such latitude is practical or desirable.

To configure the Remote Tools options, follow these steps:

1. From the client's Control Panel, double-click on the Remote Control applet to display the Remote Control Properties window, shown in Figure 10-11.

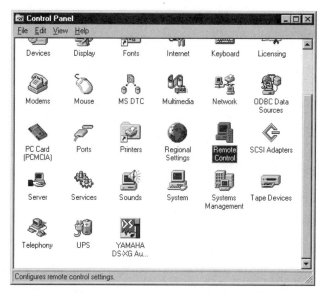

Figure 10-10. *The Remote Control applet added to the client's Control Panel.*

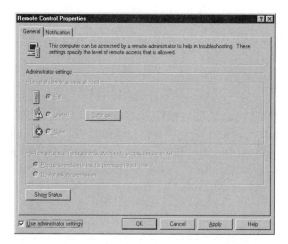

Figure 10-11. *The Remote Control Properties window.*

The settings on the General and Notification tabs will reflect those configured in the SMS Administrator Console.

2. To make a change, clear the Use Administrator Settings check box at the bottom of either tab, and configure the policy and notification settings as described in the previous section.

3. Click the Show Status button on the General tab to display the Remote Control Status dialog box, shown in Figure 10-12, which contains connection information regarding the agent. This information will include the IP address and name of the client, the level of compression and acceleration used, and whether a session is currently active. From this screen, the user can also click Close Session to terminate the session. Users running Windows 3.x will see a different Remote Control Status dialog box with similar information provided.

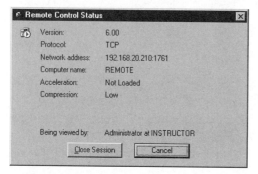

Figure 10-12. *The Remote Control Status dialog box.*

If the Show High-Security Indicator On Desktop visual indicator notification is enabled, users can display the same screen by double-clicking on the face of the indicator.

4. Click OK to save your settings.

When the Remote Tools Client Agent has been correctly configured and installed on your SMS clients, you should be able to establish remote control sessions. However, one of the client requirements mentioned earlier was that the client and the SMS Administrator Console computer both use the same protocol. This requirement is not always as clear cut as we might think, as we'll see in the next section.

Client Protocol Considerations

When you use Remote Tools, the SMS Administrator Console computer and the client computer must share a common protocol. At first glance, this requirement probably seems obvious. However, it is important to note that when the client agent is installed, it automatically binds to the primary protocol on the client computer, and this is the protocol under which the Remote Tools session will be attempted.

The SMS Administrator Console computer will search through its first eight loaded protocols (LANA 0 through 7) looking for the one that matches the primary protocol of the client computer. The values for the eight default protocols are stored in the registry under HKEY_LOCAL_MACHINE\SOFTWARE\ Microsoft\SMS\Components\SightNT\Lana. You can change the order of these protocols or add protocols by modifying this entry.

Caution   Never make modifications to the registry unless you know what you are doing and what effects, if any, your change will produce. Refer to the documentation for Windows NT before modifying this particular key.

Figure 10-13 shows an example of the message box displayed in the SMS Administrator Console while this protocol negotiation takes place.

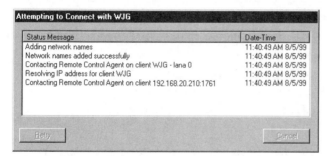

Figure 10-13. *Message box showing the SMS Administrator Console computer's attempts to find and negotiate a protocol for establishing the Remote Tools session.*

For example, suppose that the SMS Administrator Console computer has only TCP/IP installed and the client computer has NetBEUI and TCP/IP installed, with NetBEUI as the primary protocol. In this case, the Remote Tools Client Agent will use NetBEUI as its protocol. When a Remote Tools session is attempted, it won't be established because the SMS Administrator Console computer and the client do not have a common Remote Tools protocol.

You can either change the protocol order on the client or reconfigure the settings on the Advanced tab in the Remote Tools Client Agent Properties window to use a different LANA number. The problem, of course, is that these settings are sitewide, and perhaps not all your clients experience the same problem. Changing the LANA number may clear up the issue for some clients and introduce it for other clients. Fortunately, there is now a *Microsoft BackOffice 4.5 Resource Kit* utility, RCCliopt.exe, that allows you to set the LANA number on a per-client basis. You can also find this utility in the Support\Reskit\Bin*Platform*\Diagnose directory on the SMS 2.0 CD. We'll look at this utility in the section "Remote Control Settings (RCCliopt.exe)" later in this chapter.

> **Note** When you upgrade the site server with SMS Service Pack 1, the support directory files and folders mentioned above are replaced with a single executable setup. When you execute this setup file, the support tools are expanded and written to a new folder named SMS 2.0 Supportability Tools, created under C:\Program Files by default. The RCCliopt.exe tool can be found here in the subfolder mentioned above.

Clients with Multiple Network Interface Cards

A similar issue may arise if your network has clients with more than one NIC installed. By default, the Remote Tools Client Agent binds to the first NIC in the binding order. Changing the NIC to which the client agent binds varies depending on platform

On Windows 3.x clients, in each client's Windows or Windows\System directory, create a file named Imp.ini that includes the following section:

```
[Protocol]
Subnet = xxx.xxx.xxx.xxx
SubnetMask = xxx.xxx.xxx.xxx
```

The IP addresses you specify should be those of the NIC to which you want the Remote Tools Client Agent to bind.

On Windows 95, Windows 98, Windows NT, and Windows 2000 clients, using the Registry Editor, locate the key HKEY_LOCAL_MACHINE\Software\SMS\ Client\Client Components\Remote Control. Add new string type values to this key named *Subnet* and *SubnetMask*, each containing the appropriate address value for the NIC you want the agent to bind to. This forces the client agent to bind to the NIC specified by the subnet and subnet mask.

Remote Tools and TCP/IP

In most sites today, you will be configuring Remote Tools for use over TCP/IP. TCP/IP must be configured to communicate with other network components. The SMS Remote Tools function communicates over NetBIOS. This protocol allows Remote Tools to register and use unique NetBIOS names for communication between the SMS Administrator Console computer and the client. So for SMS to establish a Remote Tools session with a client, it must be able to resolve the client's NetBIOS name with an IP address. The easiest way to ensure that this resolution can occur is to configure your network to use WINS or DNS to provide name resolution services.

Note   It should go without saying that we are, of course, talking about Microsoft WINS and DNS services here. Other implementations won't work.

If your network environment does not include a WINS server for NetBIOS name registration and you want to use NetBIOS over TCP/IP, it may be necessary to configure an LMHOSTS file on the SMS Administrator Console computer. As you know, this is a text file that contains a list of clients and their IP addresses. This file will also provide the name-to-IP address resolution required for Remote Tools to function properly. When configuring the LMHOSTS file entries, consider the following requirements:

- Each entry will include the IP address, client name, and remote function code, as shown here:

  xxx.xxx.xxx.xxx "clientname A"

- The client name and remote function code must be enclosed in quotation marks.

- Each client name and remote function code entry must be exactly 16 characters in length. Add spaces between the client name and remote function code as necessary.

- The remote function code is the 16th (last) character and can be either A (enables chat), C (enables remote control), or E (enables file transfer).

Note   The default LMHOSTS file on Windows NT systems is located in the WINNT\System32\Drivers\Etc directory on the SMS Administrator Console computer and can be configured using a text editor.

The LMHOSTS file would need to be configured on every SMS Administrator Console computer that would be performing Remote Tools tasks. If you were enabling remote control, file transfer, and chat for a 1000 clients, that would entail 3000 entries for each LMHOSTS file. (We'll look at Remote Tools in detail in the section "Remote Functions" later in this chapter.) The moral of this story: use WINS or DNS.

Using Remote Tools over RAS Connections

As an SMS administrator, you may need to diagnose a problem or assist a client over a RAS connection. Remote Tools enables you to connect to client computers over such connections. Consider the following requirements when you are using Remote Tools over RAS:

- To use Remote Tools over a RAS connection, the link should be at least 28.8 Kbps. Keep in mind that this is a minimum specification—as with any remote connection, faster is better. Also, remember to disable any wallpaper settings.
- The SMS Administrator Console computer will connect to the remote RAS server, so you must install and configure the RAS client software on this computer.
- The SMS Administrator Console computer, the RAS server, and the remote client computer must be running the same NetBIOS transport protocol.
- At the site containing the remote client, a RAS server must be located on the same LAN as the remote client computer.

SMS can dial the remote site automatically before connecting to the destination client on another SMS site. This is accomplished through Gateway.dll. Gateway.dll initiates the RAS connection to the remote LAN and authenticates the user by communicating with a RAS server that exists on the same LAN as the remote client. When the Remote Tools session is terminated, Gateway.dll disconnects the target LAN and closes the session.

Note Remote Tools sessions with NetWare clients are not supported over RAS connections.

Exploring Remote Tools Functions

The SMS administrator is frequently called on to diagnose problems on client computers. Remote Tools enables you to run diagnostics on Windows 3.x, Windows 95, Windows 98, Windows NT (3.51 and 4.0), and Windows 2000 clients. This diagnostic information can then be used to help analyze and troubleshoot client hardware and other problems. Although most of the more recent Windows client versions are supported in SMS, there are some differences in the diagnostic procedures and test results for the various Windows clients.

Running Diagnostic Tools for Windows NT and Windows 2000 Clients

The diagnostic tools for Windows NT and Windows 2000 clients are based on the standard Windows NT Diagnostics utility (WinMsd). The Diagnostics utility provides a static view of the system configuration parameters, services, resources, environment settings, and other system information.

To run the Diagnostics utility, follow these steps:

1. In the SMS Administrator Console, navigate to Collections and select the collection that contains the Windows NT or Windows 2000 client for which you want to initiate remote diagnostics.

2. Select the client, right-click on it, choose All Tasks from the context menu as shown in Figure 10-14, and then choose Start Windows NT Diagnostics.

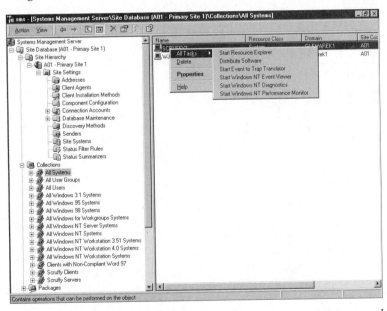

Figure 10-14. *Choosing All Tasks from the context menu to access the Start Windows NT Diagnostics utility.*

3. The Windows NT Diagnostics window appears, as shown in Figure 10-15. This is the same Windows NT Diagnostics window you would see if you were logged on at the client and executed the utility there. You can select one of the nine tabs to view information about the hardware connected to the computer and identify device drivers and services that should be started when you start the computer. For more information about running this utility, see the Windows NT product documentation.

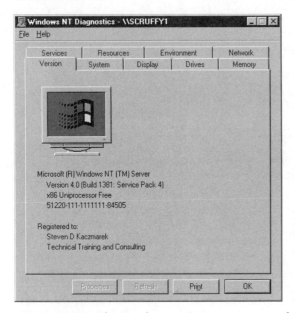

Figure 10-15. *The Windows NT Diagnostics window.*

4. When you have finished, click OK to close the window.

> **Note** You can also run the Windows NT Event Viewer and Performance Monitor utilities remotely for Windows NT and Windows 2000 clients by choosing All Tasks from the context menu.

Running Diagnostic Tools for Windows 3.x, Windows 95, and Windows 98 Clients

The diagnostic tools for Windows 3.x, Windows 95, and Windows 98 clients are run from the Remote Tools window, shown in Figure 10-16.

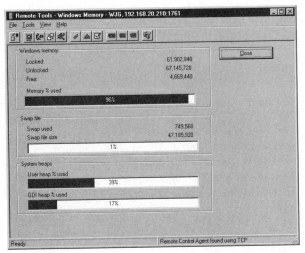

Figure 10-16. *The Remote Tools window, showing the result of running the Windows Memory diagnostic for the client WJG.*

From the toolbar or the Tools menu, you can run diagnostic routines on the client computer to view information about memory allocation, CMOS data, interrupt usage, and so on.

To start a Remote Tools session, follow these steps:

1. In the SMS Administrator Console, navigate to Collections, and select the collection that contains the client for which you want to initiate remote tools.

2. Select the client, right-click on it, choose All Tasks from the context menu, and then choose Start Remote Tools to display the Remote Tools window, shown in Figure 10-16.

On the toolbar in the Remote Tools window, the diagnostic tools for Windows clients begin with the sixth icon from the left. They are, in order: Windows Memory, Windows Modules, Windows Tasks, CMOS Information, ROM Information, and DOS Memory Map. If you are running SMS 2.0 but have not yet applied SMS Service Pack 1, you'll see additional options on the toolbar, including Windows Heap Walk, GDI Heap Walk, Windows Classes, Device Drivers, and Interrupt Vectors. SMS Service Pack 1 has streamlined this information and rolled it into the six options visible in Figure 10-16. Table 10-1 lists the diagnostic tools for Windows 3.x, Windows 95, and Windows 98 clients.

Table 10-1. **Diagnostic tools for Windows 3.x, Windows 95, and Windows 98 clients**

Diagnostic Test	Description
Windows Memory	Displays the allocation of memory on the client, providing information about locked, unlocked, and free memory on the remote client; swap file size; user and GDI heap usage; and the largest amount of contiguous memory available on the remote client
Windows Modules	Displays the drivers and libraries loaded on the client at the time the diagnostic was run and provides information such as the module handle, use count, path to the module, and memory objects reserved by the module
Windows Tasks	Displays the tasks currently running on the client, providing information such as handle, instance, queue location and size, waiting events, current directory, and command-line options in effect
CMOS Information	Displays the data stored in the client CMOS for only Intel-based AT-class and later chip sets
ROM Information	Displays the IRQ hooks (if they exist) and ASCII strings for ROM entries on the client
DOS Memory Map	Displays which programs are loaded into conventional (first 640-KB) and upper memory only

When you select one of these diagnostic tools, the client will first be asked to allow permission if that option was enabled for the Remote Tools Client Agent, as shown in Figure 10-17. When permission is granted, or if that option was not enabled for the agent, the Remote Tools window will display the desired information.

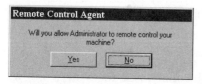

Figure 10-17. *The Remote Control Agent dialog box.*

Ping Test

Another useful Remote Tools function is the Ping Test utility. This utility can be used to determine whether a client is accessible for a Remote Tools session. The Ping Test icon is the rightmost icon on the Remote Tools window toolbar; the utility can also be run from the Tools menu. Ping Test generates and sends packets to the client, waits for a response, and then sends additional packets over a 4-second period to determine the reliability and speed of the connection.

Figure 10-18 shows the results of running a sample ping test. These results include test statistics and a thermometer that visually represents the effectiveness of the connection—red means poor connectivity, yellow means fair, and green means good. To the right of the thermometer, two level indicators can be seen. The yellow (top) arrow indicates the maximum number of packets per second that the test generated; the green (bottom) arrow indicates the average number.

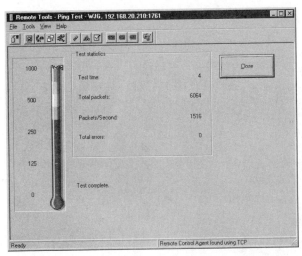

Figure 10-18. *The results of running a sample ping test.*

Remote Functions

Five remote functions are available to the SMS administrator. In order of their position on the toolbar and on the Tools menu, they are (from left to right): Remote Control, Remote Reboot, Remote Chat, Remote File Transfer, and Remote Execute. All of these functions are initiated from the Remote Tools window, but before we can use any of them, SMS must establish a remote connection with the client. If the client session cannot be established, the Remote Tools window will be closed. Remember that the inability to establish a Remote Tools session is typically due to network or client agent configuration problems, as we discussed in the sections "Client System Requirements" and "Client Protocol Considerations" earlier in this chapter. In this section, we'll look more closely at each of these functions.

Remote Control

To initiate a Remote Control session through the Remote Tools window, either click on the first toolbar icon, or choose Remote Control from the Tools menu. The client will first be asked to grant permission for the Remote Control session if that option was enabled for the Remote Tools Client Agent. When permission is granted, or if permission is not required, the Remote Control window appears on the SMS Administrator Console computer, bordered with a moving yellow and black marquee. Figure 10-19 shows an example of a Remote Control window for a Windows 95 client.

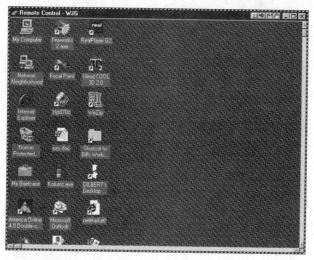

Figure 10-19. *A Remote Control window for a Windows 95 client.*

Here you are viewing the actual desktop of the client computer, and you can manipulate that client's mouse and keyboard. Currently, there is no way to lock the keyboard and mouse from user input. If both the administrator and the user are manipulating the keyboard and mouse, some fascinating control wars can result. To avoid this conflict, it's a good idea to present some kind of visual or audible signal to the user, and probably to require user permission as well, to notify the user that you are establishing the Remote Control session. Otherwise, you could end up creating a whole new set of problems on the client.

Note All mouse and key sequences are passed to the client except Ctrl+Alt+Del, Ctrl+Esc, Alt+Tab, and any hot-key sequences you identify.

The Remote Control window may not be large enough to display the entire client desktop. With SMS 2.0, however, the window can now be fully maximized. To help facilitate control of the desktop, the Remote Control window includes four toolbar buttons in the top right corner for Windows 3.x, Windows 95, and Windows 98 clients and five toolbar buttons for Windows NT and Windows 2000 clients.

The first button displays the Start menu on the client. The second button (an arrow) acts like the Alt+Tab combination on the client and toggles between active windows. The third button allows Alt-key combinations to be passed through to the client instead of being run locally. The fourth button (a hand) activates an area box that can be used to navigate in the Remote Control window when maximizing the screen is not sufficient or practical.

If you established a Remote Control session with a Windows NT client, you will also see a gold key button. Under certain circumstances, it is necessary to log onto a Windows NT–based client as well as lock and unlock the desktop. For example, you might have a Windows NT server system acting as an application server. Servers are usually in a locked or "unlogged-in" state, making any user intervention to the Remote Tools function unavailable. Locking or unlocking a Windows NT system and logging on require a Ctrl+Alt+Del sequence, which we know we cannot initiate from the SMS Administrator Console computer. This is what that gold key button is for. When you click the gold key button, you send a Ctrl+Alt+Del sequence to the Windows NT client. Pretty neat!

> **Caution**   After the Remote Tools Client Agent has been installed on a Windows NT client, it is necessary to restart the Windows NT client at least once before all remote functionality, like the gold key button, becomes enabled. This extra step is needed because a new KBStuff.sys driver is written to the registry and it can only be read and enabled.

In addition to the toolbar buttons, configuration options are available through the Remote Control window's control menu, sometimes referred to as the system menu. This menu is displayed when you click the icon on the left in the title bar. The system menu contains the usual Minimize and Maximize options and also provides Configure, Hot Keys, and Help options.

If you choose Configure, the Control Parameters dialog box will appear, as shown in Figure 10-20.

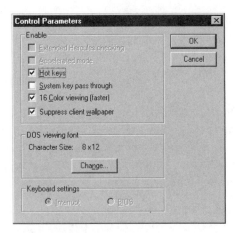

Figure 10-20. *The Control Parameters dialog box.*

From this dialog box, you can set configuration options. These options, which will vary slightly based on your clients, include:

- **Extended Hercules Checking** Monitors a Hercules-based client for text or graphics mode. Available only to support SMS 1.2 MS-DOS clients.

- **Accelerated Mode** Sends screen refreshes from the client at the fastest speed supported by the network. Available only to support SMS 1.2 MS-DOS clients.

- **Hot Keys** Enables hot-key sequences defined under the Hot Keys option to be passed to the client.

- **System Key Pass Through** Disables passing of system key sequences to the client.

- **16 Color Viewing (Faster)** Forces 16-color display resolution on the client to help speed screen transfer.

- **Suppress Client Wallpaper** Disables the client's wallpaper during the Remote Control session—again to help speed screen transfer and minimize network traffic.

- **DOS Viewing Font** Modifies the display font size for Windows 3.x, Windows 95, and Windows 98 clients.

- **Keyboard Settings** Switches between BIOS and interrupt methods of sending key sequences to Windows 3.x, Windows 95, and Windows 98 clients.

If you choose Hot Keys from the system menu, the Hot Key Settings dialog box will appear, as shown in Figure 10-21. In this dialog box, you can define hot-key sequences for seven remote control commands, all of which are fairly self-explanatory.

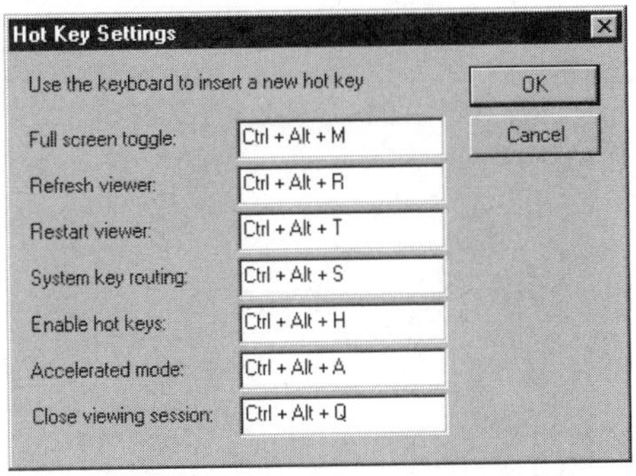

Figure 10-21. *The Hot Key Settings dialog box.*

To end the Remote Control session, simply close the Remote Control window.

Remote Reboot

The client computer can be restarted a couple of ways. One way is to establish a Remote Control session and then, through the Remote Control window, choose Shutdown from the client's Start menu. The advantage of this method is that you can follow the shutdown process and see any messages that may appear, such as a request to close a file or a message indicating an error shutting down a service.

You can also click the Remote Reboot button or choose the Remote Reboot option from the Tools menu in the Remote Tools window. This method has the same result, but since you do not have a Remote Control window open, you will not see the shutdown process. Indeed, you might not know for sure whether the client actually shut down—it might be waiting for some kind of user input.

Remote Chat

Remote Chat is similar to a chat room on the Internet. It provides an avenue through which the SMS administrator can communicate with the user. It can be used when a voice connection is not available, for example. When you start a chat session, the user is prompted first for permission, if that option was enabled. Then the SMS administrator and the user are presented with a chat window similar to the one shown in Figure 10-22. The top text box always represents the remote person, and the bottom text box represents the local person. When the session is over, either party can click Exit Chat to terminate the session.

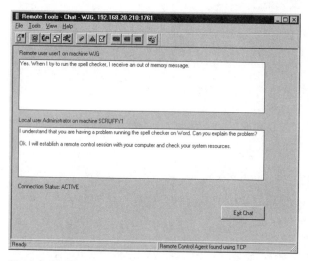

Figure 10-22. *A sample Remote Chat session.*

Remote File Transfer

The Remote File Transfer tool provides a means to initiate file, folder, and tree copies between the SMS Administrator Console computer and the client computer. This feature has been greatly enhanced in SMS 2.0. In addition to the change in the interface itself, SMS 2.0 now allows copies of folders and directories.

When the Remote File Transfer feature is engaged, and after the user has given permission (if necessary), the Remote Tools screen displays a Windows Explorer–type window, as shown in Figure 10-23. The SMS Administrator Console computer's directories are controlled through the top pane, and the remote client's directories are controlled through the bottom pane. You navigate this window in the same way you would Windows Explorer. File transfer is effected simply by dragging files from one pane to the other. This tool is especially effective when the client does not have file sharing enabled or does not have the necessary shares available to create network mappings.

Figure 10-23. *The Remote File Transfer interface.*

Remote Execute

The Remote Execute tool enables the SMS administrator to run a program on the client, such as a disk defragmentation program or a virus scan—or even a game of solitaire. When the Remote Execute option is selected and user permission is granted, a simple dialog box named Run Program At User's Workstation is displayed. Enter the path and name of the program and click Run to execute that program on the client.

Remote Tools Session Process Flow

Now that we have examined how to configure and run a Remote Tools session on an SMS client, let's take some time to explore the process of initiating a Remote Tools session. An understanding of this process will enable you to analyze problem situations when you are attempting to remotely control a client computer.

When the SMS administrator starts a Remote Tools session, a specific sequence of events occurs. This flow of events will allow the communication between the SMS Administrator Console computer and the remote client computer. This section will guide you through the steps that take place in the SMS Administrator

Console computer and on the primary site server when a Remote Tools session is initiated with a client computer. It will also give you a fair indication of the network traffic that is generated.

As you know, a Remote Tools session is initiated by selecting a client in the Collection folder in the SMS Administrator Console. So really the first step that occurs is that SMS determines whether the SMS administrator has permission to start a Remote Tools session through that collection. This permission is different from the Permitted Viewers list that can be configured as part of the Remote Tools settings; it involves object security set on the collection itself through SMS security. This type of security allows you to create customized SMS Administrator Consoles and delegate specific tasks, such as remote troubleshooting, to specific individuals without having to give them access to everything else. (This aspect of security is discussed in detail in Chapter 16.)

Now when the SMS administrator begins a Remote Tools session, Remote.exe makes a connection via the SMS Provider to the SMS site database using the resource ID of the client in question. The SMS Provider returns the IP and/or IPX address and NetBIOS name of the client. This information is passed to LDWMNT.dll, which attempts to connect to the client. LDWMNT.dll resolves the NetBIOS name through WINS or DNS, for example, and attempts a connection over each protocol (connection point).

> **Note** SMS 2.0 now establishes a TCP session with the client by default, instead of the User Datagram Protocol (UDP) sessions used by earlier versions of SMS. This guaranteed connection ensures that communications exist between the SMS Administrator Console and the client and should result in fewer lost session events.

In the meantime, the client agent is "listening," using the protocol to which Remote Tools was bound (by default, the primary protocol, or LANA 0). When a connection is attempted using this protocol, the client agent responds, and returns the Permitted Viewers list to Remote.exe. The list is evaluated to determine whether it includes the logged-on SMS administrator. If not, the logged-on SMS administrator is prompted for the name of a valid user. If the administrator is included, the client determines which remote tools are enabled, and Remote.exe displays the Remote Tools window to the SMS administrator with the appropriate tools enabled or disabled.

The SMS administrator initiates a remote tool such as Remote Chat or Remote Control. If user permission is required, the client displays a Remote Control Agent dialog box, as shown in Figure 10-17, asking the user for permission.

If user permission is granted, the appropriate tool is launched. If permission is denied, a message box similar to the one shown in Figure 10-24 is displayed on the SMS administrator's desktop.

Figure 10-24. *Message box notifying the SMS administrator that user permission has been denied.*

As you can see, a fair amount of network traffic is involved in establishing the Remote Tools session. In addition, the Remote Tools session itself can generate a rather significant amount of CPU usage on the client. For example, on a computer running Windows NT 4.0 with compression set to high and screen acceleration enabled, it is not uncommon to experience a CPU usage increase of between 90 and 100 percent. Setting compression to low can bring that down to the 50 to 65 percent range, but changing the compression setting may also generate additional network bandwidth usage.

Monitoring Status and Flow

As we've seen, when the Remote Tools Client Agent is configured, SMS status messages are generated at the site server by the site update process— Hierarchy Manager, Site Control Manager, and so on. These status messages will help you determine whether the Remote Tools Client Agent is available for installation on the client. Additionally, status messages are generated for each Remote Tools session between a user at an SMS Administrator Console and a client computer. Status messages will provide the necessary information for tracking Remote Tools sessions. Unfortunately, no log files are generated for the Remote Tools session itself.

Monitoring Installation

Two log files can be viewed at the SMS site server to verify that the Remote Tools Client Agent is ready for installation at the client: SMS\Logs\Cidm.log (Client Install Data Manager) and SMS\Logs\Inboxmgr.log (Inbox Manager). These log files can be viewed using a text editor or the SMS Trace utility. Search for entries with the text string "Remctrl," as shown in the sample log in Figure 10-25.

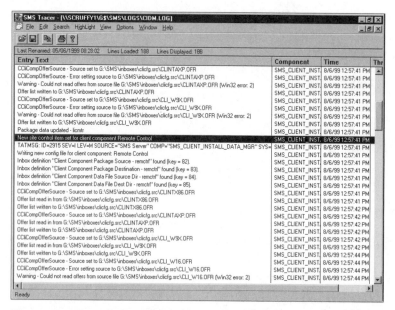

Figure 10-25. *Sample Cidm.log file with the reference to Remote Control selected.*

Log activity is also generated at the client computer when the Remote Tools Client Agent is installed or updated, just as with any other client agent. At the Windows NT client, for example, you can view the \MS\Sms\Logs\Ccim32.log. Open this log using any text editor or SMS Trace, and search for a wake-up event. In other words, look for specific entries that record when the Remote Control Client Agent was found, when the offer for Remote Control was read, and when the offer was submitted to Advertised Programs Manager for installation (Launch32).

You can also view the Advertised Programs Manager log file for remote control activity. Open *systemroot*\MS\Sms\Logs\Smsapm32.log, and search for the string "remote control". You should see a request to schedule Remote Control, an attempt to execute Remctrl.exe for service context, and the reporting of installation status.

As we've seen, you can also open the Remote Control log file, \MS\Sms\Logs\ Remctrl.log. You can use this log file to identify the following events that occur during the Remote Tools Client Agent installation:

- Detection of the operating system on an Intel processor

- Installation of appropriate language support for the client's installed languages

- Installation of the discovered platform's remote control files

- Configuration of registry settings, including security and permissions
- Configuration of hardware-specific Remote Tools settings from the registry
- Registration of the agent with the SMS application launcher (Launch32 or Launch16)
- Start-up of the agent

If you come across any problems during the installation of the Remote Tools Client Agent, remember to review this file on the client computer. You can also monitor the Remote Tools session itself, as we'll see in the next section.

Monitoring a Remote Tools Session

When the SMS administrator initiates a Remote Tools session of any kind with the client, the Remote Tools Client Agent will generate status messages. These messages can of course be viewed through the Status Message Viewer. However, while SMS log activity will be generated on the client computer as a result of installing the agent, the act of establishing and terminating a Remote Control session is recorded as part of the Windows NT Security Event log on Windows NT clients. Relying on the Status Message Viewer in this case will give you more useful information.

You can view status messages specific to a Remote Tools session by executing one of the following status message queries related to Remote Tools sessions:

- Remote Tools Activity Initiated At A Specific Site
- Remote Tools Activity Initiated By A Specific User
- Remote Tools Activity Initiated From A Specific System
- Remote Tools Activity Targeted At A Specific System

The status messages displayed by these queries are in the range $300xx$ and will provide you with the following details:

- The domain name and user account of the user that is viewing the client
- The machine name of the SMS Administrator Console that is being used
- The machine name of the client computer on which remote functions are being carried out
- The types of functions being performed

Figure 10-26 shows an example of the status messages returned by the status message query Remote Tools Activity Targeted At A Specific Site. Notice the entries in the Description column for initiating and ending each type of remote function.

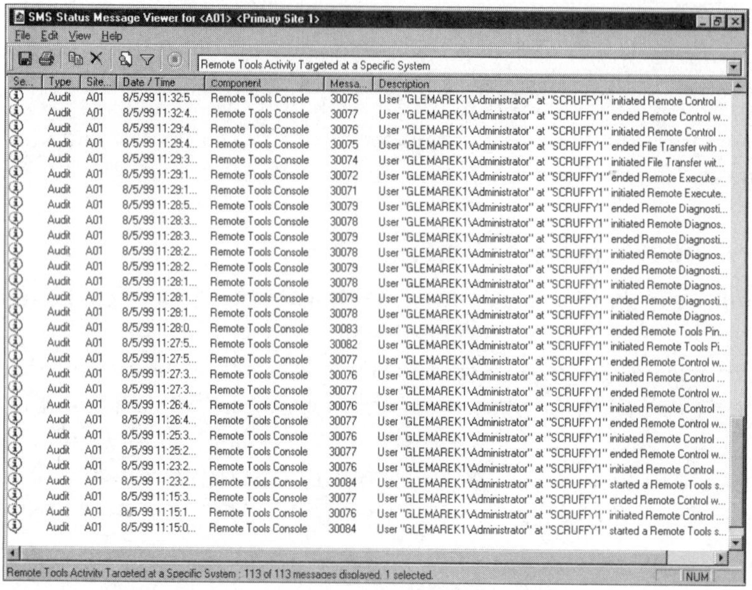

Figure 10-26. *Sample status message query results.*

To view the client log activity generated by a Remote Tools session recorded in the Windows NT Security Event log, follow these steps:

1. In the SMS Administrator Console, navigate to the Collections folder, expand it, and then select All Windows NT Workstation Systems or another collection that contains the Windows NT client.

2. In the Details pane, right-click on the client entry, and choose All Tasks from the context menu.

3. Choose Start Windows NT Event Viewer. The Event Viewer window displays the System log from the client computer, as shown in Figure 10-27. Navigate the Windows NT Event Viewer as you normally would.

4. Choose Security from the Log menu to open the Security log, and display the details for Event ID 5. The Event Detail dialog box appears, as shown in Figure 10-28. Notice that the text for the event indicates a Remote Control session with the client started by the SMS administrator using Windows NT security.

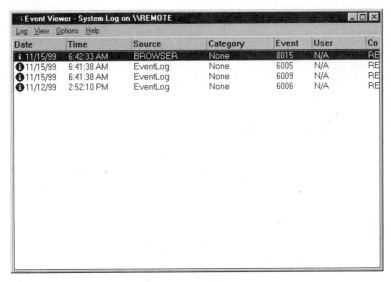

Figure 10-27. *The Event Viewer System log.*

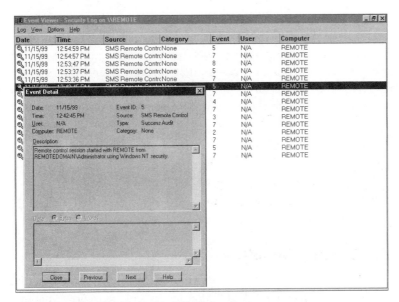

Figure 10-28. *The Event Detail dialog box.*

Table 10-2 shows the Remote Tools session events that can be recorded in the Windows NT Security log.

Table 10-2.   **Windows NT security events generated by a remote function**

Event ID	Remote Function
1	Remote Reboot
2	Remote Chat
3	Remote File Transfer
4	Remote Execute
5	Remote Control Session Start
6	Remote Control Session End
7	Local User Granted Permission For Remote Session
8	Local User Denied Permission For Remote Session

Resource Kit Utilities

The *Microsoft BackOffice 4.5 Resource Kit* offers the three utilities described below to facilitate the configuration of the Remote Tools Client Agent.

Remote Control Settings (RCCliopt.exe)

This utility actually performs two tasks. It can be used to set the default protocol or LANA number (if the protocol is NetBIOS) for each client agent by sending this utility as an SMS package or running it on individual clients. It also has the capability of disabling the client update process so that you can set individual options, such as Permission Required, for each client, without fear that the Hardware Munger or Security Munger will reset the client agent settings to their original values.

Set NIC (Multinic.exe)

This utility allows you to identify which NIC the Remote Tools Client Agent will bind to on a client with more than one NIC. Again, this utility overrides the process followed by the Hardware Munger when determining which NIC takes precedence for Remote Control.

Stop Remote Control (StopRC.exe)

This utility allows you to stop and start the Remote Tools Client Agent on a 32-bit client to force it to reestablish a valid TCP/IP address to listen with. This utility is useful for clients currently connected to the network through RAS because SMS components start before the RAS IP addresses are assigned. Thus, the agent will be incorrectly listening with IP address 0.0.0.0. The Stop Remote Control utility forces the agent to stop and then restart once you determine that the client has a valid IP address assigned.

Real World   Using RCCliopt.exe

It's not uncommon within a network environment using SMS to include various Windows NT servers as SMS clients. The benefits of being able to use Remote Tools to monitor, manage, and diagnose our servers are obvious. And because Remote Tools settings are sitewide settings, if we require permissions as a Remote Tools Client Agent setting, then *all* our SMS clients—including our servers—will receive the same setting.

Not many of us have administrators logged in and sitting in front of our servers. When that permission dialog box pops up on a server, who is going to click Yes to allow the Remote Tools session to be initiated? You could always change the Permission Required setting, but that would turn off the option on all your users' desktops, which might not be your intention either.

In SMS 2.0, you can enable or disable sitewide remote control security settings using one of two methods: you can either modify the registry on each server or run the RCCliopt.exe utility at the server.

In each 32-bit client's registry, SMS creates the following key when the Remote Tools Client Agent is installed: HKEY_LOCAL_MACHINE\SOFTWARE\ Microsoft\SMS\Client\Client Components\Remote Control. This key contains all of the client agent settings. A hidden registry value named *UpdateEnabled* is also added, with a default value of *Yes*. This value needs to be set to *No* to prevent the Security Munger from ensuring that sitewide settings are forced to each client.

Refer to Chapter 2 for details on the process for adding values to the registry. We don't review the process here—except to remind you to do so with extreme caution. You must add the *UpdateEnabled* string value parameter to the registry key with the value set to *No* on each server that needs to be configured individually. This process entails going to each server and modifying the registry.

The RCCliop.exe utility is a command-line utility that can be run at each server to safely modify the registry entry for you. Execute it at the server with the command-line option *RCCliopt No*. Then, in the Control Panel, double-click on the Remote Control applet to reset the permission required option to *No*. The RCCliopt.exe utility can be sent to each affected server as an SMS package that is part of a script that performs the entire process, resetting the values for you without requiring a stop at each server.

Checkpoints

If you've been reading carefully and experimenting with Remote Tools as we go along, you should already be aware of the most frequent problem areas. Let's recap the main "gotchas."

Configuring the Client as an SMS Client

Remember that in SMS 2.0, unlike earlier versions of SMS, the SMS client is not required to collect any kind of inventory to the SMS site database. Nevertheless, the client does have to be discovered and installed as an SMS client.

Using NetBIOS Names for Session Communication

All of the remote tasks you can perform have been enhanced or rewritten in SMS 2.0. However, one fact remains the same as in earlier versions of SMS: Remote Tools sessions are still NetBIOS-based. This means that SMS will require a NetBIOS name resolution server such as WINS or DNS to successfully initiate the session.

Remote Control Protocol

The SMS Administrator Console computer and the client computer must share a common protocol. Although the SMS administrator's Windows NT workstation will attempt to use any one of the first eight LANA bound protocols to establish the Remote Tools session, by default the client listens and establishes the session only on the primary protocol or the LANA 0 protocol. This default can be changed directly on the client through its registry or by using the *Microsoft BackOffice 4.5 Resource Kit* utility RCCliopt.exe, as described in the section "Remote Control Settings (RCCliopt.exe)" earlier in this chapter.

Multiple-Site Considerations

Recall that when a client belongs to more than one SMS site, the Remote Tools Client Agent settings are determined by the Hardware Munger and Security Munger. For example, if user permission is required by at least one SMS site, the client agent will require user permission regardless of the settings of the other SMS sites.

Reconfiguring the Client Agent

Normally, if you make a change to any client agent setting, that change is propagated to the client at its next maintenance cycle. This is true for most Remote Tools settings. However, changes to settings made on the Advanced tab in the Remote Tools Client Agent Properties window after the client agent has been installed on the client will propagate only to new clients.

To update existing clients, you need to either uninstall and then reinstall Remote Tools from all the clients, run the Repair Installation procedure through the Systems Management applet in Control Panel on each client, or create an SMS package to force an update of the client agent settings. The SMS package program should contain the command line *%WIN%\MS\SMS\Clicomp\Remctrl\Rchwcfg.exe* with the command option *Install*. (*%WIN%* is an environmental variable that returns the system root on the client.)

Service Pack 1 Issues

SMS 2.0 Service Pack 1 has resolved several difficulties related to Remote Tools sessions, but nevertheless several entries in the Microsoft Systems Management Server Version 2.0 Service Pack 1 Release Notes are worth mentioning. For example, the Remote Tools Client Agent will not install correctly on clients currently running Intel's LAN Desk product or Novell's ZEN Works. You must uninstall these applications before you install the client agent. In general, although not explicitly stated in the Release Notes, SMS Remote Tools does not like to compete with any other remote control product.

Because you should be running SMS 2.0 with Service Pack 1 applied, which gives you access to the Release Notes, there's no point in repeating that information here. Many of the other "gotchas" described in the Release Notes involve the use of incompatible video cards, accelerators, or drivers. If you experience a failed or problematic Remote Tools session, the basic workaround involves disabling the video driver or setting acceleration to None and then retrying the Remote Tools session.

Tip   Read the Microsoft Systems Management Server Version 2.0 Service Pack 1 Release Notes!

Summary

In this chapter, we have explored the various Remote Tools as well as the configuration settings for the Remote Tools Client Agent. We have also explored the process for installing and initiating a Remote Tools session with a client, monitoring the session's status, and troubleshooting potential problems. We've looked at three useful *Microsoft BackOffice 4.5 Resource Kit* utilities and at additional technical details regarding the remote control process. In Part III, we'll shift our focus to another set of SMS functions that deal more specifically with program management on client computers.

Part III
Software and Package Management

Chapter 11
Collections

In Part III, we'll explore application management on Microsoft Systems Management Server (SMS) clients. In particular, we will look at how to deploy packages to SMS clients and then manage or track their usage. Fundamental to the package distribution process in SMS 2.0 is the creation and use of collections. So before we begin our examination of the package distribution process in earnest, we need to turn our attention to collections. In this chapter, you'll learn how to define, create, and update collections; how collections are handled in an SMS site hierarchy; and how to troubleshoot potential problems.

Defining Collections

Although our primary focus here is on the use of collections in the package distribution process, collections have many other uses. Collections are groups of SMS resources and can consist not only of computers, but also of Microsoft Windows NT users and user groups, as well as any resources discovered through the Network Discovery method, as we discussed in Chapter 7. Package programs can be advertised to collections that consist of users, user groups, or computers. Computer collections, however, are the starting point for performing many client management tasks. For example, the Remote Tools, Resource Explorer, and Event to Trap Translator configurations for each client are initiated by selecting the client through a collection. For Windows NT client computers, you can also initiate remote diagnostics such as viewing a client's Event Viewer or Windows NT Diagnostics utility through the client entry in a collection.

Caution Collections represent discovered resources. The computer resources that are discovered and displayed in a collection may not actually be installed as SMS clients. If a client has not been installed and the appropriate client component has not been enabled, you will not be able to initiate a Remote Tools session, collect inventory, and so on, even though the discovery data record (DDR) exists.

We know that if a computer is discovered but not installed as an SMS client, that computer cannot be the recipient of an advertisement since the Advertised Programs Client Agent (also sometimes referred to as the Advertised Programs Agent) is an SMS client component. On the other hand, a discovered Windows NT *user* obviously cannot be installed as an SMS client, since there is no equivalent user installation method. However, a discovered user can be the recipient of an advertisement when that user is logged on at an SMS client. For example, suppose that the auditing department of a company has developed a spreadsheet that their auditors use when auditing other departments. If SMS has discovered the auditors' user accounts, those user accounts can be grouped into a collection called *Auditors*. The audit spreadsheet can then be advertised to the *Auditors* collection and would subsequently be available to each auditor at whatever SMS client they log on to, in whatever department they are visiting.

In many ways, collections are similar to Windows NT global groups. You use Windows NT groups to organize users into easily managed units. Groups are used to assign access permissions to Windows NT resources such as printers, folders, files, and shares. When a new user joins a group, that user automatically inherits all the permissions assigned to that group.

The same concept applies to SMS collections. You use collections to organize your SMS discovered resources into manageable units. For example, suppose you have installed 1000 clients as SMS clients. These clients will appear as part of the *All Systems* collection in the SMS Administrator Console. If each of these clients belongs to a different business unit or department within your organization and you need to send these computers packages based on their affiliation with their business unit or department, you could create a collection for each business unit or department and add each client to the appropriate collection. Your clients are now grouped into manageable units to which you can easily target packages.

Collections can contain subcollections to give the SMS administrator more flexibility (or more headaches, depending on your point of view). Subcollections work in much the same way as nested groups in Windows NT. Actions performed on a main collection can also be performed on its subcollections. The most common use for subcollections is in connection with advertisements. Package programs are advertised to collections, but you can also advertise to a collection's subcollections.

Subcollections are not considered to be *members* of the collection that contains them. Think of subcollections more as a convenient way to link several different collections so that they can be treated as one unit. Membership rules are unique for each subcollection and don't affect any other collection. We'll look at collection membership in the next section.

Collection Membership

Collection membership rules can be either direct or query-based. *Direct membership* is a manual membership method, meaning that you define which resources are to be members of the collection. You are also responsible for maintaining the collection over time. If, for example, computers are added or removed from the business group or department, you will need to add or remove those computers from their corresponding collections.

Query-based membership, on the other hand, is more dynamic in nature. You define the rules by which the collection membership is established, and then SMS keeps the collection up-to-date by periodically rerunning the query. For example, suppose your company standard for naming computers is to include a business unit or departmental code—say, all computers in the finance department are named FIN203-PCx, where x is a value that's incremented each time a new computer name is needed. You could create a collection named *Finance* whose membership rule is based on a query that searches the database for all computers whose names begin with FIN203. SMS would automatically populate the collections with the appropriate computers. If computers are added or removed from the finance department, the collection would be updated automatically when the collection query was next executed.

As you can see, query-based collections are generally more practical and efficient than those based on direct-membership rules.

Real World   Automating Collections and Packages

Let's build on our query-based collection example, in which all computers in the finance department are named FIN203-PCx and a *Finance* collection has been created whose membership rule is based on a query that searches the database for all computers whose names begin with FIN203. Since package programs are always advertised to collections, all members of the *Finance* collection would receive any advertisement to that collection. If computers are added or removed from the finance department, the next time the *Finance* collection is (automatically) updated, this change will be reflected to the collection and any new computers that were added to the collection will receive advertisements made to the collection. Similarly, if a computer has been removed from the *Finance* collection, that computer will no longer receive any advertisements made to the collection.

This process makes it easier for the SMS administrator to automate some client management tasks, such as applying virus updates. Suppose your advertisement is to copy a new virus update to each client in the finance department once a month. You already have the *Finance* collection, so all you need to do is create a recurring advertisement (you'll learn how to do this in Chapter 12) that copies a new virus update file to the clients on a specified day of each month.

Working together, the advertisement and the collection ensure that all computers in the finance department will receive the virus update file once a month. If new computers are added to the finance department, the next time the collection is automatically updated they will automatically receive the same advertisement for the virus update file that every other member of the *Finance* collection will receive. Similarly, if a computer is moved to another department, the next time the collection is automatically updated that computer will no longer receive advertisements for the virus update. The only administrative task that you need to worry about is obtaining the virus update file once a month and making it available to the advertised package.

Predefined Collections

As mentioned, collections represent discovered resources that have not necessarily been installed as SMS clients. For example, Windows NT users and user groups can be discovered as resources for an SMS site and the discovered users and user groups are automatically made members of the *All Users* and *All User Groups* collections—two examples of predefined collections.

Collections are used to group resources into more easily managed units. When you install SMS 2.0, twelve default collections are created. These default collections are described in Table 11-1.

Table 11-1. Default collections created during SMS site server installation

Collection	Description
All Systems	Displays all computers and IP-addressable resources discovered through any discovery method except Windows NT User Account Discovery and Windows NT User Group Discovery
All User Groups	Displays all Windows NT users discovered through the Windows NT User Group Discovery method

Table 11-1.   *continued*

Collection	Description
All Users	Displays all Windows NT users discovered through the Windows NT User Account Discovery method
All Windows 3.1 Systems	Displays all discovered computers running the Microsoft Windows 3.1 operating system
All Windows 95 Systems	Displays all discovered computers running the Windows 95 operating system
All Windows 98 Systems	Displays all discovered computers running the Windows 98 operating system
All Windows For Workgroups Systems	Displays all discovered computers running the Windows for Workgroups operating system
All Windows NT Server Systems	Displays all discovered server computers running the Windows NT Server 3.51 or 4.0 or Windows 2000 operating system
All Windows NT Systems	Displays all discovered server or workstation computers running the Windows NT operating system
All Windows NT Workstation 3.51 Systems	Displays all discovered computers running the Windows NT Workstation 3.51 operating system
All Windows NT Workstation 4.0 Systems	Displays all discovered computers running the Windows NT Workstation 4.0 operating system
All Windows NT Workstation Systems	Displays all discovered workstation computers running the Windows NT Workstation 3.51 or 4.0 or Windows 2000 operating system

As you can see, these default collections are designed to group resources by operating system. The collections can be used as targets for receiving advertisements. They are updated once per hour by default, but you can change that frequency by clicking the Schedule button on the Membership Rules tab in the collection's Properties window, as we'll see in the section "Creating a Query-Based Collection" later in this chapter. Note that you can manage the default collections only from the central site. They can't be modified from child sites.

Creating Collections

The default collections provide some basic resource groupings, but these will not always be the best way to manage your resources, especially when it comes to advertising package programs to SMS clients. Instead, you can create your own collections, grouping together your resources in as many logical units as makes sense within your SMS site or site hierarchy.

Part of creating a collection involves defining who the collection members will be using membership rules. Recall that a collection's membership rules can be either direct, a manual method that requires more maintenance, or query-based, which provides greater flexibility and less maintenance. In this section, we'll look at how to create collections with both types of membership rules.

Creating a Direct Membership Collection

To create a direct membership collection, follow these steps:

1. Navigate to the Collections folder in the SMS Administrator Console.
2. Right-click on the Collections folder, choose New from the context menu, and then choose Collection to display the Collection Properties window, shown in Figure 11-1.

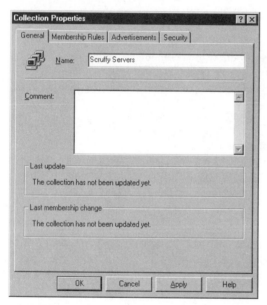

Figure 11-1. *The Collection Properties window.*

3. On the General tab, enter a descriptive name for your collection along with a descriptive comment if you like.
4. Click on the Membership Rules tab, and click the Direct Membership button (the PC with the yellow star) to launch the Create Direct Membership Rule Wizard. Figure 11-2 shows the Create Direct Membership Rule Wizard welcome screen.

Figure 11-2. *The Create Direct Membership Rule Wizard welcome screen.*

5. Click Next to display the Search For Resources screen, shown in Figure 11-3. Select the resource class for the resource you want to add to the collection. On the Resource Class list, the User Group Resource and User Resource options will let you add members discovered by the Windows NT User Account Discovery and Windows NT User Group Discovery methods. The System Resource option relates to discovered computers. The IP Network Resource option relates to IP-addressable devices discovered through the Network Discovery method. For this example, select System Resource.

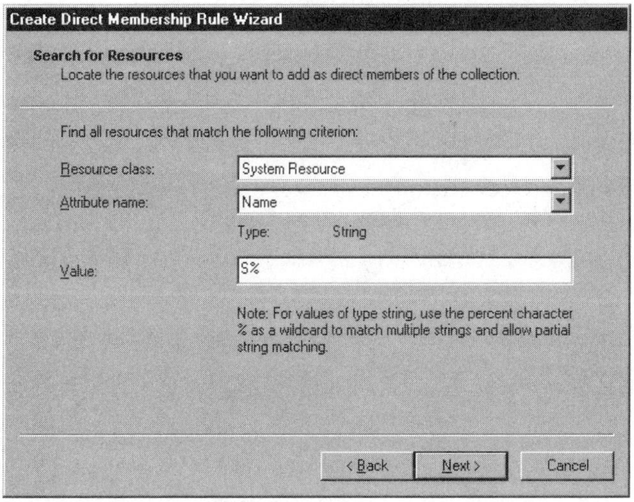

Figure 11-3. *The Search For Resources screen.*

6. Select the resource attribute on which you will base your membership choice. Attributes include resource name, resource ID, IP information, domain information, and so on. The attributes listed reflect the discovery data collected for that class of resource. For this example, specify Name.

7. Enter the appropriate attribute value to look for when selecting members for this group. The % sign is a wildcard character. In this case, we are looking for all computers whose name begins with the letter "S."

8. Click Next to display the Collection Limiting screen, shown in Figure 11-4. From this screen, you specify which existing collection to use to look for the resources you identified. You can leave the field blank if you have sufficient permissions to search the entire SMS database. Otherwise, you must enter the name of a collection that you have permissions to view.

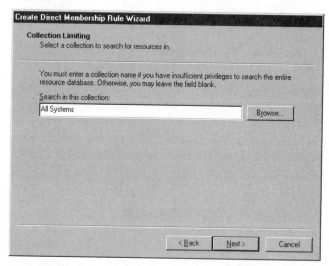

Figure 11-4. *The Collection Limiting screen.*

9. Click Next to display the Select Resources screen, as shown in Figure 11-5. This screen shows a list of the resources that match your membership criteria—in this case, a list of all the computer names that begin with the letter "S." Select the resources you want to include in the collection.

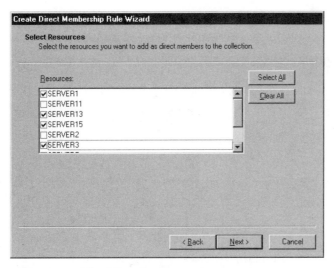

Figure 11-5. *The Select Resources screen.*

10. Click Next to display the Completing The Create Direct Membership Rule Wizard screen, shown in Figure 11-6. You can also click the Back button to review or change your settings. Review your choices and then click Finish.

Figure 11-6. *The Completing The Create Direct Membership Rule Wizard screen.*

11. The resources you selected will now appear on the Membership Rules tab of the Collection Properties window, as shown in Figure 11-7.

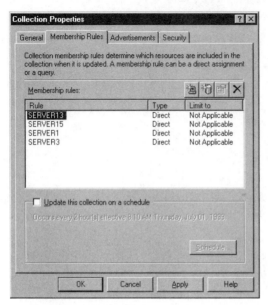

Figure 11-7. *The Membership Rules tab of the Collection Properties window.*

12. In step 8 you specified a collection to use to look for resources you identified. On the Membership Rules tab, the Update This Collection On A Schedule check box indicates the frequency with which Collection Evaluator will browse the collection you specified to see if the resource still exists. If the resource is no longer a member of the specified collection, it will be removed from this new collection. *Collection Evaluator* is the SMS thread component that performs collection management tasks such as updating or refreshing collection data. By default, the collection will be updated once every two hours. Click the Schedule button to modify the collections update schedule.

Note The minimum update interval is every 15 minutes. If you specify an update interval of less than 15 minutes, the collections won't be updated at that interval. In addition, if you change the membership update schedule, the first evaluation will have a delay up to 15 minutes.

13. Click OK to create the collection and add it to the Collections folder.

The Advertisements tab of the Collection Properties window lists all advertisements that have targeted that collection. The Security tab lets you specify who can access this collection—and collections in general—and to what extent they can administer the collections. Security will be discussed in detail in Chapter 17.

Creating a Query-Based Collection

To create a query-based collection, follow these steps:

1. Navigate to the Collections folder in the SMS Administrator Console.

2. Right-click on the Collections folder, choose New from the context menu, and then choose Collection to display the Collection Properties window, shown in Figure 11-1.

3. On the General tab, enter a descriptive name for your collection along with a descriptive comment if you like.

4. On the Membership Rules tab, click the Query Rules button (the database with the yellow star) to display the Query Rule Properties window, shown in Figure 11-8.

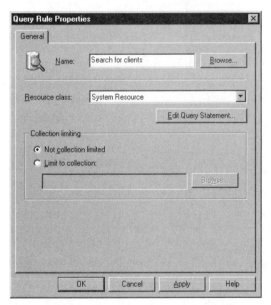

Figure 11-8. *The Query Rules Properties window.*

5. On the General tab, enter a name for your query, or click Browse to choose from a list of existing SMS queries.

6. Select the resource class for a set of related objects you want to add to the collection. The Systems Resource option is selected by default. In the Collection Limiting section, select Limit To Collection if you want to narrow the query to a specific collection's membership. Click Browse to select from a list of existing collections.

7. Click Edit Query Statement to display the Client Query Statement Properties window, shown in Figure 11-9.

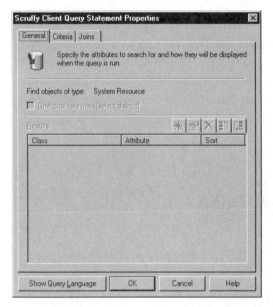

Figure 11-9. *The Client Query Statement Properties window.*

8. On the General tab, you'll notice that you do not have the ability to create or modify a Query Results window. This is because the query is being used to populate a collection membership instead of displaying resource attributes.

9. Select the Criteria tab, as shown in Figure 11-10, where you can define how to populate the collection.

10. Click the New button (the yellow star) to display the Criterion Properties window, shown in Figure 11-11.

Figure 11-10. *The Criteria tab.*

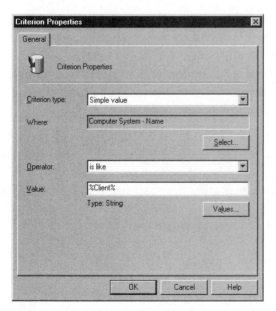

Figure 11-11. *The Criterion Properties window.*

11. Select the criterion type. The available choices are Null Value, Simple Value, Attribute Reference, Subselected Values, and List of Values. (See Chapter 15 for a description of each criterion type.)

12. Click the Select button to define the attribute class and attribute on which you are basing the query.

13. Select an operator and enter a value appropriate to the attribute class and attribute you defined, or click Values to make your selection from a list of values recorded in the SMS database. When you have finished, click OK.

Caution String values require an exact value entry. If you wish to use a wildcard character, use the operator Is Like or Is Not Like, and then use the percent sign (%) like you see in Figure 11-11 or one of the other wildcard characters described in Chapter 15.

14. Repeat steps 10 through 13 to add selection criteria.

Note As mentioned, a collection can be mixed—that is, it can contain computers, users, and groups.

15. Click OK to return to the Query Rule Properties window. Click OK again to return to the Collection Properties window.

16. Click on the Membership Rules tab, shown in Figure 11-12. Select the Update This Collection On A Schedule option to define the frequency at which you want Collection Evaluator to run the query and update the collection. By default, the collection will be updated once every two hours.

17. Click OK to create the collection and add it to the Collections folder.

As with direct membership collections, the Advertisements tab of the Collection Properties window lists all advertisements that have targeted that collection. The Security tab lets you specify who can access this collection—and collections in general—and to what extent they can administer the collections. Security will be discussed in detail in Chapter 16.

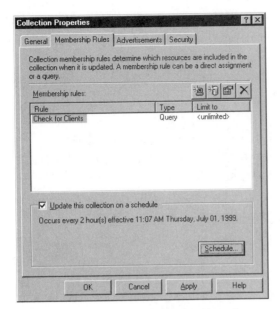

Figure 11-12. *The Membership Rules tab.*

Creating Subcollections

When a collection has one or more subcollections associated with it, any actions (such as advertisements) performed on the collection can also be performed on the subcollection. However, each subcollection is still its own collection and as such is governed by its own membership rules. Placing them as subcollections within a new collection provides a way to link different collections rather than as a method of nesting collections.

Suppose a particular business unit can be further subdivided into smaller units. Management Information Services (MIS), for example, might be divided into various support areas—say, PC Support, Network Support, and Server Support. Let's say that you create a collection for each of these groups—*MIS, PC Support, Network Support,* and *Server Support.* The last three collections could become subcollections of the *MIS* collection. This reclassification enables you to advertise packages to the *MIS* collection, which includes the members of the three subcollections. If you don't need to hit all the collections, you can opt not to when you create the advertisement. And you still have the ability to advertise to each collection directly.

To link one collection to another, thus creating a subcollection, follow these steps:

1. Navigate to the Collections folder in the SMS Administrator Console and expand it.

2. Right-click on the collection that you want to associate with a subcollection, choose New from the Context menu, and then choose Link To Collection to display the Browse Collection dialog box, shown in Figure 11-13.

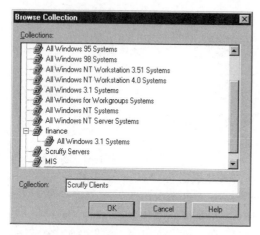

Figure 11-13. *The Browse Collection dialog box.*

3. The Browse Collection dialog box contains a list of all the available collections. Select the collection you want to add as a subcollection—and then click OK.

You can easily view which collections have subcollections and what those subcollections are by expanding the collection entries in the SMS Administrator Console, shown in Figure 11-14. In this example, the *Scruffy Clients* collection has a subcollection named *Finance* that itself has a subcollection named *All Windows 3.1 Systems*, which is one of the default collections.

Tip Subcollections of a collection can be viewed by clicking the plus sign (+) preceding the collection name.

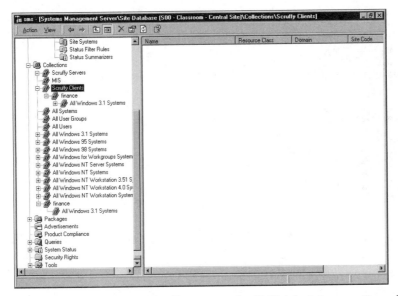

Figure 11-14. *Viewing subcollections in the SMS Administrator Console.*

Unlinking Subcollections

If you need to "un-link" a subcollection to reorganize your collection structure, follow these steps:

1. Navigate to the Collections folder, expand it, and highlight the subcollection you want to delete.

2. Right-click on the subcollection, and then choose Delete from the context menu to initiate the Delete Collection Wizard, as shown in Figure 11-15.

3. Verify the subcollection name, and then click Next to display the Delete Collection Instance screen, as shown in Figure 11-16.

4. Select Yes to delete this instance of the collection. Note that you will be deleting only this instance of the collection. You will not delete any other instance of the same collection that appears elsewhere in the Collections folder.

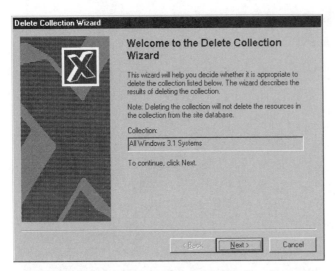

Figure 11-15. *The Delete Collection Wizard welcome screen.*

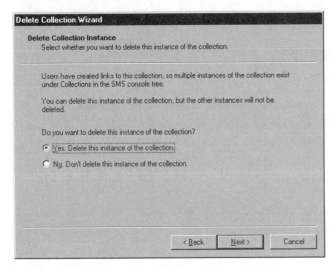

Figure 11-16. *The Delete Collection Instance screen.*

5. Click Next and then click Finish. The Collections folder will be refreshed, and the subcollection will no longer be displayed or linked.

Now that we have created and deleted collections and subcollections, let's take a look at how we can keep them up-to-date through SMS.

Updating Collections

As we've seen, collections that are based on direct-membership rules need to be maintained by the SMS administrator since they are manually created and defined. Collections that are based on queries, however, can be updated automatically based on the schedule that you define. The SMS component responsible for carrying out this updating task is Collection Evaluator.

Collection Evaluator will execute the query and update the collection whenever the scheduled interval occurs, or when the SMS administrator forces an update through the SMS Administrator Console. When the SMS administrator forces an update or modifies a collection, creates a new collection, or deletes an existing collection, Collection Evaluator is notified of the event by SQL Monitor.

Forcing an Update

Collection Evaluator will execute a collection's query and update the collection membership according to whatever schedule you define. However, sometimes you need or want to update the collection membership outside of that schedule. The SMS administrator can force Collection Evaluator to update all the collections or any individual collection at any point in time.

Updating All Collections

To update all the collections at once, follow these steps:

1. Navigate to the Collections folder in the SMS Administrator Console and expand it.

2. Right-click on the Collections folder, choose All Tasks from the context menu, and then choose Update Collection Membership.

3. A message box will appear confirming the update of all collections. Choose OK. This update may take some time to complete depending on the number of collections, network traffic if the SMS database is on another computer, and so on.

4. When the update is complete, all the collections in the SMS Administrator Console will show an hourglass alongside the collection icon in the SMS Administrator Console, as in Figure 11-17. These hourglasses indicate that the collection was updated, but that the SMS Administrator Console window needs to be refreshed.

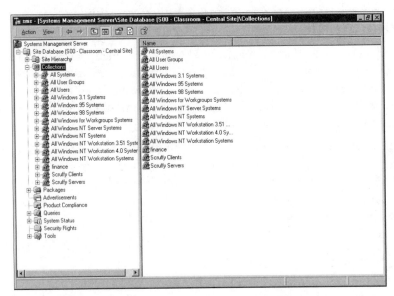

Figure 11-17. *The SMS Administrator Console with updated collections before being refreshed.*

5. To refresh the SMS Administrator Console window, right-click on the Collections folder again, and choose Refresh from the context menu. The collections will now display their updated memberships.

Updating an Individual Collection

To update an individual collection, follow these steps:

1. Navigate to the Collections folder in the SMS Administrator Console and expand it.

2. Right-click on the collection you want to update, choose All Tasks from the context menu, and then choose Update Collection Membership.

3. As shown in Figure 11-18, a message box appears confirming the update of this collection and giving you the option of simultaneously updating the collection's subcollections. If you want the subcollections updated as well, select the Update Subcollection Membership check box. Click OK to begin the update.

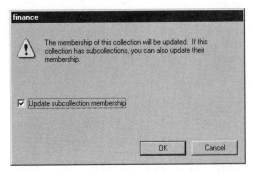

Figure 11-18. *Message box confirming the collection update.*

4. When the update is complete, the collection in the SMS Administrator Console will show an hourglass icon alongside the collection entry. This indicates that the collection was updated, but that you still need to refresh the SMS Administrator Console window.

5. To refresh the SMS Administrator Console window, right-click on the collection again, and choose Refresh from the context menu. The collection will then display its updated membership.

Deleting a Collection

That which the SMS administrator gives, the SMS administrator can take away. This of course is true of collections. While you maintain collections, you might need to reorganize your collection structure by creating new collections and deleting existing ones. Deleting a collection can have consequences other than just removing that collection. When you delete a collection, you will also effect the following events:

- Any advertisements that have targeted only this collection will also be deleted. (If an advertisement is also targeting another collection, it will not be affected.)

- When you create a query, you can limit its scope by associating it with a particular collection. When the collection is deleted, the query's scope is no longer limited.

- Any collections whose membership rules (queries) are limited to the collection that is being deleted will still process the rule, but will display no resources.

- Through the object class or instance security (discussed in Chapter 16) you can identify which SMS administrators have the ability to view the membership of each collection. After you remove a collection, the administrators you identified will no longer be able to view that collection's resources if the resources aren't in other collections that the administrators can view.

Fortunately, when you delete a collection, the Delete Collection Wizard warns you of these effects and shows you what properties of the collection might be affected.

Follow these steps to delete a collection:

1. Navigate to the Collections folder in the SMS Administrator Console and expand it.

2. Right-click on the collection you want to delete, and choose Delete from the context menu. The Delete Collection Wizard welcome screen is displayed, as shown previously in Figure 11-15. Verify the name of the collection to be deleted.

3. Click Next to display the Effects Of Deleting This Collection screen, shown in Figure 11-19. This screen warns you about the effects of deleting a collection and lets you choose whether to display details about the effects.

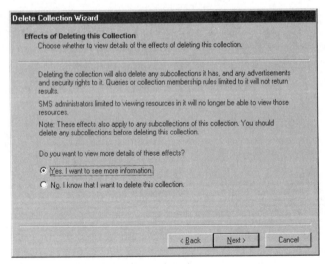

Figure 11-19. *The Effects Of Deleting This Collection screen.*

4. Select the Yes option to view individual screens describing what will be affected by the deletion. Select the No option to proceed with the deletion.

   If you selected the No option, you would proceed to step 11, where you would simply delete the collection. For this example, select the Yes option.

5. Click Next to display the Subcollections screen, as shown in Figure 11-20. This screen displays a list of this collection's subcollections. Note the warning that deleting this collection will also delete the subcollections.

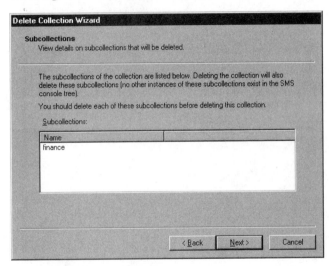

Figure 11-20. *The Subcollections screen.*

6. Click Next to display the Advertisements screen, as shown in Figure 11-21, which displays a list of all the advertisements that have targeted this collection. Again, note the warning that deleting this collection could also delete the advertisements (if they are not also targeted to another collection).

7. Click Next to display the Queries screen, shown in Figure 11-22, which lists any queries that have been limited to this collection. A similar warning message is provided.

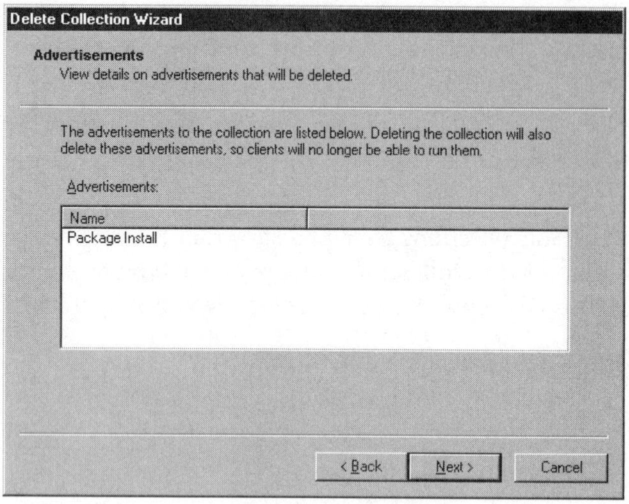

Figure 11-21. *The Advertisements screen.*

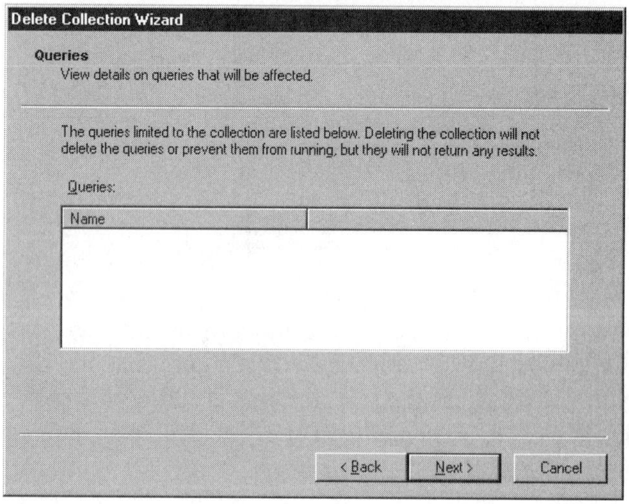

Figure 11-22. *The Queries screen.*

8. Click Next to display the Collection Membership Rules screen, shown in Figure 11-23. This screen displays a list of collections whose membership rules are limited to this collection and warns of possible effects.

9. Click Next to display the Administrators screen, shown in Figure 11-24, which lists the administrators who have permissions to view resources in this collection and the effect that the deletion may have on them.

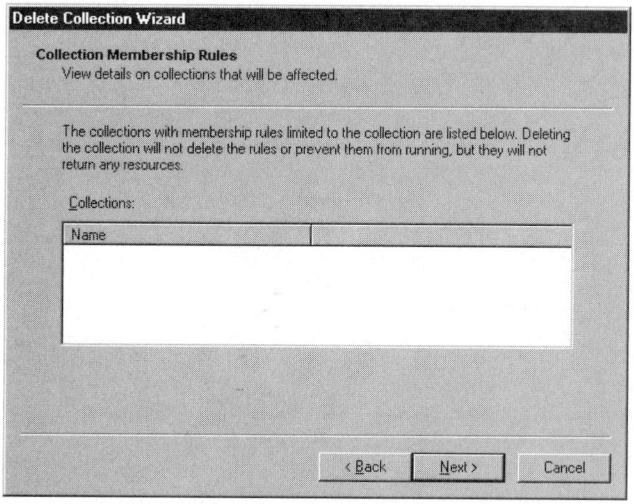

Figure 11-23. *The Collection Membership Rules screen.*

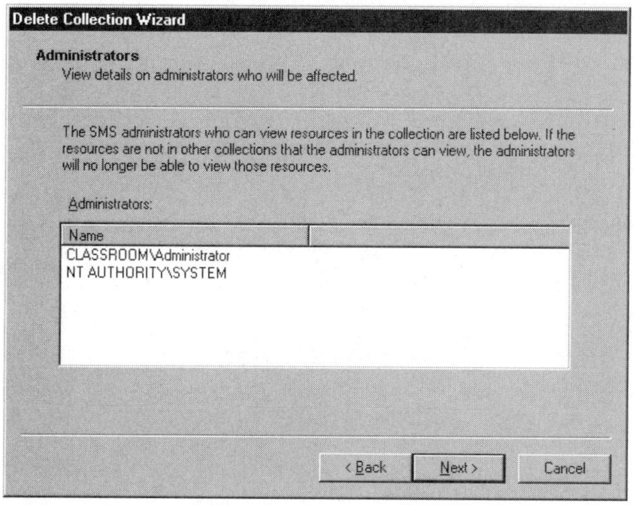

Figure 11-24. *The Administrators screen.*

10. Click Next to display the Choose Whether To Delete This Collection screen, shown in Figure 11-25. This final confirmation screen asks whether you want to proceed with the deletion. Select the Yes option to continue.

11. Click Next to display the Completing The Delete Collection Wizard screen, shown in Figure 11-26. Click Finish to delete the collection.

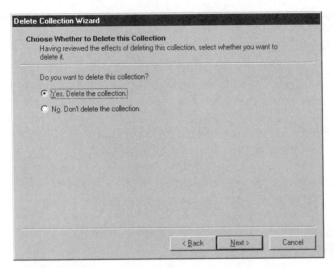

Figure 11-25. *The Choose Whether To Delete This Collection screen.*

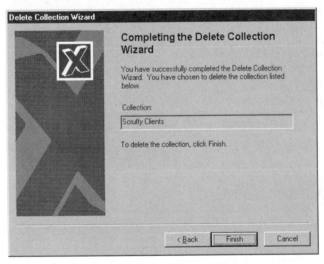

Figure 11-26. *The Completing The Delete Collection Wizard screen.*

In this section, we have seen SMS administrators update and maintain collections and subcollections. Next, let's discuss how SMS itself can update your collections automatically.

Collection Evaluator Update Process Flow

Collection Evaluator assigns resources to collections according to the most recent data about the resources. Collection Evaluator waits for a file change notification from SQL Monitor before the update process starts. As shown in Figure 11-27,

SQL Monitor writes a wake-up file to Collection Evaluator's inbox (SMS\Inboxes\Colleval.box). SQL Monitor writes an update collection (.UDC) file when the update is forced or a collection is modified, an add collection (.ADC) file when a new collection is created, and a delete collection (.DC) file when a collection is deleted. SQL Monitor, like so many other components in SMS 2.0, is driven by SQL trigger events that cause the component ultimately to wake up and perform its task. Collection Evaluator then executes the query and updates the membership results in the SMS database.

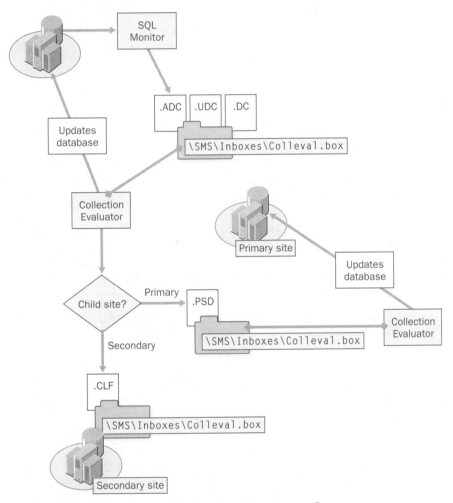

Figure 11-27. *The Collection Evaluator update process flow.*

If the SMS site has child sites, Collection Evaluator also creates a .PSD file that contains the collection definition and membership. It writes this file to Replication Manager's inbox (SMS\Inboxes\Replmgr.box) so that the file can be scheduled and copied to Collection Evaluator's inbox on the child site. If the child site is a secondary site, the file is rewritten to disk as a .CLF file and contains only the collection memberships. If the child site is a primary site, the collection will be processed in much the same fashion as described in the beginning of this section.

When a child site changes its parent site affiliation, Collection Evaluator is responsible for removing any collections that were created by the parent (and are therefore locked at the child site). When the child site joins the new parent site, the collections created at the parent site are passed down to the child site, and Collection Evaluator locks them and keeps them updated.

Status Messages

As with all SMS components, Collection Evaluator generates status messages as it processes collections and subcollections, as well as a log file if you have enabled logging for this component. The Status Message Viewer window shown in Figure 11-28 displays typical status messages generated by Collection Evaluator. Notice that this component's message IDs lie within the 25xx range. For example, message ID 2516 indicates that Collection Evaluator was notified that a new collection was added (by the SMS administrator, of course). The .ADC file is a wake-up file written by SQL Monitor.

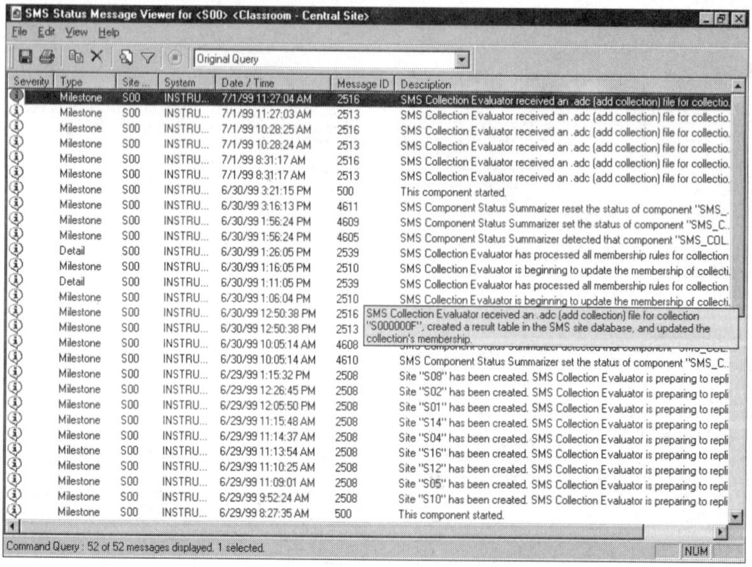

Figure 11-28. *Sample status messages generated by Collection Evaluator as it processes SMS collections.*

Notice also the 2508 messages, in which Collection Evaluator is set to replicate the site's collections and subcollections to child sites. The pairing of messages 2539 and 2510 indicates when the membership rules for a collection were processed and when the collection was updated.

In addition to these status messages, Collection Evaluator writes its thread activity to a log file named Colleval.log, if you enabled logging for this component. Figure 11-29 displays log entries as viewed through the SMS Trace utility. As you can see, there's really nothing remarkable here, except that you can view on a per-thread basis when Collection Evaluator processes each collection, updates or deletes wake-up files, and so on.

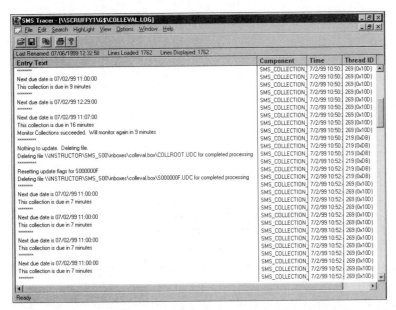

Figure 11-29. *Sample log entries generated by Collection Evaluator during normal processing.*

Collections and the SMS Site Hierarchy

Because the manner in which collections are handled within an SMS site hierarchy can be confusing, let's take a brief look at this topic. Collections created at a parent site will be propagated to that parent's child sites. However, the configurations of such collections will be locked to the child site's SMS administrator. As shown in Figure 11-30, a small lock icon appears next to these collections in the SMS Administrator Console showing that the collections are locked and can't be modified. The lock feature is by design. Collections created at the parent site can be modified only at the parent site. Child sites that receive these collections will evaluate them and populate them based on their SMS database, if they are also primary sites. All the members of a locked collection can be deleted by right-clicking the locked collection and choosing Delete Special from the context menu. However, if the deleted members are still valid at the parent site, they will reappear the next time the collection is evaluated and updated.

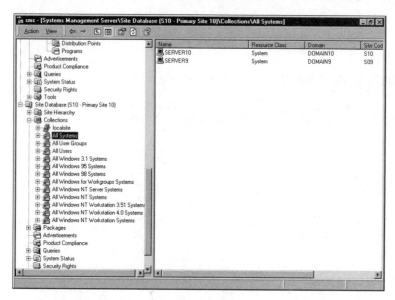

Figure 11-30. *Sample locked collections in the SMS Administrator Console.*

Child sites can create their own collections. These collections are fully manageable by the child site's SMS administrator and are not forwarded back up to the parent site. They will be propagated to their child sites and of course will be locked at the child sites.

Because secondary child sites do not maintain an SMS database of their own, their collections will be created and maintained at their parent sites. The secondary child sites will receive only the list of collection members that belong to their secondary site.

Note If a collection hasn't been updated for a week, SMS will automatically send the entire collection from a primary site to its child sites to synchronize the collections.

Checkpoints

There's not much danger lurking as far as collections are concerned. Any potential problems lie mostly in the setup of the collection. For example, remember that the most useful collections are those based on queries. Query-based membership rules allow the collection to be updated on a regular schedule that you define, ensuring that the collection will be kept up-to-date. However, this regular updating will not take place unless you enable that option on the Membership Rules tab of the Collection Properties window. Since this option is not enabled by default, it can be easily missed.

Another "gotcha" comes through the SMS Administrator Console. To view the members in a collection, you expand the Collections folder and highlight the collection entry. Remember that the collection members are not updated in the window automatically. After Collection Evaluator reevaluates the collections' memberships, you still need to refresh the screen by right-clicking on the Collections folder and choosing Refresh from the context menu. And if you force an update to one or all of the collections, you still need to refresh the screen—an update does not also refresh.

Summary

In this chapter, we've seen how much easier the life of the SMS administrator can become when the appropriate collections have been created, updated, and evaluated. Good collections, like properly configured Windows NT groups, can facilitate other SMS management activities, such as accessing clients for remote control, targeting clients for package distribution, troubleshooting remote clients, and so on. Chapter 12 will build on this management theme as we begin our examination of the package distribution capabilities of SMS 2.0.

Chapter 12
Package Distribution and Management

One of the primary features of Microsoft Systems Management Server (SMS) 2.0 is its ability to distribute packages to and run programs on SMS client computers. This process consists of three main elements:

- Creating and distributing the package
- Advertising a package program to a collection
- Receiving the advertisement and executing the program on a client

The package distribution process is the focus of this chapter—let's begin with a discussion of what package distribution is all about. First we'll define some terms and outline just what SMS does throughout the distribution process. Then we'll explore the administrative tasks involved in the creation of packages and advertisements. Finally we'll learn how to monitor status messages and log files for the appropriate SMS components involved, and how to test the package and its programs to ensure that they execute properly on the target clients.

Defining Package Distribution

The package distribution process is often misunderstood or mislabeled somehow by SMS administrators and users. It's important to remember that SMS 2.0 is fundamentally a package delivery tool. Basically, SMS is designed to make a package that you create available to a specified target or targets. The key here is that you are responsible for creating the package. You are also responsible for ensuring that the package will execute as intended when it reaches its target. SMS will get it there for you, but SMS will not "error-correct" it for you—nor should it be expected to.

Look at it this way. Suppose you are sending a bicycle to your nephew. You box it up carefully, go to your nearest package delivery service office, fill out the appropriate forms, pay the appropriate fees, and hand over the box. The responsibility of the package delivery service now is to get the box containing the bicycle to your nephew's house within the time frame you specified and paid for. Once the package arrives at your nephew's house, the delivery person may be kind enough to open the box and take the bicycle out but is under no obligation to do so. Nor is the delivery person expected to assemble the bicycle or teach your nephew how to ride it.

SMS works in much the same way. You, the SMS administrator, are responsible for creating the package and ensuring that all the appropriate pieces are assembled: source files, scripts, executables, command switches, and so on. You identify where the package must go and who should receive it. SMS carries out your instructions, and even "opens" the package when it arrives at the target. However, the ability of the package to execute—or the user's ability to use the application, for that matter—are not SMS's responsibility.

Terminology

This description of the basic package distribution process uses some terms that you are probably familiar with. Let's take a moment here to review these terms in more detail.

An *SMS package* generally represents a software application that needs to be installed on an SMS client computer. However, a package might also contain update programs or software patches, single files such as a virus update file, or no files at all—just a command to execute a program already resident on the client. You need to identify to SMS exactly what the package consists of.

Every package must contain at least one program. An *SMS program* identifies what should occur on the client when the package is received. Perhaps a setup routine is executed, or a virus scan is performed, or a file is copied to a particular directory. Perhaps the user needs to supply information such as the program directory, or perhaps no user intervention is required at all. A package may have several programs associated with it, allowing for the application to be run in a variety of ways on different clients. Consider your Microsoft Office 2000 installation. You can choose to perform a Typical, Custom, or Laptop installation of the software. If this software were an SMS package—and it could be—you would have to include a program for each of these installation methods if you intended to use them. Once again, you must define the program to SMS and include any and all appropriate references to script files or command switches. The program also defines the platform and environment within which the package can run.

For instance, can the package run on any platform, or only on Microsoft Windows NT 4.0 computers with Service Pack 4 installed? Can the program be executed by any user, or can it run only in an administrator context?

Some applications include predefined scripts called package definition files (PDFs) that can be used with SMS. *PDFs* contain all the package and program information required for SMS to successfully distribute the package and, usually, to deploy it. PDFs often come with the application's source file, or they can be obtained from the developer. You can also create PDFs using various tools and utilities from Microsoft. We'll return to PDFs in the section "Creating a Package from a Definition File" later in this chapter.

An *advertisement* makes the program and package available to a specified collection. Recall from Chapter 11 that collections can contain not only SMS client computers, but also Windows NT users and groups. This means that a program can be advertised to clients as well as to users and groups. So before you create the advertisement, you will need to have created the appropriate collections.

Advertisements are often used to schedule when a program runs and to specify whether the user can reschedule the program. Advertisements can also be configured to recur—that is, to make a program available on a recurring basis. For example, if you distribute virus update files on a monthly basis, you might create a virus update package and program and then an advertisement that makes the virus update file available on a monthly basis.

The Advertised Programs Client Agent (also sometimes referred to as the Advertised Programs Agent) is installed and started on the SMS client. As with other client agents, this agent is optional and must be configured and enabled by the SMS administrator. The Advertised Programs Client Agent's job is to monitor the client access point (CAP) for available advertised programs that target the client or the user at the client. When an advertisement is found and the program is ready to be run, the agent connects to an available distribution point—as defined in the package details—to execute the program. If the program runs an existing file on the client, the agent executes the program appropriately.

Two SMS site systems, in addition to the site server, are involved in the package distribution process: CAPs and distribution points. The CAP is always the point of interchange between the site server and the SMS clients. In this exchange, package detail information and advertisements are copied to the CAP for access by the Advertised Programs Client Agent on the client. The actual source files that constitute the package are copied to distribution points. Both CAPs and distribution points need to have been assigned before you can distribute any packages.

Remember that the site server becomes a CAP and a distribution point by default when you install SMS 2.0. (The role of site systems and how they are assigned is discussed in Chapter 3.)

Preparing for Package Distribution

As you can see from the previous section, many components are involved in package distribution. Before we continue our discussion of package distribution, let's outline the actions required for the distribution process:

- Define your CAPs and distribution points for the package
- Create appropriate collections
- Gather all source files, setup routines, scripts, and so on needed for the package
- Create the SMS package
- Define at least one program for the package
- Advertise the programs to one or more collections
- Distribute the package to the distribution points
- Execute the advertised program on the client

After reviewing these elements of the distribution process, you'll have a solid foundation to build on. The following sections of this chapter will cover how to configure various components for package distribution.

Creating Packages for Distribution

Now we can delve into the package distribution process in more detail, beginning with package creation itself. In this section, we will explore the package creation process, including identifying distribution points and creating programs.

Gathering Source Files

If your package involves the accessing of source files, such as performing a software installation, you must define a location for the source files. The location can be a shared folder on the site server or on a remote server, including a CD-ROM drive. The most important characteristic of the source file location is that it must be accessible to the SMS Service account. If your program involves using a script file or files, be sure to include them as part of your source files as well or the program will fail.

Creating a Package from Scratch

As in all things SMS, you will begin in the SMS Administrator Console. A package can be created either from scratch—one for which you provide all the configuration details—or from a package definition file that already contains all the package details. In this section, we'll look at the former technique.

To create a package from the ground up, follow these steps:

1. Navigate to the Packages folder, right-click on it, and choose New from the context menu, and then choose Package to display the Package Properties window, shown in Figure 12-1.

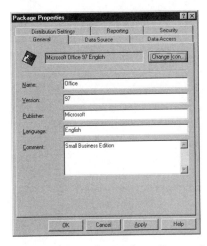

Figure 12-1. *The Package Properties window.*

2. On the General tab, enter the name of the package, its version, its publisher, its language, and a descriptive comment if desired. The only required value here is Name. Notice that the full package name is displayed in the text box to the left of the Change Icon button.

3. Click the Change Icon button to enter or browse for an icon file or Setup.exe file to display the correct icon for the package. The default icon is the SMS package icon.

4. Click on the Data Source tab, shown in Figure 12-2. This tab lets you define details concerning the source files for the package. If the package contains source files—even a single file—check the This Package Contains Source Files check box to enable the options in the Source Directory section.

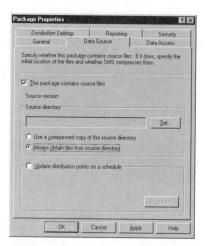

Figure 12-2. *The Data Source tab.*

5. Click the Set button to display the Set Source Directory dialog box, shown in Figure 12-3. In this dialog box, you define the location of the source files. The location can either be a local drive path or a UNC path to a remote share. Enter the location or click Browse to look for the directory. Then click OK to return to the Data Source tab.

Figure 12-3. *The Set Source Directory dialog box.*

6. If your source files are not likely to change or are on a removable medium such as CD-ROM, or if the source path is likely to change, select the Use A Compressed Copy Of The Source Directory option.

This option causes SMS to create and store a compressed version of the source files on the site server. When the package needs to be sent to a new distribution point or updated on existing distribution points, SMS will access the compressed files, uncompress them, and send them to the distribution points.

7. If your source files are likely to change periodically—for example, if they include a monthly virus update file—select Always Obtain Files From Source Directory. Selecting this option also allows you to check the Update Distribution Points On A Schedule check box. Setting an update schedule ensures that as the source files change, the distribution points will be updated regularly.

8. Click on the Data Access tab, shown in Figure 12-4. The Data Access tab defines how SMS will store the package source files on the distribution points. The default setting is Access Distribution Folder Through Common SMS Package Share. With this setting, SMS will define a share point on the distribution points and place the source files in a folder in that share. The share will always be SMSPKGx\$$, where x represents the drive with the most free disk space. This share is a hidden share to keep prying eyes from browsing for it. When SMS runs out of disk space, it will find the next drive with the most free space and create an additional SMSPKGx\$$ directory and share there.

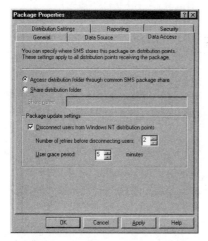

Figure 12-4. *The Data Access tab.*

9. If you prefer to create your own folder organization and access shares, you may do so first and then reference the share by selecting the option Share Distribution Folder and entering the UNC path to the share. This

value can be a share or a share and a path, but whatever value you enter must be unique among all packages. If you enter only a share name (in the form *server**appshare*), any file or subfolders created within the share will be deleted and re-created whenever the package is updated or refreshed. If you enter a share that includes a path (*server**appshare**word*), only the down-level folder will be deleted and re-created.

10. Check the Disconnect Users From Windows NT Distribution Points to do just that. If you want to ensure that no users are connected to the package folder on the distribution points when files are being refreshed or updated, this option will cause SMS to inform users that they will be disconnected. Users will be disconnected after the time period you specify in the User Grace Period text box. The default value is 5 minutes, but you can specify from 0 to 59 minutes. The Number Of Retries Before Disconnecting Users option indicates how many times SMS will attempt to refresh the distribution points before disconnecting users. This value can range from 0 to 99.

11. Click on the Distribution Settings tab, shown in Figure 12-5. On this tab, you identify the sending priority and preferred sender to use when sending this package to distribution points in a child site. If you have no child sites, these settings will have no effect. (Refer to Chapter 4 for a discussion of parent-child relationships and the role of the sender in transferring information between sites in the hierarchy.)

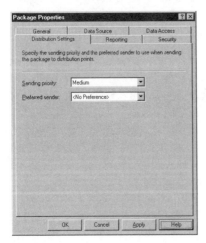

Figure 12-5. *The Distribution Settings tab.*

12. Click on the Reporting tab, shown in Figure 12-6. This tab lets you identify how SMS reports installation status Management Information Format (MIF) files from the client when the package is run. Select Use Package Properties For Status MIF Matching to simply use the values you supplied on the General tab to identify status MIF files generated during installation. Or, select Use These Fields For Status MIF Matching and fill in the fields if you want to specify different values.

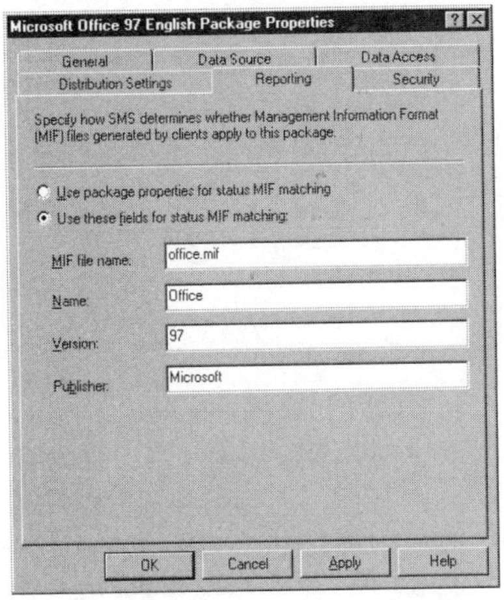

Figure 12-6. *The Reporting tab.*

13. Click on the Security tab to set class and instance security for the package. This type of security is discussed in Chapter 16.

14. Click OK to create the package.

We haven't quite finished creating this package. If you expand the new package entry you just created in the SMS Administrator Console, as in the example shown in Figure 12-7, you'll see that three areas of configuration remain. The first area, defining access accounts, allows you to further secure who has access to the distribution source files. The other two areas are absolutely essential to the successful distribution of the package: defining distribution points, without which the client has no access to the source files, and defining programs, which specifies how to install or run the source files. Let's configure the access account first.

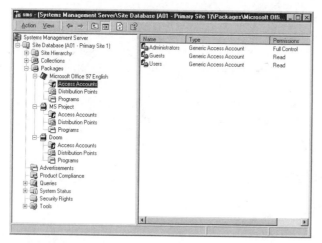

Figure 12-7. *A sample expanded package entry.*

Defining Access Accounts

By default, when SMS creates the SMSPKGx\$ share, it grants Read access to the local Users and Guests groups, and Full Control to the Administrators group. The default Users, Guests, and Administrators entries map to the local Users, Guests, and Administrators groups for Windows NT distribution points. On NetWare distribution points, Users and Guests map to the Everyone group, and Administrators maps to the Supervisor account. The Administrators, Users, and Guests accounts are known as generic accounts.

Since the default share is a hidden share, the only way a client should know that a package is available to it is through the package distribution process. In other words, the client agent will see an advertisement for that package that targets a collection the client is a member of. Bear in mind that users will be users, and it is possible that they will find the hidden share, navigate to a package folder, and execute any programs they find there. This could also happen if you create your own shares.

There are a couple of ways to deal with this little breach of security. One would be for you to evaluate the share (or NTFS) security for the SMS shares or for the package folders within the share. This is a time-consuming and potentially destructive process if you happen to lock out SMS from accessing the share. The other solution is to define access accounts for the package through the SMS Administrator Console. When you define an access account, you also define the level of access or permission for the specified user or group. This is very much like creating access control lists (ACLs) in Windows NT.

To define an access account, follow these steps:

1. Navigate to the Packages folder, find your package entry, and expand it.
2. Right-click on Access Accounts, choose New from the context menu, and then choose the type of access account you want to create.
3. The four types of access accounts are listed here:

   - **Windows NT access account**   Defines a Windows NT user or group account and the level of permission to allow
   - **NetWare NDS access account**   Defines a NetWare NDS user or group account and the level of permission to allow
   - **NetWare Bindery access account**   Defines a NetWare Bindery user or group account and the level of permission to allow
   - **Generic access account**   Defines additional or replacement user, guest, or administrator accounts and the level of permission to allow

   Select the appropriate option to display the Access Account Properties window, shown in Figure 12-8.

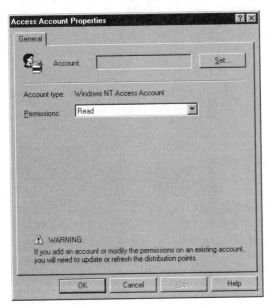

Figure 12-8. *The Access Account Properties window.*

4. Click the Set button to specify the account information as follows:

   - For a Windows NT account, the Windows NT Account dialog box will appear, as shown in Figure 12-9. Enter the user or group account in *Domain\user* format, and select User or Group.

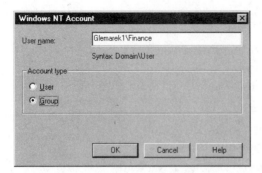

Figure 12-9. *The Windows NT Account dialog box.*

- For a NetWare NDS account, the NetWare NDS Account dialog box will appear, as shown in Figure 12-10. Enter the tree and user name information, and select User or Group.

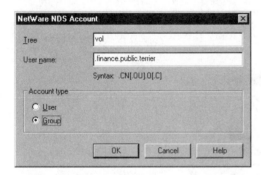

Figure 12-10. *The NetWare NDS Account dialog box.*

- For a NetWare Bindery account, the NetWare Bindery Account dialog box will appear, as shown in Figure 12-11. Enter the user or group account in *Server\User* format, and select User or Group.

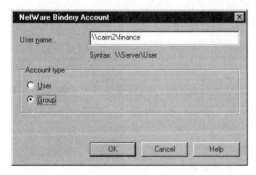

Figure 12-11. *The NetWare Bindery Account dialog box.*

- For a Generic account, the Generic Account dialog box will appear, as shown in Figure 12-12. Select the account type.

Figure 12-12. *The Generic Account dialog box.*

5. Click OK to return to the Access Account Properties window. Select the appropriate level of permissions from the Permissions list, as shown in Figure 12-13. For most applications, Read permission will be sufficient. However, if the program requires any kind of writing back to the source directory, you will need to assign at least Change permission.

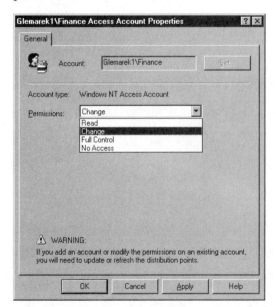

Figure 12-13. *The Permissions list on the General tab of the Access Account Properties window.*

6. Click OK to create the account.

Defining Distribution Points

An essential configuration detail for any package is identifying the distribution points on which the package can be found. You should have already assigned the distribution point role to one or more site systems in your SMS site, as well as at any child sites. You now need to tell SMS which of those distribution points will host the package.

> **Note** If you are distributing the package to a child site, even if the SMS administrator for that site will ultimately distribute the package to its clients, you still must identify at least one distribution point at that child site when you create the package.

To define distribution points, follow these steps:

1. Navigate to the Packages folder, find your package entry, and expand it.

2. Right-click on Distribution Points, choose New from the context menu, and then choose Distribution Points to activate the New Distribution Points Wizard, shown in Figure 12-14.

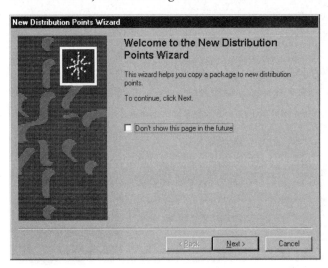

Figure 12-14. *The New Distribution Points Wizard welcome screen.*

3. Click Next to display the Copy Package screen, shown in Figure 12-15. This screen shows a list of available distribution points. Scroll through the list and select the distribution points you want.

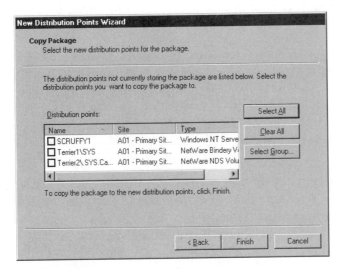

Figure 12-15. *The Copy Package screen.*

4. Click the Select Group button to open the Browse Distribution Point Group dialog box, shown in Figure 12-16. Here you can view a list of distribution point groups and their member site systems. If you select one of the distribution point groups and click OK, all the site systems that are members of that group will be selected in the Copy Package screen.

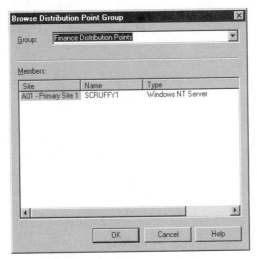

Figure 12-16. *The Browse Distribution Point Group dialog box.*

5. Click Finish to add the distribution points you selected to the package details.

Once you have added a distribution point to the package, that distribution point will no longer appear in the list of available distribution points if you run the New Distribution Points Wizard again—the wizard displays only distribution points that are available. If you need to remove a distribution point from the package, select it, right-click on it, and choose Delete from the context menu. When you delete a distribution point, you will also delete the package source directory on that distribution point.

It is often desirable to group distribution points so that packages can be distributed to them as a block rather than having to name the distribution points individually. Distribution point groups are defined through the site settings of your site—in the same place that you assign the distribution point role.

To define a distribution point group, follow these steps:

1. In the SMS Administrator Console, navigate to the Site Systems folder under Site Settings.

2. Right-click on one of the distribution points you defined, and choose Properties from the context menu to display the Site System Properties window. Click on the Distribution Point tab, shown in Figure 12-17.

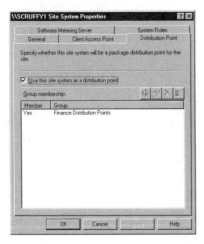

Figure 12-17. *The Distribution Point tab of the Site System Properties window.*

3. To add a new distribution point group, in the Group Membership section click the New button (the yellow star) to display the Distribution Point Group Properties window, shown in Figure 12-18. Enter the name of the group and indicate whether this site system is to be a member of the group. Then click OK to return to the Site System Properties window.

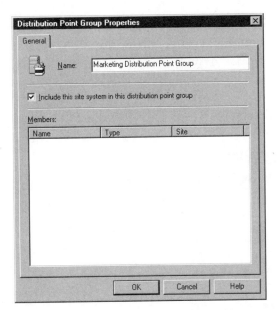

Figure 12-18. *The Distribution Point Group Properties window.*

4. Select the next site system you want to include in the distribution point group, right-click on it, choose Properties from the context menu, and click on the Distribution Point tab. Notice that any distribution point groups you have created will be listed on this tab for each site system, as shown in Figure 12-19.

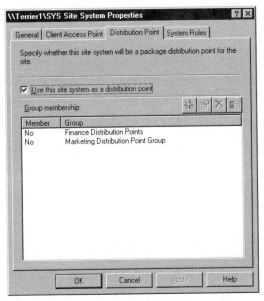

Figure 12-19. *The updated Group Membership list on the Distribution Point tab.*

5. Select the distribution point group that this site system should be a member of and click the Properties button (the hand holding a piece of paper) to display the Distribution Point Group Properties window, shown in Figure 12-20. Select the Include This Site System In This Distribution Point Group check box, and then click OK to return to the Distribution Point tab. The site system will now show that it is a member of the distribution point group. Click OK again.

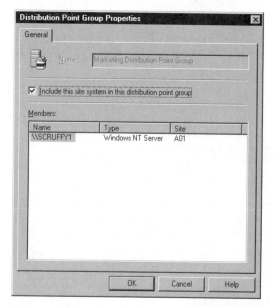

Figure 12-20. *The updated Distribution Point Group Properties window.*

6. Repeat step 5 for every site system that needs to be a member of a distribution point group.

If you need to remove a site system from a distribution point group, simply repeat step 5 of this procedure, but clear the Include This Site System In This Distribution Point Group check box. If you need to remove a distribution point group altogether, select any site system, open its Site Systems Properties window, and click on the Distribution Point tab. Select the distribution point group in the Group Membership list and click the Delete button (the black "X").

Creating Programs

Finally, it is necessary to create at least one program for each package. This program specifies how the package is to be executed at the client. Many packages can have more than one program associated with them. For example, a package might have different installation methods such as Custom, Typical, and Compact. This is where you really have to know your package. The command-line information you provide here will either make or break the package when it is run on the client.

To create a program, follow these steps:

1. Navigate to the Packages folder, find your package entry, and expand it.

2. Right-click on Programs, choose New from the context menu, and then choose Program to display the Program Properties window, shown in Figure 12-21.

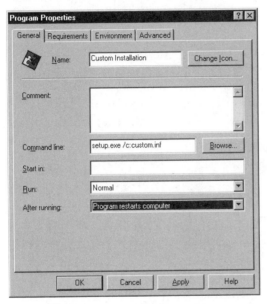

Figure 12-21. *The Program Properties window.*

3. On the General tab, enter a descriptive name for the program—for example, *Custom Installation* or *Unattended Installation*. Enter additional descriptive information in the Comment text box.

4. In the Command Line text box, enter the command that should be executed at the client. This could be a Setup.exe file or a batch file; however, you must include any and all command-line arguments required for successful execution. For example, if you run the Setup program, which uses a script file called Custom.inf, and this script file is invoked by the Setup program through a "/c" command-line switch, you must enter the full command as it references the script: setup.exe /c:custom.inf.

5. In the Start In text box, enter the name and path of the directory in which you want the program to start. This field is optional, and by default the distribution folder on the distribution point is used.

6. From the Run drop-down list, select an option—Normal, Minimized, Maximized, or Hidden—to specify how the program will be displayed to the user. Hidden does mean that nothing will be displayed; this option is best used with fully unattended, or silent, installations.

7. From the After Running drop-down list, select an option—No Action Required, SMS Restarts Computer, Program Restarts Computer, or SMS Logs User Off—to specify what action, if any, will be performed after the program completes.

8. Click on the Requirements tab, shown in Figure 12-22. This tab lets you specify descriptive elements regarding the program's estimated size and installation run time. More importantly, it allows you to identify which operating system platforms the program can run on. This enables you to filter out those clients on whose platform the program can't run.

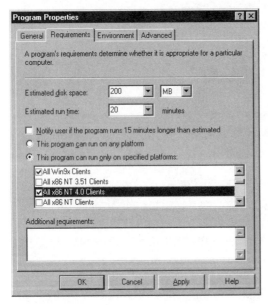

Figure 12-22. *The Requirements tab.*

9. Click on the Environment tab, shown in Figure 12-23. On this tab, user level and drive mode requirements are defined. First specify when the program can run. The drop-down list options are Only When A User Is Logged On, which would apply to all Windows 98 and earlier clients;

Whether Or Not A User Is Logged On; and Only When No User Is Logged On. These last two options are specific to Windows NT computers. If either of these options is selected, the User Input Required check box and the Run With User's Rights Run Mode option are automatically disabled.

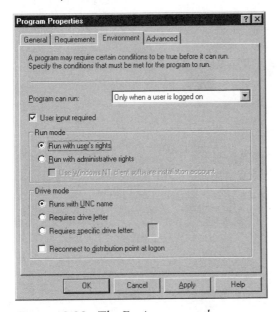

Figure 12-23. *The Environment tab.*

10. If the program requires the user to click even a single OK button, you must select Only When A User Is Logged On from the Program Can Run drop-down list, and then select the User Input Required option. Clear this option only if the program is fully scripted. If the program must be run in the local administrative account, select the Run With Administrative Rights option in the Run Mode section. If you have specified a particular account to use on Windows NT computers when running programs that require administrative privileges, select the Use Windows NT Client Software Installation Account check box.

11. In the Drive Mode section, select the option that best fits the program. As you have no doubt experienced, while most programs understand UNC paths, some do not and require at least a drive letter mapping. If you need to have the client reconnect to the distribution point each time the user logs on, check the Reconnect To Distribution Point At Logon check box. This option could be useful if the application needs to write

information back to the distribution folder on the distribution point, retrieve startup files, and so on. Just remember that 16-bit clients do not support this feature.

12. Click on the Advanced tab, shown in Figure 12-24, which provides several additional options. If you need to run another program before this one—for example, to install a service pack or a patch, select the Run Another Program First check box and then select the appropriate package and program. This assumes, of course, that you have already created the other package and program. In this example you won't need to advertise the other program separately.

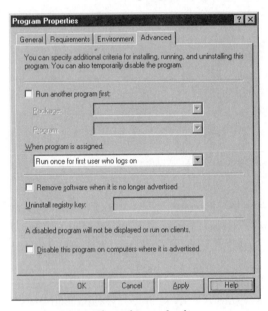

Figure 12-24. *The Advanced tab.*

13. Some applications, especially those that register using Add/Remove Programs in Control Panel, write uninstall information to a key in the registry under HKEY_LOCAL_MACHINE\Software\Microsoft\Windows\ CurrentVersion\Uninstall. If this is true of your program, select the Remove Software When It Is No Longer Advertised check box and then enter the name of the key that the program writes in the Uninstall Registry Key text box. The effect of this setting is that when the program is

no longer advertised to the client—say, the advertisement was deleted, it expired, or its collection membership no longer includes the client—the application will be uninstalled from the client automatically.

14. To temporarily disable the program from being run—even if it has been assigned a specific time—select the Disable This Program On Clients Where It Is Advertised check box. This option can be handy if you need to update files, test an installation, and so on.

15. Click OK to save the program.

If you later decide to delete a program, you would do so by right-clicking on the program in the SMS Administrator Console and choosing Delete from the context menu to activate the Delete Program Wizard. This wizard walks you through the process and helps you decide whether to delete the program. Deleting a program does produce a ripple effect for other SMS components. Any advertisements of the program will also be deleted and will no longer be made available to the client. If you selected the Remove Software When It Is No Longer Advertised option on the Advanced tab, you could end up removing the application from the client computers. The wizard displays all the affected advertisements and prompts you once more to confirm the deletion.

In Chapter 11, we examined the advantages of using collections whose membership rules are query-based when advertising programs. When a new member joins the collection, it automatically receives any advertisements made to that collection. In general, you should leave programs advertised until they are no longer needed or until they should be retired.

Creating a Package from a Definition File

We've seen what's involved in creating a package from the ground up. Now let's see how much simpler the process becomes when you're creating a package from a package definition file.

To create a package from a predefined definition file, follow these steps:

1. Navigate to the Packages folder, right-click on it, choose New from the context menu, and choose Package From Definition. This will initiate the Create Package From Definition Wizard, shown in Figure 12-25.

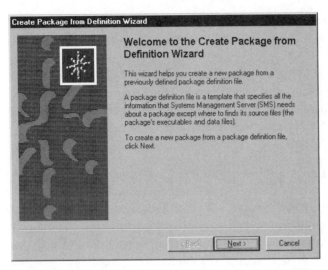

Figure 12-25. *The Create Package From Definition Wizard welcome screen.*

2. Click Next to display the Package Definition screen, shown in Figure 12-26. Select one of the definitions provided by SMS 2.0 from the Package Definition list, click the Browse button to search for an SMS 2.0 compatible .SMS or .PDF file, or select SMS 1.x PDF from the Publisher drop-down list to browse for or select an earlier version definition file.

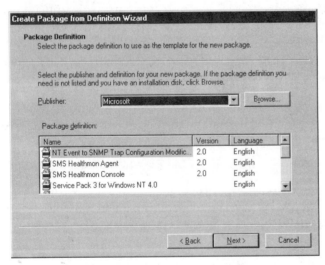

Figure 12-26. *The Package Definition screen.*

3. Click Next to display the Source Files screen, shown in Figure 12-27. Here you specify how SMS should manage source files.

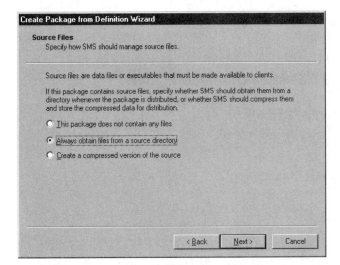

Figure 12-27. *The Source Files screen.*

4. If you select This Package Does Not Contain Any Files and click Next, you will proceed directly to step 5. If you select one of the other options and click Next, the Source Directory screen will appear, as shown in Figure 12-28. In this screen, identify either the network or local drive location of the source files and click Next.

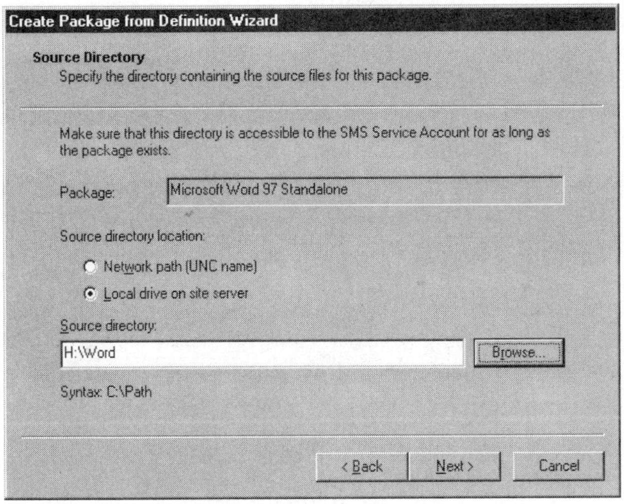

Figure 12-28. *The Source Directory screen.*

5. The Completing The Create Package From Definition Wizard screen will appear, as shown in Figure 12-29. Review your choices, and then click Finish.

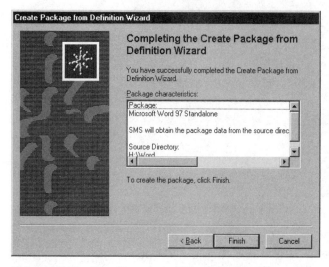

Figure 12-29. *The Completing The Create Package From Definition Wizard screen.*

Right-clicking on the package you just created in the SMS Administrator Console will display the Package Properties window. The end result will be the creation of a package with the essential package details filled in and the appropriate programs created with their essential details filled in on the General, Data Source, and Reporting tabs of the Package Properties window. The Data Access and Distribution Settings tabs are left with the default values. Figures 12-30 through 12-37 will give you an idea of the type of information generated by the package definition file provided with SMS 2.0 for distributing Microsoft Windows 2000 Professional. Of course, while SMS 2.0 or any other application developer provides the package definition file itself, you will still need to obtain a copy of the source files for the application.

The General tab of the Package Properties window, shown in Figure 12-30, contains the package detail information.

The settings on the Data Source tab, shown in Figure 12-31, are based on the parameters you defined using the Create Package From Definition Wizard.

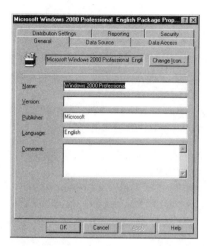

Figure 12-30. *The General tab of the Package Properties window.*

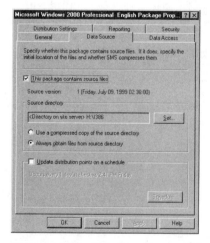

Figure 12-31. *The Data Source tab of the Package Properties window.*

Package definition files do not always provide status MIF information for the Reporting tab. However, the package definition file for Windows 2000 Professional provided with SMS 2.0 does fill in some information, as shown in Figure 12-32. You need to enter the MIF filename that should be used.

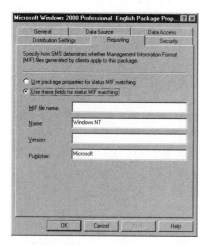

Figure 12-32. *The Reporting tab of the Package Properties window.*

The package definition file is designed to generate all appropriate programs for the application package. The package definition file for Windows 2000 Professional creates four programs, as shown in Figure 12-33.

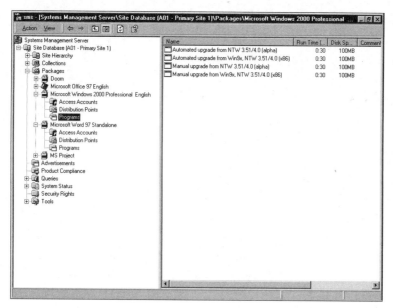

Figure 12-33. *The SMS Administrator Console showing programs generated for Windows 2000 Professional.*

Right-clicking on the automated upgrade for the x86 platforms entry will display the General tab of the Automated Upgrade Program Properties window, shown in Figure 12-34, which provides the appropriate command-line executable and switches.

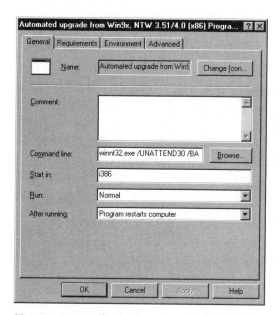

Figure 12-34. *The General tab of the Automated Upgrade Program Properties window.*

The Requirements tab, shown in Figure 12-35, displays the estimated disk space and estimated run-time settings—all provided by the package definition file.

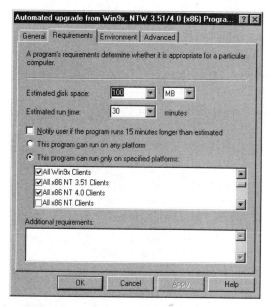

Figure 12-35. *The Requirements tab of the Automated Upgrade Program Properties window.*

Because the upgrade to Windows 2000 Professional requires administrative level access at the client, the program definition file specifies that option on the Environment tab, as shown in Figure 12-36.

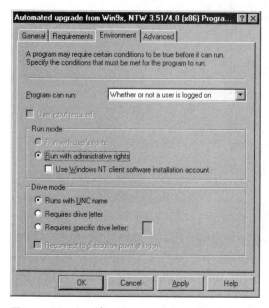

Figure 12-36. *The Environment tab of the Automated Upgrade Program Properties window.*

As for the Advanced tab, shown in Figure 12-37, the package definition file doesn't provide any property settings for you. Again, it's up to you to decide whether to run another program first, remove the program when it is no longer available, or temporarily disable the advertisement.

In general, the package definition file will provide package details for the General and Data Source tabs of the Package Properties window, which should make sense. Distribution settings, for example, define how a package is sent from one site to another, and only the SMS administrator for each site can modify those settings. On the other hand, most of the property settings in the Automated Upgrade Program Properties window usually will be provided by the package definition file. The exceptions are the options on the Advanced tab, where you'll need to set the options that apply to your package on your own.

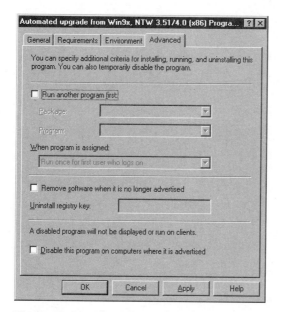

Figure 12-37. *The Advanced tab of the Automated Upgrade Program Properties window.*

Package Distribution Process Flow

The process behind the creation and distribution of a package, illustrated in Figure 12-38, is fairly straightforward. We begin, as always, with the SMS administrator defining the package, distribution points, and programs. This information is written to the SMS database by the SMS Provider. This action triggers SQL Monitor to write a package notification wake-up file to Distribution Manager's inbox (\SMS\Inboxes\Distmgr.box). The wake-up file takes the form of a site code and package ID as the filename with a .PKN extension. For example, a package notification file for site A01 might be named A0100003.pkn.

The Distribution Manager component wakes up and processes the package based on the package details you provided. Distribution Manager performs the following general tasks:

- Compresses the source files, if necessary
- Copies the package source directory to the specified distribution points
- Creates various instruction files for clients that are copied to the CAPs by Inbox Manager
- Creates replication files for sending the package to child sites

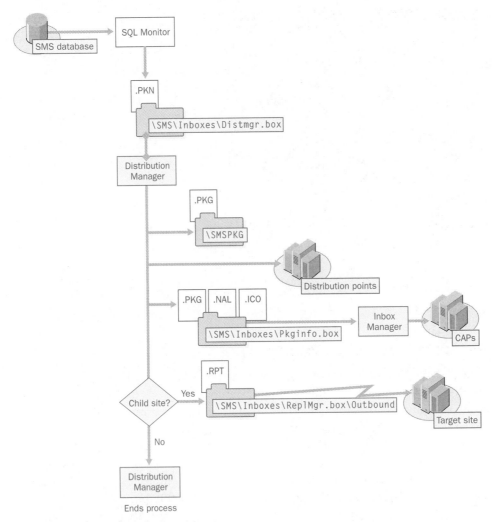

Figure 12-38. *The package distribution process flow.*

If you specified that a compressed version of the files should be used, Distribution Manager will compress the files and store them either in the location specified when the Software Distribution component was configured (this process is discussed in the next section) or by default in the SMSPKG folder created on the drive on which SMS was installed on the site server, with the same filename and the extension .PKG.

Distribution Manager then copies the source file directory to the SMSPKG*x*$ folder created on each specified distribution point within the site. If the package files were compressed, Distribution Manager uncompresses them first.

Distribution Manager generates three files and writes them to the SMS\Inboxes\ Pkginfo.box folder on the site server. These files (with filenames as described earlier) are:

- **.PKG**   Package program detail information
- **.NAL**   Location of distribution points
- **.ICO**   Icon file information

The Inbox Manager component, as it is wont to do, copies these files to the Pkginfo.box folder on each CAP. These files serve as instruction files for the client after it receives an advertisement. At this point, the process stops unless the package needs to be sent to a child site.

If the package does need to be sent to a child site, Distribution Manager writes a package replication file (.RPT) to Replication Manager's inbox (SMS\Inboxes\ Replmgr.box\Outbound). If a compressed copy of the package source directory does not already exist, Distribution Manager also compresses the source directory into a temporary directory on the site server and then moves the file to the SMSPKG folder (on the SMS installation drive on the site server or the drive you specified when configuring the Software Distribution component).

Now Replication Manager takes over and begins the sending process. This process is discussed in detail in Chapter 4, so we'll look at only the highlights here. Replication Manager creates a minijob for the Scheduler and places it in the Scheduler's inbox (SMS\Inboxes\Schedule.box). The Scheduler creates the package and instruction files needed for sending the data in question, as well as a send request file for the sender. The package and instruction files are placed in the SMS\ Inboxes\Schedule.box\Tosend directory. The send request file is written to the preferred sender's outbox (SMS\Inboxes\Schedule.box\Outboxes*sender*, where *sender* is the sender folder, such as LAN, RASAsynch, RASISDN, and so on). Recall that both the sending priority and the preferred sender are identified in the Package Properties window.

When the send request file is written, the sender wakes up and reads the file. It also examines whether the address properties have placed any restrictions on when requests of this priority can be sent and whether there are any bandwidth limits. It then changes the extension of the send request file to .SRS and writes status information to it.

The sender connects to the target site's SMS_SITE share—the SMS\Inboxes\ Despoolr.box\Receive directory—where the Despooler component on the target site will complete processing of the information at the target site. When the data has been completely transferred, the send request file is updated to a status of "completed," and the file is then deleted. Distribution Manager on the target site will carry out any necessary tasks. For example, if you identified distribution points at the target site, the Despooler will decompress the package and pass it to Distribution Manager, which will process the package for those distribution points.

Configuring the Software Distribution Component

Additional settings can be configured for the package distribution process if the SMS defaults are not appropriate within your environment.

To access these settings, in the SMS Administrator Console, navigate to the Component Configuration folder under Site Settings, expand it, right-click on Software Distribution, and select Properties to display the Software Distribution Properties window, shown in Figure 12-39.

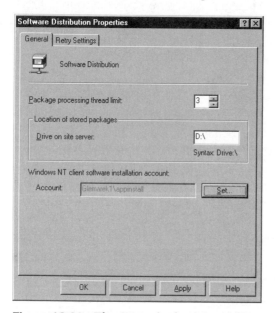

Figure 12-39. *The General tab of the Software Distribution Properties window.*

The Package Processing Thread Limit option on the General tab lets you identify how many threads to allocate to Distribution Manager to process packages for the site. The default value is 3, but it can range from 1 through 7. In this case, more is not always better. If your site server were only processing packages—and not performing any other functions—you might bump up this number, monitor the performance of the site server, and determine what value achieves an optimum level of performance between package processing and other server functions. A higher number of allocated threads may be appropriate and assignable.

However, if the site server has all SMS functions enabled—package distribution, software metering, Remote Tools, inventory collection, all site system roles, and so on—increasing the number of threads may prove to be detrimental to the overall performance of the site server. The best rule of thumb would be to try adjusting the number if you feel you need to improve package processing performance and then use the various tools available to monitor the performance of the site server and its other functions to find the best balance.

Two other options you can configure on the General tab are Location Of Stored Packages, which identifies for SMS the drive on which it should create the compressed package folder (SMSPKG), and the SMS Windows NT Client Software Installation account. When programs are executed at the client computer, they will run under the local user account's security context. Since most users are logged on as users and not as administrators, this means that these programs will run under the local user context. As you have probably discovered, most application software installs .DLL files, modifies registry entries, stops and starts services, and performs other tasks that require an administrative security context on the client. For Windows 95 and Windows 98 clients, this security context is not usually a big issue. However, it is a big issue for Windows NT clients since they maintain a local account database and provide more security over system modifications.

Security poses a problem when you're dealing with SMS packages. One of our main objectives here is to be able to remotely install software on clients without the users'—or the administrator's—intervention. Earlier versions of SMS simply had no way to deal with this problem, and eventually resource kit and third-party utilities were created to assist the SMS administrator.

SMS 2.0, however, does provide two solutions to the security issue. The first involves the use of an internal account that SMS creates on the client when a higher level of security access is required to run a program. This account, named SMSCliToknAcct&, is created automatically and is granted Act As Part Of The Operating System, Log On As A Service, and Replace Process Level Token user rights on the client. The SMSCliToknAcct& account will be sufficient in most cases. However, if the program execution requires that the program connect to network resources other than the distribution point, SMSCliToknAcct& will fail because it is created as a local account rather than a domain account. In this case, you should use the second solution, the Windows NT Client Software Installation account.

You create the Windows NT Client Software Installation account in the Windows NT domain (or domains) your clients are members of. The easiest thing to do, of course, would be to make the account a member of the Domain Admins global group in the domain that the Windows NT client is a member of. As you know, when a computer running Windows NT joins a Windows NT domain, the Domain Admins global group is made a member of the local Administrators group on that computer. Making the account a member of the Domain Admins group would give it the appropriate level of local rights on the Windows NT client (provided you haven't altered the local Administrator group memberships to exclude the Domain Admins group), but this arrangement is not very secure. Ideally, this account should be made a direct member of the local Administrator's group on each client computer or be given the appropriate level of security access required to run the programs you create.

After you create and configure the account appropriately, identify it to SMS on the General tab of the Software Distribution Properties window by clicking the Set button next to the Windows NT Client Software Installation Account text box and entering the name of the account in the Windows NT Account dialog box.

The Retry Settings tab of the Software Distribution Properties window is fairly self-explanatory, as shown in Figure 12-40. It lets you alter the retry settings for Distribution Manager's attempts to deliver packages and for Advertisement Manager's attempts to advertise programs and specify the delay between attempts.

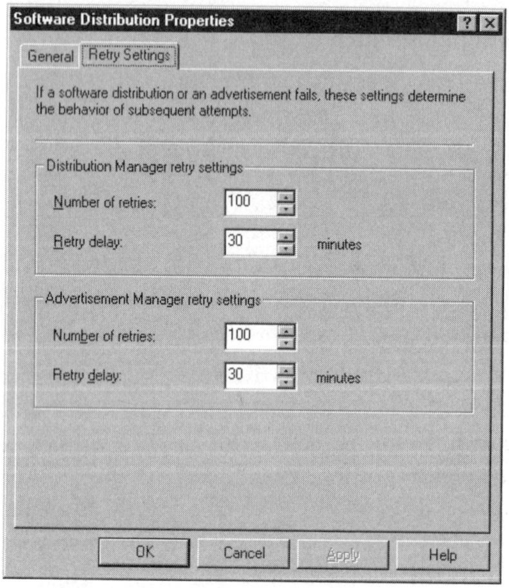

Figure 12-40. *The Retry Settings tab.*

Distribute Software Wizard

In addition to the methods described earlier in this chapter for creating and distributing a package and an advertisement, SMS 2.0 includes an alternative tool called the Distribute Software Wizard. This wizard walks you through each step in the process of creating or identifying a package and program, defining a distribution point, creating or identifying a collection to a target, and creating an advertisement.

To run the Distribute Software Wizard, follow these steps:

1. Right-click on any collection, resource, package, program, or advertisement in the SMS Administrator Console, choose All Tasks from the context menu, and then choose Distribute Software to launch the Distribute Software Wizard, shown in Figure 12-41.

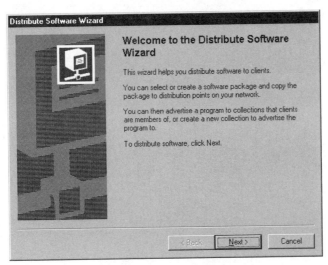

Figure 12-41. *The Distribute Software Wizard welcome screen.*

2. Click Next to display the Package screen, shown in Figure 12-42. Here you can create a new package and program from scratch or from a definition file or you can select an existing package.

3. Click Next. The next few Distribute Software Wizard screens will vary depending on whether you are creating a new program from scratch or from a package definition or by selecting an existing program. If you selected an existing package, the Distribution Points screen is displayed, as shown in Figure 12-43. Select the distribution point that should receive the package source files.

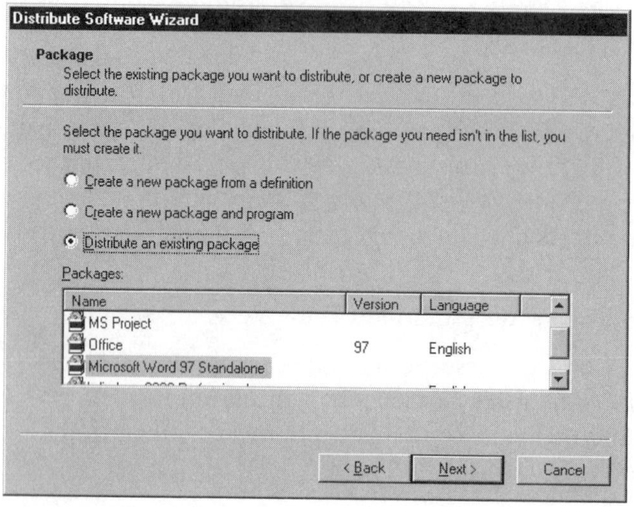

Figure 12-42. *The Package screen.*

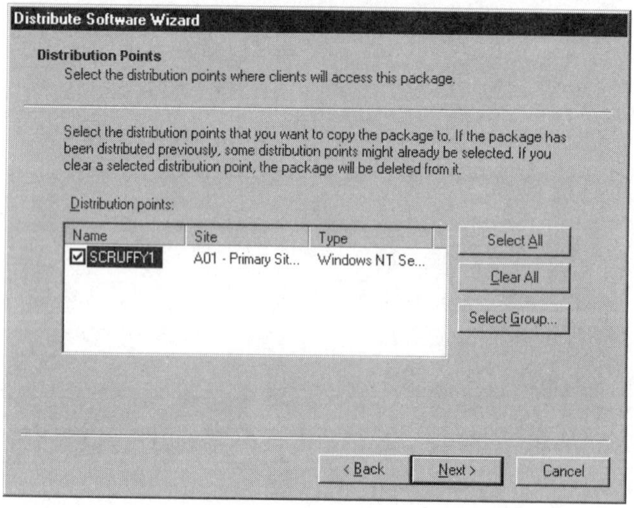

Figure 12-43. *The Distribution Points screen.*

If you selected Create A New Package From A Definition, you will be presented with screens asking you to select the package definition file and define the source file directory.

If you selected Create A New Package And Program, the wizard will prompt you for a package name and identification, the location of source files, if there are any, the program name and command line, as well as ask whether user input is required or administrative rights are needed.

Eventually, you will see a screen similar to the Advertise A Program screen shown in Figure 12-44 asking whether you want to advertise the program to a collection.

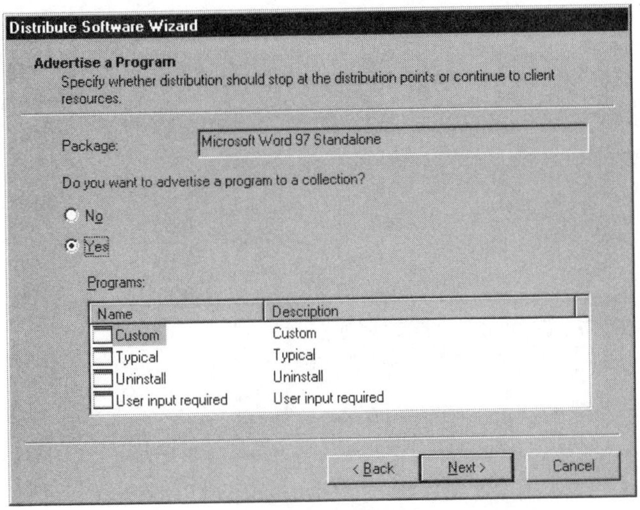

Figure 12-44. *The Advertise A Program screen.*

4. If you choose No and click Next, you'll go directly to the Completing The Distribute Software Wizard screen. If you choose Yes and click Next, the Advertisement Target screen is displayed, as shown in Figure 12-45.

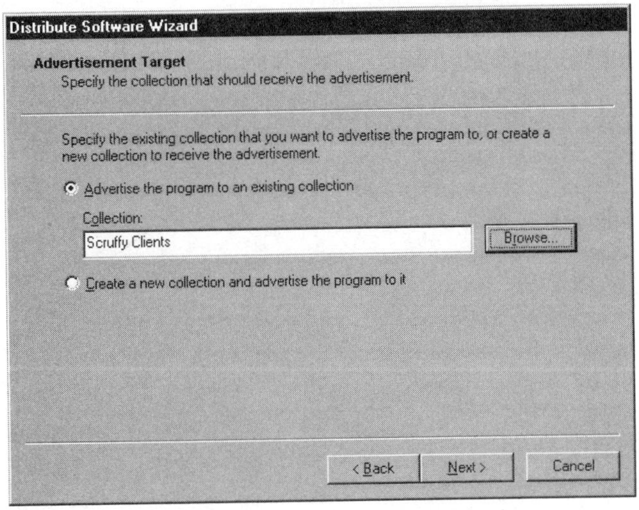

Figure 12-45. *The Advertisement Target screen.*

5. From this screen, you can create a new collection and advertise a program to it or enter an existing collection. If you choose to create a new collection, the wizard will prompt you for the collection name and membership rules.

6. Click Next. The next few screens prompt for advertisement properties. On the Advertisement Name screen, shown in Figure 12-46, enter a descriptive name and comment for the advertisement.

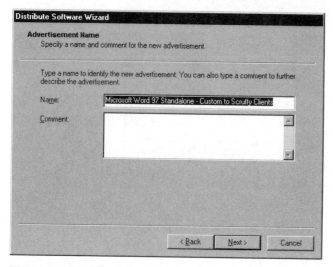

Figure 12-46. *The Advertisement Name screen.*

7. Click Next to display the Advertise To Subcollections screen, shown in Figure 12-47. Here you can specify whether to advertise to the collection's subcollections if any exist.

8. Click Next to display the Advertisement Schedule screen, shown in Figure 12-48. This screen lets you specify when the advertisement should be offered and whether it expires.

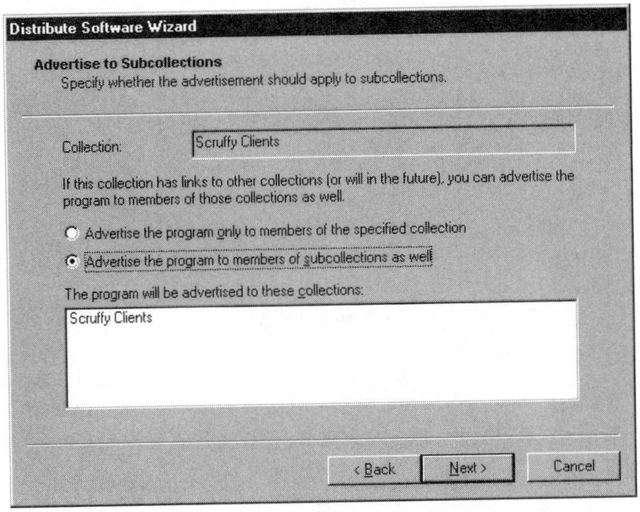

Figure 12-47. *The Advertise To Subcollections screen.*

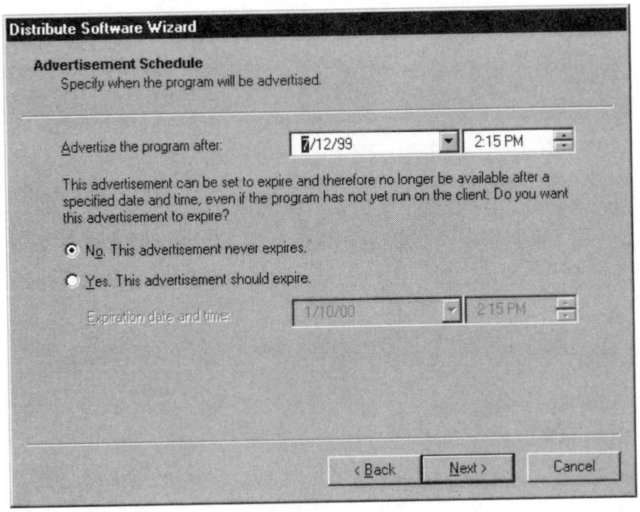

Figure 12-48. *The Advertisement Schedule screen.*

9. Click Next to display the Assign Program screen, shown in Figure 12-49. Here you can specify an assigned time if necessary.

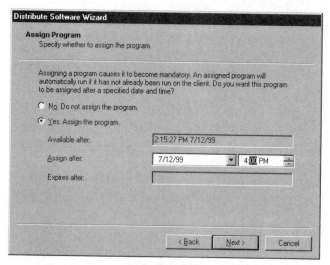

Figure 12-49. *The Assign Program screen.*

10. Click Next to display the Completing The Distribute Software Wizard screen, shown in Figure 12-50. Review your selections, and then click Finish to begin the package distribution and advertisement processes.

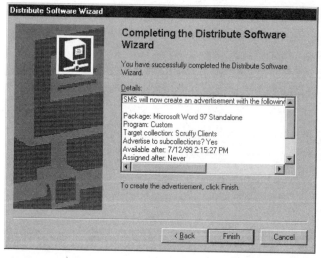

Figure 12-50. *The Completing The Distribute Software Wizard screen.*

As you've probably noticed, the Distribute Software Wizard does not present you with all possible options available for packages, programs, and advertisements. For example, you cannot create a recurring advertisement using this wizard. However, the wizard does provide a fine method for generating general packages, programs, collections, and advertisements. There's also a neat technique for targeting one computer without having to create a collection of one: use the wizard to create the collection for you. Simply launch the wizard by right-clicking on the computer resource you want to target.

> **Note** In case you were wondering, you cannot use Ctrl+click to select more than one client at a time in a collection. There is currently no way to target a group of two or three computers that are part of a larger membership without creating a separate collection for them. Perhaps we'll see this functionality in a future release of SMS.

Creating an Advertisement

After you have created your packages and programs, the next step is to create an advertisement. Remember, before you configure an advertisement, you must have identified and created the collections that you will advertise the programs to. Programs are always advertised to collections—even if it is a collection of one.

To create an advertisement, follow these steps:

1. In the SMS Administrator Console, navigate to the Advertisements folder, right-click on it, choose New from the context menu, and then choose Advertisement to display the Advertisement Properties window, as shown in Figure 12-51.

2. On the General tab, begin by entering a descriptive name for the advertisement. Enter a descriptive comment to add more detail. Select the package and program to advertise from their respective list boxes. Enter the collection name, or browse for it by clicking the Browse button. If the collection has subcollections and you want to include them in the advertisement, check the Include Members Of Subcollections check box.

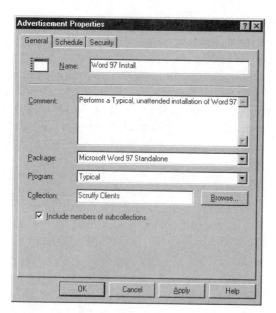

Figure 12-51. *The Advertisement Properties window*

3. Click the Schedule tab, shown in Figure 12-52. Begin by selecting the start time and date for the advertisement. This setting represents the time at which the program is advertised and made available for the client to run. By default, the advertisement will be made available in all time zones at the same time, meaning that if the advertisement start time is 3:00 in New York, it is made available in New York at 3:00, in Chicago at 2:00, in London at 8:00, and so on. If you want the advertisement to be made available at a specific hour in each time zone—for example, at 3:00 in New York, Chicago, and London, check the Greenwich Mean Time check box.

4. If the advertisement will be available for only a specific period of time, check the Advertisement Will Expire check box, select an expiration date, and check Greenwich Mean Time if desired. The priority you specify is a sending priority only and is used when the advertisement is sent to a child site.

5. You can also assign a run time to the advertisement. To configure this option, click the New button in the Mandatory Assignments section of the Schedule tab to display the Assignment Schedule dialog box, shown in Figure 12-53. Here you can assign a mandatory time and date for the advertised program to run. If the program is not run by this time and date, the Advertised Programs Client Agent on the client will execute it.

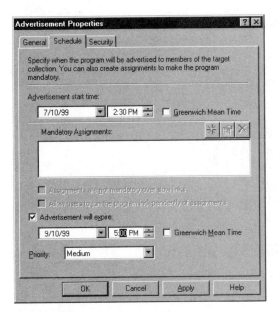

Figure 12-52. *The Schedule tab.*

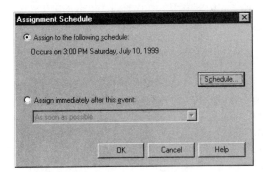

Figure 12-53. *The Assignment Schedule dialog box.*

6. If you select Assign To The Following Schedule and click the Schedule button, the Schedule dialog box will appear, as shown in Figure 12-54. In this dialog box, you can specify exactly when you want to run the advertised program. You can also set a recurrence interval for advertisements such as monthly virus file updates.

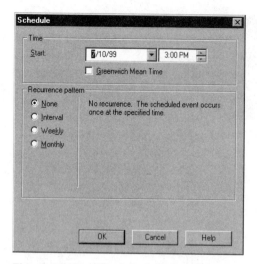

Figure 12-54. *The Schedule dialog box.*

7. If you select the Assign Immediately After This Event option in the Assignment Schedule dialog box, you can choose to have the advertised program execute as soon as possible—meaning as soon as the program reaches the client and all program requirements (correct platform, user logged on, administrator access, and so on) are met; at logoff—the next time a user logs off the client; or at logon—the next time a user logs on to the client.

8. Click OK to return to the Schedule tab. If you configure a mandatory assignment, two additional options become available. Select the Assignments Are Not Mandatory Over Slow Links check box to prevent a potentially large program from running if the Advertised Programs Client Agent discovers that the network is overutilized. Check the Allow Users To Run The Program Independently Of Assignments check box if you want to give the user the option of canceling a mandatory advertisement when it is scheduled to run or to reschedule when the advertisement runs.

9. Click OK to create the advertisement.

Note   If you have not yet identified a distribution point for the package, you will be notified of that fact when you click OK. Also, if you have not yet enabled the Advertised Programs Client Agent for the clients, you will be given the option to do so.

Real World   Recurring Assignments

As we've seen, you can specify a recurring schedule for your advertisement. This setting can be useful for programs that need to be executed on a regular basis. Let's return to our virus update file example. Suppose you have created a package that distributes a virus update file once a month. On the 14th of every month, you obtain a virus update file and replace the old file in the package source file directory with the new file. You also configure the package to refresh its distribution points once a month, say on the 15th.

When you create the advertisement, give it an assigned schedule. Set it to run on the 16th, maybe at 11:00 PM. Now all you have to do is remember to update the source file directory once a month. The package and advertisement process will take care of the rest.

You might also consider creating a package that executes the virus scanning program on the client. Again, a recurring advertisement could be assigned to run the virus scan at regular intervals. Here's another twist on this scenario: let's say that you want the virus scan to run immediately after the virus update file is installed. You've seen that when you create a program, you have an advanced option to run another program first. You would then create a program that executes the virus scan but first copies the update file. Then create a recurring advertisement that runs that program once a month at the appropriate time.

Recurring advertisements can be used to handle a variety of these kinds of events. Use them to periodically synchronize the system time on your SMS clients with the site server. Use them to perform disk maintenance tasks such as monthly defragmentation or optimization routines. With a little creativity and imagination, you can automate many such tasks and make your job as a system administrator more productive.

Configuring the Client

Of course, life would not be complete if we did not have a client component to configure, and we do. In order for the client to receive any advertisements we are targeting to it, we must configure the Advertised Programs Client Agent and have it installed on each client. As with other client agents, this agent can be found in the Client Agents folder under Site Settings in the SMS Administrator Console.

To configure the Advertised Programs Client Agent, follow these steps:

1. Navigate to the Client Agents folder, select Advertised Programs Client Agent, right-click on it, and choose Properties from the context menu to display the Advertised Programs Client Agent Properties window, shown in Figure 12-55.

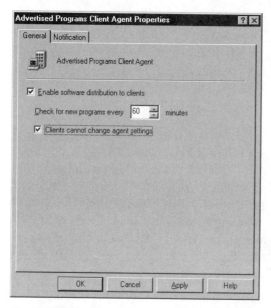

Figure 12-55. *The Advertised Programs Client Agent Properties window.*

2. On the General tab, select the Enable Software Distribution To Clients check box. Note that by default the Advertised Programs Client Agent will check the CAP for new advertisements every 60 minutes (just like the old Package Command Manager from SMS 1.x). You can substitute a value from 5 to 1440 minutes.

Caution Enter a value appropriate to the frequency at which you advertise programs and the urgency of those advertisements. In general, the default 60 minutes or even longer should be appropriate. The client can always force a check for new advertisements at any time.

3. The other option on the General tab—Clients Cannot Change Agent Settings—ensures that the settings you configure for the client agent stay that way. Select this option if desired.

4. Select the Notification tab, shown in Figure 12-56. This tab provides several options for defining how the client is notified of an advertisement.

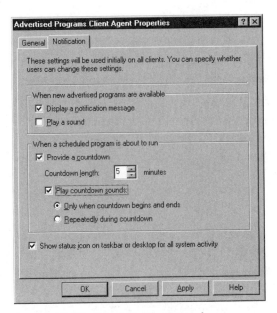

Figure 12-56. *The Notification tab.*

5. The options on the Notification tab are fairly self-explanatory. Select the options that fit your needs, and then click OK to save the configuration and begin the site update process.

If you don't select any options on this tab, the Advertised Programs Client Agent will check for an advertisement but will never notify the user that an advertisement has been received. The user would have to periodically run the Advertised Programs Wizard from Control Panel to find and run advertisements. If the advertised program had a mandatory assignment, it would simply run, again without notification to the user. In general, it is not a good idea to not notify the user when an advertisement has been received. Notifying the user can prevent unfortunate occurrences such as the user logging off or shutting down before the program finishes running.

Recall from Chapter 8 that the newly enabled and configured agent will not be installed automatically on your SMS clients until the next Client Component Installation Manager (CCIM) maintenance cycle (once every 23 hours) or until you select Update Configuration through the Systems Management applet in the Control Panel of each client.

When the client is updated, two new applets will be added to the Control Panel on each client—Advertised Programs Wizard and Advertised Programs Monitor.

Advertised Programs Wizard

The Advertised Programs Wizard is used to display available advertisements, select advertisements to run, and execute advertisements. When accessed through the Control Panel, this wizard causes the Advertised Programs Client Agent to check the CAP for new advertisements. When an advertised program is available on the client, the New Advertised Programs icon appears on the taskbar (if you enabled this type of notification). You can also access the wizard through the New Advertised Programs icon.

To run the Advertised Programs Wizard, follow these steps:

1. Click on the Advertised Programs Wizard applet in the Control Panel, or double-click on the New Advertised Programs icon on the taskbar (if that option was enabled), or right-click on the New Advertised Programs icon and choose Run Advertised Programs Wizard from the context menu. The Advertised Programs Wizard welcome screen is displayed, as shown in Figure 12-57.

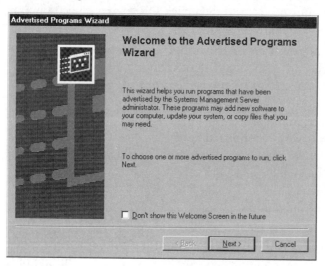

Figure 12-57. *The Advertised Programs Wizard welcome screen.*

2. Click Next to display the Select Programs To Run screen, shown in Figure 12-58. All available advertised programs are listed on this screen. Select the program you want to run.

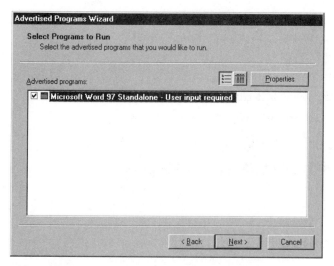

Figure 12-58. *The Select Programs To Run screen.*

3. You can view the properties of each program by clicking the Properties button to display the Program Properties window, shown in Figure 12-59. This window provides information such as whether the program is scheduled to run, whether it has an expiration date, whether user input is required, and the running time of the program. Click Close to return to the Select Programs To Run screen.

Figure 12-59. *The Program Properties window.*

4. The two buttons to the left of the Properties button switch between a simple list of programs and a list that displays the following properties in columnar fashion:

  - When the program is scheduled to run
  - When the program was last run
  - When the program was advertised

The alternative Advertised Programs list is shown in Figure 12-60.

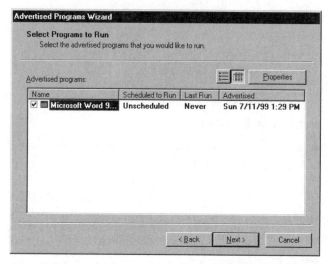

Figure 12-60. *The alternative Advertised Programs list.*

5. Click Next to display the Run Programs Now Or Later screen, shown in Figure 12-61. You can either let the program run now (the default) or select the Schedule This Program To Run On option and then specify a date and time for the program to run.

6. Click Next to display the Completing The Advertised Programs Wizard screen, shown in Figure 12-62. Review your selection, and then click Finish.

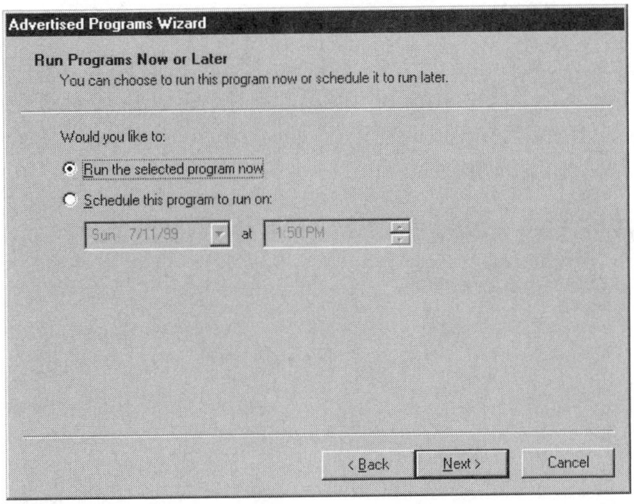

Figure 12-61. *The Run Programs Now Or Later screen.*

Figure 12-62. *The Completing The Advertised Programs Wizard screen.*

Advertised Programs Monitor

The Advertised Programs Monitor provides audit information about programs that have run on the client. When you launch the Advertised Programs Monitor from the Control Panel (or from the taskbar), it displays advertised programs that have run, are running, or are scheduled to run, as shown in Figure 12-63.

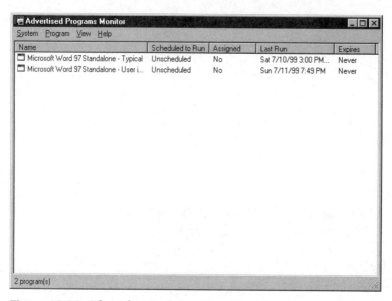

Figure 12-63. *The Advertised Programs Monitor.*

Through the Advertised Programs Monitor, you can view the program's properties and reschedule the program if you have permission to do so. You can also modify monitor settings such as the polling cycle for the agent to check the CAP for new advertisements—again, if you have permission to do so.

After a program is run, depending on whether you enabled SMS reporting either through the package details or through a script, the Advertised Programs Client Agent will write its success or failure status back to the CAP.

If a program is assigned to run as mandatory and notification to the client has not been disabled, the user will see a dialog box similar to the one shown in Figure 12-64. As you can see, depending on the countdown that was configured for the client agent, the user can opt to run the package immediately or click OK and let the package execute when the countdown completes. The user can also view a list of all scheduled programs and the details for this program.

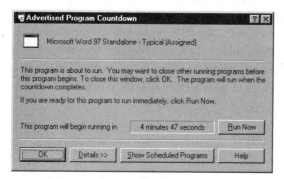

Figure 12-64. *The Advertised Program Countdown dialog box.*

Real World   Synchronizing System Time on Clients

When you schedule an advertised program to run at a predefined time, the Advertised Programs Client Agent on the client will check the assigned time against the system time *as reported on the client*. This can cause significant problems for you if the client's system clock is off. For example, if the client's system clock is set for a different time zone, the package may not run when you expect it to.

Another scenario involves trial software. Suppose a user obtains a trial software application that is timed to run for a specific period—say, 120 days. The user likes the product but doesn't want to actually buy it (a license no-no!) or has not finished evaluating it. So the user simply sets the system clock back a month, or a year, or even two years. This can really muck up your package distribution.

To avoid this problem, be sure to build in some kind of time synchronization routine for your clients that periodically synchronizes their time with the site server or some other designated time server. This goes for site systems and the SQL server as well. Several third-party utilities are available to help automate this task, or you can simply add a time synchronization command to the users' logon scripts.

Advertised Programs Process Flow

The advertisement and its associated files are generated in a process even more straightforward than the package distribution process, as illustrated in Figure 12-65. Just as with the package distribution process, when the advertisement is created and written to the SMS database, a SQL trigger causes the SMS SQL Monitor service to write a wake-up file (.OFN) to Offer Manager's inbox (SMS\Inboxes\Offermgr.box).

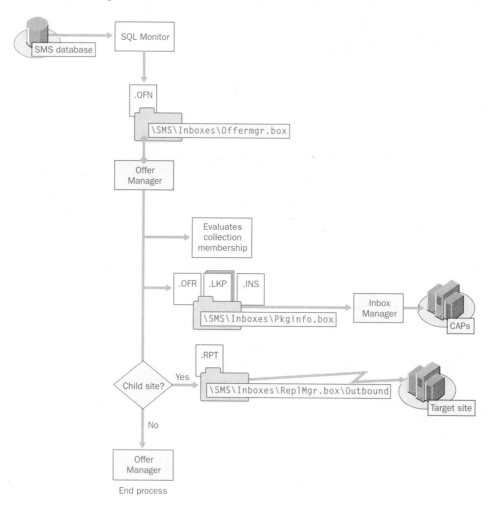

Figure 12-65. *The advertised programs process flow on the server side.*

The Offer Manager component generates instruction files for the Advertised Programs Client Agent on the target client computers and writes these to the SMS\Inboxes\Offerinf.box directory on the site server. These instruction files consist of an offer file (with a name similar to that of the package but with an .OFR extension), which is the actual advertisement; an installation file (.INS) that references the advertisement ID and the collection ID it is targeting; and up to three lookup files (.LKP) depending on the collection membership. These lookup files act as filters to determine whether the client (*sitecode*systm.lkp), the user (*sitecode*usr.lkp), or user group (*sitecode*usrgrp.lkp) should receive the advertisement. At this time, Offer Manager also evaluates the collection membership to determine which lookup files to create. Once again, ever-faithful Inbox Manager copies these instruction files to the Offerinf.box folder on the CAPs.

> **Note** As you peruse the documentation for SMS 2.0, you will probably find that the terms "advertisement" and "offer" are often used to refer to the same elements. This is because at some point during the development process for SMS 2.0 it was decided to change the term "offer" to "advertisement" to better coordinate with Windows 2000. Internal component and filenames were not modified, however.

On the client, when the Advertised Programs Client Agent runs, it uses the file Launch32.exe to begin the process, as shown in Figure 12-66. Launch32.exe itself starts two other threads called Offer Data Providers (ODPs)(ODPsys32.exe and ODPusr32.exe for Windows NT 4.0 systems, and ODPWin9x.exe for Windows 95 and Windows 98 systems). These threads read the lookup files that were created by Offer Manager and copied to the Offerinf.box on the CAP by Inbox Manager. These files specify whether the client computer, user, or user group should receive the advertisement.

If the client, user, and user group should receive the advertisement, the Advertised Programs Client Agent then reads the instruction and offer file for the advertisement to collect more detailed information. It checks parameters such as the operating system platform on the client and the system time to determine whether to receive the offer. If all is fine, the client agent receives the offer, passes it to the Advertised Programs Manager, generates a status message to that effect, and writes the status message back to the CAP.

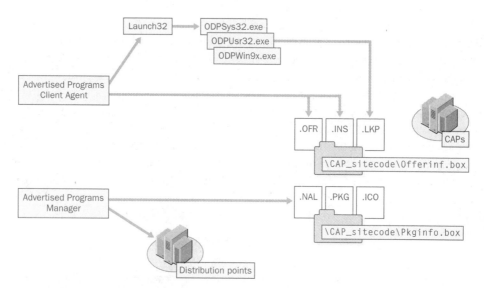

Figure 12-66. *The advertised programs process flow on the client side.*

The Advertised Programs Manager then reads the .PKG, .ICO, and .NAL files for the package in question from the Pkginfo.box folder on the CAP. Based on the information stored there, the client agent connects to an appropriate distribution point and executes the program. When the program is completed—successfully or unsuccessfully—the client agent again generates a program status message that it writes to the CAP. You can view this status message using the Status Message Viewer in your SMS Administrator Console.

Monitoring Status

Both the package distribution process and the advertised programs process generate status messages. You can monitor status in the same place you have monitored other SMS functions—the System Status folder in the SMS Administrator Console. You can also expand the Component Status folder and view the messages for Distribution Manager and Offer Manager.

You've probably noticed two other folders in the SMS Administrator Console: Package Status and Advertisement Status. These folders pertain specifically to packages and advertisements and are more useful for monitoring their status. As with Component Status, both Package Status and Advertisement Status have status summarizers, which consolidate status messages generated by the SMS components involved in the package and advertisement processes.

In Figure 12-67, the Advertisement Status and Package Status folders have been expanded to demonstrate the information they summarize. Package status detail is summarized at two levels—by site and by distribution point. Advertisement status detail is summarized by site. At each level, you can view the detailed messages that were generated for that particular package or advertisement by right-clicking on an entry, choosing Show Messages from the context menu, and then choosing All. After you specify a view data and time range, the Status Message Viewer will display the messages related to the package or advertisement.

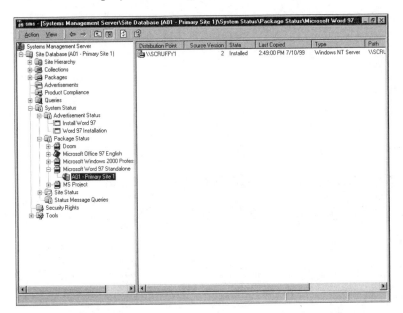

Figure 12-67. *The expanded Advertisement Status and Package Status folders.*

The summary information displayed when a site entry is selected, as in Figure 12-67, shows when the package was copied to the distribution point and last refreshed. The summary information displayed when a distribution point is selected, as in Figure 12-68, shows at a glance how many clients installed the package, how many failed, and how many are retrying.

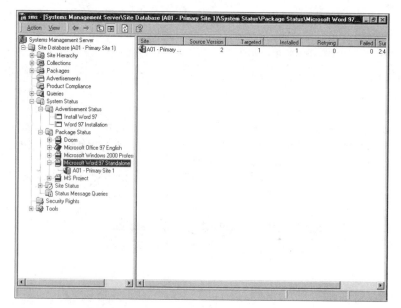

Figure 12-68. *Sample summary information displayed when a distribution point is selected in the SMS Administrator Console.*

Figure 12-69 shows the status messages generated at the site level for a package.

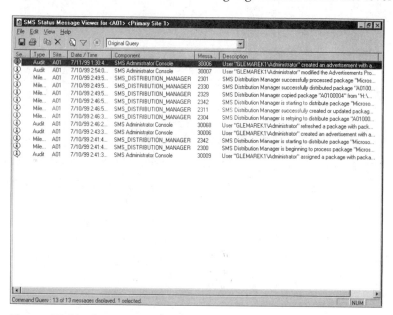

Figure 12-69. *Status messages for a package generated at the site level.*

Figure 12-70 shows the detailed messages for a specific distribution point in the site.

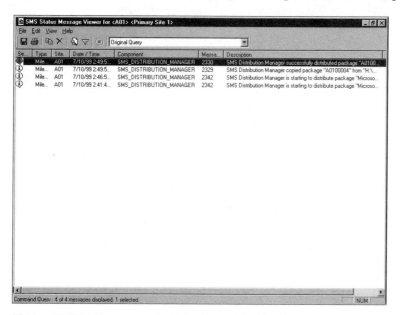

Figure 12-70. *Status messages for a specific distribution point in a site.*

Notice the difference in messages summarized for each. Messages for the distribution point are specific to that distribution point. Messages in the 23*xx* range refer to Distribution Manager tasks.

Figure 12-71 shows the summary information displayed in the SMS Administrator Console when you select an advertisement. This summary information includes success and failure status generated by the program as it is run on the targeted clients.

Figure 12-72 shows the detailed messages generated for an advertisement associated with one of the package's programs. As you can see, messages generated by the Offer Manager component fall within the 39*xx* range. The messages generated by the Available Programs Manager came from the client agent. The complete message text (under Description) tells you when the advertisement was received, when the program started, and when the program completed.

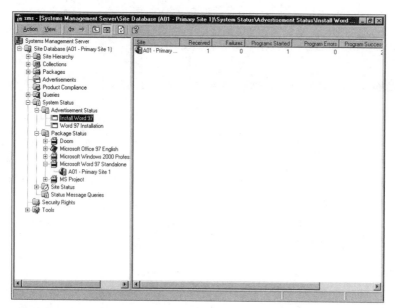

Figure 12-71. *Advertisement summary showing successful and failed program executions on the targeted clients.*

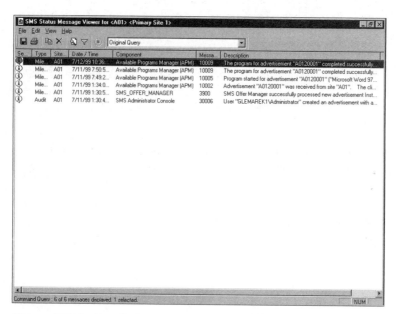

Figure 12-72. *Detailed messages generated for an advertisement associated with one of the package's programs.*

When a program executes at the client and a status MIF is generated, you can determine whether the program completed, how the program ran, and if it failed, what caused the problem.

Those of you who monitored job status in SMS 1.x will recall that the Package Command Manager client component reported when a program was executed. However, Package Command Manager could not really report whether a program ran successfully, and if it did not, why not. The status message system in SMS 2.0, on the other hand, is quite robust, with nearly every SMS component generating a host of detailed messages. (Chapter 5 provides a complete discussion of the status message system and its components.)

It should be no surprise, therefore, that we can determine not only whether a program ran, but also how it ran, whether it was successful, and if it was unsuccessful, why it failed, as shown in Figure 12-72. The degree to which a program can generate this information depends on whether the program generates a status MIF for SMS reporting and the exit codes that are generated. SMS interprets any nonzero exit code as an error or a failure. For example, a Setup.bat file may simply execute an XCOPY of a file to a directory on the client. Even though the XCOPY command is successful, the exit code that it generates is interpreted as an error. Nevertheless, the detailed message is still far more useful and informative than its counterpart in SMS 1.x.

As always, you can also view the log files associated with the Distribution Manager and Offer Manager—Distmgr.log and Offermgr.log. These logs will provide thread activity details, but they are more useful for determining why a source file could not be copied to a distribution point or why a program could not be advertised—in other words, to troubleshoot the package distribution and advertised program processes. For monitoring the package distribution and program execution process, the Status Viewer will be more than sufficient and probably more efficient.

Checkpoints

As we've seen, the process flows for package distribution and advertised programs are quite straightforward. Outside of normal network traffic issues that may interfere with the copying of source files to a distribution point or the copying of instruction files to a CAP, not much can go wrong. The amount of network traffic generated by updating the CAPs with package and advertisement files is relatively small, as these files are generally no more than 1 KB to 2 KB in size.

The real traffic comes with the copying or refreshing of source files to the distribution points. Remember that distribution points receive their files in an uncompressed format. That 200-MB application is generating 200 MB worth of network traffic when the source files are copied to the distribution point, and this traffic increases proportionally to the number of distribution points you are targeting. Although you can schedule when the distribution points are refreshed, the initial copy will take place at the time you create the package and identify the distribution points.

Also, keep in mind that when a client accesses a distribution point to run a program, the installation may also generate a significant amount of traffic between the distribution point and the client. The more clients accessing the distribution point at the same time, the more traffic generated, and the greater the performance hit taken by the distribution point. In general, if you are targeting large numbers of clients, you should consider distributing the package load across several distribution points, perhaps local to the clients in question.

This same issue of source file size is a reminder to be sure that the proposed distribution points have enough free disk space to host the source files. The client computer needs about 900 KB of space to install the Advertised Programs Client Agent and, of course, enough space to carry out the installation of the application.

If a program fails, start your troubleshooting with the status message system or the log files. Often, simply retracing your steps will be sufficient to spot the problem. Check the package and program parameters. Test the package yourself. Check the clients' system time to be sure that they are receiving the advertisements when you think they should. Check the Advertised Programs Client Agent polling cycle to be sure that the client agent is checking for new advertisements in a timely fashion. And so on.

Summary

In this chapter, we have covered one of the most significant functions of SMS 2.0—distributing and advertising packages and programs to clients. This function facilitates remote installation, updating, and maintenance of SMS client computers.

However, SMS should be thought of as more than a delivery system. As we've seen, it is still your responsibility as the SMS administrator to create (and script, if necessary) the packages you distribute. Scripting an installation is a significant requirement for most organizations that want their client maintenance to be "hands-off" to the user. Chapter 13 introduces a utility that can assist you in creating a fully scripted and unattended installation package for SMS to distribute— the SMS Installer 2.0.

Chapter 13
Microsoft Systems Management Server Installer 2.0

As we saw in Chapter 12, SMS 2.0's package distribution function is primarily a delivery tool. It is ultimately the SMS administrator's responsibility to create the package, including all scripts and information files, and to test the veracity of the package. Thus the ability to create scripts and somehow bundle the package to ease the installation becomes an integral part of the package distribution process for many organizations and administrators.

For software applications that need to be installed on client computers, the most sought after characteristic of the script is that it be fully unattended—in other words, you don't want the user to have any interaction with the installation process. This separation ensures a standard installation and minimizes questions and confusion on the part of the user. SMS 2.0, of course, does not offer this kind of functionality natively. Installation is not the responsibility of the SMS package distribution process. Remember our package delivery example in Chapter 12. Package delivery services such as Federal Express and United Parcel Service are entrusted with getting your package to its destination, but not with the assembly of its contents—the same holds true for SMS.

Fortunately, several third-party applications are available whose main function is to create package bundles. The Sysdiff utility in Windows NT, for example, essentially takes before and after snapshots of a system in order to bundle application installation with operating system installation. Microsoft provides a package scripting utility for SMS called SMS Installer.

> **Note** The SMS 2.0 CD includes SMS Installer 2.0, an upgrade to the earlier version of this utility. Throughout this chapter, when we refer to SMS Installer we are referring to SMS Installer 2.0

In this chapter, we'll look first at SMS Installer and its initial installation; then we'll explore the software repackaging process. Next we'll focus on modifying installation scripts using the Installation Expert and Script Editor. Finally, we will explore rolling back and uninstalling a scripted installation and look at some of the updates to SMS Installer.

Overview

SMS Installer enables you to create customized, self-extracting, software installation files. The SMS Installer–generated executable files let you install software with the SMS package distribution feature. Scripted installation makes installing software easier and less prone to error. The self-extracting executable files contain everything necessary to install the software, including an installation script to control the installation process. The SMS Installer compiler creates the self-extracting files. SMS package distribution is generally used to deliver these files to users. However, these files could certainly be distributed using other methods—for example, by packaging the files on disks, placing them on a Web site, or even attaching them to an e-mail message.

SMS Installer is really more than a developer's tool, and as such it requires intensive study to truly master. The basic process lets you quickly run through an application installation, repackage the application into a script, and distribute it. This basic process is actually quite intuitive and can be learned and accomplished in relatively short order. However, usually you will want something more elegant than a simple repackaging of the script, and to accomplish this you can use one of two tools: the Installation Expert or Script Editor. Using Script Editor requires a higher level of expertise.

It may take several months of practice creating, testing, and modifying scripts using SMS Installer before you feel truly comfortable. Don't let this scare you off. SMS Installer 2.0 is a fine, well thought out, and useful tool for amateur and expert script developers alike. At its high end, however, it is certainly not simple and requires effort and motivation on your part. In this chapter, we focus on the Repackage and Installation Expert components of SMS Installer—the two components that are easiest to master. For more specific information, especially regarding use of Script Editor, refer to the *Systems Management Server Administrator's Guide*.

Installing Systems Management Server Installer 2.0

SMS Installer is an optional component. To use SMS Installer, you must first install the SMS Installer files at the site server using the normal SMS 2.0 installation methods. If you choose the Express Setup to install SMS, the SMS Installer files are copied to the primary site server automatically. If you choose Custom Setup, you must select SMS Installer as an installation option. SMS Installer consists of a single self-extracting file, Smsinstl.exe; this file can be found in the \SMSSetup\SMS_Instl\i386 folder on the SMS 2.0 CD. You can also find this file in the \SMS\SMS_Instl*platform* folder on the site server. Smsinstl.exe includes all of the SMS Installer support files needed to set up the utility on a reference computer.

Identifying and Configuring a Reference Computer

The next phase is to configure a reference computer. SMS Installer supports any Microsoft Windows platform and requires about 8 MB of RAM and at least 6 MB of hard disk space for the installation. The reference computer must be a standard desktop configuration that is representative of your target computers. This computer contains the applications and registry settings that are configured on the end-user systems. It is critical that the reference computer be identical to the computer systems on which you will be installing the final software package. Be sure to check the following system components:

- **Hardware devices**   The devices installed on the reference computer should match those installed on prospective target clients, including video controllers, modems, I/O configurations, and disk drive configurations, especially if the application references these components during its installation.

- **Operating system**   The operating system of the reference computer should match that of all target systems, including version number and perhaps even service packs installed, especially if the application is platform specific.

- **Installed applications**   The reference computer and all target computers should have the same applications installed. Unless the repackaged application has a specific dependency on an existing application, the reference computer should contain only software that is directly needed by the repackaging process.

- **Directory structure**   If your script includes telling the application where to place the application's installation files, it is imperative that the reference computer's directory structure and the directory structures of the prospective target clients be standardized. Any changes, however insignificant they may be in the mind of the user—for example, moving or renaming the Program Files directory—can result in failure to run the script.

As you can see, the choice and configuration of the reference computer is one of the keys to creating a successful script using SMS Installer.

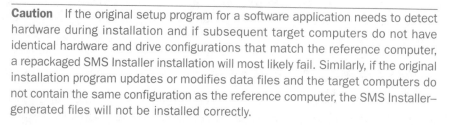

Caution If the original setup program for a software application needs to detect hardware during installation and if subsequent target computers do not have identical hardware and drive configurations that match the reference computer, a repackaged SMS Installer installation will most likely fail. Similarly, if the original installation program updates or modifies data files and the target computers do not contain the same configuration as the reference computer, the SMS Installer-generated files will not be installed correctly.

Installing Systems Management Server Installer 2.0 on the Reference Computer

Once the reference computer has been selected and properly configured, SMS Installer can be installed. Remember, the more closely the reference computer resembles the proposed target computers, the higher the rate of success for using SMS Installer.

To install SMS Installer, follow these steps:

1. From the reference computer, attach to the *siteserver*\SMS_*sitecode* share.

2. Navigate to the SMS_Instl\i386 directory, and run Smsinstl.exe to start the Microsoft SMS Installer Wizard, shown in Figure 13-1.

Figure 13-1. *The Microsoft SMS Installer Wizard Welcome screen.*

3. Click Next to display the Select Destination Directory screen, shown in Figure 13-2. Specify the destination directory for the SMS Installer files. By default, they will be placed in a folder named Microsoft SMS Installer under the Program Files directory.

Figure 13-2. *The Select Destination Directory screen.*

4. Click Next to display the Backup Replaced Files? screen, shown in Figure 13-3. From this screen, you specify whether to create a backup of all files replaced during the installation. Select Yes to keep a copy of the files that are changed during the SMS Installer installation. Select No to overwrite these files.

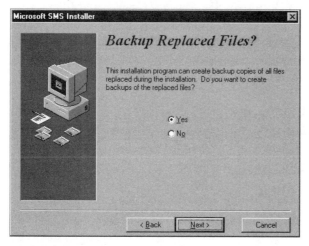

Figure 13-3. *The Backup Replaced Files? screen.*

5. Click Next to display the Select Backup Directory screen, shown in Figure 13-4, and select a location for the backup files to be written to. (This screen will not appear if you selected No in the previous screen.) By default, the backup files will be written to a folder named \Backup in the installation folder you defined in step 3.

Figure 13-4. *The Select Backup Directory screen.*

6. Click Next to display the Select Installation Type screen, shown in Figure 13-5, and select a development environment. SMS Installer supports both 16-bit and 32-bit environments, which means that the SMS Installer–generated executables can run on all Microsoft Windows operating systems. If you are creating an SMS Installer–generated file in a 16-bit environment such as Microsoft Windows 3.1 or if you are creating an MS-DOS application that runs in Windows 3.1, you will use the 16-bit environment. Otherwise, choose the 32-bit version. Notice that an option to support both environments is also provided for package flexibility.

7. Click Next to copy the files and display the Installation Completed screen, shown in Figure 13-6. Click Finish to exit the SMS Installer installation process.

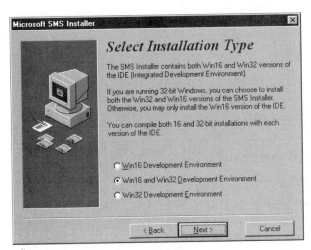

Figure 13-5. *The Select Installation Type screen.*

Figure 13-6. *The Installation Completed screen.*

Once the installation of SMS Installer is complete, the utility is ready for use. When SMS Installer is installed, it creates its own program group on the Start menu. You can access the utility by choosing Programs from the Start menu and then selecting the Microsoft SMS Installer program group. Alternatively, you can navigate directly to the SMS Installer directory through Windows Explorer. With either method, you will be able to select the appropriate development environment by selecting the appropriate program entry in the SMS Installer program group or by clicking on either the Smsins32 icon or the SMSinstl icon through Windows Explorer for the 32-bit or 16-bit environment.

Systems Management Server Installer 2.0 Tools

Before we go into the details of actually using the SMS Installer utility, let's look at the tools that SMS Installer uses to create and customize the SMS Installer executable files. To create and customize the installation scripts, SMS Installer uses two interfaces: the Installation Expert and Script Editor.

Installation Expert

The Installation Expert automatically creates a basic installation script using the configuration of the reference computer. The installation script contains commands that perform the actions necessary to carry out the installation. You can modify the actions performed within the script by configuring the installation attributes; we'll discuss these attributes in the section "Installation Attributes" later in this chapter.

Once the basic script has been created, Script Editor (discussed in the next section) can be used to customize the installation script for specific end-user functions. However, you will find it much easier to generate the installation script using the Installation Expert. This technique allows you to create a basic installation script and switch between the Installation Expert and Script Editor to perform modifications. This approach also prevents potential loss of data that can occur if you initially create the installation script using Script Editor and then switch to the Installation Expert. The Installation Expert provides two methods for packaging script files: the Repackage Installation Wizard and the Watch Application Wizard. The application for which you are creating the script file will determine which of these wizards you will use. The Installation Expert also provides several other tools to test and compile the installation script and to run the installation package. We'll look at each tool in the following sections.

Repackage Installation Wizard

If the application you are attempting to install currently contains a setup file, you may need to repackage the setup file along with the source files and any other support files for distribution to the target clients. The Repackage Installation

Wizard is used to accomplish this task. In a single-computer environment, installation of an application typically requires running a setup program. More often than not, during the installation you will be asked for specific input concerning the setup. For a single workstation setup, this situation is fine. When we talk about distributing these applications to hundreds of users and we want to have control over the input selection, however, we need to provide the input to the setup by some other means. The repackaging process allows us to provide the answers to installation questions and set specific configurations that will apply to all of our client machines. When we run the Repackage Installation Wizard, the reference computer is monitored for changes and a script file is generated from the changes made during setup.

Watch Application Wizard

The Watch Application Wizard can be used to create a customized installation file for those applications that do not have their own setup programs by "watching" the files used while the application is run and creating a script from them. In many cases, such as with custom or proprietary applications, a setup file has not been created for the application, and we're faced with the problem of how to successfully distribute the application to the clients. The Watch Application Wizard creates an SMS Installer–generated executable file that is used to install the program and all of its supporting components, such as DLLs. The wizard runs the existing application on the reference computer and tracks the files being used by the application. Using this list of files, an installation script is created for the application.

The Watch Application Wizard is also useful for applications that make calls for Microsoft Visual Basic support files or run-time files. The repackaging process will catch all the application files, but not necessarily those called from outside the application directory. In this case, you can use the Watch Application Wizard to look for these files and add them to the installation script for the application.

The Compiler

The SMS Installer compiler is used to create the self-extracting installation file. After you have created your installation script and made all of the necessary modifications to the installation attributes, the script file is compiled into an executable file. This SMS Installer–generated file contains the script and all of the necessary application files. It is the final file that is distributed throughout your organization.

Files created at compile time include the following:

- **Testapp.exe**   The installation executable, including the script and all necessary application files in a compressed format.

- **Testapp.pdf and Testapp.sms**   The standard SMS package definition file (PDF) used to distribute the SMS Installer–generated file to the target computers through SMS package distribution. Two versions of this file are created: one with the old .PDF extension used with earlier versions of SMS and supported in SMS 2.0, and one with the new, preferred .SMS extension adopted by Microsoft to avoid confusion with other market applications that use the .PDF extension.

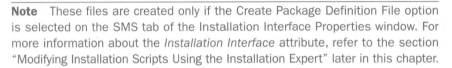

Note   These files are created only if the Create Package Definition File option is selected on the SMS tab of the Installation Interface Properties window. For more information about the *Installation Interface* attribute, refer to the section "Modifying Installation Scripts Using the Installation Expert" later in this chapter.

- **Testapp.ipf**   Text version of the installation script used when making modifications to the script through the SMS Installer utility.

- **Testapp.wsm**   Additional working file used by the installation script to maintain changes made to the script before it gets compiled.

The Test Program

The Test program is used to test the installation executable file without actually installing it. By running Test from the Installation Expert, you can preview how your setup script will actually run. Are the correct menus presented? Does the installation run unattended? These are the things we can test locally before distributing the installation package.

Keep in mind that Test does not really install the application and run it. Test simply copies needed files such as help files and DLL files to the \Temp directory. As always, it is good practice to select a pilot test group for testing the installation before distributing the package to your entire organization.

The Run Program

The Run program lets you run the installation program on the reference computer. Run will test the SMS Installer–generated file exactly as it will run on the target computers. Run will install the application and make any changes to the system that are required, including registry modifications.

Caution   If you plan to run the installation on the reference computer, you will need to remove the application (along with any registry settings that were created or modified) that was installed during the repackaging process. Otherwise, the installation may fail when it attempts to create or write to directories needed for the installation.

Script Editor

Script Editor is used to edit the basic installation script generated by the Installation Expert. Script Editor allows you to tune the installation script for customization and optimization. You can also modify such items as file locations, registry settings, and user prompts. Many of the functions that can be manually configured through Script Editor can also be added to the script by configuring them in the Installation Expert. Some functions can be added only through the Script Editor window. For example, uninstall support can be configured using either method, but support for rollback (which enables you to remove patches rather than uninstalling the application outright) can be configured only through Script Editor. We'll discuss uninstall and rollback support in the section "Rolling Back and Uninstalling a Scripted Installation" later in this chapter.

Script Editor provides a much higher level of control over the action of the script. Learning to use this tool effectively takes a long time. It also requires an intimate understanding of how the application's installation routine works—including what files and directories are modified, what registry entries are added or configured, what external DLL support is required, whether a restart is required, and what happens as a result.

Now that you have a working knowledge of the SMS Installer tools, let's look at how to use SMS Installer to create the installation script.

Creating Installation Scripts

To begin the process of creating an installation script, start SMS Installer to launch the Installation Expert window, as shown in Figure 13-7.

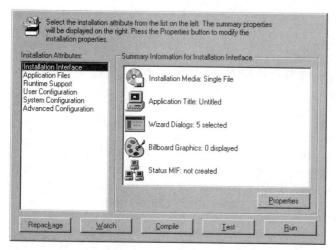

Figure 13-7. *The Installation Expert window.*

We'll begin the process of creating an SMS Installer–generated executable by running the Repackage Installation Wizard. In this example, we'll create the Microsoft Office 97 installation executable.

Caution   The setup routines of some of the newer Microsoft applications, such as Microsoft Office 2000, use the Microsoft Windows Installer Service to perform product installation. Using SMS Installer to repackage applications that use the Microsoft Windows Installer Service is not recommended because you must use the setup options bundled with these applications to install these applications.

To create the Office 97 installation executable, follow these steps:

1. In the Installation Expert window, click the Repackage button to launch the Repackage Installation Wizard, shown in Figure 13-8.

2. On the Repackage Installation Wizard screen, you configure the name and path of the setup program used by the application for installation. You may also need to add any other command-line arguments that might be needed by the setup program.

3. In the Directory list, configure any directories you want to be included in the list of directories to be scanned during the installation process. For this example, we'll be installing to drive D, so we need to add this drive to our list. To add a drive, click the Change button to open the Repackage Advanced Settings window, shown in Figure 13-9.

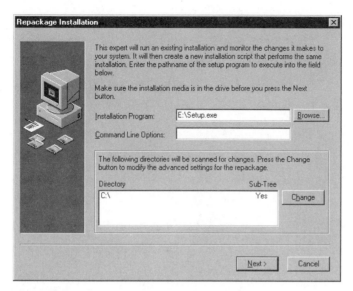

Figure 13-8. *The Repackage Installation Wizard screen.*

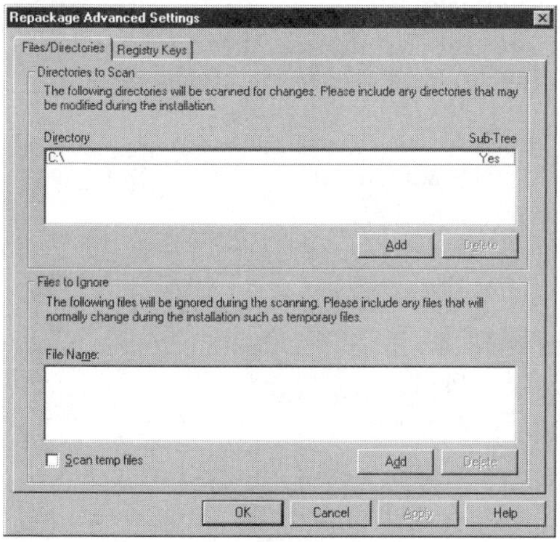

Figure 13-9. *The Repackage Advanced Settings window.*

4. In the Directories To Scan section of the Files/Directories tab, click Add to display the Select Directory dialog box, shown in Figure 13-10.

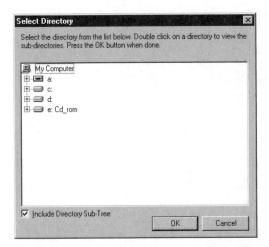

Figure 13-10. *The Select Directory dialog box.*

5. In the Select Directory dialog box, we can select the root directory D or we can select only the specific subdirectories we want to scan. Narrowing the scan can save significant time during the repackaging process. As a general rule, you do not want to scan every directory if you know some directories will not be affected during the installation. For our example, since our reference computer has little installed on drive D, we can add the root of this partition to our list.

6. When you have added all the directories you want to scan, click OK. The directories are added to the Directory list.

7. Next we will configure the directories and files we want to ignore during the scan process. Again, being selective here can improve the performance of the installation process. In the Files To Ignore section of the Files/Directories tab, click Add to display the Open dialog box, as shown in Figure 13-11.

8. For this example, the D:\junk directory will not contain any files pertaining to our installation of Office 97, so we can ignore this entire directory. Select the D:\junk directory by double-clicking on it, and then enter *.* in the File Name text box to include all files in this directory.

9. Click Open to add the directory to the File Name list, as shown in Figure 13-12.

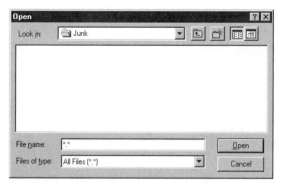

Figure 13-11. *The Open dialog box.*

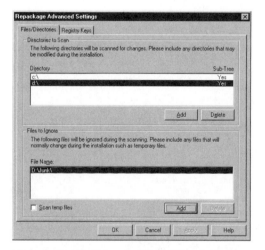

Figure 13-12. *The modified File Name list.*

10. You can also specify whether to ignore scanning of any temporary files during the installation process. To scan temporary files, check the Scan Temp Files check box.

11. To specify the registry keys and values to scan or ignore during the installation process, click on the Registry Keys tab, shown in Figure 13-13.

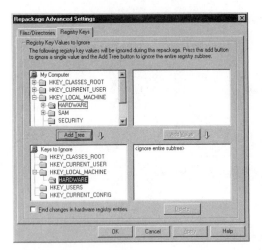

Figure 13-13. *The Registry Keys tab.*

Caution Selecting registry keys to scan or ignore can be a tricky business. Be especially careful not to overlook or choose to ignore a key that is altered during the setup process—doing so would invariably render your installation script worthless. On the other hand, the installation can change something such as a DHCP address setting by releasing and renewing an IP setting during a system restart, which is unrelated to the installation itself and should not be included in the installation script. Your best bet is to get to know the keys that your installation will affect, and once you have created the final script, test, test, test!

12. The Registry Keys tab contains four panes. The top two panes represent the current registry settings read from the reference computer. The lower two panes represent the registry settings that are to be ignored. In the top left pane, under My Computer, select the registry trees or values you want to ignore. To add the registry subtree to the list of subtrees to ignore, click Add Tree. To add a key you want to ignore, select the key in the upper right pane, and then click Add Value. The lower left pane shows where the selected keys are located on the reference computer; the lower right pane lists their values. Check the Find Changes In Hardware Registry Entries check box to have the repackaging process ignore any changes made in the hardware registry.

13. Click OK to return to the Repackage Installation Wizard screen, shown in Figure 13-14, and then click Next to begin the scanning and installation process of our application.

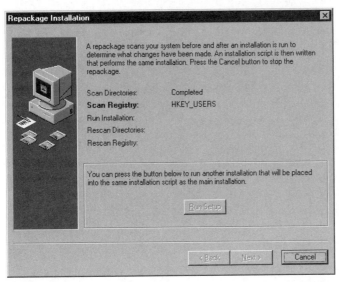

Figure 13-14. *The Repackage Installation screen showing the scanning process.*

During the installation phase, the Repackage Installation Wizard will run Setup.exe. With switches provided in the initial configuration of the wizard, the setup will run exactly as it normally does. Remember that you are providing the installation options that will be used during the actual setup of the application on the target computers.

14. After the Repackage Installation Wizard has completed the setup of the application, click Next to rescan the directories and registry settings, as shown in Figure 13-15. The wizard will compare the system image before and after the installation of the software.

Note You might also want to add application setups during this repackaging process—for example, you might want to distribute several applications within one silent install process. To accomplish this, click the Run Setup button to run the next setup and add the additional software. Keep in mind the size of these packages as we begin to install larger, more complex applications or multiple applications in a single SMS Installer–generated executable.

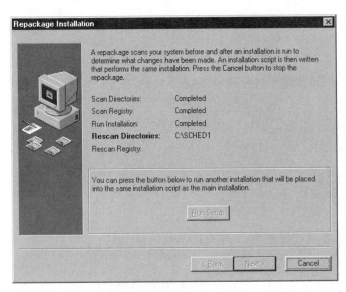

Figure 13-15. *The Repackage Installation screen showing the rescanning process.*

15. When the rescan of the directories and registry keys is complete, click Finish to complete the repackaging process.

At this point, clicking Compile in the Installation Expert window will generate a basic script that, while not elegant, may certainly be adequate for distribution. You could use the Installation Expert to verify the installation configuration that was created during the repackaging process and then modify and customize the script to meet the particular needs of your users and organization.

Caution   If the setup routine for the application you are repackaging requires a system restart, SMS Installer will not automatically restart the repackaging process. You will need to restart SMS Installer and the repackaging process and then continue repackaging.

Modifying Installation Scripts Using the Installation Expert

After we have created the installation script, we can begin the process of modifying and customizing it to fit our specific needs. As we've seen, the Installation Expert and Script Editor allow us to modify our installation scripts. In this section, we'll look at how to modify installation scripts using the Installation Expert. But first let's look at the installation attributes.

Installation Attributes

Six sets of installation attributes need to be considered when modifying installation scripts, as follows:

- **Installation Interface**   Enables you to configure the settings used by the SMS Installer–generated executable during installation.

- **Application Files**   Enables you to configure specific components to install based on the type of installation you select.

- **Runtime Support**   Enables you to configure uninstall support and to add additional components for Microsoft Visual Basic or Visual FoxPro. The Visual Basic components you select will affect how the Watch Application Wizard performs.

- **User Configuration**   Enables you to set up the program groups and icons and to configure file associations for the installation.

- **System Configuration**   Enables you to change or reconfigure the system environment during the installation process.

- **Advanced Configuration**   Enables you to configure such items as the screen settings that will be displayed during the installation, language settings, and patch settings, as well as global attributes that will control the actual installation file.

You can configure these attribute sets in the Installation Expert window, shown in Figure 13-7. Select an installation attribute, and click Properties to display its Properties window, where you can customize the installation script through a relatively user-friendly graphical interface.

Modifying the Script

In this section, we'll customize the settings for our SMS Installer–generated executable file using the Installation Expert. In this example, we will also modify the script by editing the installation attributes to facilitate an "unattended" installation.

To modify the script using the Installation Expert, follow these steps:

1. From the Installation Expert window, select Installation Interface from the Installation Attributes pane and click the Properties button or double-click on Installation Interface to display the Installation Interface Properties window, shown in Figure 13-16.

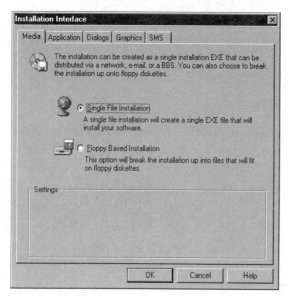

Figure 13-16. *The Installation Interface Properties window.*

2. On the Media tab, you can specify whether the SMS Installer–generated executable file will be a single file, used for network or Web distribution; or multiple files, used for floppy-based installation. For this example, verify that the Single File Installation option is selected. This will cause SMS Installer to generate a single executable file when we compile our script.

3. Click on the Application tab, shown in Figure 13-17. On this tab, you can specify the application name that will be used in wizard screens and in the welcome screen. This name is also displayed with the program icon. The name you use should be descriptive of the product being installed. You can also enter or modify the default directory that the application will be installed to. This option should be set to the top-level directory used for the application installation. If appropriate, select

the Place Default Directory Under Program Files check box to place
the default directory in the Program Files folder on Windows 95,
Windows 98, and Windows NT 4.0 systems.

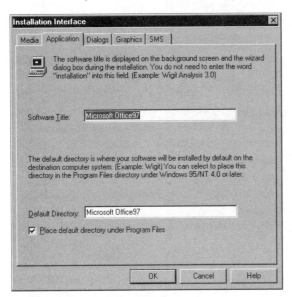

Figure 13-17. *The Application tab of the Installation Interface Properties*
window.

4. Click on the Dialogs tab, shown in Figure 13-18. This tab represents
   the dialog boxes the user will see when the script is run at a client computer. (You can also create your own custom dialog boxes and have them
   displayed through Script Editor.) To suppress all the dialog boxes that
   are displayed to the user for an unattended installation, clear all the
   screen options on this tab. The only item that the user will see will be a
   progress bar indicating that the installation script for the application is
   running. To enable uninstall or rollback support, select the Back Up
   Replaced Files option. If you want to facilitate a "silent" installation,
   you can also enable this option through Script Editor. For a detailed discussion on enabling this option, refer to the section "Enabling Rollback
   Support" later in this chapter.

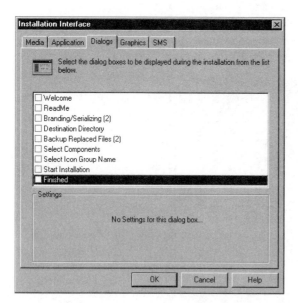

Figure 13-18. *The Dialogs tab of the Installation Interface Properties window.*

Note   A fully silent installation—one that does not display the progress bar or any dialog boxes—can be effected by running the compiled script on the client with a "/s" switch. If you are using SMS to distribute the SMS Installer file, be sure to include the "/s" switch on the command line for the program you create. Fully silent installations are best used on Windows NT computers, such as servers, which are rarely in a logged on state. Performing a silent installation on a user's workstation can cause problems because the user will be unaware that anything is happening. Unpredictable results can occur if, for example, the user decides to log off or restart the system while the script is running.

5. Click on the Graphics tab, shown in Figure 13-19. You can configure this tab to display custom graphics, such as a custom logo, text boxes that display animation or tips, and so on, in the form of .BMP files during the installation. Figure 13-19 shows a sample bitmap added, although in our example we will not add any additional graphics.

6. Click on the SMS tab, shown in Figure 13-20. These settings are used during a rollout of our application using the SMS distribution process. On this tab, you can specify whether to have the installation process generate a status MIF file for status reporting to SMS 2.0. If you choose to create an MIF file, enter the name for the status MIF files for installation and deinstallation of the application. You must supply a filename and the .MIF extension for both installation and deinstallation if you

enable rollback or uninstall support. Select the Create Package Definition File check box if you want to create a package definition file (.PDF
and .SMS) when creating the package for distribution through SMS 2.0.

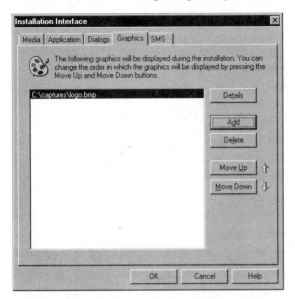

Figure 13-19. *The Graphics tab of the Installation Interface Properties window.*

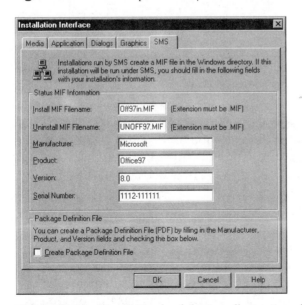

Figure 13-20. *The SMS tab of the Installation Interface Properties window.*

7. Click OK to return to the Installation Expert window. Select Application Files and then click Properties to display the Application Files Properties window, shown in Figure 13-21.

Figure 13-21. *The Application Files Properties window.*

8. On the Components tab, you can select a list of optional components for the installation. These options represent components the user can install during execution of the installation of the script. For example, suppose a custom Microsoft Access database installation contains three different database files that can be installed. You can identify each database as a component on this tab. (Then, on the Files tab, you can identify which database files are associated with each component.) Components are listed for the user during the execution of the installation script in the order in which they appear on this tab. You can add, sort, or modify the list of components using the Move Up, Move Down, Add, and Delete buttons.

9. Click on the Files tab, shown in Figure 13-22. The Files tab contains four panes. In the top two panes, locate the folders or files you want to include in your script. In the lower two panes, select a location on the destination computer at which to install these folders or files. You can add or remove files to your installation. For example, if you needed to include customized Word templates as part of the installation, you could add them here. This example shows the files added during the installation of Office 97.

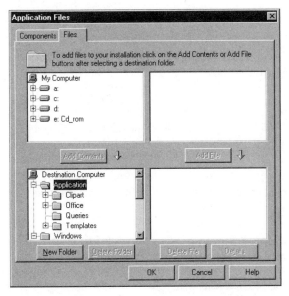

Figure 13-22. *The Files tab of the Application Files Properties window.*

10. Click OK to return to the Installation Expert window, select Runtime Support, and click Properties to display the Runtime Support Properties window, shown in Figure 13-23.

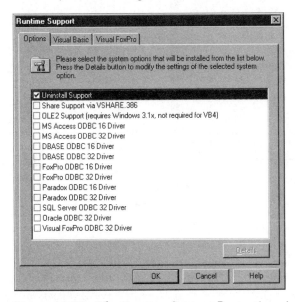

Figure 13-23. *The Runtime Support Properties window.*

11. On the Options tab, you can configure uninstall support, which is enabled by default, and specify the support drivers needed for the SMS Installer–generated executable file. For this example, we've left the default setting for Uninstall Support selected for rollback support.

Note Two additional tabs are available for the *Runtime Support* attribute: the Visual Basic tab and the Visual FoxPro tab. On the Visual Basic tab, you can configure Visual Basic support, including the Visual Basic directory and application type. You can also select Visual Basic options such as runtime support. On the Visual FoxPro tab, you can configure Visual FoxPro support, including the Visual FoxPro directory and other options such as runtime support and OCX support. Refer to the *Systems Management Server Administrator's Guide* for more information about these tabs.

---

12. Click OK, select User Configuration , and click Properties to display the User Configuration Properties window, shown in Figure 13-24.

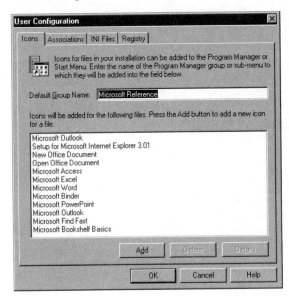

Figure 13-24. *The User Configuration Properties window.*

13. On the Icons tab, specify the name of the program group to which icons will be added. You can also specify additional icons to be added to the program group or even delete icons that should not be added to the program group. For example, you might choose to remove the Setup For Microsoft Internet Explorer 3.01 icon if you already have Internet Explorer 5.0 installed. Notice the icons added for Office 97.

14. To verify modifications to file associations and INI files, click on the Associations tab and the INI Files tab. The Associations tab allows you to specify and modify file associations for files being installed; the INI Files tab allows you to specify the INI files and their entries requiring modification during setup. For example, if you know that you need to modify the net heap size entry in the System.ini file on a Windows 98 computer after an application is installed, you could do so on the INI Files tab as part of the installation script.

15. To display the registry changes made during execution of the installation script, select the Registry tab, shown in Figure 13-25.

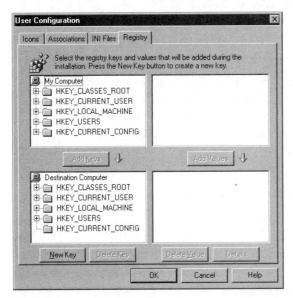

Figure 13-25. *The Registry tab of the User Configuration Properties window.*

16. You can modify certain registry settings from this tab. For example, in this Office 97 installation, we want to change the setting for the product ID. Under Destination Computer, navigate to the HKEY_LOCAL_MACHINE\SOFTWARE\Microsoft\MS Office 97 Professional\97.0.0.1117(1033)\Registration key, and select Product ID.

17. Click Details to display the Registry Key Settings dialog box, shown in Figure 13-26. In this dialog box, you can make changes to the registry key settings. Click OK to close the dialog box, and click OK once more to return to the Installation Expert window.

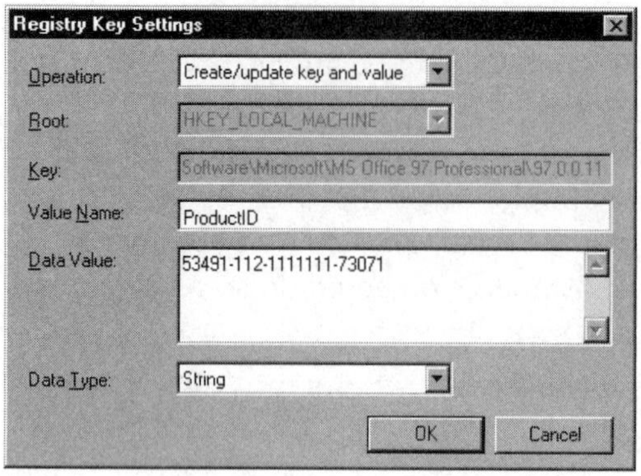

Figure 13-26. *The Registry Key Settings dialog box.*

The two remaining installation attributes—*System Configuration* and *Advanced Configuration*—should be verified and modified according to your specific target computer needs Although our Office 97 installation example does not make any modifications to these attributes, let's look at the two installation attribute Properties windows briefly. Keep in mind that you need to verify these settings just as we have verified our other attribute settings. To configure these Properties windows, follow these steps:

1. In the Installation Expert window, select System Configuration, and click Properties to display the System Configuration Properties window, shown in Figure 13-27.

2. On the Devices tab, add or delete devices or modify device properties on 16-bit Windows systems. This tab modifies the [386enh] section of the System.ini file.

3. Click on the Services tab, shown in Figure 13-28. Here you can add system services to or modify system services in the Control Panel.

4. Click on the Autoexec.bat tab, shown in Figure 13-29. On this tab, you can produce a script that will modify the system's Autoexec.bat file by adding new lines or appending to existing lines, such as altering the PATH statement or adding SET variable statements.

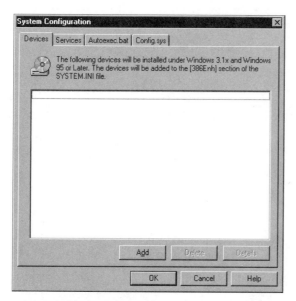

Figure 13-27. *The System Configuration Properties window.*

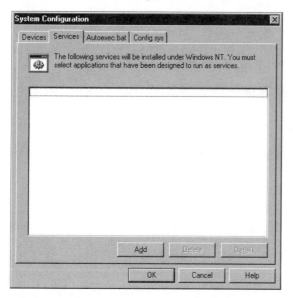

Figure 13-28. *The Services tab of the System Configuration Properties window.*

Figure 13-29. *The Autoexec.bat tab of the System Configuration Properties window.*

5. Select the Config.sys tab, shown in Figure 13-30. On this tab, you can produce a script to modify the Config.sys file. After you configure each of these tabs, click OK to return to the Installation Expert window.

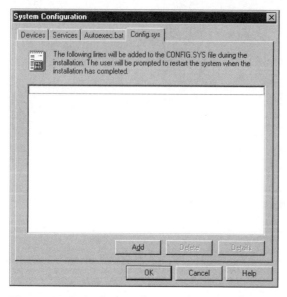

Figure 13-30. *The Config.sys tab of the System Configuration Properties window.*

6. Select Advanced Configuration and click Properties to display the Advanced Configuration Properties window, shown in Figure 13-31.

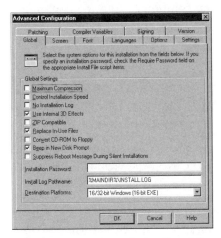

Figure 13-31. *The Advanced Configuration Properties window.*

7. On the Global tab, you can modify the installation file settings, such as compression, log settings, suppression of reboot message during silent installs, and use of an installation password.

8. Click on the Screen tab, where you can select options for the installation progress bar settings and display background gradient of installation dialog boxes. Display color options used during the installation can also be selected here.

9. Click on the Font tab to specify the default font used to display all installation screens and dialog boxes.

10. Click on the Languages tab to configure the language settings used for the installation.

11. Click on the Options tab, where you can specify the Script Editor, compiler, and Watch Application Wizard settings to be used by SMS Installer. You can also set options for specific DLLs to be ignored by the Watch Application Wizard.

12. Click on the Patching tab, where you can create patching versions of files. You can select patching threshold levels based on a percentage of change to an existing file, configure memory settings used during the patch process, and configure the compression level for patch files.

13. Click on the Compiler Variables tab, where you can configure the compiler used during the compilation of the installation script and enable user-prompted compiler variables when compiling from the command prompt.

14. Click on the Signing tab, where you can set up a secure installation environment used in 32-bit installations. From this tab, you can also create a CAB-formatted installation file and supply the contents of Setup.inf, commonly used during setup to provide installation settings.

> **Note** If you have applied SMS 2.0 Service Pack 1, you will see one more tab in the Advanced Configuration Properties window: the Version tab. Refer to the section "Updates to SMS 2.0 Installer" later in this chapter for more information about this tab.

As you can see, these installation attributes will enable you to modify your installation script and help it to compile and run more smoothly. Although you can configure these options prior to running the Repackage Installation Wizard or the Watch Application Wizard, it is usually a good idea to return to the Installation Expert after running either wizard and verify all of your configuration options and settings.

> **More Info** Refer to the *Systems Management Server Administrator's Guide* for more information about each tab in the installation attribute Properties windows.

Modifying Installation Scripts Using Script Editor

As we've seen, we can use SMS Installer's graphical menus and attribute settings to configure our installation scripts to suit our specific needs. Under different circumstances, however, these tools may not give us all of the control needed to fully customize our SMS Installer–generated script file. Likewise, specific situations may arise in which it is more efficient or just faster and easier to use a scripting method to make changes.

It really doesn't matter how we go about creating our scripted installation. Remember, we can generate our initial script using either the Repackage Installation Wizard or the Watch Application Wizard. These two methods are probably preferred, as they give us a good basic script that we can customize using the Script Editor utility. Or we can open the Script Editor window to modify an existing script or even begin scripting from scratch. In this section, we'll explore Script Editor variables and actions and then look at how to modify installation scripts using Script Editor.

Script Editor Variables and Actions

The Script Editor provided by SMS Installer is a powerful scripting utility. It provides a vast array of variables and actions (SMS Installer commands) that let you optimize the script files used by the installation process. Script variables contain information about the installation being performed. We can use these variables to hold the information gathered from users about where to place files. Script variables can also be used to hold information about which files users want to install. Additionally, a number of predefined variables contain information about the target computer system on which you are installing software.

Before we look at how to make modifications to a script using Script Editor, let's review some common scripting variables and actions. The following tables are not intended as a comprehensive list of all the available variables and actions, but rather as a short list of those more commonly used.

> **More Info**   Refer to the *Systems Management Server Administrator's Guide* for a comprehensive list of scripting variables and actions.

Table 13-1 lists several predefined variables and the values they are designed to return.

Table 13-1.   Predefined variables

Variable	Returns
WIN	The path of the Windows directory—for example, C:\Windows.
SYS32	The system directory for Win32 files under Windows NT—for example, C:\Winnt\System32.
TEMP	The path of the temporary directory on the reference computer. This directory is often used by an application to store DLLs before referencing them.
CMDLINE	The command-line options that are passed to the SMS Installer–generated file.
PASSWORD	The installation password assigned to a password-protected installation.

As we write our script, we can have SMS assign values to existing variables or generate additional variables to perform functions or hold values. During the installation, we can create the variables SMS uses to perform various functions. For example, we can define the values for the four variables listed in Table 13-2 as part of the installation script or have SMS prompt for the values during execution of the installation script. These variables are frequently used by SMS—note especially the *DOBACKUP* variable, which is used to support the SMS Installer rollback feature.

Table 13-2. **Functional variables**

Variable	Function
BACKUPDIR	Defines where the backup files should be located.
DOBACKUP	Enables the performance of a backup of all files replaced during an installation.
HELPFILE	Identifies the help file to be read and displayed during installation when the user clicks Help.
RESTART	Causes the system to be restarted when the script terminates. This variable is generally set automatically.

Defining Variables

As mentioned, you can also define your own variables in the script. You can use the Set Variable action or the Prompt For Text action from Script Editor. To create variables, follow these steps:

1. In the Installation Expert window, choose Script Editor from the View menu to display the Script Editor window, shown in Figure 13-32.

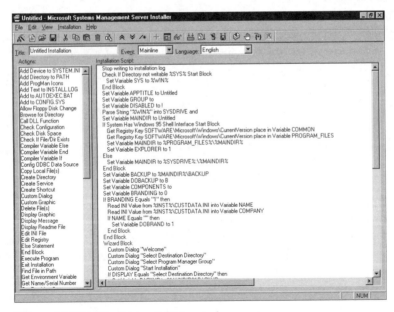

Figure 13-32. *The Script Editor window.*

> **Note**   If you previously closed SMS Installer from the Script Editor window, when you next open SMS Installer, Script Editor will appear with the Installation Script pane blank. If you open SMS Installer in the Installation Expert window, it loads a default script, which is displayed in the Installation Script screen when you switch to Script Editor.

2. In the Actions list, double-click on the Set Variable action to display the Set Variable dialog box, shown in Figure 13-33.

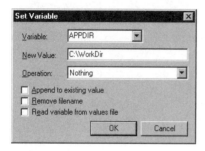

Figure 13-33. *The Set Variable dialog box.*

3. Enter the name of the variable you want to create. Variable names must always begin with a letter, must be no longer than 14 characters, and must contain no special characters except underscores.

4. In the New Value text box, enter the value you want to set the variable to.

5. Select an operation that you want performed on the new value from the Operation drop-down list, if required. Operations include incrementing or decrementing a numeric value by 1, removing trailing backslashes, converting a value to all uppercase or lowercase, converting the path and filename to a short or long filename, or simply performing no action—the default.

> **More Info**   Refer to the SMS Installer 2.0 help for examples of how to use the different operations.

6. Three check boxes appear at the bottom of the Set Variable dialog box: Append To Existing Value, Remove Filename, and Read Variable From Values File. If the variable you entered is a counter and you choose to increment or decrement its value, select the Append To Existing Value check box. You can also use this option to append a string value to the current string value. If you want to remove the filename from a value

that has a full path, select the Remove Filename check box. If you want SMS Installer to read the variable's value from a file, select the Read Variable From Values File select box. Selecting this option will cause the entered value to be ignored, so select this option only if you are running your script from the command line.

7. Click OK to close the Set Variable dialog box.

To create a variable named APPDIR, for example, in which you set the location of the application's working directory, enter APPDIR as the variable name and an appropriate path such as C:\WorkDir as the value. When you need to invoke this value in your script, reference the variable's value by enclosing the variable name in percent signs. To create a BACKUP directory for rollback that is a subdirectory of the path you entered for APPDIR, your script line would look like this:

Set Variable BACKUP to %APPDIR%\BACKUP

Set Variable is just one of the SMS Installer Script Editor actions. In the next section, we'll look at the more common Script Editor actions.

Common Script Editor Actions

The Script Editor window, shown in Figure 13-32, contains a list of SMS Installer Script Editor actions that the installation script can perform. In this section, we'll look at some of the more common actions and their functions. Table 13-3 lists these actions.

Table 13-3. SMS Installer Script Editor actions

Action	Description
Add to AUTOEXEC.BAT	Adds or replaces commands and environment variables in the Autoexec.bat file other than the PATH command.
Add to CONFIG.SYS	Adds device driver and other statements to the Config.sys file.
Call DLL Function	Calls specific Win16 and Win32 DLLs.
Check Disk Space	Performs a check of disk space to verify that there is enough space to complete the installation.
Check If File/Dir Exists	Checks whether a specified file or directory exists on the target computer.
Create Directory	Creates a new directory on the target computer.
Create Service	Creates a service on a target Windows NT computer.

Table 13-3. *continued*

Action	Description
Delete Files	Deletes specified files and directories from the target computer.
Edit Registry	Creates or deletes new keys and values in the registry on Windows 95, Windows 98, Windows NT, and Windows 2000 computers.
Else Statement	Inserts a logical ELSE statement into the script.
Execute Program	Calls an executable to run outside the actual scripted installation.
Exit Installation	Terminates and exits the installation.
If/While Statement	Inserts IF/WHILE logic into the script.
Install Files	Finds the source files used during installation and compresses them into the installer executable file. These files are uncompressed on the target computer when the script is run.
Prompt For Text	Generates a dialog box to prompt the user for text input such as a filename or directory path.
Remark	Adds comments to the script.
Rename File/Directory	Finds and renames a file or directory on the target computer.
Set Variable	Creates or modifies a script variable.

As you can see, variables and actions can be set in your script. You can find more details about these options in the *Systems Management Server Administrator's Guide* and in the SMS Installer help file accessible through the SMS Installer interface. Don't expect to become proficient at scripting in a couple of hours or even a couple of days. We're talking about a development language here, and that takes time to learn and appreciate. But with a little perseverance you will become proficient at using many of these options.

Modifying the Script

Now let's take a look at how to make some simple modifications to our script using Script Editor. To do so, follow these steps:

1. In the Installation Expert window, choose Script Editor from the View menu to display the Script Editor window, shown in Figure 13-32.

2. Choose Open from the File menu to display the Open dialog box, shown in Figure 13-34, and then select a script (.IPF) file to open for editing. For this example, we will use the Office 97 script we created earlier. Click Open to open the script for editing.

Figure 13-34. *The Open dialog box.*

3. Next we will edit the variable that specifies the installation directory the program will use. In this example, we are installing to the Microsoft Office 97 directory. We will change this to Office97.

Choose Find from the Edit menu to display the Find Text In Installation Script dialog box, shown in Figure 13-35. Enter *Maindir* in the Find What text box, and then click Find Next. The first instance of a script line containing "Maindir" is selected. This is the variable setting for the directory location of the Office installation we want to modify. Click Close to close the dialog box.

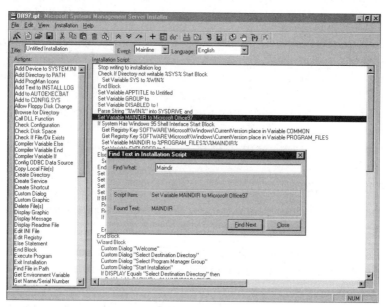

Figure 13-35. *The Find Text In Installation Script dialog box.*

4. Choose Edit Script Item from the Installation menu or double-click on the Set Variable statement containing "Maindir" to display the Set Variable dialog box, shown in Figure 13-36. In the New Value text box, enter Office97, and then click OK. The variable setting is modified in the Installation Script pane of the Script Editor window.

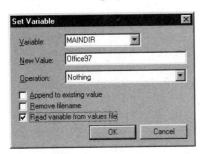

Figure 13-36. *The Set Variable dialog box.*

Any additional script modifications would be accomplished in much the same manner. After we have completed our editing of the script, we are ready to test and compile the installation script file. This will give us the SMS Installer–generated executable file.

Real World   Sample Script

Occasionally, you may encounter a situation in which you do not want to install an application or run the installation script if certain elements are not in place on the target computer. For example, you might want to verify that there is enough disk space available before proceeding or that a particular program file exists. This example uses a file to indicate whether a computer should execute the installation script. This is a simple text file that you create and copy to all the computers that should not execute the script. If the file is found on the computer, the script will be terminated. If the file is not found, the script will continue.

The sample SMS Installer script routine shown in Figure 13-37 demonstrates how to test for the existence of a file and can be incorporated into larger scripts. It provides a basic structure that can be easily modified to meet other needs.

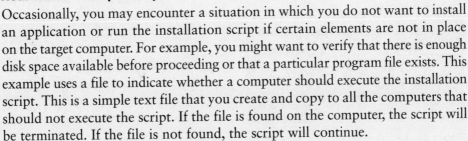

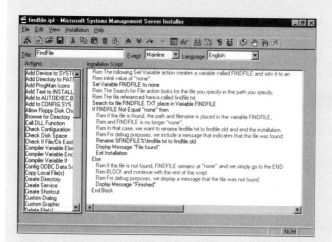

Figure 13-37. *Sample SMS Installer script designed to find a file and perform an action.*

This script is designed to look for a specific file identified in the script as Findfile.txt using the Search For File action. In the Actions list, double-click on Search For File to display the Search For File Settings dialog box, shown in Figure 13-38.

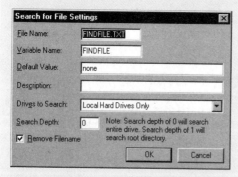

Figure 13-38. *The Search For File Settings dialog box.*

In the Search For File Settings dialog box, specify the file and path to search for and whether to search all local drives, all network drives, or both. The path that is searched is determined by the Search Depth value. A value of 0 indicates that the entire drive will be searched. A value of 1 indicates that the root drive will be searched. Values of 2, 3, and higher indicate that the first directory level, second directory level, and so on will be searched. In this example, we will search all local drives.

Select the Remove Filename check box. If the file is found, the file and its path will be stored in the variable *FINDFILE*. This option will remove the file entry and keep just the path, which can be useful if you are trying to capture a specific path or need to rename a file, as we do in this script.

The script begins by using Set Variable to define a variable named *FINDFILE*. This variable is set to a default value of None to indicate that no file has been found. The Search For File action looks for the file on all local drives on the target computer. If the file is found, the file and its full path are placed in *FINDFILE*, and the value of *FINDFILE* is no longer None. Simple IF/THEN logic tests to determine whether *FINDFILE* is still None. If it is not, the file has been found, and we will rename it Findfile.old. If the file has not been found, we simply continue on with the rest of the script. The script also includes display messages for debugging purposes to alert us when the file has been found. These messages can be removed after the existence of the file has been tested.

This basic script routine can be easily modified to perform any number of actions or tasks—for example, deleting the file, moving the file to a new location, or creating a new file with the same name as an existing file if that file is not found.

Testing and Compiling the Installation Script

Now that we have verified and modified our installation settings, we are ready to test and finally compile—or recompile, as the case may be—the installation script. To accomplish this, follow these steps:

1. In the Installation Expert window, shown in Figure 13-7, click the Test button. (You can also choose Test from the Installation menu in the Script Editor window.)

2. If you haven't already saved the script, a Save As dialog box will appear, prompting you to provide a name for the script (IPF) file that will be created during the test run of the installation.

3. The SMS Installer–generated script should now run successfully, displaying any dialog boxes you defined. The Test program will notify you of any syntactical problems within the script. If an error is encountered,

the Script Editor window can be opened, with the offending line highlighted and waiting to be edited. Correct any problems and continue to retest the script until it runs without error.

4. After you have successfully tested the script file, you can run the installation script in much the same manner as you did when you tested it. The significant difference in running the script is that it will actually perform the installation. Recall that to avoid potential conflicts, you may want to remove the version of the application that was installed during the repackaging process.

5. To run the script file from the Installation Expert window, click Run. You can also choose Run from the Installation menu in the Script Editor window.

6. The script will run completely and, as with the Test program, will prompt you with any syntactical errors that are found, giving you the option to correct them. Correct any errors, and repeat the run process until no errors are found.

7. After the installation script has run successfully, click the Compile button to create the SMS Installer–generated executable file. You can also choose Compile from the Installation menu in the Script Editor window. Once again, any errors will be noted and should be corrected.

Tip Remember to recompile the script after each change you make, either through the Installation Expert or through Script Editor. You might also want to make a copy of the old script before modifying and recompiling it.

After the final testing has been completed, the SMS Installer–generated executable is ready to distribute to your target systems. Using SMS or any other method of distribution, our scripted package is ready to be rolled out to the client computers.

Rolling Back and Uninstalling a Scripted Installation

Occasionally, it may be necessary to remove a software application from the client computers after it has been installed. This may be due to configuration issues or because the application was rolled out to a group of clients that should not have received it. Whatever the reason, at some point, you will likely be faced with the task of uninstalling an application.

In most applications today, the Setup program is used to perform the deinstallation as well as the installation of the application. The biggest problem administrators encounter with these types of uninstall routines is that they usually don't remove everything that was installed with the application. It isn't uncommon to have an uninstall routine leave behind directories, abandoned files, and even unwanted registry entries. This isn't necessarily the application's fault. Install programs are usually not written to keep track of what is or isn't installed.

SMS Installer has both an uninstall and a rollback feature to help alleviate these types of problems. Recall that SMS doesn't actually perform the application's install routine on the target computer. Instead, the Repackage Installation Wizard performs a before and after scan of the reference computer and creates a script that defines what should be modified on the target computers. Uninstall and rollback support help to restore the reference computer to the condition it was in before an SMS Installer–generated executable file made any modifications to the system by logging what the script did. Uninstall support is designed for complete removal of an application, including its files, registry modifications, and so on. Rollback support is designed more as a restoration tool—to restore any replaced files and any changed registry entries, such as removing a patch that was applied to an application.

Enabling Uninstall Support

Enabling uninstall support came up in our discussion of modifying the script from Installation Expert earlier in this chapter. Let's recap here. To enable uninstall support, you must configure it from the Installation Expert prior to compiling your Installer executable file. To do so, follow these steps:

1. Select the *Runtime Support* installation attribute in the Installation Expert window.

2. In the Summary Information For Runtime Support section, click on Runtime Options, and then click Properties to display the Runtime Support Properties window, shown in Figure 13-23.

3. On the Options tab, verify that Uninstall Support is selected—which it should be by default.

4. Click OK. Uninstal.exe will be included in the installation package and copied to the client computer during the package execution, and an uninstall log file will be maintained on the target computers.

Enabling Rollback Support

Enabling rollback support requires one additional change to the process used to enable uninstall support. To properly restore settings and files, those settings and files must be saved somewhere during the installation of the software package. SMS Installer's trick for rolling back a file such as a patch is to copy the original to a backup location before performing any modifications. To accomplish this, you must specify the backup directory into which to save replaced files.

We also touched on enabling rollback support when we discussed modifying installation scripts using the Installation Expert. To enable rollback support, follow these steps:

1. In the Installation Expert window, select the Installation Interface installation attribute.

2. In the Summary Information For Installation Interface section, click on Wizard Dialogs, and then click Properties to display the Dialogs tab of the Installation Interface Properties window, shown in Figure 13-18.

3. On the Dialogs tab, select Backup Replaced Files. Selecting this option will cause two dialog boxes to be displayed to the user during the SMS Installer executable file execution. The first will prompt the user to specify whether to back up the files. The second will prompt for the location of the backup files.

If rollback support is required but your intention is to provide an unattended installation script with dialog boxes suppressed, you need to manually edit the Set Variable DOBACKUP script action as shown here:

1. From the Script Editor window, choose Find from the Edit menu. In the Find What text box of the Find Text In Installation Script dialog box, enter *Set Variable DOBACKUP To B*, and click Find Next.

2. Double-click on the selected script action line to display the Set Variable dialog box, and change this variable value from B to A. This change causes any replaced files to be backed up during the installation script execution.

3. Click OK to return to the Script Editor window, shown in Figure 13-39.

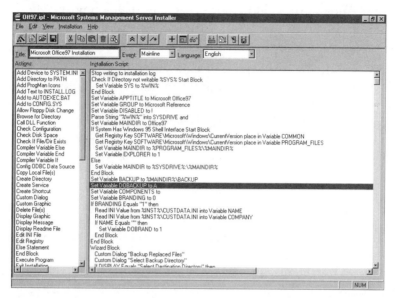

Figure 13-39. *The Script Editor window, with a modified script action line selected.*

4. Verify the location of the backup files by searching for the variable Set Variable Backup To. This variable will show the location of the backup files. Modify this value as appropriate for the target computers.

Note   Rollback support is meant for restoring specific files and values and not for uninstalling an application—that's what uninstall support is for. Using rollback to uninstall implies that every file or setting that is modified needs to be backed up, which is not always practical or desirable.

Performing Uninstall and Rollback

The Uninstal.exe file that is copied to the target computer during the SMS Installer–generated executable file execution is used to perform the actual rollback. Two methods can be used to uninstall or roll back the client computer to its original configuration. If the installation is an application installation, it is automatically added to Add/Remove Programs in Control Panel. All we have to do is select the application in the Add/Remove Programs dialog box and click Remove. The SMS Installer Uninstall Wizard will appear, enabling you to perform both the uninstall and the rollback.

The second method is to manually run Uninstal.exe from the application's main directory. The Uninstall routine will prompt for the name of the installation log generated by the installation package—usually Install.log—and then begin the removal process. Uninstal.exe also supports a silent mode using the /s parameter from the command line—all of which means, of course, that you could create an unattended SMS package that removes the application for you.

Installation Log

If an uninstall or a rollback has been configured for an SMS Installer–generated executable file, a log file (Install.log) is generated during the installation process and saved in the application directory created on the target computer. This log file contains entries for the files that were copied or installed as well as every registry entry that is created or modified. Additional changes—including icons that were created, shortcuts, and any files that were replaced, such as DLL files—will be archived to the backup location if rollback support is enabled. This log file will be used in the uninstall or rollback process to return files to their original versions and to return all registry settings to their prior configuration.

Also, when the script needs to modify existing INI files, it comments out the line that needs to be modified by adding ";SMS" at the beginning of the line and then writing the new line above it. This way, when an uninstall or a rollback occurs, the process simply searches for the ;SMS entries, deletes the line above, and removes the comment prefix. Clever, eh?

Creating an Uninstall Status MIF File

As with package installation, SMS Installer can also be configured to generate an uninstall status MIF file to indicate that the application has been removed. As we've seen in the section "Modifying Installation Scripts Using the Installation Expert," the configuration of the uninstall status MIF file is done from the SMS tab of the Installation Interface Properties window. To create the uninstall MIF file, you must have configured an uninstall MIF filename, as shown in Figure 13-20, before compiling the SMS Installer–generated executable file.

Updates to Systems Management Server Installer 2.0

The basic functionality of SMS Installer 2.0 as described in this chapter remains unchanged with the application of SMS 2.0 Service Pack 1. However, some new features have been added to facilitate your use of SMS Installer.

> **Caution**   Scripts created with the SMS 2.0 Service Pack 1 version of SMS Installer should not be opened with earlier versions of SMS Installer. If you used any of the new functions of the SMS 2.0 Service Pack 1 version of SMS Installer, such as the new *Syswin* predefined variable, you might lose that support when you save the script.

When you view installation scripts through the Script Editor window, you will notice an added option on the Installation menu: the Debug option. This option enables you to test the entire script, set breakpoints, and test the script one line at a time.

The Options tab of the Advanced Configuration Properties window now includes a Set Color button that lets you assign colors to highlight script elements such as logical statements or remarks. This feature can help you more easily scan and sort your installation script. In addition, a Version tab has been added, which enables you to identify version information for the Setup program (not the application). This feature is useful for tracking multiple Setup versions.

Some actions have been enhanced, and several new actions have been added to Script Editor. The Set Variable, Wizard Block, and If/While actions have been enhanced to support more complex expressions and operators. The Call DLL Function action has been enhanced to call functions written for SMS Installer or functions that have variable parameters unknown to SMS Installer. A new Sleep action can be used to pause the execution of the installation script for a specified period of time. This action is useful if you want to invoke an external program during script execution and you need to stop execution until the external program has completed.

A new variable, named *Syswin*, has also been added. This variable returns the path of the system directory on computers running Windows 95, Windows 98, Windows NT, and Windows 2000.

This version of SMS Installer also installs support for all language versions supported by Windows NT and SMS 2.0. As always, refer to the updated *Systems Management Server Administrator's Guide* for more information, as well as the Microsoft Systems Management Server Version 2.0 Service Pack 1 Release Notes. The online help for SMS Installer 2.0 is also updated with the service pack.

After you update your site server with the service pack, simply reinstall SMS Installer to upgrade it to the Service Pack 1 version.

Tip   Consider participating in the SMS Installer newsgroup *microsoft.public. sms.installer*, accessible through the *msnews.microsoft.com* news server. In this newsgroup, you can have unmonitored discussions about SMS Installer and the new features available.

Summary

SMS Installer is a powerful graphical tool as well as a formidable script-editing utility used to generate executable files that can be distributed through SMS or by any other means you may choose. Ideally, the use of SMS Installer will help you in creating and distributing installation script files with a minimal amount of effort and error.

As we've seen, various levels of scripting are supported, each requiring a higher level of learning. Very basic scripts using the Repackage Installation Wizard are sufficient for installations that are uncomplicated or that don't need to be fully unattended or scripted. The Installation Expert can be used to make the basic script perform more specific tasks, such as modifying registry entries or suppressing dialog boxes. Elegant scripts can be created using Script Editor actions. The technique you choose should depend on your needs and the amount of time you are willing to invest.

In Chapter 12, we examined the process of creating and delivering packages that install applications to SMS clients. In this chapter, we looked at creating application installation scripts using SMS Installer that could then be delivered to and installed on SMS clients using the package delivery feature of SMS. In Chapter 14, we will explore the software metering feature of SMS and you'll learn how to monitor application use on your SMS clients.

Chapter 14
Software Metering

Microsoft introduced a new application management utility with Microsoft Systems Management Server (SMS) 2.0 called Software Metering. This feature enables the SMS administrator to monitor the use of applications among SMS clients, track license usage, place restrictions on running applications based on time or permissions, and spot unauthorized applications when they are run.

Tip If you have not already applied Microsoft Systems Management Server Version 2.0 Service Pack 1, you should certainly do so now if you intend to use the Software Metering tool. Service Pack 1 has updated this feature, and it appears to run much more smoothly than it did in its original release.

In this chapter, we'll look at the components that participate in the software metering process. We'll begin by examining in more detail just what software metering is and how it works. We'll explore the roles of the site server, the software metering server, and the Software Metering Client Agent (also sometimes referred to as the Software Metering Agent). You'll also learn how to manage metered applications beyond simply tracking usage. As always, we will investigate the status messages that are generated by various components and review network traffic considerations. Finally, we'll learn how to create reports and charts to analyze program and license usage data, and review troubleshooting issues.

Note Software metering is not supported for Microsoft Windows 3.x or Microsoft Windows for Workgroups clients. Although it is supported for Alpha clients, Alpha site systems cannot function as software metering servers. Novell NetWare servers also do not support this feature.

Overview

The SMS 2.0 Software Metering tool provides application tracking support in two related areas: software usage and software restrictions. "Software usage" refers to when an application starts on the client, who started it, how long the application ran, how many instances of the application were run, and so on. "Software restrictions" refer to the actual licenses available for the application and license usage, stopping unauthorized applications from running, and placing time and user restrictions on an application, much like creating an access control list (ACL) for a file or folder in Windows NT.

Four main systems participate in the software metering process, whether you are tracking usage or restricting access: the site server, the software metering server and its data cache, the software metering database server, and the SMS client running the Software Metering Client Agent.

The site server, as always, acts as the configuration point for software metering. The site server is where you configure the SMS components that support software metering, including defining which site system will become the software metering server. The site server is also where you will configure, register, or exclude applications for metering and where you will define the number of licenses available and how to balance license information across the software metering servers.

The software metering server is itself the point of contact for the SMS clients. It receives configuration and license information from the site server, it stores usage information reported by the client agents, and it responds to client requests for application access and licenses. The software metering server maintains this license and usage data in its own local data cache (a FoxPro database engine), which it makes available to the site server on a periodic basis.

The software metering data is stored in its own SQL database. This database is separate from the SMS database; unlike the SMS database, it does not require Windows Management Instrumentation (WMI) access or support. The data is viewed through the Software Metering tool, which is installed on the SMS Administrator Console when you select Software Metering as one of the SMS Custom Setup options.

The Software Metering Client Agent is configured through the site server and installed on the SMS clients in much the same fashion as other client agents. Its purpose is to report usage data to the software metering server, request licenses, and update component information on the client such as the excluded programs list.

Software Metering Process Flow

The software metering process, shown in Figure 14-1, begins at the site server, of course. From the SMS Administrator Console on the site server, you configure the Software Metering component and assign the software metering server role to designated site systems. When you select the Software Metering component from the SMS Administrator's Console on the site server, you configure the License Metering process thread. License Metering is responsible for maintaining product configurations such as permitted users, time restrictions, license checkouts, and so on; determining license usage trends; balancing licenses among software metering servers in the same site and across sites; maintaining and forwarding a list of excluded products for the software metering server; copying metered and configuration data from and to the software metering server; and summarizing the metered data.

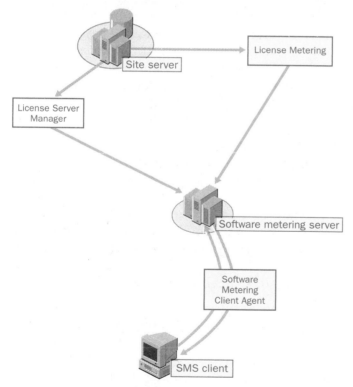

Figure 14-1. *Software metering process flow.*

More Info You can also find detailed flowcharts that outline the various tasks performed by the Software Metering tool and its components in the *Systems Management Server Administrator's Guide,* and also in Chapter 22 of the SMS 2.0 Resource Guide (part of the *Microsoft BackOffice 4.5 Resource Kit,* available through Microsoft Press).

When you assign the software metering server role to a site system, the License Server Manager component is responsible for installing the appropriate support components on that site system. License Server Manager creates and installs the software metering data cache in the SWMTR folder, shares the folder as LICMTR, creates the *SWMAccount* service account, and starts and loads the SMS License Service on the software metering server. The service account will then be used by the SMS License Service.

Once it has been configured, the software metering server makes license and other reporting configuration information available to the SMS clients and receives metered data from the clients. This server does not itself make any connections to either the SMS client or the site server as part of the software metering process. Instead, the Software Metering Client Agent connects to the software metering server to download license and other configuration information to the client and to copy metered data, callback requests, and other data to the software metering server's data cache. The main function of the SMS License Service on the software metering server is to provide or decline software access to the client agent.

If you have configured the Software Metering component to track software usage on the client, the client agent is directed to collect information about the applications running on the client computers. When an application is started—and if it has not been excluded—the client agent gathers its usage information and sends the information to the software metering server. The client agent reports the client on which the application was executed, when the client was started, when the client was stopped, how long the application ran, and the logged on user that initiated the program. This data is then stored as part of the software metering server's data cache.

Software metering operates in one of the two modes: offline and online. If you are running the client agent in offline mode, this usage information is stored on the client and reported to the software metering server on a periodic schedule. Operating in offline mode means that you have not enabled real-time license verification for the client agent. Offline mode is the default; it provides passive monitoring of application usage. If the client cannot connect to the software metering server for whatever reason—for example, if the client is a laptop and is not currently connected to the local network—the usage data is stored locally on the client until a connection to the software metering server can be made.

Online mode is enabled by turning on real-time license verification for the client agent. In this case, software usage is reported by the client agent dynamically. In addition, through online mode, the Software Metering Client Agent checks the software metering server for any restrictions or available licenses for the application that is being started. As mentioned, the SMS License Service on the software metering server is responsible for granting or denying access. If user restrictions or time restrictions exist, or if not enough licenses are available for the application, the application will be prevented from running by the client agent.

If no licenses are available, the Software Metering Client Agent displays a message to that effect on the client computer, asking whether the user would like a callback, as shown in Figure 14-2. If the user accepts the callback, the SMS License Service monitors the application licenses in question.

Figure 14-2. *A callback request to the user when a program cannot be run due to unavailable licenses.*

The callback request is placed in a callback queue and remains in the queue for a specified period of time—by default, 30 minutes. After the specified period of time has passed, the request is dropped from the queue, and the user who requested the callback must generate another license request. During the time the request is in the queue, the client agent periodically checks the software metering server (every 5 minutes by default) to see whether a license has become available and has been reserved for the user. When it finds that a license has been made available, the client agent displays another message to the user to that effect, as shown in Figure 14-3, which also notes the grace period during which the license will be reserved for the user. If the user does not start the application within that grace period—by default, 10 minutes—the reserved license goes back into the pool of available licenses and is fair game to any other client.

Figure 14-3. *Message box notifying user that a license has become available.*

As mentioned, usage and license data are copied to the software metering server by the Software Metering Client Agent. The License Metering process thread on the site server copies software usage and callback data as well as license usage and restrictions data from the software metering server and updates the software metering database.

Software metering configuration data such as new product licenses and excluded programs is passed from a parent site to its child sites. Data about application and license usage, callback requests, and so on is passed from the child site to its parent. Software metering servers can be shared among sites, or they can be installed as site systems on each site. When licenses need to be balanced across sites, you can specify when and how by enabling intersite license balancing. The License Metering process thread component keeps track of license usage at each software metering server and redistributes licenses among them as necessary.

 Caution Product license information moves only from parent to child and not vice versa. If the software product is installed on the child site, its product license information cannot be propagated to the parent site. Usage data about that product is reported to the site for which the product was installed. Thus, intersite license balancing cannot take place unless the product was registered at the parent site.

Mobile Users

Users that are not always connected to the network—such as laptop users, or those with unreliable network connections—are considered mobile users by SMS. When the Software Metering Client Agent cannot connect to the software metering server to report software usage and other data to the data cache, it will store this information in a file on the client until the next time it can complete the connection. Also, if you have configured real-time license enforcement and the client agent is unable to connect to the software metering server, the client agent will allow the program to run if it is installed locally.

You do have the ability to allow users to check out licenses for a specific period of time. Users can thus check out and hold "legal" licenses while they are away from the network. This feature and other configuration options will be discussed in detail in the sections that follow.

Configuring Software Metering

Software metering is configured in two areas of reference: server components and the client agent. Let's begin by looking at the server components because without these, the client agent is useless. The two server components that need to be configured are the Software Metering component and the software metering site system. Both are definable through the Site Settings folder in the SMS Administrator Console.

Software Metering Component

The Software Metering component controls policy settings used for tracking software and summarizing metered data, defines the frequency at which license balancing and other management tasks occur, and defines rules and schedules for summarizing data. This configuration information is used by the License Metering process thread to carry out management tasks related to software metering.

Note As for all SMS components, the settings you apply for the Software Metering component are sitewide settings.

To configure the Software Metering component, follow these steps:

1. In the SMS Administrator Console, navigate to the Component Configuration folder under Site Settings.

2. Right-click on Software Metering, and choose Properties from the context menu to display the Software Metering Properties window, as shown in Figure 14-4.

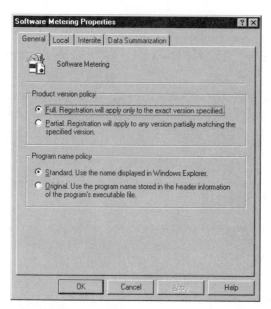

Figure 14-4. *The Software Metering Properties window.*

3. On the General tab, select the product version policy appropriate for your organization. Product version policy defines how SMS will register and refer to an application.

   Partial registration, the default, will register and monitor any version of a software application that partially matches the major version number. Full registration registers each version of the application as a separate program to monitor. For example, Solitaire installed on Windows NT and Windows 95 workstations are versions 4.00 and 4.00.950, respectively. Under partial registration, both versions would be recognized and monitored as the same program. Under full registration, each version would be considered a separate application and thus would have to be registered and monitored separately.

4. Select the program name policy most appropriate to your organization. Your selection defines how SMS should identify the program when it is monitored.

   Standard, the default, indicates that the filename for the executable will be used to identify the program. If a user renames the executable, SMS would potentially no longer recognize the application as one to monitor.

Original, on the other hand, directs SMS to read the application's name from the header information contained in the application's executable file. Thus even if the user renamed the file, SMS would still recognize the application as one to monitor.

Caution   Not all applications are written to contain the program name in the header information of the executable file. Games, for example, tend not to do this.

5. Click on the Local tab, shown in Figure 14-5. This tab allows you to set the schedule for three server management tasks carried out by the License Metering process thread on the site server.

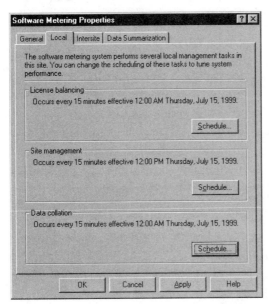

Figure 14-5. *The Local tab.*

6. Recall that within a site, the site server periodically checks the software metering servers to determine whether they have an appropriate number of licenses assigned to each. The License Balancing option defines how often the site server checks license usage at the software metering servers to determine whether to transfer licenses from underutilized to overutilized servers. You can have the site server balance licenses one time only—for example, if you have one software metering server and

you have defined all the licenses up front—or you can set a recurrence pattern. To do so, click the Schedule button to display the Schedule dialog box, make the appropriate choices, and click OK. The default is every 4 hours.

7. The Site Management option defines the frequency with which the site server updates the software metering servers with new licensed programs, excluded programs lists, and registered programs. To modify the frequency, click the Schedule button, make the appropriate choices in the displayed dialog box, and click OK. The default setting is once per hour.

8. The Data Collation option process defines how frequently the License Metering thread on the site server copies usage data from the software metering server to the site server for update to the software metering database. To modify the frequency with which the data is collated, click the Schedule button to display the Schedule dialog box, make the appropriate choices, and click OK. The default setting is once per hour. Usage data, you might recall, is written to the data cache stored on the software metering server (in the SWMTR folder). After the data is updated to the software metering database, it is deleted from the data cache. This data can also be sent to a parent site in a site hierarchy if the product is registered at the parent site.

Note Although it might appear that you can set any of these schedule values to less than 15 minutes, the minimum value is, in fact, 15 minutes.

9. Although your organization may consist of several SMS sites, licenses for your organization may be managed as a group. For this and other reasons, software metering servers can be established at each SMS site and share the total available licenses for the organization. You can either distribute the licenses yourself or have SMS balance licenses among the software metering servers at each site, much as it does within its own site. To enable intersite license balancing, select the Schedule Intersite License Management option on the Intersite tab, shown in Figure 14-6. This tab also lets you specify when and how often this balancing occurs and the receipt time period, which is the maximum time that a "donating" site waits for the "receiving" site to acknowledge receipt of the licenses. If the transfer does not complete within this time period, the licenses revert back to the donating server. You can modify the license

balancing schedule by clicking the Schedule button and specifying the appropriate time period in the displayed dialog box. Click OK to close the dialog box.

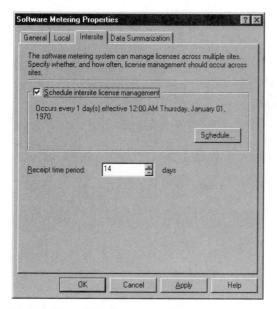

Figure 14-6. *The Intersite tab.*

Caution License balancing may be difficult to monitor outside of a production environment. External influences such as network traffic and bandwidth can certainly affect whether a receiving server can acknowledge balanced licenses within the receipt time period. You will probably need to monitor license balancing under various conditions to obtain the optimum values for the license balancing settings.

10. The Software Metering component is an inclusive rather than exclusive usage tracker. By default, it records usage information about every executable program file that runs on the client unless you specifically exclude files. This allows you to record any and all versions of programs that are executed at the clients. If all this information is written to the software metering database, the database could quickly become very large, eventually resulting in reduced performance. The Data Summarization tab, shown in Figure 14-7, lets you specify how often software metering

data is summarized, much like the component summarizers described in Chapter 5, and what criteria are used. Like other status summarizers, the License Metering process thread summarizes usage data by condensing multiple references to a program's usage to a single general record of use for that product. For example, if five clients each run two instances of Solitaire for five days, 50 records of usage for Solitaire will have been reported. Data summarization can condense this to one record per program per day, per week, and so on.

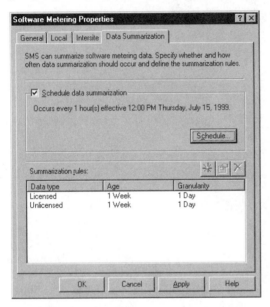

Figure 14-7. *The Data Summarization tab.*

11. To enable data summarization, select the Schedule Data Summarization check box. Click the Schedule button to display the Schedule dialog box to configure the frequency at which summarization takes place. Click OK to return to the Data Summarization tab.

12. In the Summarization Rules section, click the New button (the yellow star), to display the Summarization Rule Properties window, shown in Figure 14-8.

In this Properties window, you can specify the age and granularity for both licensed and unlicensed usage. *Age* refers to the length of time data is recorded before it is summarized. *Granularity* refers to how records are condensed. The Granularity setting must be less than or equal to the Age setting. If you set Age to 1 Day and Granularity to 1 Hour, the data will be summarized as 24 records each day—one record per program per hour. If you set Age to 1 Week and Granularity to 1 Day—the defaults—after one week of collected usage data, one record will be generated per program per day. Click OK to return to the Data Summarization tab.

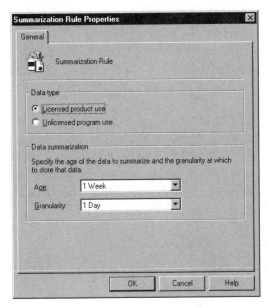

Figure 14-8. *The Summarization Rule Properties window.*

13. Click OK to apply your selections and begin the site update process.

Real World   Partial vs. Full Registration

Sometimes it is essential to determine the difference between the Partial registration and the Full registration of program policy options when configuring the Software Metering component.

As we've seen, it's important to recognize that Solitaire is not always Solitaire when it comes to software metering. Consider the following scenario: Suppose that when you first enabled the Software Metering component options, you selected Full as the registration option. You then updated your clients

(Windows NT and Windows 95) and began to experiment with restrictions, exclusions, and licenses. One of the applications you registered with license enforcement was Solitaire. If you purposely create situations in which you will run out of licenses for Solitaire, you should generate a callback request on your clients. For some reason, the callback will appear on your Windows NT client but never on your Windows 95 client, even though both would record usage information for Solitaire.

So how do you stop Solitaire from executing on the Windows 95 client? If you examine the Summary view in the Software Metering tool that we'll discuss in the section "Using the Software Metering Tool" later in this chapter, you'll notice that Solitaire on the Windows 95 client is returning a version number of 4.00.950, whereas Solitaire on the Windows NT client is returning a version number of 4.00.

Like every good administrator, your next step would be to check your component settings. Here you'll discover that the Product Version Policy option was set to Full, which means that Solitaire version 4.00 running on the Windows NT client, from SMS's point of view, was entirely different from Solitaire version 4.00.950 running on the Windows 95 client. As you instructed it to, SMS was duly tracking the license usage for Solitaire on the Windows NT client, and blissfully ignoring license usage for Solitaire on the Windows 95 client.

The moral of this story? Full registration is highly specific to the version. Product versions must match exactly for tracking and monitoring to take place. Full registration is a powerful tool for the SMS administrator and gives you a great deal of control. It is also a sitewide setting for the Software Metering component, which means that if you want to track programs that register different version numbers on different operating system platforms, you'll need to either register each program separately or switch back to Partial registration.

Local License Balancing

Let's take a moment to clarify how local license balancing works within the site. The License Metering process thread on the site server checks the license balancing schedule configured through the SMS Administrator Console for the Software Metering component. When license balancing is scheduled to run, the License

Metering process thread retrieves usage information from the data cache on each software metering server, including statistics about license grants and denials, peak activity, and callbacks. Based on calculated trends, it may take available licenses from an underutilized software metering server and distribute them to software metering servers that are overutilized.

When the site server is notified of a license denial, the License Metering process thread sends the software metering server an additional license or licenses within 15 minutes if it has them available—this is known as *instant license balancing*. You may have defined additional licenses, or the site server may have licenses it obtained from other software metering servers during the license balancing process. If the site server does not have any licenses, the License Metering process thread will query each software metering server every 15 minutes to determine whether any has a free license or if any require additional licenses. When the License Metering process thread obtains a license, it forwards the license to the software metering server that needed the license at the next license balancing cycle, or the next time a license is denied.

Defining the Software Metering Site System

In Chapter 3, we examined the site server roles you can assign and the process of creating a site server and assigning it one or more roles. In this section, we'll focus on configuring a site system for the software metering server role.

As with all site systems, you begin by identifying which servers will become a site system for your site and then assign the appropriate roles to that site system. To assign the role of software metering server to the site system, follow these steps:

1. In the SMS Administrator Console, navigate to the Site Systems folder under Site Settings.

2. Right-click on the site system that will be assigned the software metering server role, and choose Properties to display the Site System Properties window.

3. Click on the Software Metering Server tab, shown in Figure 14-9, and check the Use This Site System As A Software Metering Server check box.

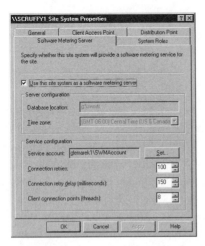

Figure 14-9. *The Software Metering Server tab of the Site System Properties window.*

4. In the Server Configuration section, enter a location for the SWMTR database directory. This should be a drive that has at least 10 MB of free space plus about 100 bytes for each client that will be metered. Also be sure that the correct time zone is selected; otherwise, balancing and other maintenance tasks may not occur when expected.

5. In the Service Configuration section, identify the name of the service account you want to use. The default service account name is *SWM-Account*, and there's no particular reason to change it unless your organization requires specific naming conventions. Click the Set button to display the Windows NT Account dialog box, shown in Figure 14-10, and reenter the account name, including the Windows NT domain name. This removes any confusion as to the domain membership of the account. Enter and confirm a password for the account, and then click OK.

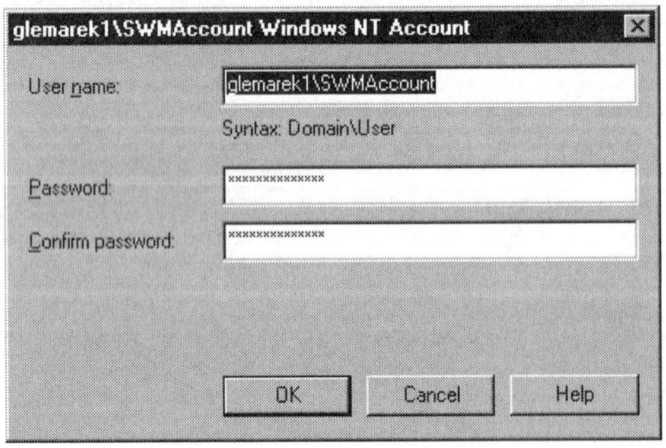

Figure 14-10. *The Windows NT Account dialog box.*

6. The Connection Retries option represents the number of times the service account will attempt to connect to the data cache on the site server. This setting can be any value from 1 through 1000. The Connection Retry Delay option represents the interval in milliseconds between connection attempts. The Client Connection Points option represents the number of simultaneous client connections that can be made to the data cache on the site server. If the number of clients connecting exceeds this value, their requests are queued and processed as threads become available. This setting can be any value from 1 through 100; the default is 8.

7. Click OK to begin the site system setup process.

Caution   Resist the urge to set Client Connection Points to a high value. You are, after all, defining the number of clients that can simultaneously connect to the software metering server's data cache. Setting it to a high value can really bog down the site system, especially if it is performing other roles as well. As with all SMS options, try a value, monitor performance, and test!

At this point, License Server Manager creates and installs the data cache in the SWMTR folder on the site system, loads and starts the SMS License Service on the site system, and copies component configuration information and support files to the site system. As we've discussed, the SWMTR folder will be shared as LICMTR. This is the share that the Software Metering Client Agent will use to request configuration and license information and to write its product usage information.

Caution   The data cache in the SWMTR folder cannot be installed on a compressed drive. If you try to do so, you will experience the SMS disappearing directory trick: the directory will be built to a point, and then the process will fail and the directory will be removed. SMS retries rebuilding the directory until it times out. If you peruse the log file associated with License Server Manager (Licsvcfg.log), you'll see a message to the effect that an attempt to copy *Product*DB.dll failed and that License Server Manager will remove the directory.

Always use the Software Metering Server tab of the Site System Properties window to change the Software Metering Service account password. All references that SMS or the software metering server makes to this account are controlled through this setting. If you change the password on your own through User Manager For Domains and change its reference in the SMS License Service through the Control Panel Services utility, you will not have properly informed SMS that a change has been made, and license updates and other configuration information may not be correctly reported.

However, when you remove the software metering server role from a site system (by simply clearing that option on the Software Metering Server tab of the Site System Properties window), the Software Metering Service account is *not* automatically removed. This you will have to do manually through User Manager For Domains.

Configuring the Software Metering Client Agent

After—and only after—you have successfully configured both the License Metering process thread and the software metering site system, you can configure the Software Metering Client Agent and update the client computers.

Caution This is extremely important! The client agent will not configure correctly unless at least one software metering server has been successfully and completely configured for the site.

To configure the Software Metering Client Agent, follow these steps:

1. In the SMS Administrator Console, navigate to the Client Agents folder under Site Settings.

2. Right-click on Software Metering Client Agent, and choose Properties from the context menu to display the Software Metering Client Agent Properties window, shown in Figure 14-11.

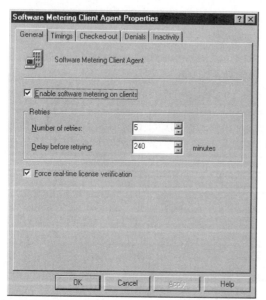

Figure 14-11. *The Software Metering Client Agent Properties window.*

3. On the General tab, select the Enable Software Metering On Clients check box.

4. In the Retries section, enter the number of times that the client agent will attempt to connect to the software metering server to transfer data and the number of minutes to wait between attempts. The default values are 5 retries with a delay of 2 hours (240 minutes).

   If the client agent cannot connect after the specified number of retries, it will attempt to contact another software metering server in the site. If it is still unable to connect, it will return to offline mode and proceed to maintain usage information on the client, which it will forward to the software metering server the next time it can connect.

5. If you intend to enable license and restriction tracking instead of just usage tracking, be sure to select the Force Real-Time License Verification check box. This option switches the client agent from offline monitoring to online monitoring and enables license balancing and real-time license verification.

6. Click on the Timings tab, shown in Figure 14-12. This tab contains options that let you control how the Software Metering Client Agent communicates with the software metering server. The Client Time-Out Settings and Callback Settings options are active only if you selected Force Real-Time License Verification on the General tab to enable on-line monitoring.

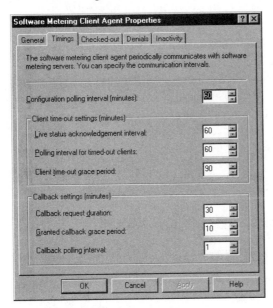

Figure 14-12. *The Timings tab.*

7. The Configuration Polling Interval option defines how frequently the client agent contacts the software metering server to check for updated configuration information such as the excluded programs list as well as how frequently the client forwards usage data when the client is in offline monitoring mode. The default interval is 240 minutes, but this value can range from 1 through 10,080 minutes.

8. The Client Time-Out Settings options define how frequently the client agent connects to the software metering server before the client agent is considered to be timed-out. The Live Status Acknowledgement Interval setting specifies how often, in minutes, the client agent connects and acknowledges that it is running. By default, this happens every 60 minutes, but you can specify any value in the range from 30 through 10,080 minutes. The Polling Interval For Timed-Out Clients setting represents the frequency with which the software metering server checks for timed-out clients as determined by the Client Time-Out Grace Period setting. The default setting is 60 minutes, but you can specify any value in the range from 60 through 20,160 minutes and should be set to a value at least as large as the Live Status Acknowledgement Interval. Client Time-Out Grace Period represents the maximum length of time the client agent can go without acknowledging that it is running. If the client agent fails to acknowledge itself as running within this period, it is considered timed-out at the next polling interval. By default, the client is given 90 minutes, but you can choose a value in the range from 90 through 30,240 minutes.

9. The Callback Settings options define the callback parameters. Recall that callbacks occur when a client requests a license and none are available. The client agent displays a Callback Request dialog box asking whether the user wants to be notified when a license becomes available. If the user does request a callback, the client agent will periodically check with the software metering server to see whether a license has become available. The Callback Polling Interval setting represents the frequency with which the client agent will check with the software metering server. The default value is 5 minutes and can range from 1 through 60 minutes. If the user requested a callback and a license becomes available, the License Service on the software metering server will add that license to a pending callback list and hold it there for the period of time specified in Callback Request Duration. The default value is 30 min-

utes, but it can range from 10 through 1,440 minutes. If the user does not accept the callback within this time, the license is given back to the pool of available licenses. When the client agent determines that a license is available, it will display a message to that effect to the user. If the user accepts the callback, the user must launch the application in question within the time specified by the Granted Callback Grace Period setting; otherwise, the license will be returned to the pool of available licenses. The Granted Callback Grace Period default value is 10 minutes, and can range from 1 through 1,440 minutes.

10. Click on the Checked-Out tab, shown in Figure 14-13. The License Expiration Message text box contains the message displayed by the client agent when a license the user has checked out is nearing its due date. You can enter whatever text you like, including the name and number of an administrator to call. Just remember that because you are configuring a client agent, all clients will receive the same message text.

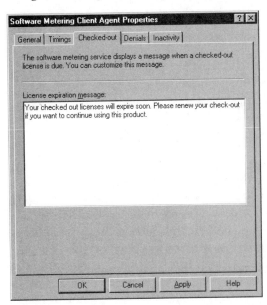

Figure 14-13. *The Checked-Out tab.*

11. Click on the Denials tab, shown in Figure 14-14. The Product Use Denial Message text box contains the message displayed by the client agent when a license has been denied due to a restriction other than

unavailable licenses. Again, you can enter whatever text you like, but remember that this is a sitewide setting. The Denial Message Time value represents the length of time in seconds that the denial message will be displayed. The default setting is 30 seconds, but this value can range from 1 through 86,400 seconds (24 hours).

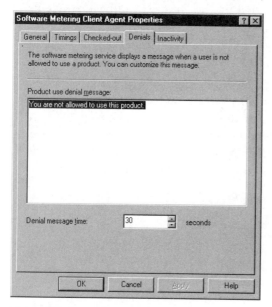

Figure 14-14.   *The Denials tab.*

12. Click on the Inactivity tab, shown in Figure 14-15. The Inactive Product Message text box contains the message displayed by the client agent when an application has been determined to be inactive due to a prolonged lack of keyboard or mouse activity or as defined by the SMS administrator in the Software Metering tool (on the Alerts tab of the registered application's Properties window).

13. Click OK to save your settings and begin the site update process.

The Software Metering Client Agent will be installed on the client computer at the next CCIM maintenance cycle (every 23 hours) or when an update configuration is performed on the client computer. (Refer to Chapter 8 for a complete discussion of the client update process.)

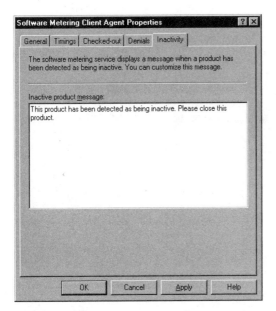

Figure 14-15. *The Inactivity tab.*

Using the Software Metering Tool

The Software Metering tool provides both viewing and configuration options for the applications you are tracking. You can view usage data, set restrictions and licenses, and generate simple usage reports. To access the Software Metering tool, follow these steps:

1. In the SMS Administrator Console, navigate to the Tools folder and expand it.

2. Right-click on Software Metering, choose All Tasks from the context menu, and then choose Start Software Metering to display the Software Metering tool, shown in Figure 14-16.

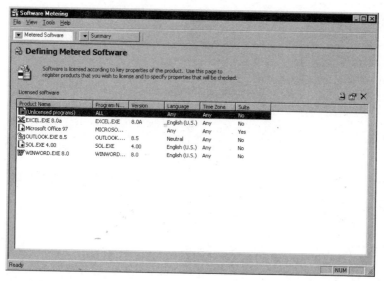

Figure 14-16. *The Software Metering tool.*

Tracking Usage

As shown in Figure 14-16, the Software Metering tool opens to the Metered Software view by default. In this window, you will see a list of all the applications you have registered and for which you have set specific license data, restrictions, or other properties. The Summary view window contains two tabs for displaying usage data: Unlicensed and Licensed. The Unlicensed tab, shown in Figure 14-17, displays all applications that have been metered from your SMS clients. By default, the Software Metering Client Agent records and forwards usage information for every executable run on the client with the exception of those listed in the Excluded Programs list. The information recorded and displayed here includes the name, version, and language of the program that was executed; the user that executed the program; the name of the computer on which the program was executed; when the program was started; and how long the program ran. Each instance of each program running on each SMS client will be reported, including, of course, any instance of any executable called by another application. Consequently, this list can quickly become quite large.

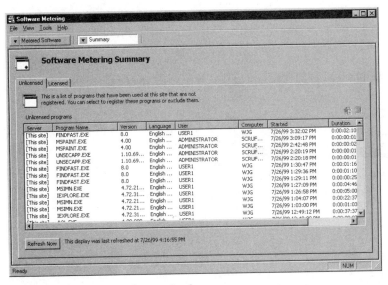

Figure 14-17. *The Unlicensed tab.*

The amount of data recorded here can be controlled in several ways. Recall that the Data Summarization tab of the Software Metering Component Properties window lets you define rules for summarizing this usage information. Following your criteria, the SMS License Service summarizes usage data by condensing multiple references to a program's usage in a single general record of use for that product. Recall the Solitaire example cited previously. If five clients each run two instances of Solitaire for five days, 50 records of usage for Solitaire will have been reported. Data summarization can condense this information to one record per program per day, per week, and so on.

Another way to control the amount of usage data that is monitored and recorded is to exclude programs you don't want to monitor. For example, you might not want to know or even care whether a user runs the Calculator tool or what executables were called by a program when the user ran a spell-check. These types of programs can—and should—be excluded from tracking by the Software Metering Client Agent.

The Software Metering tool is configured with a default Excluded Programs list. This list includes most of the SMS client agent executables, some Windows NT operating system program files and .DLLs and some programs such as Notepad,

Program Manager, and Microsoft Management Console (MMC). To view the Excluded Programs list (shown in Figure 14-18), choose Excluded Programs from the Tools menu in the Software Metering window.

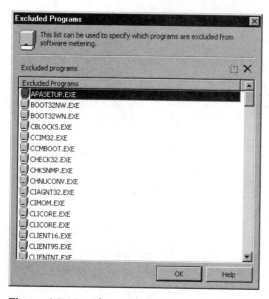

Figure 14-18. *The Excluded Programs list.*

There are two ways to add programs to the Excluded Programs list. The first is to find the programs you want to exclude in the Unlicensed Programs list on the Unlicensed tab. Right-click on a program and choose Exclude from the context menu, or select the program and click the Exclude button (the one that looks like a software box with a bag over it). This will add the program to the Excluded Programs list. However, you will need to let the Software Metering Client Agent monitor and record all the programs you want to exclude at least once before you can exclude them in this fashion because the Unlicensed Programs list is created as the Software Metering Client Agent reports application usage. An application will not appear in the list until it has been reported by the client agent at least once.

Another way to exclude programs is through the Excluded Program list itself. To use this technique, follow these steps:

1. Start the Software Metering tool from the SMS Administrator Console.

2. Select Excluded Programs from the Tools menu to display the Excluded Programs list (shown in Figure 14-18).

3. Click the New button to display the New Excluded Program dialog box, shown in Figure 14-19.

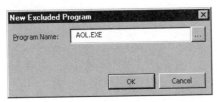

Figure 14-19. *The New Excluded Program dialog box.*

4. Enter the name of the program you want to add to the list, or click the Browse button to browse for the program name. Then click OK.

5. Click OK again to update the Excluded Program list.

The updated Excluded Programs list is copied to the software metering server by the License Metering process thread on the site server. At the next component polling cycle for the Software Metering Client Agent, the updated Excluded Programs list is downloaded to the SMS client. From this point forward, the client agent will ignore any instance of the excluded programs that are run on the client.

Registering, Restricting, and Licensing Programs

Beyond simply tracking application usage on your clients, you may want to establish other usage policies and restrictions. This process involves registering a program and configuring more specific usage policies for that program. You can accomplish this task in several ways using the Software Metering tool.

The first method is to find the programs you want to register in the Unlicensed Programs list on the Unlicensed tab. Right-click on the program, and choose Register from the context menu, or click the Register button (the yellow star on a software box). The New Product dialog box will appear, as shown in Figure 14-20. Notice that some product and file details are already filled in. Most of these were derived from header information contained in the executable file. Make any modifications you want to these fields. The purchase date will always be the date on which you registered the product.

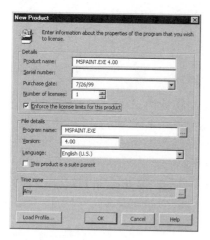

Figure 14-20. *The New Product dialog box.*

In particular, be sure to enter the number of licenses available for this product. This number will be used to grant or deny licenses to your SMS clients running the Software Metering Client Agent if you also enable the Enforce The License Limits For This Product option. If you do not select that option, the license number will be strictly informational.

As with excluding programs through the Unlicensed tab, you will need to let the Software Metering Client Agent monitor and record all the programs that you want to register at least once before you can register them in this fashion.

The other method of registering programs is accomplished through the Metered Software view window of the Software Metering tool.

1. Start the Software Metering tool from the SMS Administrator Console.

2. In the Metered Software view window, click the New button (the yellow star on a software box) to display the Add Product dialog box, shown in Figure 14-21.

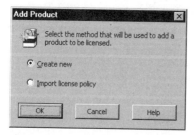

Figure 14-21. *The Add Product dialog box*

3. Select Create New and then click OK to display the New Product dialog box, shown in Figure 14-20. Enter the product details, including the product name, the serial number, and the purchase date. Enter the number of licenses and select Enforce The License Limits For This Product if you intend to track license usage for this program.

4. Enter the file details, including the program name, version, and language. If the product is a suite parent (discussed in detail in the section "Registering Product Suites" later in this chapter), select This Product Is A Suite Parent. Click the Browse button to browse for the program file. If you select a program file using this method, product and file details will be filled in to the extent that they can be read from the header information of the program file.

5. Adjust the Time Zone as necessary, and then click OK to complete the registration.

Policies and Profiles

Occasionally, software developers include a license policy or profile generated as a Management Information Format (MIF) file during the setup of the application. These files usually include product and file details and the number of licenses granted. If the product you are registering includes such a file, you can use it to fill in the New Product dialog box.

To do so, copy the policy or profile file to the SMS\Inboxes\License.box\Local\Miflp folder on the site server. In the Metered Software view window, click the New button to display the Add Product dialog box. Choose Import License Policy and then click OK to display the Import License Policy dialog box. Select the product from the list and click Import. Alternatively, you can click the New button and then choose Create New. In the New Product dialog box (shown in Figure 14-20), click the Load Profile button to display the Load Profile dialog box. Select the profile from the list, and click Load Profile to return to the New Product dialog box. The New Product dialog box will reflect the product, file, and license entries contained in the policy or profile.

Registering Product Suites

You have no doubt noticed in the New Product dialog box the This Product Is A Suite Parent option. *Product suites* consist of two or more applications that are functionally related or that work together. Microsoft Office and Lotus Smart Suite are examples of product suites. For example, Microsoft Office represents the suite parent, and Microsoft Word, Microsoft Excel, Microsoft PowerPoint, and so on, represent the applications that belong to Microsoft Office. You can register suites by first registering each application that belongs to the suite and then registering the suite and adding the individual applications to the suite.

Licenses obtained for suite products apply to the members of the suite. For example, if you purchase 50 Microsoft Office Professional licenses, they apply equally to Word, Excel, PowerPoint, and Microsoft Access—all members of the suite. When you register the individual applications within the suite, set the number of licenses to 0.

Note If you obtained extra licenses for any member of the suite, specify the number of extra licenses when you register that member. For example, if you have 50 Microsoft Office Professional licenses and you then purchased 10 extra Access licenses, set the number of licenses for Access to 10 when you register it.

Register the suite parent as you would any other new product through the Metered Software view window as outlined earlier. The product name entered in the New Product dialog box should reflect the suite name—for example, Microsoft Office 97—as shown in Figure 14-22. Enter any additional details you want except the version number, and select the option This Product Is A Suite Parent. Be sure to enter the number of licenses available for the suite members.

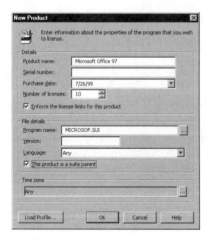

Figure 14-22. *Defining a suite parent in the New Product dialog box.*

To add the individual programs to the suite parent, follow these steps:

1. Select the suite entry from the Licensed Software list in the Metered Software view window. Right-click on the entry and choose Properties from the context menu to display the Program Properties window, shown in Figure 14-23.

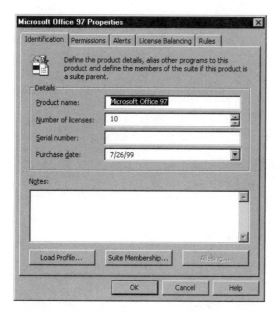

Figure 14-23. *The Program Properties window.*

2. On the Identification tab, click Suite Membership to display the Suite Membership dialog box, shown in Figure 14-24. Select each program in the Available Resources list that should be a member of the suite, and click the Add button to add it to the Members list.

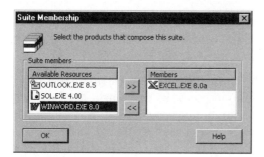

Figure 14-24. *The Suite Membership dialog box.*

3. Click OK, and then click OK again to add the programs to the suite parent.

Modifying Registered Product Properties

Once a product has been registered, you can set additional policies and restrictions on it by modifying its properties. To do so, follow these steps:

1. In the Metered Software view window, select the program whose properties you want to configure from the Licensed Software list.

2. Right-click on the entry, and then choose Properties from the context menu to display the Program Properties window, shown in Figure 14-25.

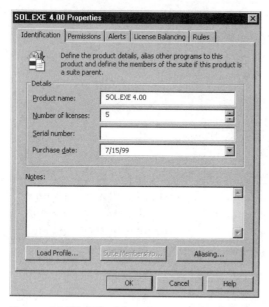

Figure 14-25. *The Identification tab of the Program Properties window.*

3. The Identification tab displays the product details you entered when you registered the program. You can modify these as necessary. The Number Of Licenses setting represents the number of licenses that are currently available at the site server and have not yet been distributed, or balanced, to the software metering servers. Once all available licenses have been balanced, this value will be 0. If you have purchased additional licenses, enter the number of licenses here.

Note You can only increase the number of licenses using the technique described above. If you need to decrease the number of licenses, you must first delete the registered program, wait for the site server to update the software metering servers, and then reregister the program with the new (lower) number of licenses.

4. Click on the Permissions tab, shown in Figure 14-26. Here you can set two types of restrictions on the application: you can identify which users and computers can access the program and specify which times of day the application can be run.

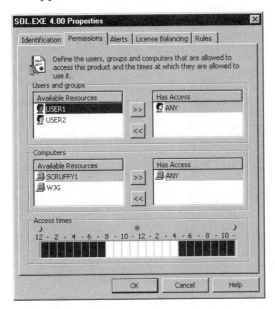

Figure 14-26. *The Permissions tab.*

5. Specifying users and computers is much like configuring an ACL in Windows NT. Anyone you explicitly identify in the Has Access list will be able to run the program. To give a specific user or computer access to the program, select it from the Available Resources list and click the Add button to add it to the Has Access list. Be sure to remove the entry ANY from the Has Access list, as this acts much like the Everyone group in Windows NT. The list of users and computers is generated through a Tools menu option in the Software Metering tool and is discussed in the section "Resource Manager" later in this chapter.

6. To disallow access at specific times of the day, highlight the range or ranges of time when the program cannot be run in the Access Times section, and then click OK.

7. Click on the Alerts tab, shown in Figure 14-27. These settings allow you to define events that will generate system messages as well as define how computer inactivity is managed.

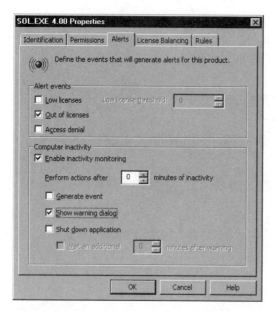

Figure 14-27. *The Alerts tab.*

8. In the Alert Events section, select the event option for which you want an alert generated. If you select Low Licenses, you can also specify the threshold number of licenses that must be reached before the alert is generated.

9. In the Computer Inactivity section, you can enable monitoring for inactivity by selecting Enable Inactivity Monitoring. Enter the number of minutes of inactivity (lack of mouse or keyboard movement) that must be detected before an action is performed, and then select one or more actions. If you select Generate Event, an event will be written to the Application log in the Windows NT Event Viewer of the computer in question. If you select Show Warning Dialog, the Software Metering Client Agent will display the warning message you defined on the Inactivity tab of the Software Metering Client Agent Properties window. If you select Shut Down Application, you can optionally define a grace period during which the user can save data files before the application is shut down.

10. Click on the License Balancing tab, shown in Figure 14-28. Here you can specify license balancing percentages within the site and among sites.

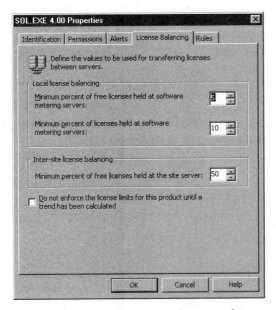

Figure 14-28. *The License Balancing tab.*

11. The Minimum Percent Of Free Licenses Held At Software Metering Servers setting in the Local License Balancing section represents the minimum number of peak usage licenses to keep at the software metering server. If the number of licenses falls below this threshold, the license balancing process will attempt to locate available licenses in other sites.

12. The Minimum Percent Of Licenses Held At Software Metering Servers setting represents the minimum percentage of free and used licenses that should be maintained by the software metering server at all times. If the site server is balancing licenses, it will not take licenses from a software metering server if it will breach this threshold.

13. The Minimum Percent Of Free Licenses Held At The Site Server setting in the Inter-Site License Balancing section indicates that you want at least that percentage of licenses kept available at the site server to distribute to software metering servers should they require additional licenses. When the percentage of free licenses falls below this threshold, the site server will attempt to obtain available licenses from other software metering servers through its load balancing process.

14. By default, license restrictions will not be enforced until SMS has determined how licenses are being used at each software metering server. License usage is monitored for seven days, after which licenses are reapportioned—that is, balanced—according to usage statistics. License restrictions are then enforced on the clients. If you want to begin enforcing license restrictions immediately, especially if you have only one software metering server, clear the Do Not Enforce License Limits For This Product Until A Trend Has Been Calculated check box.

15. To configure additional policy options, click on the Rules tab, shown in Figure 14-29.

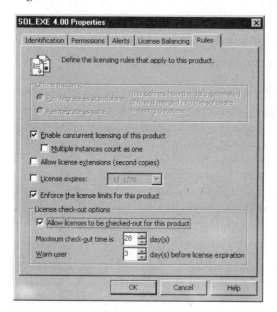

Figure 14-29. *The Rules tab.*

16. If the program you have selected is a member of a suite, the options in the Offline Metering section are activated. These options define how data will be collected and reported for individual programs that are also members of a suite while in offline mode. You can specify that offline data should be reintegrated using the individual product's license data by selecting Reintegrate As Standalone or using the suite parent's license data by selecting Reintegrate As Suite.

17. The Enable Concurrent Licensing Of This Product option allows the simultaneous use of one product on one computer using one license. When this is selected (by default), you can also select Multiple Instances Count As One, which means that a single license allows the user to run

multiple instances of the product. For example, if you are licensing Calculator, you can initiate several instances of it but use only one license and track all instances as one.

18. The Allow License Extensions option allows for licenses that permit the program to be run on more than one computer using the same license—for example, programs that can be installed legally on both a business and home computer.

19. If the program is an evaluation copy of software, or if for some other reason the license period is short, select License Expires and enter an expiration date.

20. If you intend to grant and deny licenses through the software metering server based on the license rules you configured, select the Enforce The License Limits For This Product check box.

21. In the License Check-Out Options section, you can enable your user to check out a license for this product for a specified maximum period of time (from 1 to 365 days). After the maximum number of days is reached, the license is revoked and returned to the available pool of licenses. The Warn User value indicates the number of days before the license will expire that the Software Metering Client Agent will begin to warn the user that the license will expire. The message displayed to the user is the message you configured on the Checked-Out tab of the Software Metering Client Agent Properties window.

22. Click OK to save the program configuration.

This configuration data will be forwarded to the software metering server and will be updated for the client by the Software Metering Client Agent at its next configuration polling interval.

Aliasing Registered Programs

On the Identification tab of the registered program's Properties window, you might recall seeing a button labeled Aliasing. In software metering, *aliasing* a program enables you to identify one or more programs to be monitored as another registered program.

The following example of aliasing is adapted from the *Systems Management Server Administrator's Guide*. The Software Metering Client Agent for Windows 95 and Windows 98 clients is named Liccli95.exe; for Windows NT clients, it is named Licclint.exe. If client agents are monitored separately, they are tracked by their filenames. However, both of these client agents are 32-bit agents. You could register one of those programs—say, Licclint.exe—as "32-bit Software Metering Client", and then alias Liccli95.exe. When Liccli95.exe or Licclint.exe is started, a license for "32-bit Software Metering Client" is used. To alias a program, follow these steps:

1. Open the Properties window for the program you just registered.

2. On the Identification tab, click the Aliasing button to display the Aliasing dialog box, shown in Figure 14-30.

Figure 14-30. *The Aliasing dialog box.*

3. Click the New button to display the Add A New Alias dialog box, shown in Figure 14-31.

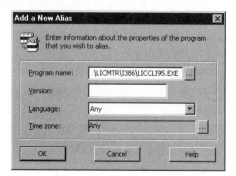

Figure 14-31. *The Add A New Alias dialog box.*

4. Enter the program name for the program you want to alias or click the Browse button. Specify version, language, and time zone information if necessary, and then click OK.

5. Click OK again to save the alias.

6. Click OK to close the registered program's Properties window.

Now when either program is run, it will be monitored and recorded under a single alias—the registered program you created. This alias can help facilitate your analysis of programs that are run.

Real World   **Restricting Unlicensed Software**

As mentioned, any application that you have not either registered or excluded using the Software Metering tool will be tracked by the Software Metering Client Agent. Usage data for these applications is displayed on the Unlicensed tab in the Summary view window of the Software Metering tool. Unlicensed programs of this type can also be restricted. Notice that the Licensed Software list in the Metered Software view window contains an Unlicensed Programs entry, as shown in Figure 14-15.

Right-click on Unlicensed Programs and choose Properties from the context menu to display the same Program Properties window you see for any other registered program, where you can set user and computer restrictions, time restrictions, alerts, and concurrent license options. You cannot set any policies that deal with licenses or license balancing, however, as those can be set only for registered programs.

Also, all the options that you configure here will apply to *all* unlicensed programs. Unless you have been meticulous about the programs you have registered and excluded, restricting the unlicensed software may not always be practical. However, if you have been scrupulous, you could use this feature of the Software Metering tool to intentionally set restrictions on or lock out specific programs that have not been explicitly excluded or registered.

Consider the following example: If your organization maintains desktop standards that do not allow users to install their own software, you would register all the standard programs that are supported by your organization and exclude the little applets like Clock and Calculator. Perhaps you have purposely removed the Games folder from the Accessories folder because it is not a company standard. Theoretically, the only programs that should now appear in the Unlicensed Programs list are nonstandard programs—those that are unsupported or that shouldn't run on clients' workstations.

You could then set a global restriction for all these unlicensed and therefore nonstandard or unsupported programs such that they should not be run at all at any time. This would effectively prevent a user from being able to run these kinds of applications.

Resource Manager

One of the program property restrictions you can set is which users and computers can explicitly run a particular registered program. The users and computers that can be added to this list are configured using the Software Metering tool's Resource Manager. Resource Manager also lets you identify a callback priority for each user. By default, callbacks are granted on a first come, first served basis. Let's say that user A is denied a license and requests a callback. User B tries to run the same program next, is also denied a license, and requests a callback. When a license becomes available, user A will receive the first callback. User B will receive the next callback, and so on.

The default callback priority is 5, with 1 the lowest priority and 9 the highest. Revisiting the same scenario, let's set the callback priority for user B to 7. In this case, user A is denied a license and requests a callback. User B tries to run the same program next, is also denied a license, and requests a callback. When a license becomes available, user B will receive the first callback because user B's callback priority is higher than user A's. Similarly, the user with the next highest callback priority will receive the next callback, and so on.

You configure Resource Manager in the following manner:

1. From the Software Metering window, choose Resource Manager from the Tools menu to display the Resource Manager window, shown in Figure 14-32.

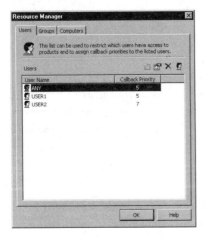

Figure 14-32. *The Resource Manager window.*

2. On the Users tab, you can create a list of users that you can reference when setting access permission for a registered program. To add a user,

click the New button to display the Add New User dialog box, shown in Figure 14-33.

Figure 14-33. *The Add New User dialog box.*

3. Enter the Windows NT user name in the User Name text box. Enter the Callback Priority, if necessary, for this user, and then click OK.

4. Click on the Groups tab, shown in Figure 14-34. Here you can create a list of groups that you can reference when setting access permission for a registered program.

Figure 14-34. *The Groups tab.*

5. Click the New button to display the Add New Group dialog box, shown in Figure 14-35.

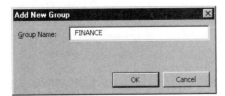

Figure 14-35. *The Add New Group dialog box.*

6. Enter the Windows NT group name in the Group Name text box, and then click OK.

7. Click on the Computers tab, shown in Figure 14-36. Here you can create a list of computers that you can reference when setting access permission for a registered program. By default, all your SMS client computers will be listed here.

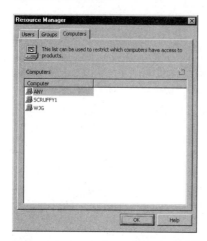

Figure 14-36. *The Computers tab.*

8. Click the New button to display the Add New Computer dialog box, shown in Figure 14-37.

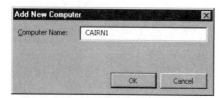

Figure 14-37. *The Add New Computer dialog box.*

9. Enter the Windows NT computer name in the Computer Name text box. Then click OK.

Note   Although the steps for adding a new group have been included here for completeness, the Software Metering tool, even with SMS 2.0 Service Pack 1 applied, does not recognize groups. The Software Metering tool cannot validate access based on group resources; it can validate access only based on users or computers.

Monitoring Status and Flow

Status messages are reported by both License Server Manager and the License Metering component on the site server and can be viewed through the Status Message Viewer. Recall that License Server Manager is responsible for the setup or uninstall of the software metering server as well as maintaining configuration information on the software metering server. The License Metering process thread is the real workhorse, maintaining the registered program properties, performing trend analysis and license balancing among software metering servers within the site and across SMS sites, maintaining the excluded programs list, retrieving usage information from and updating license and configuration information to the software metering servers, and summarizing usage data for the Software Metering tool.

Status Messages

Status messages generated by these two components tend to be of the start and stop variety, although the License Metering process thread does generate useful messages when licenses are low, when balancing fails for some reason, or when no more licenses are available, as shown in Figure 14-38.

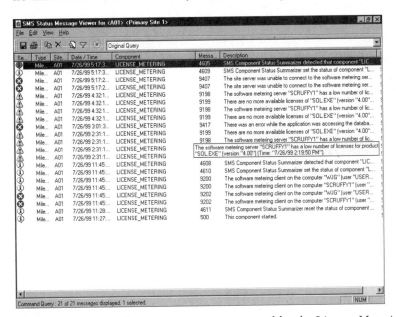

Figure 14-38. *Sample status messages generated by the License Metering process thread.*

Each of these components also writes data to its log files if logging has been enabled on the site server. The log files for License Server Manager and the License Metering process thread are Licsvcfg.log and Licsrvc.log. Through these log files, you can more clearly follow the process threads involved with the activity of the two components. Figure 14-39 illustrates how licenses were balanced for a specific product for which the software metering server was out of licenses.

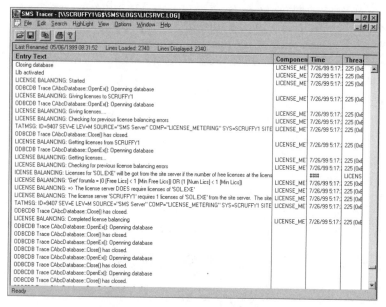

Figure 14-39. *Sample License Metering log file.*

On the SMS client, the Software Metering Client Agent also generates a log file, named Liccli.log, as shown in Figure 14-40. Through this file you can watch as the client agent updates the Excluded Programs list on the client, checks for callbacks, copies offline data to the software metering server, tracks product instances, grants and denies licenses, and more.

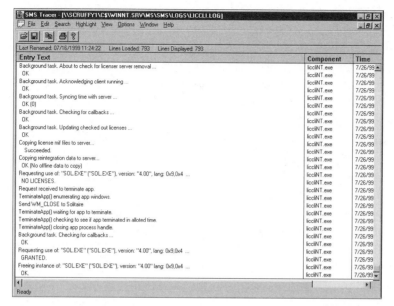

Figure 14-40. *Sample Software Metering Client Agent log file.*

Network Performance Considerations

Outside of the obvious network traffic involved in installing the software metering server and the Software Metering Client Agent, traffic will occur whenever the software metering server is contacted. The software metering server does not make any network connections of its own. Instead, the License Metering process thread on the site server connects to the software metering server periodically to carry out the maintenance tasks for the software metering server, as outlined earlier in this chapter in the section "Software Metering Component." And the client agent contacts the software metering server to copy usage information to it and to retrieve callbacks, licenses, excluded programs, and other configuration updates.

The amount of traffic that is generated depends on the extent to which you plan to monitor your clients. For example, if you choose to monitor just software usage in offline mode, instances of programs run at the client are periodically copied to the software metering server. Since licenses and other restrictions are not being monitored, the License Metering process thread on the site server does not need to perform license balancing. Thus, the amount of network traffic is minimized and controlled.

On the other hand, if you enable online mode by enforcing license tracking and other restrictions, the client agent will notify the software metering server each time an application is started on the client, check for licenses and callbacks periodically, grant or deny access, and so on. Also, the License Metering process thread will perform license balancing according to the schedule you configure, perform instant license balancing when licenses are unavailable on a software metering server, and so on. This corresponds to a proportionately higher amount of network traffic generated—a significant portion of which is out of your control.

One way to help minimize the amount of traffic generated is to exclude the programs that you do not need to license or track. It takes only 12 KB per excluded program to download the list to each client. Also, schedule local and intersite balancing to occur on a less frequent basis, and let SMS calculate license balancing trends for you to minimize occurrences of instant license balancing.

Creating Reports and Interpreting Data

The Software Metering tool includes some basic reports and charts that can help you analyze program and license usage data. These can be accessed through the Tools menu in the Software Metering window. The Tools menu contains two wizards that are designed to generate statistical reports: the Report Wizard and the Graph Wizard. Summary data for licensed and unlicensed programs can also be viewed and analyzed through the Summary view window.

> **Note** You must have defined a default printer, preferably of PostScript quality, for reports and graphs to display correctly. You do not need to actually have the print device installed—unless, of course, you need printed output.

Viewing Licensed and Unlicensed Program Usage

As we've seen, the Summary view window contains two tabs: Licensed and Unlicensed. The Unlicensed tab displays usage data for each instance of a program that is run if it has not been either excluded or registered, including the name, version, and language of the program that was executed; the user that executed the program; the name of the computer on which the program was run; when the program was started; how long the program ran; and how many copies ran.

This list can grow to be quite large, and as we have seen, you can set summarization rules for condensing this data. After summarization has taken place, each instance of a program is rolled into a single entry, which is displayed in the Unlicensed Programs list, as shown in Figure 14-41. In this example, unlicensed programs are monitored for one week, after which data is summarized for each day.

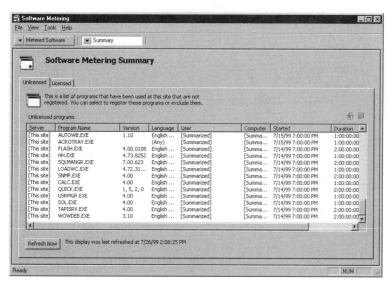

Figure 14-41. *Sample Unlicensed Programs list.*

Each entry includes the tag [Summarized] to show that summarization has taken place. Unfortunately, the Started and Duration entries reflect the summarization schedule rather than the start and stop times of the program, which would be more useful.

On the Licensed tab, each licensed product is displayed in the Products list, as shown in Figure 14-42. As you select each entry, you can change the data displayed in the right pane by clicking the Reports button (the far right button). Six different report views are available. The default is the Active Summary Of License Use view.

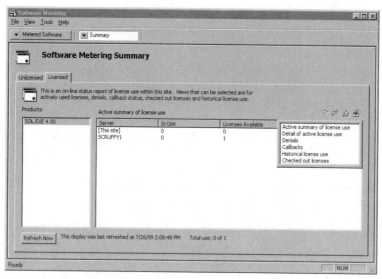

Figure 14-42. *Report views available on the Licensed tab.*

Table 14-1 lists the six report views.

Table 14-1.   Report views for the Licensed tab

View	Description
Active Summary Of License Use	Displays licenses available for balancing at the site server, licenses available at each software metering server, and the number of licenses in use. The number of licenses shown as being in use includes licenses reserved through callbacks.
Detail Of Active License Use	Displays the registered products for which a license is currently in use, including the computer and user that are running the program and when it was started.
Denials	Displays when the program was denied and which user and computer received the denial.
Callbacks	Displays current callback status for this product, including which computers and users have requested or received a callback.
Historical License Use	Displays detailed program license usage for the program if summarization rules have not been defined. If they have been defined, displays detailed usage for the summarization age interval defined and summarized entries based on the summarization granularity defined.
Checked Out Licenses	Displays current licenses that have been checked out, the user and computer that checked out the license, and the length of time the license is checked out.

As on the Unlicensed tab, summary data displayed using the Historical License Use report view includes the time and date when summarization occurred.

Report Wizard

The Report Wizard offers 15 different reports, as follows:

- Callback Priority
- Detailed Product Use (Grouped By Product)
- Detailed Product Use (Grouped By User)
- Excluded Programs
- Last Client Run Time Sorted By Age
- Last Client Run Time Sorted By Computer
- Licensed Products
- Multiple Site Summary
- Product Denials
- Single Site Summary
- Software Metering Server Configuration
- Suites
- Total Use of Product (Grouped By Product)
- Total Use of Product (Grouped By User)
- Unlicensed Program Usage

These reports can help to supplement usage data by organizing the information by user, by product, by site, and so on. Figures 14-43 and 14-44 show two examples of reports generated by the Report Wizard. Each report can be printed, resized, or even exported to one of several export formats, such as Crystal Reports, comma-separated values(CSVs), Excel, Word, and a variety of ODBC-compliant formats.

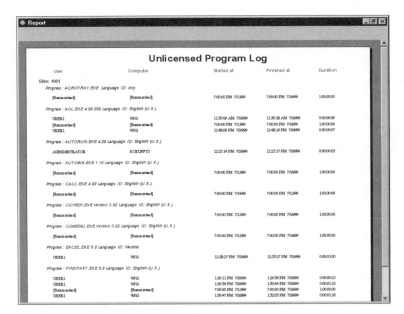

Figure 14-43. *Sample Unlicensed Program Log.*

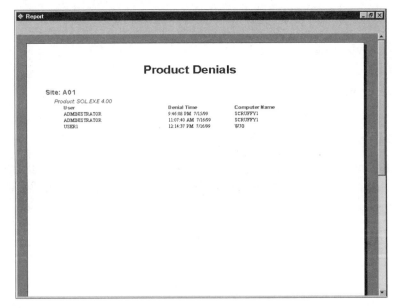

Figure 14-44. *Sample Product Denials report.*

The Software Metering Server Configuration report is particularly handy for documentation purposes. As shown in Figure 14-45, it gives you an overview of current server settings.

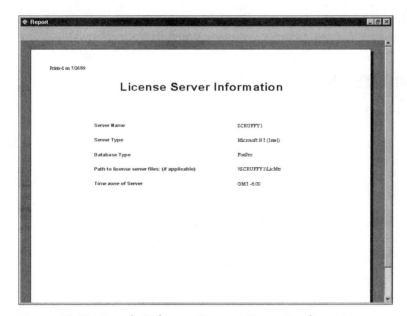

Figure 14-45. *Sample Software Metering Server Configuration report.*

To generate a report using the Report Wizard, follow these steps.

1. From the SMS Administrator Console, start the Software Metering tool.
2. Choose Report Wizard from the Tools menu to launch the Report Wizard, shown in Figure 14-46.

Figure 14-46. *The Report Wizard welcome screen.*

3. Click Next to display the Available Reports screen, shown in Figure 14-47. Select the report you want to generate from the Available Reports list.

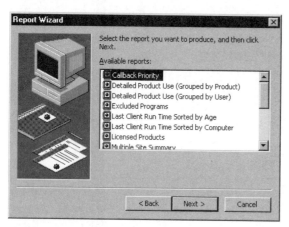

Figure 14-47. *The Available Reports screen.*

4. Click Next to display the Report Range screen, shown in Figure 14-48. Depending on the report you chose, select the appropriate product, site, user, and computer ranges.

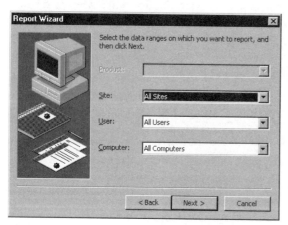

Figure 14-48. *The Report Range screen.*

5. Click Next to display the Date Range screen, shown in Figure 14-49. Enter an appropriate date and time range.

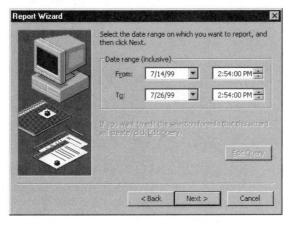

Figure 14-49. *The Date Range screen.*

6. Click Next to display the Finish screen, shown in Figure 14-50, and click Finish to generate the report and display it.

Figure 14-50. *The Finish screen.*

Graph Wizard

The Graph Wizard lets you chart usage data using any of five different graph types, as follows:

- 2-D Bar Graph
- 3-D Bar Graph
- 3-D Perspective Graph
- Area Graph
- Line Graph

These graphs can help to supplement usage data by displaying product usage data by user, by computer, and by site. Figures 14-51 and 14-52 show two examples of graphs generated by the Graph Wizard. Like the reports generated by the Report Wizard, these graphs can be printed, resized, or even exported to a variety of export formats.

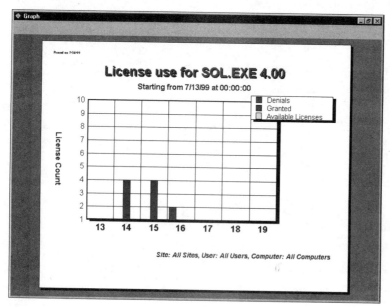

Figure 14-51. *Sample 2-D bar graph.*

Figure 14-52. *Sample 3-D perspective graph.*

To generate a graph using the Graph Wizard, follow these steps:

1. From the SMS Administrator Console, start the Software Metering tool.

2. Choose Graph Wizard from the Tools menu to launch the Graph Wizard, shown in Figure 14-53.

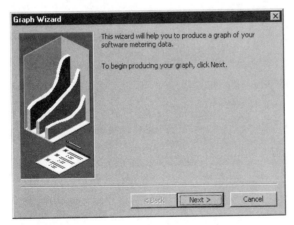

Figure 14-53. *The Graph Wizard welcome screen.*

3. Click Next to display the Available Graphs screen, shown in Figure 14-54. Select the type of graph you want to generate from the Available Graphs list.

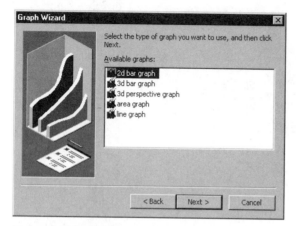

Figure 14-54. *The Available Graphs screen.*

4. Click Next to display the Graph Range screen, shown in Figure 14-55. Select the product, site, user, and computer ranges for which you want to generate the graph.

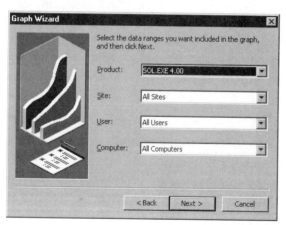

Figure 14-55. *The Graph Range screen.*

5. Click Next to display the Date/Time/Unit screen, shown in Figure 14-56. Enter an appropriate date and time range, as well as the number of units to graph and the time period for each unit.

Figure 14-56. *The Date/Time/Unit screen.*

6. Click Next to display the Finish screen, shown in Figure 14-57, and click Finish to generate the report and display it.

Figure 14-57. *The Finish screen.*

Checkpoints

The Software Metering tool is a new feature in SMS 2.0, and as such it is still experiencing some growing pains. As mentioned, SMS 2.0 Service Pack 1 resolves some of the anomalous activity some SMS administrators have experienced when they've used the Software Metering feature.

Several "notes" and "cautions" have appeared throughout this chapter. These represent the most significant "gotchas" you may experience when you are configuring and using the Software Metering tool. Let's review some of these issues.

Remember that the software metering server and the Software Metering process thread must both be completely configured before you configure and install the Software Metering Client Agent. The software metering server data cache requires about 10 MB at the start and additional space to store metered data. Be sure that you have ample disk space, as always, and that the drive on which you are installing the data cache is not compressed.

When you register a product to enforce license restrictions, the default setting is for SMS to calculate product trends for seven days, balance licenses across software metering servers based on these trends, and only *then* begin to enforce licenses for clients. If you intend to begin enforcing licenses right away, be sure to clear that option. However, clearing that option also means disabling SMS from performing license balancing for you—it's a trade-off.

Otherwise, check your license settings, check to see whether licenses have been properly balanced, be sure that your software metering servers are accessible to the clients, and don't forget to monitor your status messages and log files.

Summary

Software metering, the newest feature of SMS 2.0, is still being refined, but nevertheless it does offer the SMS administrator some powerful program tracking tools. Remember to install SMS 2.0 Service Pack 1 to really make it shine.

As you've seen, you can manage client software in two ways. You can simply meter the applications as they are run on the client and report usage data periodically to the software metering server. Or you can report program execution dynamically and check for license or other restrictions that may have been placed on a registered program.

Recorded usage data can be summarized, analyzed, and reported. Licenses can be automatically load-balanced across software metering servers within the local site as well as across SMS sites. You can track all programs, exclude programs, or register specific programs with specific properties and policies.

In this part of the book, we have examined various ways to manage client applications. The package distribution process showed us how we can remotely install programs on our SMS clients and how the package distribution process can be maximized through the use of collections. With the SMS Installer, we can fully script our packages to require little or no user input during the package's execution. In this chapter, we have seen how to monitor the usage of client applications. In Part IV, we'll explore various ways to retrieve and present information from the SMS database, as well as site database maintenance and recovery.

Part IV

Site Database Maintenance and Recovery

Chapter 15
Queries and Reports

In the first three parts of this book, we've covered the primary functions of Microsoft Systems Management Server (SMS) 2.0. We've explored the inventory collection process, package distribution and management, software metering, and remote client management. Along the way, a lot of information has made its way into the SMS database, and you've seen periodic references to using a query to extract information from the SMS database—for example, a query might be used as a membership rule to populate a collection or to view status messages generated by various client agents. This section of the book focuses on database maintenance tasks including extracting and analyzing data, setting security, and recovering data.

Queries are an efficient and relatively easy way to retrieve information from the SMS database. SMS also makes Crystal Info available as a reporting tool within the SMS Administrator Console. We will explore both methods of accessing SMS database information in this chapter, and you'll be introduced to another *Microsoft Backoffice 4.5 Resource Kit* utility to facilitate the analysis of such data. We'll also see how we can use applications such as Microsoft Excel and Microsoft Access to extract and analyze SMS data.

Queries

As you know, the premise behind any database query is the return of information based on a set of criteria. In other words, you define what information you are trying to obtain in the form of a query statement. The query engine then searches the database for entries that match your criteria. The query result then displays the data that matched your criteria.

The same is true for SMS queries. To define a simple SMS query, you would specify an SMS object to search on, one or more attributes of the object, an operator of some kind, and a value. For example, suppose you are querying for computers with processors greater than 155 MHz. In this case, *computer* is an object, *processor* is an attribute of the object, *greater than* is the relational operator, and *155 MHz* is the value.

SMS queries can be used for a variety of purposes. Generally, we think of queries as a means of reporting on data in the database. Indeed, we might use SMS queries to find all the computers that meet a certain memory, disk space, and platform requirement before sending out a package to them. And as we've seen, queries are particularly useful in defining collection memberships. Collections whose members are based on the results of a query can be updated periodically to keep them current. Any programs advertised to a collection are automatically made available to the collection's members. As the query runs and updates the collection, new members automatically receive any advertisements that targeted the collection, and deleted members no longer receive the advertisements.

SMS queries can be generated a couple of different ways. The easiest way to create and run a query—and the easiest method to learn—is using SMS Query Builder, which is built into the SMS Administrator Console. This interface provides you with a point-and-click method for building your query. You could also write the query statements yourself; however, this method entails learning a query language—specifically, WBEM Query Language (WQL).

Unlike other SQL Server databases, SMS relies on the Windows Management Instrumentation (WMI) layer to expose its database information to the SMS Administrator Console and other tools. Therefore, you cannot use regular SQL queries or commands to extract data from the SMS database.

> **Caution** Don't even try using SQL queries against your SMS database. If you do, you might corrupt the database.

What you need is a tool that can connect to WMI to access the SMS Provider and collect the information you require. Any utility that is WBEM ODBC–compliant can be used for this purpose. Because the SMS Administrator Console uses WMI and the SMS Provider to manage the database, its query functions and its installation of Crystal Info for SMS are probably the easiest way to display information contained in the SMS database. However, you could use a reporting tool such as Microsoft Excel 97 or Microsoft Access 2000 with the WBEM ODBC drivers to report on SMS data. We will review those methods in the section "Other Reporting Tools" later in this chapter.

SMS 2.0 loads 33 predefined queries, some of which are shown in Figure 15-1. As you can see, these predefined queries are fairly general in scope and are meant to be more globally oriented, perhaps as the target of an advertisement. However, you can certainly create your own queries—for example, to assist with certain management tasks, including populating and updating collections and viewing client status messages.

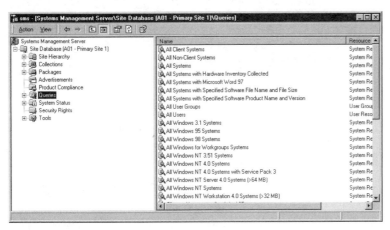

Figure 15-1. *Some of the predefined queries in SMS 2.0.*

Query Elements

Before we review the steps for creating a query, let's take a look at the individual elements that make up a query. The relationship between these elements is illustrated in Figure 15-2. As mentioned, you begin your query definition by selecting an object to query on. SMS provides several object types for generating queries. An *object type* has specific attribute classes that describe it. For example, the *System Resource* object type is defined by its *memory, environment, logical disk, processor,* and *network* attribute classes, and so on. An *attribute class* is essentially a category of attributes and contains an attribute list. For example, the *System Resource* attribute class includes the *IP Addresses, IP Subnets, NetBIOS Name, Operating System Name and Version,* and *SMS Assigned Sites* attributes.

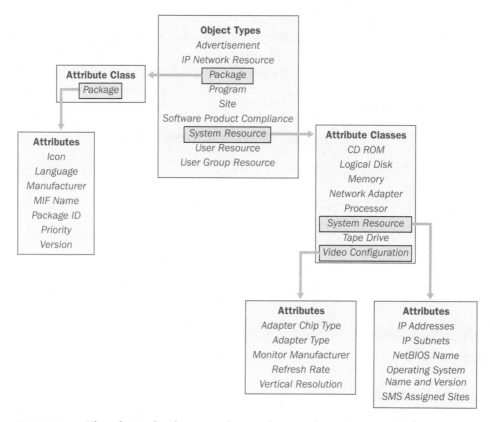

Figure 15-2. *The relationship between objects, their attribute classes, and the attributes of each class.*

Table 15-1 lists the more frequently used object types, some of their attribute classes, and a short list of attributes.

Table 15-1.   SMS objects and some of their attribute classes and attributes

Object Type	Attribute Classes	Attributes
Advertisement	*Advertisement*	*Advertisement ID* *Advertisement Name* *Collection ID* *Package ID* *Program Name*
Package	*Package*	*Description* *Manufacturer* *Name* *Package ID* *Priority*

Table 15-1.   *continued*

Object Type	Attribute Classes	Attributes
Program	Program	Command Line Comment Disk Space Required Package ID Working Directory
Site	Site	Build Number Install Directory Server Name Site Code Site Name
Software Product Compliance	Software Product Compliance	Category Product Company Product Name Product Version Type
System Resource	Collected File	Collection Date File Name File Path
	Logical Disk	File System Free Space Volume Name
	Memory	Total Pagefile Space Total Physical Memory Total Virtual Memory
	Network Adapter	Adapter Type MAC Address Manufacturer
	Operating System	Build Number Manufacturer Version
	Processor	Family Manufacturer Max Clock Speed
	System Resource	IP Addresses NetBIOS Name Operating System Name And Version
User Group Resource	User Group Resource	Name Resource ID SMS Assigned Sites User Group Name Windows NT Domain
User Resource	User Resource	Full User Name Resource ID SMS Assigned Sites User Name Windows NT Domain

More Info For a complete list of objects, attribute classes, and their attributes, refer to Appendix E in the *Systems Management Server Administrator's Guide*. When you define your query to SMS, in addition to a name you will need to supply the object type, attribute class, and attributes you want to search on. You will usually need to supply criterion types and values; relational and logical operators; and sometimes attribute class joins, order of preference, or WBEM Query Language.

The *criterion type* defines what you are comparing the attribute with. The six criterion types are listed in Table 15-2.

Table 15-2.   Criterion types

Type	Description
Null Value	Used when the attribute value may or may not be null
Simple Value	Constant value against which the attribute is compared
Prompted Value	Prompts you to enter a value before the query is evaluated
Attribute Reference	Lets you compare the query attribute to another attribute that you identify
Subselected Values	Lets you compare the query attribute to the results of another query
List Of Values	List of constant values against which the attribute is compared

Along with the criterion type, you will select a relational operator and supply a value to search for. This value can be null, numeric, a string, or a date/time. The list of relational operators is pretty much what you would expect: Is Equal To, Is Not Equal To, Is Greater Than, Is Less Than, and so on. However, the kinds of operators that are available depend on whether the attribute is null, numeric, string, or date/time. Table 15-3 outlines the subtle differences between these operators.

Table 15-3.   Relational operators

Data Type	Relational Operators
Null	Is Null Is Not Null
Numeric	Is Equal To Is Not Equal To Is Greater Than Is Less Than Is Greater Than Or Equal To Is Less Than Or Equal To

Table 15-3.   *continued*

Data Type	Relational Operators
String	Is Equal To Is Not Equal To Is Like Is Not Like Is Greater Than Is Less Than Is Greater Than Or Equal To Is Less Than Or Equal To
Date/Time	*Unit* Is Equal To *Unit* Is Not Equal To *Unit* Is Greater Than *Unit* Is Less Than *Unit* Is Greater Than Or Equal To *Unit* Is Less Than Or Equal To *Unit* Is
Date/Time	*Unit* Is Not *Unit* Is After *Unit* Is Before *Unit* Is On Or After *Unit* Is On Or Before

(*Unit* is a date or time unit—millisecond, second, minute, hour, day, week, month, or year.)

When string values are used in a query, the exact string must be provided, without quotation marks unless the quotation marks are part of the string. If you use either the Is Like or Is Not Like relational operator, you can use wildcard characters as part of the string. Acceptable wildcard characters include those shown in Table 15-4.

Table 15-4.   Wildcard characters

Symbol	Meaning
% (percent)	Any string of characters
_ (underscore)	Any single character
[ ](brackets)	Any character within a specified range of characters
^ (caret)	Any character *not* within the specified range of characters

For example, if we wanted to query the database for all SMS clients that contained the string *FIN* in the client name, we might use the value %*FIN*%. String operators are not case-sensitive unless the SQL code page you are using uses case-sensitive comparisons.

In real life, your queries will probably be more complex and will consist of several query statements. These statements are connected using logical operators and are grouped for evaluation using parentheses. The three primary logical operators used with SMS queries are AND, OR, and NOT.

An AND operation finds all data that matches two query statements connected by the AND. AND operations generally result in a more restricted search since every expression must be satisfied to generate a result.

An OR operation finds all the data that matches any portion of the two statements connected by the OR. As you might expect, OR operations generally result in a broader search since any expression may be satisfied to generate a result.

A NOT operation finds all the data that does not satisfy the statement preceded by the NOT. For instance, in our sample query we might have wanted to exclude all the computers running a lower version number of Windows 95 for upgrade purposes.

Creating a Query

Now that you've gotten your feet wet, let's put some of these SMS query elements to use by creating a query. Our test query will search for all computers running Windows 95 that have at least 300 MB of free disk space (perhaps so that we can install Microsoft Office 2000 or upgrade to Windows NT or Windows 2000).

As we've seen in previous chapters, you can create a query from a number of locations—for example, you can create or reference a query when you define the membership of a collection, or you can create a status message query in the Status Message Queries folder in the SMS Administrator Console. The process is essentially the same wherever the query is created. For this example, we'll create a query from the Queries folder in the SMS Administrator Console. To do so, follow these steps:

1. In the SMS Administrator Console, navigate to the Queries folder and expand it to view the existing queries.

2. Right-click on the Queries folder, choose New from the context menu, and then choose Query to display the Query Properties window, shown in Figure 15-3.

3. On the General tab, enter a name for your query. This name can be up to 127 characters so can be quite descriptive (see Figure 15-1). You can also select an existing query to copy and modify, by clicking Browse.

4. Enter a more detailed description of the query in the Comment text box if desired.

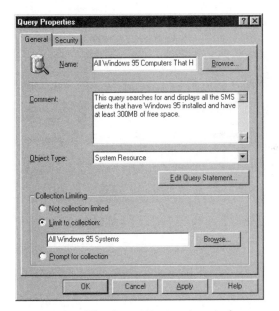

Figure 15-3. *The Query Properties window.*

5. In the Collection Limiting section, you can narrow the scope of the query by selecting Limit To Collection and then typing in or browsing for the collection name. You can also make the query more interactive and there-fore more useful by selecting Prompt For Collection, in which case you will need to supply the collection name whenever the query is run. If you leave the default Not Collection Limited option selected, the query will be run against the entire database, assuming that the administrator executing the query has access to the entire database.

Note As described in Chapters 11 and 16, you can create SMS security rights so that administrators have access to various objects in the database, includ-ing specific collections. If an administrator cannot access a collection, the query will not run.

6. Select the object type you want to run the query on, and then click the Edit Query Statement button to display the Query Statement Properties window, shown in Figure 15-4.

7. On the General tab, you will define the query results window—that is the data (the attributes) displayed in the SMS Administrator Console when the query is run. To add a class and an attribute, click the New button (the yellow star) to display the Result Properties window, shown in Figure 15-5.

Figure 15-4. *The Query Statement Properties window.*

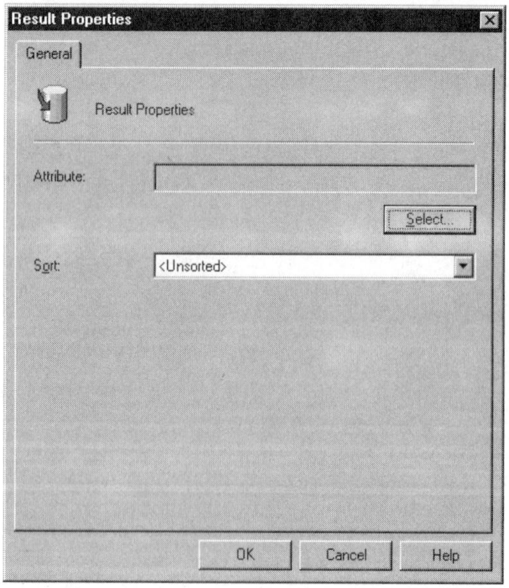

Figure 15-5. *The Result Properties window.*

8. Click Select to display the Select Attribute dialog box, shown in Figure 15-6, where you define an attribute class and an attribute.

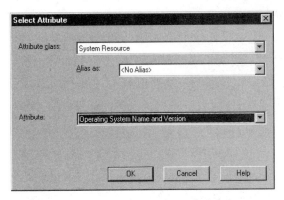

Figure 15-6. *The Select Attribute dialog box.*

9. Enter or select an alias if desired. This must be a valid SQL alias. (Refer to your SQL documentation for more information about aliases.) Click OK to save your selections and return to the Result Properties window (Figure 15-5).

10. Select a sort order if desired, and then click OK to return to the Query Statement Properties window (Figure 15-4).

11. Repeat steps 7 through 10 to add as many attributes as you want displayed when the query is run. Remember, the query results displayed are based on your query criteria.

12. Click on the Criteria tab. On this tab, you will actually define your query statement. Click the New button to display the Criterion Properties window, shown in Figure 15-7. Here you will define the specific query elements.

13. Select a criterion type from the drop-down list. To select an attribute class and an attribute to fill the Where text box, click Select to display the Select Attribute dialog box and choose the appropriate entries from the drop-down lists. In this example, because we are looking for computers with at least 300 MB of free space, our Attribute Class setting will be Logical Disk and the Attribute setting will be Free Space (Mbytes).

14. Click on OK to return to the Criterion Properties window, and select an appropriate operator from the drop-down list.

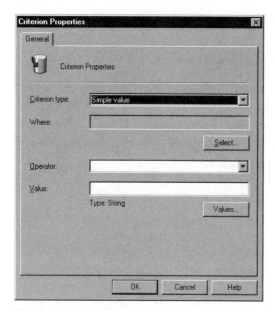

Figure 15-7. *The Criterion Properties window.*

15. Next enter a value. If you click the Values button, SMS will display the Values dialog box, shown in Figure 15-8, which lists all the *Free Space* values currently recorded in the SMS database. You can select one of these values or enter the appropriate value (300, in this case) in the Value text box and then click OK. Notice that the value will then be added automatically to the Value text box in the Criterion Properties window.

16. The completed Criterion Properties window is shown in Figure 15-9. Click OK to save your settings and return to the Criteria tab.

17. Repeat steps 12 through 16 to add additional query statements and use the logical operator buttons listed on the Criteria tab (shown in Figure 15-10) to connect these query statements. The New button, used to add a query statement, creates an AND connection by default. Selecting the AND operator and clicking the &l button will change the AND to an OR, and clicking the ! button will change the AND to a NOT. The two Parentheses buttons are for grouping (or ungrouping) two or more selected statements.

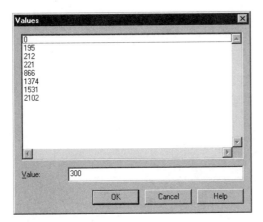

Figure 15-8. *The Values dialog box.*

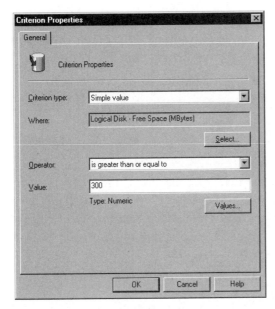

Figure 15-9. *The completed Criterion Properties window.*

18. Group your statements together using parentheses to define the order of evaluation. For example, Figure 15-10 shows what the query statement would look like if we had not restricted the query to the All Windows 95 Computers collection.

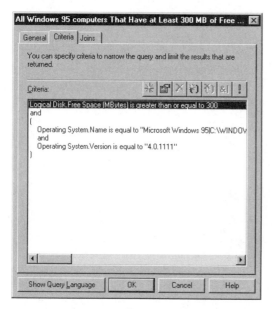

Figure 15-10. *A sample query statement using logical operators and parentheses.*

Notice that this example also specifies more precisely the version number of computers running Windows 95 and that the collection is more generic. Notice too that the operating system name and version are grouped together to ensure that we evaluate clients as those running Windows 95 version 4.0.1111 instead of clients that are running Windows 95 and clients that have any operating system whose version is 4.0.1111.

Combining Attributes

The Joins tab of the Query Statement Properties window, shown in Figure 15-11, displays the links made between the attribute classes. This linking is done for the most part automatically by SMS as you select attributes from different attribute classes. Sometimes, however, because of the nature of the query, you may need to create joins between different attribute classes manually.

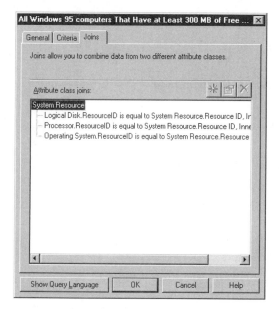

Figure 15-11. *The Joins tab.*

To create your own joins to different attribute classes, follow these steps:

1. Select the Joins tab and click the New button to display the Attribute Class Join Properties window, shown in Figure 15-12.

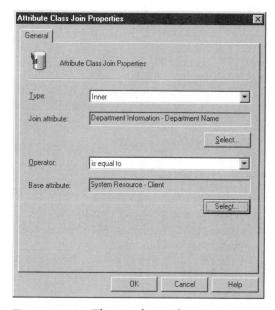

Figure 15-12. *The Attribute Class Join Properties window.*

2. In the Type drop-down list, select the join type. Four types of attribute class joins exist in SMS:

   * **Inner**   Displays only matching results

   * **Left**   Displays all results for the base attribute and matching results for the join attribute

   * **Right**   Displays all results for the join attribute and matching results for the base attribute

   * **Full**   displays all results for both the base and the join attributes

3. To select an attribute class and attribute for the Join Attribute text box, click the Select button to display the Select Attribute dialog box, where you can select appropriate entries from the drop down lists. The attribute you specified will be connected to the base attribute and becomes a child of the base attribute.

4. Choose an appropriate relational operator from the Operator drop-down list.

5. To fill in the Base Attribute text box, click Select to display the Select Attribute dialog box and choose the appropriate base attribute. The *base attribute class* is an existing attribute class on which you based the query. Notice that you cannot change the base attribute class; you can change the base attribute only.

6. Click OK to close and save your query configuration.

7. Click OK again to save the query.

More Info   Working with joins requires a better than good understanding of SMS attribute classes and attributes. For a complete treatment of joins, refer to Chapter 11 in the *Systems Management Server Administrator's Guide*. You should also refer to the SMS 2.0 Toolkit for a complete discussion of WQL. A sample of the toolkit is included with the *Microsoft BackOffice 4.5 Resource Kit*.

Viewing the Query Language

Figure 15-13 shows our sample query using WQL. You can display the WQL version of any query by clicking the Show Query Language button on the General, Criteria, or Join tab of the Query Statement Properties window. As you can see, writing an SMS 2.0 query using WQL is not trivial.

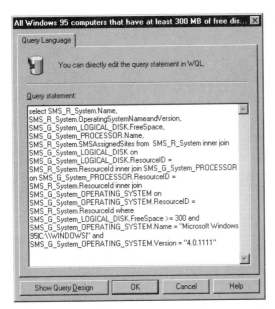

Figure 15-13. *The WQL version of our sample query.*

Prompted Queries

The query we just created will satisfy our immediate quest for information from the SMS database. However, it is static in the sense that it will always check the database for the same information—that is, all computers running Windows 95 that have at least 300 MB of free disk space.

A more useful query would be one that prompts us for value information as the query is being evaluated. For example, instead of hard-coding the value *300*, it might be more useful to have the query prompt us for the *Size* value. This way, we can use the query repeatedly to find computers with different amounts of free space for different packages and purposes.

To change our query to a prompted query, we need to open it and modify it. You can modify any query by right-clicking on it in the SMS Administrator Console and choosing Properties from the context menu to display the Query Properties window. Click the Edit Query Statement button to return to the Query Statement Properties window, and select the Criteria tab, and then double-click on the element you want to modify to display the Criterion Properties window. In the example shown in Figure 15-14, we are modifying the *Size* value. The criterion type has been changed from Simple Value to Prompted Value.

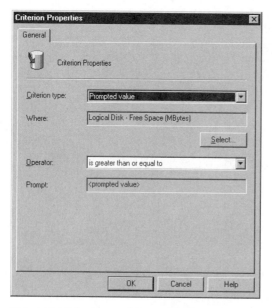

Figure 15-14. *A sample prompted query.*

Compare this figure with Figure 15-9, and you'll see that the Value field has changed to indicate a prompted value. When this query is executed, it will first ask us to provide the value for Logical Disk - Free Space (Mbytes).

> **Note** The following statement is taken directly from the Microsoft Systems Management Server Version 2.0 Service Pack 1 Release Notes: "Running queries that include prompted value criteria that also use an alias for an attribute class is not supported in this release of SMS."

Executing Queries

Now that we have seen how to create a query, it's time to explore how to run a query. All SMS queries are run through the SMS Administrator Console. The results of the queries will also be displayed in the SMS Administrator Console. To execute our sample query, follow these steps:

1. In the SMS Administrator Console, navigate to the Queries folder.

2. Right-click on the query you want to run, and choose Run Query from the context menu.

3. If the query contains any prompts, the Input Query Value dialog box will appear, as shown in Figure 15-15. Enter the appropriate value, and click OK.

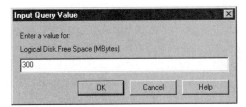

Figure 15-15. *The Input Query Value dialog box.*

4. The results of the query can be viewed in the result pane of the SMS Administrator Console interface, shown in Figure 15-16. You'll need to scroll to the right to see all the result fields you chose to display.

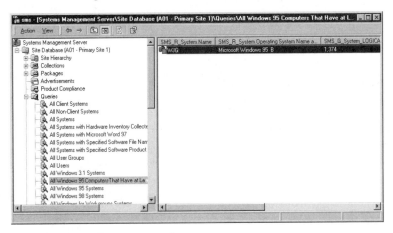

Figure 15-16. *The query results.*

As with other SMS-managed objects such as collections, packages, and advertisements, only users that have access to the database objects will be able to run the query. The user must have rights to execute the SMS Administrator Console, rights to access the Queries folder, and rights to access data in the SMS database. This permission is assigned by applying object security through the SMS Administrator Console, or sometimes through the WMI itself. SMS security is discussed in more detail in Chapter 16.

Reports

SMS 2.0 includes an installation option called Crystal Reports which is an SMS 2.0 snap-in provided by Seagate Corporation. The version supplied with SMS 2.0 is Crystal Info 6.0. Crystal Info is a useful reporting tool that can generate a variety of reports based on information stored in the SMS database such as inventory, product compliance, and system status. Because Crystal Info is integrated as a Microsoft Management Console (MMC) snap-in, it is fully integrated into the SMS Administrator Console. In addition to running the default reports provided with Crystal Info, you can create your own reports or customize the defaults. The reports can be scheduled to run at a particular time or even on a recurring basis. Report types include the following:

- Standard chart
- Form letter
- Form
- Cross-tab
- Subreport
- Mail label
- Drill-down
- Online Analytical Processing (OLAP)

When you choose Crystal Info as an option during setup, SMS installs several default reports. These reports can be found in the Reports folder under Tools in the SMS Administrator Console. The default reports are broken into five categories: Configuration, Hardware Inventory, Product Compliance, Queries, and Status. Each category includes one or more reports that you can run or customize. When you select one of these folders, the reports it contains will be listed in the right pane, preceded by one of three icons, shown in Figure 15-17.

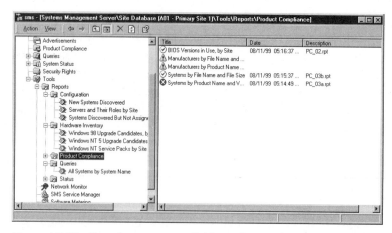

Figure 15-17. *Sample reports available in the Product Compliance folder.*

The green check mark (an OK indicator) shows that the report is ready to view, meaning that it has run successfully. The yellow triangle with an exclamation point (a Warning indicator) shows that the report is currently unscheduled and so has not yet been run. A red "x" (a Critical indicator) shows that the report experienced a failure and did not run properly. Additional information about the status of each report can be obtained by right-clicking on the report and choosing Properties from the context menu to display the Report Properties window.

Running a Crystal Info Report

Running a Crystal Info report is relatively straightforward and involves telling SMS when the report should run and under what security context. The administrators who will run Crystal Info reports must have access to the WMI data classes used by the SMS Provider, which itself accesses the SMS database. Remember, at no time do you ever query the SMS database directly—you always go through the WMI via the SMS Provider.

To create reports, your user account could be a member of the SMS Admins group, which of course does have appropriate access. If you do not want to add your user account to this group, you must specify an account that does have appropriate access permission. Accessing resources through another user account is known as "impersonation." However, for impersonation to work under Windows NT, your user account must have the Act As Part Of The Operating System user right assigned at your Windows NT workstation.

To run a Crystal Info report through the SMS Administrator Console, follow these steps:

1. In the SMS Administrator Console, navigate to the Reports folder under Tools and expand it.

2. Select the report you want to run, right-click on it, choose All Tasks from the context menu, and then choose Schedule Report to display the Schedule Report Properties window for that report, shown in Figure 15-18.

3. On the General tab, click Refresh to display the report filename in the Description text box. Click Modify if you need to change the appearance of the displayed report. The Modify button launches the Info Report Designer, which we will discuss in the section "Creating a Report" later in this chapter.

4. Click on the Schedule tab, shown in Figure 15-19. On this tab, you specify when the report should be run. You can have it run immediately or at a defined time, and you can also set a recurrence pattern.

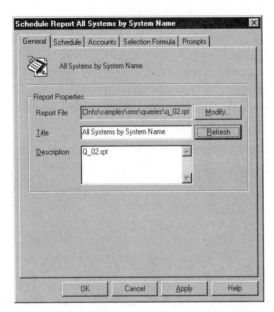

Figure 15-18. *The Schedule Report Properties window.*

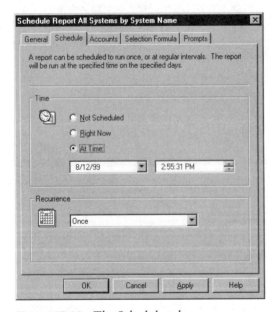

Figure 15-19. *The Schedule tab.*

5. Click on the Accounts tab, shown in Figure 15-20. The name of the user who is logged in at the workstation is displayed in the Logon User Name text box. If this account has appropriate rights to run the report, enter the logon password. If the account does not have appropriate rights, enter the name of an account that does and supply the appropriate password. The Server and Database entries are read-only and can be modified only when you are modifying an existing report or creating a new report.

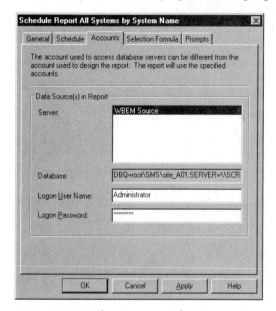

Figure 15-20. *The Accounts tab.*

6. Click on the Selection Formula tab, shown in Figure 15-21. On this tab, you can either view or modify the query statement used to generate the report and display data. Click the Edit Selection Formula button if you want to modify the query statement.

7. Click on the Prompts tab, shown in Figure 15-22. On this tab, you can specify the parameters a user must supply before the report can run. Like using prompted queries, this technique provides a more useful report format.

8. Click on OK to save your settings.

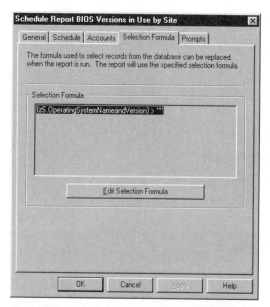

Figure 15-21. *The Selection Formula tab.*

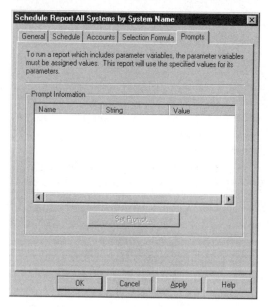

Figure 15-22. *The Prompts tab.*

The report will run at the scheduled time. To view the report, select the report entry under its report folder. The report is initially displayed in the right pane of the SMS Administrator Console. Viewing of this report (as shown in Figure 15-23) was facilitated by suppressing the view of the console tree. By resizing the screen, changing the zoom percentage, and using the scroll bars, you can view various parts of the report. You can also print the report if you want.

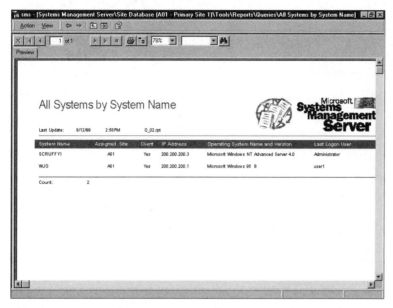

Figure 15-23. *Sample report generated using Crystal Info.*

Tip To generate a Crystal Info report, you must have installed a printer driver on your workstation. The reports display much better—and print better too—if you install a high-resolution print driver such as a PostScript printer.

Creating a Report

The three main tasks involved in creating a new Crystal Info report are as follows:

- Creating the new report
- Creating a report folder if no appropriate folder exists in the SMS Administrator Console
- Adding the report to the folder

Unlike SMS queries, to create a Crystal Info report you need a more extensive knowledge of the WMI object classes that compose the SMS database. To create a new report, you should start the Info Report Designer, which enables you to control the layout, data, and style of the report. While the Info Report Designer is a point-and-click interface, you must still select items from lists of classes and attributes. (Appendix E of the *Systems Management Server Administrator's Guide* will prove useful for you in this regard, as will the Microsoft Systems Management Server Resource Guide, part of the *Microsoft BackOffice 4.5 Resource Kit*.)

To create a report, follow these steps:

1. In the SMS Administrator Console, navigate to any report in the Reports folder, right-click on the report, choose All Tasks from the context menu, and then choose Design New Report to launch the Info Report Designer. The Info Report Designer welcome dialog box will display, as shown in Figure 15-24.

Figure 15-24. *The Info Report Designer welcome dialog box.*

2. Click New Report to create a new report (or click Open Report to modify an existing report). The Report Gallery dialog box will appear, as shown in Figure 15-25.

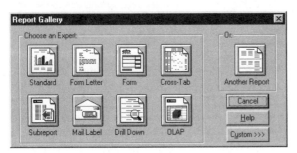

Figure 15-25. *The Report Gallery dialog box.*

3. In the Report Gallery dialog box, select the type of report you want to generate. The Create Report Expert opens to guide you through the process of laying out the report, as shown in Figure 15-26.

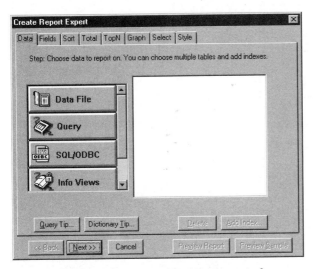

Figure 15-26. *The Create Report Expert window.*

4. On the Data tab, specify a data source by clicking SQL/ODBC to display the Log On Server dialog box, shown in Figure 15-27. In this dialog box, select ODBC-WBEM Source as the data source and click OK.

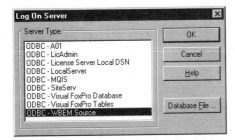

Figure 15-27. *The Log On Server dialog box.*

5. In the Configure Connection dialog box (shown in Figure 15-28), which appears automatically after you've selected the data source from the Log On Server dialog box, enter the name of the user account that has access to the data (as described in the previous section). Enter or browse for the SMS database server name, and click Connect. If the connection is successful, the Namespace Selection box on this screen will display a tree structure that begins with the entry *Root*. Expand this structure until you find your site-code entry, and then select it.

Figure 15-28. *The Configure Connection dialog box.*

6. Click OK. If the logon is successful, the Choose SQL Table dialog box is displayed, as shown in Figure 15-29.

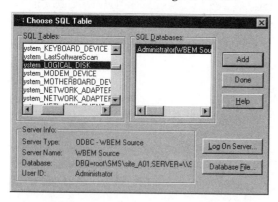

Figure 15-29. *The Choose SQL Table dialog box.*

7. Select each table you want to use for your report, and then click Add. When you have finished, click Done to return to the Create Report Expert window.

8. The Create Report Expert now displays the Links tab, shown in Figure 15-30. On this tab, the fields that are common to the tables you selected are displayed as links. Select the link that is most appropriate for your report, such as Resource ID, and delete the others by selecting each link, and then clicking Delete.

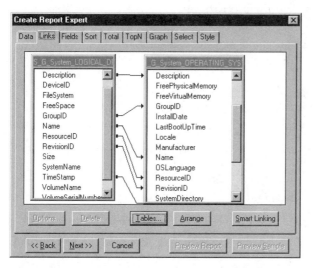

Figure 15-30. *The Links tab.*

9. After selecting the link most appropriate for your report, click Options to display the Link Options dialog box, shown in Figure 15-31. Choose the type of join you want to create between the tables you selected. (Crystal Info help describes these joins in detail, including examples.) These joins are somewhat different from those involved with query creation. A Left Outer join is the recommended option for most reports. It returns all records in which the linked value in both tables is an exact match, as well as a separate row for every entry that does not have an exact match. Click OK to return to the Links tab.

10. Click on the Fields tab or click Next to display the Fields tab, shown in Figure 15-32, and select the fields you want to display when the report is run.

11. Click on the remaining tabs—Sort, Total, TopN, Graph, Select, and Style— to complete any additional settings for your report. You can use these options to sort, sum, or filter the data that is displayed; choose a graph style and layout style; and preview the report layout. The Style tab is shown in Figure 15-33.

12. Click Preview Report to see what your report will look like. Make any changes you want by choosing Format from the Info Report Designer menu, and then choosing Report Style Expert. You can also use the preview screen to modify how the report will look—by changing headers, removing totals, and so on.

Save the report template you just created by clicking Preview Report, File, and then choosing Save from the Info Report Design menu. By default, your report will be saved in the \SMS\CInfo\Winnt folder on the site server.

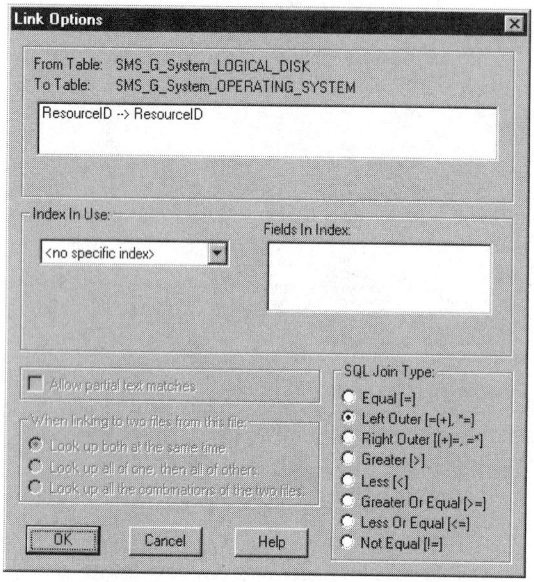

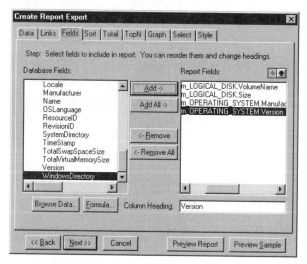

Figure 15-31. *The Link Options dialog box.*

Figure 15-32. *The Fields tab.*

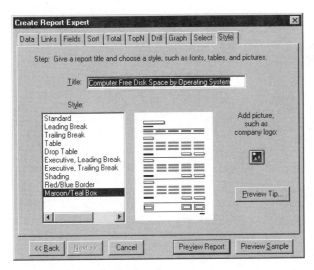

Figure 15-33. *The Style tab.*

Creating a Report Folder

Your new report needs to be added to a folder under Reports in the SMS Administrator Console. You can create a report folder to organize your reports. To create a new folder, follow these steps:

1. In the SMS Administrator Console, navigate to the Reports folder, right-click on it, choose New from the context menu, and then choose Folder to display the Seagate Crystal Info dialog box, shown in Figure 15-34.

2. Enter a name for your new folder, and then click OK. The new folder will be displayed under Reports.

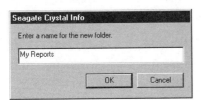

Figure 15-34. *The Seagate Crystal Info dialog box.*

Adding a Report to the Folder

To add your report to the new folder or to an existing folder, follow these steps:

1. In the SMS Administrator Console, navigate to the folder to which you want to add the report you created or modified, right-click on it, choose New from the context menu, and then choose Report Object to display the New Report Object Properties window, shown in Figure 15-35.

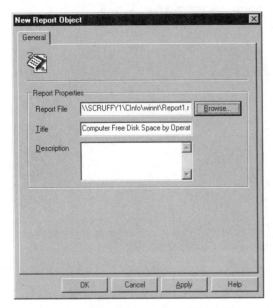

Figure 15-35. *The New Report Object Properties window*

2. In the Report File text box, enter the full path to the report you want to add.

3. Enter a descriptive title for the report as well as any additional comments, and then click OK.

Note Remember to close the report in the Info Report Designer before you add it to a report folder; otherwise a sharing violation will occur.

Modifying Reports

To modify an existing report, follow these steps:

1. Right-click on the report, choose All Tasks from the context menu, and then choose Modify Report to launch the Info Report Designer tool. The report will be loaded.

   You must connect to the WBEM data source server before you make any changes to the report data. For details on how to connect to the WBEM data source server, refer to the section "Creating a Report" earlier in this chapter.

2. Make whatever modifications you want. Before saving the report, choose Options from the File menu to display the File Options Properties window. On the Reporting tab, shown in Figure 15-36, verify that Save Data With Report is not selected, and then save the report.

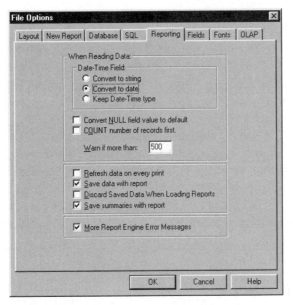

Figure 15-36. *The Reporting tab of the File Options Properties window.*

3. In the SMS Administrator Console, right-click on the report and choose All Tasks from the context menu, and then choose Schedule Report to display the Schedule Report Properties window. On the General tab, click Refresh to update the report with your changes.

4. Schedule and run the report to generate a new report with the design changes you implemented.

More Info   Refer to the *Systems Management Server Administrator's Guide* and the online help for the Info Report Designer for more details on creating, modifying, and updating reports.

Other Reporting Tools

You can use any reporting tool you want to extract information from the SMS database. The most important requirement is that your tool be WBEM ODBC–compliant—in other words, the reporting tool must use the WBEM ODBC driver installed with the SMS Administrator Console to access the SMS database via the SMS Provider and WMI. Microsoft Access 97 and later is one such tool; another is Microsoft Excel 97 and later using the Query Extract tool included in the *Microsoft BackOffice 4.5 Resource Kit*. Let's look first at the Excel 97 Query Extract tool as an alternative way of creating and generating reports.

Microsoft Excel 97 Query Extract Tool

As mentioned, the Query Extract tool is provided as part of the *Microsoft BackOffice 4.5 Resource Kit* utilities. This tool consists of an Excel workbook and template that contain macros designed to use the WMI Scripting API to access the database via the SMS Provider. You provide the name of the site server and a valid access account, and Query Extract in turn finds the SMS database server. Here's the really neat part: Query Extract displays for you a list of all the current SMS queries to choose from so you don't have to worry about learning a query language. You select the query or queries that you want to execute. The results of each query are placed on a separate workbook page. You are then free to analyze this data as you see fit. You can create charts, pivot tables, or export the data to another database or application format such as Microsoft PowerPoint.

As mentioned, Excel contains both a workbook version and a template version of this tool. If you import the workbook version, it functions as a stand-alone file—meaning that when you import SMS data into this tool and save the file, you need to import another Query Extract worksheet for the next set of reports you want to create. However, if you use the template version to generate a new report, you can simply open a new workbook based on the template, without the need to import another Query Extract worksheet.

The Query Extract tool workbook and template files are named SMSExtract.xls and SMSExtract.xlt. When the *Microsoft BackOffice 4.5 Resource Kit* utilities are installed, these files can be found under the Resource Kit\SMS\Report directory. Copy the two files into the appropriate folder on your SMS Administrator Console computer—for example, C:\Program Files\Microsoft Office\Templates.

Let's walk through the basic steps for using the Query Extract tool with Excel 97:

1. Start Excel, and either open the SMSExtract.xls workbook file, or create a new workbook using the SMSExtract.xlt template.

2. Depending on how your installation of Excel handles macros, you may see a message asking whether you want to enable macros. Click the Enable Macros button to initiate the tool.

3. The SMS Login dialog box appears, as shown in Figure 15-37. Enter the name of the site server in the Server text box, enter the name and password of a user account that has access to the database, and then click OK. These values will be saved in the Windows NT registry and will be displayed automatically the next time you run the tool.

4. In the Select Site Query To Import dialog box that appears automatically (Figure 15-38), you will see all the currently available SMS queries.

Check the query you want to run. You can select two or more queries to import by holding down the Ctrl key and clicking on the queries.

Figure 15-37. *The SMS Login dialog box.*

5. Click OK. If the query requires user input, a dialog box is displayed asking you to enter the appropriate value. Close the dialog box after entering the value.

6. The results of each query will be displayed on a separate workbook page, as shown in Figure 15-39.

7. Save the workbook, and work with the data as you please.

Note A version of this tool, named SMSQuery.xlt, is included with SMS 2.0 and can be found in the Support\Reskit\Bin*platform*\Diagnose folder on the SMS 2.0 CD or in the same folder when you install the Supportability Tools with SMS 2.0 Service Pack 1. Aside from some formatting differences, this version works the same way as the Resource Kit tool; however, it does not support prompted queries.

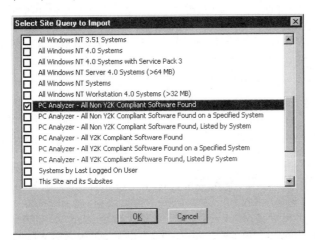

Figure 15-38. *The Select Site Query To Import dialog box.*

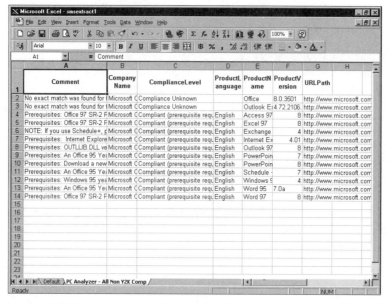

Figure 15-39. *A sample results workbook page.*

Microsoft Access

Using Access to extract SMS database information requires that the WBEM ODBC driver first be installed on the Access workstation. If you installed the SMS Administrator Console on this computer, you have already installed this driver by default. If not, you can install it from the SMS 2.0 CD or from the SMS_*SiteCode* share (the \SMS folder) on the primary site server. On the CD, it can be found in \SMSSetup\Bin*platform*\Wbemsdk.exe; on the site server, it can be found in \SMS\bin*platform*\Wbemsdk.exe. When you launch this program, a simple wizard is displayed that will walk you through the installation. You will need to restart your computer when the installation is complete.

You can then use Access configuration options to point to the SMS database using the WBEM ODBC driver. You will need to have a valid account and password, as described earlier. Refer to your Access documentation for instructions regarding the configuration of Access to import data from SQL databases.

More Info Chapter 15 of the SMS 2.0 Resource Guide (part of the *Microsoft BackOffice 4.5 Resource Kit*, available through Microsoft Press) offers several approaches to extracting information from the SMS database using Microsoft Access, such as creating links to the SMS data and creating SQL pass-through queries. Refer to that chapter for a detailed discussion of these approaches.

Checkpoints

The main issues you would encounter when running a report, aside from creating the wrong query statement, involve security. It's important to remember that for someone to run a report, they must have access permission to the SMS Administrator Console, the folder containing the query (such as the Queries, Reports, or Status Message Queries folders), and the database information the query is searching for; otherwise, the query will fail. As mentioned, you'll learn more about security in Chapter 16.

The other "gotcha" pertinent to this chapter involves Crystal Info and comes from the Microsoft Systems Management Server Version 2.0 Service Pack 1 Release Notes (which by now you've discovered contain a wealth of useful information of the "gotcha" variety). This tool has a built-in limitation. If your site will have more than 500 clients reporting data, Crystal Info will unnecessarily bog down the server, causing significant performance problems. The published workaround involves creating a separate (or new) central site that your current site will report to. On this new central site, you will install SMS 2.0 in a custom installation, selecting *only* Crystal Info as a component option and clearing all other component choices. Refer to the Microsoft Systems Management Server Version 2.0 Service Pack 1 Release Notes for a complete explanation of this limitation and its workaround.

A more effective workaround is to purchase the newest version of Crystal Info from Seagate Corporation. It is fully SMS-compatible and will offer you more options for creating and manipulating reports, without the same strain and overhead.

Also, like other SMS components, once you have installed Crystal Info you cannot uninstall it properly without also uninstalling SMS. It is true that you can select Crystal Info and remove it through Add\Remove Programs in the Control Panel, but once it is removed in this way it can never be reinstalled, even if you perform a site update, without first uninstalling SMS.

Summary

As you can see, there are several ways to extract and use the data collected and stored in the SMS database. Throughout this book, we've looked at examples of queries for various reporting purposes, and now you should have a better understanding of how to create—and improve—them and how to generate queries of your own to view status messages, populate collections, and otherwise search for data based on your specific criteria. Chapter 16 focuses on another database management issue—security.

Chapter 16
Security

This chapter will summarize some of the security-related issues we've looked at in earlier chapters, such as Microsoft Systems Management Server (SMS) accounts, and introduce a few new topics. We'll begin with an overview of the NTFS security SMS itself places on various directories. Then we'll review the use of internal and manually created SMS accounts and group accounts. You'll also learn how to set permissions on SMS objects through the SMS Administrator Console and how to create a custom SMS Administrator Console that incorporates SMS object security.

SMS builds several levels of security into its overall security model. At the top layer, SMS of course uses Microsoft Windows NT security—NTFS and share permissions, internal and system accounts, and internal groups. Next, the SMS Provider and Windows Management Instrumentation (WMI) security are established, including access control over SMS objects in the SMS Administrator Console. This level of security can be applied at the class or instance level, as we'll see in the section "Security Objects and Permissions" later in this chapter. Finally, security is enforced at the SQL server level through the use of integrated or standard security, as discussed in Chapter 2.

NTFS Security

As you know, an SMS 2.0 site server requires the existence of an NTFS partition that is at least 1 GB in size. This requirement extends to the main SMS directory, of course, but it also includes the client access point (CAP) and SMSLogon directories. You should invest some time in reviewing the permissions set by SMS both on the directories and on the shares SMS creates to learn why various connection accounts need to be created and how the permissions set by SMS affect the ability of these accounts to carry out a task.

SMS 2.0 Service Pack 1 makes some modifications to the permissions on the CAP directory originally set by the release to market (RTM) version of SMS 2.0. When you use SMS 2.0 with Service Pack 1 to install a new SMS site server, the new permissions will be automatically applied. However, if you apply the service pack to an existing SMS 2.0 site server, the CAP permissions are not automatically updated. Tables 16-1 through 16-5 can be used to verify the permissions on the CAP, as well as on the other SMS directories.

Table 16-1. Service Pack 1 CAP permission updates

Share or Directory Name	Adminis-trators	Guests	Users	Windows NT Everyone	NetWare Bindery Everyone	Netware NDS OU
CAP_*sitecode* (share)	Not assigned	Not assigned	Not assigned	Full	Folder not shared in NetWare environ-ment	Folder not shared in NetWare environ-ment
CAP_*sitecode*	Full	Read	Read	Not assigned	Read	Read
Ccr.box	Full	Write	Write	Not assigned	Write	Write
Clicomp.box	Full	Read	Read	Not assigned	Read	Read
Clicomp.box subfolders	Full	Read	Read	Not assigned	Read	Read
Clidata.box	Full	Read	Read	Not assigned	Read	Read
Clifiles.box	Full	Read	Read	Not assigned	Read	Read
Clifiles.box subfolders	Full	Read	Read	Not assigned	Read	Read
Ddr.box	Full	Write	Write	Not assigned	Write	Write
Inventory.box	Full	Write	Write	Not assigned	Write	Write
Offerinf.box	Full	Read	Read	Not assigned	Read	Read
Pkginfo.box	Full	Read	Read	Not assigned	Read	Read
Sinv.box	Full	Write	Write	Not assigned	Write	Write
Statmsgs.box	Full	Write	Write	Not assigned	Write	Write

Table 16-2. SMS logon points folder and share permissions

Share or Directory Name	Administrators	Windows NT Everyone	NetWare Bindery Everyone	NetWare NDS OU
SMSLogon (share)	Full	Read	Folder not shared in NetWare environment	Folder not shared in NetWare environment
SMSLogon	Full	Read	Read	Read
Alpha	Full	None	None	None
Alpha.bin	Full	Read	Folder not created in NetWare environment	Folder not created in NetWare environment
Alpha.bin subfolders	Full	Read	Folders not created in NetWare environment	Folders not created in NetWare environment
Config	Full	Read	Read	Read
Ddr.box	Full	Write	Write	Write
i386	Full	None	None	None
Logs	Full	None	None	None
Sites	Full	Read	Read	Read
Sites subfolders	Full	Read	Read	Read
Sitescfg	Full	None	None	None
X86.bin	Full	Read	Read	Read
X86.bin subfolders	Full	Read	Read	Read

Table 16-3. SMS distribution points folder and share permissions

Share or Directory Name	Administrators	Guests	Users	Windows NT Everyone	NetWare Bindery Everyone	Netware NDS OU
SMSPKGx$ (share)	Not assigned	Not assigned	Not assigned	Full	Folder not shared in NetWare environment	Folder not shared in NetWare environment
SMSPKGx$	Full	Read	Read	Not assigned	Read	Read
<package id>	Full	Read	Read	Not assigned	Read	Read

Table 16-4. SMS site server folder and share permissions

Share or Directory Name	Description	Administrators	Everyone	SMSServer_*sitecode* (Internal Account)
SMS_*sitecode* (share)	This share is associated with the \SMS directory —the installation directory for SMS on a site server.	Not assigned	Full	Not assigned
SMS	The directory into which SMS is installed on a site server.	Full	Not assigned	Read
SMS_SITE (share)	This share is associated with the SMS\Inboxes\Despoolr. box\Receive directory.	Not assigned	Full	Not assigned
SMS\Inboxes\ Despoolr.box\ Receive	This directory is used when data is transferred from a child site to its parent site.	Full	Not assigned	Full
CINFO (share)	This share is associated with the \SMS\Cinfo directory.	Not assigned	Full	Not assigned
SMS\Cinfo	This directory is used to store predefined report information created by users using Crystal Reports.	Full	Not assigned	Read
SMS_CPS*x*$ (share)	This share is associated with the \SMSPKG.Stores directory and stores compressed package source. The directory for this share is \SMSPKG.	Not assigned	Full	Not assigned
SMSPKG	This directory is used to store the compressed package source file created during the package distribution process.	Full	Not assigned	Read

Table 16-5. SMS software metering server folder and share permissions

Share or Directory Name	Administrators	Everyone
LICMTR (share)	Full	Full
SWMTR	Full	Read
DLL files	Full	Read
EXE files	Full	Read

Accounts and Groups

As we've seen throughout this book, SMS uses a variety of accounts to perform various tasks. Some of these accounts must be created by you, such as a NetWare Site System Connection account; others are created by SMS automatically, such as the SMS Server Connection account. The user accounts and user group accounts used by SMS for various tasks fall into seven categories, as follows:

- Site server service accounts
- Server connection account
- Site system connection accounts
- Remote site system service accounts
- Client service accounts
- Client installation accounts
- Group accounts

In this section, we'll review each of these account categories in more detail.

> **Tip**   In this instance, the original release of the *Systems Management Server Administrator's Guide* is ineffective. For the most up-to-date information regarding SMS user accounts and user group accounts, you should refer to the online version of the *Systems Management Server Administrator's Guide* installed with SMS 2.0 Service Pack 1. You should also refer to the Microsoft Systems Management Server Version 2.0 Service Pack 1 Release Notes for additional information.

Site Server Service Accounts

Three site server service accounts enable SMS to carry out its primary tasks: the SMS Service account, the SQL Server account, and the SMS Site Address account. Both the SMS Service and the SQL Server accounts are required; the SMS Site Address account, while not required, is usually desired.

SMS Service Account

By now, you should be familiar with this account. The SMS Service account is the primary account created by SMS. This account is used by site server services to create shares and directories on site systems, set permissions, copy files, install services and components, and verify operation of the site system. Specifically, this account is used by the SMS Executive, SMS Site Component Manager, SMS Site

Backup (new with Service Pack 1), SMS SQL Monitor, and SMS Client Configuration Manager. If Crystal Info is installed, the three Crystal Info services—Info Agent, Info APS, and Info Sentinel—also use the SMS Service account.

The SMS Service account is created when the SMS site server is installed. By default, it is named *SMSService* and made a member of the local Administrators group on the site server as well as the Domain Admins and Domain Users groups in the Windows NT domain the site server belongs to. Because the account is a domain administrator, you should probably rename it and provide password protection with a unique password composed of alphanumeric and special characters. (Just don't forget what the password is.)

Tip One way to increase security for your Windows NT domain is to remove the SMS Service account from the Domain Admins group and add it directly to the local Administrators groups on the site server, SQL server, CAP, logon point, and software metering server. If you are not using an SMS Windows NT Client Software Installation account, add the SMS Service account to the local Administrators group on every Windows NT SMS client as well.

If your SMS site systems are members of trusted Windows NT domains, the same SMS Service account can be used throughout your site hierarchy for convenience. However, if SMS sites and site systems are in untrusted Windows NT domains, you must create the account separately in each domain. For example, the SMS Service account is used to access the SMS database on the SQL server. If the SQL server happens to be in a different, untrusted Windows NT domain than the SMS site server, SMS will need to use Windows NT's pass-through authentication method to gain access to the SQL server. This means that you will need to create the SMS Service account in the SQL server's domain using the same account name and password as are used on the site server.

Caution Do not change this account through the User Manager For Domains utility in Windows NT. If you need to rename the account or change the password, do so using the Reset function of SMS Setup. This method will ensure that all the SMS services are properly updated with the changed account information.

SQL Server Account

The SQL Server account, created by SQL Server during its installation, is used to provide SMS services with access to the SMS database and the software metering database. The type of account that is used depends on whether you are using standard security or integrated security when accessing SQL Server. Recall from Chapter 2 that you need to tell SMS which security method you have enabled for SQL Server in order for SMS to establish the correct account to use.

By and large, SQL Server accounts are managed through the SQL Server Enterprise Manager utility. If you need to change the account for SMS, first establish the account in SQL Server, and then update SMS with the new account information, as shown here:

1. In the SMS Administrator Console, navigate to the *site code - site name* entry under Site Hierarchy.

2. Right-click on the site entry, and choose Properties from the context menu to display the Site Properties window.

3. Select the Accounts tab, shown in Figure 16-1. In the SQL Server Account section, click the Set button, and supply the new account name and password in the SQL Server Account dialog box.

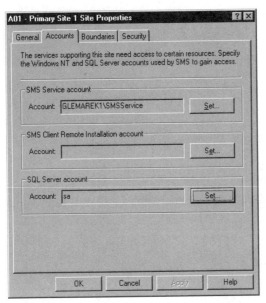

Figure 16-1. *The Accounts tab of the Site Properties window.*

4. Choose OK to save the change and update SMS.

SMS Site Address Account

The SMS Site Address account is used to establish communications between a parent site and a child site in an SMS hierarchy for the purpose of forwarding data such as discovery data records (DDRs), site control information, inventory, and packages. (Refer to Chapter 4 for more information about the communications process). Although the SMS Service account can be used to accomplish this task, it is generally recommended that a separate account be created by the SMS administrator specifically for the purpose of intersite communications. This account can be made fairly secure as well because it need not be a member of Domain Admins. In fact, the account needs only Read, Write, Execute, and Delete permissions on the SMS_SITE share (SMS\Inboxes\Despoolr.box\Receive), so it could be simply a guest account with the appropriate permissions to the share.

Server Connection Account

The SMS Server Connection account is created by SMS automatically during installation of the site server and is used by remote site systems to connect back to the site server to transfer information. For example, the SMS NT Logon Discovery Agent service running on logon points uses this account to forward DDRs generated during Windows NT logon discovery. The Inbox Manager Assistant component on CAPs uses this account to transfer client data to appropriate inboxes on the site server. The SMS Provider also uses this account to access SMS directories on the site server as well as the package definition file (PDF) store.

The SMS Server Connection account is named SMSServer_*sitecode* and is assigned a randomly generated password. *Do not modify this account in any way.* Figure 16-2 shows some of the accounts typically used by SMS through the User Manager For Domains utility. Notice that some of these accounts have "DO NOT MODIFY" in the Description field. In general, do not modify *any* account created and maintained by SMS itself.

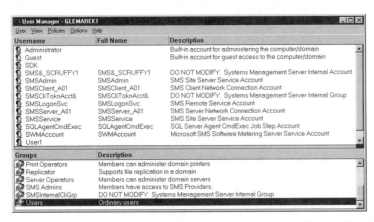

Figure 16-2. *Windows NT accounts and groups typically used by SMS.*

If you change the password for the SMS Server Connection account, it can be reset by running the Reset routine through SMS Setup. However, if you delete the account, calling Reset will not restore it. Instead, you will need to reinstall SMS.

Site System Connection Accounts

Site system connection accounts are almost the opposite of a server connection account. Site system connection accounts are accounts created on site systems such as CAPs and logon points and are used by the Logon Server Manager, Inbox Manager, and Distribution Manager (on Windows NT site systems only) components running on the site server to connect to and transfer information such as client configuration information, advertisements, and logon script updates to these site systems. The three types of site system connection accounts are: Windows Networking Site System Connection, NetWare Bindery Site System Connection, and NetWare NDS Site System Connection.

As with the SMS Site Address account, the Windows Networking Site System Connection account is not required, since the SMS Service account can perform the same tasks. The same is true for the NetWare Bindery Site System Connection account. For security purposes, however, it is recommended that you do create specific site system connection accounts for NetWare Bindery, CAPs, distribution points, and logon points to perform these tasks. The accounts can be created through the Connection Accounts folder under Site Settings in the SMS Administrator Console. (Refer to Chapter 3 for a complete discussion of creating and using these accounts.)

> **More Info**   For more information, see the white paper "Integrating Microsoft Systems Management Server 2.0 with Novell NetWare," on the companion CD; this white paper is also available through the SMS Web site, at *http://www.microsoft.com/smsmgmt*.

Remote Site System Service Accounts

Remote site system service accounts are service accounts used by SMS services that are installed and run on remote site systems such as the SMS Executive running on a CAP or the SMS NT Logon Discovery Agent service running on a logon point. The three Remote Site System Service accounts are: the SMS Logon Service account, the SMS Remote Service account, and the Software Metering Service account.

SMS Logon Service Account

The SMS Logon Service account is required; it is created automatically on all logon points when the Windows Networking Logon Discovery method is enabled. The account is named *SMSLogonSvc* and is assigned a randomly generated password. It is made a member of the Domain Users group and the local Administrators group and is assigned the Log On As A Service user right on each logon point.

Remember, do not modify this account in any way. If you do modify the account, SMS will eventually fix it, but the key word here is "eventually." The process could take anywhere from several hours to several days.

SMS Remote Service Account

The SMS Remote Service account is also required and is created automatically on each CAP when that site system role is assigned. The SMS Executive installed on each CAP uses this account to start up and carry out various SMS tasks, such as running Inbox Manager Assistant. This account is named SMSSvc_*sitecode_xxxx* (where *xxxx* represents a number increment assigned by SMS and is different on each CAP), is a member of the local Administrators group on each CAP, and is assigned the Log On As A Service user right.

Software Metering Service Account

As we saw in Chapter 14, the Software Metering Service account is used by the SMS License Service installed on each software metering server to manage license usage. The account's default name is *SWMAccount*, but you can name it anything you want as well as assign it a password. Like the SMS Service account, the Software Metering Service account should be modified through the SMS Administrator Console rather than through the User Manager For Domains utility. To do so, change the appropriate settings on the Software Metering tab of the Site System Properties window.

Client Service Accounts

Four required internal accounts are created by SMS: the Client Services DC account, the Client Services Non-DC account, the Client User Token account, and SMS Client Connection account. These accounts are used by SMS services running on those clients to carry out various tasks.

Client Services DC Account

The Client Services DC account is created and used by SMS client services specifically on domain controllers that are also SMS clients. The account is named *SMS&_domain_controller_name*. It is a member of the local Administrators group and is assigned the Log On As A Service, Act As Part Of The Operating System, and Replace A Process Level Token user rights.

Client Services Non-DC Account

The Client Services Non-DC account is created and used by SMS client services specifically on Windows NT SMS clients that are not domain controllers. The account is named *SMSCliSvcAcct&*. It is a member of the local Administrators group and is assigned the Log On As A Service, Act As Part Of The Operating System, and Replace A Process Level Token user rights. It is created by Client Configuration Manager or when SMSMan.exe or the SMSls.bat script is run.

Client User Token Account

When programs are executed at the client computer, they will run under the local user account's security context. Since most users are logged on as users and not as administrators, these programs will run under the local user context. While this is not such a big deal for non–Windows NT systems, it can be a big issue on Windows NT clients because they maintain a local account database and provide more security over system modifications such as program installation. Thus, the security context poses a problem when dealing with SMS packages.

When you identify a program to SMS as requiring an administrator context to execute it, SMS uses the Client User Token account, named *SMSCliToknAcct&*, to create a user token on the client with sufficient access to run the program. This internal account is created automatically, assigned a random password, and granted the Act As Part Of The Operating System, Logon As A Service, and Replace Process Level Token user rights on the client. This account will be sufficient in most cases. Recall from Chapter 12, however, that if the program execution requires that the program connect to network resources other than the distribution point, *SMSCliToknAcct&* will fail because it is created as a local account rather than as a domain account. In this case, you should use the SMS Windows NT Client Software Installation account. (See Chapter 12 for a complete discussion of installation accounts.)

SMS Client Connection Account

The SMS Client Connection account functions much the same as the server connection account and site system connection accounts on their respective systems. SMS Client Connection account is used by SMS client components running on Windows NT clients to connect to CAPs and distribution points to transfer data such as inventory or client configuration updates. For the Windows NT domain, SMS creates one account named *SMSClient_sitecode* with a random password that is propagated to each Windows NT client.

If you have Windows NT clients that access NetWare CAPs or distribution points, you need to create a NetWare Bindery or NetWare NDS client connection account. Again, this would be an account you have already created on your NetWare server that has appropriate permissions to the site system directories. (To review these permissions, refer to Tables 16-1 and 16-3.)

Real World   Creating Additional Client Connection Accounts

Since client connection account information such as the randomly generated password is propagated to each Windows NT computer that is an SMS client, you may encounter account lockout problems in Windows NT networks that have enabled account policies such as account lockout. When SMS updates a client connection account password, that information is normally passed on to the client computers at the next logon if Windows Networking Logon Client Installation method has been enabled.

But what if a client computer has been shut down for a period of time—say, while a user was on vacation—and in the interim SMS updated the client account password? In this scenario, the client computer would have no way of knowing about the password change. When the client computer was restarted, the client connection account would try to reconnect using the old password and would be locked out—effectively disabling SMS client components from sending or receiving updates to the CAP. This problem is especially likely when the client computer was installed using the Windows NT Remote Client Installation method.

The solution to this problem involves creating additional client connection accounts through the site server. You can create two or more client connection accounts for which you control the passwords. Rotate these accounts within the password aging cycle of your Windows NT account policy so that the client will always have access to a valid account. As you create a new client connection account, you can delete the oldest account. This technique ensures that the client computers will always have current account information and minimizes the possibility of the client connection account being locked out.

More Info   Refer to the Microsoft Systems Management Server Version 2.0 Service Pack 1 Release Notes article "Avoiding Client Lockouts when Working with SMS Client Connection Accounts" for a detailed discussion of the need for and method of creating these additional client connection accounts.

Client Installation Accounts

Two kinds of client installation accounts are available: the SMS Client Remote Installation account and the SMS Windows NT Client Software Installation account. Each is used for a slightly different purpose; both are specifically for Windows NT clients on which a higher security context than that of the logged on user is required for carrying out an installation task. The first account is used to install SMS components on an Windows NT client; the other is used to run an advertised program in the correct security context on a Windows NT SMS client.

SMS Client Remote Installation Account

As you know, when SMS needs to be installed on a Windows NT client, it requires an account that has local administrative rights on that client. By default, SMS will use the SMS Service account to accomplish this since that account is automatically made a member of the Domain Admins group, which is by default made a member of the local Administrators group on every Windows NT computer that joins that domain. However, this setting implies that the SMS Service account has a rather broad scope of security.

For enhanced security, you can create a separate client installation account for SMS to use when installing the SMS components on a Windows NT client; this account is called the SMS Client Remote Installation account. This process involves creating an account through User Manager For Domains and ensuring that it is made a member of the local Administrator's group on the Windows NT client in question. After you create this account, you then need to tell SMS to use the account when installing the SMS components on Windows NT clients by configuring the Accounts tab of the Site Properties window. (Refer to Chapter 8 for details.)

SMS Windows NT Client Software Installation Account

The SMS Windows NT Client Software Installation account created by you, the SMS administrator, is used in lieu of the *SMSCliToknAcct&* account described in the section "Client User Token Account" earlier in this chapter. You create this account either for the Windows NT domain or on each Windows NT client; you should give this account the appropriate level of permissions to install software successfully on the Windows NT client. The account is then identified to SMS through the Software Distribution Properties window, which you can display by right-clicking on the Software Distribution component under Component Configuration in the Site Settings folder in the SMS Administrator Console. Refer to Chapter 12 for a detailed discussion of this account.

Group Accounts

As you know, group accounts in Windows NT are used to provide permissions and set security on a global level for a large number of user accounts by virtue of their membership in a group account. Similarly, SMS also makes use of group accounts to satisfy and provide additional security within the Windows NT environment. In addition to the accounts described above, SMS creates two internal group accounts: SMS Admins and *SMSInternalCliGrp*.

SMS Admins Group Account

The SMS Admins local group provides its members access to the SMS Provider through WMI, and thus provides access to the SMS database. The local Administrator account on the site server is automatically made a member of this group. You will need to populate this group with the accounts of any administrators who will be using the SMS Administrator Console remotely to access the SMS database and carry out tasks such as creating and distributing packages or initiating Remote Tools sessions.

SMSInternalCliGrp Group Account

The *SMSInternalCliGrp* global group is created on domain controllers and contains the *SMSCliToknAcct&* and *SMS&_domain_controller_name* accounts. This group provides a global group membership (required by Windows NT) for these two internal accounts without having to make them a member of any other existing Windows NT global groups that may inadvertently assign a higher level of permissions than the accounts require.

Permissions and Security Objects

In addition to the security provided by Windows NT and through SQL Server, SMS 2.0 maintains its own object-level security for the SMS site database using the SMS Provider and Web-Based Enterprise Management (WBEM) security. By assigning specific permissions to Windows NT users and groups, the SMS Provider controls access to specific SMS objects such as packages, advertisements, and collections.

The SMS database is accessed through the SMS Administrator Console, and it is here that SMS object security is defined. The user must have a valid Windows NT account in the domain in which the site server resides. When a user launches the SMS Administrator Console, the user's account automatically logs onto WBEM, which validates the user's permission. The user must be a member of the local SMS Admins group on the SMS Administrator Console computer, be a local Administrator, or be specifically granted WBEM user rights through the WbemPerm utility, which is installed in the WINNT\System32\WBEM folder when SMS is installed on the site server. This utility provides a GUI for assigning users and groups Read or Write permission to WBEM objects. The user must also be a member of the SMS Admins group on the site server or on the SQL server if the SMS Provider was installed there.

After the user is validated by WBEM security, the SMS Provider validates the account and launches the SMS Administrator Console, displaying those objects for which the user has been given permission. By default, permission to all SMS objects is granted to the local system account (the Windows NT Authority/System account) and the administrator who first installed the site server, as shown in Figure 16-3. To view the object security of any SMS object, select the Security tab in the object's Properties window.

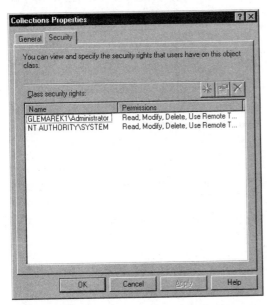

Figure 16-3. *The Security tab of the Collections Properties window.*

Security Objects

Security can be established for the following six SMS object classes:

- *Advertisements*
- *Collections*
- *Packages*
- *Queries*
- *Sites*
- *Status Messages*

Two kinds of security configuration are possible: class and instance. *Class security* is similar to NTFS folder permissions. Just as a folder's NTFS permissions apply by default to all the files within the folder, so is class security applied to all members of the object class. In other words, any permissions you set for the object class *Collections* will apply to each collection, whether they are the default collections or new collections you create.

Instance security is similar to NTFS file security. Just as you can set permissions on files different from those set at the folder level, you can also set security on individual members of an object class. For example, you might give the Windows NT group Finance Helpdesk no permission to the object class *Collections* yet still allow the group to read and manage the specific collection *Finance Clients*.

Establishing class and instance security for SMS objects is much the same as creating access control lists (ACLs) for Windows NT files, folders, and printers. In fact, many of the same principles apply: Permissions are always assigned to users or groups. Members of a group implicitly inherit the permissions for that group. No permissions granted is the same as No Access—you cannot access the object class.

For each class, you will identify which Windows NT users or user groups have what level of access. You will then refine that access at the instance level for each object. The permissions list reads much like NTFS permissions, with the addition of some permissions specific to SMS tasks and functions, such as remote control. Table 16-6 describes the available permissions and their object types.

Table 16-6.   Object permissions

Permission	Object Type	Description
Administer	All security object types	Administers all object classes, including assigning or modifying security rights
Advertise	*Collections*	Advertises existing programs to a collection
Create	All security object types	Creates an instance of an object type, such as a new query or collection
Delete	All security object types except *Status Messages*	Deletes an instance of an object type, such as a package or an advertisement
Delete Resource	*Collections*	Deletes a resource form a collection, such as a computer
Distribute	*Packages*	Deploys a package to a distribution point
Modify	All security object types except *Status Messages*	Makes changes to an object, such as editing the query statement for a query
Modify Resource	*Collections*	Modifies a resource in a collection
Read	All security object types except *Status Messages*	Views an instance and its properties
Read Resource	*Collections*	Views a resource in a collection
Use Remote Tools	*Collections*	Initiates a Remote Tools session with a client in a collection
View Collected Files	*Collections*	Views the files collected from a client through the Resource Explorer

Each object type must have at least one account granted Administer permission to prevent the possibility that SMS administrators could be locked out of the SMS Administrator Console. In fact, SMS does not allow you to remove the last account with Administer permission from an object type, nor can you delete your own Administer permission on any given object.

When a user creates a new instance of an object, the user is automatically assigned Read, Modify, and Delete permissions for that instance. Granting Administer permission does not automatically grant the other three permissions.

Assigning Permissions

Permissions can be assigned to an object in two ways: you can use the Security Rights folder in the SMS Administrator Console to assign permissions to object classes and instances, or you can assign permissions at the specific object class or instance. Figure 16-4 shows the list of object classes and specific instances and their permissions that is displayed when you open the Security Rights folder. Notice that you can see the default permission as well as specific instances created.

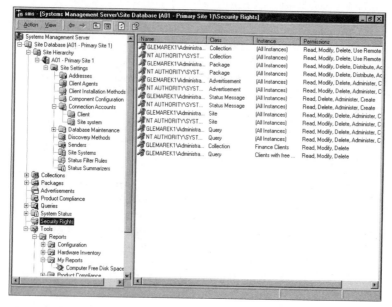

Figure 16-4. *Permissions displayed in the Security Rights folder.*

To assign permissions through the Security Rights folder, follow these steps:

1. In the SMS Administrator Console, navigate to the Security Rights folder, select it, right-click on it, and choose New from the context menu.

2. Choose Class Security Right to assign permissions to an existing object class, or choose Instance Security Right to assign permissions to an existing object instance.

3. If you choose Class Security Right, the Security Right Properties window for the class is displayed, shown in Figure 16-5.

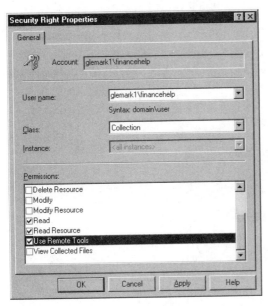

Figure 16-5. *The Security Right Properties window for a class.*

Enter the user name (or group name), select the object class, and select the permissions you want to assign. The permissions listed will vary depending on the object class you select.

Notice that the Instance field is disabled here. If you had chosen Instance Security Right in step 2, the Instance field would be available for you to specify an instance of an SMS security object.

4. Choose OK to save your security configuration.

Tip   You can modify any entry in the Security Rights folder simply by double-clicking on it to display its Properties window. Also, once you enter a user or group name, the name is saved for future modifications and can be selected from the User Name drop-down list.

You can also assign or modify permissions at the individual object class or instance level. This technique is preferable because it forces you to specifically choose the object whose permissions you want to modify. Follow the steps on the next page to assign or modify permissions at the object class level.

1. In the SMS Administrator Console, navigate to the folder whose class permissions you want to modify, right-click on it, and choose Properties from the context menu to display the object's Properties window. For this example, we will select the *Queries* object to display the Queries Properties window.

2. Select the Security tab, shown in Figure 16-6. Note the existing class-level security permissions.

Figure 16-6. *The Security tab of the Queries Properties window.*

3. To add a new user or group to the list, click the New button (the yellow star) to display the Object Class Security Right Properties window, shown in Figure 16-7.

4. Supply a user or group name, and select the permissions you want to apply. (As mentioned, selecting no permissions is like selecting No Access in NTFS.) Click OK to return to the Security tab of the Queries Properties window.

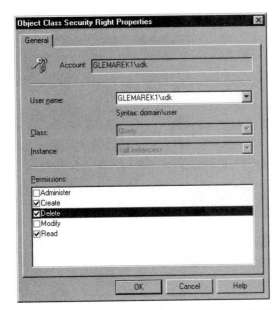

Figure 16-7. *The Object Class Security Right Properties window.*

5. To modify an existing entry, select that entry in the Class Security Rights list, and click the Properties button (the hand holding a piece of paper) to display the Object Class Security Right Properties window. Make the appropriate permission changes, and then click OK.

6. Click OK again to save your changes.

In the preceding example, we modified the permissions for the user SDK so that SDK has no permissions at the object class level for *Queries*. Now let's modify permissions at a specific object instance. To do so, follow these steps:

1. In the SMS Administrator Console, navigate to the specific object instance you want to modify, select it, and choose Properties from the context menu to display the Properties window for that instance. For this example, we will select an instance of the *Queries* object—Clients With Free Disk Space—to display the Clients With Free Disk Space Query Properties window.

2. Select the Security tab, shown in Figure 16-8. Notice the existing class and instance security permissions—SDK [No Permission] has "trickled down" to this instance.

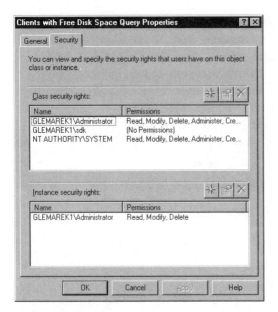

Figure 16-8. *The Security tab of the Query Properties window.*

On this tab, you can modify both the class permissions for the *Queries* object (by clicking the New button, as we did in the preceding example) and the specific permissions for this instance.

3. To modify the instance permissions, click the New button in the Instance Security Rights section of the dialog box to display the Object Instance Security Right Properties window, shown in Figure 16-9.

4. Supply a user or group name, select the appropriate permissions, and then click OK.

5. Click OK again to save your configuration.

Figure 16-10 demonstrates how, in the preceding examples, instance security rights take precedence over class security rights. Notice that even though the user SDK has no permissions for the *Queries* object class, SDK can nevertheless read, modify, and delete the specific query Clients With Free Disk Space. This is wholly consistent with the NTFS security system. Even if you deny a user access to a folder, if the user has permissions to read a file within that folder, the user will be able to access that file through an application or from the command prompt.

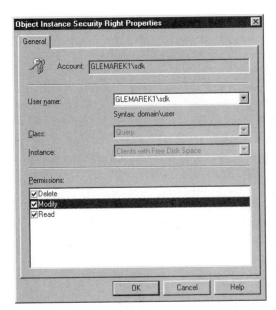

Figure 16-9. *The Object Instance Security Right Properties window.*

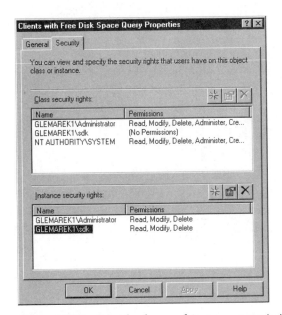

Figure 16-10. *Sample class and instance permissions.*

Real World   Using Security

Consider the SMS site hierarchy illustrated in Figure 16-11. In this model, SMS administrators are present at each site in the hierarchy. For organizational reasons, the third-level sites are secondary sites. Recall that secondary sites do not have their own SQL Server databases. Therefore, for the administrators at the secondary sites to be able to manage their sites, their SMS Administrator Console computers need to connect to the SQL Server database for their parent site. Using default security, every administrator at every secondary site can manage not only his or her own site, but also any other secondary site that is a child of the same parent.

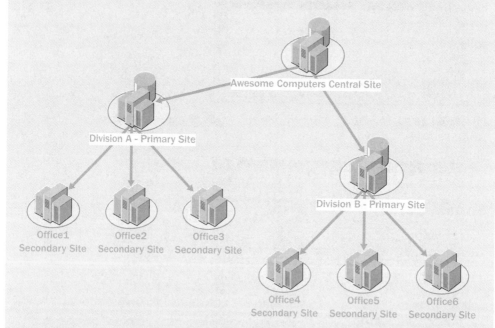

Figure 16-11. *Sample site hierarchy model.*

To remedy this situation, you can set security on each of the secondary site entries under the Site Hierarchy folder in the SMS Administrator Console so that only that site's administrator has access to that site's settings. In this way, you have preserved security for each site and can still maintain the desired site structure.

Custom SMS Administrator Consoles

The SMS Administrator Console is a Microsoft Management Console (MMC) snap-in, and as such it is customizable. You can create a custom SMS Administrator Console that displays only the SMS objects to which a particular administrator needs access to perform delegated tasks such as package distribution, advertising, or initiating remote diagnostic sessions.

Perhaps the most common form of delegation is the help desk function. In a large organization, it would not be unusual to have an administrator or a group whose help desk responsibility is focused on specific departments or regions. It may not be desirable or practical for these individuals to have full access to every object in the SMS database. They really need access only to their assigned department's collection and the ability to initiate remote sessions with their assigned clients.

We can start by providing a custom SMS Administrator Console that displays only the *Collections* objects. This limitation narrows down what the administrator sees when the SMS Administrator Console is launched. However, this is only a surface modification—any savvy user could restore the other SMS objects to the SMS Administrator Console. The complete solution is to create a custom console and apply appropriate security to all the SMS objects and instances so that administrators see and have access only to what they should.

Setting Security

You begin the process of creating a custom console by applying the appropriate security to the SMS objects. Consider, for example, a help desk group assigned to the finance department of your organization. Help desk administrators belong to a Windows NT group named Finance Help. You have also created an SMS collection named *Finance Clients* that contains all the SMS client computers in the finance department.

> **Note** The membership rules for this collection are based on a query so that as new computers are implemented in the finance department, they are automatically added to the *Finance Clients* collection when they are discovered and installed by SMS.

You set security on all SMS objects such that the Finance Help group has no permissions on any SMS object class. This effectively restricts the Finance Help group members from viewing any SMS objects other than what they need access to—the *Finance Clients* collection. For that one collection, you will give Finance Help the permissions the members need to initiate Remote Tools sessions—Read, Read Resource, and Use Remote Tools—shown in Figure 16-12.

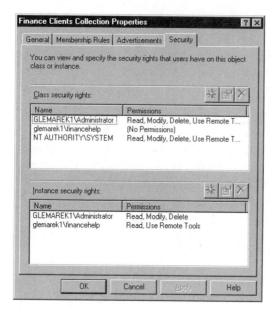

Figure 16-12. *Setting security for the* Finance Clients *collection.*

Notice that for the *Collections* object class, Finance Help has no permissions. However, for the *Collections* object instance *Finance Clients*, Finance Help has the permissions necessary to initiate a Remote Tools session. (Note that Read Resource is not displayed even if you selected it.) The end result is that the group has no access to any other collection except this one.

Creating the Custom Console

The next step is to create a custom console to the Finance Help administrators that displays only the *Finance Clients* collection. To create a customized SMS Administrator Console, follow these steps:

1. From the Start menu on the desktop taskbar of your SMS Administrator Console computer, choose Run and enter MMC to launch a generic MMC, shown in Figure 16-13.

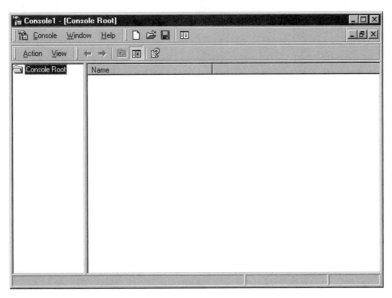

Figure 16-13. *A generic MMC.*

2. Choose Add/Remove Snap-In from the Console menu to display the Add/ Remove Snap-In Properties window, shown in Figure 16-14.

Figure 16-14. *The Add/Remove Snap-In Properties window.*

3. On the Standalone tab, click the Add button to display the Add Standalone Snap-In dialog box, shown in Figure 16-15. This dialog box lists the MMC snap-ins currently available.

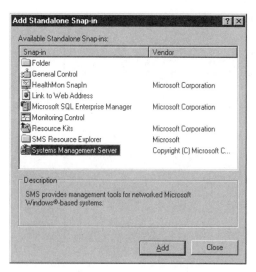

Figure 16-15. *The Add Standalone Snap-In dialog box.*

4. Select Systems Management Server from the list, and then click Add to launch the Site Database Connection Wizard, shown in Figure 16-16.

Figure 16-16. *The Site Database Connection Wizard welcome screen.*

5. Click Next to display the Locate Site Database screen, shown in Figure 16-17. Specify the site server to which you want the console to connect. Remember, this should be the SMS site that the Finance Help administrators need access to.

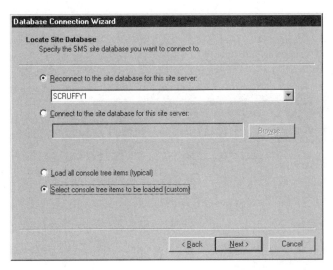

Figure 16-17. *The Locate Site Database screen.*

6. Select the Select Console Tree Items To Be Loaded (Custom) option.

7. Click Next to display the Console Tree Items screen, shown in Figure 16-18. Select the SMS console tree entries you want to display in the custom console. In this example, you will choose SMS Collections only.

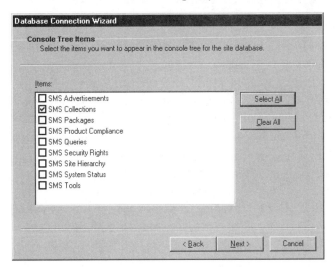

Figure 16-18. *The Console Tree Items screen.*

8. Click Next to display the Completing The Database Connection Wizard screen. Review your selections, and then click Finish.

9. Click Close in the Add Standalone Snap-In dialog box, and then click OK on the Standalone tab in the Add/Remove Snap-In Properties window to save your configuration. The console screen shown in Figure 16-19 demonstrates that the only SMS object this console will display is *Collections*.

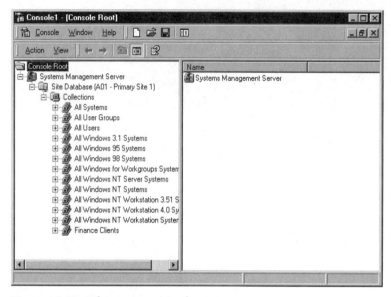

Figure 16-19. *The custom console screen.*

10. Choose Options from the Console menu to display the Options Properties window, shown in Figure 16-20.

11. On the User tab, confirm that the option Always Open Console Files In Author Mode is disabled. This setting will ensure that the user cannot make modifications to this custom console once they are using it.

12. Select the Console tab, as shown in Figure 16-21. Click Change Icon if you want to switch to the SMS Administrator Console icon (the tool icon). Enter a name for the console. Under Console Mode, select User Mode - Delegated Access, Single Window. This option ensures that the top-level console menus (Console, Window, and Help) are hidden when the console is open and effectively prevents the user from modifying the console in any way. Click OK to save your settings and return to the console window.

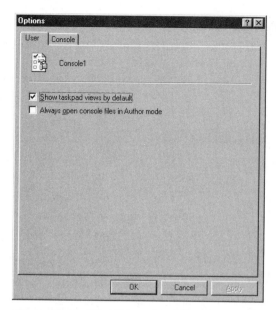

Figure 16-20. *The User tab of the Options Properties window.*

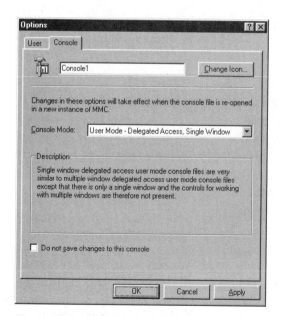

Figure 16-21. *The Console tab.*

13. Choose Save As from the Console menu to display the Save As dialog box. By default, the file will be saved in a new Programs folder named My Administrative Tools. Retain that folder, or select or create your own. Enter a filename for the console—for example, Finance.msc. Then choose Save.

14. Close the new console.

Distributing the Custom Console

The next step is to distribute the custom console to the administrators in the Finance Help group. Begin by installing the SMS Administrator Console on their Windows NT workstations. Next replace the default SMS.msc file with the console you just created. You can rename the console SMS.msc so that when administrators click on the shortcut in the Systems Management Server program group, the correct console is launched.

Caution Remember that the users in the Finance Help group must be able to access the SMS database, as discussed earlier. One way to do this is to add the Finance Help group to the local SMS Admins group on the site server or the SQL server (wherever the SMS Provider is installed).

When a administrator in the Finance Help group launches the customized SMS Administrator Console, he or she will see only the *Collections* object, and because of the security you applied, only one object instance—the *Finance Clients* collection, shown in Figure 16-22.

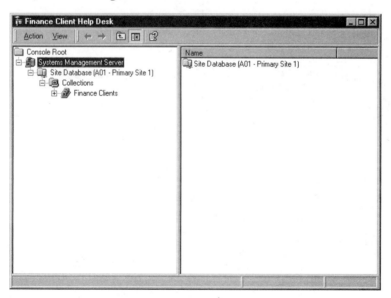

Figure 16-22. *Sample custom console with security applied.*

Summary

As we've seen, the combination of a custom console with SMS object class and instance security can provide a high level of secure access to the SMS database. Achieving the correct balance of customization and security is not trivial and, like most aspects of SMS, requires a fair amount of planning. However, the final result can be quite rewarding. Equally rewarding is the recovery of your site server in the event of a problem, as we'll see in Chapter 17.

Chapter 17
Disaster Recovery

Disaster recovery! Which of you never wants to experience it, but nevertheless needs to be prepared for the possibility? Presumably you all raised your hands. If you didn't, by the end of this chapter you will.

The key to a successful disaster recovery effort is, of course, a sound backup strategy. The focus of this chapter is just that—the establishment of a useful backup strategy and strategies for recovering your Microsoft Systems Management Server (SMS) database server, site server, and site systems. This chapter and Chapter 18, which focuses on database maintenance strategies, provide you with the resources you need to be amply prepared for disaster recovery, but more importantly, teach you how to avoid disaster in the first place.

We'll begin by establishing sound database maintenance practices, including a regular backup process, and then you'll learn how to recover or move the SMS database server, recover or move the SMS site server, and restore an SMS site system.

Database Maintenance

Perhaps the most obvious way to keep your SMS site systems from experiencing failure is to keep them running in top form, much like you might develop an exercise and diet program for yourself or change the oil in your car regularly. In addition to developing a backup and restore strategy, there are several things you can do for your SMS servers on a regular basis both to keep them running well and to spot problems before they cause damage. For the most part, these maintenance tasks can be broken down into four groups: general, daily, weekly, and monthly maintenance tasks.

General Maintenance Tasks

Probably the most important general task you can perform for any Microsoft Windows NT system is to develop a backup plan for your servers. At a minimum, you want to develop a backup strategy for your SMS site server and SMS database server, as these are your key systems. Much has been written about backup strategies—full vs. differential, daily vs. weekly, and so on.

For example, one backup strategy might be that you perform a full, or complete, backup of your database once a week, say on Friday nights, while you perform a differential backup of the database Mondays through Thursdays. The *differential backup* only backs up data that had changed since the last full backup and will result in reduced backup time and less backup space used.

It all comes down to one ultimate question: How important is it that you recover your data, and how current must that data be? We'll look at the recommended procedure for backing up SMS in the section "Backup Process Flow" later in this chapter.

Other general maintenance tasks might more properly be called troubleshooting assistance tasks, such as configuring the Status Message Viewer, configuring the Performance Monitor and SQL Server alerts, performing a database and site backup, and monitoring the performance of the site systems. We've looked at some of these tasks in previous chapters, such as the following:

- **Configure the Status Message Viewer to view status messages.** Recall from Chapter 5 that the status message system is your first and often best source of information regarding the state of your SMS site systems. You can configure the display interval for status messages, set filters, have programs such as pager alerts executed based on message events, and so on. Take some time to determine how the Status Message Viewer might figure into your overall maintenance—and ultimately disaster recovery—strategy.

- **Configure Performance Monitor alerts for key events.** You can set up alerts for the events such as low disk space, overutilization of the processor and memory, excessive pagefile access, and so on. The HealthMon utility, described in Chapter 6, is designed to monitor and record these and other significant performance events.

- **Configure SQL Server alerts.** You can set up the alerts in the SQL Server Enterprise Manager to monitor database space usage, user locks, and connections. (For more information about setting up SQL Server alerts, refer to the SQL Server product documentation.)

- **Configure Event to Trap Translator.** If your network uses an SNMP management system, consider whether the Event to Trap Translator might be of benefit to you as a monitoring tool (see Chapter 6).

- **Determine a fault tolerance strategy.** If your server supports a fault tolerance method such as RAID 1 (disk mirroring) or RAID 5 (striping with parity) either through a hardware method or through Windows NT, consider configuring one of these fault tolerance methods. Maintaining data redundancy is a hallmark of disaster recovery.

You will undoubtedly think of many other troubleshooting assistance tasks to add to this list. Be as creative—and redundant—as you like. In the following sections we'll explore some specific daily, weekly, and monthly tasks you can perform as an SMS site administrator.

Daily Maintenance Tasks

As the SMS administrator, you decide when various maintenance tasks should be performed within your organization and with what frequency. No single blueprint will provide a perfect fit for every SMS site or site structure. Microsoft recommends that the following tasks be performed daily to protect your SMS servers. You can modify this list to suit your needs.

- **Perform a site backup.** This task ensures that you can recover to at least the previous day's state.
- **Review status messages.** Especially important if SMS generates a status message alert indicating a potential problem with a component. By default, the Status Message Viewer displays only messages generated since the previous midnight. If you skip a couple of days, you might miss significant status messages. Consider changing the display interval or setting up custom filters so that you will be alerted about serious events.
- **Monitor the Windows NT Event logs and SQL Server Error logs.** Check for errors or warnings that might be indicative of an impending failure of your SMS site. You can view the SQL Server Error logs in SQL Enterprise Manager.
- **Monitor system health and performance through the Performance Monitor, HealthMon, and SMS Service Manager tools.**
- **Monitor network utilization using a network traffic analysis tool such as Network Monitor.** This task is especially important if package distribution or intersite communication appears to be poor, to determine when and where traffic congestion is occurring.

Weekly Maintenance Tasks

Microsoft recommends that the following tasks be performed weekly. Again, you can modify this list to fit your needs.

- **Monitor the size and percentage of database growth of the SMS site database, as well as the software metering database if you have implemented that feature.** If you are using SQL Server 7.0, you're in luck. This version of SQL Server can be set to automatically grow to accommodate an increasing database. Of course, this does not absolve you from monitoring the database on a regular basis to determine how fast the database is growing and especially whether you might run out of disk space. However, you might not need to look at the database so frequently, and you can set a SQL Server alert to let you know when and how much the database grows.

   If you are using SQL Server 6.5, a more frequent database size check will be imperative, especially with an active SMS site. In general, if the database or log device gets to be more than 80 percent full, consider expanding its size. Similarly, expand the tempdb device or log when it gets to be more than 60 percent full.

- **Monitor the amount of free disk space on the SMS database server, the site server, and the site systems (CAPs, logon points, distribution points, and software metering servers).** Remember, with very few exceptions, SMS components will just stop working if they run out of disk space.

- **Purge data that is no longer needed or relevant.** Remove bad Management Information Format (MIF) files, duplicate computer records, aged inventory records, and so on.

- **Perform regular disk cleanup tasks.** This cleanup would include your weekly full virus check or disk optimization routine, or monitoring for unused or old Temp files. Check the SMS directories as well for folders that have an unusually high number of files, such as a BadMIFs folder or an inbox with files that are not being processed, and cross-check these folders with status messages and logs for the specific components involved.

Monthly Maintenance Tasks

Here are some of the recommended maintenance tasks that might be performed on a monthly or an as-needed basis:

- Verify and test your ability to restore the database or the site server.
- Modify SMS accounts and passwords for those accounts you have control over. Refer to Chapter 16 for a discussion of SMS accounts.
- Review SMS object permissions.
- Review SMS site boundaries and component configuration.

You can protect your SMS site by scheduling and performing these maintenance tasks regularly. In the following section we'll look at how to schedule these tasks.

Scheduling Maintenance Tasks

Several of the maintenance tasks mentioned above can be scheduled to run on your timetable through the SMS Administrator Console. These tasks can be found in the Database Maintenance folder under Site Settings. Two types of database maintenance objects can be configured: SQL commands and tasks.

Scheduling SQL Commands

No predefined SQL commands are available for you to schedule; you must configure these commands yourself. For example, among the recommended weekly tasks is a database size check. Database size can be viewed using the SQL Enterprise Manager, of course, but it can also be determined by executing the SQL stored procedure SP_SPACEUSED.

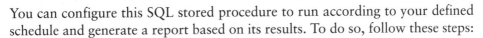

Caution Before running any SQL stored procedure, be sure to consult the SQL Server documentation for correct syntax and usage.

You can configure this SQL stored procedure to run according to your defined schedule and generate a report based on its results. To do so, follow these steps:

1. Navigate to the SQL Commands folder under Database Maintenance in the SMS Administrator Console and select it.
2. Right-click on the folder, choose New from the context menu, and then choose SQL Command to display the SQL Command Properties window, shown in Figure 17-1.
3. Enter a descriptive name for the command.

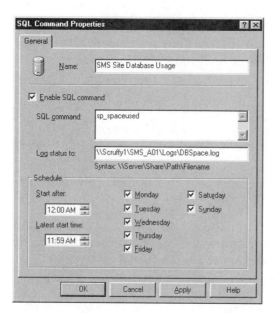

Figure 17-1. *The SQL Command Properties window.*

4. Verify that Enable SQL Command is selected. Enter the command name in the SQL Command text box. Be sure to use the appropriate syntax or the command will fail.

5. In the Log Status To text box, enter the path and filename of the text file you want the command results written to. This must be an existing share and path.

6. Define your schedule, and then click OK.

The SQL command you created will now be listed in the SMS Administrator Console when you select the SQL Commands folder. You might consider scheduling other SQL maintenance commands such as DBCC CHECKDB, DBCC CHECKALLOC, DBCC CHECKCATALOG, and DBCC UPDATEUSAGE. For example, if you recently reindexed the database, you may want to run the DBCC UPDATEUSAGE command to reset space usage reporting so that SP_SPACEUSED returns accurate data. You could schedule this command to run with SP_SPACEUSED or separately, under its own schedule.

When the SQL command is run, it will write the results of its execution to the log file you specified. Figure 17-2 shows the results of the SQL command created in the previous example.

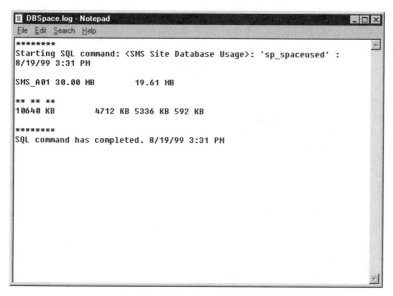

```
DBSpace.log - Notepad
File  Edit  Search  Help
********
Starting SQL command: <SMS Site Database Usage>: 'sp_spaceused' :
8/19/99 3:31 PM

SMS_A01 30.00 MB        19.61 MB

** ** **
10640 KB          4712 KB 5336 KB 592 KB

********
SQL command has completed. 8/19/99 3:31 PM
```

Figure 17-2. *Results of running the SP_SPACEUSED SQL stored procedure as a SQL command.*

The first line of data (beginning with *SMS_A01*) indicates the total database size and the available free space. The second line of data indicates the amount of reserved space, breaking this value down into the amount of space used by data, the index size, and unused space.

Scheduling Tasks

The other type of database maintenance objects you can schedule, tasks, are found in the Tasks folder in the SMS Administrator Console. The Tasks folder contains twelve predefined tasks; you cannot add tasks to this list. Table 17-1 describes these predefined tasks.

Notice that seven of these tasks are already enabled by default to ensure that vital tasks such as rebuilding indexes are carried out on a regular schedule. All the deletion tasks are designed to keep the database from becoming too large and unwieldy. You can, of course, modify the schedule and disable or enable any of these tasks as you choose. (To enable or disable a task in the Tasks folder, right-click on the task and choose Properties from the context menu. In the Task Properties window, then check or clear the Enable This Task option.) For example, you could enable the Export Site Database and Export Site Database Transaction Log tasks to schedule a regular backup of the SMS database without having to do so in SQL Server. However, as indicated in Table 17-1, you must have already defined a backup device through the SQL Server Enterprise Manager. We'll discuss how to define a backup device in the section "Backing Up the Site Database" later in this chapter.

Table 17-1.   Database maintenance tasks

Task	Description
Export Site Database	Exports the SMS site database to a predefined SQL backup device.
Export Site Database Transaction Log	Exports the SMS Site Transaction log to a predefined SQL backup device. Do not use this command if Truncate Log On Checkpoint is enabled for the database (the default).
Export Software Metering Database	Exports the SMS software metering database to a predefined SQL backup device.
Export Software Metering Transaction Log	Exports the SMS Software Metering Transaction log to a predefined SQL backup device. Do not use this command if Truncate Log On Checkpoint is enabled for the database (the default).
Backup SMS Site Server	Performs a comprehensive backup of the SMS site database, the software metering database, the \SMS directory on the site server, and the SMS and NAL registry keys on the site server.
Update Statistics	Rebuilds statistics created by SQL Server about data contained in indexes that enables the SQL Query Optimizer to determine the most efficient way to run a query. Enabled by default.
Rebuild Indexes	Rebuilds indexes created on database tables that are used to more efficiently retrieve data. Enabled by default.
Monitor Keys And Recreate Views	Monitors the integrity of primary keys used to uniquely identify all SMS database tables. Enabled by default.
Delete Aged Inventory History	Deletes all hardware inventory that has not been updated within a specified period of days (by default, 90 days). By default, this task is enabled and runs every Saturday.
Delete Aged Status Messages	Deletes status messages older than 7 days by default, and runs every day. Enabled by default.
Delete Aged Discovery Data	Deletes all discovery data records (DDRs) that have not been updated within a specified period of days (by default, 90 days). By default, this task is enabled and runs every Saturday.
Delete Aged Collected Files	Deletes all collected files that have not been updated within a specified period of days (90 days, by default). By default, this task is enabled and runs every Saturday.

The most powerful of these tasks is Backup SMS Site Server. This is by far the most comprehensive backup routine available for SMS. It backs up not only the SMS site database and software metering database, but also the full SMS directory structure on the site server and the SMS and NAL keys in the Windows NT registry on the site server—all necessary to fully recover a failed site server. This task is discussed in more detail in the section "Backing Up the Site Server" later in this chapter.

Backup Process Flow

The process for completely backing up your SMS site server involves the same basic steps whether you are automating this task through the SMS Administrator Console or carrying out the procedure yourself. In either case, you should have successfully backed up the following data:

- SMS site database
- SMS directory on the site server
- Master site control file (SMS\Inboxes\Sitectrl.box\Sitectrl.ct0)
- SMS and NAL registry keys on the site server

The following sections explore how to back up the data types listed above. We'll begin by discussing SMS Service Manager, first discussed in Chapter 3 and then again in Chapter 5, to stop all SMS services and components.

Stopping All Services and Components

Before you initiate any backup steps, you must of course stop any SMS services and components that may be running so that they do not leave open any files or lock any portion of the database. This includes ending any remote SMS Administrator Console sessions that may be active.

SMS services and components are best managed through the SMS Service Manager tool in the SMS Administrator Console. We discussed how to use this tool in Chapter 5 and we'll review briefly here. To stop a service or component, follow these steps:

1. In the SMS Administrator Console, navigate to the Tools folder, select SMS Service Manager, right-click on it, choose Select All Tasks, and then choose Start SMS Service Manager.

2. Expand the site server entry, and select Components to display a list of available components, as shown in Figure 17-3.

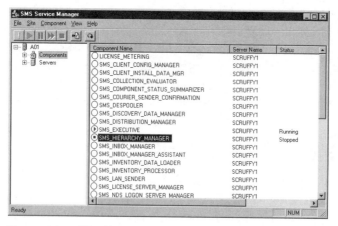

Figure 17-3. *The SMS Service Manager window, showing available services and components.*

3. To view the current status of a component, select it and click the Query Component button (an exclamation point). To disable the component, select it and click the Stop button (the red square).

4. Click the Query Component button again to verify that the component has stopped.

5. To start a component, select it and click the Start button (the green triangle).

> **Tip** You can stop or start all the components at one time by choosing Select All from the Component menu and then clicking the Stop or Start button.

By stopping the SMS Executive first through the SMS Service Manager, you will stop most of the other SMS components, as many of these components are themselves started by the SMS Executive. After you have stopped all SMS services and components using this technique, verify that the following services have indeed stopped by running the Services applet in the Control Panel:

- Info APS, Info Sentinel, and Info Agent (if Crystal Info is installed)
- SMS Executive
- SMS License Server Manager
- SMS NT Logon Discovery Agent
- SMS Site Component Manager
- SMS SQL Monitor
- SQL Executive

- SQL Server Agent (SQL Server 7.0)
- Windows Management

Only after you have stopped all the services and components should you back up the SMS site database.

Backing Up the Site Database

You can back up this database using a number of techniques. You could use SQL Server's BACKUP command through the SQL Server Enterprise Manager. (This process is described in Chapter 18.) You could use your favorite third-party backup system, such as Seagate's Backup Exec, which includes add-ons that back up SQL Server databases.(Review your backup product's documentation to learn how.) You could also use the Export Site Database or Backup SMS Site Server maintenance tasks available through the SMS Administrator Console. These tasks are described in the section "Backing Up the Site Through Systems Management Server" later in this chapter.

Backing Up Registry Keys and the Directory Structure

Next you back up the SMS and NAL registry keys by choosing Save Key from the Windows NT Registry Editor's Registry menu and then the SMS directory structure. When you back up these elements, you should give the backups similar names. Use the site code in the name, and perhaps add a number indicating the date or iteration of the backup. For example, you could name the registry keys SMS*xxx*.reg and NAL*xxx*.reg, where *xxx* represents the three-digit site code for your site.

Save your backups in a single directory for easy reference. This directory can then itself be backed up by your favorite server backup program for added redundancy. Again, consider your naming convention carefully. For example, you could name the directory something like SMSBackup*xxx*.*ddd*, where *xxx* represents the site code of your site and *ddd* represents a date or iteration reference.

If you were backing up the site A01 on August 31, for instance, you could create a directory named SMSBackupA01.aug31. You would save the SMS database backup file here, perhaps as SMSDBA01, as well as the registry keys (SMSA01.reg and NALA01.reg) and the SMS directory (SMSA01.dir). This master backup location should be maintained on another server; the master backup folder itself should also be backed up as part of your normal network server backup routine.

The Backup SMS Site Server database maintenance task included in the SMS Administrator Console includes most of these steps in one automated package. Because you don't have to perform these backups manually, it is a more effective backup routine. For a detailed discussion of this database maintenance task, refer to the section "Backing Up the Site Server" later in this chapter.

Backing Up the Site Through Systems Management Server

As mentioned, the SMS Administrator Console provides backup tasks among its database maintenance tasks. These backup tasks fall into two categories: backing up the site database (or the software metering database) and backing up the site server. Let's look at both options in this section.

Backing Up the Site Database

The site database backup consists of two parts: the backup of the database transaction log using the Export Site Database Transaction Log task and the backup of the database itself using the Export Site Database task.

The transaction log maintains an audit of database transactions that have taken place to aid in recovery of the database in the event of failure. Because the transaction log contains this audit trail of activity, it is sometimes used by SQL Server administrators as an alternative to performing frequent full database backups. They can perform a full backup once a week, say, and back up the transaction log on a daily basis. In the event the database needs to be recovered, it is an easy matter to restore the database and the appropriate transaction logs.

Before you back up the transaction log, you must turn off the Truncate Log On Checkpoint option in SQL Server Enterprise Manager. The Truncate Log On Checkpoint option is set through the Properties window for the database (SQL Server 7.0) or for the transaction log device (SQL Server 6.5) and is accessible through the SQL Server Enterprise Manager. By default, this option is enabled and causes the transaction log to be frequently flushed to keep it from growing too large too quickly. If you leave this option enabled, backing up the transaction log does not produce any added benefit, as it will most likely contain few, if any, recent transactions.

Note   As the database transaction log backup is currently configured, it doesn't provide much useful information. It is up to you, the administrator, to consider the SQL Server backup procedures you may already have in place for other databases. If you already backup the transaction logs for your current databases, you may choose to turn off Truncate Log on Checkpoint and back up the site database transaction logs as well. It is not necessary, however, to back up the site database transaction log in order to have a complete backup of the site.

If you turn off the Truncate Log On Checkpoint option, you must then build into your daily or weekly task list a disk space check of the transaction log to ensure that it does not run out of space or, as in the case of SQL Server 7.0 autosizing, consume too much disk space.

> **More Info** Please refer to your SQL Server documentation for detailed informa-tion regarding how to modify database options, create backup devices, and con-figure backup and restore options through the SQL Server Enterprise Manager.

The Export Site Database maintenance task exports the site database to a pre-defined backup device or file. Thus, before you can enable this task, you must have created a backup device through the SQL Server Enterprise Manager. To create a backup device using SQL Server 7.0, follow these steps:

1. In the SQL Server Enterprise Manager, expand the server entry, navigate to the Management folder, expand it, and select Backup, as shown in Figure 17-4.

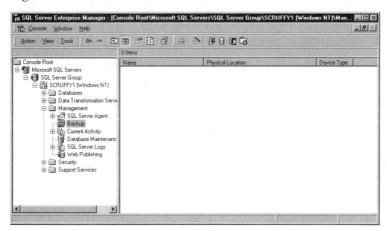

Figure 17-4. *The SQL Server Enterprise Manager window.*

2. Right-click on Backup, and choose New Backup Device from the con-text menu to display the Backup Device Properties window, shown in Figure 17-5.

3. Enter the name of the backup device you want to create—for example, SMS*xxx*, where *xxx* represents the site code of your SMS site.

4. Specify whether your backup device resides on tape or as a file. If you have installed a tape device on your server, you will be able to select it from the drop-down list for the Tape Drive Name option. Otherwise this option will be unavailable. If your backup device resides as a file, a filename will be created for you, or you can specify where to create the device.

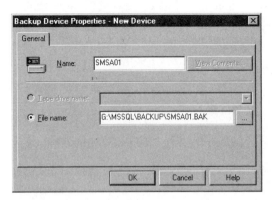

Figure 17-5. *The Backup Device Properties window.*

5. Click OK to create the device. Your new device will now appear in the Details pane of the SQL Server Enterprise Manager window when you select Backup.

Once the backup device has been created, you can enable the Export Site Database task through the SMS Administrator Console. To do so, follow these steps:

1. In the SMS Administrator Console, navigate to the Database Maintenance folder under Site Settings, expand it, and select the Tasks folder.

2. Right-click on Export Site Database, and choose Properties to display the Export Site Database Task Properties window, shown in Figure 17-6.

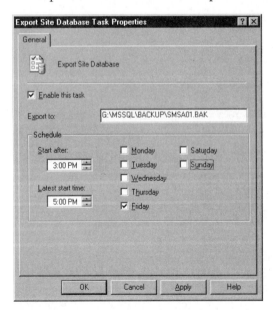

Figure 17-6. *The Export Site Database Task Properties window.*

3. Select the Enable This Task check box. Enter the name of the backup device, including any paths, in the Export To text box, and specify a schedule for the backup.

4. Click OK to save your configuration.

At the scheduled time, SMS will perform the site database backup task. Until the backup has occurred, the backup device file you created will not be displayed in the actual folder. You can view the contents of the backup device using Enterprise Manager by double-clicking on the device to display the Backup Device Properties window, shown in Figure 17-5. Click on the View Contents button to display the View Backup Media Contents dialog box, shown in Figure 17-7. This dialog box displays details about the backup, including when the backup took place, the type of backup that was performed, the database name, and its size at the time of backup.

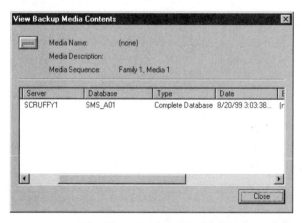

Figure 17-7. *The View Backup Media Contents dialog box.*

Repeat this procedure to enable the backup maintenance tasks for the site database transaction log if you have disabled the Truncate Log On Checkpoint option and for the software metering database and transaction logs if you have installed that feature.

Backing Up the Site Server

A far more comprehensive backup routine is contained in the Backup SMS Site Server maintenance task. This maintenance task essentially performs all the required backups outlined earlier in this chapter in the section "Backup Process Flow," plus backs up some additional information including the SMS directory structure and files, the SMS-related Windows NT registry keys and values, and the site control file.

This task was available in SMS 2.0 prior to SMS 2.0 Service Pack 1, but Service Pack 1 has added some significant enhancements to its performance. To facilitate the processing of this task, SMS 2.0 Service Pack 1 installs and loads a new SMS service named SMS Site Backup. Like other SMS service components, this service comes with a log file (Smsbkup.log) that you can enable through SMS Service Manager (see Chapter 3). Unlike the other log files, which are best used for troubleshooting tasks, the SMS Site Backup log should be enabled because it maintains a record of what you ran for site backup. When you restore a site, you can use the log to verify that you are restoring from a valid backup. Like other logs, as this log reaches its maximum size (1 MB by default), it is written to Smsbkup.lo_, and a new Smsbkup.log file is created. For a complete backup history, and for redundancy, back up these two files as well. Figure 17-8 shows an example Smsbkup.log file created after the Backup SMS Site Server task is run. Notice that the task first stops SMS components and services before beginning its copy process.

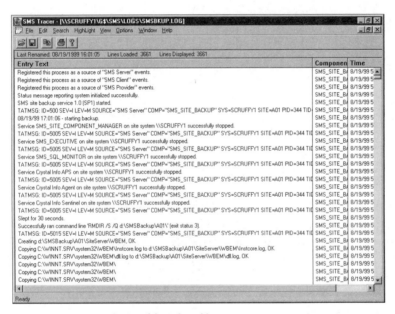

Figure 17-8. *Sample Smsbkup.log file.*

It's not necessary to have predefined a backup device when you enable the Backup SMS Site Server task. You must, however, provide the name of a backup folder location where the SMS Site Backup service will write the backed up data. This location can actually serve as the main backup location for several site servers because when the task is run, the SMS Site Backup service creates a subdirectory named by the site code, and all backup data is written there.

It should be of no little significance then that the location of the backup folder must be on a partition with adequate disk space to accommodate the data being written there. Microsoft recommends at least 2 GB of available space. However, a more accurate accounting of the space required can be determined by considering the following factors:

- Amount of disk space used by the entire SMS directory structure
- Amount of space used by the following SQL Server databases: master, MSDB, site server, and software metering server
- At least 10 MB additional space for miscellaneous files such as saved registry keys

At each subsequent scheduled backup, the SMS Site Backup service will first remove the old backed up data before writing the new data. It will also record each backup event in the Smsbkup.log file, viewable using the SMS Trace utility.

> **Note** If you enabled the Backup SMS Site Server task prior to installing SMS 2.0 Service Pack 1, you should remove the old backup files before enabling the task under Service Pack 1, as the task will not overwrite old backup files.

The Backup Control File

The entire Backup SMS Site Server task is actually governed by a backup control file named Smsbkup.ctl, contained in the SMS\Inboxes\SMSbkup.box folder. This file outlines exactly what will be backed up and where. Smsbkup.ctl is a text file, and as such it is fully customizable. It is also well annotated, which will assist you in reading and understanding its flow, as well as in customizing it.

The backup control file is based on the Express Setup option for SMS—that is, it assumes that all default components have been installed. If you selected specific components and chose not to install others during a Custom setup, the backup control file will try to stop and start SMS services and components that have not been installed, resulting in the recording of superfluous errors. These errors will not affect the actual backup process; however, to avoid recording them you should consider modifying the backup control file so that it deals only with those components you did install. Be sure to edit the file again if you decide to add SMS components in the future.

Appendix A presents the code for the backup control file for your reference. Refer also to the Microsoft Systems Management Server Version 2.0 Service Pack 1 Release Notes for additional information regarding the use and customization of this file.

Configuring Backup SMS Site Server

To configure the Backup SMS Site Server maintenance task, follow these steps:

1. In the SMS Administrator Console, navigate to the Database Maintenance folder under Site Settings and expand it.

2. Select the Tasks folder, select Backup SMS Site Server, right-click on it, and choose Properties to display the Backup SMS Site Server Task Properties window, shown in Figure 17-9.

Figure 17-9. *The Backup SMS Site Server Task Properties window.*

3. Select the Enable This Task check box.

4. In the Export To text box, enter the name of the drive and directory where you have already created a backup folder or where you want SMS to create the folder for you. This name cannot contain any extended ASCII characters.

5. Specify a schedule for the backup. For active databases, a daily backup is recommended.

6. Click OK to save your configuration and enable the backup.

At the scheduled time, the SMS Site Backup service will find or create the backup destination folders, stop appropriate SMS site server services, and perform the backup. After the backup is complete, you can view the contents of the backup folder through the Windows Explorer. Figure 17-10 shows the contents of a sample backup folder.

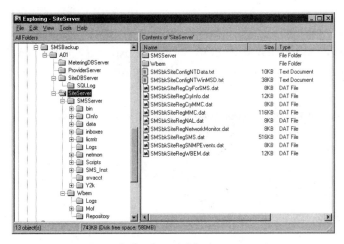

Figure 17-10. *Sample backup folder contents.*

Notice that the SMS Site Backup service created a subdirectory named with the site code. Within this directory are directories containing information relating to the software metering and site database servers (MeteringDBServer and SiteDBServer), the SMS Provider server (ProviderServer), and the SMS site server (SiteServer), which itself contains the entire site directory structure and also the WBEM directory entries. Notice too that the SiteServer folder contains two server configuration data files, the result of running Srvinfo.exe and Winmsd.exe, and many more registry keys than the recommended SMS and NAL registry backups (SMSbkSiteRegSMS.dat and SMSbkSiteRegNAL.dat). In fact, the following registry keys are backed up from the Windows NT Registry on the SMS site server:

- HKEY_LOCAL_MACHINE\Software\Microsoft\MMC
- HKEY_LOCAL_MACHINE\Software\Microsoft\NAL
- HKEY_LOCAL_MACHINE\Software\Microsoft\NetworkMonitor
- HKEY_LOCAL_MACHINE\Software\Microsoft\SMS
- HKEY_LOCAL_MACHINE\Software\Microsoft\SNMPEvents
- HKEY_LOCAL_MACHINE\Software\Microsoft\WBEM
- HKEY_LOCAL_MACHINE\Software\Microsoft\Seagate Software\Crystal Info
- HKEY_LOCAL_MACHINE\Software\Microsoft\Seagate Software\Crystal MMC SnapIn
- HKEY_LOCAL_MACHINE\Software\Microsoft\Seagate Software\Seagate Crystal Info for SMS

The SiteDBServer directory, shown in Figure 17-11, contains configuration information about the Windows NT server on which SQL Server is installed and about the SQL Server installation in particular. If SQL Server is installed on the same server as SMS, the Windows NT server configuration is the same as that written to the SiteServer directory.

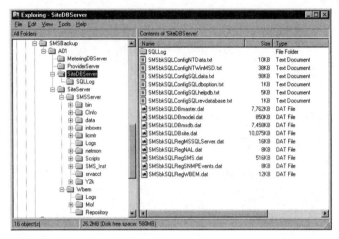

Figure 17-11. *The SiteDBServer directory.*

Notice that this directory contains duplicate backups of the main SQL Server database files, as follows:

- Master (SMSbkSQLDBmaster.dat)
- Model (SMSbkSQLDBmodel.dat)
- MSDB (SMSbkSQLDBmsdb.dat)
- SMS site database (SMSbkSQLDBsite.dat)

It also contains the HKEY_LOCAL_MACHINE\Software\Microsoft\MSSQLServer registry key (SMSbkSQLRegMSSQLServer.dat) and copies of the NAL, SMS, SNMPEvents, and WBEM keys on the SQL server. If SQL Server is installed on the same server as SMS, these last four keys are the same as those written to the SiteServer directory.

The registry value saved under ProviderServer is a redundant copy of the HKEY_LOCAL_MACHINE\Software\Microsoft\SMS key written to either the SiteDBServer or the SiteServer folder, depending on whether the SQL server or the SMS site server was installed with the SMS Provider. Typically, the SMS Provider is installed on the SQL server if the SQL server is a different Windows NT server from the SMS site server.

As you can see, this backup routine is quite comprehensive, and should be more than adequate to act as your SMS backup routine.

> **Tip** You can change the scheduled time for the Backup SMS Site Server task to whenever you want, but the SMS Site Backup service is engineered to check the schedule only once per day. If you need to execute this maintenance task immediately, configure the task and then stop and start the SMS Site Backup service by running the Services applet in the Control Panel on the site server.

Real World   Connection Accounts and Backup

As we saw in Chapter 16, the SMS Client Connection account is used by SMS client components running on Windows NT clients to connect to client access points (CAPs) and distribution points to transfer data such as inventory or client configuration updates. SMS creates one such account for the Windows NT domain named SMSClient_*sitecode*, with a random password that is propagated to each Windows NT client. This is an internal account that should not be manually modified in any way.

When a site is restored from a backup, the password for the default SMS Client Connection account is reset. If you have not created any client connection accounts in addition to the default, the SMS clients will effectively be unable to connect to a CAP or distribution point because the password recognized by the client will be different from that reassigned as a result of the restore process. The change in password is copied to all site CAPs so that the clients can be updated. Ironically, since the client will be unable to connect to the CAP in the first place, it will not be able to update itself with the new SMS Client Connection account password. There is no way to set the password back to the original, because there is no way of knowing what the original password was.

If you have additional client connection accounts specified for the Windows NT clients and they cannot connect using one account, they will try using the others. You control the passwords for the manually created client connection accounts. The site backup and restore scenario is a perfect example of why you should consider creating at least one additional client connection account for your site (preferably before you back up the site).

Recovering the SMS Site

Recovery of an SMS site generally falls into two categories: recovering the site database and recovering the site server. If the SMS database fails for some reason, you can restore it from its backup using SQL Server Enterprise Manager. You need to have access to a current backup, of course, as well as to the SQL Server Enterprise Manager interface. There is no restore function in SMS because, presumably, if you need to restore the site in some fashion, you probably cannot open the SMS Administrator Console.

Recovering the Site Database

Recovering the SMS database itself is a fairly straightforward task—which is not to imply that it is a mundane or trivial matter, but rather that it is cut and dried. You recover the site database by restoring it from a current backup. For example, if you need to move the SMS database to another SQL server for some reason, you would follow these steps:

1. Close all SMS-related tools, such as all SMS Administrator Consoles, that are accessing the current database, as well as all SMS site server services (including the SQL Monitor service on the SQL server). You don't want anything trying to update the database while you are managing it.

2. Start SQL Server in single-user mode and back up the SMS database, or schedule a database backup through the SMS Administrator Console. The single-user mode option is set through the Properties window for the database accessible through the SQL Server Enterprise Manager.

3. Locate (or install) the other SQL server, ensuring that the same database sort order has been used as on the original SQL server, as well as the same hardware platform.

4. Create database and log devices or files (depending on the SQL Server version) that are at least as large as the backed up database.

5. Restore the backed up SMS database to the new SQL server.

6. Use the Reset option of the SMS Setup program on the site server to point the site server to the location of the new SQL server and the database.

You would follow similar steps if the database needed to be restored for any other reason, although if you were restoring to the same SQL server, you might not need to perform step 6.

Recovering the Site Server

If you encounter a situation in which the SMS site server itself needs to be recovered—perhaps it crashed or it had be moved to a different physical computer—the steps for recovery are somewhat more involved. First of all, your situation would probably be hopeless if you had not already created a current backup of your SMS database, so let's assume that you have been backing it up regularly.

As we've seen, other significant elements of the site server in addition to the SMS database need to be backed up in order to completely restore the site server to its previous state. These elements include the SMS and NAL registry keys, the site control file (\SMS\Inboxes\Sitectrl.box\Sitectrl.ct0), and the SMS directory structure and files.

The recovery process begins with the restoration of the SMS site database of course. However, it will also involve the restoration of the backed up elements. For example, if you need to reinstall SMS on the site server or install it on a new computer, you will restore the previous site by copying the backed up SMS directory and site control file over the new install or over the reinstall. Similarly, you can restore the SMS-related registry keys by using the Windows NT Registry Editor to replace the existing SMS keys (created when you reinstalled SMS or installed it to a new server) with the backed up versions of those keys.

You could restore just the database itself and let the SMS site server rebuild itself—which it will do eventually. However, any changes you made that were written to the registry but not yet updated to the database will probably be lost. Restoring the SMS site server completely, as described here, will ensure that all elements of the site server are properly synchronized.

Note If you need to completely reinstall the SMS site server, all vestiges of the old site server must be cleaned off the server first. This includes uninstalling the SMS client software, removing the registry keys, and removing the remainder of the SMS directories and setup files not removed through the Remove SMS option of the Setup program. Then reinstall SMS, and restore the previous site as outlined above.

Real World Using Preinst.exe

As you've seen throughout this book, the *Microsoft BackOffice 4.5 Resource Kit*, available through Microsoft Press, includes several useful tools designed to facilitate your administration of the SMS site. Pertinent to this chapter's discussion is the Site Utilities tool (Preinst.exe). This tool must be installed on a site server and is used to help diagnose problems, repair the site control file, delete incorrectly removed sites, or stop SMS site server services, among other things.

You'll find a complete explanation of the many functions of this tool in the Microsoft Systems Management Server 2.0 Resource Guide, one of the four volumes in the *Microsoft BackOffice 4.5 Resource Kit*. Let's look at three of this tool's command-line options here that can be of particular use in the SMS site server recovery and maintenance process: /DUMP, /DELSITE, and /DELJOB. You can run this Windows NT command-line tool through the SMS 2.0 Resource Kit Tools Management Console created when you install the *Microsoft BackOffice 4.5 Resource Kit* or by changing the path to the appropriate directory through a Windows NT command window and executing the tool.

Executing the PREINST /DUMP command causes a new site control image to be written to the root of the partition on which SMS was installed, shown in Figure 17-12. An *image* is a binary representation of the site control file. This image is based on the current site control data stored in the SMS database and is named SMS_*sitecode*.scf. This file can then be copied to the Site Control Manager's inbox (SMS\Inboxes\Sitectrl.box) and renamed Sitectrl.ct0 to rebuild the site's properties. This function is useful if the site control file becomes corrupted or if you do not have a current backup of it.

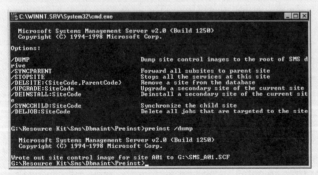

Figure 17-12. *Sample site control binary image written by PREINST /DUMP.*

PREINST /DELSITE can be used to remove a "phantom" child site. When a child site is to be removed from a parent site, the correct process is to break the parent-child relationship through the child site's properties, wait for the parent and child sites to update their respective databases, and then remove the addresses. A *phantom* child site occurs if the child site is removed from the parent site before the relationship has been broken or before the databases can be correctly updated, and references to the deleted child site may remain at the parent.

To delete the removed site from the parent site, execute PREINST /DELSITE: {*childsitecode*, *parentsitecode*}, where *childsitecode* represents the site code of the site that needs to be deleted and *parentsitecode* represents the parent's site code for the site that needs to be deleted. Once executed, the change will be replicated up the SMS site hierarchy.

Last, PREINST /DELJOB is designed to remove jobs or commands targeted to a specific site. This command can be used to remove jobs that may still be in the queue for the removed site but keep trying to be sent or executed, resulting in error status messages. Executing PREINST /DELJOB:*sitecode* will delete all commands that are targeting the specified site code.

Restoring Site Systems

Compared to recovering a site server, restoring an SMS site system such as a CAP, logon point, distribution point, or software metering server is rather elemental. Recall from Chapter 3 that SMS site systems are built by the SMS site server. You identify the site systems and assign their roles through the SMS Administrator Console. Consequently, if a site system should need to be rebuilt or replaced, it is merely a matter of reassigning that server through the site server.

For example, suppose that a site system such as a CAP goes down and needs to be replaced. When you bring the failed server back on line, SMS will simply restore the appropriate files and components to that site system. If the site system itself needs to be replaced and its computer name has changed, you would remove the old server as a site system from the site server and then add the new server to the SMS site as a site system and assign it the appropriate role.

SMS logon points are always domain controllers for the Windows NT domain you specify. When you need to replace an existing domain controller or add a new domain controller to the Windows NT domain, the SMS site server will automatically discover it and configure it appropriately to become a logon point for the site.

In a similar fashion, distribution points actually assume their role as packages are distributed and refreshed to these distribution points. Consequently, replacing or recovering a distribution point is simply a matter of refreshing the packages for that distribution point. To do so, follow these steps:

1. In the Packages folder of the SMS Administrator Console, select the package you need to redistribute, right-click on it, choose All Tasks from the context menu, and then choose Manage Distribution Points to launch the Manage Distribution Points Wizard, shown in Figure 17-13.

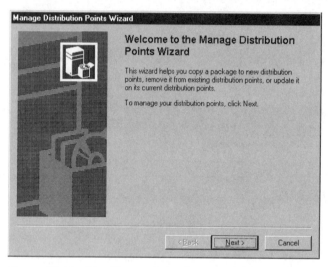

Figure 17-13. *The Manage Distribution Points Wizard welcome screen.*

2. Click Next to display the Manage Distribution Points screen, shown in Figure 17-14. Select the Refresh The Package On Selected Distribution Points option.

3. Click Next to display the Refresh Package screen, shown in Figure 17-15. In the Distribution Points list, find the distribution point you just recovered and select it.

4. Click Next to display the Completing The Manage Distribution Points Wizard screen, and click Finish to begin the update process.

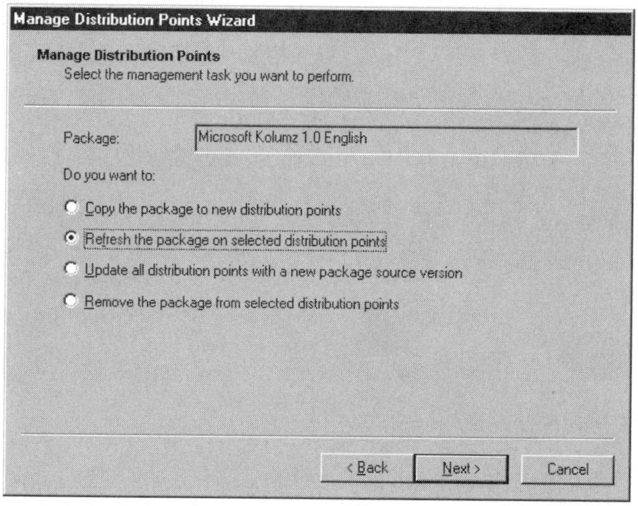

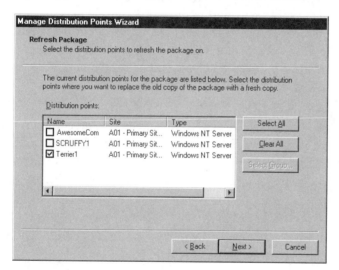

Figure 17-14. *The Manage Distribution Points screen.*

Figure 17-15. *The Refresh Package screen.*

Caution   If you are recovering a distribution point that has gone down, the packages must be redistributed to the same drive and directory on which they were originally configured. For example, if you created your own shared folders to which the package was originally distributed, re-create the shares before redistributing the packages.

Software metering servers are also recovered by reassigning them through the SMS Administrator Console. If the site maintains other software metering servers, licenses will be balanced to the recovered system according to the balancing options you configured for the site. Refer to Chapter 14 for a detailed discussion of the configuration and implementation of software metering servers.

Tip If the SQL server or site server fails, SMS components running on site systems will continue to function correctly, although status messages and data updates will not be forwarded to the site server until it is restored. This means that SMS clients will continue to report inventory data, run advertised programs, and meter software.

Summary

At this point, you have developed sound strategies for maintaining, backing up, and restoring SMS within your site. You have configured the database maintenance tasks and scheduled these tasks within appropriate time periods—daily, weekly, or monthly. You have established a regular backup plan that includes backing up not only the SMS database, but also the strategic files, folders, and registry keys contained on the site server. You have outlined and practiced recovery procedures to be followed in the event the SMS database server or site server fails or needs to be moved or a site system needs to be replaced.

Chapter 18 takes us a step further, as we explore maintenance and configuration from the point of view of SQL Server. These two chapters combined provide the groundwork necessary to keep your SMS site optimized and well-prepared should you ever encounter a recovery event.

Chapter 18
Maintaining the Database Through Microsoft SQL Server

In Chapter 2, we outlined the prerequisites for the SQL server to successfully host the Microsoft Systems Management Server (SMS) 2.0 database. Let's recap those requirements here. Recall that to use SMS 2.0, you must have installed either Microsoft SQL Server 6.5 with Service Pack 4 or later or Microsoft SQL Server 7.0. SQL Server can be installed either on its own server or on the same computer as the site server. The decision as to which location is more appropriate depends on many factors, not the least of which are the performance capabilities of the server itself.

The same decision also affects the way in which the SMS 2.0 installation will proceed. If SQL Server is installed on the same server as SMS 2.0, the SMS Setup program can create the necessary database devices and files for you. If SQL Server is installed on a different server, you will need to define those devices and files prior to installing SMS.

There are several SQL parameters which affect the way the SMS database is handled by SQL Server. Some of those parameters, such as the number of open connections and the amount of memory allocated, were discussed in Chapter 2. Other parameters will be discussed in this chapter.

In this chapter we will focus on some specific tasks and terms, beginning with the SQL Server components used by the SMS database. Then we'll look at the management tools available in SQL Server and discuss how to maintain the SMS database using SQL Server 6.5 and 7.0. Last we'll explore how to modify SQL Server parameters and how to solve the problems that might occur in your SQL server. The intent of this chapter is not to teach you all there is to know about SQL Server. Plenty of good books and courses on SQL Server are available to provide you with that information. Here, however, we will explore how to maintain the SMS database through SQL Server.

Tip   It is possible to install and use SMS 2.0 without a working knowledge of SQL Server, but in the long run you will need to master at least SQL Server administration tasks. SMS 2.0 is not itself a database server; instead, it acts as a front end to the SMS database maintained in SQL Server. Therefore, many database maintenance tasks will need to be initiated through SQL Server. Consider taking a class about SQL Server administration, such as Microsoft Official Curriculum (MOC) 832, "System Administration for Microsoft SQL 7.0," or MOC 867, "System Administration for Microsoft SQL 6.5" prior to implementing a multitiered SMS site structure. *Microsoft SQL Server 7.0 Administrator's Companion* (available through Microsoft Press) is also a good source of information regarding the execution of administrative tasks.

SQL Server Components

In this section, we'll review some basic terminology and see how it relates to the SMS database. Every entity we call a database actually consists of two components: the database and its transaction log. The *database* is a collection of data records, object tables, and indexes organized in a specific structure designed to facilitate the displaying, sorting, updating, and analysis of the information it contains. The *transaction log* is used to record each action performed on the database, such as adding a new record or updating or deleting an existing record.

In SQL Server 6.5, databases and their corresponding transaction logs are created and maintained in devices. A *SQL device* is a placeholder, or predefined storage space, for the database and for its transaction log. SMS requires separate devices for the SMS database and for the transaction log. If SQL Server is installed on the same computer as the SMS 2.0 site server, SMS can create the database and log devices for you during its setup. If not, you must create the database and log devices before you install SMS 2.0. This requirement applies to the software metering data and transaction log devices as well.

SQL Server 7.0, on the other hand, does not require the creation of devices for the database and log files. Instead, the database and transaction logs are each maintained in their own files. Again, if SQL Server is installed on the same computer as SMS 2.0, SMS 2.0 can create the database and log files for you during its setup. If not, you will need to create the files in advance. This requirement too applies to the software metering data and transaction log devices.

> **Note** If you install SMS using the Express Setup option, SMS will use the names SMSDATA and SMSLOG for the SMS database and log devices and LIC_DATA and LIC_LOG for the software metering database and log devices. If you use the Custom Setup option and SQL Server is installed on the same server, SMS will use the names SMSDATA_*sitecode*, SMSLOG_*sitecode*, LIC_DATA_*sitecode*, and LIC_LOG_*sitecode* to identify these devices.

If you install SMS 2.0 on the same computer as SQL Server, SMS 2.0 will not only create the devices for you, but it will also tune SQL Server for use with SMS 2.0. This feature does not, of course, relieve you of all responsibility in the maintenance of the SQL server, but it does ease some of the setup concerns regarding SQL Server, especially if you've had little experience with it.

If SQL Server is not already installed on the proposed site server, the SMS 2.0 installation process will prompt you for the SQL Server 6.5 or 7.0 source files and install a dedicated SQL Server database for itself. In the case of SQL Server 6.5, the installation will also automatically apply SQL Server Service Pack 4. This process is outlined in Chapter 2.

Most of the actions you will need to perform on the SQL server can be accomplished through the SQL Server Enterprise Manager. Through this utility, you can create databases and transaction logs, set security, back up and restore the database, perform routine database maintenance tasks, and optimize SQL Server parameters for the SMS database. Enterprise Manager for SQL Server 6.5 and Enterprise Manager for SQL Server 7.0 use different interfaces, and the procedures for performing these tasks are somewhat different for each interface. Let's explore the process of creating devices in each SQL Server version.

Creating a Device in SQL Server 6.5

The Enterprise Manager for SQL Server 6.5, shown in Figure 18-1, groups its managed objects into four main categories:

- Database devices
- Backup devices
- Databases
- Logins (accounts)

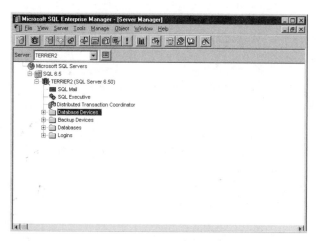

Figure 18-1. *SQL Server 6.5 Enterprise Manager.*

To create a new device, follow these steps:

1. In Enterprise Manager, choose Database Devices from the Manage menu to display the Manage Database Devices window, shown in Figure 18-2.

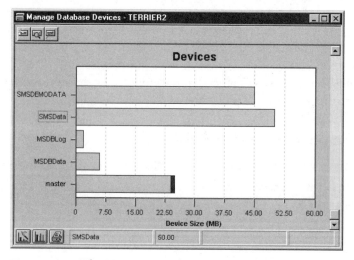

Figure 18-2. *The Manage Database Devices window.*

2. Click the New Device button (the disk drive with the yellow star) on the toolbar to display the New Database Device dialog box, shown in Figure 18-3. (Alternatively, in Enterprise Manager, navigate to the Database Devices folder, right-click on it, and choose New Device from the context menu to display the same dialog box, shown in Figure 18-3.)

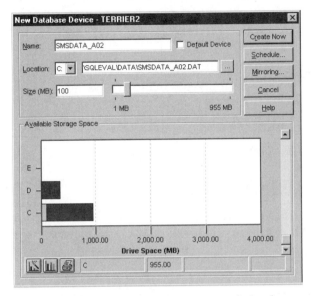

Figure 18-3. *The New Database Device dialog box.*

3. Enter a name for the device, such as SMSDATA_*xxx*, where *xxx* represents the site code of your new site. Specify the drive and path where the device will be created and stored, as well as the size of the database. The Available Storage Space graph will show how much space you have allocated and how much is left on the specified drive.

4. Click Create Now to generate the device. If SQL Server successfully created a device, it will display a message to that effect. Click OK.

5. Repeat steps 1 through 4 to create the corresponding transaction log device.

As shown in Figure 18-4, two new devices now appear but are currently empty. (The dark bars indicate that the device is empty.)The database itself, with its tables, views, objects, and so on, will be created by SMS during its setup. The entries for SMSDATA and SMSLOG visible (the light bars) in Figure 18-4 indicate that these devices contain databases.

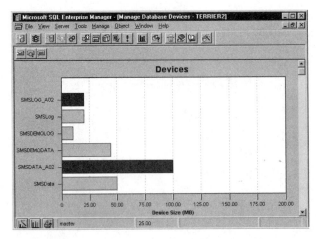

Figure 18-4. *Used and unused data and log devices.*

Creating a Device in SQL Server 7.0

The SQL Server 7.0 Enterprise Manager, shown in Figure 18-5, is a Microsoft Management Console (MMC) snap-in. It groups its managed objects into five main categories:

- Databases
- Data transformation services
- Management
- Security
- Support services

SQL Server 7.0 does not require the creation of separate devices before the database can be generated. Instead, it requires the creation of database files that will contain both the actual database objects and the transaction log data. Follow these steps to create a SQL Server 7.0 database file:

1. In Enterprise Manager, navigate to the Databases folder, right-click on it, and choose New Database from the context menu to display the Database Properties window, shown in Figure 18-6.

2. On the General tab, enter a name for the database, such as SMS_*xxx*, where *xxx* represents the site code for your new site.

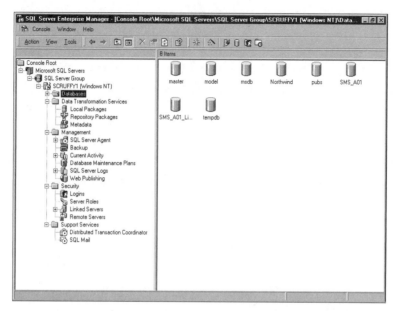

Figure 18-5. *SQL Server 7.0 Enterprise Manager.*

Figure 18-6. *The Database Properties window.*

3. The database file name will appear as SMS_*xxx*_Data in the Database Files list. You can click the Browse button (found in the Location column) to display the Locate Database File window where you can modify the location of the file. You can also change the initial size through this entry.

4. In the File Properties section, the Automatically Grow File option is enabled by default. This option ensures that SQL Server monitors the size of your database and expands it as necessary according to the File Growth parameter you specify. You can also allow the growth to be unrestricted or set a maximum size.

5. Click on the Transaction Log tab, shown in Figure 18-7, and configure the same parameters for the transaction log. The transaction log file will be named SMS_*xxx*_Log.

Figure 18-7. *The Transaction Log tab.*

6. Click OK to create the files.

SQL Server 7.0 considers the database and transaction log files combined as representing the database and displays a single database entry, rather than listing individual devices as is done in SQL Server 6.5.

SMS Database Components

The SMS database contains data objects and their attributes arranged in an organized fashion. Each database consists of five main elements, as follows:

- Tables
- Indexes
- Views
- Event triggers
- Stored procedures

A *table* is a database object that contains all the data in the database organized as a collection of rows and columns. Each row in the table represents a data record, and each column represents an associated field for that record. Generally, each table defines one or more columns (fields) as a key entry that can be used to link tables for the purpose of sorting, searching, and reporting on data in the database. SMS 2.0 contains more than 200 predefined tables.

An *index* can be thought of as a companion object to a table. Separate from the table, an index functions much like an index in a book, providing a quick way to search and locate data. If an index is available for a table, your queries will exhibit better performance. If no index is available, the entire table must be searched. The two index types, clustered index and nonclustered index, determine how the data records are searched. The nonclustered index is similar to a book index—each entry contains a bookmark that tells the database where to find the data that corresponds to the key in the index. For example, when you look up an entry such as *site-server* in a book index, you might be directed to several different locations in the book. The index does not represent the order in which the data is stored in the book. The clustered index is similar to a telephone directory—it contains the data itself, not just the index keys. The clustered indexes are usually based on a primary key defined in each table. Each index entry corresponds to the order in which the data is stored in the book. Like looking up a name in the phone book, when you find the name you also find the address and phone number.

When you execute a query, you are searching tables for a specific value based on the criteria you enter, using indexes whenever possible. The query result represents the records or data values obtained from records contained in one or more tables. SMS 2.0 contains more than 250 predefined indexes.

A *view* represents a specific, predefined query that can be used to generate reports. This type of database object was used extensively in SMS 1.2 to support Crystal Reports (known in SMS 2.0 as Crystal Info) and other report access tools. Although SMS 2.0 supports views and maintains them if you are upgrading from SMS 1.2, SMS 2.0 itself does not include views. Rather, data access must be secured through Open Database Connectivity (ODBC) and Windows Management Instrumentation (WMI) for management reporting purposes.

An *event trigger* is a Transact-SQL statement that is executed whenever a specific event occurs in a given table. The Transact-SQL language is used for communication between applications and SQL Server. It is an enhancement to structured query language (SQL) and provides a comprehensive language for defining tables, maintaining tables, and controlling access to data in the tables. If data is added, deleted, or modified within a specific table, an event trigger will be executed. SMS uses event triggers to notify its components that an event has occurred that a particular component needs to attend to. Event triggers cause components to "wake up" in response to an event rather than waiting for a specific polling cycle to occur. Obviously, this translates to better performance for the site server. For example, when you change a site setting, an event trigger causes SQL Monitor to write a wake-up file in the Hierarchy Manager inbox (see Chapter 3). SMS 2.0 uses over 200 different event triggers.

A *stored procedure* is a group of Transact-SQL statements that have been compiled into a single executable routine. You could think of a stored procedure as a kind of batch file for SQL Server. When a SQL Server event activates a trigger, a corresponding stored procedure is executed that writes the wake-up file into the appropriate SMS component's inbox on the site server. Two common stored procedures you might execute are *SP_SPACEDUSED*, which displays the amount of reserved and actual disk space used by a table in the database or by the entire database, and *SP_WHO*, which identifies SQL Server connections (users and processes) currently in use.

SQL Server Management Tools

A quick scan of the SQL Server 6.5 and 7.0 program groups will reveal that many tools are installed to assist the SQL Server administrator in maintaining the SQL server. Unless you are the SQL Server administrator as well as the SMS administrator or you get the necessary education to fully understand and appreciate the product, you will probably use only two or three of these tools. The SQL Server 6.5 program tools are described in Table 18-1; the SQL Server 7.0 program tools are described in Table 18-2.

Table 18-1.   SQL Server 6.5 program tools

Tool	Description
ISQL/w	Graphical query interface used to execute maintenance tasks by running Transact-SQL statements or stored procedures.
Microsoft ODBC SQL Server Driver	Online help for configuring and using the Microsoft ODBC SQL Server driver.
MS Query	Graphical interface designed to allow users to build SELECT query statements against any ODBC-compliant database, including SQL Server databases. SMS 2.0 does not allow access to the database in this manner, as it uses the WMI exclusively. Database access can be achieved outside the SMS Administrator Console through any Web-Based Enterprise Management (WBEM)ODBC-compliant application such as Crystal Info 7.0 or Microsoft Access 2000.
Readme.txt	Provides documentation to supplement that included in the Books Online tool.
SQL Client Configuration Utility	Used to set the default server connection and Net-Library configuration for clients.
SQL Distributed Management Objects	Online help outlining the SQL Server Distributed Management Object (SQL-DMO) model.
SQL Enterprise Manager	Graphical interface that facilitates the configuration of the SQL server and the management of SQL Server databases, including devices and databases, space usage, backups, and restores.
SQL Performance Monitor	Runs Windows NT Performance Monitor with performance objects and counters specific to the SQL server.
SQL Security Manager	Enables management of user access to database objects.
SQL Server Books Online	Provides an online version of the documentation set *SQL Server Books Online* with full searching capabilities.
SQL Server Web Assistant	Converts SQL Server data to HTML format.
SQL Service Manager	Starts, stops, and pauses the SQL Server, SQL Executive, and Microsoft Distributed Transaction Coordinator (MS DTC) services.
SQL Setup	Accesses the setup program used to reconfigure, rebuild, or remove SQL Server.
SQL Trace	Similar to SMS Trace. Used to monitor statements, procedure calls, and so on sent to the server and to follow the corresponding activity of the server.

Table 18-2. SQL Server 7.0 program tools

Tool	Description
Books Online	Provides an on-line version of the documentation set *SQL Server Books Online* with full searching capabilities.
Client Network Utility	Used to set the custom server connection, DB-Library, and Net-Library configuration for clients.
Enterprise Manager	MMC snap-in that facilitates the configuration of the SQL server and the management of SQL Server databases, including devices and databases, space usage, backups and restores, permissions, data import and export, and so on through object-level folders.
Import And Export Data	Launches the Data Transformation Service Wizard, designed to facilitate the import, export, and conversion of data from various data formats.
MS DTC Administrative Console	Launches the MS DTC Administrative Console.
Performance Monitor	Runs Windows NT Performance Monitor with performance objects and counters specific to the SQL server.
Profiler	Used to monitor server events, procedure calls, and other real-time server activity; Profiler can also filter events and direct output to the screen, file, or table.
Query Analyzer	Graphical query interface used to execute maintenance tasks such as Transact-SQL statements or stored procedures.
Readme.txt	Provides documentation to supplement the documentation included in the Books Online tool.
Server Network Utility	Used to configure SQL Server to use Net-Libraries and to specify the network protocol stacks on which the server will listen for SQL Server clients' requests.
Service Manager	Starts, stops, and pauses the SQL Server, SQL Server Agent, and MS DTC services. Also implemented as a taskbar program.
Uninstall SQL Server 7.0	Initiates the Uninstall routine for SQL Server.

Many SQL Server maintenance tasks specific to the SMS database can be configured and scheduled to run through the SMS Administrator Console, including a complete site server backup (see Chapter 17). Database backups can also be effected by using a third-party backup program capable of including SQL Server databases as part of its backup routine. Consequently, as an SMS administrator, you are most likely to use Enterprise Manager to perform any additional or advanced maintenance tasks. Through this interface you can create database devices, manage space usage, configure the server, schedule events, backup and restore the database, and so on.

You can also use the SQL Server 6.5 ISQL/w tool or the SQL Server 7.0 SQL Server Query Analyzer to execute maintenance tasks such as those described in Chapter 17. You can use the SQL Server Security Manager to provide a more granular level of security to the SMS database through SQL Server, and you can use the Performance Monitor tool to analyze server performance and resource allocation.

As with most Microsoft BackOffice applications, when you install SQL Server several performance objects and counters are included to assist you in evaluating the ongoing performance and resource use of your SQL server as well as facilitate the troubleshooting of specific performance-related problems. To view the available SQL Server performance objects and counters, you can start the Windows NT Performance Monitor utility.

However, both versions of SQL Server include a Performance Monitor tool. This tool is linked directly to the Windows NT Performance Monitor and launches a Performance Monitor chart that tracks common counters. Figure 18-8 shows an example Performance Monitor chart generated using the SQL Server 6.5 Performance Monitor tool, and Figure 18-9 shows an example Performance Monitor chart generated using SQL Server 7.0's Performance Monitor tool.

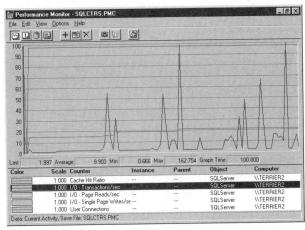

Figure 18-8. *Sample SQL Server 6.5 Performance Monitor chart.*

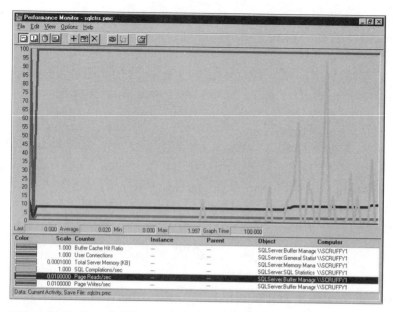

Figure 18-9. *Sample SQL Server 7.0 Performance Monitor chart.*

These are live Performance Monitor sessions and can be modified to display additional counters, change the intervals, switch to Log or Report view, and so on. These charts can be helpful as you perform your periodic database maintenance tasks (described in Chapter 17). For example, the *SQL Server:Database* object has a counter called named *Data File Size (KB)* which will help you monitor the cumulative size of your databases, such as tempdb.

Database Maintenance

As we've seen, some database maintenance tasks should be carried out on a regular basis—either daily, weekly, or monthly. For example, every day you might execute a database backup and review status messages and system performance. Once a week, you might monitor database size usage and purge old data out of the database. Once a month, you might verify the integrity of the database backup by testing a restore of the database. Once a month, you might also review security and make appropriate adjustments such as resetting account passwords.

Most of these tasks can be performed or configured and scheduled to run through the SMS Administrator Console. However, many of these same tasks, and database backup and restores, can be performed through SQL Server. In this section, we'll review the commands used for performing the essential maintenance tasks, and how to perform these tasks in SQL Server 6.5 and SQL Server 7.0.

Commands Used for Performing Essential Maintenance Tasks

Some of the database integrity checking and space monitoring commands you might consider running on a weekly or monthly basis are listed below. These database consistency checker (DBCC) commands are certainly not the only ones available, but they are among the commands most often recommended by Microsoft.

- **DBCC CHECKALLOC (DBCC NEWALLOC in SQL Server 6.5)**
  Checks the specified database to verify that all pages have been correctly allocated and used; reports the space allocation and usage.

- **DBCC CHECKDB**   Checks every database table and index to verify that they are linked correctly, that their pointers are consistent, and that they are in the proper sort order.

- **DBCC CHECKCATALOG**   Checks consistency between tables and reports on defined segments.

- **DBCC UPDATEUSAGE**   Used with a recently reindexed database to reset space usage reporting so that *SP_SPACEUSED* returns accurate data. You could schedule this command to run with *SP_SPACEUSED* or to run separately under its own schedule.

Tip   To obtain a complete list and explanation of all Transact-SQL statements and stored procedures, including the DBCC commands, query the online help for both SQL Server 6.5 and 7.0.

Before you run any DBCC command, remember to set SQL Server to single-user mode. We'll look at how to start SQL Server in single-user mode in the section "Backing Up and Restoring the Database" later in this chapter. We'll discuss how to run these commands in the following sections.

Executing a Maintenance Command Using SQL Server 6.5

To execute a database maintenance command in SQL Server 6.5, launch the ISQL/w program tool, found in the SQL Server 6.5 programs group, to display the Connect Server dialog box (shown in Figure 18-10) and follow these steps:

1. In the Connect Server dialog box, enter the name of the SQL server to which you want to connect by selecting it from the drop-down list, or by clicking the List Servers button and selecting the server from that list.

Figure 18-10. *The Connect Server dialog box.*

2. Select either the Use Trusted Connection or Use Standard Security option, depending on the security mode you enabled for your SQL server. Supply a login ID and password if appropriate.

3. Click Connect to display the Query window, shown in Figure 18-11. Enter the command you want to execute—in this case, DBCC CHECKDB.

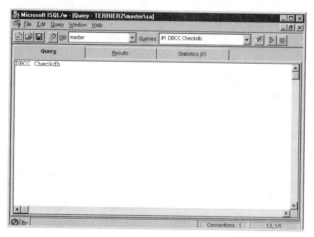

Figure 18-11. *The Query window.*

4. Choose Execute from the Query menu, or click the Execute Query button (the green arrow). The results of the query are displayed in the Results window, shown in Figure 18-12.

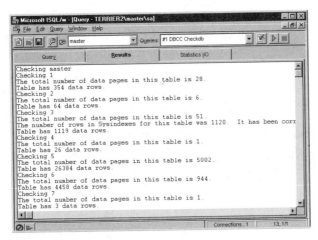

Figure 18-12. *The Results window.*

Executing a Maintenance Command Using SQL Server 7.0

To execute a database maintenance command in SQL Server 7.0, launch the Query Analyzer tool found in the SQL Server 7.0 programs group to display the Connect To SQL Server dialog box, shown in Figure 18-13, and follow these steps:

1. In the Connect To SQL Server dialog box, if the SQL server is the local server, verify that the Local option is selected. Otherwise, click the Browse button to choose from a list of SQL servers located on the network. If you need to start the SQL Server service, select the Start SQL Server If Stopped check box.

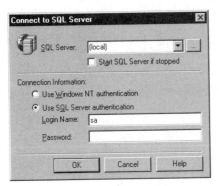

Figure 18-13. *The Connect To SQL Server dialog box*

2. Select either Use Windows NT Authentication or Use SQL Server Authentication, depending on the security mode you enabled for your SQL server. Supply a login ID and password if appropriate.

3. Click OK to display the Query window, shown in Figure 18-14, and enter the command that you want to execute—in this case, DBCC CHECKALLOC.

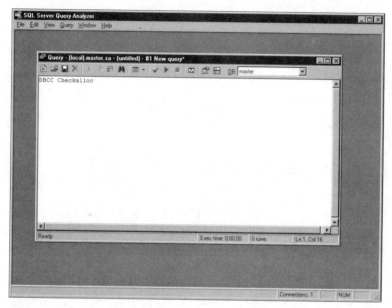

Figure 18-14. *The Query window.*

4. Choose Execute from the Query menu, or click the Execute Query button (the green arrow) on the toolbar. The results of the query are displayed in the Results window, shown in Figure 18-15.

Tip Each of the DBCC commands and stored procedures may have additional syntax options that will affect how the command is executed. Refer to your SQL Server documentation for a complete description of each command and its syntax.

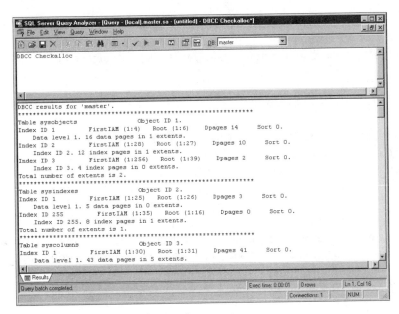

Figure 18-15. *The Results window.*

Backing Up and Restoring the Database

We began our discussion of backing up and restoring the database in Chapter 17, when we explored some of the built-in database maintenance routines configurable through the SMS Administrator Console. In this section, we'll review the procedure for backing up and restoring the database directly through SQL Server.

The contents of the database and transaction log can be backed up to a device such as a tape drive or to another file location on the server. The frequency of the backup is up to you, the SMS administrator. Generally, you will back up the SMS database as frequently as necessary to ensure a current and accurate restoration of the data. A common database strategy involves performing a complete backup of the database once a week, with incremental backups of the data that has changed each day between full backups.

Tip As you've seen throughout this book, SMS components have frequent communication with the SMS database. Before implementing a production site, develop and test a backup and restore strategy that will adequately protect your data.

Remember that you should turn off the Truncate Log On Checkpoint option before you back up the transaction log. This option is enabled by default and causes the transaction log to contain only few, if any, recent transactions. For most of the time, the default Truncate Log On Checkpoint option setting will be appropriate, and you will need to turn off this option only when backing up the SMS database.

Note Several third-party backup programs, such as Seagate's Backup Exec 7.2 for Windows NT, include modules designed specifically for backing up SQL Server databases. If you have access to such a product, you can have it perform the backup as part of its systemwide backup routine, eliminating the need to configure a backup redundantly through SQL Server or through the SMS Administrator Console.

To preserve the integrity of the data, it is important that no SMS components try to access the SMS database when the backup or restore is taking place. Be sure that no SMS Administrator Consoles are running and that all SMS components on the site server have been stopped. In addition, when you are restoring the database be sure to set the database to single-user mode. This is set as a property of the database. Note that you will not be able to set the single-user mode option if any open connections exist to the database.

Backing Up and Restoring Using SQL Server 6.5

Let's begin with backing up and restoring the database using SQL Server 6.5. Recall from Chapter 17 that to back up the database, you must identify a backup device. You can do this ahead of time, or you can create one as you configure the backup.

To back up the database, follow these steps:

1. In Enterprise Manager, navigate to the Databases folder and expand it.
2. Select your SMS site database, right-click on it, and choose Backup/Restore from the context menu to display the Database Backup/Restore Properties window, shown in Figure 18-16.

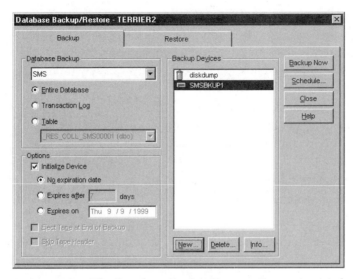

Figure 18-16. *The Database Backup/Restore Properties window.*

3. On the Backup tab, verify that your SMS database has been selected, and that the Entire Database option is enabled.

4. If you want to add this backup to existing backups on the backup device, enable the Initialize Device option in the Options section. If you want to overwrite what is already on the device, do not enable this option. If you do enable the Initialize Device option, you can also define an expiration interval for the backup.

5. If you have already created a backup device, select it from the Backup Devices list. To identify a new backup device, click New to display the New Backup Device dialog box, shown in Figure 18-17.

Figure 18-17. *The New Backup Device dialog box.*

6. Enter a name for the device, confirm or define a location, and specify whether the backup device is a disk or a tape. Click Create to create the device and return to the Backup tab of the Database Backup/Restore Properties window. The new backup device will now be shown in the window.

7. With the backup device selected, click Backup Now to begin the backup process. If you enabled the Initialize Device option, a dialog box will appear allowing you to confirm or modify a volume label for the backup. If previous backups exist for the device, you will be prompted to confirm their deletion. Then click OK.

8. When the backup is complete, a message to that effect will be displayed. Click OK.

The restore process is essentially the reverse of the backup process. To restore the database, follow these steps:

1. In Enterprise Manager, navigate to the Databases folder and expand it.

2. Select your SMS database, right-click on it, and choose Edit from the context menu to display the Edit Database Properties window.

3. Click on the Options tab, shown in Figure 18-18. Check the Single User check box, and then click OK to return to Enterprise Manager.

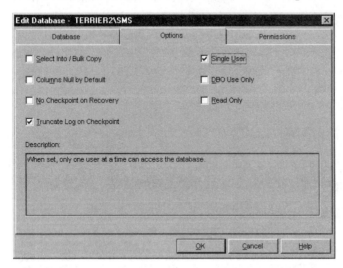

Figure 18-18. *The Options tab of the Edit Database Properties window.*

4. Right-click on the SMS database, and choose Backup/Restore to display the Database Backup/Restore Properties window.

5. Click on the Restore tab, shown in Figure 18-19. Verify that your SMS database has been selected and that the Database And/Or Transaction Logs option is enabled.

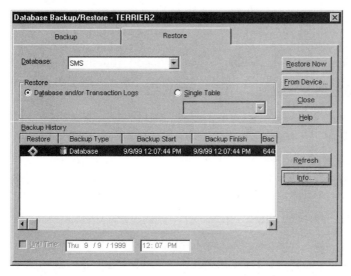

Figure 18-19. *The Restore tab of the Database Backup/Restore Properties window.*

6. Select the backup you want to restore from the Backup History list, and then click the Info button to display the Backup History Information dialog box, shown in Figure 18-20.

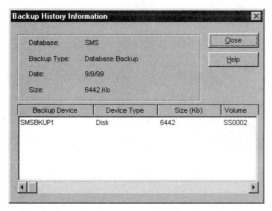

Figure 18-20. *The Backup History Information dialog box.*

7. Verify the backup device and volume label, and click Close to return to the Restore tab.

8. Click Restore Now to begin the restoration process.

9. When the restore process has completed successfully, SQL Server will display a message to that effect. Click OK.

> **Note** This process represents the basic configuration procedure for backing up and restoring the SMS database; it should in no way be considered exhaustive of every backup/restore option available. As mentioned, you should consider adding SQL Server to your ongoing professional training goals if you will be managing the SMS database extensively through SQL Server.

Backing Up and Restoring Using SQL Server 7.0

The backup and restore process for SQL Server 7.0 is similar to that for SQL Server 6.5. As with SQL Server 6.5, you can either create a backup device ahead of time through Enterprise Manager or while you configure the backup.

To back up the SMS database using SQL Server 7.0, follow these steps:

1. In Enterprise Manager, navigate to the Databases folder and expand it.

2. Select the SMS database you want to back up, right-click on it, and choose Properties to display the Database Properties window.

3. Click on the Options tab, shown in Figure 18-21. Select the Single User check box, and click OK to return to Enterprise Manager.

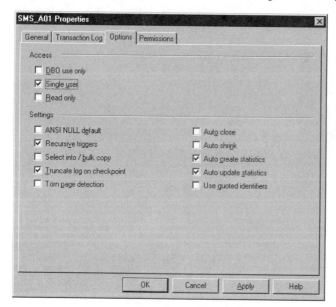

Figure 18-21. *The Options tab of the Database Properties window.*

4. Right-click on the database entry again, choose All Tasks from the context menu, and then choose Backup Database to display the SQL Server Backup Properties window, shown in Figure 18-22.

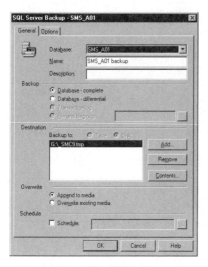

Figure 18-22. *The SQL Server Backup Properties window.*

5. On the General tab, confirm that your SMS database is selected. Modify the name of the backup if you want, and verify that the Database - Complete option has been selected.

Note   Unlike a backup using SQL Server 6.5, here you do have the option of also performing a differential backup.

---

6. To specify a backup device, click the Add button to display the Choose Backup Destination dialog box, shown in Figure 18-23. Enter a filename and select an existing backup device from the Backup Devices list or select New Backup Device to create a new device.

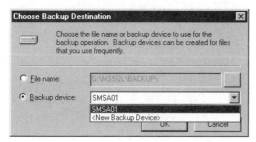

Figure 18-23. *The Choose Backup Destination dialog box.*

7. If you select New Backup Device, the Backup Device Properties - New Device window will appear, as shown in Figure 18-24. Enter a name for the device, and then click OK to return to the Choose Backup Destination dialog box.

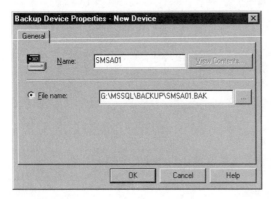

Figure 18-24. *The Backup Device Properties - New Device window.*

8. Click OK again to accept the device destination and return to the SQL Server Backup Properties window.

9. Remove any other backup devices that may be listed in the Backup To list on the General tab, such as a temp file. Set whatever other options you want on the General and Options tabs, and then click OK to begin the backup process. (You can click the Help button for more information about each of the options available on these tabs.)

10. When the backup is complete, a message to that effect will be displayed. Click OK.

To restore the database, follow these steps:

1. In Enterprise Manager, navigate to the Databases folder and expand it.

2. Select your SMS site database, right-click on it, choose All Tasks from the context menu, and then choose Restore Database to display the Restore Database Properties window, shown in Figure 18-25.

3. On the General tab, verify that the correct database is selected and that the Database option in the Restore section has been enabled.

4. In the Parameters section, select the appropriate backup device from the Show Backups Of Database drop-down list. The First Backup To Restore

drop-down lists displays in chronological order the database backups for this device. This option allows you to restore selective differential backups if you performed them. Select the appropriate entry.

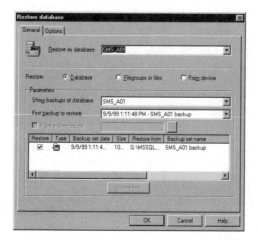

Figure 18-25. *The Restore Database Properties window.*

5. Click OK to begin the restore process.

6. When the restore process has completed successfully, SQL Server will display a message to that effect. Click OK.

In this section, we've looked at the procedures for backing up and restoring SMS databases using SQL Server. Note that what we discussed are only essential procedures. You should consult the SQL Server documentation for other configuration options.

Modifying SQL Server Parameters

Recall from Chapter 2 that if you install SQL Server as part of the SMS 2.0 setup process, SMS will set the SQL Server parameters to their optimum values for you. If you choose to install SQL Server yourself, however, you should pay attention to the following SQL Server configuration parameters and set them appropriately before installing SMS 2.0: *User Connections*, *Open Objects*, *Memory*, *Locks*, and *Tempdb Size*. Table 18-3 provides guidelines for setting these parameters for SQL Server 6.5 and SQL Server 7.0.

Table 18-3. SQL Server configuration parameters

Parameter	Guidelines
User Connections	SMS 2.0 requires a minimum of 40 user connections for the site server and 2 connections for each SMS Administrator Console you plan to install. It also requires 5 additional user connections for each instance of the SMS Administrator Console, if more than five consoles will be running concurrently on your site. You can set SMS 2.0 to calculate this number and configure it automatically during setup. Each installation of SMS 2.0 requires 20 user connections. In SQL Server 6.5, each user connection allocates 40 KB of RAM. In SQL 7.0, this allocation is made dynamically at the time of the connection, providing more efficient memory management.
Open Objects	This parameter indicates the number of tables, views, stored procedures, and the like that can be open at a time. If you exceed the specified number of open objects, SQL Server must close some objects before it can open others, resulting in a performance hit. For most sites, although the default is *500*, you may want to set this parameter to *1000*. For large sites, this number could be *5000* or more. Use SQL Server Performance Monitor counters to track the number of open objects in use to determine the optimum number for the SMS site. Note that SQL Server 7.0 sizes this number automatically.
Memory	This parameter indicates the amount of RAM that should be used for database caching and management. SMS automatically allocates 16 MB of RAM for SQL Server use. In SQL Server 6.5, memory is allocated in memory units of 2 KB. Set this value to at least *8192* (16 MB). Increasing this number may improve SQL Server performance, but it may also detract from other server operations (such as SMS site server). SQL Server 7.0 allocates memory dynamically in 8-KB units. You can define a range for SQL Server to use.
Locks	This parameter prevents users from accessing and updating the same data at the same time. Because of the volume of information contained in the database, Microsoft recommends setting this value from *5000* to *10,000* depending on the size of the database and the number of SMS Administrator Consoles.
Tempdb Size	This temporary database and log are used to manage queries and sorts. By default, the tempdb database and log information are maintained in the same SQL device. (Please see Chapter 18 for details on the SQL device.) For best performance, both should be kept in this default location. Note that this is contrary to what the *Systems Management Server Administrator's Guide* recommends for high volumes of activity. This recommendation was later corrected in the Microsoft Systems Management Server Version 2.0 Release Notes. Set the tempdb data device size in SQL Server 6.5 to at least 20 percent of the SMS database device size. Set the tempdb log device size to at least 20 percent of the tempdb data device size. In SQL Server 7.0, as you have by now surmised, the tempdb database is sized dynamically.

Modifying Parameters for SQL Server 6.5

To modify these parameters settings for SQL Server 6.5, follow these steps:

1. In Enterprise Manager, select your SQL server entry, right-click on it, and choose Configure from the context menu to display the Server Configuration/Options Properties window.

2. Click on the Configuration tab, shown in Figure 18-26. Scroll through the parameter list to locate the parameter you want to modify. In the Current column for the parameter, enter the new value. Repeat this process for each parameter you want to modify.

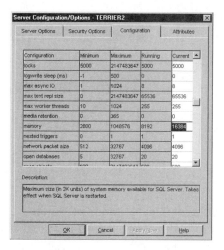

Figure 18-26. *The Configuration tab of the Server Configuration/Options Properties window.*

3. Click OK to save your changes.

As you select each parameter, an explanation appears in the Description text box at the bottom of the Configuration tab describing the parameter and indicating when the change will take effect. Most changes require that you stop and restart SQL Server. If you need to stop and restart SQL Server to effect your changes, simply right-click on the server entry in Enterprise Manager, and choose Stop from the context menu. To restart SQL Server, right-click on the server entry again, and choose Start.

Modifying Parameters for SQL Server 7.0

To modify these parameter settings for SQL Server 7.0, follow these steps:

1. In Enterprise Manager, select your SQL server entry, right-click on it, and choose Properties from the context menu to display the SQL Server Properties window, shown in Figure 18-27.

Figure 18-27. *The SQL Server Properties window.*

2. The SQL Server Properties window contains tabs for those parameters for which you can modify settings. (Recall from Table 18-3 that most SMS-specific parameters are dynamically managed by SQL Server 7.0.)

3. Click on the Memory tab, shown in Figure 18-28. Notice that the Dynamically Configure SQL Server Memory option is enabled by default, although you can modify the memory range within which SQL Server should manage memory allocation. You can also specify a fixed amount of memory as well as identify the amount of RAM to allocate per user for query execution.

4. Click on the Connections tab, shown in Figure 18-29. This tab displays the maximum number of user connections that were configured for SQL Server during the SMS setup. SQL Server will dynamically allocate connections and appropriate resources to support them up to this maximum number. The allocation of user connections is a value you should monitor. If you add additional SMS Administrator Consoles or define additional site systems, you may need to increase the maximum number of connections to accommodate the increased resource demand by modifying this setting.

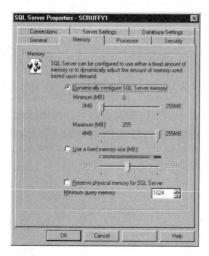

Figure 18-28. *The Memory tab.*

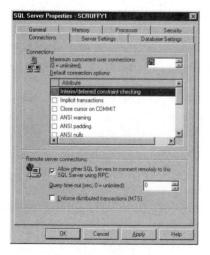

Figure 18-29. *The Connections tab.*

5. When you have finished making your changes, click OK to save them. As with SQL Server 6.5, you may need to stop and then restart SQL Server to implement your changes. If this step is necessary, a message box will display to that effect.

More Info For more information about performance tuning SQL Server 7.0, download the SQL Server 7.0 Performance Tuning white paper at *http://www.microsoft.com/sql/productinfo/perftuning.htm*.

The topic of time synchronization is significant enough to bear revisiting here (you can refer to the "Synchronizing System Clocks" Real World section in Chapter 2 for a specific example) especially if SQL server and the SMS site server are installed on two different servers. Because the time stamp of data objects created will generally be that of the SQL server, it's important that the SMS site server and the SQL server synchronize their system times on a regular basis.

It is also important that the SMS clients synchronize their time with the SMS site server and the SQL server. SMS client computers will check their own system clocks when determining when to execute a program or run an agent. You can see how easily things can go awry if the SQL server, site server and client computer system clocks are all set to different times. A package may not execute at the time you expected, or an inventory collection may not take place because the scheduled times and the system clock are out of synch.

One way to overcome this situation is to identify one server as your time server for the SMS site. Have all your site systems, the SMS client computers, and the SQL server synchronize their times with the time server. Or, you might even consider making the SQL server the time server for the SMS site.

Checkpoints

If you're using SQL Server 6.5 with Service Pack 4, you may need to add a patch to your SQL server if you encounter random general protection faults or lock-ups related to WMI or the SMS Administrator Console. To do so, locate the file \SQLSetup\SQLHotfix*platform*\Sqlctr60.dll on the SMS 2.0 CD and copy it to the \MSSQL\Binn folder on the SQL server. SQL Server 6.5 with Service Pack 5 and SQL Server 7.0 are not affected.

Along similar lines, you may find that the SQL Server Performance Monitor counters are disabled by default when the SMS Provider is installed on a server running SQL Server 6.5. You will see no SQL Server–related objects when you run the Windows NT Performance Monitor, nor will the SQL Server Performance Monitor display any data. The SQL Server Performance Monitor counters must be enabled through the registry on the SQL server. In the Registry Editor, navigate to the following key: HKEY_LOCAL_MACHINE\System\CurrentControl-Set\Services\Performance. Locate the parameter entry *Library*, double-click on the entry to display the String Editor dialog box, and change the value to *Sqlctr60.dll* to enable the counters. To disable the counters when you have finished your analysis, reset the *Library* value to " " (empty quotation marks) by double-clicking on the *Library* entry and deleting the reference to *Sqlctr60.dll* in the displayed

String Editor dialog box. (This scenario does not apply to SQL Server 6.5 with Service Pack 5 and SQL Server 7.0.)

However, making this change may result in random WMI or SMS Administrator Console errors. You can clear up the problem by restarting the SMS Administrator Console. However, for this reason, you should enable the SQL Server performance counters only when it is necessary to analyze a suspected performance-related problem.

Summary

After reading Chapters 17 and this chapter, you should be well aware of the importance of creating and following an ongoing maintenance schedule for your SMS database. Chapter 17 focused on tasks that can be performed directly through the SMS Administrator Console. This chapter focused specifically on the SQL server and the tools and procedures that facilitate the management and maintenance of the server and the SMS database.

Part IV of this book focused mainly on the SMS database. We explored ways to extract and report on data in the database, how to secure that data, and how to recover in the event of a failure of some kind. We also discussed ways to maintain the integrity of the SMS database and optimize the SQL server hosting that database.

Part V, the final part of this book, enables the administrator to look both forward and backward in providing SMS 2.0 support. Chapter 19 examines the process of migrating from an SMS 1.2 environment to an SMS 2.0 environment. You'll learn how to support both versions of SMS within the same hierarchy and how to upgrade from SMS 1.2 to SMS 2.0. Chapter 20 compares SMS 2.0 features to similar features contained in Microsoft Windows 2000, and examines how SMS 2.0 can be used to support the Microsoft Windows 2000 environment.

Part V

Supporting Microsoft Systems Management Server 1.2 and Microsoft Windows 2000

Chapter 19
Migration Issues

This chapter is designed for those of you who currently maintain Microsoft Systems Management Server (SMS) 1.2 sites and need to either upgrade to SMS 2.0 or have the two versions of SMS coexist in the same site structure. Microsoft has published a body of good, detailed information concerning the topic of migration, including the *Systems Management Server Administrator's Guide* and two excellent white papers, "Microsoft Systems Management Server Version 1.2 to 2.0 Interoperability" and "Systems Management Server Version 1.2 to 2.0 Upgrade," available on Microsoft's SMS Web site at *http://www.microsoft.com/smsmgmt*.

This chapter supplements the above information. In this chapter, we will explore the most significant aspects of the two migration scenarios—interoperability and upgrading—to help you determine which approach is appropriate for your needs and what the main issues are. Our examination of migration is divided into four sections: planning the site structure, maintaining SMS 1.2 and 2.0 sites within the same site structure, upgrading from SMS 1.2 to SMS 2.0, and reviewing the tasks to be performed after the upgrade.

Planning the Site Structure

Whether you need to upgrade all your SMS 1.2 servers to SMS 2.0 or maintain a mixed SMS 1.2 and 2.0 environment, you will need to spend some time thinking through the two scenarios. Both bring up issues that tend to split into server-related and client-related concerns. A checklist of premigration considerations should include the following tasks:

- Review the current SMS site structure
- Determine which client platforms need to be supported within your upgraded site structure
- Review server hardware and software currently in use
- Explore site limitations between SMS 1.2 servers and SMS 2.0 servers

- Review and clean up the database to be converted
- Document current site settings that need to be re-created
- Back up the site and the server

Of course, you must also apply SMS 1.2 Service Pack 4. For a detailed discussion about this service pack, refer to the section "Applying Systems Management Server 1.2 Service Pack 4" later in this chapter. You will no doubt add items specific and unique to your own SMS installation, but this checklist should serve as a good starting point as you prepare your SMS 2.0 migration strategy. We'll look at each of these tasks in detail in the sections that follow.

Reviewing the Current Site Structure

The first step in developing a migration strategy is to review your current SMS site structure. The current SMS site structure can play a more significant role in determining your migration strategy than you might realize. In general, the clearer your understanding of the current site structure, the easier it will be for you to manage upgrading the sites and maintaining a mixed site. This means documenting all aspects of your current structure, site by site.

Identify the location of your sites' logon servers, distribution servers, site servers, and helper servers—all of these will be affected by an upgrade in one way or another. You should check to see whether any SMS 1.2 sites are overlapping Microsoft Windows NT domains. Since SMS 2.0 is more concerned with site boundaries than with domain structure, overlapping sites can pose some challenges dring an upgrade.

If your system currently supports SMS 1.2 secondary sites, consider whether you need to retain this support. Perhaps the needs of that site or your organization have changed since the secondary sites were implemented. Once you have upgraded an SMS 1.2 secondary site's parent from SMS 1.2 to SMS 2.0, that secondary site can no longer be managed by the parent. It is easier to join one SMS 1.2 site to another than it is to attach an SMS 1.2 site to an SMS 2.0 site. It is also easier to delete an SMS 1.2 secondary site from its original parent SMS 1.2 site than it will be once the parent site is upgraded.

Also, most SMS 1.2 database objects are not completely migrated or upgraded from SMS 1.2 to 2.0. It will be necessary to re-create objects such as custom queries or site security, and that task will much easier if you have adequately documented those settings prior to migration.

> **Tip** If your site would benefit by reconfiguring the site structure, especially where secondary site servers are concerned, it would be easier to make the modifications prior to beginning the upgrade process. This technique gives the sites a chance to propagate their updated information, including inventory data, up through the reconfigured structure. The databases will then be ready for conversion.

Determining Which Client Platforms Need to Be Supported

You already know that certain client operating system platforms that are supported in SMS 1.2 are not supported in SMS 2.0. These platforms include MS-DOS 5.0 and later, Apple Macintosh System 7.*x*, and IBM OS/2 2.11. Prior to upgrading any existing site servers to SMS 2.0 or implementing any new site servers using SMS 2.0, you need to revisit those clients and determine whether they still need to be managed by an SMS site. If not, you should remove the old SMS client components from those clients before upgrading the site server they belong to.

If these clients still need to participate in an SMS site, they can be managed only by an SMS 1.2 site and you will still be looking at implementing a mixed site of SMS 1.2 and SMS 2.0 servers. While this is not an impossible situation, it is also not without challenges. Mixed-site interoperability will be discussed in detail in the section "Maintaining Mixed Sites Within the Same Site Structure" later in this chapter.

> **Tip** Take this opportunity to review the hardware components for your proposed SMS 2.0 clients to be sure that you have adequate resources to support installation of the SMS 2.0 client components. For example, installation of all SMS 2.0 client components will require at least 16 MB of free disk space.

Reviewing Hardware and Software Currently in Use

Now is an excellent time for you to review the hardware and software currently in use on your Windows NT servers. Recall from Chapter 2 that some minimum and recommended hardware and software requirements must be met to successfully upgrade to or install SMS 2.0 on a Windows NT server. For example, you should have at least 128 MB of RAM and 2 GB of available disk space on an NTFS partition, and your server's processor must be at least an Intel Pentium 166 MHz.

By now, you certainly understand that RAM, disk space and I/O, and processor speed are all important factors in maintaining acceptable performance for SMS 2.0

site systems, particularly the site server and SMS database server. You must upgrade your servers accordingly before beginning an upgrade or install process.

In terms of software, some simple, non-negotiable terms must be met in order to upgrade to or install SMS 2.0. The proposed site server must be running Windows NT 4.0 with Service Pack 4 or later, and it must be fully Y2K-compliant. This means that, in addition to Service Pack 4, you must install the Y2K components and updated Microsoft Data Access Components (MDAC) as well as Microsoft Internet Explorer 4.01 with Service Pack 1. All of these items can be found on the SMS 2.0 CD and are appropriately updated through the SMS 2.0 Service Pack 1 installation process.

Also, Windows NT 4.0 supports Microsoft SQL Server 6.5 or later, and SMS 2.0 requires SQL Server 6.5 with Service Pack 4 or later applied. SQL Service Pack 4 also is included on the SMS 2.0 CD. SQL Server 7.0 is highly recommended for use with SMS 2.0 because of its significant performance enhancements and improved database handling.

> **Caution** If you are upgrading from SMS 1.2 to SMS 2.0 and also upgrading from SQL Server 6.5 to 7.0, perform the SMS upgrade first. SMS 1.2 does not support SQL Server 7.0, and if you perform the SQL Server upgrade first, you will lose database support for the existing SMS 1.2 site.

Exploring Site Limitations in a Mixed-Version Environment

If you need to maintain a mixed SMS 1.2 and SMS 2.0 site structure, you need to be aware of several limitations as you reorganize the structure and roll out the upgrade. Although SMS 1.2 sites can report to SMS 2.0 sites, the reverse is not supported—that is, SMS 2.0 sites can report only to other SMS 2.0 sites and not to SMS 1.2 sites. Be sure your proposed mixed-site structure reflects this reporting path. This limitation also almost guarantees the necessity of performing a top-down upgrade of SMS 1.2 sites. Begin your upgrade with the SMS 1.2 central site and work your way down to ensure that all SMS 2.0 sites always report to another SMS 2.0 site.

> **Note** If you will be supporting a mixed SMS 1.2 and SMS 2.0 site structure, the SMS 1.2 site servers must be upgraded with SMS 1.2 Service Pack 4. This service pack implements several performance and component enhancements that deal specifically with interoperability between SMS 1.2 and SMS 2.0 sites.

SMS 1.2 components cannot be installed or run on an SMS 2.0 site system. For example, you could not define an SMS 2.0 logon point to be a helper server for an SMS 1.2 site server. Similarly, SMS 2.0 client access points (CAPs) cannot be installed on SMS 1.2 logon servers. However, SMS 1.2 and SMS 2.0 sites can share distribution points because there are no SMS components installed on those servers. Also, SMS 2.0 no longer supports servers running MIPS or LAN Manager. If you need to maintain these platforms, plan on keeping an SMS 1.2 site around to do so.

Perhaps the most important of these limitations is that SMS 1.2 and SMS 2.0 cannot share the same SQL Server database, although both sites can maintain separate SMS databases on the same SQL server.

Any SMS 1.2 servers within an SMS 2.0 site will themselves become SMS 2.0 clients, including the SMS 1.2 site server. For example, a distribution point can be shared by both an SMS 1.2 and SMS 2.0 site, but the distribution point will become a client to the SMS 2.0 site only.

SMS 1.2 site properties can be administered only through the SMS 1.2 Administrator window. The SMS 1.2 Administrator window cannot be installed on the same Windows NT workstation as the SMS 2.0 Administrator Console. This means that you will need to maintain a separate administrator's workstation to support the SMS 1.2 site.

> **Tip** The Add/Remove 1.2 Console tool (V12Admin.ipf) in the *Microsoft BackOffice 4.5 Resource Kit* allows the support of both the SMS 2.0 Administrator Console and the SMS 1.2 Administrator window on the same Windows NT workstation. This utility is described in the section "Systems Management Server 1.2 Administrator Window" later in this chapter.

SMS 1.2 supports intersite communications via Microsoft SNA servers using the SNA Sender. SMS 2.0 does not support this mode of communication. Instead, it supports SNA over RAS to connect these sites. If you need to maintain SNA connectivity, be sure to configure the site server to use SNA over RAS.

SMS 2.0 also does not support the concept of the helper server in the manner in which SMS 1.2 does. You must move SMS components from the helper servers back to the site server before you begin the upgrade process. If you do not, once the upgrade has been completed those helper servers will be "orphaned" and SMS components will have to be removed manually—a messy project.

Reviewing and Cleaning Up the Database

Although the actual SMS 2.0 upgrade process does a fairly good job of converting the SMS 1.2 database, performing whatever maintenance and cleanup tasks are necessary to make the database as error-free as possible before the upgrade is strongly recommended. Otherwise, you could run the risk of migrating "bad" data into the new site, and what's the point of doing that?

Reviewing the Database

Before you upgrade, you should perform the usual recommended SQL Server database maintenance tasks. As we saw in Chapter 18, Microsoft recommends the following database maintenance commands for consistency checks:

- **DBCC CHECKDB**   Verifies that index and data pages are correctly linked for each database table, indexes are in the proper sort order, pointers are consistent, and page information and offsets are reasonable

- **DBCC CHECKALLOC (DBCC NEWALLOC in SQL Server 6.5)**   Verifies that all data pages are appropriately allocated and used

- **DBCC CHECKCATALOG**   Verifies consistency in and between system tables

- **DBCC UPDATEUSAGE**   Reports on and corrects inaccuracies in the Sysindexes table that could result in incorrect space usage reports

For details about how to execute these commands using the SQL Server 6.5 ISQL/w graphical query interface, refer to Chapter 18. Also refer to your SQL Server documentation for complete information about these and other database maintenance commands.

Removing Duplicate Records

As mentioned, the upgrade process has been designed to deal positively with some database inconsistencies. For example, if the upgrade process encounters a duplicate data key that should be unique after conversion, it removes all instances of the duplicate key as well as any unused data keys to ensure consistency. The deleted data should be regenerated after the next inventory update cycle is performed.

If you suspect that your database is in poor shape—that it contains duplicate records—you should clean up those records before the upgrade. Figure 19-1 shows an example of duplicate records displayed in the SMS 1.2 Administrator window—in this case, the same computer name appears with different SMSIDs. Obviously, with a small database you can clean up these duplicates quickly simply by selecting the relevant records and pressing the Delete key. However, this task would be much more daunting in a database consisting of hundreds or thousands of records.

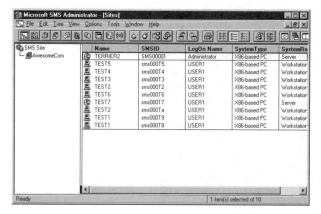

Figure 19-1. *Sample duplicate records displayed in the SMS 1.2 Administrator window.*

Fortunately, duplicate records can also be identified and removed using the SMS 1.2 database maintenance utility DBClean.exe. DBClean.exe should be in the \SMS\Site.Srv\X86.bin directory on the SMS 1.2 site server. If you don't find it there, look for it on the SMS 1.2 CD.

To use DBClean.exe to remove duplicate records, follow these steps:

1. Using the Windows Explorer, find DBClean.exe and double-click on it.
2. The SMS Database Manager SQL Login dialog box will appear, as shown in Figure 19-2. Enter the name of the SQL server on which the SMS database can be found, and enter the name of the SMS database. Provide the SQL login ID—usually the default, *sa*—as well as the password for that account.

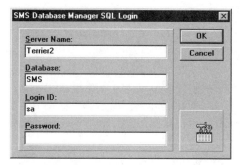

Figure 19-2. *The SMS Database Manager SQL Login dialog box.*

3. Click OK to display the SMS Database Manager window, shown in Figure 19-3.

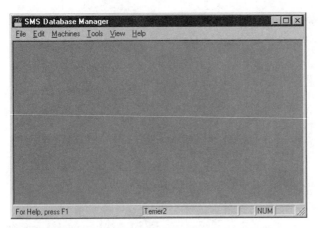

Figure 19-3. *The SMS Database Manager window.*

4. Choose Display Duplicate Personal Computers from the Machines menu to display the Duplicate Machines window, shown in Figure 19-4.

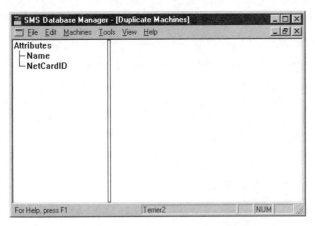

Figure 19-4. *The Duplicate Machines window.*

5. If the database contains duplicate records, the window will display the Attributes entries Name and NetCardID. Double-click on either to display the duplicate records by name or network card address, as shown in Figure 19-5.

6. Select a duplicate record name to display the actual records in the right pane, as shown in Figure 19-6. Each record will display the date and time of the last hardware scan, the computer's name, its SMSID, the site it belongs to, the Windows NT and SMS domains it is a member of, and its system role, such as *server* or *workstation*.

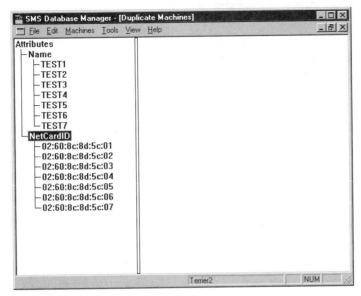

Figure 19-5. *Duplicate records listed by name or network card address.*

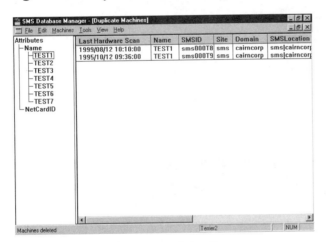

Figure 19-6. *Duplicate record details.*

7. To delete a record, select that record in the right pane and then choose
Delete Selected PCs from the Edit menu or press the Delete key. A mes-
sage box will appear asking you to confirm the deletion, as shown in
Figure 19-7. Click Yes.

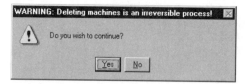

Figure 19-7. *Warning message that appears before you delete a record.*

 Note You may need to switch back from the SMS Database Manager window to the SMS 1.2 Administrator window to cross-reference the computers listed in Figure 19-6 by their SMSIDs to be sure you are deleting the appropriate records.

8. It may happen that the two records actually reference the same physical computer. In this case, you can choose to merge the two records to create a single "good" record instead of deleting the duplicate.

   To merge two records, select the records to be merged in the right pane by Ctrl-clicking on each, and choose Merge History For Selected PCs from the Edit menu. A message box will appear, asking you to confirm the merge, as shown in Figure 19-8. Click Yes.

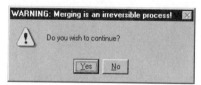

Figure 19-8. *Warning message that appears before you merge records.*

9. The duplicate records will now appear as one record, as shown in Figure 19-9.

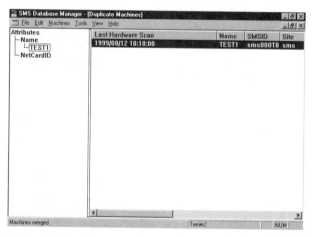

Figure 19-9. *The merged record.*

10. Repeat steps 6 though 9 for each duplicate entry, until all duplicate records have been dealt with. When you have finished, choose Refresh from the View menu to rescan the database. If all duplicate records have been removed, a message box will appear, as shown in Figure 19-10, notifying you that no duplicate records were found.

Figure 19-10. *Message box that appears when no duplicate records are found.*

11. Close the SMS Database Manager utility.

As shown in Figure 19-11, our SMS 1.2 Administrator window now contains only one entry for each computer, indicating that the duplicate entries have indeed been cleaned up.

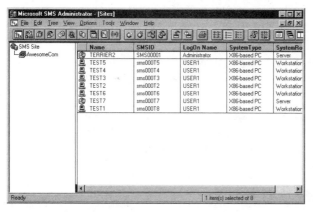

Figure 19-11. *The cleaned-up database shown in the SMS 1.2 Administrator window.*

> **Note**   The SMS Database Manager utility (DBClean.exe) can also remove collected files for computers that have been deleted, and it can group classes and unused common and specific records created through custom MIF files and associated with computers that no longer exist in the database. Deleting these elements should also be considered part of the cleanup process for the SMS database.

Removing Obsolete Records

To ensure that database conversion occurs quickly and efficiently, consider removing out-of-date records. For example, records that haven't been updated for 60 or 90 days could probably be eliminated from the database with little effect. If these records are still active, they will be added back to the database when they are discovered or inventoried by SMS 2.0.

To remove old records from the database in SMS 1.2, follow these steps:

1. In the SMS Administrator Sites window, choose Delete Special from the Edit menu to display the Delete Special dialog box, shown in Figure 19-12. This option is available only in the Sites, Jobs, and Events windows.

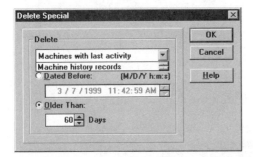

Figure 19-12. *The Delete Special dialog box.*

2. Select the criterion for deleting computer records from the drop-down list. Your choices are Machines With Last Activity or Machine History Records.

3. Select a specific cut-off date from the Dated Before drop-down list, or enter a specific number of days in the Older Than text box, and then click OK. A message box will appear, as shown in Figure 19-13, asking you to confirm the deletion. Click Yes.

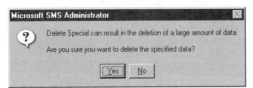

Figure 19-13. *Message box that appears before you delete a record.*

SMS will indicate the number of items deleted from the database, and the SMS Administrator Sites window will be refreshed, as shown in Figure 19-14.

Caution   Once again, it is imperative that you review the records you intend to delete to be sure that it is appropriate to do so. Otherwise, you may unintentionally lose data records.

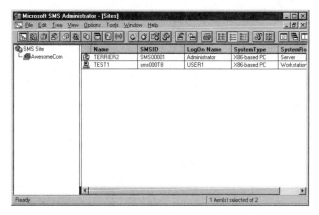

Figure 19-14. *The updated Sites window.*

Checking Database Size

Part of your database review should include a look at the current size of the database. Remember that SMS 2.0 will require about 100 KB to 200 KB per client to store discovery and inventory data, depending on how much inventory you choose to collect. You current database size may have been appropriate for the SMS 1.2 site server, but the database could be woefully undersized for use by SMS 2.0.

Use Chapter 2 as a guide to assist you in determining the appropriate database size. Modify the current database size to accommodate the larger amount of data collected. For example, if you will be supporting 1000 clients, the database size needs to be at least 1000 × 100 KB, or 100 MB. The transaction log also should be resized if necessary to be at least 10 percent of the database size. Using the same example, the transaction log should be at least 10 MB.

Additionally, the SQL Server tempdb database—used to support the database for queries, sorts, and other tasks—should be at least 20 percent of the database size, and its transaction log should be 20 percent of that. Using our sample database size of 100 MB, the tempdb database should be at least 20 MB (100 MB × 20%) and the tempdb transaction log should be at least 4 MB (20 MB × 20%).

To resize a database in SQL Server 6.5, follow these steps:

1. From the Microsoft SQL Server 6.5 program group, launch SQL Server Enterprise Manager.

2. Navigate to the Database Devices folder and expand it, as shown in Figure 19-15.

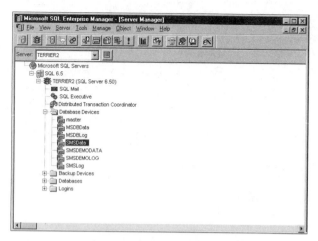

Figure 19-15. *The expanded Database Devices folder.*

3. Select the database device entry for your SMS database, right-click on it, and choose Edit from the context menu to display the Edit Database Device dialog box, shown in Figure 19-16. For this example, we will select SMSData.

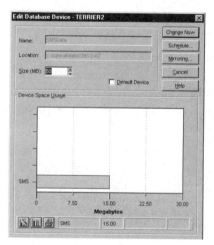

Figure 19-16. *The Edit Database Device dialog box.*

4. Increase the database size to a value appropriate for the upgrade, and then click Change Now.

5. Repeat steps 3 and 4 for the database log device.

6. In the Enterprise Manager, navigate to the Databases folder and expand it, as shown in Figure 19-17.

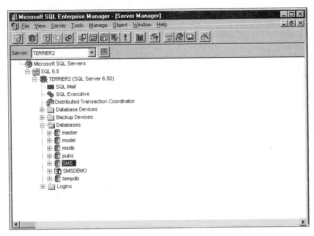

Figure 19-17. *The expanded Databases folder.*

7. Select the database entry for your SMS database, right-click on it, and choose Edit from the context menu to display the Edit Database Properties window, shown in Figure 19-18.

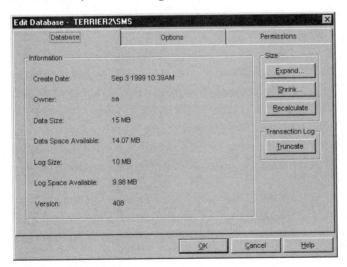

Figure 19-18. *The Edit Database Properties window.*

8. Click the Expand button to display the Expand Database dialog box, shown in Figure 19-19. Select the data device and log device you modified previously. The Size values represent the amount of free space available in the devices. Click Expand Now.

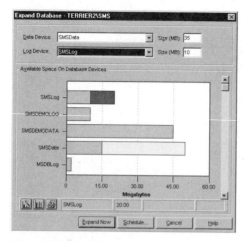

Figure 19-19. *The Expand Database dialog box.*

9. When the expansion process is complete, the Edit Database dialog box is displayed with the new data and log sizes reflected, as shown in Figure 19-20. Click OK.

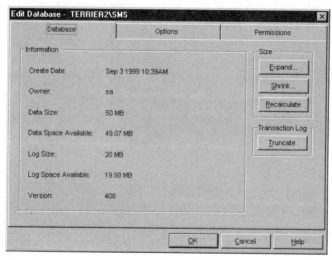

Figure 19-20. *The updated Edit Database Properties window.*

The review and cleanup tasks we've performed on the database are essential to the upgrade process. Refer to your SQL Server 6.5 documentation for complete information about the other options available for editing your database and its devices.

Documenting Current Site Settings

SMS 1.2 has fewer site properties than SMS 2.0. Most of these properties are static by nature and are handled quite differently than they are in SMS 2.0. Consequently, most SMS 1.2 site properties are not carried over to the new SMS 2.0 site. If you need to preserve any properties or settings, especially customized MIF files, queries, or security settings, document them prior to performing the upgrade or they will be lost. In this section, we'll look at some of the more significant items you should consider documenting prior to upgrade.

Machine Groups

The SMS 2.0 upgrade process converts existing SMS 1.2 machine groups to SMS 2.0 collections. The only real issue for you is to be sure that you haven't used any of the default collection names as machine group names, as these will be over-written with the SMS 2.0 default collection membership. The default collection names are listed here:

- *All Systems*
- *All Users*
- *All User Groups*
- *All Windows 3.1 Systems*
- *All Windows 95 Systems*
- *All Windows 98 Systems*
- *All Windows For Workgroups Systems*
- *All Windows NT Server Systems*
- *All Windows NT Systems*
- *All Windows NT 3.51 Workstation Systems*
- *All Windows NT 4.0 Workstation Systems*
- *All Windows NT Workstation Systems*

Queries

Because SMS 2.0 database objects are so different from SMS 1.2 database objects, any queries you created in SMS 1.2 will be discarded. If you want to be able to create similar queries for use with SMS 2.0, you will need to document each query before the upgrade.

Jobs

The upgrade process deletes all SMS 1.2 active jobs except system jobs. If you have created jobs that you want to maintain under SMS 2.0, including recurring jobs, be sure to document the job settings and targets so that you can create similar advertisements in SMS 2.0.

Custom MIF Files

Any custom MIF files you created on your own or any custom MIF files you created using the SMS 1.2 MIF Form Generator can also be used under SMS 2.0. The SMS 1.2 MIF Form Generator saves the custom MIF file with an .XNF extension. However, if you store these files in the \SMS directory structure, they will be overwritten when the directory is upgraded. If you want to keep these files, copy them to a directory other than \SMS.

Package Definition Files and Wrapper Programs

As with custom MIF files, package definition files (PDFs) and wrapper programs used to create packages under SMS 1.2 can be used in SMS 2.0. Here too, if you store these files in the \SMS directory structure, they will be overwritten when the directory is upgraded. If you want to keep these files, copy them to a directory other than \SMS.

Collected Files

Along the same lines, files collected through the SMS 1.2 software inventory collection process are stored in the \SMS directory structure. Consequently, these files will be overwritten when the new \SMS directory structure is created. If you need to retain copies of these files, copy them to a directory other than \SMS.

> **Tip** Consider discarding the old versions of these collected files and collecting new versions using the SMS 2.0 software inventory process. This will ensure that you have the newest copies of the files and that they are viewable through the SMS Administrator Console.

Logon Scripts

If you use the standard logon script files that come with SMS 1.2, there is really nothing to concern yourself with here. During the upgrade process, SMS 1.2 logon script files and user profiles are removed. When an SMS 2.0 logon discovery or logon installation method is enabled, the SMS 2.0 site server will automatically overwrite the old version of the logon script files with the new version of the script files. However, if you have created customized versions of these files, you should document the changes you made—and why—and make backup copies of the customized logon scripts so that you can re-create them in SMS 2.0 if necessary.

Security Settings

SMS 1.2 allows you to allocate security based on roles—for example, help desk, package administrator, and so on. These roles are tied to the SQL Server database security you set. As we've seen, SMS 2.0 handles database objects and their security in a decidedly different manner. In fact, SMS 2.0 object security is far more robust and granular than the object security provided through SMS 1.2.

If you want to create security levels in SMS 2.0 that are similar to those under SMS 1.2, be sure to document them carefully. You can then use object class and instance security through SMS 2.0 to re-create those security levels and enhance and improve them.

Physical Disk Inventory

All data regarding physical disks collected from SMS 1.2 client computers is discarded during the database upgrade process. A more current and complete inventory of the physical disk is generated during SMS 2.0's hardware inventory process. This data will then be added to the existing client record. However, this process can take time to complete. If you need access to physical disk data for your existing clients, consider running a report to document that information prior to upgrading.

Backing Up the Site and the Server

While not entirely necessary, especially if you like to live on the wild side, it is a good idea to back up your SMS 1.2 site, including not only the site database but also the SMS directory structure and registry keys. This backup can assist you mightily if you encounter problems with the upgrade and need to restore your site—as will all the other documentation procedures we've discussed.

In addition, consider creating or updating the emergency repair disk for the Windows NT server on which your site is installed. This disk will assist you in restoring registry keys and SMS services should you need to do so. After the upgrade is successfully completed, update the emergency repair disk again, as SMS 2.0 makes extensive changes to the registry, services, and components installed.

Tip   You should consider creating a lab environment in which you can test the database upgrade process—and recovery, if need be—outside of a production environment. This testing environment can help you to identify problem records, old settings that need to be documented, and other issues that can and will be unique to your installation.

Maintaining Mixed Sites
Within the Same Site Structure

The most pressing reason for maintaining an SMS 1.2 site as part of an SMS 2.0 site hierarchy is to enable you to manage those clients that are not supported by SMS 2.0—namely, MS-DOS, Apple Macintosh, and IBM OS/2 clients. SMS 2.0 certainly supports having SMS 1.2 site servers as part of the hierarchy.

Maintaining a friendly relationship between the sites, however, creates more work for you, the SMS administrator. For example, in a perfect network, the SMS 1.2 and SMS 2.0 sites would be separate and isolated, meaning that their boundaries would not overlap, they would not share servers, and most especially clients belonging to one site would *never* log on to a different SMS site. This separation would create more administrative work for you.

The most significant issue you may have to deal with occurs when clients log on to different sites. You want to be sure that you don't accidentally try to upgrade an SMS 1.2 client with SMS 2.0 client software when that would be inappropriate. In this section, we'll explore this and other interoperability issues.

SMS 2.0 supports the existence of SMS 1.2 primary and secondary sites. However, it deals with them slightly differently. Remember that SMS 1.2 sites can report to other SMS 1.2 sites or to SMS 2.0 sites but that SMS 2.0 sites can never report to SMS 1.2 sites. As mentioned, it is important that your SMS 2.0 migration strategy take this limitation into consideration. In general, a top-down upgrade approach, starting with the central site, will be the cleanest approach.

Applying Systems Management Server 1.2 Service Pack 4

It is imperative that any SMS 1.2 sites, primary or secondary, that will participate in a mixed SMS hierarchy have the SMS 1.2 Service Pack 4 applied. This service pack includes enhanced features that, among other things, improve the relationship between SMS 1.2 and SMS 2.0 sites.

One significant enhancement provided by the service pack affects the installation of SMS software on clients. Service Pack 4 upgrades the SMS 1.2 logon script files to include functionality that will determine whether a client computer executing the script has already been installed as an SMS 2.0 client. If a client computer has been installed, the script will essentially ignore that client computer. If a computer has not already been installed as an SMS 2.0 client, the script will proceed to install the SMS 1.2 client software on the computer. Later, the client could be upgraded to SMS 2.0 when one of the SMS 2.0 installation methods is employed.

A similar enhancement has been added to the SMS 1.2 site server. When the site server attempts to manage a domain or a list of servers, it wants to load its own client services—namely, Inventory Agent NT and Package Command Manager. If the client server is already an SMS 2.0 client, the functionality provided by these services is accomplished through other components. With Service Pack 4 applied, the SMS 1.2 site server can determine whether the server is already an SMS 2.0 client by noting the presence of the SMS Client Service, and if so, like the logon script update, the site server will effectively ignore the server.

The service pack also adds support for handling database updates to the parent SMS 2.0 site, as well as for reducing the number of duplicate data keys and other database inconsistencies that sometimes occur within the SMS 1.2 database.

The SMS 1.2 Service Pack 4 is available as a downloadable file from such sources as the Microsoft TechNet CD series or the Microsoft Developer's Network. It is a self-extracting executable file named SMS12SP4.exe. To apply the service pack to an existing SMS 1.2 site server, follow these steps:

1. Copy SMS12SP4.exe to a folder on your site server.

2. Double-click on the filename to extract the service pack files. The default target directory is generally C:\Temp. Place the files in a directory on a partition other than the partition in which SMS is installed.

3. Navigate to that folder and expand it.

Tip The Readme.txt file contains detailed information regarding the execution of the service pack. For example, Readme.txt contains the procedure for running the service pack from the same partition as that in which SMS is installed.

4. Double-click on Setup.exe to launch the Systems Management Server Setup program, shown in Figure 19-21.

5. Click Continue. A message box will appear, notifying you that an existing installation of SMS 1.2 was discovered, as shown in Figure 19-22. (This is a good thing.)

6. Click Continue to display the Installation Options screen, shown in Figure 19-23.

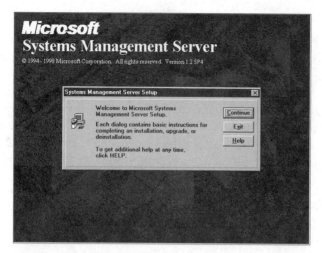

Figure 19-21. *The Systems Management Server Setup program welcome screen.*

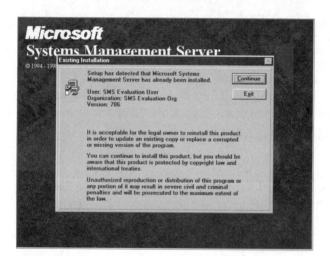

Figure 19-22. *A message box notifying you of an existing installation of SMS 1.2.*

7. Click the Operations button to display the Site Operations screen, shown in Figure 19-24.

8. Click Upgrade to begin the upgrade process. A progress bar dialog box will be displayed. You will notice SMS services stopping, files being copied, and services being restarted.

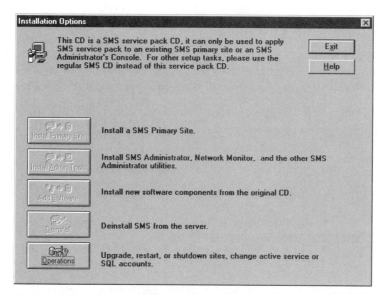

Figure 19-23. *The Installation Options screen.*

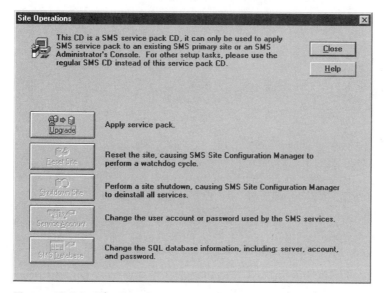

Figure 19-24. *The Site Operations screen.*

9. A message box will be displayed when the update process is complete.

Real World   **Distributing the Service Pack**

Updates such as applying a service pack to a site affect only the site itself. Changes will be propagated to the site's site systems (logon servers and so on), secondary sites, and clients. However, the changes will not propagate to other child sites.

To distribute the service pack update to all child sites, you can use the PDF SMS12SP4.pdf. The obvious strategy is to distribute the package from the central site.

To distribute the service pack upgrade, follow these general steps:

1. In the SMS Administrator window, switch to the Packages window, shown in Figure 19-25.

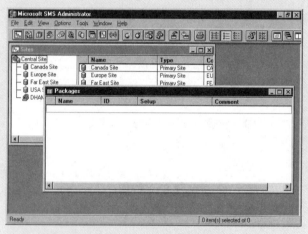

Figure 19-25. *The Packages window.*

2. Create a new package by choosing New from the File menu or by clicking the New button (the globe with a star) on the toolbar to display the Package Properties dialog box, shown in Figure 19-26.

3. Click the Import button to display the File Browser dialog box, shown in Figure 19-27, and navigate to the folder from which you extracted the service pack files.

4. In this case, locate the file SMS12SP4.pdf, select it, and then click OK. The Package Properties dialog box will be filled in with service pack information, shown in Figure 19-28.

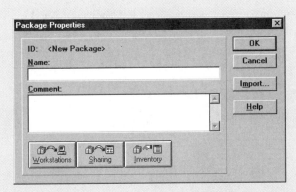

Figure 19-26. *The Package Properties dialog box.*

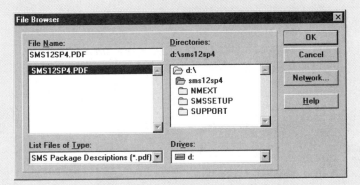

Figure 19-27. *The File Browser dialog box.*

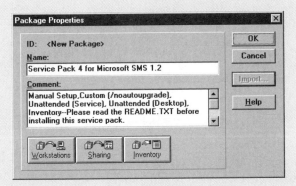

Figure 19-28. *The updated Package Properties dialog box.*

5. Click the Workstations button to display the Setup Package For Workstations dialog box, shown in Figure 19-29. Enter the name of the folder containing the service pack source files or click the Browse button to locate the folder.

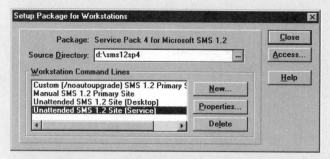

Figure 19-29. *The Setup Package For Workstations dialog box.*

6. If you want, select one of the command-line entries and click Properties to display the Command Line Properties dialog box, shown in Figure 19-30. Here you can familiarize yourself with the command that will be executed or modify the command if necessary.

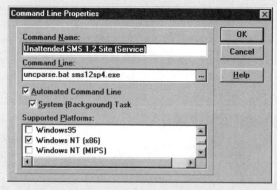

Figure 19-30. *The Command Line Properties dialog box.*

7. Click OK, and then click Close to save your changes.

You may see a message to the effect that the source file path may not be accessible to other SMS machines. Depending on the configuration of your site, you may need to refer to the source file path as a UNC path rather than a local path. You will need to test which path works within your environment.

8. Click OK in the Package Properties dialog box to update the package at all sites, and click OK again in the confirmation screen.

9. Switch to the Jobs window in the SMS Administrator window.

10. Create a new job by choosing New from the File menu or by clicking the New button on the toolbar to display the Job Properties dialog box, shown in Figure 19-31.

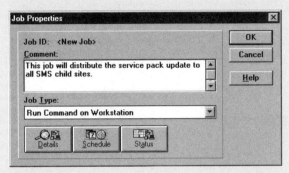

Figure 19-31. *The Job Properties dialog box.*

11. In the Job Properties dialog box, enter a descriptive comment for the job.

12. Click Details to display the Job Details dialog box, shown in Figure 19-32. Select the Service Pack 4 For Microsoft SMS package, and select the appropriate SMS site or site group to target. Verify that the Only If Not Previously Sent option has been selected and that both check boxes in the Distribute Phase section have been checked. This will ensure that the package is copied completely.

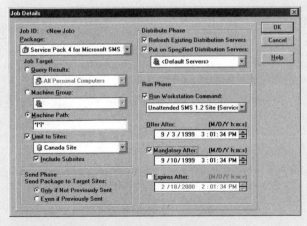

Figure 19-32. *The Job Details dialog box.*

13. In the Run Phase section, select the appropriate command to execute from the drop-down list. Refer to the service pack Readme.txt file for information about the use of each command. In this example, the command selected is Unattended SMS 1.2 Site (Service) Intended For SMS Site Servers Running Package Command Manager As A Service. If you have chosen an unattended installation, you should also make the job mandatory by checking Mandatory After and entering a date and time.

14. Click OK to return to the Job Properties dialog box, and then click the Schedule button to display the Job Schedule dialog box, shown in Figure 19-33. Modify the Start After, Priority, and Repeat entries if necessary. The only option you are likely to modify is Priority. Higher priority jobs will always be processed ahead of lower priority jobs. Click OK.

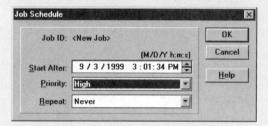

Figure 19-33. *The Job Schedule dialog box.*

15. Click OK again to save and schedule your job.

You can follow the status of the job by refreshing the Jobs window periodically and then double-clicking on the job entry and clicking the Status button. You will probably want to double-check each site server, or at least do a spot check, to verify that the site servers have been upgraded.

Database Support

If your migration strategy involves upgrading an existing SMS 1.2 site hierarchy to SMS 2.0 and you have taken all the necessary steps to ensure a clean transition as outlined earlier in this chapter, your databases should be up-to-date and all information should have been passed up through the hierarchy. Assuming a top-down upgrade approach, after the central site has been upgraded to SMS 2.0 its SMS 1.2 child sites will continue to forward delta MIF files from their databases that the central site will successfully process and add to the database. This procedure will be followed for each subsequent site level as well; it is also the cleanest approach.

You can attach an SMS 1.2 site to a new or an existing SMS 2.0 site, however, as may be appropriate in some organizations. In this scenario, the SMS 1.2 site will send a complete inventory of its database to the new SMS 2.0 parent site. The SMS 2.0 parent site is unable to process this data because of its different structure. In the preceding example, we started our upgrade with an existing database that included all child site records. Subsequent updates to those records are successfully processed. In this case, the child site records do not already exist; therefore, the parent site does not recognize them and discards the information.

The good news is that over time the SMS 1.2 child site will continue to send delta MIF files for its clients to the parent site. The parent site, having received a delta MIF file for a record it does not already have, will of course generate a resynchronization request that will pass to the child site, causing it to generate a new inventory for each client that is passed back up to the parent site and into the database. *Voilà!*

The bad news is that this process can take a good long time, especially if the inventory frequency set at the clients is long or if the clients are not logged on all the time. Also, the initial attempt by the SMS 1.2 site to send its complete inventory will almost certainly result in network congestion and performance stresses at both site servers.

SMS 1.2 Service Pack 4 makes available at the SMS 1.2 site a new registry key designed to suppress the replication of its database on the SMS 2.0 site. Because the SMS 2.0 parent site cannot process the complete database anyway, this key would be a good parameter to set. To do so, in the Windows NT Registry Editor navigate to the key HKEY_Local_Machine\Software\Microsoft\SMS\Components\ SMS_Hierarchy_Manager. Add the following entry as type REG_DWORD: *Don't Send DB To Parent Site*. Set the key's value to *1*, which enables it. The SMS 1.2 site will no longer forward its complete database to the SMS 2.0 parent site.

Now, if you understand and accept that inventory records for SMS 1.2 clients will not immediately pass but will instead eventually trickle into the SMS 2.0 database, just sit back and wait. Let's say that the inventory frequency for those clients is set to the default value of 7 days. You will wait on average at least 7 days for the inventory to be received and updated in the SMS 2.0 database because you are waiting for a resynchronization event to occur.

If you want to populate the SMS 2.0 database more quickly, you can delete all the .HMS and .SMH files stored in the SMS\Site.srv\Inventry.box\History directory on the SMS 1.2 site server. This will cause the Inventory Data Loader to treat each client inventory as a new record, thus forwarding a complete inventory for each client as a delta MIF file to the parent SMS 2.0 site. Again, the good news is that the inventory data will be forwarded more quickly. The bad news is that you are once again looking at potential network congestion as well as performance degradation on the SMS site servers and SQL servers involved.

Another option is to create an intermediary SMS 1.2 site for the sole purpose of collecting the target SMS 1.2 site's database inventory. This sleight of hand works as follows: Suppose you want SMS 1.2 site ABC to connect to SMS 2.0 site XYZ. Instead of directly attaching site ABC to site XYZ, you create an intermediary SMS 1.2 site named TMP and attach ABC to it. Since both are SMS 1.2 sites, site ABC can successfully forward its complete inventory to site TMP. After this transfer is accomplished, you upgrade site TMP to SMS 2.0, thus converting the database, and then attach site TMP to site XYZ. Because TMP and XYZ are now both SMS 2.0 sites, the database is forwarded successfully from TMP to XYZ. Later, you can attach site ABC to site XYZ (with the aforementioned registry key configured). Because XYZ will now include the records from site ABC, delta MIF files sent from ABC to XYZ will be received and processed successfully.

No matter how you look at it, a lot of planning and work is involved when you need to maintain the SMS 1.2 site and its database in a mixed-site hierarchy.

Client Support

Clients maintained by SMS 1.2 sites will continue to be maintained by those sites in a mixed-site environment with little difference. You will need to be able to access these sites through SMS 1.2 Administrator windows, as noted earlier. We will discuss some specific issues regarding the SMS Administrator window in the section "Systems Management Server 1.2 Administrator Window" later in this chapter. For now, let's look at three areas of concern for clients participating in a mixed-site environment: package distribution, Program Group Control (PGC) support, and logon contention.

Package Distribution

Obviously, the package distribution process has changed significantly from SMS 1.2 to SMS 2.0. For one thing, the concept of an SMS 1.2 "job" does not exist in SMS 2.0. In SMS 1.2, we target a package to a client by creating and scheduling a job. Once that job is completed, any new clients that need the package require the creation and scheduling of a new job.

As we've seen, SMS 2.0 begins with the creation of a package and a program. Programs are advertised to collections of clients (or users, or user groups). Any new collection member automatically receives all advertisements targeted to that collection. You cannot directly distribute a package from an SMS 2.0 site to an SMS 1.2 client. However, you can originate the package and job from the SMS 1.2 site if it is a primary site. Alternatively, you can advertise programs to SMS 1.2 child sites, which can in turn send these programs to target clients by means of a job.

For this technique to work, you must have created an address in the parent site (or sites) to every SMS 1.2 child site below the parent in the hierarchy to which you will be distributing programs. Then you must determine whether the program needs to be run as a Run Command On Workstation job at the SMS 1.2 site or as the alternative Share Package On Server job.

Making this distinction is actually quite easy, as the type of job you choose depends solely on how you are sharing the package files. If you choose to originate a Run Command On Workstation job from an SMS 2.0 site server, you begin by creating the package just as you normally would (see Chapter 12). In the Package Properties window, select the Data Access tab, and enable the Access Distribution Folder Through Common SMS Package Share option.

In SMS 1.2, the Run Command On Workstation job can be accessed only from the default SMSPKG*x* share. The Share Package On Server job, on the other hand, implies that the package is being copied to a specific share point on a server from which the client can access it using PGC. It should be no surprise, then, that the way to initiate a Share Package On Server job from an SMS 2.0 site is to create the package as you normally would and then, in the Package Properties window, switch to the Data Access tab, and enable the Enable Share Distribution Folder *share name* option, having created the share ahead of time.

Using either of these methods, you can distribute the programs to the SMS 1.2 child site. The child site treats the package accordingly, and it can then be targeted to the clients as usual through SMS 1.2 jobs.

Program Group Control

As long as we've mentioned the Share Package On Server job, we should also talk about PGC support. This feature does not change for SMS 1.2 clients managed by SMS 1.2 sites. However, when an SMS 1.2 client is upgraded, it loses PGC support since SMS 2.0 does not provide that feature on the client to share applications from a network server. You must determine ahead of time whether you need to continue providing this type of functionality to your users.

You can provide similar support for your SMS 2.0 clients. In general, you should consider creating the four elements on the following page when you are implementing PGC support.

- The shared application image that will be distributed to distribution points. As with SMS 1.2, creating this image may require an administrative or a network installation of the application first.

- A package script that creates a shortcut to the application on the user's desktop. This script takes the place of the PGC in SMS 1.2.

- A package script or setup program that copies appropriate client files, registry values, and so on that may be required on the client computer and that are usually accomplished through the application's normal client setup routine (sometimes referred to as a one-time setup). This program is usually referenced on the configuration command line for the SMS 1.2 Sharing package type.

- A package or script that can make any needed modifications to the application image on each distribution point, such as a client installation update file.

Tip Consider creating a new SMS 2.0 site rather than upgrading an existing SMS 1.2 site that is providing PGC functionality. Once the upgrade begins, PGC functionality will not be available to your users until you have configured it successfully through SMS 2.0. This could result in an inappropriate period of downtime for your clients. Instead, create a new SMS 2.0 site, configure similar functionality and test it, and then configure your site boundaries and installation methods to begin upgrading your SMS 1.2 clients. This way you can more seamlessly migrate the clients with little or no loss of application access.

Although the procedure will vary somewhat from application to application, here are the basic steps for configuring SMS 2.0 to support shared application functionality:

1. Distribute the installed application to the designated distribution points or shares.

Tip Remember that if the application is distributed to a specific share rather than to the default share, it can also be advertised to down-level SMS 1.2 sites as a Share Package On Server job.

2. Create a script using SMS Installer that creates a shortcut to the application, copies any files that are needed on the client computer, and modifies appropriate registry entries, .INI files, and so on. Use SMS Installer to create a PDF to facilitate the package creation process.

3. Create a collection that identifies clients that need this type of access to a shared application. To more closely simulate PGC, you might consider

creating a collection based on user or user group membership rather than computer resources.

4. Create a new package using the PDF you created in step 2, including all appropriate programs that install the client as necessary.

5. Test your package and programs before going to production.

6. Advertise the programs to the collection you created as a mandatory assignment that runs immediately.

7. Create and advertise any additional programs that may be required to update the applications themselves.

This procedure will provide your clients with basic functionality that mimics that provided by PGC. Refer to Chapter 5 in the SMS 2.0 Resource Guide for more detailed information regarding various types of shared application and client scenarios.

SMS 2.0 includes a PGC Migration Wizard, which can be effective in helping you migrate PGC applications already defined in an SMS 1.2 database that you are upgrading. This wizard provides both a simple migration for applications that do not require extensive modifications (or any modifications) at the client and a manual page-by-page method that enables you to identify more challenging items such as configuration command-line commands that need to be run on the client. Again, this wizard is explored thoroughly in the Microsoft Systems Management Server 2.0 Resource Guide (part of the *Microsoft BackOffice 4.5 Resource Kit*, available through Microsoft Press).

Logon Contention

If SMS 1.2 and SMS 2.0 sites participating in the same site structure rely on logon scripts for client discovery and installation, you need to determine whether clients from one site version would ever need to log on to a different site version. Logon contention issues can arise when SMS 1.2 clients that need to remain such have a need to periodically log on to SMS 2.0 sites and, conversely, when SMS 2.0 clients that need to remain such have a need to periodically log on to SMS 1.2 sites.

The latter case is easy to take care of, especially if you are not using a customized version of the SMSls.bat file. When you upgrade your SMS 1.2 sites with Service Pack 4, you will automatically update the SMS 1.2 logon script files to include a utility (Check20.exe) that checks for an installation of the SMS 2.0 client on a computer before executing the script.

If you have a customized SMSls.bat file, you will need to copy the SMS 2.0 client check files (SMSLS12a.bat, Check20.exe, and Checkver.exe) from the SMS 2.0

CD to the WINNT\System32\Repl\Export\Scripts directories of your SMS 1.2 logon servers. Then follow these steps to prevent contention among SMS 2.0 clients:

1. Using a text editor, in the customized SMSls.bat file, locate the following line:

```
if "OS%" == "Windows_NT" goto RUN_NT:Run_DOS
```

2. Add the following lines immediately after the line in step 1:

```
REM Call checkVer to verify that this is a supported OS for 2.0.
%0\..\checkVer
if errorlevel 1 goto RUN_DOS_2
REM Call the check20 to check whether this is a 2.0 client.
%0\..\check20
if errorlevel 1 goto RUN_DOS_2
REM This is an 2.0 client; skip processing.
goto RESTORE
:RUN_DOS_2
REM This is not an 2.0 client; process script.
```

3. Locate the line of code shown here:

```
:RUN_NT
```

4. Add these lines immediately after:

```
%0\..\check20 /v
if errorlevel 1 goto RUN_NT_2
goto RESTORE
:RUN_NT_2
```

In the case of SMS 1.2 clients logging onto SMS 2.0 sites, the process is a little more sneaky. It involves placing a "dummy" file somewhere on each SMS 1.2 client and then amending the SMS 2.0 SMSls.bat file to look for the existence of that file. If it finds the file, it essentially skips the logon script. To use this technique, follow these steps:

1. Create a dummy file containing a couple lines of descriptive text in a directory on each SMS 1.2 client. You can name the file whatever you like—in this example, our dummy file is named IAMSMS12.txt. A good place to store the file might be the C:\MS folder created on each of these clients.

> **Tip** Use SMS package distribution to copy this file to the same location on each SMS 1.2 client.

2. Modify the SMSls.bat file in the WINNT\System32\Repl\Import\Scripts folder on each SMS 2.0 logon point so that its first line reads as follows:

```
if exist C:\MS\IAMSMS12.txt goto END
```

For the special case in which SMS 1.2 and SMS 2.0 do share logon servers, as can happen if the two sites share the same Windows NT domain, you must configure the logon process so that computers with platforms not supported by SMS 2.0 are not installed with SMS 2.0 client software. SMS 2.0 provides an alternative logon point configuration file designed to list the files required by SMS 1.2 clients as well as SMS 2.0 clients. To use this configuration file, follow these steps:

1. In the \SMS\Data\NT_Logon folder on the site server, locate the file NT_Logon.pcf. This file contains a list of the files needed by SMS 2.0 clients only—the default case, in which no potential SMS 1.2 clients will be logging onto an SMS 2.0 logon server.

Note   In the case of NetWare logon points, follow the same procedure, but look for the folder and file names prefixed with "NW_" for NetWare bindery and "ND_" for NetWare NDS logon points.

---

2. Rename this file something like NT_Logon.old.
3. Locate the file NT_Logon_Interop.pcf and rename it NT_Logon.pcf. This file contains a list of the files required by both SMS 1.2 and SMS 2.0 clients. The site server will read this file and copy the files listed to all its logon points.

Caution   Be sure to turn off automatic updating of the logon script on the SMS 1.2 site that shares the logon points to prevent that site from accidentally overwriting the script files.

Systems Management Server 1.2 Administrator Window

As mentioned, running the SMS 1.2 Administrator window and the SMS 2.0 Administrator Console on the same Windows NT workstation is not supported. To maintain support for your SMS 1.2 sites, you will need to maintain a separate Windows NT workstation for each SMS Administrator window.

The *Microsoft BackOffice 4.5 Resource Kit* includes a utility designed to allow you to install both consoles on the same Windows NT workstation: the Add/Remove 1.2 Console tool (V12Admin.ipf). This tool is located in the \Resource Kit\SMS\ V12Admin folder after you install the *Microsoft BackOffice 4.5 Resource Kit*. The Add/Remove 1.2 Console tool enables you to add the SMS 1.2 Administrator window to (or remove it from) a computer already running the SMS 2.0 Administrator Console.

To install both an SMS 2.0 Administrator Console and an SMS 1.2 Administrator window on the same workstation, you must first remove the SMS 1.2 Administrator window from the workstation if it exists, then install the SMS 2.0 Administrator Console on the workstation, and then use the Add/Remove 1.2 Console tool to reinstall the SMS 1.2 Administrator window.

Those of you with a keen eye will recognize that the .IPF extension denotes an SMS Installer script file. In fact, you will need SMS Installer to create an executable file from this script to add the SMS 1.2 Administrator window to the workstation. You will also need the SMS 1.2 source files. To create an executable file, follow these steps:

1. Launch SMS Installer and open the V12Admin.ipf file, shown in Figure 19-34.

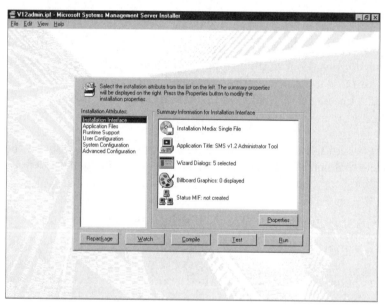

Figure 19-34. *The SMS Installer window with V12Admin.ipf open.*

2. In the Installation Expert window (the default), click the Compile button to start the Select Compile Settings program, shown in Figure 19-35. Enter the path to the SMSSetup source file folder.

3. Click Next to display the second screen of the Select Compile Settings program, shown in Figure 19-36, and select the platform type.

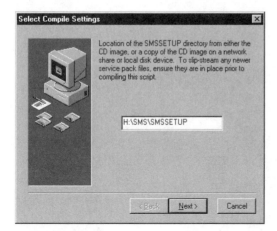

Figure 19-35. *The Select Compile Settings program.*

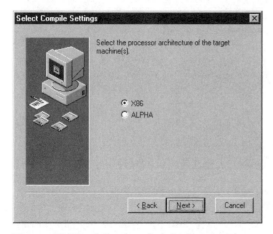

Figure 19-36. *Selecting the platform type.*

4. Click Next again. SMS Installer will proceed to create the compiled executable, which it will save in the same directory in which you stored the V12Admin.ipf file.

You can now use this executable to install the SMS 1.2 Administrator window on the Windows NT workstation computer. If you need to remove the SMS 1.2 Administrator window later, you can run the file using the /remove switch. Of course, you can also run the file in silent mode using the SMS Installer /s switch. The installation process creates a new program group named Systems Management Server v1.2 Tools. As shown in Figure 19-37, this program group includes the full range of SMS 1.2 tools required by the SMS administrator.

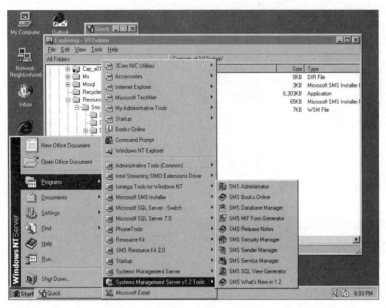

Figure 19-37. *The Systems Management Server v1.2 Tools program group.*

Upgrading to Systems Management Server 2.0

You are now ready to begin the upgrade process. Remember, a top-down upgrade is strongly recommended, as SMS 2.0 sites can report only to other SMS 2.0 sites and not to SMS 1.2 sites. In this section, we will begin with upgrading the primary site server and then explore upgrading secondary sites and SMS clients.

Object Migration

Let's begin by examining which elements of the SMS 1.2 site are migrated and which are not. Table 19-1 provides a list of these objects.

Many of these objects have been discussed earlier in this chapter, and some are listed on the premigration checklist. You might want to use Table 19-1 as a reference tool when planning your migration strategy.

Table 19-1.   SMS 1.2 object migration status

Object	Migrated?	Relationship to SMS 2.0
Alerts	No	Status messages and status message filters are used to write messages to the Windows NT Event log.
Collected Files	No	Collected files are deleted. Files must either be collected again through the software inventory feature or copied to a folder outside the SMS directory structure.
Custom Architectures	Yes	Custom architectures created under SMS 1.2—for example, through custom IDMIF files—are converted to SMS 2.0 objects.
Events	No	Status messages and status message filters are used to write messages to the Windows NT Event log.
Hardware Inventory	Yes	The Hardware Inventory Client Agent is used to collect more comprehensive data as well as physical disk data. Physical disk data should be documented prior to migration.
Software Inventory	No	The Software Inventory Client Agent is enabled through the SMS Administrator Console.
Jobs	No	Jobs, especially recurring jobs, are documented and then re-created as advertisements.
Machine Groups	Yes	Machine groups are converted to collections. (Names and membership should be documented prior to migration.)
MIF Files	No	MIF files on the site server are deleted; MIF files on the client are processed after the client upgrade. (MIF files should be saved in a folder outside the SMS directory structure if you intend to use them again.)
Packages	Yes	Packages are converted with the Compressed option enabled.
Programs	Yes	Package command lines are converted to programs; unattended command lines are converted as disabled.
Queries	No	Existing queries are documented and then re-created in the SMS Administrator Console.
Security Settings	No	Object security has been reengineered in SMS 2.0, SQL Server, and WMI. Object class and instance permissions are used to provide a more secure environment.
Site Groups	No	Site groups are not supported in SMS 2.0.
SMSID	Yes	SMS 2.0 preserves the unique identifier assigned to each client in the SMS 1.2 database.
SNA Sender	No	SMS 2.0 does not support the SMS 1.2 SNA Sender; instead, it supports an SNA RAS sender.
SQL Server Views	Yes	Views generated under SMS 1.2 are migrated; however, they are not required or used to access the data in the database. Any WBEM ODBC–compliant application, such as Crystal Info, can access the data directly.

Primary Site Upgrades

The site upgrade process for a primary site is fairly straightforward, providing you have prepared the server appropriately. Most notably, be sure that the server itself can support the resources required by SMS 2.0 and that the server has been made fully Y2K-compliant. Be sure that the version of SQL Server you are running has been updated with SQL Server 6.5 Service Pack 4 or later.

You will need to log onto the site server using an account that has administrative permissions for the SMS database as well as for the server itself. The account needs to be a member of the local Administrator group. You will also need access to the SMS 2.0 source files. For the purposes of this discussion, we will assume that you have access to SMS 2.0 source files that have been updated with SMS 2.0 Service Pack 1.

Log onto the site server and locate the SMS 2.0 source files that you will be using to upgrade the server. Then follow these steps to upgrade the primary site:

1. Locate the Autorun.exe file, and double-click on it. Choose Set Up SMS 2.0 from the Autorun menu to display the Systems Management Server Setup Wizard welcome screen, shown in Figure 19-38. (Alternatively, you can navigate to the \SMSSetup\Bin*platform* directory and run Setup.exe to launch the wizard.)

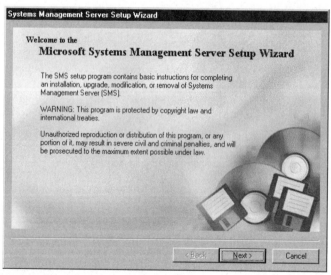

Figure 19-38. *The Systems Management Server Setup Wizard welcome screen.*

2. Click Next to display the System Configuration screen, shown in Figure 19-39, and verify that Setup has found the SMS 1.2 site. Read the screen text before you proceed with the upgrade.

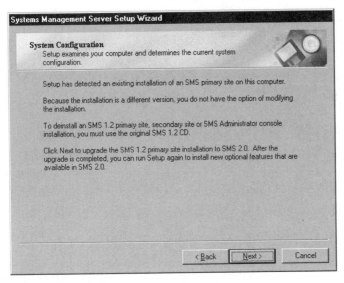

Figure 19-39. *The System Configuration screen.*

3. Click Next to display the Setup Options screen, shown in Figure 19-40. The only option available on this screen is Upgrade An Existing SMS Installation.

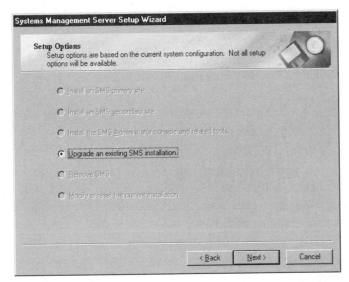

Figure 19-40. *The Setup Options screen.*

4. Click Next to display the Systems Management Server License Agreement screen, shown in Figure 19-41. After reading the license agreement, select I Agree (assuming that you do).

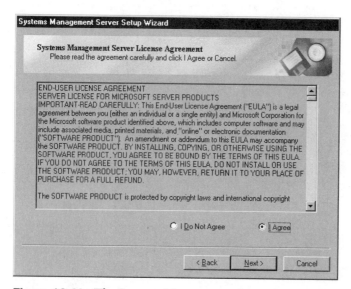

Figure 19-41. *The Systems Management Server License Agreement screen.*

5. If your installation of SQL Server is on a server other than the SMS site server, clicking Next will display the SMS Provider Information screen, shown in Figure 19-42. Select either the SMS Site Server or the SQL Server Computer option. The accompanying notes on this screen will help you decide where to place the SMS Provider. In general, for large sites with a large number of SMS administrators and because the SMS Provider's primary task is to access object data in the SMS database, you should place the SMS Provider where the database resides—on the SQL Server computer.

6. Click Next to display the Completing The Systems Management Server Setup Wizard screen, shown in Figure 19-43. Click Finish to begin the primary site upgrade process.

7. At this point, if this site has any child sites the setup process will remind you to upgrade these sites using a top-down approach, as discussed earlier. Keeping this in mind, if this site reports to an SMS 1.2 site, click Cancel to stop the migration process. Remember that SMS 2.0 sites cannot report to SMS 1.2 sites. Click Finish to continue.

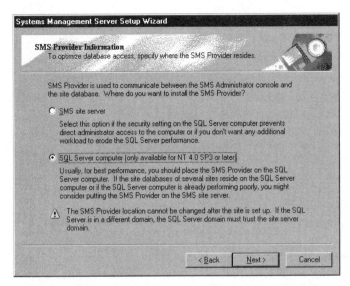

Figure 19-42. *The SMS Provider Information screen.*

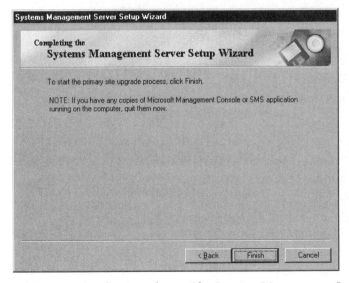

Figure 19-43. *The Completing The Systems Management Server Setup Wizard screen.*

8. One final wizard screen will be displayed, as shown in Figure 19-44. Click Start Database Conversion to launch the database conversion process. This is your last chance to back out of the upgrade—to do so, click Cancel.

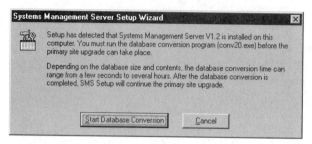

Figure 19-44. *Starting the database conversion process.*

9. A message box will appear, outlining the progress of the database conversion process, as shown in Figure 19-45. This same information can be found in the log file C:\Conv20.log.

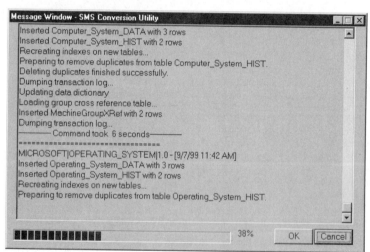

Figure 19-45. *A message box reporting on the progress of the database conversion.*

10. Finally, the old site is upgraded to SMS 2.0. Old elements are removed or upgraded, and new components and services are installed.

11. When the upgrade is complete, a message to that effect will be displayed on your screen. Click OK.

Since only a limited number of SMS 1.2 elements are upgraded to SMS 2.0, you will need to add the SMS 2.0 options and features you want to include in your new primary site. For example, you may want to add software metering or product compliance. You can add additional components to your site server the same way you would add components to a newly created SMS 2.0 site server (see Chapter 2). The basic procedure is outlined here:

1. From the SMS 2.0 source file location, launch the Systems Management Server Setup Wizard.

2. Click Next until you get to the Setup Options screen, shown in Figure 19-46. Select the Modify Or Reset The Current Installation option.

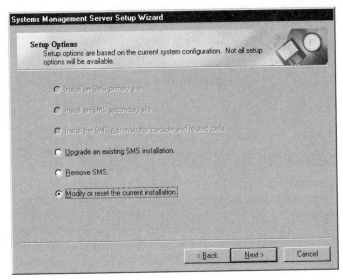

Figure 19-46. *The Setup Options screen of the Systems Management Server Setup Wizard.*

3. Click Next, and unless you need to install other platform support, click Next again to display the Setup Installation Options screen, shown in Figure 19-47. In the Options list, check the SMS 2.0 components you want to include in your SMS 2.0 site server.

4. Continue clicking Next, and if you do not need to make any changes to your SQL Server database information, such as switching to integrated security, simply accept the default values that appear on the remaining screens.

If you need to make changes, or if you chose to install the Software Metering tool, identify the SQL Server database names and account information as those screens are displayed to you.

5. Review your changes on the Completing The Systems Management Server Setup Wizard screen, shown in Figure 19-43, and then click Finish.

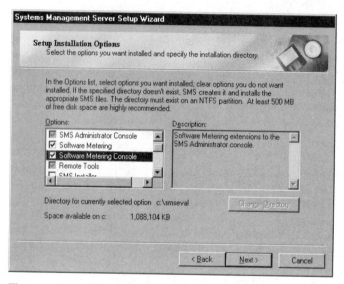

Figure 19-47. *The Setup Installations Options screen of the Systems Management Server Setup Wizard.*

Each new SMS 2.0 component is discussed in detail in a previous chapter of this book; refer to these earlier chapters for detailed information about specific SMS 2.0 features.

Site System Upgrades

SMS 2.0 introduces several new site system roles. As a matter of fact, the only SMS 1.2 site system that is not materially affected by the upgrade is the distribution server, because no SMS components or services are installed there either by SMS 1.2 or by SMS 2.0.

After a site has been upgraded to SMS 2.0, the Windows NT logon discovery and Windows NT logon installation methods are left disabled by default. When you choose to enable these methods, SMS will convert all domain controllers identified to the site to SMS 2.0 logon points. This means that any SMS 1.2 logon servers still identified as such will be overwritten. To review how to maintain both versions of the logon scripts in a mixed SMS 1.2 and SMS 2.0 environment, refer to the section "Logon Contention" earlier in this chapter. To add any other site systems to your new site, you would use the SMS Administrator Console. Refer to Chapter 3 to review this procedure.

Secondary Site Upgrades

Recall that once an SMS 1.2 secondary site's parent has been upgraded to SMS 2.0, its properties can no longer be modified. You must either make any needed changes prior to upgrading the parent or not upgrade the parent in the first place.

If you need to upgrade the secondary site, you can do so using one of the following techniques:

- Initiate the upgrade process wholly from the parent site. This procedure will take up some network bandwidth and is similar to creating a secondary site as outlined in Chapter 4—that is, you right-click on your primary site entry in the SMS Administrator Console, choose All Tasks from the context menu, and then choose Upgrade Secondary Sites to launch the Upgrade Secondary Site Wizard. This wizard is fairly self-explanatory; refer to the *Systems Management Server Administrator's Guide* for details.

- Initiate the upgrade process from the parent site, but place the source files locally at the secondary site to minimize network concerns.

- Upgrade locally at the secondary site server, using the SMS 2.0 source files and setup process. Again, this procedure is similar to that outlined in Chapter 4 for creating a new SMS 2.0 secondary site. It is almost identical to the primary site upgrade procedure discussed in the preceding section. In this case, however, there will be no database to convert, so the process should take less time.

Client Upgrades

SMS 1.2 clients will not be upgraded until you have enabled one of the following three client upgrade methods available through SMS 2.0:

- Windows Networking Logon Client Installation method
- Manual upgrade of the client by running the SMS Installation Wizard
- Windows NT Remote Client Installation method

The Windows Networking Logon Client Installation method is the most common method to enable. As discussed in Chapters 3 and 8, this method will enable the configuration of all domain controllers as SMS logon points for the site. If these domain controllers were previously SMS 1.2 logon servers, they will now be written with SMS 2.0 support files. Logon scripts will be upgraded automatically as well, and the next time the user logs on the upgraded script will also cause the SMS client to be upgraded.

> **Note** Remember that MS-DOS, Macintosh, and OS/2 clients are not supported under SMS 2.0.

If you choose not to enable Windows Networking Logon Client Installation, you could instead run the SMS Installation Wizard to manually upgrade each client or selected clients. This technique might be useful if you have a large mix of supported and nonsupported clients and want to be sure that only appropriate clients are upgraded. You will still have to configure a logon point for your site, but you would not have to enable SMS to update logon scripts. Connect to the SMSLogon share on a logon point, navigate to the X86.bin\00000409 folder, and run SMSMan.exe (or SMSMan16.exe for 16-bit Windows clients) to begin the upgrade process.

The Windows NT Remote Client Installation method can be used to push the SMS client out to computers running Windows NT. Chapter 8 outlines the client requirements and procedure for enabling this method. You specify whether to install the client on Windows NT workstations, servers, or domain controllers, and SMS essentially finds all those types of computers that reside within the site boundaries and begins the upgrade process.

> **Caution** This is an all-or-nothing option. The Windows NT Remote Client Installation method will find *all* the Windows NT computers of the type you selected within the site boundaries. As a result, you might find and install some computers running Windows NT that you did not intend to install at this time.

After the upgrade is complete, it is advisable to have the user restart the computer to ensure that all SMS components are upgraded and all agents are started. Some client agents, such as the Software Metering Client Agent and the Remote Tools Client Agent, will require a restart to fully enable their functionality. If for some reason a client component does not install correctly—for example, if when you are viewing the component status through the Systems Management applet in

Control Panel, the component displays a status of "Installation Pending" or "Failed" and a restart does not correct the problem—you should manually reinstall the client as described earlier in this section.

During the upgrade process, the old SMSID is preserved and used as the new SMSID for the new site. A new MS\SMS directory structure is created below the operating system directory, and the old MS\SMS directory structure is removed, along with all SMS 1.2 client programs and the old SMS.ini file. The exceptions are the IDMifs and NOIDMifs folders, which are moved to the new MS\SMS directory tree.

> **Tip** Since by default no client agents are enabled when you upgrade the SMS 1.2 site, you must enable and configure the SMS client agents through the SMS Administrator Console to install these components on the SMS clients during the upgrade. It is recommended that you do so prior to upgrading the clients so that as the clients are upgraded, they will not lose functionality.

Figures 19-48 and 19-49 demonstrate the extent to which an SMS 1.2 client's inventory is converted, as compared to inventory collected from an SMS 2.0 client. As you can see, the SMS 1.2 inventory is not as complete or as detailed as the SMS 2.0 inventory. Notice that physical disk information collected during the SMS 1.2 hardware inventory process is converted to logical disk information.

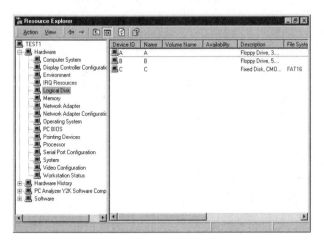

Figure 19-48. *Sample hardware inventory collected through SMS 1.2.*

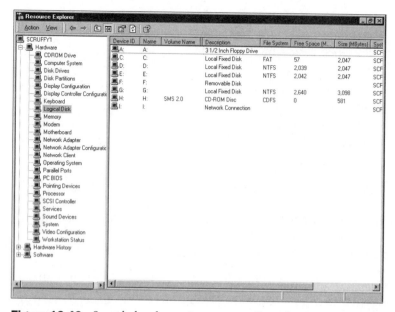

Figure 19-49. *Sample hardware inventory collected using SMS 2.0's Hardware Inventory Client Agent.*

By opening the collection containing the client, right-clicking on the client in the Details pane, and choosing Properties from the context menu, you can examine the properties of the upgraded client in the client's Properties window. Figures 19-50 and 19-51 show the Discovery Data list on the General tab of the client's Properties window. These properties will reflect the fact that the client was upgraded, the date and time of the conversion, and the client's IP information. As you can see in Figure 19-51, the client's initial domain membership and SMSID were retained.

> **Note** If you are using PGC and have not prepared for the migration of this functionality before upgrading your clients, the old PGC icons and groups will not be removed from the clients and will have to be removed manually. See the section "Program Group Control" earlier in this chapter for details.

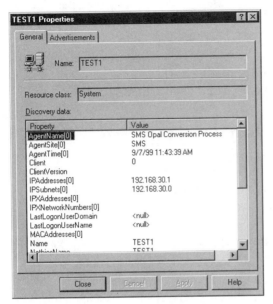

Figure 19-50. *The General tab of the Client Properties window, showing the first half of the Discovery Data list.*

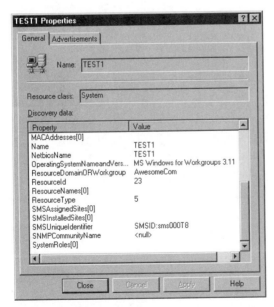

Figure 19-51. *The General tab of the Client Properties window, showing the second half of the Discovery Data list.*

Post-Upgrade Tasks

Just as this chapter began by outlining some of the more important premigration tasks that need to be considered before upgrading an SMS 1.2 site to SMS 2.0, it now ends with a checklist of post-upgrade tasks that you should consider performing as part of your overall migration strategy:

- **Revisit the converted database.** Perform consistency checks, back up the database, and test the restore process.

- **Configure site settings.** Configure site boundaries, enable and configure discovery methods, enable and configure client installation methods, enable and configure the client agents, and identify site systems and assign appropriate roles.

- **Check package and program configurations.** Consider changing the conversion default of using a compressed version of the package to Always Obtain Files From Source Directory If Applicable. Verify the source directory path, identify distribution points for the package, and confirm program settings and make any changes that are necessary, keeping in mind that unattended command lines are converted to "disabled" programs.

- **Create advertisements for your programs.** Rebuild any recurring advertisements using the documentation you gathered prior to the upgrade.

- **Confirm the membership of your collections created from converted machine groups.** Consider changing the membership rules from direct membership (or static, the default after conversion) to membership based on a query in order to make the collection more dynamic and useful. Create new collections as appropriate.

- **Re-create any queries you need for the new site.** Use the documentation you gathered prior to the upgrade to create the new queries.

- **Review your security needs.** Configure appropriate object class and instance security for the upgraded site.

As with the premigration checklist, this post-upgrade list represents the more significant items to consider. You can modify this list to suit your own needs and migration strategy.

Summary

Just as the implementation and installation of a new SMS 2.0 site requires more than a little thought and planning to be successful, in this chapter we've seen that at least as much thought and planning is necessary when migrating an existing SMS 1.2 site structure to SMS 2.0. Perhaps all your SMS 1.2 sites will be migrated. Perhaps circumstances will necessitate planning for and maintaining a mixed SMS 1.2 and SMS 2.0 environment. Whatever your needs may be, the more effort and thought you put into creating a migration strategy, the more successful and, perhaps even more important, the more uneventful your upgrade will be.

In the next and final chapter, we will look at how SMS 2.0 fits into a Windows 2000 environment and how SMS can be used to deploy Windows 2000.

Chapter 20

Microsoft Windows 2000 and Microsoft Systems Management Server 2.0

In this final chapter, we'll take a brief look at Microsoft Windows 2000 and how it relates to Microsoft Systems Management Server (SMS) 2.0. Specifically, we'll focus on a feature of Windows 2000 called IntelliMirror and see how it compares with and complements SMS 2.0 to provide a single desktop management solution for your organization. We'll also discuss how you can use SMS product compliance, inventory, and package distribution features to assist you in developing and implementing a deployment strategy for Windows 2000.

In Chapter 1, we recognized the challenge the information systems (IS) professional faces while trying to maintain a standard, well-supported computing environment within an organization. Perhaps the most formidable part of this challenge is change and configuration management, several aspects of which we have explored throughout this book using SMS 2.0's rich set of features.

Change and configuration management refers to the ability to quickly and easily diagnose, replace, or repair a computer; install and update software; and standardize the desktop—all tasks that SMS 2.0 can help with. It also refers to giving users a "follow me" technology—that is, enabling users to move from computer to computer and have their desktop settings, applications, and data files move with them. This latter piece of the management puzzle is specific to IntelliMirror technology and is the area in which SMS 2.0 and Windows 2000 can be highly complementary in their functionality.

Note This chapter is not intended to provide an exhaustive treatment of Windows 2000 and the use and implementation of IntelliMirror. Rather, it is designed to show how IntelliMirror and SMS 2.0 can work in a complementary fashion to provide an overall change and configuration management solution for your enterprise.

IntelliMirror and Systems Management Server 2.0

At first glance, some elements of IntelliMirror will probably look and feel a lot like SMS 2.0. IntelliMirror technology represents a robust set of Windows 2000 operating system features designed to facilitate desktop change and configuration management within a localized network environment. Its management focus is on user data, software installation and maintenance, user settings, and remote operating system installation. IntelliMirror is itself part of the Active Directory implementation of Windows 2000 and makes use of many Windows 2000 technologies, including Group Policy, Offline Folders, and Windows Installer.

Active Directory is the fully extensible and scalable directory service used by Windows 2000 to identify all resources on a network and make them available to users and applications. It is designed to make the physical location of a resource transparent to the user or application, thus providing a single point of logon for users and a single point of object administration.

The idea behind these powerful IntelliMirror features is to provide the Windows 2000 user with a consistent desktop environment that can follow the user from computer to computer. In this respect, rather than being an alternative to SMS 2.0, IntelliMirror is the next generation of system policy management and Microsoft's Zero Administration initiative for Windows. In this section, we'll look quickly at how these features work.

Group Policy

A key technology in implementing IntelliMirror features is the use of Group Policy to define various settings. *Group Policy* is a collection of desktop and registry configuration settings that can be applied to users and computers. Group policies allow the administrator to configure not only user settings such as which programs appear on the desktop and whether a user can access the Run option on the Start menu, but also computer-specific settings such as startup scripts, account policies, and service settings. Figure 20-1 shows an example of the Group Policy Microsoft Management Console (MMC) snap-in, with computer and user configuration options displayed.

Group policies are generally configured at the Windows 2000 site level, domain level, or organizational unit level and typically apply to objects identified within those levels. Each of the IntelliMirror features can be implemented through a Group Policy setting.

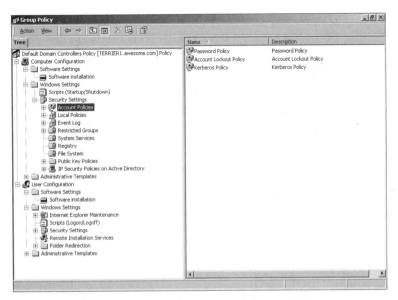

Figure 20-1. *An example configuration of Group Policy.*

User Data Management

The idea behind the user data management feature is to ensure that a user's data files are always accessible to the user regardless of whether the user has moved from one computer to another or even whether the user is logged onto the network. This accessibility is accomplished by mirroring data files to a designated network location, caching copies locally, and keeping the two versions synchronized. The My Briefcase tool, which was introduced in Microsoft Windows 95, provided similar functionality.

The user data management feature uses the following Windows 2000 technologies: Active Directory, Group Policy, Offline Folders, Synchronization Manager, and Folder Redirection. A user folder, such as My Documents, is redirected to a network server and configured for offline use. Whenever a user saves a file to the folder, it is actually saved on the network server and synchronized back to the locally cached version of the file. If for some reason the user is not connected to the network, the file can still be accessed because a copy has been saved locally. When a network connection is reestablished, Synchronization Manager synchronizes the local version with its network counterpart. This process remains mostly transparent to the user.

Figure 20-2 shows the property settings that make the My Documents folder available on line and off line. You can set up any other folder in a similar way.

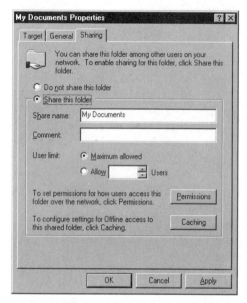

Figure 20-2. *The Sharing tab of the My Documents Properties window.*

In addition to the usual sharing permissions, you can also configure caching settings for offline access. To do so, click the Caching button on the Sharing tab of the My Documents Properties window to display the Caching Settings dialog box, shown in Figure 20-3.

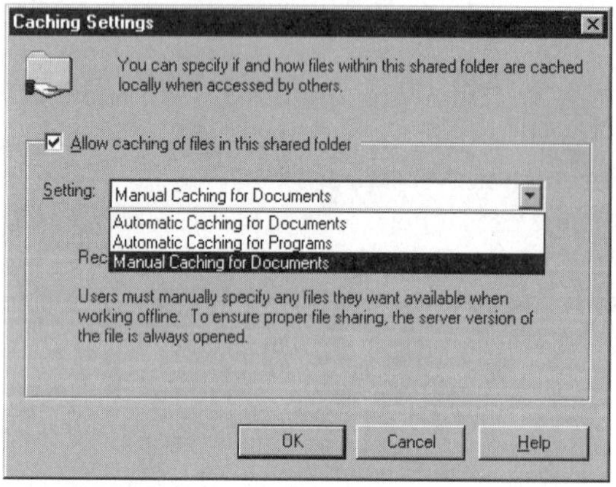

Figure 20-3. *The Caching Settings dialog box.*

The Caching Settings dialog box contains three caching options: Automatic Caching For Documents, Automatic Caching For Programs, and Manual Caching For Documents. Automatic Caching For Documents provides offline access to any file that a user opens when accessing the shared folder. Automatic Caching For Programs provides offline access to files that are read, referenced, or run but not changed in any way. This option also requires that you set the permissions on files in the shared folder to Read-Only for those users that will require offline access to them. Manual Caching For Documents provides offline access to only those files that are specifically identified by a user accessing the shared folder. Manual Caching For Documents is the default setting when a folder is configured to be used off line.

Using Group Policy, you can define a folder location so that the folder will be accessed by a Windows 2000 site, domain, or organizational unit. Figure 20-4 demonstrates that every domain user's My Documents folder is redirected to the same network share point: \\cairn1\public.

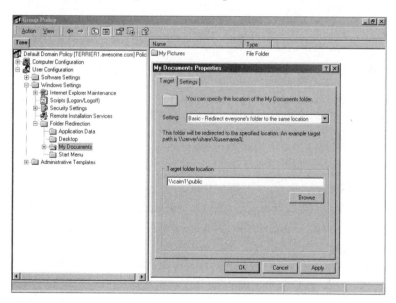

Figure 20-4. *Using the folder extension to Group Policy to redirect the My Documents folder.*

Windows Installer

Another key technology in implementing the IntelliMirror feature is the Windows Installer service. A Microsoft Installer (.MSI) package file defines the rules that govern the installation of the application. This file contains a relational database that stores all the instructions, files, and data needed to successfully install, uninstall, or repair an application. In this respect, the Microsoft Installer package file is similar to a package created using SMS Installer.

Unlike SMS Installer, however, Windows Installer runs as a Windows 2000 service on client computers. In addition to installing applications, Windows Installer can perform the following tasks:

- Restore the computer to its original state if the installation fails
- Reduce conflicts over shared resources between existing applications
- Reliably remove applications it has installed
- Repair and replace application files that are corrupt or missing
- Support on-demand installation of application subcomponents
- Support unattended installation of applications

Note   In order to use the Windows Installer feature to support a software application, the Windows Installer package files for that application must be obtained from the application's developer or manufacturer. The package files can also be created using Seagate's Veritas WinInstall program, which provides functionality similar to SMS Installer 2.0. SMS Installer 2.0, unfortunately, does not support the creation of .MSI files in its current release. At this writing, WinInstall is included on the Windows 2000 source file CD. Microsoft is developing an SMS Installer Step-Up utility that will migrate packages from SMS Installer format to Windows Installer format.

Software Installation and Maintenance

The software installation and maintenance feature is designed to make applications available to the user as a matter of policy, meaning that we can identify which applications need to be installed, upgraded, or removed from the user's desktop. This feature can be applied not only to users, but also to computers. It uses the following Windows 2000 technologies: Active Directory, Group Policy, and Windows Installer.

An application can be either assigned or published. When an application is assigned, a shortcut to the application is added to the Start menu on the user's desktop and the appropriate file associations are created in the registry. The application is fully installed the first time the user tries to open the application—or a file associated with the application. Through the Windows Installer service, all the files necessary to run the application are copied and installed from a source file location before the application is started. Similarly, if the application has already been installed but is missing some files, perhaps through user intervention, Windows Installer copies the missing files before starting the application, thus providing an automatic repair function for assigned applications.

When an application has been published, it is listed as an available program under Add/Remove Programs in Control Panel. Users can choose to install the application at their discretion. Also, if the user opens a document that requires a published application, the application will be installed at that time. Again, Windows Installer can perform an automatic repair if the application has been installed but has some files missing. Figure 20-5 shows an example of an application that has been published to all users in the domain through a group policy named *publishapps*.

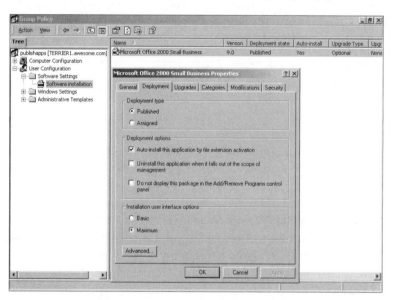

Figure 20-5. *Sample application published through a group policy.*

This sounds a lot like what SMS 2.0 can do, doesn't it? In fact, you can think of an assigned application as an SMS 2.0 program that has been advertised to run at a specified time and a published application as an SMS 2.0 program that has been advertised with no specific assigned schedule.

However, using the software installation and maintenance feature to deploy an application is highly specific and policy oriented. It represents a "just in time" type of deployment; you cannot schedule when you want the application to be deployed. It is really designed to facilitate the deployment of applications to users and computers as defined by their position in the Active Directory tree or their organizational unit membership.

Note All the IntelliMirror features discussed so far are specific to Windows 2000 systems and do not apply to computers running any other Windows operating system.

SMS 2.0, of course, supports not only Windows 2000 computers but also those running other Windows operating systems for the purpose of distributing packages. SMS 2.0 also provides you with more options for defining precisely how, when, and to whom an application is distributed.

Note SMS 2.0 does not support Windows 2000 Active Directory or Group Policy. Only Windows 2000 servers without Active Directory installed can be site servers.

User Settings

Like user data files, we can also configure user settings to follow users as they move from computer to computer. These settings might include the user's personal preferences, such as Internet Explorer favorites. They might also include administrative settings designed to lock down the system, such as hiding the Run command on the Start menu and configuring what icons the user can see through Control Panel. This user settings feature functions much like the Microsoft Windows NT 4.0 system profiles. It uses the following Windows 2000 technologies: Active Directory, Group Policy, and Roaming User Profiles. *Roaming user profiles* are those Windows NT or Windows 2000 user profiles that are stored on network servers so that the users can access their personal desktop settings from any machine on the network.

Figure 20-6 shows the list of configurable settings relating just to the Start menu and the taskbar with the Remove Run Menu From Start Menu option enabled. Again, this configuration is accomplished through the use of Group Policy and set as part of the User Configuration options.

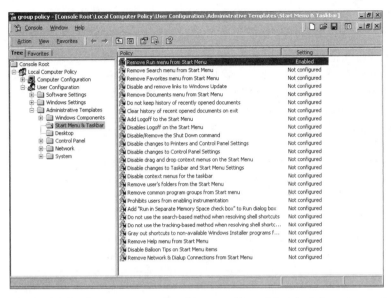

Figure 20-6. *Start menu and taskbar configurable administrative settings.*

Remote Operating System Installation

By loading and configuring DHCP and the Windows 2000 Remote Installation service, you can add the ability to install or rebuild Windows 2000 Professional on specified computers. During its initial boot sequence, the computer will request a service boot, allowing it to connect to a Windows 2000 Remote Installation server. The Remote Installation service checks Group Policy information to determine which configuration of Windows 2000 Professional should be installed on the client computer—for example, a laptop configuration or a desktop configuration.

As with the other IntelliMirror features, Active Directory and Group Policy are key technologies for the remote operating system installation feature. The client computer itself makes use of Preboot eXecution Environment (PXE) DHCP-based remote boot technology to initiate the service boot. Computers that conform to the PC98 hardware specification will support remote operating system installation. Computers whose hardware does not support remote operating system installation can still take advantage of this feature by using a remote boot disk that you can create.

Complementary Features in Systems Management Server 2.0

Whereas IntelliMirror technology is Windows 2000–based, relying specifically on Active Directory and the use of group policies to perform its tasks, SMS 2.0 is more enterprise-oriented, supporting a wider range of operating systems and providing the administrator with more flexibility and granularity in its configuration. As mentioned, IntelliMirror is designed to provide follow-me functionality for user or computer settings, including application deployment and repair. SMS 2.0 can also deploy applications—as well you know by now. As you also know, many more deployment options are available. For example, we can group users and computers into collections that can be dynamically updated, and we can specify when and where packages should be distributed and when and how programs should be run on the client computer.

SMS 2.0 also provides inventory collection and management tools, network monitoring tools, software metering functionality, and remote diagnostic utilities. Together, SMS 2.0 and IntelliMirror provide a complementary collection of system management features that neatly centralize user and computer resource management in the hands of the administrator.

Using Systems Management Server 2.0 to Deploy Windows 2000

In this section, we'll explore Windows 2000 deployment strategies using the features of SMS 2.0 that have been covered throughout this book. The process of rolling out and implementing Windows 2000 within your network is hardly a trivial operation; it can be just as complex as the development of an SMS hierarchy or the migration of an SMS 1.2 environment to SMS 2.0. A successful deployment of Windows 2000 requires planning, testing, and personnel. SMS 2.0 has the tools to assist you with this process. Let's take a look at how you can leverage your SMS 2.0 site hierarchy to smooth your rollout of Windows 2000.

As mentioned, deploying Windows 2000 on a large-scale basis requires a great deal of thought and planning. Your checklist of tasks should include the following items:

- Outlining your current and expected network infrastructure, including assessing network traffic and determining the site and domain structure

- Assessing hardware and software requirements, including identifying computers for hardware and software upgrades

- Defining organizational units, including locating users and computers
- Upgrading computers where appropriate, including upgrading servers to Windows 2000 and upgrading workstations to Windows 2000 Professional
- Monitoring status and generating documentation

As you can see, SMS 2.0 fits in well as a means to facilitate the planning process—in fact, it can be used quite effectively to accomplish most of the tasks listed here. For example, SMS 2.0 can help you gather information about network infrastructure, estimate hardware and software requirements, determine off-peak hours for performing the upgrade, and so on. In this section, we'll look at some of the ways SMS features can assist you as you develop an upgrade strategy for Windows 2000.

Outlining Network Infrastructure

The Network Discovery method in SMS 2.0 gathers information about network resources and infrastructure. This information will help you determine where your computers—and users—are located and how your network is subnetted, including the location of routers, hubs, switches, and so on. Combined with data gathered using a tool such as Network Monitor, this data can help pinpoint areas of potential concern in network traffic patterns.

The Network Trace utility can be used to develop a graphical picture of the network, including locating subnets and computers, as discussed in Chapter 6. Network Trace can show at a glance whether workstations and servers are accessible and through what routes.

Network Monitor can be used to determine traffic patterns and periods of peak usage. As with SMS sites, Microsoft recommends that Windows 2000 sites not extend across slow WAN links. Also, the Windows 2000 Active Directory requires the use of the TCP/IP protocol. Network Monitor can help you determine which computers may need to have TCP/IP installed.

You'll recall from Chapter 6 that SMS 2.0 adds experts and monitors to Network Monitor to aid in your analysis of network traffic. For example, the Top Users Expert identifies the senders and recipients of frames that generated the most traffic during the capture session. This information can help you identify potential network bottlenecks and periods of peak usage. The IP Router Monitor alerts you when a specified router fails to respond, helping you identify possible weak links in your infrastructure.

Used together, these tools can help you map out a Windows 2000 site and domain structure that conforms to your network's needs and activity. They may also point out the need to restructure your network so that implementation of Windows 2000 sites is made easier.

Assessing Hardware and Software Requirements

Computers running Windows 2000 require a 32-bit, Intel-based processor rated 166 MHz or higher or an Alpha-based processor rated 200 MHz or higher. Windows 2000 Professional requires at least 32 MB of RAM (64 MB recommended) and 300 MB of available disk space. Windows 2000 requires a minimum 64 MB of RAM (128 MB recommended) for domain controllers and at least 500 MB of available disk space. Similar requirements are made for client computers. The inventory process certainly provides the data you need to determine which computers can support Windows 2000 in their current configuration and which computers need to be upgraded.

You can use an SMS predefined query or create your own query to generate lists of clients that meet Windows 2000 hardware requirements, as well as identify those that do not. These clients can be grouped into collections, using SMS queries to keep the collections dynamically updated. Refer to Chapter 15 for a detailed discussion about creating queries. As clients are upgraded, they will automatically be placed into the appropriate collection to facilitate the rollout of Windows 2000 software.

The software inventory can help to identify computers running applications that may not be supported by Windows 2000, as well as servers that may require Windows NT service pack upgrades prior to installing Windows 2000. For example, Windows NT 3.51 requires that Service Pack 5 be applied, and Windows NT 4.0 requires Service Pack 4.

Windows 2000 does support some MS-DOS–based and 16-bit applications, but those really should be tested for compatibility before you upgrade them to Windows 2000. Software inventory can help target those computers as well. Through the use of queries and collections, computers requiring upgraded or replacement software can be easily targeted with packages and advertisements.

SMS queries can be an essential and helpful tool throughout the migration process. As we've seen, collections whose membership rules are based on queries are periodically reevaluated and updated. If you use SMS 2.0 to actually deploy and initiate the Windows 2000 upgrade, it would make sense to advertise the program to appropriately configured computers. A collection that weeds out inappropriate computers—those that do not meet the prerequisites for supporting

Windows 2000—would be ideal. This collection should be based on a query so that as computers are upgraded to meet the prerequisites, they can be added to the collection automatically, and as they are upgraded to Windows 2000, they are removed from the collection.

Figure 20-7 shows an example of one such query. This query looks for Windows NT computers that have Service Pack 4 applied, have at least 64 MB of RAM and a 166 MHz Pentium processor, and have at least 500 MB of disk space—the requirements for installing Windows 2000 on a server. The query will screen out any computer that does not meet these prerequisites, and it will remove the computer from the collection after the upgrade occurs. You can create other collections by creating variations on this query.

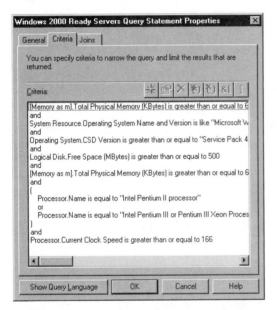

Figure 20-7. *Sample query to locate computers that meet Windows 2000 prerequisites.*

Defining Organizational Units

By enabling the Windows NT User Account Discovery and Windows NT User Group Discovery methods in SMS 2.0, you will be able to generate a list of all the users and domain groups in your network. This list, along with the information gathered using the Network Discovery method and hardware and software inventory, will make it possible for you to identify where your users are located and how they are organized. This data is essential in helping you define organizational units for your Windows 2000 Active Directory structure.

Through the intelligent use of collections to group your users, you can begin to identify which organizational units you need to create and then use the collection membership as a template for moving users into their appropriate organizational units. This same strategy can also be used for organizing client computers as you deploy Windows 2000 upgrades.

Upgrading Computers

One of the primary functions of SMS 2.0 is to distribute packages to targeted client computers. It is logical, then, to use that feature of SMS 2.0 to upgrade, remove, or install new software on potential Windows 2000 clients to make them compatible for the Windows 2000 upgrade. SMS Installer can be used to generate unattended installation scripts to get the software installed properly either before or after or even as part of the Windows 2000 upgrade process.

SMS 2.0 can also be used to initiate the actual upgrade to Windows 2000. Included with SMS 2.0 are program definition files for both Windows 2000 Professional and Windows 2000 Server. These files contain programs for manual and automated upgrades on both the Alpha and X86 platforms. Figure 20-8 shows a sample package created using the package definition file for Windows 2000 Professional. Notice that the program command line is specified for an automated upgrade on an X86 platform. You will need to supply the source files for the package, of course. For details about package distribution, refer to Chapter 12.

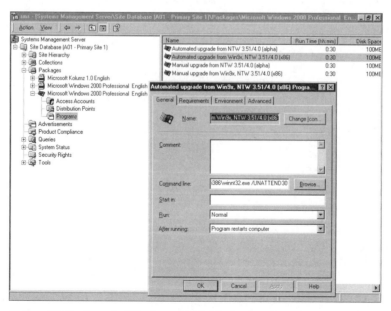

Figure 20-8. *Sample Windows 2000 Professional package.*

You will also need to identify appropriate distribution points for the Windows 2000 package. Given the size of this package, it would be appropriate to choose distribution points that are local to the computers that will be upgraded. Although package files are compressed before they are sent from one site to another, they are not compressed when they are copied to distribution points.

Also, although you can specify when and how often distribution points are refreshed, the package files are initially copied at the time you identify the distribution point. Therefore, you will want to perform the distribution point identification at a time when network traffic will be least affected.

You must also advertise the package program to the collections you created. Advertisements can be scheduled to be made available and to run at specified times. Using the data gathered through Network Monitor, you should schedule the upgrade to run at a time when network traffic will be least affected. If the target computers can select from several distribution points to initiate the upgrade, the server load will be more evenly distributed.

Monitoring Status and Generating Documentation

Through every step of the process outlined here, SMS components generate status messages and, if configured, log files. You can use the Status Message Viewer to monitor the status of the upgrade, watching the advertisement status messages in particular. Recall from Chapters 5 and 12 that status messages are generated for both package distribution and advertisements. You can identify easily which computers were upgraded and which were not, for whatever reason, and perform troubleshooting if necessary.

If you have enabled logging for your SMS site, you can use SMS Trace to view the progress of the upgrade through the log files written by the SMS components involved. For example, Distribution Manager writes its logging information to SMS\Logs\Distmgr.log. The information in the log file is generally more detailed and thread-oriented than status messages and can sometimes provide the extra detail needed to troubleshoot a problem.

Crystal Info can also be used to generate reports to help in the documentation process. In fact, as we discussed in Chapter 15, any reporting program that can access the SMS database through Web-Based Enterprise Management (WBEM) and ODBC can be used to generate supporting documentation for your upgrade.

Whatever your choice of tools, be sure to incorporate a documentation and reporting scheme into your overall upgrade strategy. As we've seen, SMS 2.0 can be helpful in providing system documentation for both the preupgrade and post-upgrade environments.

Leveraging Product Compliance

SMS 2.0 includes a product compliance database that was intended to be used with its inventory and package distribution component to create Y2K management solutions. You can use the compliance database to determine Y2K compliance among SMS client computers, or to determine other kinds of compliance for applications running in your organization.

In the previous section, we discussed the need to determine the Windows 2000 compatibility of the existing clients and software applications before you implement a Windows 2000 upgrade strategy. In this section, we will see how the product compliance feature of SMS 2.0 can be used to assist you in developing that strategy.

Customizing Product Compliance

You can customize the product compliance database by modifying existing entries or by adding new entries. Since you can use this database to test compliance of any kind within your organization, if you want to test applications for Windows 2000 compliance, you can modify or create your own product compliance database to include these products and their level of compliance. Furthermore, you can define your own method for upgrading and then use SMS to assist you in determining compliance.

To add new products to the product compliance database, follow these steps:

1. Navigate to the Product Compliance folder in the SMS Administrator Console, right-click on it, choose New from the context menu, and then choose Product Compliance to display the Product Compliance Properties window, shown in Figure 20-9.

2. On the General tab, enter the product data either by browsing for the .EXE file (whose header will contain most if not all of the required field information), selecting a product reported through software inventory from the Product Name drop-down list, or entering the information manually.

    If you choose a product from the Product Name list, some fields may be blank. You can either fill them in or leave them blank, as appropriate.

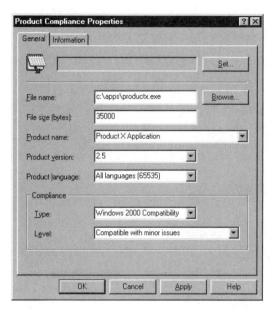

Figure 20-9. *The Product Compliance Properties window.*

Tip If you are entering the information in these fields manually, refer to the *Systems Management Server Administrator's Guide* for a complete description of each field, the data it should contain, its Windows Management Instrumentation (WMI) object name, and the type and length of the field value. Refer to this information also if you are importing product information from other sources.

3. Click the Set button to display the Set Display Name dialog box, where you can specify a friendly name that will be displayed when the product is viewed through the Product Compliance folder in the SMS Administrator Console. You can also specify version and revision information here, if desired. Click OK to return to the General tab of the Product Compliance Properties window.

4. In the Compliance section, select the compliance type from the drop-down list or enter a type of your own, such as *Windows 2000 Compatibility*. This field can contain a text string up to 30 characters long.

5. To specify the Windows 2000 Compatibility compliance type, enter a compliance level either by selecting one from the drop-down list or by entering a level of your own in the compliance level text box. For example, for Windows 2000 Compatibility you could enter one of these four levels: *Compatible, Not Compatible, Compatible With Minor*

Issues, or *Compatible With Major Issues*. This field can contain a text string up to a 40 characters long. Once you have entered your compliance type and levels, these settings will be available for any additional products you add to the product compliance database.

6. Click on the Information tab, shown in Figure 20-10, and either type in or select from the drop-down lists the appropriate entries for the company that developed the product, the languages supported, the platform the product runs on, and the data source from which the product information was obtained.

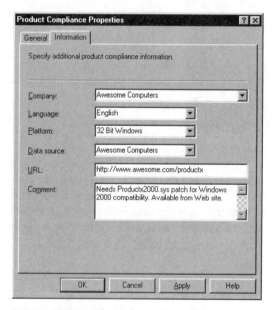

Figure 20-10. *The Information tab.*

7. Enter a URL to which the viewer can be directed to obtain more information about the product, such as compliance update files, as well as a descriptive comment that defines what needs to be updated, and perhaps how to do it. Both of these fields can contain text strings up to 255 characters long.

8. Click OK to add the product to the product compliance database.

Tip You can connect to the URL entered for the product by right-clicking on the product in the Product Compliance folder and choosing All Tasks, and then choosing Go To Web Page.

Existing entries can be modified in much the same fashion as described here. For example, you might want to modify the Comment or URL settings on the

Information tab to reflect company-specific information or the location of an intranet Web site where the update file has been stored for download.

> **More Info** For a detailed discussion about using SMS 2.0 and the product compliance database to determine Microsoft Windows 2000 compatibility among your SMS clients, refer to Chapter 8 of the document "Microsoft Windows 2000 Server Deployment and Planning Guide." This document is available from a variety of sources, including Microsoft TechNet and the *Microsoft Windows Server 2000 Resource Kit* at *http://www.microsoft.com/windows2000/library/resources/reskit*.

Exporting Data

The product compliance database can be exported to a file in Unicode format which can then be used in other applications for reporting or analysis purposes. The entire database can be exported, or you can filter what is exported by data source, compliance type, or both. To export the database, follow these steps:

1. Right-click on the Product Compliance folder in the SMS Administrator Console, choose All Tasks from the context menu, and then choose Export Product Compliance Data to display the Export Product Compliance Data dialog box, shown in Figure 20-11.

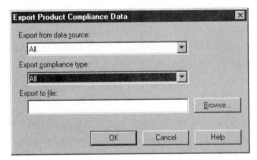

Figure 20-11. *The Export Product Compliance Data dialog box.*

2. Filter the export by selecting a particular data source and/or compliance type from their respective drop-down lists.

3. In the Export To File text box, enter the name of the file to export the data to, or click Browse to find and select an existing file.

4. Click OK to export the file.

> **Note** If you need to convert the file from Unicode format to ASCII, open and save the file using a text editor such as Microsoft Notepad.

Looking to the Future

It is important to remember that SMS 2.0 does not support Windows 2000 Active Directory or Group Policy. A Windows 2000 server with Active Directory installed cannot be installed as an SMS 2.0 site server—only Windows 2000 servers without Active Directory can be site servers. However, you can expect to see this and other functionality added in future releases of SMS. In the near future, it is reasonable to anticipate another service pack release that will continue to stabilize and enhance the current version of SMS 2.0. Several of the "gotchas" mentioned in this book may well be addressed through a future service pack.

Note Site servers that are installed on Windows 2000 servers do not support assigning site system roles to Novell NetWare NDS servers.

You can also expect at least two more versions of SMS to appear in the not-too-distant future. Since these versions are already under development, it would probably not be prudent to speculate on what they might contain in the way of feature sets or functionality; perhaps support for clients running non-Windows operating systems will be added.

Certainly as Windows Management Instrumentation (WMI) is refined, the list of SMS-manageable objects will grow. Research is underway within the microcomputer industry to develop WMI-aware computer systems. SMS could potentially take advantage of that to provide management functionality to the hardware level. We can be sure that current functionality will continue to be enhanced and that performance—already greatly improved over SMS 1.2—will continue to be enhanced as well.

Additionally, you can expect future versions of SMS to integrate more closely with Windows 2000, providing full support and synergy with IntelliMirror technology, including Active Directory and Group Policy. Microsoft is most definitely committed to this product, as this current version clearly demonstrates. Those of you who previously supported an SMS 1.2 environment can best appreciate this commitment.

Summary

As we've seen, Windows 2000 and SMS 2.0 both offer system management solutions for your enterprise network. IntelliMirror technology provides the means to leverage Active Directory and Group Policy to ensure that the user's desktop remains constant and available and that the user's settings and data are retained as the user moves from computer to computer. SMS 2.0 not only enables you to distribute software with more options and flexibility than IntelliMirror provides, but it also extends that functionality to Windows operating systems other than Windows 2000.

In addition, SMS 2.0 hosts many other features to provide a complete management solution for your organization, scaling to large enterprise networks that span the globe. Together, Windows 2000 and SMS 2.0 work in a complementary fashion to provide you with a complete strategy.

The product compliance feature of SMS 2.0 can be used with other SMS features to help you determine whether clients and applications are Windows 2000 compatible. For example, hardware inventory can be used to determine which clients may require hardware upgrades to support Windows 2000. Through software inventory and SMS 2.0 queries against the product compliance database, you can identify those applications that might not be compatible with Windows 2000 and that might require updates of some kind. Finally, you can use package distribution to send out and schedule these updates.

Microsoft has published several white papers dealing with the Windows 2000 upgrade process in general, and with integrating and leveraging SMS 2.0 functionality into the process in particular. One white paper of particular interest is "Planning, Deploying, and Managing Microsoft Windows 2000 with Systems Management Server 2.0." It can be found at Microsoft's SMS Web site (*http://www.microsoft.com/smsmgmt*). This document offers a viable blueprint for successfully implementing a Windows 2000 upgrade using existing SMS 2.0 technology, including a sample company upgrade. Combined with the information provided in this chapter, it will leave you well-prepared to design and implement your own Windows 2000 upgrade strategy.

Well, it seems we have come to the end of our exploration of SMS 2.0. This book has endeavored to provide you with a clearer understanding of SMS's many features and how to use them. Along with this understanding, you have hopefully developed a greater appreciation of the exceptional management potential this product can bring to your network environment. The inventory, package delivery, Remote Tools, and software metering features provide you with a complete management solution. Good luck as you embark on your own implementation and administration of SMS 2.0.

Part VI
Appendixes

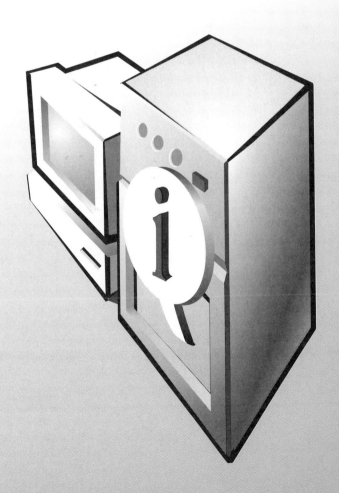

Appendix A
Backup Control File

This appendix presents the code for the backup control file (SMS\Inboxes\
SMSbkup.box\SMSbkup.ctl) used by the SMS Site Backup service when performing a site server backup scheduled through the Backup SMS Site Server database
maintenance task. This task can be enabled through the SMS Administrator Console and is discussed at length in Chapter 17.

```
# Backup Control File for automated site backup task
# Systems Management Server (SMS) version 2.0 with Service Pack 1
# Updated June 16, 1999

# Syntax help for customizing a backup control file is provided at
#  the end of this file.

# If the Site SQL Database is on a different server from the
#  Metering SQL database, remove the comments from:
#   -Any tasks that run against the METERING_DB_SERVER.
#  Also, enable the "Software Metering SQL Server" blocks in the
#  "*** SQL Data ***" and  "*** Registry Keys ***" subsections by
#  removing or commenting out their #stop and #start lines.

# Naming Conventions for Output Files:
# -----------------------------------
# Files created by "file" or "cmd" tasks are copies of original files,
#  and so and so their names are not modified.
# Files created by "reg", "sitedbdump", and "meteringdbdump" tasks
#  contain new data that requires new file names.
#
# "Config" files refer to configuration data that a task exports and saves in
#  the backup. There are 2 types of config data because a SQL server machine
#  can have both NT and SQL configuration data.
#
# The file names are built as follows:
#  -Prefix with "SMSbk" (to indicate file comes from an SMS backup.)
#  -Add the server type that the data is being backed up from:
#   "Site"  = site server,
```

(continued)

```
#    "Prov"  = site provider server,
#    "SQL"   = site SQL server,
#    "Meter" = software metering SQL server.
#  -Add the type of data the file contains:
#    "Reg"        = registry keys,
#    "DB"         = database dump,
#    "ConfigNT"   = NT configuration data,
#    "ConfigSQL" = SQL server configuration data.
#  -Add the actual data source. For example:
#    "master" = SQL server's master database
#    "NAL"     = NAL registry key
#  -Suffix with extension based on data type:
#    ".dat" = registry keys and database dumps (ie. raw data)
#    ".txt" = human readable data
#
# Samples:
#   The NAL registry key from the site server would be backed up to:
#    SMSbkSiteRegNAL.dat
#   The master database from the site SQL server would be backed up to:
#    SMSbkSQLDBmaster.dat
# ---------------------------------


[Tokens]

# Built in tokens and the values they contain:
# -------------------------------------------
#   SITE_CODE                    (3 character code for site)

#   SITE_SERVER                  (site server)
#   SITE_DB_SERVER               (site's SQL server)
#   METERING_DB_SERVER           (site's software metering SQL server)
#   PROVIDER_SERVER              (server hosting SMS provider)

#   SITE_SERVER_ROOT_DIR
#     (SMS installation's root directory on site server)
#   SITE_DB_SERVER_ROOT_DIR
#     (SQL Server installation's root directory on site's SQL server)
#   METERING_DB_SERVER_ROOT_DIR
#     (SQL Server installation's root directory on site's software
#      metering SQL server)

#   SITE_DB_NAME                 (site database name on site's SQL server)
#   METERING_DB_NAME
#     (software metering database name on site's software metering SQL server)
```

```
#  BACKUP_DEST_DIR
#  (value of "Export to" field from admin console's "Backup SMS
#    Site Server" property page)
#  -------------------------------------------


# The default destination directories allow multiple sites to share the
#  same export location.
# Destination subdirectories and their default locations:
#  --------------------------------------------------------
#  SITE_SERVER_DEST         %BACKUP_DEST_DIR%\%SITE_CODE%\SiteServer\
#  SITE_DB_SERVER_DEST      %BACKUP_DEST_DIR%\%SITE_CODE%\SiteDBServer\
#  METERING_DB_SERVER_DEST  %BACKUP_DEST_DIR%\%SITE_CODE%\MeteringDBServer\
#  PROVIDER_SERVER_DEST     %BACKUP_DEST_DIR%\%SITE_CODE%\ProviderServer\
#  --------------------------------------------------------

# These lines set the default user defined tokens:

BACKUP_DESTINATION=%BACKUP_DEST_DIR%\%SITE_CODE%

SITE_SERVER_DEST=%BACKUP_DESTINATION%\SiteServer
SITE_DB_SERVER_DEST=%BACKUP_DESTINATION%\SiteDBServer
METERING_DB_SERVER_DEST=%BACKUP_DESTINATION%\MeteringDBServer
PROVIDER_SERVER_DEST=%BACKUP_DESTINATION%\ProviderServer



[Stop]

# If the site being backed up was not installed with the express setup
#  option, some of the following services might not be installed. To avoid
#  spurious errors, comment out any services that are not installed on
#  the site.


service      \\%SITE_SERVER%\SMS_SITE_COMPONENT_MANAGER
service      \\%SITE_SERVER%\SMS_EXECUTIVE
service      \\%SITE_DB_SERVER%\SMS_SQL_MONITOR

service      `\\%SITE_SERVER%\Info APS`
service      `\\%SITE_SERVER%\Info Agent`
service      `\\%SITE_SERVER%\Info Sentinel`

# SMS services that are not being stopped because they don't interfere with
#  backup include "SMS_LICENSE_SERVER" and "SMS_NT_LOGON_DISCOVERY_AGENT".
#  They should be left running to support clients while the site is being
#  backed up.
```

(continued)

```
# The SMS Remote Control service provides a backdoor to troubleshoot
#  problems, and doesn't interfere with backup. It is safer to leave it
#  running.

# WMI (the Windows Management service) can be used by non-SMS processes, and
#  doesn't interfere with backup. To avoid interrupting operations, it is
#  better to leave it running.

# Stopping or starting the SMS client is NOT recommended in the current
#  release. Please refer to a KB article for more information.
#  service   `SMS Client Service`
#  clientapp  launch32.exe
#  clientapp  SMSMon32.exe
#  clientapp  SMSAPM32.exe

# Pause to let all writes be flushed to disk.
sleep 30




[Tasks]

# Clean out the destination directory to so old files don't get mixed up with
#  the new backup.
cmd   `RMDIR /S /Q %BACKUP_DESTINATION%\`


# *** Files ***
# ------------
# Backup is assumed to be running on the site server, and so will be backing
#  up local site server files.

# Backing up the SMS client is NOT recommended in the current release. Please
#  refer to a KB article for more information.
# file  %SystemRoot%\MS\SMS           %SITE_SERVER_DEST%\SMSClient\
file  %SystemRoot%\system32\WBEM   %SITE_SERVER_DEST%\WBEM\
file  %SITE_SERVER_ROOT_DIR%       %SITE_SERVER_DEST%\SMSServer\
# ------------


# *** Server Data ***
# ------------------
# Requirements:
#  -MACHINFO.BAT must be in SMSBKUP.EXE's (SMS_SITE_BACKUP) startup location.
#  -NT Resource Kit Tools must be in the path or in SMSBKUP.EXE's startup
#     location. The required tools are: NLTEST.EXE, NOW.EXE, SRVINFO.EXE,
#     and TLIST.EXE.
```

```
#  -WINMSD.EXE ships with the operating system and is used by MACHINFO.BAT.
#  -SMS_SITE_BACKUP runs with the site service account, which has
#    administrative rights on the site server. It also needs to have
#    administrative rights on the target server(s), and to be able to write
#    files to the destination location.

cmd   ECHO  %SITE_SERVER_DEST%\
cmd   `MACHINFO.BAT  %SITE_SERVER%          %SITE_SERVER_DEST%\➥
      SMSbkSiteConfigNT`

cmd   ECHO  %SITE_DB_SERVER_DEST%\
cmd   `MACHINFO.BAT  %SITE_DB_SERVER%       %SITE_DB_SERVER_DEST%\➥
      SMSbkSQLConfigNT`

cmd   ECHO  %METERING_DB_SERVER_DEST%\
# cmd  `MACHINFO.BAT  %METERING_DB_SERVER%  %METERING_DB_SERVER_DEST%\➥
       SMSbkMeterConfigNT`
# ------------------


# *** Registry Keys ***
# --------------------
# If the site being backed up was not installed with the express setup
#  option, some of the following registry keys might not be installed.
#  To avoid spurious errors, comment out any registry keys that are not
#  installed on the site.

# Site Server
reg   \\%SITE_SERVER%\HKEY_LOCAL_MACHINE\Software\Microsoft\MMC➥
                      %SITE_SERVER_DEST%\SMSbkSiteRegMMC.dat
reg   \\%SITE_SERVER%\HKEY_LOCAL_MACHINE\Software\Microsoft\NAL➥
                      %SITE_SERVER_DEST%\SMSbkSiteRegNAL.dat
reg   `\\%SITE_SERVER%\HKEY_LOCAL_MACHINE\Software\Microsoft\Network ➥
        Monitor`     %SITE_SERVER_DEST%\SMSbkSiteRegNetworkMonitor.dat
reg   \\%SITE_SERVER%\HKEY_LOCAL_MACHINE\Software\Microsoft\SMS➥
                      %SITE_SERVER_DEST%\SMSbkSiteRegSMS.dat
reg   \\%SITE_SERVER%\HKEY_LOCAL_MACHINE\Software\Microsoft\SNMP_EVENTS➥
                      %SITE_SERVER_DEST%\SMSbkSiteRegSNMPEvents.dat
reg   \\%SITE_SERVER%\HKEY_LOCAL_MACHINE\Software\Microsoft\WBEM➥
                      %SITE_SERVER_DEST%\SMSbkSiteRegWBEM.dat
reg   `\\%SITE_SERVER%\HKEY_LOCAL_MACHINE\SOFTWARE\Seagate Software\➥
        Crystal Info` %SITE_SERVER_DEST%\SMSbkSiteRegCryInfo.dat
reg   `\\%SITE_SERVER%\HKEY_LOCAL_MACHINE\SOFTWARE\Seagate Software\➥
        Crystal MMC SnapIn`   %SITE_SERVER_DEST%\SMSbkSiteRegCryMMC.dat
reg   `\\%SITE_SERVER%\HKEY_LOCAL_MACHINE\SOFTWARE\Seagate Software\➥
        Seagate Crystal Info for SMS`➥
                      %SITE_SERVER_DEST%\SMSbkSiteRegCryForSMS.dat
```

(continued)

```
# Site SQL Server
reg    \\%SITE_DB_SERVER%\HKEY_LOCAL_MACHINE\Software\Microsoft\MSSQLServer↵
                    %SITE_DB_SERVER_DEST%\SMSbkSQLRegMSSQLServer.dat
reg    \\%SITE_DB_SERVER%\HKEY_LOCAL_MACHINE\Software\Microsoft\NAL↵
                    %SITE_DB_SERVER_DEST%\SMSbkSQLRegNAL.dat
reg    \\%SITE_DB_SERVER%\HKEY_LOCAL_MACHINE\Software\Microsoft\SMS↵
                    %SITE_DB_SERVER_DEST%\SMSbkSQLRegSMS.dat
reg    \\%SITE_DB_SERVER%\HKEY_LOCAL_MACHINE\Software\Microsoft\SNMP_EVENTS↵
                    %SITE_DB_SERVER_DEST%\SMSbkSQLRegSNMPEvents.dat
reg    \\%SITE_DB_SERVER%\HKEY_LOCAL_MACHINE\Software\Microsoft\WBEM↵
                    %SITE_DB_SERVER_DEST%\SMSbkSQLRegWBEM.dat

# Software Metering SQL Server
#stop
reg    \\%METERING_DB_SERVER%\HKEY_LOCAL_MACHINE\Software\Microsoft\↵
        MSSQLServer    %METERING_DB_SERVER_DEST%\SMSbkMeterRegMSSQLServer.dat
reg    \\%METERING_DB_SERVER%\HKEY_LOCAL_MACHINE\Software\Microsoft\NAL↵
                    %METERING_DB_SERVER_DEST%\SMSbkMeterRegNAL.dat
reg    \\%METERING_DB_SERVER%\HKEY_LOCAL_MACHINE\Software\Microsoft\SMS↵
                    %METERING_DB_SERVER_DEST%\SMSbkMeterRegSMS.dat
reg    \\%METERING_DB_SERVER%\HKEY_LOCAL_MACHINE\Software\Microsoft\↵
        SNMP_EVENTS    %METERING_DB_SERVER_DEST%\SMSbkMeterRegSNMPEvents.dat
reg    \\%METERING_DB_SERVER%\HKEY_LOCAL_MACHINE\Software\Microsoft\WBEM↵
                    %METERING_DB_SERVER_DEST%\SMSbkMeterRegWBEM.dat
#start

# Presently, the Provider Server is either the Site or Site SQL Server. This
#  registry key has therefore already been backed up. Backing it up again
#  here helps ensure future compatibility.
reg    \\%PROVIDER_SERVER%\HKEY_LOCAL_MACHINE\Software\Microsoft\SMS↵
                    %PROVIDER_SERVER_DEST%\SMSbkProvRegSMS.dat
# --------------------


# *** SQL Data ***
# ----------------
# Requirements:
#  -SMSSQLINFO.BAT and the SQL script SMSSQLINFO.SQL must be in SMSBKUP.EXE's
#   (SMS_SITE_BACKUP) start location.
#  -The SQL utility ISQL.EXE must be in the path or in SMSBKUP.EXE's
#   start location.
#  -SMS_SITE_BACKUP runs with the site service account which has administrative
#   rights on the site server. This account must also have administrative
#   rights on the target server(s) and database(s), and write access to
#   the destination location.
```

```
# Consider running the following before backup to reduce the risk of a
#   corrupted backup:
#      DBCC CHECKDB
#      DBCC CHECKCATALOG
#      DBCC NEWALLOC (6.5 only)
#      DBCC TEXTALLOC (6.5 only)


# Site SQL Server
cmd  `SMSSQLINFO.BAT    %SITE_DB_SERVER%  %SITE_DB_NAME%➡
                        %SITE_DB_SERVER_DEST%\  SMSbkSQLConfigSQL`

sitedbdump   master               %SITE_DB_SERVER_DEST%\SMSbkSQLDBmaster.dat
sitedbdump   msdb                 %SITE_DB_SERVER_DEST%\SMSbkSQLDBmsdb.dat
sitedbdump   model                %SITE_DB_SERVER_DEST%\SMSbkSQLDBmodel.dat
sitedbdump   %SITE_DB_NAME%  %SITE_DB_SERVER_DEST%\SMSbkSQLDBsite.dat


# Software Metering SQL Server
# Always dump metering database if metering is installed.
meteringdbdump  %METERING_DB_NAME%➡
                %METERING_DB_SERVER_DEST%\SMSbkMeterDBmeter.dat

# By default, the metering database is installed on the site SQL server. In
#  that case, all the SQL configuration information has already been
#  collected.If the metering database is on a separate SQL server, enable
#  the following block.
#stop
cmd  `SMSSQLINFO.BAT    %METERING_DB_SERVER%  %METERING_DB_NAME%➡
                        %METERING_DB_SERVER_DEST%\  SMSbkMeterConfigSQL`

meteringdbdump   master   %METERING_DB_SERVER_DEST%\SMSbkMeterDBmaster.dat
meteringdbdump   msdb     %METERING_DB_SERVER_DEST%\SMSbkMeterDBmsdb.dat
meteringdbdump   model    %METERING_DB_SERVER_DEST%\SMSbkMeterDBmodel.dat
#start


# These log files should be backed up after the SQL related tasks have run,
#  to record any SQL server errors that might effect the integrity of backup.
file  %SITE_DB_SERVER_ROOT_DIR%\LOG        %SITE_DB_SERVER_DEST%\SQLLog\
# file  %METERING_DB_SERVER_ROOT_DIR%\LOG  %METERING_DB_SERVER_DEST%\SQLLog\
# ----------------


# Create a record of the whole backup cycle
# ---------------------------------------
```

(continued)

```
#  This takes a snapshot of the backup log (if backup logging is enabled.)
#   It should be used to verify the quality and completeness of a backup
#   before restoring. Be sure to enable SMS logging for SMS_SITE_BACKUP
#   so these files can be saved with the backup, or there won't be any way
#   to verify the backup before restoring a failed site.
file  %SITE_SERVER_ROOT_DIR%\Logs\smsbkup.log  %BACKUP_DESTINATION%\
file  %SITE_SERVER_ROOT_DIR%\Logs\smsbkup.lo_  %BACKUP_DESTINATION%\


[Start]

# If the site being backed up was not installed with the express setup
#  option, some of the following services might not be installed. To avoid
#  spurious errors, comment out any services that are not installed on the
#  site.

service       \\%SITE_DB_SERVER%\SMS_SQL_MONITOR
service       \\%SITE_SERVER%\SMS_EXECUTIVE
service       \\%SITE_SERVER%\SMS_SITE_COMPONENT_MANAGER

service       `\\%SITE_SERVER%\Info APS`
service       `\\%SITE_SERVER%\Info Agent`
service       `\\%SITE_SERVER%\Info Sentinel`

# Stopping or starting the SMS client is NOT recommended in the current
#  release. Please refer to a KB article for more information.
#  service     `SMS Client Service`
#  clientapp  %SystemRoot%\MS\SMS\core\bin\launch32.exe
#  "SMS Client Service" and launch32.exe will start SMSAPM32.exe and
#  automatically, so there is no need to manually start them.




#  SYNTAX HELP
#  ----------
# Most of the syntax is used by working tasks in the default backup control
#  file, so if unsure about usage, find a line, make a copy, and edit it.

#  Using White space:
#   A space character separates each of the 3 sections of a task (that is, the
#    task type, source, and destination.) Use the back quote character, " ` ",
#    to quote a source or destination that contains spaces.
#   For example, the following two lines will cause errors:
#     file  C:\Program Files\Common Files  %BACKUP_DESTINATION%
#     file  C:\`Program Files`\`Common Files`  %BACKUP_DESTINATION%
#   Use this line instead:
#     file  `C:\Program Files\Common Files`  %BACKUP_DESTINATION%
```

```
# Destination Syntax Rules:
#  All tasks will implicitly create the directory where their destination
#   component goes, if it doesn't already exist. Note that the "cmd" task
#   creates any path needed for its destination component, (the third
#   component on the line), and NOT any directories used by the command line
#   itself (the second component on the line.) For example, "cmd" tasks
#   won't create a destination directory just because the BACKUP_DEST_DIR
#   token is used in the task's source section.
#  To create a directory that must exist for a later "cmd" task, use either
#    of the following syntaxes:
#       cmd   ECHO   %BACKUP_DEST_DIR%\NewDir\
#       cmd   `mkdir %BACKUP_DEST_DIR%\NewDir\`
#  A destination need not be specified for "cmd" tasks, but is required by
#   every other task type.
#  "reg", "sitedbdump", and "meteringdbdump" tasks require a file name to be
#   specified as a destination.
#  "file" tasks require a directory name to be specified as a destination.
#   Source files are copied into the dest directory. Source directories'
#   contents, but not the directory itself, are copied into the dest
#   directory. For example, the following task:
#     file  c:\winnt  c:\saved_winnt
#   creates a directory "c:\saved_winnt" that has the same contents as
#   "c:\winnt", including subdirectories. It does NOT create a directory
#   "c:\saved_winnt\winnt" with the same contents as "c:\winnt".

# Verifying Token Contents:
#  To check the value of a token (especially if there is a question about a
#   user defined token) use this syntax. This saves the token's value so that
#   it can be it can be verified after the backup cycle finishes:
#     cmd   `echo %SITE_DB_NAME%`  %BACKUP_DEST_DIR%\SiteDBName.txt

# When troubleshooting syntax errors, it's possible to save time by making a
#  copy of the control file and commenting out tasks that are running properly.
# If the backup is being run on a test site, manually stop the site services,
#  comment out the control file's "[Stop]" and "[Start]"
#  sections, and manually start backup.
# Start backup by starting the SMS_SITE_BACKUP service. If enough tasks are
#  commented out, a backup cycle can take only a few seconds.

# The backup task's default directory is on the site server, in the same
#  directory as the SMSBKUP.EXE that runs backups. If the site server's
#  machine type is i386, the default directory is "\sms\bin\i386\".
#  When custom executables are used in backup "cmd" tasks without providing
#  an explicit directory location, backup will first look in its default
#  directory and then in the path.
# ----------
```

Appendix B
Recommended Web Sites

By now, you should have the insight and information you need to implement and begin managing your network using Microsoft Systems Management Server (SMS) 2.0. As you venture forth into the exciting world of systems management using SMS 2.0, it will be important for you to stay on top of the product and to continue to develop your knowledge. The Internet sites and products described here can help you in this regard.

http://www.microsoft.com/smsmgmt

This site is of course Microsoft's own Web site, dedicated to SMS in all its versions. At this site, you will find the latest information about SMS, including updates and service packs, downloadable products, patches, and so on, as well as links to deployment and technology white papers (several of which have been referenced throughout this book). This site also offers information about SMS 2.0 training options.

Some of the articles you can find at this site are listed here:

- Microsoft Systems Management Server 2.0 Server Sizing in an Organization
- Integrating Microsoft Systems Management Server 2.0 with Novell NetWare
- Analyzing Year 2000 Compliance with Systems Management Server 2.0
- Microsoft Systems Management Server Version 1.2 and 2.0 Interoperability
- Systems Management Server Version 1.2 to 2.0 Upgrade
- Guide to Deploying the Windows 98 Client Operating System Using Systems Management Server
- Planning, Deploying, and Managing Microsoft Windows 2000 with Systems Management Server 2.0

http://www.microsoft.com/windows2000/

This Microsoft Web site hosts links to technical white papers supporting Microsoft Windows 2000 technology as well as links to other Windows 2000 support sites. For example, you can find the white papers listed below by navigating to *http://www.microsoft.com/windows2000/library/howitworks*. These white papers can help you draw distinctions between Windows 2000 and SMS 2.0, and that can help clarify how the two products work together.

- Introduction to Change and Configuration Management
- Introduction to IntelliMirror
- Introduction to Windows Management Services
- Introduction to Windows 2000 Group Policy

http://www.swynk.com

The SWYNK Web site is dedicated to providing Microsoft BackOffice administrative support for SMS, Microsoft SQL Server, Microsoft Exchange, Microsoft Windows NT, Windows 2000, Internet Information Server (IIS), Transaction Server, and Remote Access Server (RAS). This site hosts several public discussion boards through which administrators and "experts" can ask questions and share information. It is also host to several regular columnists, who share their experiences and offer tips and techniques.

This site is a good SMS support site. Its articles and discussion boards can be extremely helpful in resolving unusual problems. It also keeps updated lists of bugs and fixes—some of which are published by Microsoft, and others of which are discovered and published by peers—SMS Installer sample scripts, third-party support utilities for SMS, and SMS Knowledge Base articles. You can subscribe to this Web site to receive monthly notices of updates, articles, and so on.

http://www.computingedge.com

Computing Edge is a Microsoft Certified Solution Provider (MCSP) specializing in the development of products that enhance and add value to SMS 2.0 as well as previous versions of SMS. Computing Edge, founded in 1994, started out by primarily developing and consulting in management products with SMS. Over time, this development led to a line of products called +Plus Pack. Some of the Computing Edge products that many SMS administrators have found useful are described in the following sections. Additional information about these and other products can be found at Computing Edge's Web site. Computing Edge also sponsors a well-attended annual SMS User Conference as well as product road shows; it posts information relating to these events on its Web site.

Notification Server

Notification Server is a companion product for the SMS site server. It extends the reach of SMS by providing an integration method for UNIX systems and remote/mobile users, as well as stand-alone environments. Notification Server also extends the features of SMS by providing support for Active Management solutions that enable real-time detection, notification, and correction of problems.

Web Administrator

Web Administrator extends the management interface to UNIX and any other platform that supports a Web browser, making it a unique enterprise management tool. For instance, using Web Administrator a UNIX administrator can manage any UNIX system from his or her workstation simply by using a Netscape Web browser.

Computing Edge is committed to providing UNIX administrators and managers with a management interface that is easy to use from their local machine. For example, Web Reports is integrated with Web Administrator to support server-side rendering for graphs in support of Netscape.

Web Administrator for Microsoft SMS enables administrators and help desk personnel to access the functions of SMS 2.0, including remote control, from any Web browser. Additionally, in Windows 95 and Windows 98 environments help desk personnel can use the same operating system as their end-users and still run SMS to manage inventory and remote control functions. The Web Administrator interface can be customized and integrated with the help desk for quick access to common end-user issues. A demo version of this product is included on the companion CD for this book.

Web Reports

Web Reports provides administrators and their managers with a means of accessing database information about SMS resources by integrating over 100 report templates with the functions provided by Web Administrator. All of the reports, including presentation-quality graphs, are linked to the systems whose information is shown in the report. Also, reports are automatically scheduled to run at times when the database is inactive, thereby reducing the overhead and load on the SMS site server. A demo version of this product is included on the companion CD for this book.

UNIX Inventory +Solution

UNIX Inventory +Solution tracks hardware and software inventories for multiple-vendor UNIX systems and integrates this information with the SMS database. Standard inventory groups include: Operating System, Patches, Processors, Memory, Swap Space, Disk, File System, Network, Print Queues, Cron Queue, Users, Groups, and Software Audit. A toolkit permits extensions and customization of the inventory data.

UNIX SW Delivery +Solution

UNIX SW Delivery +Solution enables SMS administrators to distribute software to UNIX systems. It provides full support for SMS packages and advertisements.

Baseline +Plus

Baseline +Plus provides a means for detecting machines with nonstandard configurations. After creating the standard configuration of machines or groups of machines, you can run a scan of the SMS database to determine which clients deviate from the set standard. This product detects what applications are missing, what settings are different, and what programs should be removed.

Serial Number +Plus

Serial Number +Plus retrieves the manufacturer, model, model number, serial number, BIOS manufacturer, BIOS version, and memory module configuration from SMS clients without having to install any other software, such as Desktop Management Interface (DMI). Serial Number +Plus also enables you to import leasing information such as the start and end dates of leases and provides a variety of lease management reports—for example, listing machines with less than three months left on their lease and listing the average age of leased machines by department. A demo version of this product is included on the companion CD.

Index

Note: Page numbers in italics refer to figures.

Steven D. Kaczmarek is an independent consultant, trainer, and author. Since 1982, he has provided a variety of client PC support services for several organizations in the Chicago region, including Continental Bank, McDonald's Corporation, Heller International, and most recently Productivity Point International. His responsibilities have included purchase and installation of PC hardware and software, network implementation, management and troubleshooting, computer maintenance and help desk support, and customized end-user and network administrator training.

Steve holds training and professional certifications (MCT and MCP) from Microsoft Corporation for several products, including Microsoft Windows NT 4.0 and Microsoft Windows 2000, Microsoft Systems Management Server (SMS) 1.2 and 2.0, and TCP/IP, as well as the Microsoft Certified Systems Engineer (MCSE) certification. He has been involved in training and support for SMS since its initial release (version 1.0) and has been active in the beta testing programs for subsequent versions. Current client support projects include migration from SMS 1.2 to SMS 2.0, new implementations of SMS 2.0 sites, and customized SMS training for clients. He is also creating a computer-based training (CBT) program for the SMS Installer 2.0 application, designed to help administrators configure SMS Installer 2.0 and create custom installation scripts.

Steve is the author or a contributing author of three books: *Windows NT Workstation 4.0 Exam Guide* (Indianapolis: QUE Corporation, 1997); *Windows NT Server 4.0 in the Enterprise Exam Guide* (Indianapolis: QUE Corporation, 1997); and *Windows NT Server 4.0 Exam Guide* (Indianapolis: QUE Corporation, 1998). He has also been involved in a number of other authoring projects, including producing questions for ReviewNet Corporation designed to assist organizations in the screening of potential applicants for positions as Windows NT 4.0 network administrators.

Steve has a master of science degree from Loyola University with a specialization in computational mathematics.

Steve can be reached through e-mail, at Sdkacz@aol.com, and through his Web site, *http://www.skaczmarek.com*.

The manuscript for this book was prepared and galleyed using Microsoft Word 2000. Pages were composed by Microsoft Press using Adobe PageMaker 6.52 for Windows, with text in Garamond Light and display type in ITC Franklin Gothic. Composed pages were delivered to the printer as electronic prepress files.

Cover Designer:	Greg Hickman
Interior Graphic Designer:	James D. Kramer
Principal Compositors:	Daniel Latimer and Elizabeth Hansford
Principal Proofreader:	Cheryl Penner
Indexer:	Bill Meyers

Microsoft® Resource Kits—powerhouse resources to minimize costs while maximizing performance

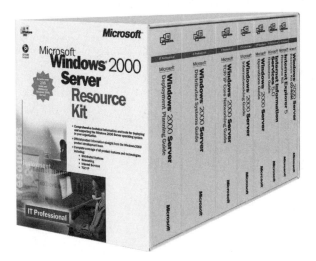

Deploy and support your enterprise business systems using the expertise and tools of those who know the technology best—the Microsoft product groups. Each RESOURCE KIT packs precise technical reference, installation and rollout tactics, planning guides, upgrade strategies, and essential utilities on CD-ROM. They're everything you need to help maximize system performance as you reduce ownership and support costs!

mspress.microsoft.com

Gain work-ready expertise as you prepare for the Microsoft Certified Professional (MCP) exam.

Learn by doing—learn for the job—with official Microsoft self-paced training kits. Whether you choose a book-and-CD TRAINING KIT or the all-multimedia learning experience of an ONLINE TRAINING KIT, you'll gain hands-on experience building essential systems support skills—as you prepare for the corresponding MCP exam. It's Microsoft Official Curriculum—how, when, and where you study best.

Microsoft® Certified Systems
Engineer Core Requirements
Training Kit
ISBN 1-57231-905-4

MCSE Training Kit, Microsoft
Windows® 2000 Server
ISBN 1-57231-903-8

MCSE Online Training Kit,
Microsoft Windows 2000
Server
ISBN 0-7356-0954-3
COMING SOON

MCSE Training Kit, Microsoft
Windows 2000 Professional
ISBN 1-57231-901-1

MCSE Online Training Kit,
Microsoft Windows 2000
Professional
ISBN 0-7356-0953-5
COMING SOON

MCSE Training Kit, Microsoft
Windows 2000 Active
Directory™ Services
ISBN 0-7356-0999-3

MCSE Online Training Kit,
Microsoft Windows 2000
Active Directory Services
ISBN 0-7356-1008-8
COMING SOON

Microsoft SQL Server™ 7.0
Database Implementation
Training Kit
ISBN 1-57231-826-0

Microsoft SQL Server 7.0
Database Implementation
Online Training Kit
ISBN 0-7356-0679-X

Microsoft SQL Server 7.0
System Administration
Training Kit
ISBN 1-57231-827-9

Microsoft SQL Server 7.0
System Administration Online
Training Kit
ISBN 0-7356-0678-1

MCSE Training Kit,
Networking Essentials Plus,
Third Edition
ISBN 1-57231-902-X

MCSE Online Training Kit,
Networking Essentials Plus
ISBN 0-7356-0880-6

Upgrading to Microsoft
Windows 2000 Training Kit
ISBN 0-7356-0940-3

MCSE Training Kit, Microsoft
Windows 2000 Network
Infrastructure Administration
ISBN 1-57231-904-6
COMING SOON

Microsoft®

mspress.microsoft.com

Practical, *portable guides for* **troubleshooters**

For hands-on, immediate references that will help you troubleshoot and administer Microsoft Windows NT Server 4.0, Microsoft SQL Server 7.0, or Microsoft Exchange 5.5, get:

Microsoft® Windows NT® Server 4.0 Administrator's Pocket Consultant
ISBN 0-7356-0574-2 $29.99 ($44.99 Canada)

Microsoft SQL Server™ 7.0 Administrator's Pocket Consultant
ISBN 0-7356-0596-3 $29.99 ($44.99 Canada)

Microsoft Exchange 5.5 Administrator's Pocket Consultant
ISBN 0-7356-0623-4 $29.99 ($44.99 Canada)

Ideal at the desk or on the go, from workstation to workstation, these fast-answers guides focus on what needs to be done in specific scenarios to support and manage mission-critical IT products. Great software and great learning solutions: Made for each other. Made by Microsoft.

Microsoft®
mspress.microsoft.com

There's no *substitute* for *experience.*

System Requirements for the Microsoft Systems Management Server 2.0 Evaluation Software

This CD contains the Systems Management Server 2.0 120-Day Evaluation Software and online documentation for SMS 2.0. To use the evaluation software, you will need at least two computers—one server and one client. You can have more than one client.

Server Computer

Your site server must meet the following requirements:

- Pentium 120-MHz or higher processor
- New installation of Microsoft Windows NT 4.0 Server with Service Pack 4 (recommended) or later
- Minimum 128 MB of RAM
- 100 MB free space on the system hard drive
- 500 MB free space on an NTFS partition
- CD-ROM drive
- Microsoft Internet Explorer 4.01 or later

Supported Network Operating Systems

Before you install the evaluation software, your network should be configured with one of the following network operating systems:

- Microsoft Windows NT 4.0
- Novell NetWare 3.x Bindery
- Novell NetWare 4.x Directory Services
- LAN Manager

Supported Client Operating Systems

Before you install the evaluation software, the computer that you configure as your client should be running one of the following operating systems:

- Microsoft Windows NT 3.51 or later
- Microsoft Windows 95
- Microsoft Windows 98
- Microsoft Windows for Workgroups 3.11
- Microsoft Windows 3.x

Installation Concerns

There may be rare instances in which the Systems Management Server software will not install properly. These issues have been addressed in the SMS 2.0 Service Pack 1 (SP1). However, you will not be able to install SP1 if you are running the evaluation version of SMS 2.0. The service pack requires the full retail version of the software.

For a complete list of fixes that SP1 provides, please review the following Knowledge Base article on the Microsoft Web site:

> SMS: Systems Management Server 2.0 Service Pack 1 Fixlist
> http://support.microsoft.com/support/kb/articles/Q235/9/91.ASP

System Requirements for the Companion CD

The companion CD includes an electronic version of the book, white papers, and third-party software. For installation information, refer to the Readme.txt file in the root of the companion CD.

Electronic Version of the Book

The complete text of the print book, *Microsoft Systems Management Server 2.0 Administrator's Companion*, is included on the CD as a fully searchable electronic book (eBook). To view the eBook, you must have Microsoft Internet Explorer 4.01 or later installed on your system. If you do not have Internet Explorer 4.01 or later, the setup wizard will offer to install Internet Explorer 5. Internet Explorer setup has been configured to install the minimum files necessary and will not change the user's current settings or associations.

System Requirements

To install and run an eBook, your system must meet the following requirements:

- 486/66 or higher processor
- One of the following operating systems:
  - Microsoft Windows 95
  - Microsoft Windows 98
  - Microsoft Windows NT 4.0 with Service Pack 3 or later

- Memory:
  - Microsoft Windows 95: 12 MB RAM
  - Microsoft Windows 98: 16 MB RAM
  - Microsoft Windows NT 4.0: 16 MB RAM
- Disk space:
  - To install and run an eBook from a network (network installation): 10 MB
  - To install an eBook to the hard drive (local installation): 20 - 31 MB
  - To install Microsoft Internet Explorer to the hard drive (local installation) and install and run an eBook from a network (network installation): 110 MB
  - To install Microsoft Internet Explorer to the hard drive (local installation) and install and run an eBook from the hard drive (local installation): 120 - 131 MB

White Papers

For the user's convenience, the CD includes two white papers: Integrating Microsoft Systems Management Server 2.0 with Novell NetWare, and Microsoft Windows Management Instrumentation: Background and Overview. You need Microsoft Word 97 or later to view the former and a browser that supports frames to view the latter. For more information about these white papers, please see the Introduction of this book.

Third-Party Software

The CD also includes third-party software to be used with Systems Management Server 2.0. Please note that these products are not under the control of Microsoft Corporation, and Microsoft is not responsible for their content, nor should their inclusion on this CD be construed as an endorsement of a product or Web site. Additional hardware and software may be required to use some of these resources. You need a browser that supports frames to view the Web page that accesses the software demos. Please see the Introduction of this book for more information about the Computing Edge demo products available on the CD.

Microsoft Press Support Information

Every effort has been made to ensure the accuracy of this book and the contents of the companion disc. Microsoft Press provides corrections for books through the Web at the following address:

http://mspress.microsoft.com/support/

If you have comments, questions, or ideas regarding this book or the companion CD, please send them to Microsoft Press using either of the following methods:

Postal Mail:

Microsoft Press
Attn: Systems Management Server 2.0 Administrator's Companion
One Microsoft Way
Redmond, WA 98052-6399

E-mail:

mspinput@microsoft.com

Please note that product support is not offered through the above mail addresses. The Systems Management Server 2.0 evaluation software is not supported by Microsoft Technical Support.

MICROSOFT LICENSE AGREEMENT
Book Companion CD

IMPORTANT—READ CAREFULLY: This Microsoft End-User License Agreement ("EULA") is a legal agreement between you (either an individual or an entity) and Microsoft Corporation for the Microsoft product identified above, which includes computer software and may include associated media, printed materials, and "on-line" or electronic documentation ("SOFTWARE PRODUCT"). Any component included within the SOFTWARE PRODUCT that is accompanied by a separate End-User License Agreement shall be governed by such agreement and not the terms set forth below. By installing, copying, or otherwise using the SOFTWARE PRODUCT, you agree to be bound by the terms of this EULA. If you do not agree to the terms of this EULA, you are not authorized to install, copy, or otherwise use the SOFTWARE PRODUCT; you may, however, return the SOFTWARE PRODUCT, along with all printed materials and other items that form a part of the Microsoft product that includes the SOFTWARE PRODUCT, to the place you obtained them for a full refund.

SOFTWARE PRODUCT LICENSE

The SOFTWARE PRODUCT is protected by United States copyright laws and international copyright treaties, as well as other intellectual property laws and treaties. The SOFTWARE PRODUCT is licensed, not sold.

1. **GRANT OF LICENSE.** This EULA grants you the following rights:

    a. **Software Product.** You may install and use one copy of the SOFTWARE PRODUCT on a single computer. The primary user of the computer on which the SOFTWARE PRODUCT is installed may make a second copy for his or her exclusive use on a portable computer.

    b. **Storage/Network Use.** You may also store or install a copy of the SOFTWARE PRODUCT on a storage device, such as a network server, used only to install or run the SOFTWARE PRODUCT on your other computers over an internal network; however, you must acquire and dedicate a license for each separate computer on which the SOFTWARE PRODUCT is installed or run from the storage device. A license for the SOFTWARE PRODUCT may not be shared or used concurrently on different computers.

    c. **License Pak.** If you have acquired this EULA in a Microsoft License Pak, you may make the number of additional copies of the computer software portion of the SOFTWARE PRODUCT authorized on the printed copy of this EULA, and you may use each copy in the manner specified above. You are also entitled to make a corresponding number of secondary copies for portable computer use as specified above.

    d. **Sample Code.** Solely with respect to portions, if any, of the SOFTWARE PRODUCT that are identified within the SOFTWARE PRODUCT as sample code (the "SAMPLE CODE"):

    i. **Use and Modification.** Microsoft grants you the right to use and modify the source code version of the SAMPLE CODE, *provided* you comply with subsection (d)(iii) below. You may not distribute the SAMPLE CODE, or any modified version of the SAMPLE CODE, in source code form.

    ii. **Redistributable Files.** Provided you comply with subsection (d)(iii) below, Microsoft grants you a nonexclusive, royalty-free right to reproduce and distribute the object code version of the SAMPLE CODE and of any modified SAMPLE CODE, other than SAMPLE CODE (or any modified version thereof) designated as not redistributable in the Readme file that forms a part of the SOFTWARE PRODUCT (the "Non-Redistributable Sample Code"). All SAMPLE CODE other than the Non-Redistributable Sample Code is collectively referred to as the "REDISTRIBUTABLES."

    iii. **Redistribution Requirements.** If you redistribute the REDISTRIBUTABLES, you agree to: (i) distribute the REDISTRIBUTABLES in object code form only in conjunction with and as a part of your software application product; (ii) not use Microsoft's name, logo, or trademarks to market your software application product; (iii) include a valid copyright notice on your software application product; (iv) indemnify, hold harmless, and defend Microsoft from and against any claims or lawsuits, including attorney's fees, that arise or result from the use or distribution of your software application product; and (v) not permit further distribution of the REDISTRIBUTABLES by your end user. Contact Microsoft for the applicable royalties due and other licensing terms for all other uses and/or distribution of the REDISTRIBUTABLES.

2. **DESCRIPTION OF OTHER RIGHTS AND LIMITATIONS.**

    - **Limitations on Reverse Engineering, Decompilation, and Disassembly.** You may not reverse engineer, decompile, or disassemble the SOFTWARE PRODUCT, except and only to the extent that such activity is expressly permitted by applicable law notwithstanding this limitation.

    - **Separation of Components.** The SOFTWARE PRODUCT is licensed as a single product. Its component parts may not be separated for use on more than one computer.

    - **Rental.** You may not rent, lease, or lend the SOFTWARE PRODUCT.

    - **Support Services.** Microsoft may, but is not obligated to, provide you with support services related to the SOFTWARE PRODUCT ("Support Services"). Use of Support Services is governed by the Microsoft policies and programs described in the user manual, in "on-line" documentation, and/or in other Microsoft-provided materials. Any supplemental software code provided to you as part of the Support Services shall be considered part of the SOFTWARE PRODUCT and subject to the terms and conditions of this EULA. With respect to technical information you provide to Microsoft as part of the Support Services, Microsoft may use such information for its business purposes, including for product support and development. Microsoft will not utilize such technical information in a form that personally identifies you.

- **Software Transfer.** You may permanently transfer all of your rights under this EULA, provided you retain no copies, you transfer all of the SOFTWARE PRODUCT (including all component parts, the media and printed materials, any upgrades, this EULA, and, if applicable, the Certificate of Authenticity), **and** the recipient agrees to the terms of this EULA.

- **Termination.** Without prejudice to any other rights, Microsoft may terminate this EULA if you fail to comply with the terms and conditions of this EULA. In such event, you must destroy all copies of the SOFTWARE PRODUCT and all of its component parts.

3. **COPYRIGHT.** All title and copyrights in and to the SOFTWARE PRODUCT (including but not limited to any images, photographs, animations, video, audio, music, text, SAMPLE CODE, REDISTRIBUTABLES, and "applets" incorporated into the SOFTWARE PRODUCT) and any copies of the SOFTWARE PRODUCT are owned by Microsoft or its suppliers. The SOFTWARE PRODUCT is protected by copyright laws and international treaty provisions. Therefore, you must treat the SOFTWARE PRODUCT like any other copyrighted material **except** that you may install the SOFTWARE PRODUCT on a single computer provided you keep the original solely for backup or archival purposes. You may not copy the printed materials accompanying the SOFTWARE PRODUCT.

4. **U.S. GOVERNMENT RESTRICTED RIGHTS.** The SOFTWARE PRODUCT and documentation are provided with RESTRICTED RIGHTS. Use, duplication, or disclosure by the Government is subject to restrictions as set forth in subparagraph (c)(1)(ii) of the Rights in Technical Data and Computer Software clause at DFARS 252.227-7013 or subparagraphs (c)(1) and (2) of the Commercial Computer Software—Restricted Rights at 48 CFR 52.227-19, as applicable. Manufacturer is Microsoft Corporation/One Microsoft Way/Redmond, WA 98052-6399.

5. **EXPORT RESTRICTIONS.** You agree that you will not export or re-export the SOFTWARE PRODUCT, any part thereof, or any process or service that is the direct product of the SOFTWARE PRODUCT (the foregoing collectively referred to as the "Restricted Components"), to any country, person, entity, or end user subject to U.S. export restrictions. You specifically agree not to export or re-export any of the Restricted Components (i) to any country to which the U.S. has embargoed or restricted the export of goods or services, which currently include, but are not necessarily limited to, Cuba, Iran, Iraq, Libya, North Korea, Sudan, and Syria, or to any national of any such country, wherever located, who intends to transmit or transport the Restricted Components back to such country; (ii) to any end user who you know or have reason to know will utilize the Restricted Components in the design, development, or production of nuclear, chemical, or biological weapons; or (iii) to any end user who has been prohibited from participating in U.S. export transactions by any federal agency of the U.S. government. You warrant and represent that neither the BXA nor any other U.S. federal agency has suspended, revoked, or denied your export privileges.

6. **NOTE ON JAVA SUPPORT.** THE SOFTWARE PRODUCT MAY CONTAIN SUPPORT FOR PROGRAMS WRITTEN IN JAVA. JAVA TECHNOLOGY IS NOT FAULT TOLERANT AND IS NOT DESIGNED, MANUFACTURED, OR INTENDED FOR USE OR RESALE AS ON-LINE CONTROL EQUIPMENT IN HAZARDOUS ENVIRONMENTS REQUIRING FAIL-SAFE PERFORMANCE, SUCH AS IN THE OPERATION OF NUCLEAR FACILITIES, AIRCRAFT NAVIGATION OR COMMUNICATION SYSTEMS, AIR TRAFFIC CONTROL, DIRECT LIFE SUPPORT MACHINES, OR WEAPONS SYSTEMS, IN WHICH THE FAILURE OF JAVA TECHNOLOGY COULD LEAD DIRECTLY TO DEATH, PERSONAL INJURY, OR SEVERE PHYSICAL OR ENVIRONMENTAL DAMAGE. SUN MICROSYSTEMS, INC. HAS CONTRACTUALLY OBLIGATED MICROSOFT TO MAKE THIS DISCLAIMER.

DISCLAIMER OF WARRANTY

NO WARRANTIES OR CONDITIONS. MICROSOFT EXPRESSLY DISCLAIMS ANY WARRANTY OR CONDITION FOR THE SOFTWARE PRODUCT. THE SOFTWARE PRODUCT AND ANY RELATED DOCUMENTATION ARE PROVIDED "AS IS" WITHOUT WARRANTY OR CONDITION OF ANY KIND, EITHER EXPRESS OR IMPLIED, INCLUDING, WITHOUT LIMITATION, THE IMPLIED WARRANTIES OF MERCHANTABILITY, FITNESS FOR A PARTICULAR PURPOSE, OR NONINFRINGEMENT. THE ENTIRE RISK ARISING OUT OF USE OR PERFORMANCE OF THE SOFTWARE PRODUCT REMAINS WITH YOU.

LIMITATION OF LIABILITY. TO THE MAXIMUM EXTENT PERMITTED BY APPLICABLE LAW, IN NO EVENT SHALL MICROSOFT OR ITS SUPPLIERS BE LIABLE FOR ANY SPECIAL, INCIDENTAL, INDIRECT, OR CONSEQUENTIAL DAMAGES WHATSOEVER (INCLUDING, WITHOUT LIMITATION, DAMAGES FOR LOSS OF BUSINESS PROFITS, BUSINESS INTERRUPTION, LOSS OF BUSINESS INFORMATION, OR ANY OTHER PECUNIARY LOSS) ARISING OUT OF THE USE OF OR INABILITY TO USE THE SOFTWARE PRODUCT OR THE PROVISION OF OR FAILURE TO PROVIDE SUPPORT SERVICES, EVEN IF MICROSOFT HAS BEEN ADVISED OF THE POSSIBILITY OF SUCH DAMAGES. IN ANY CASE, MICROSOFT'S ENTIRE LIABILITY UNDER ANY PROVISION OF THIS EULA SHALL BE LIMITED TO THE GREATER OF THE AMOUNT ACTUALLY PAID BY YOU FOR THE SOFTWARE PRODUCT OR US$5.00; PROVIDED, HOWEVER, IF YOU HAVE ENTERED INTO A MICROSOFT SUPPORT SERVICES AGREEMENT, MICROSOFT'S ENTIRE LIABILITY REGARDING SUPPORT SERVICES SHALL BE GOVERNED BY THE TERMS OF THAT AGREEMENT. BECAUSE SOME STATES AND JURISDICTIONS DO NOT ALLOW THE EXCLUSION OR LIMITATION OF LIABILITY, THE ABOVE LIMITATION MAY NOT APPLY TO YOU.

MISCELLANEOUS

This EULA is governed by the laws of the State of Washington USA, except and only to the extent that applicable law mandates governing law of a different jurisdiction.

Should you have any questions concerning this EULA, or if you desire to contact Microsoft for any reason, please contact the Microsoft subsidiary serving your country, or write: Microsoft Sales Information Center/One Microsoft Way/Redmond, WA 98052-6399.